Compilers

Principles, Techniques, and Tools

Compilers

Principles, Techniques, and Tools

ALFRED V. AHO

AT&T Bell Laboratories
Murray Hill, New Jersey

RAVI SETHI

AT&T Bell Laboratories
Murray Hill, New Jersey

JEFFREY D. ULLMAN

Stanford University
Stanford, California

ADDISON-WESLEY PUBLISHING COMPANY
Reading, Massachusetts • Menlo Park, California
Don Mills, Ontario • Wokingham, England • Amsterdam • Sydney
Singapore • Tokyo • Mexico City • Bogotá • Santiago • San Juan

Mark S. Dalton/Publisher
James T. DeWolf/Sponsoring Editor

Bette J. Aaronson/Production Supervisor
Hugh Crawford/Manufacturing Supervisor
Jean Depoian/Cover Design and Illustration
Karen Guardino/Managing Editor

This book is in the Addison-Wesley series in Computer Science
Michael A. Harrison/Consulting Editor

Library of Congress Cataloging in Publication Data

Aho, Alfred V.
  Compilers, principles, techniques, and tools.

    Bibliography: p.
    Includes index.
    1. Compiling (Electronic computers)   I. Sethi,
Ravi. II. Ullman, Jeffrey D., 1942-   . III. Title.
QA76.76.C65A37 1985   005.4'53   85-15647
ISBN 0-201-10088-6

Reprinted with corrections June, 1987

Reproduced by Addison-Wesley from camera-ready copy supplied by the authors.

DEFGHIJK-HA-8987

Preface

This book is a descendant of *Principles of Compiler Design* by Alfred V. Aho and Jeffrey D. Ullman. Like its ancestor, it is intended as a text for a first course in compiler design. The emphasis is on solving problems universally encountered in designing a language translator, regardless of the source or target machine.

Although few people are likely to build or even maintain a compiler for a major programming language, the reader can profitably apply the ideas and techniques discussed in this book to general software design. For example, the string matching techniques for building lexical analyzers have also been used in text editors, information retrieval systems, and pattern recognition programs. Context-free grammars and syntax-directed definitions have been used to build many little languages such as the typesetting and figure drawing systems that produced this book. The techniques of code optimization have been used in program verifiers and in programs that produce "structured" programs from unstructured ones.

Use of the Book

The major topics in compiler design are covered in depth. The first chapter introduces the basic structure of a compiler and is essential to the rest of the book.

Chapter 2 presents a translator from infix to postfix expressions, built using some of the basic techniques described in this book. Many of the remaining chapters amplify the material in Chapter 2.

Chapter 3 covers lexical analysis, regular expressions, finite-state machines, and scanner-generator tools. The material in this chapter is broadly applicable to text-processing.

Chapter 4 covers the major parsing techniques in depth, ranging from the recursive-descent methods that are suitable for hand implementation to the computationally more intensive LR techniques that have been used in parser generators.

Chapter 5 introduces the principal ideas in syntax-directed translation. This chapter is used in the remainder of the book for both specifying and implementing translations.

Chapter 6 presents the main ideas for performing static semantic checking. Type checking and unification are discussed in detail.

Chapter 7 discusses storage organizations used to support the run-time environment of a program.

Chapter 8 begins with a discussion of intermediate languages and then shows how common programming language constructs can be translated into intermediate code.

Chapter 9 covers target code generation. Included are the basic "on-the-fly" code generation methods, as well as optimal methods for generating code for expressions. Peephole optimization and code-generator generators are also covered.

Chapter 10 is a comprehensive treatment of code optimization. Data-flow analysis methods are covered in detail, as well as the principal methods for global optimization.

Chapter 11 discusses some pragmatic issues that arise in implementing a compiler. Software engineering and testing are particularly important in compiler construction.

Chapter 12 presents case studies of compilers that have been constructed using some of the techniques presented in this book.

Appendix A describes a simple language, a "subset" of Pascal, that can be used as the basis of an implementation project.

The authors have taught both introductory and advanced courses, at the undergraduate and graduate levels, from the material in this book at AT&T Bell Laboratories, Columbia, Princeton, and Stanford.

An introductory compiler course might cover material from the following sections of this book:

introduction	Chapter 1 and Sections 2.1-2.5
lexical analysis	2.6, 3.1-3.4
symbol tables	2.7, 7.6
parsing	2.4, 4.1-4.4
syntax-directed translation	2.5, 5.1-5.5
type checking	6.1-6.2
run-time organization	7.1-7.3
intermediate code generation	8.1-8.3
code generation	9.1-9.4
code optimization	10.1-10.2

Information needed for a programming project like the one in Appendix A is introduced in Chapter 2.

A course stressing tools in compiler construction might include the discussion of lexical analyzer generators in Sections 3.5, of parser generators in Sections 4.8 and 4.9, of code-generator generators in Section 9.12, and material on techniques for compiler construction from Chapter 11.

An advanced course might stress the algorithms used in lexical analyzer generators and parser generators discussed in Chapters 3 and 4, the material on type equivalence, overloading, polymorphism, and unification in Chapter 6, the material on run-time storage organization in Chapter 7, the pattern-directed code generation methods discussed in Chapter 9, and material on code optimization from Chapter 10.

Exercises

As before, we rate exercises with stars. Exercises without stars test understanding of definitions, singly starred exercises are intended for more advanced courses, and doubly starred exercises are food for thought.

Acknowledgments

At various stages in the writing of this book, a number of people have given us invaluable comments on the manuscript. In this regard we owe a debt of gratitude to Bill Appelbe, Nelson Beebe, Jon Bentley, Lois Bogess, Rodney Farrow, Stu Feldman, Charles Fischer, Chris Fraser, Art Gittelman, Eric Grosse, Dave Hanson, Fritz Henglein, Robert Henry, Gerard Holzmann, Steve Johnson, Brian Kernighan, Ken Kubota, Dave MacQueen, Dianne Maki, Alan Martin, Doug McIlroy, Charles McLaughlin, John Mitchell, Elliott Organick, Robert Paige, Phil Pfeiffer, Rob Pike, Kari-Jouko Räihä, Dennis Ritchie, Sriram Sankar, Paul Stoecker, Bjarne Stroustrup, Tom Szymanski, Kim Tracy, Peter Weinberger, and Reinhard Wilhelm.

This book was phototypeset by the authors using the excellent software available on the UNIX system. The typesetting command read

    pic *files* | tbl | eqn | troff -ms

pic is Brian Kernighan's language for typesetting figures; we owe Brian a special debt of gratitude for accommodating our special and extensive figure-drawing needs so cheerfully. tbl is Mike Lesk's language for laying out tables. eqn is Brian Kernighan and Lorinda Cherry's language for typesetting mathematics. troff is Joe Ossana's program for formatting text for a photo-typesetter, which in our case was a Mergenthaler Linotron 202/N. The ms package of troff macros was written by Mike Lesk. In addition, we managed the text using make due to Stu Feldman. Cross references within the text were maintained using awk created by Al Aho, Brian Kernighan, and Peter Weinberger, and sed created by Lee McMahon.

The authors would particularly like to acknowledge Patricia Solomon for helping prepare the manuscript for photocomposition. Her cheerfulness and expert typing were greatly appreciated. J. D. Ullman was supported by an Einstein Fellowship of the Israeli Academy of Arts and Sciences during part of the time in which this book was written. Finally, the authors would like to thank AT&T Bell Laboratories for its support during the preparation of the manuscript.

A. V. A., R. S., J. D. U.

Contents

CHAPTER 1

Introduction
to Compiling

The principles and techniques of compiler writing are so pervasive that the ideas found in this book will be used many times in the career of a computer scientist. Compiler writing spans programming languages, machine architecture, language theory, algorithms, and software engineering. Fortunately, a few basic compiler-writing techniques can be used to construct translators for a wide variety of languages and machines. In this chapter, we introduce the subject of compiling by describing the components of a compiler, the environment in which compilers do their job, and some software tools that make it easier to build compilers.

1.1 COMPILERS

Simply stated, a compiler is a program that reads a program written in one language – the *source* language – and translates it into an equivalent program in another language – the *target* language (see Fig. 1.1). As an important part of this translation process, the compiler reports to its user the presence of errors in the source program.

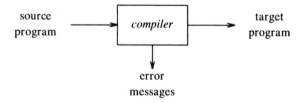

Fig. 1.1. A compiler.

At first glance, the variety of compilers may appear overwhelming. There are thousands of source languages, ranging from traditional programming languages such as Fortran and Pascal to specialized languages that have arisen in virtually every area of computer application. Target languages are equally as varied; a target language may be another programming language, or the machine language of any computer between a microprocessor and a supercomputer. Compilers are sometimes classified as single-pass, multi-pass, load-and-go, debugging, or optimizing, depending on how they have been constructed or on what function they are supposed to perform. Despite this apparent complexity, the basic tasks that any compiler must perform are essentially the same. By understanding these tasks, we can construct compilers for a wide variety of source languages and target machines using the same basic techniques.

Our knowledge about how to organize and write compilers has increased vastly since the first compilers started to appear in the early 1950's. It is difficult to give an exact date for the first compiler because initially a great deal of experimentation and implementation was done independently by several groups. Much of the early work on compiling dealt with the translation of arithmetic formulas into machine code.

Throughout the 1950's, compilers were considered notoriously difficult programs to write. The first Fortran compiler, for example, took 18 staff-years to implement (Backus et al. [1957]). We have since discovered systematic techniques for handling many of the important tasks that occur during compilation. Good implementation languages, programming environments, and software tools have also been developed. With these advances, a substantial compiler can be implemented even as a student project in a one-semester compiler-design course.

The Analysis-Synthesis Model of Compilation

There are two parts to compilation: analysis and synthesis. The analysis part breaks up the source program into constituent pieces and creates an intermediate representation of the source program. The synthesis part constructs the desired target program from the intermediate representation. Of the two parts, synthesis requires the most specialized techniques. We shall consider analysis informally in Section 1.2 and outline the way target code is synthesized in a standard compiler in Section 1.3.

During analysis, the operations implied by the source program are determined and recorded in a hierarchical structure called a tree. Often, a special kind of tree called a syntax tree is used, in which each node represents an operation and the children of a node represent the arguments of the operation. For example, a syntax tree for an assignment statement is shown in Fig. 1.2.

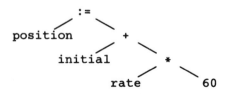

Fig. 1.2. Syntax tree for `position := initial + rate * 60`.

Many software tools that manipulate source programs first perform some kind of analysis. Some examples of such tools include:

1. *Structure editors.* A structure editor takes as input a sequence of commands to build a source program. The structure editor not only performs the text-creation and modification functions of an ordinary text editor, but it also analyzes the program text, putting an appropriate hierarchical structure on the source program. Thus, the structure editor can perform additional tasks that are useful in the preparation of programs. For example, it can check that the input is correctly formed, can supply keywords automatically (e.g., when the user types while, the editor supplies the matching do and reminds the user that a conditional must come between them), and can jump from a begin or left parenthesis to its matching end or right parenthesis. Further, the output of such an editor is often similar to the output of the analysis phase of a compiler.

2. *Pretty printers.* A pretty printer analyzes a program and prints it in such a way that the structure of the program becomes clearly visible. For example, comments may appear in a special font, and statements may appear with an amount of indentation proportional to the depth of their nesting in the hierarchical organization of the statements.

3. *Static checkers.* A static checker reads a program, analyzes it, and attempts to discover potential bugs without running the program. The analysis portion is often similar to that found in optimizing compilers of the type discussed in Chapter 10. For example, a static checker may detect that parts of the source program can never be executed, or that a certain variable might be used before being defined. In addition, it can catch logical errors such as trying to use a real variable as a pointer, employing the type-checking techniques discussed in Chapter 6.

4. *Interpreters.* Instead of producing a target program as a translation, an interpreter performs the operations implied by the source program. For an assignment statement, for example, an interpreter might build a tree like Fig. 1.2, and then carry out the operations at the nodes as it "walks" the tree. At the root it would discover it had an assignment to perform, so it would call a routine to evaluate the expression on the right, and then store the resulting value in the location associated with the identifier position. At the right child of the root, the routine would discover it had to compute the sum of two expressions. It would call itself recursively to compute the value of the expression rate * 60. It would then add that value to the value of the variable initial.

    Interpreters are frequently used to execute command languages, since each operator executed in a command language is usually an invocation of a complex routine such as an editor or compiler. Similarly, some "very high-level" languages, like APL, are normally interpreted because there are many things about the data, such as the size and shape of arrays, that cannot be deduced at compile time.

Traditionally, we think of a compiler as a program that translates a source language like Fortran into the assembly or machine language of some computer. However, there are seemingly unrelated places where compiler technology is regularly used. The analysis portion in each of the following examples is similar to that of a conventional compiler.

1. *Text formatters.* A text formatter takes input that is a stream of characters, most of which is text to be typeset, but some of which includes commands to indicate paragraphs, figures, or mathematical structures like subscripts and superscripts. We mention some of the analysis done by text formatters in the next section.

2. *Silicon compilers.* A silicon compiler has a source language that is similar or identical to a conventional programming language. However, the variables of the language represent, not locations in memory, but, logical signals (0 or 1) or groups of signals in a switching circuit. The output is a circuit design in an appropriate language. See Johnson [1983], Ullman [1984], or Trickey [1985] for a discussion of silicon compilation.

3. *Query interpreters.* A query interpreter translates a predicate containing relational and boolean operators into commands to search a database for records satisfying that predicate. (See Ullman [1982] or Date [1986].)

The Context of a Compiler

In addition to a compiler, several other programs may be required to create an executable target program. A source program may be divided into modules stored in separate files. The task of collecting the source program is sometimes entrusted to a distinct program, called a preprocessor. The preprocessor may also expand shorthands, called macros, into source language statements.

Figure 1.3 shows a typical "compilation." The target program created by the compiler may require further processing before it can be run. The compiler in Fig. 1.3 creates assembly code that is translated by an assembler into machine code and then linked together with some library routines into the code that actually runs on the machine.

We shall consider the components of a compiler in the next two sections; the remaining programs in Fig. 1.3 are discussed in Section 1.4.

1.2 ANALYSIS OF THE SOURCE PROGRAM

In this section, we introduce analysis and illustrate its use in some text-formatting languages. The subject is treated in more detail in Chapters 2-4 and 6. In compiling, analysis consists of three phases:

1. *Linear analysis*, in which the stream of characters making up the source program is read from left-to-right and grouped into *tokens* that are sequences of characters having a collective meaning.

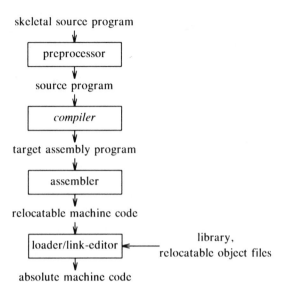

skeletal source program

preprocessor

source program

compiler

target assembly program

assembler

relocatable machine code

loader/link-editor

library,
relocatable object files

absolute machine code

Fig. 1.3. A language-processing system.

2. *Hierarchical analysis*, in which characters or tokens are grouped hierarchically into nested collections with collective meaning.

3. *Semantic analysis*, in which certain checks are performed to ensure that the components of a program fit together meaningfully.

Lexical Analysis

In a compiler, linear analysis is called *lexical analysis* or *scanning*. For example, in lexical analysis the characters in the assignment statement

```
position := initial + rate * 60
```

would be grouped into the following tokens:

1. The identifier `position`.
2. The assignment symbol `:=`.
3. The identifier `initial`.
4. The plus sign.
5. The identifier `rate`.
6. The multiplication sign.
7. The number `60`.

The blanks separating the characters of these tokens would normally be eliminated during lexical analysis.

Syntax Analysis

Hierarchical analysis is called *parsing* or *syntax analysis*. It involves grouping the tokens of the source program into grammatical phrases that are used by the compiler to synthesize output. Usually, the grammatical phrases of the source program are represented by a parse tree such as the one shown in Fig. 1.4.

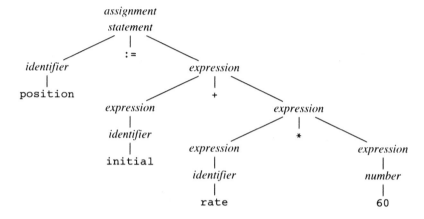

Fig. 1.4. Parse tree for `position := initial + rate * 60`.

In the expression `initial + rate * 60`, the phrase `rate * 60` is a logical unit because the usual conventions of arithmetic expressions tell us that multiplication is performed before addition. Because the expression `initial + rate` is followed by a `*`, it is not grouped into a single phrase by itself in Fig. 1.4.

The hierarchical structure of a program is usually expressed by recursive rules. For example, we might have the following rules as part of the definition of expressions:

1. Any *identifier* is an expression.
2. Any *number* is an expression.
3. If *expression*₁ and *expression*₂ are expressions, then so are

$$expression_1 \; + \; expression_2$$
$$expression_1 \; * \; expression_2$$
$$(\; expression_1 \;)$$

Rules (1) and (2) are (nonrecursive) basis rules, while (3) defines expressions in terms of operators applied to other expressions. Thus, by rule (1), `initial` and `rate` are expressions. By rule (2), `60` is an expression, while by rule (3), we can first infer that `rate * 60` is an expression and finally that `initial + rate * 60` is an expression.

Similarly, many languages define statements recursively by rules such as:

1. If *identifier*$_1$ is an identifier, and *expression*$_2$ is an expression, then

    identifier$_1$: = *expression*$_2$

    is a statement.

2. If *expression*$_1$ is an expression and *statement*$_2$ is a statement, then

    while (*expression*$_1$) **do** *statement*$_2$
    if (*expression*$_1$) **then** *statement*$_2$

    are statements.

The division between lexical and syntactic analysis is somewhat arbitrary. We usually choose a division that simplifies the overall task of analysis. One factor in determining the division is whether a source language construct is inherently recursive or not. Lexical constructs do not require recursion, while syntactic constructs often do. Context-free grammars are a formalization of recursive rules that can be used to guide syntactic analysis. They are introduced in Chapter 2 and studied extensively in Chapter 4.

For example, recursion is not required to recognize identifiers, which are typically strings of letters and digits beginning with a letter. We would normally recognize identifiers by a simple scan of the input stream, waiting until a character that was neither a letter nor a digit was found, and then grouping all the letters and digits found up to that point into an identifier token. The characters so grouped are recorded in a table, called a symbol table, and removed from the input so that processing of the next token can begin.

On the other hand, this kind of linear scan is not powerful enough to analyze expressions or statements. For example, we cannot properly match parentheses in expressions, or **begin** and **end** in statements, without putting some kind of hierarchical or nesting structure on the input.

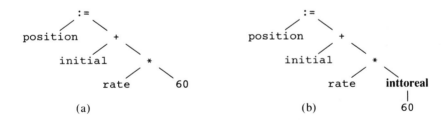

(a)   (b)

Fig. 1.5. Semantic analysis inserts a conversion from integer to real.

The parse tree in Fig. 1.4 describes the syntactic structure of the input. A more common internal representation of this syntactic structure is given by the syntax tree in Fig. 1.5(a). A syntax tree is a compressed representation of the parse tree in which the operators appear as the interior nodes, and the operands of an operator are the children of the node for that operator. The construction of trees such as the one in Fig. 1.5(a) is discussed in Section 5.2.

We shall take up in Chapter 2, and in more detail in Chapter 5, the subject of *syntax-directed translation*, in which the compiler uses the hierarchical structure on the input to help generate the output.

Semantic Analysis

The semantic analysis phase checks the source program for semantic errors and gathers type information for the subsequent code-generation phase. It uses the hierarchical structure determined by the syntax-analysis phase to identify the operators and operands of expressions and statements.

An important component of semantic analysis is type checking. Here the compiler checks that each operator has operands that are permitted by the source language specification. For example, many programming language definitions require a compiler to report an error every time a real number is used to index an array. However, the language specification may permit some operand coercions, for example, when a binary arithmetic operator is applied to an integer and real. In this case, the compiler may need to convert the integer to a real. Type checking and semantic analysis are discussed in Chapter 6.

Example 1.1. Inside a machine, the bit pattern representing an integer is generally different from the bit pattern for a real, even if the integer and the real number happen to have the same value. Suppose, for example, that all identifiers in Fig. 1.5 have been declared to be reals and that 60 by itself is assumed to be an integer. Type checking of Fig. 1.5(a) reveals that ∗ is applied to a real, rate, and an integer, 60. The general approach is to convert the integer into a real. This has been achieved in Fig. 1.5(b) by creating an extra node for the operator **inttoreal** that explicitly converts an integer into a real. Alternatively, since the operand of **inttoreal** is a constant, the compiler may instead replace the integer constant by an equivalent real constant. □

Analysis in Text Formatters

It is useful to regard the input to a text formatter as specifying a hierarchy of *boxes* that are rectangular regions to be filled by some bit pattern, representing light and dark pixels to be printed by the output device.

For example, the TEX system (Knuth [1984a]) views its input this way. Each character that is not part of a command represents a box containing the bit pattern for that character in the appropriate font and size. Consecutive characters not separated by "white space" (blanks or newline characters) are grouped into words, consisting of a sequence of horizontally arranged boxes, shown schematically in Fig. 1.6. The grouping of characters into words (or commands) is the linear or lexical aspect of analysis in a text formatter.

Boxes in TEX may be built from smaller boxes by arbitrary horizontal and vertical combinations. For example,

```
\hbox{ <list of boxes> }
```

Fig. 1.6. Grouping of characters and words into boxes.

groups the list of boxes by juxtaposing them horizontally, while the \vbox operator similarly groups a list of boxes by vertical juxtaposition. Thus, if we say in T_EX

    \hbox{\vbox{! 1} \vbox{@ 2}}

we get the arrangement of boxes shown in Fig. 1.7. Determining the hierarchical arrangement of boxes implied by the input is part of syntax analysis in T_EX.

Fig. 1.7. Hierarchy of boxes in T_EX.

As another example, the preprocessor EQN for mathematics (Kernighan and Cherry [1975]), or the mathematical processor in T_EX, builds mathematical expressions from operators like sub and sup for subscripts and superscripts. If EQN encounters an input text of the form

    BOX sub *box*

it shrinks the size of *box* and attaches it to *BOX* near the lower right corner, as illustrated in Fig. 1.8. The sup operator similarly attaches *box* at the upper right.

Fig. 1.8. Building the subscript structure in mathematical text.

These operators can be applied recursively, so, for example, the EQN text

```
    a sub {i sup 2}
```

results in a_{i^2}. Grouping the operators sub and sup into tokens is part of the lexical analysis of EQN text. However, the syntactic structure of the text is needed to determine the size and placement of a box.

1.3 THE PHASES OF A COMPILER

Conceptually, a compiler operates in *phases*, each of which transforms the source program from one representation to another. A typical decomposition of a compiler is shown in Fig. 1.9. In practice, some of the phases may be grouped together, as mentioned in Section 1.5, and the intermediate representations between the grouped phases need not be explicitly constructed.

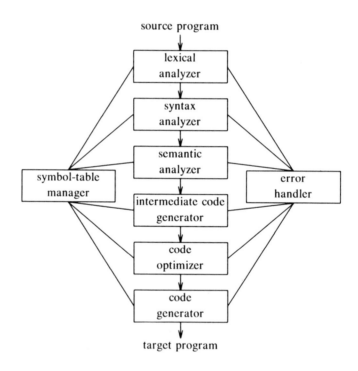

Fig. 1.9. Phases of a compiler.

The first three phases, forming the bulk of the analysis portion of a compiler, were introduced in the last section. Two other activities, symbol-table management and error handling, are shown interacting with the six phases of lexical analysis, syntax analysis, semantic analysis, intermediate code generation, code optimization, and code generation. Informally, we shall also call the symbol-table manager and the error handler "phases."

Symbol-Table Management

An essential function of a compiler is to record the identifiers used in the source program and collect information about various attributes of each identifier. These attributes may provide information about the storage allocated for an identifier, its type, its scope (where in the program it is valid), and, in the case of procedure names, such things as the number and types of its arguments, the method of passing each argument (e.g., by reference), and the type returned, if any.

A *symbol table* is a data structure containing a record for each identifier, with fields for the attributes of the identifier. The data structure allows us to find the record for each identifier quickly and to store or retrieve data from that record quickly. Symbol tables are discussed in Chapters 2 and 7.

When an identifier in the source program is detected by the lexical analyzer, the identifier is entered into the symbol table. However, the attributes of an identifier cannot normally be determined during lexical analysis. For example, in a Pascal declaration like

```
    var position, initial, rate : real ;
```

the type real is not known when position, initial, and rate are seen by the lexical analyzer.

The remaining phases enter information about identifiers into the symbol table and then use this information in various ways. For example, when doing semantic analysis and intermediate code generation, we need to know what the types of identifiers are, so we can check that the source program uses them in valid ways, and so that we can generate the proper operations on them. The code generator typically enters and uses detailed information about the storage assigned to identifiers.

Error Detection and Reporting

Each phase can encounter errors. However, after detecting an error, a phase must somehow deal with that error, so that compilation can proceed, allowing further errors in the source program to be detected. A compiler that stops when it finds the first error is not as helpful as it could be.

The syntax and semantic analysis phases usually handle a large fraction of the errors detectable by the compiler. The lexical phase can detect errors where the characters remaining in the input do not form any token of the language. Errors where the token stream violates the structure rules (syntax) of the language are determined by the syntax analysis phase. During semantic analysis the compiler tries to detect constructs that have the right syntactic structure but no meaning to the operation involved, e.g., if we try to add two identifiers, one of which is the name of an array, and the other the name of a procedure. We discuss the handling of errors by each phase in the part of the book devoted to that phase.

The Analysis Phases

As translation progresses, the compiler's internal representation of the source program changes. We illustrate these representations by considering the translation of the statement

```
position := initial + rate * 60
```
(1.1)

Figure 1.10 shows the representation of this statement after each phase.

The lexical analysis phase reads the characters in the source program and groups them into a stream of tokens in which each token represents a logically cohesive sequence of characters, such as an identifier, a keyword (`if`, `while`, etc.), a punctuation character, or a multi-character operator like `:=`. The character sequence forming a token is called the *lexeme* for the token.

Certain tokens will be augmented by a "lexical value." For example, when an identifier like `rate` is found, the lexical analyzer not only generates a token, say **id**, but also enters the lexeme `rate` into the symbol table, if it is not already there. The lexical value associated with this occurrence of **id** points to the symbol-table entry for `rate`.

In this section, we shall use $\mathbf{id}_1$, $\mathbf{id}_2$, and $\mathbf{id}_3$ for `position`, `initial`, and `rate`, respectively, to emphasize that the internal representation of an identifier is different from the character sequence forming the identifier. The representation of (1.1) after lexical analysis is therefore suggested by:

$$\mathbf{id}_1 := \mathbf{id}_2 + \mathbf{id}_3 * 60$$
(1.2)

We should also make up tokens for the multi-character operator `:=` and the number `60` to reflect their internal representation, but we defer that until Chapter 2. Lexical analysis is covered in detail in Chapter 3.

The second and third phases, syntax and semantic analysis, have also been introduced in Section 1.2. Syntax analysis imposes a hierarchical structure on the token stream, which we shall portray by syntax trees as in Fig. 1.11(a). A typical data structure for the tree is shown in Fig. 1.11(b) in which an interior node is a record with a field for the operator and two fields containing pointers to the records for the left and right children. A leaf is a record with two or more fields, one to identify the token at the leaf, and the others to record information about the token. Additional information about language constructs can be kept by adding more fields to the records for nodes. We discuss syntax and semantic analysis in Chapters 4 and 6, respectively.

Intermediate Code Generation

After syntax and semantic analysis, some compilers generate an explicit intermediate representation of the source program. We can think of this intermediate representation as a program for an abstract machine. This intermediate representation should have two important properties; it should be easy to produce, and easy to translate into the target program.

The intermediate representation can have a variety of forms. In Chapter 8,

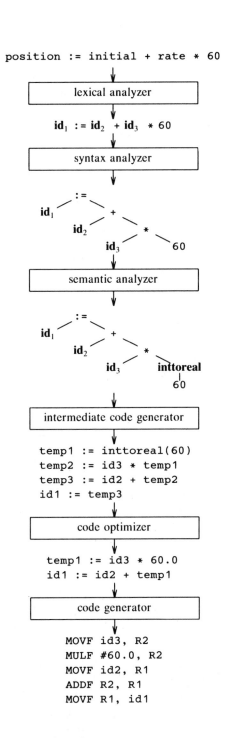

Fig. 1.10. Translation of a statement.

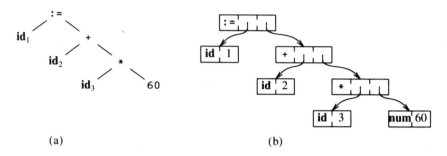

(a)   (b)

Fig. 1.11. The data structure in (b) is for the tree in (a).

we consider an intermediate form called "three-address code," which is like the assembly language for a machine in which every memory location can act like a register. Three-address code consists of a sequence of instructions, each of which has at most three operands. The source program in (1.1) might appear in three-address code as

```
temp1 := inttoreal(60)
temp2 := id3 * temp1
temp3 := id2 + temp2
id1 := temp3
```
(1.3)

This intermediate form has several properties. First, each three-address instruction has at most one operator in addition to the assignment. Thus, when generating these instructions, the compiler has to decide on the order in which operations are to be done; the multiplication precedes the addition in the source program of (1.1). Second, the compiler must generate a temporary name to hold the value computed by each instruction. Third, some "three-address" instructions have fewer than three operands, e.g., the first and last instructions in (1.3).

In Chapter 8, we cover the principal intermediate representations used in compilers. In general, these representations must do more than compute expressions; they must also handle flow-of-control constructs and procedure calls. Chapters 5 and 8 present algorithms for generating intermediate code for typical programming language constructs.

Code Optimization

The code optimization phase attempts to improve the intermediate code, so that faster-running machine code will result. Some optimizations are trivial. For example, a natural algorithm generates the intermediate code (1.3), using an instruction for each operator in the tree representation after semantic analysis, even though there is a better way to perform the same calculation, using the two instructions

```
temp1 := id3 * 60.0
id1  := id2 + temp1
```
                                                                (1.4)

There is nothing wrong with this simple algorithm, since the problem can be fixed during the code-optimization phase. That is, the compiler can deduce that the conversion of 60 from integer to real representation can be done once and for all at compile time, so the `inttoreal` operation can be eliminated. Besides, `temp3` is used only once, to transmit its value to `id1`. It then becomes safe to substitute `id1` for `temp3`, whereupon the last statement of (1.3) is not needed and the code of (1.4) results.

There is great variation in the amount of code optimization different compilers perform. In those that do the most, called "optimizing compilers," a significant fraction of the time of the compiler is spent on this phase. However, there are simple optimizations that significantly improve the running time of the target program without slowing down compilation too much. Many of these are discussed in Chapter 9, while Chapter 10 gives the technology used by the most powerful optimizing compilers.

Code Generation

The final phase of the compiler is the generation of target code, consisting normally of relocatable machine code or assembly code. Memory locations are selected for each of the variables used by the program. Then, intermediate instructions are each translated into a sequence of machine instructions that perform the same task. A crucial aspect is the assignment of variables to registers.

For example, using registers 1 and 2, the translation of the code of (1.4) might become

```
MOVF id3, R2
MULF #60.0, R2
MOVF id2, R1                                                     (1.5)
ADDF R2, R1
MOVF R1, id1
```

The first and second operands of each instruction specify a source and destination, respectively. The F in each instruction tells us that instructions deal with floating-point numbers. This code moves the contents of the address[1] id3 into register 2, then multiplies it with the real-constant 60.0. The # signifies that 60.0 is to be treated as a constant. The third instruction moves id2 into register 1 and adds to it the value previously computed in register 2. Finally, the value in register 1 is moved into the address of id1, so the code implements the assignment in Fig. 1.10. Chapter 9 covers code generation.

---

[1] We have side-stepped the important issue of storage allocation for the identifiers in the source program. As we shall see in Chapter 7, the organization of storage at run-time depends on the language being compiled. Storage-allocation decisions are made either during intermediate code generation or during code generation.

1.4 COUSINS OF THE COMPILER

As we saw in Fig. 1.3, the input to a compiler may be produced by one or more preprocessors, and further processing of the compiler's output may be needed before running machine code is obtained. In this section, we discuss the context in which a compiler typically operates.

Preprocessors

Preprocessors produce input to compilers. They may perform the following functions:

1. *Macro processing.* A preprocessor may allow a user to define macros that are shorthands for longer constructs.

2. *File inclusion.* A preprocessor may include header files into the program text. For example, the C preprocessor causes the contents of the file `<global.h>` to replace the statement `#include <global.h>` when it processes a file containing this statement.

3. *"Rational" preprocessors.* These processors augment older languages with more modern flow-of-control and data-structuring facilities. For example, such a preprocessor might provide the user with built-in macros for constructs like while-statements or if-statements, where none exist in the programming language itself.

4. *Language extensions.* These processors attempt to add capabilities to the language by what amounts to built-in macros. For example, the language Equel (Stonebraker et al. [1976]) is a database query language embedded in C. Statements beginning with `##` are taken by the preprocessor to be database-access statements, unrelated to C, and are translated into procedure calls on routines that perform the database access.

Macro processors deal with two kinds of statement: macro definition and macro use. Definitions are normally indicated by some unique character or keyword, like `define` or `macro`. They consist of a name for the macro being defined and a *body*, forming its definition. Often, macro processors permit *formal parameters* in their definition, that is, symbols to be replaced by values (a "value" is a string of characters, in this context). The use of a macro consists of naming the macro and supplying *actual parameters*, that is, values for its formal parameters. The macro processor substitutes the actual parameters for the formal parameters in the body of the macro; the transformed body then replaces the macro use itself.

Example 1.2. The TEX typesetting system mentioned in Section 1.2 contains a general macro facility. Macro definitions take the form

$$\text{\textbackslash define } <\text{macro name}> \quad <\text{template}> \quad \{<\text{body}>\}$$

A macro name is any string of letters preceded by a backslash. The template is any string of characters, with strings of the form #1, #2, ... , #9 regarded as formal parameters. These symbols may also appear in the body, any number of times. For example, the following macro defines a citation for the *Journal of the ACM*.

```
\define\JACM #1;#2;#3.
        {{\sl J. ACM} {\bf #1}:#2, pp. #3.}
```

The macro name is \JACM, and the template is "#1;#2;#3."; semicolons separate the parameters and the last parameter is followed by a period. A use of this macro must take the form of the template, except that arbitrary strings may be substituted for the formal parameters.[2] Thus, we may write

```
\JACM 17;4;715-728.
```

and expect to see

J. ACM **17**:4, pp. 715-728.

The portion of the body {\sl J. ACM} calls for an italicized ("slanted") "*J. ACM*". Expression {\bf #1} says that the first actual parameter is to be made boldface; this parameter is intended to be the volume number.

TₑX allows any punctuation or string of text to separate the volume, issue, and page numbers in the definition of the \JACM macro. We could even have used no punctuation at all, in which case TₑX would take each actual parameter to be a single character or a string surrounded by { }   □

Assemblers

Some compilers produce assembly code, as in (1.5), that is passed to an assembler for further processing. Other compilers perform the job of the assembler, producing relocatable machine code that can be passed directly to the loader/link-editor. We assume the reader has some familiarity with what an assembly language looks like and what an assembler does; here we shall review the relationship between assembly and machine code.

Assembly code is a mnemonic version of machine code, in which names are used instead of binary codes for operations, and names are also given to memory addresses. A typical sequence of assembly instructions might be

```
MOV a, R1
ADD #2, R1                                    (1.6)
MOV R1, b
```

This code moves the contents of the address a into register1, then adds the constant 2 to it, treating the contents of register 1 as a fixed-point number,

---

[2] Well, almost arbitrary strings, since a simple left-to-right scan of the macro use is made, and as soon as a symbol matching the text following a #*i* symbol in the template is found, the preceding string is deemed to match #*i*. Thus, if we tried to substitute ab;cd for #1, we would find that only ab matched #1 and cd was matched to #2.

and finally stores the result in the location named by b. Thus, it computes
b := a + 2.

It is customary for assembly languages to have macro facilities that are similar to those in the macro preprocessors discussed above.

Two-Pass Assembly

The simplest form of assembler makes two passes over the input, where a *pass*
consists of reading an input file once. In the first pass, all the identifiers that
denote storage locations are found and stored in a symbol table (separate from
that of the compiler). Identifiers are assigned storage locations as they are
encountered for the first time, so after reading (1.6), for example, the symbol
table might contain the entries shown in Fig. 1.12. In that figure, we have
assumed that a word, consisting of four bytes, is set aside for each identifier,
and that addresses are assigned starting from byte 0.

IDENTIFIER	ADDRESS
a	0
b	4

Fig. 1.12. An assembler's symbol table with identifiers of (1.6).

In the second pass, the assembler scans the input again. This time, it
translates each operation code into the sequence of bits representing that
operation in machine language, and it translates each identifier representing a
location into the address given for that identifier in the symbol table.

The output of the second pass is usually *relocatable* machine code, meaning
that it can be loaded starting at any location L in memory; i.e., if L is added
to all addresses in the code, then all references will be correct. Thus, the output of the assembler must distinguish those portions of instructions that refer
to addresses that can be relocated.

Example 1.3. The following is a hypothetical machine code into which the
assembly instructions (1.6) might be translated.

```
0001 01 00 00000000 *
0011 01 10 00000010              (1.7)
0010 01 00 00000100 *
```

We envision a tiny instruction word, in which the first four bits are the
instruction code, with 0001, 0010, and 0011 standing for load, store, and
add, respectively. By load and store we mean moves from memory into a
register and vice versa. The next two bits designate a register, and 01 refers
to register 1 in each of the three above instructions. The two bits after that
represent a "tag," with 00 standing for the ordinary address mode, where the

last eight bits refer to a memory address. The tag 10 stands for the "immediate" mode, where the last eight bits are taken literally as the operand. This mode appears in the second instruction of (1.7).

We also see in (1.7) a $*$ associated with the first and third instructions. This $*$ represents the *relocation bit* that is associated with each operand in relocatable machine code. Suppose that the address space containing the data is to be loaded starting at location L. The presence of the $*$ means that L must be added to the address of the instruction. Thus, if $L = 00001111$, i.e., 15, then a and b would be at locations 15 and 19, respectively, and the instructions of (1.7) would appear as

```
0001 01 00 00001111
0011 01 10 00000010                                      (1.8)
0010 01 00 00010011
```

in *absolute*, or unrelocatable, machine code. Note that there is no $*$ associated with the second instruction in (1.7), so L has not been added to its address in (1.8), which is exactly right because the bits represents the constant 2, not the location 2.   □

Loaders and Link-Editors

Usually, a program called a *loader* performs the two functions of loading and link-editing. The process of loading consists of taking relocatable machine code, altering the relocatable addresses as discussed in Example 1.3, and placing the altered instructions and data in memory at the proper locations.

The link-editor allows us to make a single program from several files of relocatable machine code. These files may have been the result of several different compilations, and one or more may be library files of routines provided by the system and available to any program that needs them.

If the files are to be used together in a useful way, there may be some *external* references, in which the code of one file refers to a location in another file. This reference may be to a data location defined in one file and used in another, or it may be to the entry point of a procedure that appears in the code for one file and is called from another file. The relocatable machine code file must retain the information in the symbol table for each data location or instruction label that is referred to externally. If we do not know in advance what might be referred to, we in effect must include the entire assembler symbol table as part of the relocatable machine code.

For example, the code of (1.7) would be preceded by

```
a    0
b    4
```

If a file loaded with (1.7) referred to b, then that reference would be replaced by 4 plus the offset by which the data locations in file (1.7) were relocated.

1.5 THE GROUPING OF PHASES

The discussion of phases in Section 1.3 deals with the logical organization of a compiler. In an implementation, activities from more than one phase are often grouped together.

Front and Back Ends

Often, the phases are collected into a *front end* and a *back end*. The front end consists of those phases, or parts of phases, that depend primarily on the source language and are largely independent of the target machine. These normally include lexical and syntactic analysis, the creation of the symbol table, semantic analysis, and the generation of intermediate code. A certain amount of code optimization can be done by the front end as well. The front end also includes the error handling that goes along with each of these phases.

The back end includes those portions of the compiler that depend on the target machine, and generally, these portions do not depend on the source language, just the intermediate language. In the back end, we find aspects of the code optimization phase, and we find code generation, along with the necessary error handling and symbol-table operations.

It has become fairly routine to take the front end of a compiler and redo its associated back end to produce a compiler for the same source language on a different machine. If the back end is designed carefully, it may not even be necessary to redesign too much of the back end; this matter is discussed in Chapter 9. It is also tempting to compile several different languages into the same intermediate language and use a common back end for the different front ends, thereby obtaining several compilers for one machine. However, because of subtle differences in the viewpoints of different languages, there has been only limited success in this direction.

Passes

Several phases of compilation are usually implemented in a single *pass* consisting of reading an input file and writing an output file. In practice, there is great variation in the way the phases of a compiler are grouped into passes, so we prefer to organize our discussion of compiling around phases rather than passes. Chapter 12 discusses some representative compilers and mentions the way they have structured the phases into passes.

As we have mentioned, it is common for several phases to be grouped into one pass, and for the activity of these phases to be interleaved during the pass. For example, lexical analysis, syntax analysis, semantic analysis, and intermediate code generation might be grouped into one pass. If so, the token stream after lexical analysis may be translated directly into intermediate code. In more detail, we may think of the syntax analyzer as being "in charge." It attempts to discover the grammatical structure on the tokens it sees; it obtains tokens as it needs them, by calling the lexical analyzer to find the next token. As the grammatical structure is discovered, the parser calls the intermediate code generator to perform semantic analysis and generate a portion of the code. A compiler organized this way is presented in Chapter 2.

Reducing the Number of Passes

It is desirable to have relatively few passes, since it takes time to read and write intermediate files. On the other hand, if we group several phases into one pass, we may be forced to keep the entire program in memory, because one phase may need information in a different order than a previous phase produces it. The internal form of the program may be considerably larger than either the source program or the target program, so this space may not be a trivial matter.

For some phases, grouping into one pass presents few problems. For example, as we mentioned above, the interface between the lexical and syntactic analyzers can often be limited to a single token. On the other hand, it is often very hard to perform code generation until the intermediate representation has been completely generated. For example, languages like PL/I and Algol 68 permit variables to be used before they are declared. We cannot generate the target code for a construct if we do not know the types of variables involved in that construct. Similarly, most languages allow goto's that jump forward in the code. We cannot determine the target address of such a jump until we have seen the intervening source code and generated target code for it.

In some cases, it is possible to leave a blank slot for missing information, and fill in the slot when the information becomes available. In particular, intermediate and target code generation can often be merged into one pass using a technique called "backpatching." While we cannot explain all the details until we have seen intermediate-code generation in Chapter 8, we can illustrate backpatching in terms of an assembler. Recall that in the previous section we discussed a two-pass assembler, where the first pass discovered all the identifiers that represent memory locations and deduced their addresses as they were discovered. Then a second pass substituted addresses for identifiers.

We can combine the action of the passes as follows. On encountering an assembly statement that is a forward reference, say

```
GOTO target
```

we generate a skeletal instruction, with the machine operation code for GOTO and blanks for the address. All instructions with blanks for the address of target are kept in a list associated with the symbol-table entry for target. The blanks are filled in when we finally encounter an instruction such as

```
target: MOV foobar, R1
```

and determine the value of target; it is the address of the current instruction. We then "backpatch," by going down the list for target of all the instructions that need its address, substituting the address of target for the blanks in the address fields of those instructions. This approach is easy to implement if the instructions can be kept in memory until all target addresses can be determined.

This approach is a reasonable one for an assembler that can keep all its output in memory. Since the intermediate and final representations of code for an assembler are roughly the same, and surely of approximately the same length, backpatching over the length of the entire assembly program is not infeasible. However, in a compiler, with a space-consuming intermediate code, we may need to be careful about the distance over which backpatching occurs.

1.6 COMPILER-CONSTRUCTION TOOLS

The compiler writer, like any programmer, can profitably use software tools such as debuggers, version managers, profilers, and so on. In Chapter 11, we shall see how some of these tools can be used to implement a compiler. In addition to these software-development tools, other more specialized tools have been developed for helping implement various phases of a compiler. We mention them briefly in this section; they are covered in detail in the appropriate chapters.

Shortly after the first compilers were written, systems to help with the compiler-writing process appeared. These systems have often been referred to as *compiler-compilers*, *compiler-generators*, or *translator-writing systems*. Largely, they are oriented around a particular model of languages, and they are most suitable for generating compilers of languages similar to the model.

For example, it is tempting to assume that lexical analyzers for all languages are essentially the same, except for the particular keywords and signs recognized. Many compiler-compilers do in fact produce fixed lexical analysis routines for use in the generated compiler. These routines differ only in the list of keywords recognized, and this list is all that needs to be supplied by the user. The approach is valid, but may be unworkable if it is required to recognize nonstandard tokens, such as identifiers that may include certain characters other than letters and digits.

Some general tools have been created for the automatic design of specific compiler components. These tools use specialized languages for specifying and implementing the component, and many use algorithms that are quite sophisticated. The most successful tools are those that hide the details of the generation algorithm and produce components that can be easily integrated into the remainder of a compiler. The following is a list of some useful compiler-construction tools:

1. *Parser generators.* These produce syntax analyzers, normally from input that is based on a context-free grammar. In early compilers, syntax analysis consumed not only a large fraction of the running time of a compiler, but a large fraction of the intellectual effort of writing a compiler. This phase is now considered one of the easiest to implement. Many of

the "little languages" used to typeset this book, such as PIC (Kernighan [1982]) and EQN, were implemented in a few days using the parser generator described in Section 4.7. Many parser generators utilize powerful parsing algorithms that are too complex to be carried out by hand.

2. *Scanner generators.* These automatically generate lexical analyzers, normally from a specification based on regular expressions, discussed in Chapter 3. The basic organization of the resulting lexical analyzer is in effect a finite automaton. A typical scanner generator and its implementation are discussed in Sections 3.5 and 3.8.

3. *Syntax-directed translation engines.* These produce collections of routines that walk the parse tree, such as Fig. 1.4, generating intermediate code. The basic idea is that one or more "translations" are associated with each node of the parse tree, and each translation is defined in terms of translations at its neighbor nodes in the tree. Such engines are discussed in Chapter 5.

4. *Automatic code generators.* Such a tool takes a collection of rules that define the translation of each operation of the intermediate language into the machine language for the target machine. The rules must include sufficient detail that we can handle the different possible access methods for data; e.g., variables may be in registers, in a fixed (static) location in memory, or may be allocated a position on a stack. The basic technique is "template matching." The intermediate code statements are replaced by "templates" that represent sequences of machine instructions, in such a way that the assumptions about storage of variables match from template to template. Since there are usually many options regarding where variables are to be placed (e.g., in one of several registers or in memory), there are many possible ways to "tile" intermediate code with a given set of templates, and it is necessary to select a good tiling without a combinatorial explosion in running time of the compiler. Tools of this nature are covered in Chapter 9.

5. *Data-flow engines.* Much of the information needed to perform good code optimization involves "data-flow analysis," the gathering of information about how values are transmitted from one part of a program to each other part. Different tasks of this nature can be performed by essentially the same routine, with the user supplying details of the relationship between intermediate code statements and the information being gathered. A tool of this nature is described in Section 10.11.

BIBLIOGRAPHIC NOTES

Writing in 1962 on the history of compiler writing, Knuth [1962] observed that, "In this field there has been an unusual amount of parallel discovery of the same technique by people working independently." He continued by observing that several individuals had in fact discovered "various aspects of a technique, and it has been polished up through the years into a very pretty algorithm, which none of the originators fully realized." Ascribing credit for techniques remains a perilous task; the bibliographic notes in this book are intended merely as an aid for further study of the literature.

Historical notes on the development of programming languages and compilers until the arrival of Fortran may be found in Knuth and Trabb Pardo [1977]. Wexelblat [1981] contains historical recollections about several programming languages by participants in their development.

Some fundamental early papers on compiling have been collected in Rosen [1967] and Pollack [1972]. The January 1961 issue of the *Communications of the ACM* provides a snapshot of the state of compiler writing at the time. A detailed account of an early Algol 60 compiler is given by Randell and Russell [1964].

Beginning in the early 1960's with the study of syntax, theoretical studies have had a profound influence on the development of compiler technology, perhaps, at least as much influence as in any other area of computer science. The fascination with syntax has long since waned, but compiling as a whole continues to be the subject of lively research. The fruits of this research will become evident when we examine compiling in more detail in the following chapters.

CHAPTER 2

A Simple
One-Pass
Compiler

This chapter is an introduction to the material in Chapters 3 through 8 of this book. It presents a number of basic compiling techniques that are illustrated by developing a working C program that translates infix expressions into postfix form. Here, the emphasis is on the front end of a compiler, that is, on lexical analysis, parsing, and intermediate code generation. Chapters 9 and 10 cover code generation and optimization.

2.1 OVERVIEW

A programming language can be defined by describing what its programs look like (the *syntax* of the language) and what its programs mean (the *semantics* of the language). For specifying the syntax of a language, we present a widely used notation, called context-free grammars or BNF (for Backus-Naur Form). With the notations currently available, the semantics of a language is much more difficult to describe than the syntax. Consequently, for specifying the semantics of a language we shall use informal descriptions and suggestive examples.

Besides specifying the syntax of a language, a context-free grammar can be used to help guide the translation of programs. A grammar-oriented compiling technique, known as *syntax-directed translation*, is very helpful for organizing a compiler front end and will be used extensively throughout this chapter.

In the course of discussing syntax-directed translation, we shall construct a compiler that translates infix expressions into postfix form, a notation in which the operators appear after their operands. For example, the postfix form of the expression 9−5+2 is 95−2+. Postfix notation can be converted directly into code for a computer that performs all its computations using a stack. We begin by constructing a simple program to translate expressions consisting of digits separated by plus and minus signs into postfix form. As the basic ideas become clear, we extend the program to handle more general programming language constructs. Each of our translators is formed by systematically extending the previous one.

In our compiler, the *lexical analyzer* converts the stream of input characters into a stream of tokens that becomes the input to the following phase, as shown in Fig. 2.1. The "syntax-directed translator" in the figure is a combination of a syntax analyzer and an intermediate-code generator. One reason for starting with expressions consisting of digits and operators is to make lexical analysis initially very easy; each input character forms a single token. Later, we extend the language to include lexical constructs such as numbers, identifiers, and keywords. For this extended language we shall construct a lexical analyzer that collects consecutive input characters into the appropriate tokens. The construction of lexical analyzers will be discussed in detail in Chapter 3.

Fig. 2.1. Structure of our compiler front end.

2.2 SYNTAX DEFINITION

In this section, we introduce a notation, called a context-free grammar (grammar, for short), for specifying the syntax of a language. It will be used throughout this book as part of the specification of the front end of a compiler.

A grammar naturally describes the hierarchical structure of many programming language constructs. For example, an if-else statement in C has the form

  if (expression) statement **else** statement

That is, the statement is the concatenation of the keyword **if**, an opening parenthesis, an expression, a closing parenthesis, a statement, the keyword **else**, and another statement. (In C, there is no keyword **then**.) Using the variable *expr* to denote an expression and the variable *stmt* to denote a statement, this structuring rule can be expressed as

  stmt → **if** (*expr*) *stmt* **else** *stmt*   (2.1)

in which the arrow may be read as "can have the form." Such a rule is called a *production*. In a production lexical elements like the keyword **if** and the parentheses are called *tokens*. Variables like *expr* and *stmt* represent sequences of tokens and are called *nonterminals*.

A *context-free grammar* has four components:

1. A set of tokens, known as *terminal* symbols.

2. A set of nonterminals.

3. A set of productions where each production consists of a nonterminal, called the *left side* of the production, an arrow, and a sequence of tokens and/or nonterminals, called the *right side* of the production.

4. A designation of one of the nonterminals as the *start* symbol.

We follow the convention of specifying grammars by listing their productions, with the productions for the start symbol listed first. We assume that digits, signs such as <=, and boldface strings such as **while** are terminals. An italicized name is a nonterminal and any nonitalicized name or symbol may be assumed to be a token.[1] For notational convenience, productions with the same nonterminal on the left can have their right sides grouped, with the alternative right sides separated by the symbol |, which we read as "or."

Example 2.1. Several examples in this chapter use expressions consisting of digits and plus and minus signs, e.g., 9-5+2, 3-1, and 7. Since a plus or minus sign must appear between two digits, we refer to such expressions as "lists of digits separated by plus or minus signs." The following grammar describes the syntax of these expressions. The productions are:

$$
\begin{array}{ll}
list \;\rightarrow\; list + digit & \text{(2.2)} \\
list \;\rightarrow\; list - digit & \text{(2.3)} \\
list \;\rightarrow\; digit & \text{(2.4)} \\
digit \;\rightarrow\; 0 \mid 1 \mid 2 \mid 3 \mid 4 \mid 5 \mid 6 \mid 7 \mid 8 \mid 9 & \text{(2.5)}
\end{array}
$$

The right sides of the three productions with nonterminal *list* on the left side can equivalently be grouped:

$$list \;\rightarrow\; list + digit \;\mid\; list - digit \;\mid\; digit$$

According to our conventions, the tokens of the grammar are the symbols

+ - 0 1 2 3 4 5 6 7 8 9

The nonterminals are the italicized names *list* and *digit*, with *list* being the starting nonterminal because its productions are given first.   □

We say a production is *for* a nonterminal if the nonterminal appears on the left side of the production. A string of tokens is a sequence of zero or more tokens. The string containing zero tokens, written as ϵ, is called the *empty* string.

A grammar derives strings by beginning with the start symbol and repeatedly replacing a nonterminal by the right side of a production for that

---

[1] Individual italic letters will be used for additional purposes when grammars are studied in detail in Chapter 4. For example, we shall use X, Y, and Z to talk about a symbol that is either a token or a nonterminal. However, any italicized name containing two or more characters will continue to represent a nonterminal.

nonterminal. The token strings that can be derived from the start symbol form the *language* defined by the grammar.

Example 2.2. The language defined by the grammar of Example 2.1 consists of lists of digits separated by plus and minus signs.

The ten productions for the nonterminal *digit* allow it to stand for any of the tokens 0, 1, . . . , 9. From production (2.4), a single digit by itself is a list. Productions (2.2) and (2.3) express the fact that if we take any list and follow it by a plus or minus sign and then another digit we have a new list.

It turns out that productions (2.2) to (2.5) are all we need to define the language we are interested in. For example, we can deduce that 9−5+2 is a *list* as follows.

a)   9 is a *list* by production (2.4), since 9 is a *digit*.

b)   9−5 is a *list* by production (2.3), since 9 is a *list* and 5 is a *digit*.

c)   9−5+2 is a *list* by production (2.2), since 9−5 is a *list* and 2 is a *digit*.

This reasoning is illustrated by the tree in Fig. 2.2. Each node in the tree is labeled by a grammar symbol. An interior node and its children correspond to a production; the interior node corresponds to the left side of the production, the children to the right side. Such trees are called parse trees and are discussed below.   □

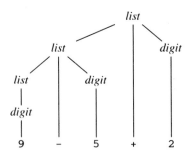

Fig. 2.2. Parse tree for 9−5+2 according to the grammar in Example 2.1.

Example 2.3. A somewhat different sort of list is the sequence of statements separated by semicolons found in Pascal begin-end blocks. One nuance of such lists is that an empty list of statements may be found between the tokens **begin** and **end**. We may start to develop a grammar for begin-end blocks by including the productions:

$$block \rightarrow \textbf{begin } opt\_stmts \textbf{ end}$$
$$opt\_stmts \rightarrow stmt\_list \mid \epsilon$$
$$stmt\_list \rightarrow stmt\_list \textbf{ ; } stmt \mid stmt$$

Note that the second possible right side for *opt_stmts* ("optional statement list") is ϵ, which stands for the empty string of symbols. That is, *opt_stmts* can be replaced by the empty string, so a *block* can consist of the two-token string **begin end**. Notice that the productions for *stmt_list* are analogous to those for *list* in Example 2.1, with semicolon in place of the arithmetic operator and *stmt* in place of *digit*. We have not shown the productions for *stmt*. Shortly, we shall discuss the appropriate productions for the various kinds of statements, such as if-statements, assignment statements, and so on.   □

Parse Trees

A parse tree pictorially shows how the start symbol of a grammar derives a string in the language. If nonterminal A has a production $A \rightarrow XYZ$, then a parse tree may have an interior node labeled A with three children labeled X, Y, and Z, from left to right:

Formally, given a context-free grammar, a *parse tree* is a tree with the following properties:

1.   The root is labeled by the start symbol.

2.   Each leaf is labeled by a token or by ϵ.

3.   Each interior node is labeled by a nonterminal.

4.   If A is the nonterminal labeling some interior node and $X_1, X_2, \ldots, X_n$ are the labels of the children of that node from left to right, then $A \rightarrow X_1 X_2 \cdots X_n$ is a production. Here, $X_1, X_2, \ldots, X_n$ stand for a symbol that is either a terminal or a nonterminal. As a special case, if $A \rightarrow \epsilon$ then a node labeled A may have a single child labeled ϵ.

Example 2.4. In Fig. 2.2, the root is labeled *list*, the start symbol of the grammar in Example 2.1. The children of the root are labeled, from left to right, *list*, +, and *digit*. Note that

> *list* → *list* + *digit*

is a production in the grammar of Example 2.1. The same pattern with – is repeated at the left child of the root, and the three nodes labeled *digit* each have one child that is labeled by a digit.   □

The leaves of a parse tree read from left to right form the *yield* of the tree, which is the string *generated* or *derived* from the nonterminal at the root of the parse tree. In Fig. 2.2, the generated string is 9–5+2. In that figure, all the leaves are shown at the bottom level. Henceforth, we shall not necessarily line up the leaves in this way. Any tree imparts a natural left-to-right order to its leaves, based on the idea that if *a* and *b* are two children with the same parent, and *a* is to the left of *b*, then all descendants of *a* are to the left of descendants of *b*.

Another definition of the language generated by a grammar is as the set of strings that can be generated by some parse tree. The process of finding a parse tree for a given string of tokens is called *parsing* that string.

Ambiguity

We have to be careful in talking about *the* structure of a string according to a grammar. While it is clear that each parse tree derives exactly the string read off its leaves, a grammar can have more than one parse tree generating a given string of tokens. Such a grammar is said to be *ambiguous*. To show that a grammar is ambiguous, all we need to do is find a token string that has more than one parse tree. Since a string with more than one parse tree usually has more than one meaning, for compiling applications we need to design unambiguous grammars, or to use ambiguous grammars with additional rules to resolve the ambiguities.

Example 2.5. Suppose we did not distinguish between digits and lists as in Example 2.1. We could have written the grammar

$$string \rightarrow string + string \mid string - string \mid 0 \mid 1 \mid 2 \mid 3 \mid 4 \mid 5 \mid 6 \mid 7 \mid 8 \mid 9$$

Merging the notion of *digit* and *list* into the nonterminal *string* makes superficial sense, because a single *digit* is a special case of a *list*.

However, Fig. 2.3 shows that an expression like 9-5+2 now has more than one parse tree. The two trees for 9-5+2 correspond to the two ways of parenthesizing the expression: (9-5)+2 and 9-(5+2). This second parenthesization gives the expression the value 2 rather than the customary value 6. The grammar of Example 2.1 did not permit this interpretation.   □

Associativity of Operators

By convention, 9+5+2 is equivalent to (9+5)+2 and 9-5-2 is equivalent to (9-5)-2. When an operand like 5 has operators to its left and right, conventions are needed for deciding which operator takes that operand. We say that the operator + *associates to the left* because an operand with plus signs on both sides of it is taken by the operator to its left. In most programming languages the four arithmetic operators, addition, subtraction, multiplication, and division are left associative.

Some common operators such as exponentiation are right associative. As another example, the assignment operator = in C is right associative; in C, the expression a=b=c is treated in the same way as the expression a=(b=c).

Strings like a=b=c with a right-associative operator are generated by the following grammar:

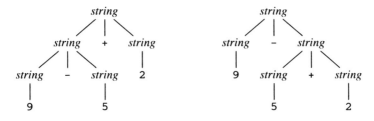

Fig. 2.3. Two parse trees for 9-5+2.

$$right \rightarrow letter = right \mid letter$$
$$letter \rightarrow a \mid b \mid \cdots \mid z$$

The contrast between a parse tree for a left-associative operator like - and a parse tree for a right-associative operator like = is shown by Fig. 2.4. Note that the parse tree for 9-5-2 grows down towards the left, whereas the parse tree for a=b=c grows down towards the right.

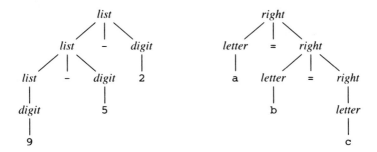

Fig. 2.4. Parse trees for left- and right-associative operators.

Precedence of Operators

Consider the expression 9+5*2. There are two possible interpretations of this expression: (9+5)*2 or 9+(5*2). The associativity of + and * do not resolve this ambiguity. For this reason, we need to know the relative precedence of operators when more than one kind of operator is present.

We say that * has *higher precedence* than + if * takes its operands before + does. In ordinary arithmetic, multiplication and division have higher precedence than addition and subtraction. Therefore, 5 is taken by * in both 9+5*2 and 9*5+2; i.e., the expressions are equivalent to 9+(5*2) and (9*5)+2, respectively.

Syntax of expressions. A grammar for arithmetic expressions can be constructed from a table showing the associativity and precedence of operators. We start with the four common arithmetic operators and a precedence table, showing the operators in order of increasing precedence with operators at the same precedence level on the same line:

> left associative: + –
> left associative: * /

We create two nonterminals *expr* and *term* for the two levels of precedence, and an extra nonterminal *factor* for generating basic units in expressions. The basic units in expressions are presently digits and parenthesized expressions.

> *factor* → **digit** | (*expr*)

Now consider the binary operators, * and /, that have the highest precedence. Since these operators associate to the left, the productions are similar to those for lists that associate to the left.

> *term* → *term* * *factor*
> | *term* / *factor*
> | *factor*

Similarly, *expr* generates lists of terms separated by the additive operators.

> *expr* → *expr* + *term*
> | *expr* – *term*
> | *term*

The resulting grammar is therefore

> *expr* → *expr* + *term* | *expr* – *term* | *term*
> *term* → *term* * *factor* | *term* / *factor* | *factor*
> *factor* → **digit** | (*expr*)

This grammar treats an expression as a list of terms separated by either + or – signs, and a term as a list of factors separated by * or / signs. Notice that any parenthesized expression is a factor, so with parentheses we can develop expressions that have arbitrarily deep nesting (and also arbitrarily deep trees).

Syntax of statements. Keywords allow us to recognize statements in most languages. All Pascal statements begin with a keyword except assignments and procedure calls. Some Pascal statements are defined by the following (ambiguous) grammar in which the token **id** represents an identifier.

> *stmt* → **id** : = *expr*
> | **if** *expr* **then** *stmt*
> | **if** *expr* **then** *stmt* **else** *stmt*
> | **while** *expr* **do** *stmt*
> | **begin** *opt_stmts* **end**

The nonterminal *opt_stmts* generates a possibly empty list of statements separated by semicolons using the productions in Example 2.3.

2.3 SYNTAX-DIRECTED TRANSLATION

To translate a programming language construct, a compiler may need to keep track of many quantities besides the code generated for the construct. For example, the compiler may need to know the type of the construct, or the location of the first instruction in the target code, or the number of instructions generated. We therefore talk abstractly about *attributes* associated with constructs. An attribute may represent any quantity, e.g., a type, a string, a memory location, or whatever.

In this section, we present a formalism called a syntax-directed definition for specifying translations for programming language constructs. A syntax-directed definition specifies the translation of a construct in terms of attributes associated with its syntactic components. In later chapters, syntax-directed definitions are used to specify many of the translations that take place in the front end of a compiler.

We also introduce a more procedural notation, called a translation scheme, for specifying translations. Throughout this chapter, we use translation schemes for translating infix expressions into postfix notation. A more detailed discussion of syntax-directed definitions and their implementation is contained in Chapter 5.

Postfix Notation

The *postfix notation* for an expression E can be defined inductively as follows:

1. If E is a variable or constant, then the postfix notation for E is E itself.

2. If E is an expression of the form E_1 *op* E_2, where *op* is any binary operator, then the postfix notation for E is $E_1'\, E_2'\, op$, where E_1' and E_2' are the postfix notations for E_1 and E_2, respectively.

3. If E is an expression of the form (E_1), then the postfix notation for E_1 is also the postfix notation for E.

No parentheses are needed in postfix notation because the position and arity (number of arguments) of the operators permits only one decoding of a postfix expression. For example, the postfix notation for (9-5)+2 is 95-2+ and the postfix notation for 9-(5+2) is 952+-.

Syntax-Directed Definitions

A *syntax-directed definition* uses a context-free grammar to specify the syntactic structure of the input. With each grammar symbol, it associates a set of attributes, and with each production, a set of *semantic rules* for computing values of the attributes associated with the symbols appearing in that production. The grammar and the set of semantic rules constitute the syntax-directed definition.

A translation is an input-output mapping. The output for each input x is specified in the following manner. First, construct a parse tree for x. Suppose a node n in the parse tree is labeled by the grammar symbol X. We write $X.a$ to denote the value of attribute a of X at that node. The value of $X.a$ at n is computed using the semantic rule for attribute a associated with the X-production used at node n. A parse tree showing the attribute values at each node is called an *annotated* parse tree.

Synthesized Attributes

An attribute is said to be *synthesized* if its value at a parse-tree node is determined from attribute values at the children of the node. Synthesized attributes have the desirable property that they can be evaluated during a single bottom-up traversal of the parse tree. In this chapter, only synthesized attributes are used; "inherited" attributes are considered in Chapter 5.

Example 2.6. A syntax-directed definition for translating expressions consisting of digits separated by plus or minus signs into postfix notation is shown in Fig. 2.5. Associated with each nonterminal is a string-valued attribute t that represents the postfix notation for the expression generated by that nonterminal in a parse tree.

PRODUCTION	SEMANTIC RULE
$expr \rightarrow expr_1 + term$	$expr.t := expr_1.t \parallel term.t \parallel '+'$
$expr \rightarrow expr_1 - term$	$expr.t := expr_1.t \parallel term.t \parallel '-'$
$expr \rightarrow term$	$expr.t := term.t$
$term \rightarrow 0$	$term.t := '0'$
$term \rightarrow 1$	$term.t := '1'$
$\cdots$	$\cdots$
$term \rightarrow 9$	$term.t := '9'$

Fig. 2.5. Syntax-directed definition for infix to postfix translation.

The postfix form of a digit is the digit itself; e.g., the semantic rule associated with the production *term* → 9 defines *term.t* to be 9 whenever this production is used at a node in a parse tree. When the production *expr* → *term* is applied, the value of *term.t* becomes the value of *expr.t*.

The production *expr* → *expr*₁ + *term* derives an expression containing a plus operator (the subscript in *expr*₁ distinguishes the instance of *expr* on the right from that on the left side). The left operand of the plus operator is given by *expr*₁ and the right operand by *term*. The semantic rule

$$expr.t := expr_1.t \parallel term.t \parallel '+'$$

associated with this production defines the value of attribute *expr.t* by concatenating the postfix forms *expr*₁*.t* and *term.t* of the left and right operands, respectively, and then appending the plus sign. The operator $\parallel$ in semantic rules represents string concatenation.

Figure 2.6 contains the annotated parse tree corresponding to the tree of Fig. 2.2. The value of the *t*-attribute at each node has been computed using the semantic rule associated with the production used at that node. The value of the attribute at the root is the postfix notation for the string generated by the parse tree.   □

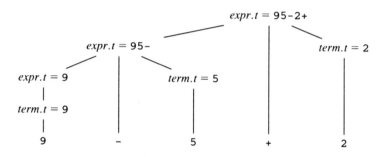

Fig. 2.6. Attribute values at nodes in a parse tree.

Example 2.7. Suppose a robot can be instructed to move one step east, north, west, or south from its current position. A sequence of such instructions is generated by the following grammar:

> *seq* → *seq instr* | **begin**
> *instr* → **east** | **north** | **west** | **south**

Changes in the position of the robot on input

> **begin west south east east east north north**

are shown in Fig. 2.7.

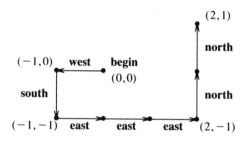

Fig. 2.7. Keeping track of a robot's position.

In the figure, a position is marked by a pair (x,y), where x and y represent the number of steps to the east and north, respectively, from the starting position. (If x is negative, then the robot is to the west of the starting position; similarly, if y is negative, then the robot is to the south of the starting position.)

Let us construct a syntax-directed definition to translate an instruction sequence into a robot position. We shall use two attributes, $seq.x$ and $seq.y$, to keep track of the position resulting from an instruction sequence generated by the nonterminal seq. Initially, seq generates **begin**, and $seq.x$ and $seq.y$ are both initialized to 0, as shown at the leftmost interior node of the parse tree for **begin west south** shown in Fig. 2.8.

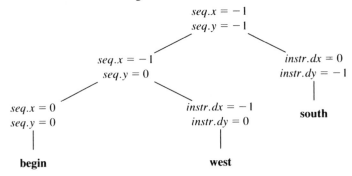

Fig. 2.8. Annotated parse tree for **begin west south**.

The change in position due to an individual instruction derived from *instr* is given by attributes $instr.dx$ and $instr.dy$. For example, if *instr* derives **west**, then $instr.dx = -1$ and $instr.dy = 0$. Suppose a sequence seq is formed by following a sequence seq_1 by a new instruction *instr*. The new position of the robot is then given by the rules

$$seq.x := seq_1.x + instr.dx$$
$$seq.y := seq_1.y + instr.dy$$

A syntax-directed definition for translating an instruction sequence into a robot position is shown in Fig. 2.9.   □

Depth-First Traversals

A syntax-directed definition does not impose any specific order for the evaluation of attributes on a parse tree; any evaluation order that computes an attribute a after all the other attributes that a depends on is acceptable. In general, we may have to evaluate some attributes when a node is first reached during a walk of the parse tree, others after all its children have been visited, or at some point in between visits to the children of the node. Suitable evaluation orders are discussed in more detail in Chapter 5.

The translations in this chapter can all be implemented by evaluating the semantic rules for the attributes in a parse tree in a predetermined order. A *traversal* of a tree starts at the root and visits each node of the tree in some

PRODUCTION	SEMANTIC RULES
$seq \rightarrow$ **begin**	$seq.x := 0$ $seq.y := 0$
$seq \rightarrow seq_1$ $instr$	$seq.x := seq_1.x + instr.dx$ $seq.y := seq_1.y + instr.dy$
$instr \rightarrow$ **east**	$instr.dx := 1$ $instr.dy := 0$
$instr \rightarrow$ **north**	$instr.dx := 0$ $instr.dy := 1$
$instr \rightarrow$ **west**	$instr.dx := -1$ $instr.dy := 0$
$instr \rightarrow$ **south**	$instr.dx := 0$ $instr.dy := -1$

Fig. 2.9. Syntax-directed definition of the robot's position.

order. In this chapter, semantic rules will be evaluated using the depth-first traversal defined in Fig. 2.10. It starts at the root and recursively visits the children of each node in left-to-right order, as shown in Fig. 2.11. The semantic rules at a given node are evaluated once all descendants of that node have been visited. It is called "depth-first" because it visits an unvisited child of a node whenever it can, so it tries to visit nodes as far away from the root as quickly as it can.

```
procedure visit(n: node);
begin
        for each child m of n, from left to right do
            visit(m);
        evaluate semantic rules at node n
end
```

Fig. 2.10. A depth-first traversal of a tree.

Translation Schemes

In the remainder of this chapter, we use a procedural specification for defining a translation. A *translation scheme* is a context-free grammar in which program fragments called *semantic actions* are embedded within the right sides of productions. A translation scheme is like a syntax-directed definition, except that the order of evaluation of the semantic rules is explicitly shown. The

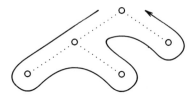

Fig. 2.11. Example of a depth-first traversal of a tree.

position at which an action is to be executed is shown by enclosing it between braces and writing it within the right side of a production, as in

$$rest \rightarrow + \; term \; \{ \, print('+') \, \} \; rest_1$$

A translation scheme generates an output for each sentence x generated by the underlying grammar by executing the actions in the order they appear during a depth-first traversal of a parse tree for x. For example, consider a parse tree with a node labeled *rest* representing this production. The action $\{ \, print('+') \, \}$ will be performed after the subtree for *term* is traversed but before the child for $rest_1$ is visited.

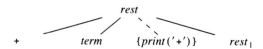

Fig. 2.12. An extra leaf is constructed for a semantic action.

When drawing a parse tree for a translation scheme, we indicate an action by constructing for it an extra child, connected by a dashed line to the node for its production. For example, the portion of the parse tree for the above production and action is drawn as in Fig. 2.12. The node for a semantic action has no children, so the action is performed when that node is first seen.

Emitting a Translation

In this chapter, the semantic actions in translations schemes will write the output of a translation into a file, a string or character at a time. For example, we translate 9−5+2 into 95−2+ by printing each character in 9−5+2 exactly once, without using any storage for the translation of subexpressions. When the output is created incrementally in this fashion, the order in which the characters are printed is important.

Notice that the syntax-directed definitions mentioned so far have the following important property: the string representing the translation of the nonterminal on the left side of each production is the concatenation of the translations of the nonterminals on the right, in the same order as in the production, with some additional strings (perhaps none) interleaved. A syntax-directed definition with this property is termed *simple*. For example, consider the first production and semantic rule from the syntax-directed definition of Fig. 2.5:

$$\text{PRODUCTION} \qquad\qquad \text{SEMANTIC RULE}$$
$$expr \rightarrow expr_1 + term \qquad expr.t := expr_1.t \parallel term.t \parallel '+' \qquad (2.6)$$

Here the translation *expr.t* is the concatenation of the translations of *expr₁* and *term*, followed by the symbol +. Notice that *expr₁* appears before *term* on the right side of the production.

An additional string appears between *term.t* and *rest₁.t* in

$$\text{PRODUCTION} \qquad\qquad \text{SEMANTIC RULE}$$
$$rest \rightarrow + term \; rest_1 \qquad rest.t := term.t \parallel '+' \parallel rest_1.t \qquad (2.7)$$

but, again, the nonterminal *term* appears before *rest₁* on the right side.

Simple syntax-directed definitions can be implemented with translation schemes in which actions print the additional strings in the order they appear in the definition. The actions in the following productions print the additional strings in (2.6) and (2.7), respectively:

$$expr \rightarrow expr_1 + term \; \{ \; print('+') \; \}$$
$$rest \rightarrow + term \; \{ \; print('+') \; \} \; rest_1$$

Example 2.8. Figure 2.5 contained a simple definition for translating expressions into postfix form. A translation scheme derived from this definition is given in Fig. 2.13 and a parse tree with actions for 9−5+2 is shown in Fig. 2.14. Note that although Figures 2.6 and 2.14 represent the same input-output mapping, the translation in the two cases is constructed differently; Fig. 2.6 attaches the output to the root of the parse tree, while Fig. 2.14 prints the output incrementally.

$$
\begin{aligned}
expr &\rightarrow expr + term &\{ \; print('+') \; \} \\
expr &\rightarrow expr - term &\{ \; print('-') \; \} \\
expr &\rightarrow term & \\
term &\rightarrow 0 &\{ \; print('0') \; \} \\
term &\rightarrow 1 &\{ \; print('1') \; \} \\
&\quad\cdots & \\
term &\rightarrow 9 &\{ \; print('9') \; \}
\end{aligned}
$$

Fig. 2.13. Actions translating expressions into postfix notation.

The root of Fig. 2.14 represents the first production in Fig. 2.13. In a depth-first traversal, we first perform all the actions in the subtree for the left operand *expr* when we traverse the leftmost subtree of the root. We then visit the leaf + at which there is no action. We next perform the actions in the

subtree for the right operand *term* and, finally, the semantic action
{ *print*('+') } at the extra node.

Since the productions for *term* have only a digit on the right side, that digit
is printed by the actions for the productions. No output is necessary for the
production *expr* → *term*, and only the operator needs to be printed in the
action for the first two productions. When executed during a depth-first
traversal of the parse tree, the actions in Fig. 2.14 print 95-2+.   □

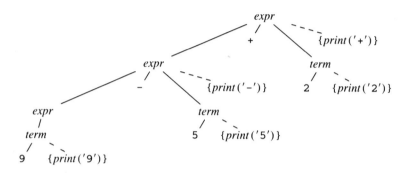

Fig. 2.14. Actions translating 9-5+2 into 95-2+.

As a general rule, most parsing methods process their input from left to
right in a "greedy" fashion; that is, they construct as much of a parse tree as
possible before reading the next input token. In a simple translation scheme
(one derived from a simple syntax-directed definition), actions are also done
in a left-to-right order. Therefore, to implement a simple translation scheme
we can execute the semantic actions while we parse; it is not necessary to construct the parse tree at all.

2.4 PARSING

Parsing is the process of determining if a string of tokens can be generated by
a grammar. In discussing this problem, it is helpful to think of a parse tree
being constructed, even though a compiler may not actually construct such a
tree. However, a parser must be capable of constructing the tree, or else the
translation cannot be guaranteed correct.

This section introduces a parsing method that can be applied to construct
syntax-directed translators. A complete C program, implementing the translation scheme of Fig. 2.13, appears in the next section. A viable alternative is
to use a software tool to generate a translator directly from a translation
scheme. See Section 4.9 for the description of such a tool; it can implement
the translation scheme of Fig. 2.13 without modification.

A parser can be constructed for any grammar. Grammars used in practice,
however, have a special form. For any context-free grammar there is a parser
that takes at most $O(n^3)$ time to parse a string of *n* tokens. But cubic time is

too expensive. Given a programming language, we can generally construct a grammar that can be parsed quickly. Linear algorithms suffice to parse essentially all languages that arise in practice. Programming language parsers almost always make a single left-to-right scan over the input, looking ahead one token at a time.

Most parsing methods fall into one of two classes, called the *top-down* and *bottom-up* methods. These terms refer to the order in which nodes in the parse tree are constructed. In the former, construction starts at the root and proceeds towards the leaves, while, in the latter, construction starts at the leaves and proceeds towards the root. The popularity of top-down parsers is due to the fact that efficient parsers can be constructed more easily by hand using top-down methods. Bottom-up parsing, however, can handle a larger class of grammars and translation schemes, so software tools for generating parsers directly from grammars have tended to use bottom-up methods.

Top-Down Parsing

We introduce top-down parsing by considering a grammar that is well-suited for this class of methods. Later in this section, we consider the construction of top-down parsers in general. The following grammar generates a subset of the types of Pascal. We use the token **dotdot** for "`..`" to emphasize that the character sequence is treated as a unit.

$$
\begin{aligned}
type \;\to\; &simple \\
\mid\; &\uparrow \textbf{ id} \\
\mid\; &\textbf{array } [\; simple \;] \textbf{ of } type \\
simple \;\to\; &\textbf{integer} \\
\mid\; &\textbf{char} \\
\mid\; &\textbf{num dotdot num}
\end{aligned}
\tag{2.8}
$$

The top-down construction of a parse tree is done by starting with the root, labeled with the starting nonterminal, and repeatedly performing the following two steps (see Fig. 2.15 for an example).

1. At node n, labeled with nonterminal A, select one of the productions for A and construct children at n for the symbols on the right side of the production.

2. Find the next node at which a subtree is to be constructed.

For some grammars, the above steps can be implemented during a single left-to-right scan of the input string. The current token being scanned in the input is frequently referred to as the *lookahead* symbol. Initially, the lookahead symbol is the first, i.e., leftmost, token of the input string. Figure 2.16 illustrates the parsing of the string

array [num dotdot num] of integer

Initially, the token **array** is the lookahead symbol and the known part of the

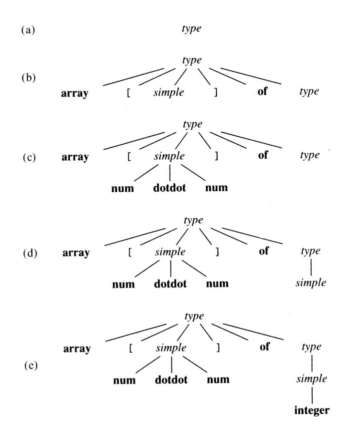

Fig. 2.15. Steps in the top-down construction of a parse tree.

parse tree consists of the root, labeled with the starting nonterminal *type* in Fig. 2.16(a). The objective is to construct the remainder of the parse tree in such a way that the string generated by the parse tree matches the input string.

For a match to occur, nonterminal *type* in Fig. 2.16(a) must derive a string that starts with the lookahead symbol **array**. In grammar (2.8), there is just one production for *type* that can derive such a string, so we select it, and construct the children of the root labeled with the symbols on the right side of the production.

Each of the three snapshots in Fig. 2.16 has arrows marking the lookahead symbol in the input and the node in the parse tree that is being considered. When children are constructed at a node, we next consider the leftmost child. In Fig. 2.16(b), children have just been constructed at the root, and the leftmost child labeled with **array** is being considered.

When the node being considered in the parse tree is for a terminal and the

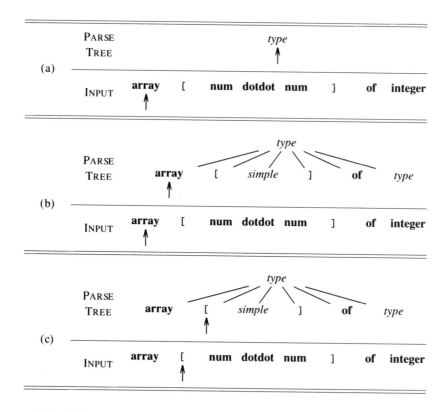

Fig. 2.16. Top-down parsing while scanning the input from left to right.

terminal matches the lookahead symbol, then we advance in both the parse tree and the input. The next token in the input becomes the new lookahead symbol and the next child in the parse tree is considered. In Fig. 2.16(c), the arrow in the parse tree has advanced to the next child of the root and the arrow in the input has advanced to the next token [. After the next advance, the arrow in the parse tree will point to the child labeled with nonterminal *simple*. When a node labeled with a nonterminal is considered, we repeat the process of selecting a production for the nonterminal.

In general, the selection of a production for a nonterminal may involve trial-and-error; that is, we may have to try a production and backtrack to try another production if the first is found to be unsuitable. A production is unsuitable if, after using the production, we cannot complete the tree to match the input string. There is an important special case, however, called predictive parsing, in which backtracking does not occur.

Predictive Parsing

Recursive-descent parsing is a top-down method of syntax analysis in which we execute a set of recursive procedures to process the input. A procedure is associated with each nonterminal of a grammar. Here, we consider a special form of recursive-descent parsing, called predictive parsing, in which the look-ahead symbol unambiguously determines the procedure selected for each non-terminal. The sequence of procedures called in processing the input implicitly defines a parse tree for the input.

```
procedure match (t : token);
begin
    if lookahead = t then
        lookahead := nexttoken
    else error
end;

procedure type ;
begin
    if lookahead is in { integer, char, num } then
        simple
    else if lookahead = '↑' then begin
        match ('↑'); match (id)
    end
    else if lookahead = array then begin
        match (array); match ('['); simple ; match (']'); match (of); type
    end
    else error
end;

procedure simple ;
begin
    if lookahead = integer then
        match (integer)
    else if lookahead = char then
        match (char)
    else if lookahead = num then begin
        match (num); match (dotdot); match (num)
    end
    else error
end;
```

Fig. 2.17. Pseudo-code for a predictive parser.

The predictive parser in Fig. 2.17 consists of procedures for the nontermi-nals *type* and *simple* of grammar (2.8) and an additional procedure *match*. We use *match* to simplify the code for *type* and *simple*; it advances to the next input token if its argument *t* matches the lookahead symbol. Thus *match* changes the variable *lookahead*, which is the currently scanned input token.

Parsing begins with a call of the procedure for the starting nonterminal *type* in our grammar. With the same input as in Fig. 2.16, *lookahead* is initially the first token **array**. Procedure *type* executes the code

$$match(\textbf{array}); \; match('\,['); \; simple\,; \; match('\,]'); \; match(\textbf{of}); \; type \qquad (2.9)$$

corresponding to the right side of the production

> *type* → **array** [*simple*] **of** *type*

Note that each terminal in the right side is matched with the lookahead symbol and that each nonterminal in the right side leads to a call of its procedure.

With the input of Fig. 2.16, after the tokens **array** and [are matched, the lookahead symbol is **num**. At this point procedure *simple* is called and the code

$$match(\textbf{num}); \; match(\textbf{dotdot}); \; match(\textbf{num})$$

in its body is executed.

The lookahead symbol guides the selection of the production to be used. If the right side of a production starts with a token, then the production can be used when the lookahead symbol matches the token. Now consider a right side starting with a nonterminal, as in

> *type* → *simple* $\qquad\qquad\qquad\qquad\qquad\qquad$ (2.10)

This production is used if the lookahead symbol can be generated from *simple*. For example, during the execution of the code fragment (2.9), suppose the lookahead symbol is **integer** when control reaches the procedure call *type*. There is no production for *type* that starts with token **integer**. However, a production for *simple* does, so production (2.10) is used by having *type* call procedure *simple* on lookahead **integer**.

Predictive parsing relies on information about what first symbols can be generated by the right side of a production. More precisely, let α be the right side of a production for nonterminal A. We define FIRST(α) to be the set of tokens that appear as the first symbols of one or more strings generated from α. If α is ϵ or can generate ϵ, then ϵ is also in FIRST(α).[2] For example,

$$\text{FIRST}(simple) = \{ \textbf{ integer, char, num } \}$$
$$\text{FIRST}(\uparrow \textbf{id}) = \{ \uparrow \}$$
$$\text{FIRST}(\textbf{array} \; [\; simple \;] \; \textbf{of} \; type) = \{ \textbf{ array } \}$$

In practice, many production right sides start with tokens, simplifying the

---

[2] Productions with ϵ on the right side complicate the determination of the first symbols generated by a nonterminal. For example, if nonterminal B can derive the empty string and there is a production $A \rightarrow BC$, then the first symbol generated by C can also be the first symbol generated by A. If C can also generate ϵ, then both FIRST(A) and FIRST(BC) contain ϵ.

construction of FIRST sets. An algorithm for computing FIRST's is given in Section 4.4.

The FIRST sets must be considered if there are two productions $A \rightarrow \alpha$ and $A \rightarrow \beta$. Recursive-descent parsing without backtracking requires FIRST(α) and FIRST(β) to be disjoint. The lookahead symbol can then be used to decide which production to use; if the lookahead symbol is in FIRST(α), then α is used. Otherwise, if the lookahead symbol is in FIRST(β), then β is used.

When to Use ϵ-Productions

Productions with ϵ on the right side require special treatment. The recursive-descent parser will use an ϵ-production as a default when no other production can be used. For example, consider:

$$stmt \rightarrow \textbf{begin} \; opt\_stmts \; \textbf{end}$$
$$opt\_stmts \rightarrow stmt\_list \mid \epsilon$$

While parsing opt_stmts, if the lookahead symbol is not in FIRST($stmt\_list$), then the ϵ-production is used. This choice is exactly right if the lookahead symbol is **end**. Any lookahead symbol other than **end** will result in an error, detected during the parsing of $stmt$.

Designing a Predictive Parser

A *predictive parser* is a program consisting of a procedure for every nonterminal. Each procedure does two things.

1. It decides which production to use by looking at the lookahead symbol. The production with right side α is used if the lookahead symbol is in FIRST(α). If there is a conflict between two right sides for any lookahead symbol, then we cannot use this parsing method on this grammar. A production with ϵ on the right side is used if the lookahead symbol is not in the FIRST set for any other right hand side.

2. The procedure uses a production by mimicking the right side. A nonterminal results in a call to the procedure for the nonterminal, and a token matching the lookahead symbol results in the next input token being read. If at some point the token in the production does not match the lookahead symbol, an error is declared. Figure 2.17 is the result of applying these rules to grammar (2.8).

Just as a translation scheme is formed by extending a grammar, a syntax-directed translator can be formed by extending a predictive parser. An algorithm for this purpose is given in Section 5.5. The following limited construction suffices for the present because the translation schemes implemented in this chapter do not associate attributes with nonterminals:

1. Construct a predictive parser, ignoring the actions in productions.

2. Copy the actions from the translation scheme into the parser. If an action
    appears after grammar symbol X in production p, then it is copied after
    the code implementing X. Otherwise, if it appears at the beginning of the
    production, then it is copied just before the code implementing the pro-
    duction.

We shall construct such a translator in the next section.

Left Recursion

It is possible for a recursive-descent parser to loop forever. A problem arises
with left-recursive productions like

$$expr \rightarrow expr + term$$

in which the leftmost symbol on the right side is the same as the nonterminal
on the left side of the production. Suppose the procedure for *expr* decides to
apply this production. The right side begins with *expr* so the procedure for
expr is called recursively, and the parser loops forever. Note that the lookahead symbol changes only when a terminal in the right side is matched.
Since the production begins with the nonterminal *expr*, no changes to the input
take place between recursive calls, causing the infinite loop.

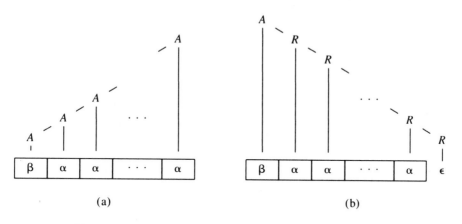

Fig. 2.18. Left- and right-recursive ways of generating a string.

A left-recursive production can be eliminated by rewriting the offending
production. Consider a nonterminal A with two productions

$$A \rightarrow A\alpha \mid \beta$$

where α and β are sequences of terminals and nonterminals that do not start
with A. For example, in

$$expr \rightarrow expr + term \mid term$$

$A = expr$, $\alpha = +\ term$, and $\beta = term$.

The nonterminal A is *left recursive* because the production $A \rightarrow A\alpha$ has A itself as the leftmost symbol on the right side. Repeated application of this production builds up a sequence of α's to the right of A, as in Fig. 2.18(a). When A is finally replaced by β, we have a β followed by a sequence of zero or more α's.

The same effect can be achieved, as in Fig. 2.18(b), by rewriting the productions for A in the following manner.

$$A \rightarrow \beta R$$
$$R \rightarrow \alpha R \mid \epsilon \qquad (2.11)$$

Here R is a new nonterminal. The production $R \rightarrow \alpha R$ is *right recursive* because this production for R has R itself as the last symbol on the right side. Right-recursive productions lead to trees that grow down towards the right, as in Fig. 2.18(b). Trees growing down to the right make it harder to translate expressions containing left-associative operators, such as minus. In the next section, however, we shall see that the proper translation of expressions into postfix notation can still be attained by a careful design of the translation scheme based on a right-recursive grammar.

In Chapter 4, we consider more general forms of left recursion and show how all left recursion can be eliminated from a grammar.

2.5 A TRANSLATOR FOR SIMPLE EXPRESSIONS

Using the techniques of the last three sections, we now construct a syntax-directed translator, in the form of a working C program, that translates arithmetic expressions into postfix form. To keep the initial program manageably small, we start off with expressions consisting of digits separated by plus and minus signs. The language is extended in the next two sections to include numbers, identifiers, and other operators. Since expressions appear as a construct in so many languages, it is worth studying their translation in detail.

$$
\begin{array}{lll}
expr & \rightarrow & expr\ +\ term \qquad \{\ print('+')\ \} \\
expr & \rightarrow & expr\ -\ term \qquad \{\ print('-')\ \} \\
expr & \rightarrow & term \\
term & \rightarrow & 0 \qquad\qquad\qquad \{\ print('0')\ \} \\
term & \rightarrow & 1 \qquad\qquad\qquad \{\ print('1')\ \} \\
& \cdots & \\
term & \rightarrow & 9 \qquad\qquad\qquad \{\ print('9')\ \}
\end{array}
$$

Fig. 2.19. Initial specification of infix-to-postfix translator.

A syntax-directed translation scheme can often serve as the specification for a translator. We use the scheme in Fig. 2.19 (repeated from Fig. 2.13) as the definition of the translation to be performed. As is often the case, the under-lying grammar of a given scheme has to be modified before it can be parsed with a predictive parser. In particular, the grammar underlying the scheme in Fig. 2.19 is left-recursive, and as we saw in the last section, a predictive parser cannot handle a left-recursive grammar. By eliminating the left-recursion, we can obtain a grammar suitable for use in a predictive recursive-descent translator.

Abstract and Concrete Syntax

A useful starting point for thinking about the translation of an input string is an *abstract syntax tree* in which each node represents an operator and the chil-dren of the node represent the operands. By contrast, a parse tree is called a *concrete syntax tree*, and the underlying grammar is called a *concrete syntax* for the language. Abstract syntax trees, or simply *syntax trees*, differ from parse trees because superficial distinctions of form, unimportant for transla-tion, do not appear in syntax trees.

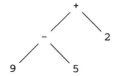

Fig. 2.20. Syntax tree for 9–5+2.

For example, the syntax tree for 9–5+2 is shown in Fig. 2.20. Since + and – have the same precedence level, and operators at the same precedence level are evaluated left to right, the tree shows 9–5 grouped as a subexpression. Comparing Fig. 2.20 with the corresponding parse tree of Fig. 2.2, we note that the syntax tree associates an operator with an interior node, rather than making the operator be one of the children.

It is desirable for a translation scheme to be based on a grammar whose parse trees are as close to syntax trees as possible. The grouping of subex-pressions by the grammar in Fig. 2.19 is similar to their grouping in syntax trees. Unfortunately, the grammar of Fig. 2.19 is left-recursive, and hence not suitable for predictive parsing. It appears there is a conflict; on the one hand we need a grammar that facilitates parsing, on the other hand we need a radically different grammar for easy translation. The obvious solution is to eliminate the left-recursion. However, this must be done carefully as the fol-lowing example shows.

Example 2.9. The following grammar is unsuitable for translating expressions into postfix form, even though it generates exactly the same language as the grammar in Fig. 2.19 and can be used for recursive-descent parsing.

$$expr \rightarrow term\ rest$$
$$rest \rightarrow +\ expr \quad | \quad -\ expr \quad | \quad \epsilon$$
$$term \rightarrow 0 \mid 1 \mid \cdots \mid 9$$

This grammar has the problem that the operands of the operators generated by $rest \rightarrow +\ expr$ and $rest \rightarrow -\ expr$ are not obvious from the productions. Neither of the following choices for forming the translation $rest.t$ from that of $expr.t$ is acceptable:

$$rest \rightarrow -\ expr \quad \{\ rest.t := \ '-' \parallel expr.t \ \} \tag{2.12}$$
$$rest \rightarrow -\ expr \quad \{\ rest.t := \ expr.t \parallel '-' \ \} \tag{2.13}$$

(We have only shown the production and semantic action for the minus operator.) The translation of 9−5 is 95−. However, if we use the action in (2.12), then the minus sign appears before $expr.t$ and 9−5 incorrectly remains 9−5 in translation.

On the other hand, if we use (2.13) and the analogous rule for plus, the operators consistently move to the right end and 9−5+2 is translated incorrectly into 952+− (the correct translation is 95−2+).   □

Adapting the Translation Scheme

The left-recursion elimination technique sketched in Fig. 2.18 can also be applied to productions containing semantic actions. We extend the transformation in Section 5.5 to take synthesized attributes into account. The technique transforms the productions $A \rightarrow A\alpha \mid A\beta \mid \gamma$ into

$$A \rightarrow \gamma R$$
$$R \rightarrow \alpha R \mid \beta R \mid \epsilon$$

When semantic actions are embedded in the productions, we carry them along in the transformation. Here, if we let $A = expr$, $\alpha = +\ term\ \{\ print('+')\ \}$, $\beta = -\ term\ \{\ print('-')\ \}$, and $\gamma = term$, the transformation above produces the translation scheme (2.14). The $expr$ productions in Fig. 2.19 have been transformed into the productions for $expr$ and the new nonterminal $rest$ in (2.14). The productions for $term$ are repeated from Fig. 2.19. Notice that the underlying grammar is different from the one in Example 2.9 and the difference makes the desired translation possible.

$$expr \rightarrow term\ rest$$
$$rest \rightarrow +\ term\ \{\ print('+')\ \}\ rest \mid -\ term\ \{\ print('-')\ \}\ rest \mid \epsilon$$
$$term \rightarrow 0\ \{\ print('0')\ \}$$
$$term \rightarrow 1\ \{\ print('1')\ \} \tag{2.14}$$
$$\cdots$$
$$term \rightarrow 9\ \{\ print('9')\ \}$$

Figure 2.21 shows how 9−5+2 is translated using the above grammar.

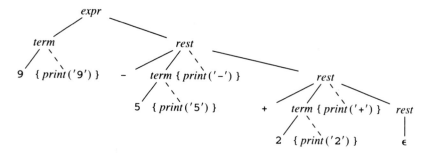

Fig. 2.21. Translation of 9-5+2 into 95-2+.

Procedures for the Nonterminals *expr,* *term,* **and** *rest*

We now implement a translator in C using the syntax-directed translation scheme (2.14). The essence of the translator is the C code in Fig. 2.22 for the functions `expr`, `term`, and `rest`. These functions implement the corresponding nonterminals in (2.14).

```
expr( )
{
     term( ); rest( );
}

rest( )
{
     if (lookahead == '+') {
          match('+'); term( ); putchar('+'); rest( );
     }
     else if (lookahead == '-') {
          match('-'); term( ); putchar('-'); rest( );
     }
     else ;
}

term( )
{
     if (isdigit(lookahead)) {
          putchar(lookahead); match(lookahead);
     }
     else error( );
}
```

Fig. 2.22. Functions for the nonterminals *expr, rest,* and *term.*

The function `match`, presented later, is the C counterpart of the code in

Fig. 2.17 to match a token with the lookahead symbol and advance through the input. Since each token is a single character in our language, match can be implemented by comparing and reading characters.

For those unfamiliar with the programming language C, we mention the salient differences between C and other Algol derivatives such as Pascal, as we find uses for those features of C. A program in C consists of a sequence of function definitions, with execution starting at a distinguished function called main. Function definitions cannot be nested. Parentheses enclosing function parameter lists are needed even if there are no parameters; hence we write expr( ), term( ), and rest( ). Functions communicate either by passing parameters "by value" or by accessing data global to all functions. For example, the functions term( ) and rest( ) examine the lookahead symbol using the global identifier lookahead.

C and Pascal use the following symbols for assignments and equality tests:

OPERATION	C	PASCAL
assignment	=	: =
equality test	==	=
inequality test	! =	<>

The functions for the nonterminals mimic the right sides of productions. For example, the production *expr → term rest* is implemented by the calls term( ) and rest( ) in the function expr( ).

As another example, function rest( ) uses the first production for *rest* in (2.14) if the lookahead symbol is a plus sign, the second production if the lookahead symbol is a minus sign, and the production *rest → ε* by default. The first production for *rest* is implemented by the first if-statement in Fig. 2.22. If the lookahead symbol is +, the plus sign is matched by the call match('+'). After the call term( ), the C standard library routine putchar('+') implements the semantic action by printing a plus character. Since the third production for *rest* has ε as its right side, the last else in rest( ) does nothing.

The ten productions for *term* generate the ten digits. In Fig. 2.22, the routine isdigit tests if the lookahead symbol is a digit. The digit is printed and matched if the test succeeds; otherwise, an error occurs. (Note that match changes the lookahead symbol, so the printing must occur before the digit is matched.) Before showing a complete program, we shall make one speed-improving transformation to the code in Fig. 2.22.

Optimizing the Translator

Certain recursive calls can be replaced by iterations. When the last statement executed in a procedure body is a recursive call of the same procedure, the call is said to be *tail recursive*. For example, the calls of rest( ) at the end of the fourth and seventh lines of the function rest( ) are tail recursive because control flows to the end of the function body after each of these calls.

We can speed up a program by replacing tail recursion by iteration. For a procedure without parameters, a tail-recursive call can be simply replaced by a jump to the beginning of the procedure. The code for rest can be rewritten as:

```
rest()
{
L:    if (lookahead == '+') {
          match('+'); term(); putchar('+'); goto L;
      }
      else if (lookahead == '-') {
          match('-'); term(); putchar('-'); goto L;
      }
      else ;
}
```

As long as the lookahead symbol is a plus or minus sign, procedure rest matches the sign, calls term to match a digit, and repeats the process. Note that since match removes the sign each time it is called, this cycle occurs only on alternating sequences of signs and digits. If this change is made in Fig. 2.22, the only remaining call of rest is from expr (see line 3). The two functions can therefore be integrated into one, as shown in Fig. 2.23. In C, a statement *stmt* can be repeatedly executed by writing

```
while(1) stmt
```

because the condition 1 is always true. We can exit from a loop by executing a break-statement. The stylized form of the code in Fig. 2.23 allows other operators to be added conveniently.

```
expr()
{
    term();
    while(1)
        if (lookahead == '+') {
            match('+'); term(); putchar('+');
        }
        else if (lookahead == '-') {
            match('-'); term(); putchar('-');
        }
        else break;
}
```

Fig. 2.23. Replacement for functions expr and rest of Fig. 2.22.

The Complete Program

The complete C program for our translator is shown in Fig. 2.24. The first line, beginning with #include, loads <ctype.h>, a file of standard routines that contains the code for the predicate isdigit.

Tokens, consisting of single characters, are supplied by the standard library routine getchar that reads the next character from the input file. However, lookahead is declared to be an integer on line 2 of Fig. 2.24 to anticipate the additional tokens that are not single characters that will be introduced in later sections. Since lookahead is declared outside any of the functions, it is global to any functions that are defined after line 2 of Fig. 2.24.

The function match checks tokens; it reads the next input token if the lookahead symbol is matched and calls the error routine otherwise.

The function error uses the standard library function printf to print the message "syntax error" and then terminates execution by the call exit(1) to another standard library function.

2.6 LEXICAL ANALYSIS

We shall now add to the translator of the previous section a lexical analyzer that reads and converts the input into a stream of tokens to be analyzed by the parser. Recall from the definition of a grammar in Section 2.2 that the sentences of a language consist of strings of tokens. A sequence of input characters that comprises a single token is called a lexeme. A lexical analyzer can insulate a parser from the lexeme representation of tokens. We begin by listing some of the functions we might want a lexical analyzer to perform.

Removal of White Space and Comments

The expression translator in the last section sees every character in the input, so extraneous characters, such as blanks, will cause it to fail. Many languages allow "white space" (blanks, tabs, and newlines) to appear between tokens. Comments can likewise be ignored by the parser and translator, so they may also be treated as white space.

If white space is eliminated by the lexical analyzer, the parser will never have to consider it. The alternative of modifying the grammar to incorporate white space into the syntax is not nearly as easy to implement.

Constants

Anytime a single digit appears in an expression, it seems reasonable to allow an arbitrary integer constant in its place. Since an integer constant is a sequence of digits, integer constants can be allowed either by adding productions to the grammar for expressions, or by creating a token for such constants. The job of collecting digits into integers is generally given to a lexical analyzer because numbers can be treated as single units during translation.

Let **num** be the token representing an integer. When a sequence of digits *postfix.c* (handwritten)

 # include <stdio.h> (handwritten)

```
#include <ctype.h> /* loads file with predicate isdigit */
int lookahead;
```
next token (handwritten)

```
main()
{
    lookahead = getchar();
    expr();
    putchar('\n'); /* adds trailing newline character */
}

expr()
{
    term();
    while(1)
        if (lookahead == '+') {
            match('+'); term(); putchar('+');
        }
        else if (lookahead == '-') {
            match('-'); term(); putchar('-');
        }
        else break;
}

term()
{
    if (isdigit(lookahead)) {
        putchar(lookahead);
        match(lookahead);
    }
    else error();
}

match(t)
    int t;
{
    if (lookahead == t)
        lookahead = getchar();
    else error();
}

error()
{
    printf("syntax error\n"); /* print error message */
    exit(1);        /* then halt */
}
```

(handwritten annotations)
eliminate recursion
expr ( )
term ( ); rest ( );
rest ( )
... ; rest ( )
R → ε
T → 0
match simply gets the next token could be eliminated

Fig. 2.24. C program to translate an infix expression into postfix form.

appears in the input stream, the lexical analyzer will pass **num** to the parser. The value of the integer will be passed along as an attribute of the token **num**. Logically, the lexical analyzer passes both the token and the attribute to the parser. If we write a token and its attribute as a tuple enclosed between $<>$, the input

    31 + 28 + 59

is transformed into the sequence of tuples

   $<$**num**, 31$>$ $<$+, $>$ $<$**num**, 28$>$ $<$+, $>$ $<$**num**, 59$>$

The token + has no attribute. The second components of the tuples, the attributes, play no role during parsing, but are needed during translation.

Recognizing Identifiers and Keywords

Languages use identifiers as names of variables, arrays, functions, and the like. A grammar for a language often treats an identifier as a token. A parser based on such a grammar wants to see the same token, say **id**, each time an identifier appears in the input. For example, the input

    count = count + increment;   (2.15)

would be converted by the lexical analyzer into the token stream

    id = **id** + **id** ;   (2.16)

This token stream is used for parsing.

When talking about the lexical analysis of the input line (2.15), it is useful to distinguish between the token **id** and the lexemes count and increment associated with instances of this token. The translator needs to know that the lexeme count forms the first two instances of **id** in (2.16) and that the lexeme increment forms the third instance of **id**.

When a lexeme forming an identifier is seen in the input, some mechanism is needed to determine if the lexeme has been seen before. As mentioned in Chapter 1, a symbol table is used as such a mechanism. The lexeme is stored in the symbol table and a pointer to this symbol-table entry becomes an attribute of the token **id**.

Many languages use fixed character strings such as begin, end, if, and so on, as punctuation marks or to identify certain constructs. These character strings, called *keywords*, generally satisfy the rules for forming identifiers, so a mechanism is needed for deciding when a lexeme forms a keyword and when it forms an identifier. The problem is easier to resolve if keywords are *reserved*, i.e., if they cannot be used as identifiers. Then a character string forms an identifier only if it is not a keyword.

The problem of isolating tokens also arises if the same characters appear in the lexemes of more than one token, as in <, <=, and <> in Pascal. Techniques for recognizing such tokens efficiently are discussed in Chapter 3.

Interface to the Lexical Analyzer

When a lexical analyzer is inserted between the parser and the input stream, it interacts with the two in the manner shown in Fig. 2.25. It reads characters from the input, groups them into lexemes, and passes the tokens formed by the lexemes, together with their attribute values, to the later stages of the compiler. In some situations, the lexical analyzer has to read some characters ahead before it can decide on the token to be returned to the parser. For example, a lexical analyzer for Pascal must read ahead after it sees the character >. If the next character is =, then the character sequence >= is the lexeme forming the token for the "greater than or equal to" operator. Otherwise > is the lexeme forming the "greater than" operator, and the lexical analyzer has read one character too many. The extra character has to be pushed back onto the input, because it can be the beginning of the next lexeme in the input.

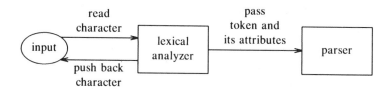

Fig. 2.25. Inserting a lexical analyzer between the input and the parser.

The lexical analyzer and parser form a *producer-consumer* pair. The lexical analyzer produces tokens and the parser consumes them. Produced tokens can be held in a token buffer until they are consumed. The interaction between the two is constrained only by the size of the buffer, because the lexical analyzer cannot proceed when the buffer is full and the parser cannot proceed when the buffer is empty. Commonly, the buffer holds just one token. In this case, the interaction can be implemented simply by making the lexical analyzer be a procedure called by the parser, returning tokens on demand.

The implementation of reading and pushing back characters is usually done by setting up an input buffer. A block of characters is read into the buffer at a time; a pointer keeps track of the portion of the input that has been analyzed. Pushing back a character is implemented by moving back the pointer. Input characters may also need to be saved for error reporting, since some indication has to be given of where in the input text the error occurred. The buffering of input characters can be justified on efficiency grounds alone. Fetching a block of characters is usually more efficient than fetching one character at a time. Techniques for input buffering are discussed in Section 3.2.

A Lexical Analyzer

We now construct a rudimentary lexical analyzer for the expression translator of Section 2.5. The purpose of the lexical analyzer is to allow white space and numbers to appear within expressions. In the next section, we extend the lexical analyzer to allow identifiers as well.

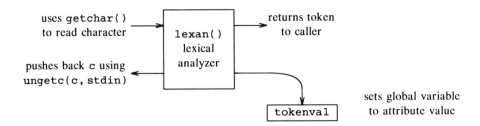

Fig. 2.26. Implementing the interactions in Fig. 2.25.

Figure 2.26 suggests how the lexical analyzer, written as the function lexan in C, implements the interactions in Fig. 2.25. The routines getchar and ungetc from the standard include-file <stdio.h> take care of input buffering; lexan reads and pushes back input characters by calling the routines getchar and ungetc, respectively. With c declared to be a character, the pair of statements

```
c = getchar(); ungetc(c, stdin);
```

leaves the input stream undisturbed. The call of getchar assigns the next input character to c; the call of ungetc pushes back the value of c onto the standard input stdin.

If the implementation language does not allow data structures to be returned from functions, then tokens and their attributes have to be passed separately. The function lexan returns an integer encoding of a token. The token for a character can be any conventional integer encoding of that character. A token, such as **num**, can then be encoded by an integer larger than any integer encoding a character, say 256. To allow the encoding to be changed easily, we use a symbolic constant NUM to refer to the integer encoding of **num**. In Pascal, the association between NUM and the encoding can be done by a **const** declaration; in C, NUM can be made to stand for 256 using a define-statement:

```
#define NUM 256
```

The function lexan returns NUM when a sequence of digits is seen in the input. A global variable tokenval is set to the value of the sequence of digits. Thus, if a 7 is followed immediately by a 6 in the input, tokenval is assigned the integer value 76.

Allowing numbers within expressions requires a change in the grammar in Fig. 2.19. We replace the individual digits by the nonterminal *factor* and introduce the following productions and semantic actions:

> *factor* → (*expr*)
> | **num** { *print*(**num**.*value*) }

The C code for *factor* in Fig. 2.27 is a direct implementation of the productions above. When lookahead equals NUM, the value of attribute **num**.*value* is given by the global variable tokenval. The action of printing this value is done by the standard library function printf. The first argument of printf is a string between double quotes specifying the format to be used for printing the remaining arguments. Where %d appears in the string, the decimal representation of the next argument is printed. Thus, the printf statement in Fig. 2.27 prints a blank followed by the decimal representation of tokenval followed by another blank.

```
factor()
{
    if (lookahead == '(') {
        match('('); expr(); match(')');
    }
    else if (lookahead == NUM) {
        printf(" %d ", tokenval); match(NUM);
    }
    else error();
}
```

Fig. 2.27. C code for *factor* when operands can be numbers.

The implementation of function lexan is shown in Fig. 2.28. Every time the body of the while statement on lines 8-28 is executed, a character is read into t on line 9. If the character is a blank or a tab (written '\t'), then no token is returned to the parser; we merely go around the while loop again. If the character is a newline (written '\n'), then a global variable lineno is incremented, thereby keeping track of line numbers in the input, but again no token is returned. Supplying a line number with an error message helps pinpoint errors.

The code for reading a sequence of digits is on lines 14-23. The predicate isdigit(t) from the include-file <ctype.h> is used on lines 14 and 17 to determine if an incoming character t is a digit. If it is, then its integer value is given by the expression t-'0' in both ASCII and EBCDIC. With other character sets, the conversion may need to be done differently. In Section 2.9, we incorporate this lexical analyzer into our expression translator.

```
(1)  #include <stdio.h>
(2)  #include <ctype.h>
(3)  int   lineno = 1;
(4)  int   tokenval = NONE;

(5)  int   lexan()
(6)  {
(7)        int t;
(8)        while(1) {
(9)              t = getchar();
(10)             if (t == ' ' || t == '\t')
(11)                   ;     /* strip out blanks and tabs */
(12)             else if (t == '\n')
(13)                   lineno = lineno + 1;
(14)             else if (isdigit(t)) {
(15)                   tokenval = t - '0';
(16)                   t = getchar();
(17)                   while (isdigit(t)) {
(18)                         tokenval = tokenval*10 + t-'0';
(19)                         t = getchar();
(20)                   }
(21)                   ungetc(t, stdin);
(22)                   return NUM;
(23)             }
(24)             else {
(25)                   tokenval = NONE;
(26)                   return t;
(27)             }
(28)       }
(29)  }
```

Fig. 2.28. C code for lexical analyzer eliminating white space and collecting numbers.

2.7 INCORPORATING A SYMBOL TABLE

A data structure called a symbol table is generally used to store information about various source language constructs. The information is collected by the analysis phases of the compiler and used by the synthesis phases to generate the target code. For example, during lexical analysis, the character string, or lexeme, forming an identifier is saved in a symbol-table entry. Later phases of the compiler might add to this entry information such as the type of the identifier, its usage (e.g., procedure, variable, or label), and its position in storage. The code generation phase would then use the information to generate the proper code to store and access this variable. In Section 7.6, we discuss the implementation and use of symbol tables in detail. In this section, we illustrate how the lexical analyzer of the previous section might interact with a symbol table.

The Symbol-Table Interface

The symbol-table routines are concerned primarily with saving and retrieving lexemes. When a lexeme is saved, we also save the token associated with the lexeme. The following operations will be performed on the symbol table.

> insert(s,t): Returns index of new entry for string s, token t.
>   lookup(s): Returns index of the entry for string s,
>   or 0 if s is not found.

The lexical analyzer uses the lookup operation to determine whether there is an entry for a lexeme in the symbol table. If no entry exists, then it uses the insert operation to create one. We shall discuss an implementation in which the lexical analyzer and parser both know about the format of symbol-table entries.

Handling Reserved Keywords

The symbol-table routines above can handle any collection of reserved keywords. For example, consider tokens **div** and **mod** with lexemes div and mod, respectively. We can initialize the symbol table using the calls

> insert("div", **div**);
> insert("mod", **mod**);

Any subsequent call lookup("div") returns the token **div**, so div cannot be used as an identifier.

Any collection of reserved keywords can be handled in this way by appropriately initializing the symbol table.

A Symbol-Table Implementation

The data structure for a particular implementation of a symbol table is sketched in Fig. 2.29. We do not wish to set aside a fixed amount of space to hold lexemes forming identifiers; a fixed amount of space may not be large enough to hold a very long identifier and may be wastefully large for a short identifier, such as i. In Fig. 2.29, a separate array lexemes holds the character string forming an identifier. The string is terminated by an end-of-string character, denoted by EOS, that may not appear in identifiers. Each entry in the symbol-table array symtable is a record consisting of two fields, lexptr, pointing to the beginning of a lexeme, and token. Additional fields can hold attribute values, although we shall not do so here.

In Fig. 2.29, the 0th entry is left empty, because lookup returns 0 to indicate that there is no entry for a string. The 1st and 2nd entries are for the keywords div and mod. The 3rd and 4th entries are for identifiers count and i.

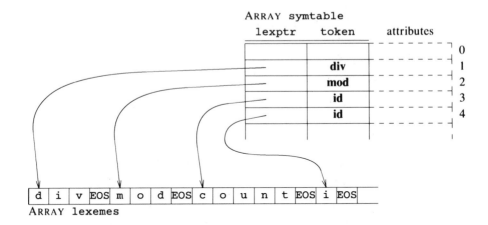

Fig. 2.29. Symbol table and array for storing strings.

Pseudo-code for a lexical analyzer that handles identifiers is shown in Fig. 2.30; a C implementation appears in Section 2.9. White space and integer constants are handled by the lexical analyzer in the same manner as in Fig. 2.28 in the last section.

When our present lexical analyzer reads a letter, it starts saving letters and digits in a buffer `lexbuf`. The string collected in `lexbuf` is then looked up in the symbol table, using the `lookup` operation. Since the symbol table is initialized with entries for the keywords `div` and `mod`, as shown in Fig. 2.29, the lookup operation will find these entries if `lexbuf` contains either `div` or `mod`. If there is no entry for the string in `lexbuf`, i.e., `lookup` returns 0, then `lexbuf` contains a lexeme for a new identifier. An entry for the new identifier is created using `insert`. After the insertion is made, `p` is the index of the symbol-table entry for the string in `lexbuf`. This index is communicated to the parser by setting `tokenval` to `p`, and the token in the `token` field of the entry is returned.

The default action is to return the integer encoding of the character as a token. Since the single character tokens here have no attributes, `tokenval` is set to NONE.

2.8 ABSTRACT STACK MACHINES

The front end of a compiler constructs an intermediate representation of the source program from which the back end generates the target program. One popular form of intermediate representation is code for an abstract stack machine. As mentioned in Chapter 1, partitioning a compiler into a front end and a back end makes it easier to modify a compiler to run on a new machine.

In this section, we present an abstract stack machine and show how code

```
function lexan: integer;
var    lexbuf :   array [0..100] of char;
       c :        char;
begin
    loop begin
        read a character into c;
        if c is a blank or a tab then
            do nothing
        else if c is a newline then
            lineno := lineno + 1
        else if c is a digit then begin
            set tokenval to the value of this and following digits;
            return NUM
        end
        else if c is a letter then begin
            place c and successive letters and digits into lexbuf;
            p := lookup (lexbuf );
            if p = 0 then
                p := insert (lexbuf, ID);
            tokenval := p;
            return the token field of table entry p
        end
        else begin    /* token is a single character */
            set tokenval to NONE;       /* there is no attribute */
            return integer encoding of character c
        end
    end
end
```

Fig. 2.30. Pseudo-code for a lexical analyzer.

can be generated for it. The machine has separate instruction and data memories and all arithmetic operations are performed on values on a stack. The instructions are quite limited and fall into three classes: integer arithmetic, stack manipulation, and control flow. Figure 2.31 illustrates the machine. The pointer *pc* indicates the instruction we are about to execute. The meanings of the instructions shown will be discussed shortly.

Arithmetic Instructions

The abstract machine must implement each operator in the intermediate language. A basic operation, such as addition or subtraction, is supported directly by the abstract machine. A more complex operation, however, may need to be implemented as a sequence of abstract machine instructions. We simplify the description of the machine by assuming that there is an

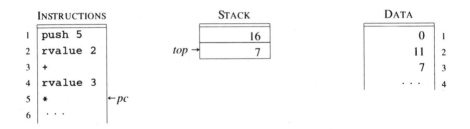

Fig. 2.31. Snapshot of the stack machine after the first four instructions are executed.

instruction for each arithmetic operator.

The abstract machine code for an arithmetic expression simulates the evaluation of a postfix representation for that expression using a stack. The evaluation proceeds by processing the postfix representation from left to right, pushing each operand onto the stack as it is encountered. When a k-ary operator is encountered, its leftmost argument is $k-1$ positions below the top of the stack and its rightmost argument is at the top. The evaluation applies the operator to the top k values on the stack, pops the operands, and pushes the result onto the stack. For example, in the evaluation of the postfix expression 1 3 + 5 *, the following actions are performed:

1.   Stack 1.
2.   Stack 3.
3.   Add the two topmost elements, pop them, and stack the result 4.
4.   Stack 5.
5.   Multiply the two topmost elements, pop them, and stack the result 20.

The value on top of the stack at the end (here 20) is the value of the entire expression.

In the intermediate language, all values will be integers, with 0 corresponding to `false` and nonzero integers corresponding to `true`. The boolean operators and and or require both their arguments to be evaluated.

L-values and R-values

There is a distinction between the meaning of identifiers on the left and right sides of an assignment. In each of the assignments

```
i := 5;
i := i + 1;
```

the right side specifies an integer value, while the left side specifies where the value is to be stored. Similarly, if p and q are pointers to characters, and

```
p↑ := q↑;
```

the right side q↑ specifies a character, while p↑ specifies where the character is to be stored. The terms *l-value* and *r-value* refer to values that are appropriate on the left and right sides of an assignment, respectively. That is, *r*-values are what we usually think of as "values," while *l*-values are locations.

Stack Manipulation

Besides the obvious instruction for pushing an integer constant onto the stack and popping a value from the top of the stack, there are instructions to access data memory:

push *v*	push *v* onto the stack
rvalue *l*	push contents of data location *l*
lvalue *l*	push address of data location *l*
pop	throw away value on top of the stack
:=	the *r*-value on top is placed in the *l*-value below it and both are popped
copy	push a copy of the top value on the stack

Translation of Expressions

Code to evaluate an expression on a stack machine is closely related to postfix notation for that expression. By definition, the postfix form of expression $E + F$ is the concatenation of the postfix form of E, the postfix form of F, and $+$. Similarly, stack-machine code to evaluate $E + F$ is the concatenation of the code to evaluate E, the code to evaluate F, and the instruction to add their values. The translation of expressions into stack-machine code can therefore be done by adapting the translators in Sections 2.6 and 2.7.

Here we generate stack code for expressions in which data locations are addressed symbolically. (The allocation of data locations for identifiers is discussed in Chapter 7.) The expression a+b translates into:

```
rvalue a
rvalue b
+
```

In words: push the contents of the data locations for a and b onto the stack; then pop the top two values on the stack, add them, and push the result onto the stack.

The translation of assignments into stack-machine code is done as follows: the *l*-value of the identifier assigned to is pushed onto the stack, the expression is evaluated, and its *r*-value is assigned to the identifier. For example, the assignment

```
day := (1461*y) div 4 + (153*m + 2) div 5 + d        (2.17)
```

translates into the code in Fig. 2.32.

```
lvalue day        push 2
push 1461         +
rvalue y          push 5
*                 div
push 4            +
div               rvalue d
push 153          +
rvalue m          :=
*
```

Fig. 2.32. Translation of day := (1461*y) div 4 + (153*m + 2) div 5 + d.

These remarks can be expressed formally as follows. Each nonterminal has an attribute *t* giving its translation. Attribute *lexeme* of **id** gives the string representation of the identifier.

> *stmt* → **id** := *expr*
>   { *stmt.t* := 'lvalue' ‖ **id**.*lexeme* ‖ *expr.t* ‖ ':=' }

Control Flow

The stack machine executes instructions in numerical sequence unless told to do otherwise by a conditional or unconditional jump statement. Several options exist for specifying the targets of jumps:

1.   The instruction operand gives the target location.

2.   The instruction operand specifies the relative distance, positive or negative, to be jumped.

3.   The target is specified symbolically; i.e., the machine supports labels.

With the first two options there is the additional possibility of taking the operand from the top of the stack.

We choose the third option for the abstract machine because it is easier to generate such jumps. Moreover, symbolic addresses need not be changed if, after we generate code for the abstract machine, we make certain improvements in the code that result in the insertion or deletion of instructions.

The control-flow instructions for the stack machine are:

label *l*	target of jumps to *l*; has no other effect
goto *l*	next instruction is taken from statement with label *l*
gofalse *l*	pop the top value; jump if it is zero
gotrue *l*	pop the top value; jump if it is nonzero
halt	stop execution

Translation of Statements

The layout in Fig. 2.33 sketches the abstract-machine code for conditional and while statements. The following discussion concentrates on creating labels.

Consider the code layout for if-statements in Fig. 2.33. There can only be one `label out` instruction in the translation of a source program; otherwise, there will be confusion about where control flows to from a `goto out` statement. We therefore need some mechanism for consistently replacing `out` in the code layout by a unique label every time an if-statement is translated.

Suppose *newlabel* is a procedure that returns a fresh label every time it is called. In the following semantic action, the label returned by a call of *newlabel* is recorded using a local variable *out*:

$$stmt \rightarrow \textbf{if } expr \textbf{ then } stmt_1 \qquad \{ \quad out := newlabel; $$
$$stmt.t := expr.t \parallel$$
$$'\texttt{gofalse}' \; out \parallel \qquad (2.18)$$
$$stmt_1.t \parallel$$
$$'\texttt{label}' \; out \}$$

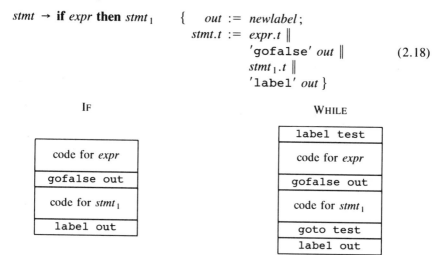

Fig. 2.33. Code layout for conditional and while statements.

Emitting a Translation

The expression translators in Section 2.5 used print statements to incrementally generate the translation of an expression. Similar print statements can be used to emit the translation of statements. Instead of print statements, we use a procedure *emit* to hide printing details. For example, *emit* can worry about whether each abstract-machine instruction needs to be on a separate line. Using the procedure *emit*, we can write the following instead of (2.18):

$$stmt \rightarrow \textbf{if}$$
$$expr \qquad \{ \; out := newlabel; \; emit('\texttt{gofalse}', \; out); \}$$
$$\textbf{then}$$
$$stmt_1 \qquad \{ \; emit('\texttt{label}', \; out); \}$$

When semantic actions appear within a production, we consider the elements on the right side of the production in a left-to-right order. For the above production, the order of actions is as follows: actions during the parsing of *expr* are done, *out* is set to the label returned by *newlabel* and the `gofalse` instruction is emitted, actions during the parsing of *stmt*₁ are done, and, finally, the `label` instruction is emitted. Assuming the actions during the parsing of *expr* and *stmt*₁ emit the code for these nonterminals, the above production implements the code layout of Fig. 2.33.

```
procedure stmt;
var test, out: integer;   /* for labels */
begin
      if lookahead = id then begin
            emit('lvalue', tokenval); match(id); match(':='); expr
      end
      else if lookahead = 'if' then begin
            match('if');
            expr;
            out := newlabel;
            emit('gofalse', out);
            match('then');
            stmt;
            emit('label', out)
      end
            /* code for remaining statements goes here */
      else error;
end
```

Fig. 2.34. Pseudo-code for translating statements.

Pseudo-code for translating assignment and conditional statements is shown in Fig. 2.34. Since variable *out* is local to procedure *stmt*, its value is not affected by the calls to procedures *expr* and *stmt*. The generation of labels requires some thought. Suppose that the labels in the translation are of the form L1, L2, ... The pseudo-code manipulates such labels using the integer following L. Thus, *out* is declared to be an integer, *newlabel* returns an integer that becomes the value of *out*, and *emit* must be written to print a label given an integer.

The code layout for while statements in Fig. 2.33 can be converted into code in a similar fashion. The translation of a sequence of statements is simply the concatenation of the statements in the sequence, and is left to the reader.

The translation of most single-entry single-exit constructs is similar to that of while statements. We illustrate by considering control flow in expressions.

Example 2.10. The lexical analyzer in Section 2.7 contains a conditional of the form:

> **if** t = **blank or** t = **tab then**   · · ·

If t is a blank, then clearly it is not necessary to test if t is a tab, because the first equality implies that the condition is true. The expression

> $expr_1$ **or** $expr_2$

can therefore be implemented as

> **if** $expr_1$ **then true else** $expr_2$

The reader can verify that the following code implements the **or** operator:

```
code for expr₁
copy                /* copy value of expr₁ */
gotrue   out
pop                 /* pop value of expr₁ */
code for expr₂
label    out
```

Recall that the `gotrue` and `gofalse` instructions pop the value on top of the stack to simplify code generation for conditional and while statements. By copying the value of $expr_1$ we ensure that the value on top of the stack is true if the `gotrue` instruction leads to a jump.   □

2.9 PUTTING THE TECHNIQUES TOGETHER

In this chapter, we have presented a number of syntax-directed techniques for constructing a compiler front end. To summarize these techniques, in this section we put together a C program that functions as an infix-to-postfix translator for a language consisting of sequences of expressions terminated by semicolons. The expressions consist of numbers, identifiers, and the operators +, -, *, /, div, and mod. The output of the translator is a postfix representation for each expression. The translator is an extension of the programs developed in Sections 2.5-2.7. A listing of the complete C program is given at the end of this section.

Description of the Translator

The translator is designed using the syntax-directed translation scheme in Fig. 2.35. The token **id** represents a nonempty sequence of letters and digits beginning with a letter, **num** a sequence of digits, and **eof** an end-of-file character. Tokens are separated by sequences of blanks, tabs, and newlines ("white space"). The attribute *lexeme* of the token **id** gives the character string forming the token; the attribute *value* of the token **num** gives the integer represented by the **num**.

The code for the translator is arranged into seven modules, each stored in a separate file. Execution begins in the module `main.c` that consists of a call

$$
\begin{aligned}
start \;&\rightarrow\; list \;\textbf{eof} \\
list \;&\rightarrow\; expr \;\; ; \;\; list \\
&\mid\; \epsilon \\
expr \;&\rightarrow\; expr \;+\; term && \{\; print('+') \;\} \\
&\mid\; expr \;-\; term && \{\; print('-') \;\} \\
&\mid\; term \\
term \;&\rightarrow\; term \;*\; factor && \{\; print('*') \;\} \\
&\mid\; term \;/\; factor && \{\; print('/') \;\} \\
&\mid\; term \;\textbf{div}\; factor && \{\; print('DIV') \;\} \\
&\mid\; term \;\textbf{mod}\; factor && \{\; print('MOD') \;\} \\
&\mid\; factor \\
factor \;&\rightarrow\; (\; expr \;) \\
&\mid\; \textbf{id} && \{\; print(\textbf{id}.lexeme) \;\} \\
&\mid\; \textbf{num} && \{\; print(\textbf{num}.value) \;\}
\end{aligned}
$$

Fig. 2.35. Specification for infix-to-postfix translator.

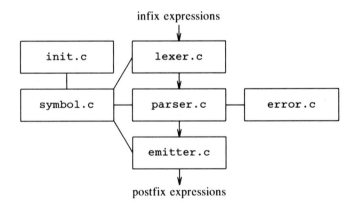

Fig. 2.36. Modules of infix-to-postfix translator.

to init( ) for initialization followed by a call to parse( ) for the translation. The remaining six modules are shown in Fig. 2.36. There is also a global header file global.h that contains definitions common to more than one module; the first statement in every module

```
#include "global.h"
```

causes this header file to be included as part of the module. Before showing the code for the translator, we briefly describe each module and how it was constructed.

The Lexical Analysis Module `lexer.c`

The lexical analyzer is a routine called `lexan()` that is called by the parser to find tokens. Implemented from the pseudo-code in Fig. 2.30, the routine reads the input one character at a time and returns to the parser the token it found. The value of the attribute associated with the token is assigned to a global variable `tokenval`.

The following tokens are expected by the parser:

  + - * / DIV MOD ( ) ID NUM DONE

Here ID represents an identifier, NUM a number, and DONE the end-of-file character. White space is silently stripped out by the lexical analyzer. The table in Fig. 2.37 shows the token and attribute value produced by the lexical analyzer for each source language lexeme.

LEXEME	TOKEN	ATTRIBUTE VALUE
white space		
sequence of digits	NUM	numeric value of sequence
div............................	DIV	
mod...........................	MOD	
other sequences of a letter		
then letters and digits	ID	index into `symtable`
end-of-file character	DONE	
any other character	that character	NONE

Fig. 2.37. Description of tokens.

The lexical analyzer uses the symbol-table routine `lookup` to determine whether an identifier lexeme has been previously seen and the routine `insert` to store a new lexeme into the symbol table. It also increments a global variable `lineno` every time it sees a newline character.

The Parser Module `parser.c`

The parser is constructed using the techniques of Section 2.5. We first eliminate left-recursion from the translation scheme of Fig. 2.35 so that the underlying grammar can be parsed with a recursive-descent parser. The transformed scheme is shown in Fig. 2.38.

We then construct functions for the nonterminals *expr*, *term*, and *factor* as we did in Fig. 2.24. The function `parse()` implements the start symbol of the grammar; it calls `lexan` whenever it needs a new token. The parser uses the function `emit` to generate the output and the function `error` to report a syntax error.

$$
\begin{aligned}
start &\rightarrow list \ \textbf{eof} \\
list &\rightarrow expr \ ; \ list \\
&\mid \ \epsilon \\
expr &\rightarrow term \ moreterms \\
moreterms &\rightarrow + \ term \ \{ \ print('+') \ \} \ moreterms \\
&\mid \ - \ term \ \{ \ print('-') \ \} \ moreterms \\
&\mid \ \epsilon \\
term &\rightarrow factor \ morefactors \\
morefactors &\rightarrow * \ factor \ \{ \ print('*') \ \} \ morefactors \\
&\mid \ / \ factor \ \{ \ print('/') \ \} \ morefactors \\
&\mid \ \textbf{div} \ factor \ \{ \ print('\text{DIV}') \ \} \ morefactors \\
&\mid \ \textbf{mod} \ factor \ \{ \ print('\text{MOD}') \ \} \ morefactors \\
&\mid \ \epsilon \\
factor &\rightarrow (\ expr \ ) \\
&\mid \ \textbf{id} \ \{ \ print(\textbf{id}.lexeme) \ \} \\
&\mid \ \textbf{num} \ \{ \ print(\textbf{num}.value) \ \}
\end{aligned}
$$

Fig. 2.38. Syntax-directed translation scheme after eliminating left-recursion.

The Emitter Module `emitter.c`

The emitter module consists of a single function `emit(t, tval)` that generates the output for token `t` with attribute value `tval`.

The Symbol-Table Modules `symbol.c` and `init.c`

The symbol-table module `symbol.c` implements the data structure shown in Fig. 2.29 of Section 2.7. The entries in the array `symtable` are pairs consisting of a pointer to the `lexemes` array and an integer denoting the token stored there. The operation `insert(s,t)` returns the `symtable` index for the lexeme `s` forming the token `t`. The function `lookup(s)` returns the index of the entry in `symtable` for the lexeme `s` or 0 if `s` is not there.

The module `init.c` is used to preload `symtable` with keywords. The lexeme and token representations for all the keywords are stored in the array `keywords`, which has the same type as the `symtable` array. The function `init()` goes sequentially through the `keyword` array, using the function `insert` to put the keywords in the symbol table. This arrangement allows us to change the representation of the tokens for keywords in a convenient way.

The Error Module `error.c`

The error module manages the error reporting, which is extremely primitive. On encountering a syntax error, the compiler prints a message saying that an error has occurred on the current input line and then halts. A better error recovery technique might skip to the next semicolon and continue parsing; the reader is encouraged to make this modification to the translator. More sophisticated error recovery techniques are presented in Chapter 4.

Creating the Compiler

The code for the modules appears in seven files: `lexer.c`, `parser.c`, `emitter.c`, `symbol.c`, `init.c`, `error.c`, and `main.c`. The file `main.c` contains the main routine in the C program that calls `init()`, then `parse()`, and upon successful completion `exit(0)`.

Under the UNIX operating system, the compiler can be created by executing the command

```
cc lexer.c parser.c emitter.c symbol.c init.c error.c main.c
```

or by separately compiling the files, using

```
cc -c filename.c
```

and linking the resulting *filename*.o files:

```
cc lexer.o parser.o emitter.o symbol.o init.o error.o main.o
```

The `cc` command creates a file `a.out` that contains the translator. The translator can then be exercised by typing `a.out` followed by the expressions to be translated; e.g.,

```
2+3*5;
12 div 5 mod 2;
```

or whatever other expressions you like. Try it.

The Listing

Here is a listing of the C program implementing the translator. Shown is the global header file `global.h`, followed by the seven source files. For clarity, the program has been written in an elementary C style.

```
/****    global.h    *********************************************/

#include <stdio.h>      /* load i/o routines */
#include <ctype.h>      /* load character test routines */

#define BSIZE   128     /* buffer size */
#define NONE    -1
#define EOS     '\0'

#define NUM     256
#define DIV     257
#define MOD     258
#define ID      259
#define DONE    260

int tokenval;       /*  value of token attribute  */
```

```
int lineno;

struct entry {      /*  form of symbol table entry  */
    char *lexptr;
    int  token;
};

struct entry symtable[];   /*  symbol table  */


/****   lexer.c   **********************************************/

#include "global.h"

char lexbuf[BSIZE];
int  lineno = 1;
int  tokenval = NONE;

int  lexan()      /*  lexical analyzer  */
{
    int t;
    while(1) {
        t = getchar();
        if (t == ' ' || t == '\t')
            ;  /*  strip out white space  */
        else if (t == '\n')
            lineno = lineno + 1;
        else if (isdigit(t)) {       /*  t is a digit */
            ungetc(t, stdin);
            scanf("%d", &tokenval);
            return NUM;
        }
        else if (isalpha(t)) {       /*  t is a letter */
            int p, b = 0;
            while (isalnum(t)) {   /*  t is alphanumeric */
                lexbuf[b] = t;
                t = getchar();
                b = b + 1;
                if (b >= BSIZE)
                    error("compiler error");
            }
            lexbuf[b] = EOS;
            if (t != EOF)
                ungetc(t, stdin);
            p = lookup(lexbuf);
            if (p == 0)
                p = insert(lexbuf, ID);
            tokenval = p;
            return symtable[p].token;
        }
        else if (t == EOF)
            return DONE;
```

```
            else {
                tokenval = NONE;
                return t;
            }
        }
}


/****    parser.c    ******************************************/

#include "global.h"

int lookahead;

parse()      /*  parses and translates expression list  */
{
    lookahead = lexan();
    while (lookahead != DONE ) {
        expr(); match(';');
    }
}

expr()
{
    int t;
    term();
    while(1)
        switch (lookahead) {
        case '+': case '-':
            t = lookahead;
            match(lookahead); term(); emit(t, NONE);
            continue;
        default:
            return;
        }
}

term()
{
    int t;
    factor();
    while(1)
        switch (lookahead) {
        case '*': case '/': case DIV: case MOD:
            t = lookahead;
            match(lookahead); factor(); emit(t, NONE);
            continue;
        default:
            return;
        }
}
```

```
factor()
{
    switch(lookahead) {
        case '(':
                match('('); expr(); match(')'); break;
        case NUM:
                emit(NUM, tokenval); match(NUM); break;
        case ID:
                emit(ID, tokenval); match(ID); break;
        default:
                error("syntax error");
    }
}

match(t)
    int  t;
{
    if (lookahead == t)
        lookahead = lexan();
    else error("syntax error");
}

/****   emitter.c  ****************************************/

#include "global.h"

emit(t, tval)    /*  generates output  */
    int  t, tval;
{
    switch(t) {
        case '+': case '-': case '*': case '/':
                printf("%c\n", t); break;
        case DIV:
                printf("DIV\n"); break;
        case MOD:
                printf("MOD\n"); break;
        case NUM:
                printf("%d\n", tval); break;
        case ID:
                printf("%s\n", symtable[tval].lexptr); break;
        default:
                printf("token %d, tokenval %d\n", t, tval);
    }
}

/****   symbol.c  ****************************************/

#include "global.h"

#define STRMAX 999    /* size of lexemes array */
#define SYMMAX 100    /* size of symtable */
```

```
char lexemes[STRMAX];
int  lastchar = - 1;  /* last used position in lexemes  */
struct entry symtable[SYMMAX];
int  lastentry = 0;   /* last used position in symtable */

int  lookup(s)        /* returns position of entry for s */
     char s[];
{
     int p;
     for (p = lastentry; p > 0; p = p - 1)
         if (strcmp(symtable[p].lexptr, s) == 0)
             return p;
     return 0;
}

int  insert(s, tok)   /* returns position of entry for s */
     char s[];
     int  tok;
{
     int len;
     len = strlen(s); /* strlen computes length of s */
     if (lastentry + 1 >= SYMMAX)
         error("symbol table full");
     if (lastchar + len + 1 >= STRMAX)
         error("lexemes array full");
     lastentry = lastentry + 1;
     symtable[lastentry].token = tok;
     symtable[lastentry].lexptr = &lexemes[lastchar + 1];
     lastchar = lastchar + len + 1;
     strcpy(symtable[lastentry].lexptr, s);
     return lastentry;
}


/****   init.c   *********************************************/

#include "global.h"

struct entry keywords[] = {
     "div", DIV,
     "mod", MOD,
     0,     0
};

init()    /*  loads keywords into symtable  */
{
     struct entry *p;
     for (p = keywords; p->token; p++)
         insert(p->lexptr, p->token);
}
```

```
/****    error.c    **********************************************/

#include "global.h"

error(m)        /*  generates all error messages  */
    char *m;
{
    fprintf(stderr, "line %d: %s\n", lineno, m);
    exit(1);      /*  unsuccessful termination  */
}


/****    main.c    ***********************************************/

#include "global.h"

main()
{
    init();
    parse();
    exit(0);      /*  successful termination  */
}


/***************************************************************/
```

EXERCISES

2.1 Consider the context-free grammar

$$S \rightarrow S\ S\ + \ |\ S\ S\ * \ |\ \text{a}$$

a) Show how the string aa+a* can be generated by this grammar.
b) Construct a parse tree for this string.
c) What language is generated by this grammar? Justify your answer.

2.2 What language is generated by the following grammars? In each case justify your answer.
a) $S \rightarrow 0\ S\ 1\ |\ 0\ 1$
b) $S \rightarrow +\ S\ S\ |\ -\ S\ S\ |\ \text{a}$
c) $S \rightarrow S\ (\ S\ )\ S\ |\ \epsilon$
d) $S \rightarrow a\ S\ b\ S\ |\ b\ S\ a\ S\ |\ \epsilon$
e) $S \rightarrow \text{a}\ |\ S\ +\ S\ |\ S\ S\ |\ S\ * \ |\ (\ S\ )$

2.3 Which of the grammars in Exercise 2.2 are ambiguous?

2.4 Construct unambiguous context-free grammars for each of the following languages. In each case show that your grammar is correct.

    a) Arithmetic expressions in postfix notation.

    b) Left-associative lists of identifiers separated by commas.

    c) Right-associative lists of identifiers separated by commas.

    d) Arithmetic expressions of integers and identifiers with the four binary operators +, -, *, /.

    e) Add unary plus and minus to the arithmetic operators of (d).

*2.5 a) Show that all binary strings generated by the following grammar have values divisible by 3. *Hint.* Use induction on the number of nodes in a parse tree.

$$num \rightarrow 11 \mid 1001 \mid num\ 0 \mid num\ num$$

    b) Does the grammar generate all binary strings with values divisible by 3?

2.6 Construct a context-free grammar for roman numerals.

2.7 Construct a syntax-directed translation scheme that translates arithmetic expressions from infix notation into prefix notation in which an operator appears before its operands; e.g., $-xy$ is the prefix notation for $x-y$. Give annotated parse trees for the inputs 9-5+2 and 9-5*2.

2.8 Construct a syntax-directed translation scheme that translates arithmetic expressions from postfix notation into infix notation. Give annotated parse trees for the inputs 95-2* and 952*-.

2.9 Construct a syntax-directed translation scheme that translates integers into roman numerals.

2.10 Construct a syntax-directed translation scheme that translates roman numerals into integers.

2.11 Construct recursive-descent parsers for the grammars in Exercise 2.2 (a), (b), and (c).

2.12 Construct a syntax-directed translator that verifies that the parentheses in an input string are properly balanced.

2.13 The following rules define the translation of an English word into *pig Latin*:

    a) If the word begins with a nonempty string of consonants, move the initial consonant string to the back of the word and add the suffix AY; e.g., pig becomes igpay.

    b) If the word begins with a vowel, add the suffix YAY; e.g., owl becomes owlyay.

    c) U following a Q is a consonant.

    d) Y at the beginning of a word is a vowel if it is not followed by a vowel.

e) One-letter words are not changed.

Construct a syntax-directed translation scheme for pig Latin.

2.14 In the programming language C the for-statement has the form:

$$\texttt{for} \ (\ expr_1 \ ; \ expr_2 \ ; \ expr_3 \ ) \ stmt$$

The first expression is executed before the loop; it is typically used for initializing the loop index. The second expression is a test made before each iteration of the loop; the loop is exited if the expression becomes 0. The loop itself consists of the statement $\{stmt \ expr_3 ;\}$. The third expression is executed at the end of each iteration; it is typically used to increment the loop index. The meaning of the for-statement is similar to

$$expr_1 \ ; \ \texttt{while} \ (\ expr_2 \ ) \ \{ \ stmt \ expr_3 ; \ \}$$

Construct a syntax-directed translation scheme to translate C for-statements into stack-machine code.

*2.15 Consider the following for-statement:

$$\textbf{for } i := 1 \ \textbf{step } 10 - j \ \textbf{until } 10 * j \ \textbf{do } \ j := j + 1$$

Three semantic definitions can be given for this statement. One possible meaning is that the limit $10 * j$ and increment $10 - j$ are to be evaluated once before the loop, as in PL/I. For example, if $j = 5$ before the loop, we would run through the loop ten times and exit. A second, completely different, meaning would ensue if we are required to evaluate the limit and increment every time through the loop. For example, if $j = 5$ before the loop, the loop would never terminate. A third meaning is given by languages such as Algol. When the increment is negative, the test made for termination of the loop is $i < 10 * j$, rather than $i > 10 * j$. For each of these three semantic definitions construct a syntax-directed translation scheme to translate these for-loops into stack-machine code.

2.16 Consider the following grammar fragment for if-then- and if-then-else-statements:

$$stmt \ \rightarrow \ \textbf{if } expr \ \textbf{then } stmt$$
$$| \ \textbf{if } expr \ \textbf{then } stmt \ \textbf{else } stmt$$
$$| \ \textbf{other}$$

where **other** stands for the other statements in the language.
a) Show that this grammar is ambiguous.
b) Construct an equivalent unambiguous grammar that associates each **else** with the closest previous unmatched **then**.

c) Construct a syntax-directed translation scheme based on this grammar to translate conditional statements into stack machine code.

*2.17 Construct a syntax-directed translation scheme that translates arithmetic expressions in infix notation into arithmetic expressions in infix notation having no redundant parentheses. Show the annotated parse tree for the input (((1 + 2) * (3 * 4)) + 5).

PROGRAMMING EXERCISES

P2.1 Implement a translator from integers to roman numerals based on the syntax-directed translation scheme developed in Exercise 2.9.

P2.2 Modify the translator in Section 2.9 to produce as output code for the abstract stack machine of Section 2.8.

P2.3 Modify the error recovery module of the translator in Section 2.9 to skip to the next input expression on encountering an error.

P2.4 Extend the translator in Section 2.9 to handle all Pascal expressions.

P2.5 Extend the compiler of Section 2.9 to translate into stack-machine code statements generated by the following grammar:

$$
\begin{aligned}
stmt \rightarrow \ & \textbf{id} \ := \ expr \\
 | \ & \textbf{if} \ expr \ \textbf{then} \ stmt \\
 | \ & \textbf{while} \ expr \ \textbf{do} \ stmt \\
 | \ & \textbf{begin} \ opt\_stmts \ \textbf{end}
\end{aligned}
$$

$$opt\_stmts \rightarrow stmt\_list \quad | \quad \epsilon$$

$$stmt\_list \rightarrow stmt\_list \ ; \ stmt \quad | \quad stmt$$

*P2.6 Construct a set of test expressions for the compiler in Section 2.9, so that each production is used at least once in deriving some test expression. Construct a testing program that can be used as a general compiler testing tool. Use your testing program to run your compiler on these test expressions.

P2.7 Construct a set of test statements for your compiler of Exercise P2.5 so that each production is used at least once to generate some test statement. Use the testing program of Exercise P2.6 to run your compiler on these test expressions.

BIBLIOGRAPHIC NOTES

This introductory chapter touches on a number of subjects that are treated in more detail in the rest of the book. Pointers to the literature appear in the chapters containing further material.

Context-free grammars were introduced by Chomsky [1956] as part of a study of natural languages. Their use in specifying the syntax of programming languages arose independently. While working with a draft of Algol 60, John Backus "hastily adapted [Emil Post's productions] to that use" (Wexelblat [1981, p.162]). The resulting notation was a variant of context-free grammars. The scholar Panini devised an equivalent syntactic notation to specify the rules of Sanskrit grammar between 400 B.C. and 200 B.C. (Ingerman [1967]).

The proposal that BNF, which began as an abbreviation of Backus Normal Form, be read as Backus-Naur Form, to recognize Naur's contributions as editor of the Algol 60 report (Naur [1963]), is contained in a letter by Knuth [1964].

Syntax-directed definitions are a form of inductive definitions in which the induction is on the syntactic structure. As such they have long been used informally in mathematics. Their application to programming languages came with the use of a grammar to structure the Algol 60 report. Shortly thereafter, Irons [1961] constructed a syntax-directed compiler.

Recursive-descent parsing has been used since the early 1960's. Bauer [1976] attributes the method to Lucas [1961]. Hoare [1962b, p.128] describes an Algol compiler organized as "a set of procedures, each of which is capable of processing one of the syntactic units of the Algol 60 report." Foster [1968] discusses the elimination of left recursion from productions containing semantic actions that do not affect attribute values.

McCarthy [1963] advocated that the translation of a language be based on abstract syntax. In the same paper McCarthy [1963, p.24] left "the reader to convince himself" that a tail-recursive formulation of the factorial function is equivalent to an iterative program.

The benefits of partitioning a compiler into a front end and a back end were explored in a committee report by Strong et al. [1958]. The report coined the name UNCOL (from universal computer oriented language) for a universal intermediate language. The concept has remained an ideal.

A good way to learn about implementation techniques is to read the code of existing compilers. Unfortunately, code is not often published. Randell and Russell [1964] give a comprehensive account of an early Algol compiler. Compiler code may also be seen in McKeeman, Horning, and Wortman [1970]. Barron [1981] is a collection of papers on Pascal implementation, including implementation notes distributed with the Pascal P compiler (Nori et al. [1981]), code generation details (Ammann [1977]), and the code for an implementation of Pascal S, a Pascal subset designed by Wirth [1981] for student use. Knuth [1985] gives an unusually clear and detailed description of the TEX translator.

Kernighan and Pike [1984] describe in detail how to build a desk calculator program around a syntax-directed translation scheme using the compiler-construction tools available on the UNIX operating system. Equation (2.17) is from Tantzen [1963].

CHAPTER 3

Lexical Analysis

This chapter deals with techniques for specifying and implementing lexical analyzers. A simple way to build a lexical analyzer is to construct a diagram that illustrates the structure of the tokens of the source language, and then to hand-translate the diagram into a program for finding tokens. Efficient lexical analyzers can be produced in this manner.

The techniques used to implement lexical analyzers can also be applied to other areas such as query languages and information retrieval systems. In each application, the underlying problem is the specification and design of programs that execute actions triggered by patterns in strings. Since pattern-directed programming is widely useful, we introduce a pattern-action language called Lex for specifying lexical analyzers. In this language, patterns are specified by regular expressions, and a compiler for Lex can generate an efficient finite-automaton recognizer for the regular expressions.

Several other languages use regular expressions to describe patterns. For example, the pattern-scanning language AWK uses regular expressions to select input lines for processing and the UNIX system shell allows a user to refer to a set of file names by writing a regular expression. The UNIX command rm *.o, for instance, removes all files with names ending in ".o".[1]

A software tool that automates the construction of lexical analyzers allows people with different backgrounds to use pattern matching in their own application areas. For example, Jarvis [1976] used a lexical-analyzer generator to create a program that recognizes imperfections in printed circuit boards. The circuits are digitally scanned and converted into "strings" of line segments at different angles. The "lexical analyzer" looked for patterns corresponding to imperfections in the string of line segments. A major advantage of a lexical-analyzer generator is that it can utilize the best-known pattern-matching algorithms and thereby create efficient lexical analyzers for people who are not experts in pattern-matching techniques.

---

[1] The expression *.o is a variant of the usual notation for regular expressions. Exercises 3.10 and 3.14 mention some commonly used variants of regular expression notations.

3.1 THE ROLE OF THE LEXICAL ANALYZER

The lexical analyzer is the first phase of a compiler. Its main task is to read the input characters and produce as output a sequence of tokens that the parser uses for syntax analysis. This interaction, summarized schematically in Fig. 3.1, is commonly implemented by making the lexical analyzer be a subroutine or a coroutine of the parser. Upon receiving a "get next token" command from the parser, the lexical analyzer reads input characters until it can identify the next token.

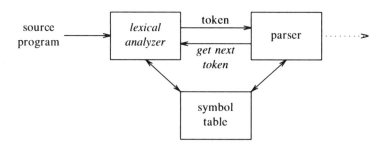

Fig. 3.1. Interaction of lexical analyzer with parser.

Since the lexical analyzer is the part of the compiler that reads the source text, it may also perform certain secondary tasks at the user interface. One such task is stripping out from the source program comments and white space in the form of blank, tab, and newline characters. Another is correlating error messages from the compiler with the source program. For example, the lexical analyzer may keep track of the number of newline characters seen, so that a line number can be associated with an error message. In some compilers, the lexical analyzer is in charge of making a copy of the source program with the error messages marked in it. If the source language supports some macro preprocessor functions, then these preprocessor functions may also be implemented as lexical analysis takes place.

Sometimes, lexical analyzers are divided into a cascade of two phases, the first called "scanning," and the second "lexical analysis." The scanner is responsible for doing simple tasks, while the lexical analyzer proper does the more complex operations. For example, a Fortran compiler might use a scanner to eliminate blanks from the input.

Issues in Lexical Analysis

There are several reasons for separating the analysis phase of compiling into lexical analysis and parsing.

1.   Simpler design is perhaps the most important consideration. The separation of lexical analysis from syntax analysis often allows us to simplify

one or the other of these phases. For example, a parser embodying the conventions for comments and white space is significantly more complex than one that can assume comments and white space have already been removed by a lexical analyzer. If we are designing a new language, separating the lexical and syntactic conventions can lead to a cleaner overall language design.

2.   Compiler efficiency is improved. A separate lexical analyzer allows us to construct a specialized and potentially more efficient processor for the task. A large amount of time is spent reading the source program and partitioning it into tokens. Specialized buffering techniques for reading input characters and processing tokens can significantly speed up the performance of a compiler.

3.   Compiler portability is enhanced. Input alphabet peculiarities and other device-specific anomalies can be restricted to the lexical analyzer. The representation of special or non-standard symbols, such as ↑ in Pascal, can be isolated in the lexical analyzer.

Specialized tools have been designed to help automate the construction of lexical analyzers and parsers when they are separated. We shall see several examples of such tools in this book.

Tokens, Patterns, Lexemes

When talking about lexical analysis, we use the terms "token," "pattern," and "lexeme" with specific meanings. Examples of their use are shown in Fig. 3.2. In general, there is a set of strings in the input for which the same token is produced as output. This set of strings is described by a rule called a *pattern* associated with the token. The pattern is said to *match* each string in the set. A lexeme is a sequence of characters in the source program that is matched by the pattern for a token. For example, in the Pascal statement

```
const pi = 3.1416;
```

the substring pi is a lexeme for the token "identifier."

TOKEN	SAMPLE LEXEMES	INFORMAL DESCRIPTION OF PATTERN
const	const	const
if	if	if
relation	<, <=, =, <>, >, >=	< or <= or = or <> or >= or >
id	pi, count, D2	letter followed by letters and digits
num	3.1416, 0, 6.02E23	any numeric constant
literal	"core dumped"	any characters between " and " except "

Fig. 3.2. Examples of tokens.

We treat tokens as terminal symbols in the grammar for the source language, using boldface names to represent tokens. The lexemes matched by the pattern for the token represent strings of characters in the source program that can be treated together as a lexical unit.

In most programming languages, the following constructs are treated as tokens: keywords, operators, identifiers, constants, literal strings, and punctuation symbols such as parentheses, commas, and semicolons. In the example above, when the character sequence pi appears in the source program, a token representing an identifier is returned to the parser. The returning of a token is often implemented by passing an integer corresponding to the token. It is this integer that is referred to in Fig. 3.2 as boldface **id**.

A pattern is a rule describing the set of lexemes that can represent a particular token in source programs. The pattern for the token **const** in Fig. 3.2 is just the single string const that spells out the keyword. The pattern for the token **relation** is the set of all six Pascal relational operators. To describe precisely the patterns for more complex tokens like **id** (for identifier) and **num** (for number) we shall use the regular-expression notation developed in Section 3.3.

Certain language conventions impact the difficulty of lexical analysis. Languages such as Fortran require certain constructs in fixed positions on the input line. Thus the alignment of a lexeme may be important in determining the correctness of a source program. The trend in modern language design is toward free-format input, allowing constructs to be positioned anywhere on the input line, so this aspect of lexical analysis is becoming less important.

The treatment of blanks varies greatly from language to language. In some languages, such as Fortran or Algol 68, blanks are not significant except in literal strings. They can be added at will to improve the readability of a program. The conventions regarding blanks can greatly complicate the task of identifying tokens.

A popular example that illustrates the potential difficulty of recognizing tokens is the DO statement of Fortran. In the statement

```
DO 5 I = 1.25
```

we cannot tell until we have seen the decimal point that DO is not a keyword, but rather part of the identifier DO5I. On the other hand, in the statement

```
DO 5 I = 1,25
```

we have seven tokens, corresponding to the keyword DO, the statement label 5, the identifier I, the operator =, the constant 1, the comma, and the constant 25. Here, we cannot be sure until we have seen the comma that DO is a keyword. To alleviate this uncertainty, Fortran 77 allows an optional comma between the label and index of the DO statement. The use of this comma is encouraged because it helps make the DO statement clearer and more readable.

In many languages, certain strings are *reserved*; i.e., their meaning is predefined and cannot be changed by the user. If keywords are not reserved, then the lexical analyzer must distinguish between a keyword and a user-defined identifier. In PL/I, keywords are not reserved; thus, the rules for distinguishing keywords from identifiers are quite complicated as the following PL/I statement illustrates:

```
IF THEN THEN THEN = ELSE; ELSE ELSE = THEN;
```

Attributes for Tokens

When more than one pattern matches a lexeme, the lexical analyzer must provide additional information about the particular lexeme that matched to the subsequent phases of the compiler. For example, the pattern **num** matches both the strings 0 and 1, but it is essential for the code generator to know what string was actually matched.

The lexical analyzer collects information about tokens into their associated attributes. The tokens influence parsing decisions; the attributes influence the translation of tokens. As a practical matter, a token has usually only a single attribute — a pointer to the symbol-table entry in which the information about the token is kept; the pointer becomes the attribute for the token. For diagnostic purposes, we may be interested in both the lexeme for an identifier and the line number on which it was first seen. Both these items of information can be stored in the symbol-table entry for the identifier.

Example 3.1. The tokens and associated attribute-values for the Fortran statement

```
E = M * C ** 2
```

are written below as a sequence of pairs:

<**id**, pointer to symbol-table entry for E>

<**assign_op**, >

<**id**, pointer to symbol-table entry for M>

<**mult_op**, >

<**id**, pointer to symbol-table entry for C>

<**exp_op**, >

<**num**, integer value 2>

Note that in certain pairs there is no need for an attribute value; the first component is sufficient to identify the lexeme. In this small example, the token **num** has been given an integer-valued attribute. The compiler may store the character string that forms a number in a symbol table and let the attribute of token **num** be a pointer to the table entry.   □

Lexical Errors

Few errors are discernible at the lexical level alone, because a lexical analyzer has a very localized view of a source program. If the string `fi` is encountered in a C program for the first time in the context

        fi (a == f(x)) $\cdots$

a lexical analyzer cannot tell whether `fi` is a misspelling of the keyword `if` or an undeclared function identifier. Since `fi` is a valid identifier, the lexical analyzer must return the token for an identifier and let some other phase of the compiler handle any error.

But, suppose a situation does arise in which the lexical analyzer is unable to proceed because none of the patterns for tokens matches a prefix of the remaining input. Perhaps the simplest recovery strategy is "panic mode" recovery. We delete successive characters from the remaining input until the lexical analyzer can find a well-formed token. This recovery technique may occasionally confuse the parser, but in an interactive computing environment it may be quite adequate.

Other possible error-recovery actions are:

1.   deleting an extraneous character
2.   inserting a missing character
3.   replacing an incorrect character by a correct character
4.   transposing two adjacent characters.

Error transformations like these may be tried in an attempt to repair the input. The simplest such strategy is to see whether a prefix of the remaining input can be transformed into a valid lexeme by just a single error transformation. This strategy assumes most lexical errors are the result of a single error transformation, an assumption usually, but not always, borne out in practice.

One way of finding the errors in a program is to compute the minimum number of error transformations required to transform the erroneous program into one that is syntactically well-formed. We say that the erroneous program has k errors if the shortest sequence of error transformations that will map it into some valid program has length k. Minimum-distance error correction is a convenient theoretical yardstick, but it is not generally used in practice because it is too costly to implement. However, a few experimental compilers have used the minimum-distance criterion to make local corrections.

3.2 INPUT BUFFERING

This section covers some efficiency issues concerned with the buffering of input. We first mention a two-buffer input scheme that is useful when look-ahead on the input is necessary to identify tokens. Then we introduce some useful techniques for speeding up the lexical analyzer, such as the use of "sentinels" to mark the buffer end.

There are three general approaches to the implementation of a lexical analyzer.

1. Use a lexical-analyzer generator, such as the Lex compiler discussed in Section 3.5, to produce the lexical analyzer from a regular-expression-based specification. In this case, the generator provides routines for reading and buffering the input.

2. Write the lexical analyzer in a conventional systems-programming language, using the I/O facilities of that language to read the input.

3. Write the lexical analyzer in assembly language and explicitly manage the reading of input.

The three choices are listed in order of increasing difficulty for the implementor. Unfortunately, the harder-to-implement approaches often yield faster lexical analyzers. Since the lexical analyzer is the only phase of the compiler that reads the source program character-by-character, it is possible to spend a considerable amount of time in the lexical analysis phase, even though the later phases are conceptually more complex. Thus, the speed of lexical analysis is a concern in compiler design. While the bulk of the chapter is devoted to the first approach, the design and use of an automatic generator, we also consider techniques that are helpful in manual design. Section 3.4 discusses transition diagrams, which are a useful concept for the organization of a hand-designed lexical analyzer.

Buffer Pairs

For many source languages, there are times when the lexical analyzer needs to look ahead several characters beyond the lexeme for a pattern before a match can be announced. The lexical analyzers in Chapter 2 used a function ungetc to push lookahead characters back into the input stream. Because a large amount of time can be consumed moving characters, specialized buffering techniques have been developed to reduce the amount of overhead required to process an input character. Many buffering schemes can be used, but since the techniques are somewhat dependent on system parameters, we shall only outline the principles behind one class of schemes here.

We use a buffer divided into two N-character halves, as shown in Fig. 3.3. Typically, N is the number of characters on one disk block, e.g., 1024 or 4096.

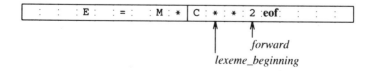

Fig. 3.3. An input buffer in two halves.

We read *N* input characters into each half of the buffer with one system read command, rather than invoking a read command for each input character. If fewer than *N* characters remain in the input, then a special character **eof** is read into the buffer after the input characters, as in Fig. 3.3. That is, **eof** marks the end of the source file and is different from any input character.

Two pointers to the input buffer are maintained. The string of characters between the two pointers is the current lexeme. Initially, both pointers point to the first character of the next lexeme to be found. One, called the forward pointer, scans ahead until a match for a pattern is found. Once the next lexeme is determined, the forward pointer is set to the character at its right end. After the lexeme is processed, both pointers are set to the character immediately past the lexeme. With this scheme, comments and white space can be treated as patterns that yield no token.

If the forward pointer is about to move past the halfway mark, the right half is filled with *N* new input characters. If the forward pointer is about to move past the right end of the buffer, the left half is filled with *N* new characters and the forward pointer wraps around to the beginning of the buffer.

This buffering scheme works quite well most of the time, but with it the amount of lookahead is limited, and this limited lookahead may make it impossible to recognize tokens in situations where the distance that the forward pointer must travel is more than the length of the buffer. For example, if we see

    DECLARE (ARG1, ARG2, . . . , ARG*n*)

in a PL/I program, we cannot determine whether DECLARE is a keyword or an array name until we see the character that follows the right parenthesis. In either case, the lexeme ends at the second E, but the amount of lookahead needed is proportional to the number of arguments, which in principle is unbounded.

```
if forward at end of first half then begin
        reload second half;
        forward := forward + 1
end
else if forward at end of second half then begin
        reload first half;
        move forward to beginning of first half
end
else forward := forward + 1;
```

Fig. 3.4. Code to advance forward pointer.

Sentinels

If we use the scheme of Fig. 3.3 exactly as shown, we must check each time we move the forward pointer that we have not moved off one half of the buffer; if we do, then we must reload the other half. That is, our code for advancing the forward pointer performs tests like those shown in Fig. 3.4.

Except at the ends of the buffer halves, the code in Fig. 3.4 requires two tests for each advance of the forward pointer. We can reduce the two tests to one if we extend each buffer half to hold a *sentinel* character at the end. The sentinel is a special character that cannot be part of the source program. A natural choice is **eof**; Fig. 3.5 shows the same buffer arrangement as Fig. 3.3, with the sentinels added.

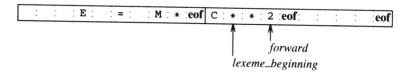

```
: : : E : : = : : M : * :eof| C : * : * : 2 :eof: : : : :eof|
```
↑   ↑
| *forward*
lexeme_beginning

Fig. 3.5. Sentinels at end of each buffer half.

With the arrangement of Fig. 3.5, we can use the code shown in Fig. 3.6 to advance the forward pointer (and test for the end of the source file). Most of the time the code performs only one test to see whether *forward* points to an **eof**. Only when we reach the end of a buffer half or the end of the file do we perform more tests. Since N input characters are encountered between **eof**'s, the average number of tests per input character is very close to 1.

```
forward := forward + 1;
if forward↑ = eof then begin
    if forward at end of first half then begin
        reload second half;
        forward := forward + 1·
    end
    else if forward at end of second half then begin
        reload first half;
        move forward to beginning of first half
    end
    else /* eof within a buffer signifying end of input */
        terminate lexical analysis
end
```

Fig. 3.6. Lookahead code with sentinels.

We also need to decide how to process the character scanned by the forward pointer; does it mark the end of a token, does it represent progress in finding a particular keyword, or what? One way to structure these tests is to use a case statement, if the implementation language has one. The test

if *forward*↑ = **eof**

can then be implemented as one of the different cases.

3.3 SPECIFICATION OF TOKENS

Regular expressions are an important notation for specifying patterns. Each pattern matches a set of strings, so regular expressions will serve as names for sets of strings. Section 3.5 extends this notation into a pattern-directed language for lexical analysis.

Strings and Languages

The term *alphabet* or *character class* denotes any finite set of symbols. Typical examples of symbols are letters and characters. The set {0,1} is the *binary alphabet*. ASCII and EBCDIC are two examples of computer alphabets.

A *string* over some alphabet is a finite sequence of symbols drawn from that alphabet. In language theory, the terms *sentence* and *word* are often used as synonyms for the term "string." The length of a string s, usually written $|s|$, is the number of occurrences of symbols in s. For example, banana is a string of length six. The *empty* string, denoted ϵ, is a special string of length zero. Some common terms associated with parts of a string are summarized in Fig. 3.7.

The term *language* denotes any set of strings over some fixed alphabet. This definition is very broad. Abstract languages like $\varnothing$, the *empty* set, or {ϵ}, the set containing only the empty string, are languages under this definition. So too are the set of all syntactically well-formed Pascal programs and the set of all grammatically correct English sentences, although the latter two sets are much more difficult to specify. Also note that this definition does not ascribe any meaning to the strings in a language. Methods for ascribing meanings to strings are discussed in Chapter 5.

If x and y are strings, then the *concatenation* of x and y, written xy, is the string formed by appending y to x. For example, if x = dog and y = house, then xy = doghouse. The empty string is the identity element under concatenation. That is, $s\epsilon = \epsilon s = s$.

If we think of concatenation as a "product", we can define string "exponentiation" as follows. Define s^0 to be ϵ, and for $i > 0$ define s^i to be $s^{i-1}s$. Since ϵs is s itself, $s^1 = s$. Then, $s^2 = ss$, $s^3 = sss$, and so on.

TERM	DEFINITION
prefix of s	A string obtained by removing zero or more trailing symbols of string s; e.g., ban is a prefix of banana.
suffix of s	A string formed by deleting zero or more of the leading symbols of s; e.g., nana is a suffix of banana.
substring of s	A string obtained by deleting a prefix and a suffix from s; e.g., nan is a substring of banana. Every prefix and every suffix of s is a substring of s, but not every substring of s is a prefix or a suffix of s. For every string s, both s and ϵ are prefixes, suffixes, and substrings of s.
proper prefix, suffix, or substring of s	Any nonempty string x that is, respectively, a prefix, suffix, or substring of s such that $s \neq x$.
subsequence of s	Any string formed by deleting zero or more not necessarily contiguous symbols from s; e.g., baaa is a subsequence of banana.

Fig. 3.7. Terms for parts of a string.

Operations on Languages

There are several important operations that can be applied to languages. For lexical analysis, we are interested primarily in union, concatenation, and closure, which are defined in Fig. 3.8. We can also generalize the "exponentiation" operator to languages by defining L^0 to be $\{\epsilon\}$, and L^i to be $L^{i-1}L$. Thus, L^i is L concatenated with itself $i-1$ times.

Example 3.2. Let L be the set $\{A, B, \ldots, Z, a, b, \ldots, z\}$ and D the set $\{0, 1, \ldots, 9\}$. We can think of L and D in two ways. We can think of L as the alphabet consisting of the set of upper and lower case letters, and D as the alphabet consisting of the set of the ten decimal digits. Alternatively, since a symbol can be regarded as a string of length one, the sets L and D are each finite languages. Here are some examples of new languages created from L and D by applying the operators defined in Fig. 3.8.

1. $L \cup D$ is the set of letters and digits.

2. LD is the set of strings consisting of a letter followed by a digit.

3. L^4 is the set of all four-letter strings.

4. $L*$ is the set of all strings of letters, including ϵ, the empty string.

5. $L(L \cup D)*$ is the set of all strings of letters and digits beginning with a letter.

6. D^+ is the set of all strings of one or more digits.   □

OPERATION	DEFINITION
union of L and M written $L \cup M$	$L \cup M = \{\, s \mid s \text{ is in } L \text{ or } s \text{ is in } M \,\}$
concatenation of L and M written LM	$LM = \{\, st \mid s \text{ is in } L \text{ and } t \text{ is in } M \,\}$
Kleene closure of L written L^*	$L^* = \bigcup_{i=0}^{\infty} L^i$ L^* denotes "zero or more concatenations of" L.
positive closure of L written L^+	$L^+ = \bigcup_{i=1}^{\infty} L^i$ L^+ denotes "one or more concatenations of" L.

Fig. 3.8. Definitions of operations on languages.

Regular Expressions

In Pascal, an identifier is a letter followed by zero or more letters or digits; that is, an identifier is a member of the set defined in part (5) of Example 3.2. In this section, we present a notation, called regular expressions, that allows us to define precisely sets such as this. With this notation, we might define Pascal identifiers as

letter (letter | digit) *

The vertical bar here means "or," the parentheses are used to group subexpressions, the star means "zero or more instances of" the parenthesized expression, and the juxtaposition of **letter** with the remainder of the expression means concatenation.

A regular expression is built up out of simpler regular expressions using a set of defining rules. Each regular expression r denotes a language $L(r)$. The defining rules specify how $L(r)$ is formed by combining in various ways the languages denoted by the subexpressions of r.

Here are the rules that define the *regular expressions over alphabet* Σ. Associated with each rule is a specification of the language denoted by the regular expression being defined.

1. ϵ is a regular expression that denotes $\{\epsilon\}$, that is, the set containing the empty string.

2. If a is a symbol in Σ, then a is a regular expression that denotes $\{a\}$, i.e., the set containing the string a. Although we use the same notation for all three, technically, the regular expression a is different from the string a or the symbol a. It will be clear from the context whether we are talking about a as a regular expression, string, or symbol.

3.   Suppose r and s are regular expressions denoting the languages $L(r)$ and $L(s)$. Then,

a) $(r)|(s)$ is a regular expression denoting $L(r) \cup L(s)$.
b) $(r)(s)$ is a regular expression denoting $L(r)L(s)$.
c) $(r)^*$ is a regular expression denoting $(L(r))^*$.
d) (r) is a regular expression denoting $L(r)$.[2]

A language denoted by a regular expression is said to be a *regular set*.

The specification of a regular expression is an example of a recursive definition. Rules (1) and (2) form the basis of the definition; we use the term *basic
symbol* to refer to ϵ or a symbol in Σ appearing in a regular expression. Rule
(3) provides the inductive step.

Unnecessary parentheses can be avoided in regular expressions if we adopt
the conventions that:

1.   the unary operator * has the highest precedence and is left associative,
2.   concatenation has the second highest precedence and is left associative,
3. | has the lowest precedence and is left associative.

Under these conventions, $(a)|((b)^*(c))$ is equivalent to $a|b^*c$. Both expres-
sions denote the set of strings that are either a single a or zero or more b's
followed by one c.

Example 3.3. Let $\Sigma = \{a,\ b\}$.

1.   The regular expression $a|b$ denotes the set $\{a,\ b\}$.

2.   The regular expression $(a|b)(a|b)$ denotes $\{aa,\ ab,\ ba,\ bb\}$, the set of all
     strings of a's and b's of length two. Another regular expression for this
     same set is $aa\ |\ ab\ |\ ba\ |\ bb$.

3.   The regular expression a^* denotes the set of all strings of zero or more
     a's, i.e., $\{\epsilon,\ a,\ aa,\ aaa,\ \cdots\ \}$.

4.   The regular expression $(a|b)^*$ denotes the set of all strings containing
     zero or more instances of an a or b, that is, the set of all strings of a's
     and b's. Another regular expression for this set is $(a^*b^*)^*$.

5.   The regular expression $a\ |\ a^*b$ denotes the set containing the string a and
     all strings consisting of zero or more a's followed by a b.   □

If two regular expressions r and s denote the same language, we say r and s
are *equivalent* and write $r = s$. For example, $(a|b) = (b|a)$.

There are a number of algebraic laws obeyed by regular expressions and
these can be used to manipulate regular expressions into equivalent forms.
Figure 3.9 shows some algebraic laws that hold for regular expressions r, s,
and t.

---

[2] This rule says that extra pairs of parentheses may be placed around regular expressions if we
desire.

AXIOM	DESCRIPTION
$r\|s = s\|r$	$\|$ is commutative
$r\|(s\|t) = (r\|s)\|t$	$\|$ is associative
$(rs)t = r(st)$	concatenation is associative
$r(s\|t) = rs\|rt$ $(s\|t)r = sr\|tr$	concatenation distributes over $\|$
$\epsilon r = r$ $r\epsilon = r$	ϵ is the identity element for concatenation
$r* = (r\|\epsilon)*$	relation between * and ϵ
$r** = r*$	* is idempotent

Fig. 3.9. Algebraic properties of regular expressions.

Regular Definitions

For notational convenience, we may wish to give names to regular expressions and to define regular expressions using these names as if they were symbols. If Σ is an alphabet of basic symbols, then a *regular definition* is a sequence of definitions of the form

$$d_1 \rightarrow r_1$$
$$d_2 \rightarrow r_2$$
$$\cdots$$
$$d_n \rightarrow r_n$$

where each d_i is a distinct name, and each r_i is a regular expression over the symbols in $\Sigma \cup \{d_1, d_2, \ldots, d_{i-1}\}$, i.e., the basic symbols and the previously defined names. By restricting each r_i to symbols of Σ and the previously defined names, we can construct a regular expression over Σ for any r_i by repeatedly replacing regular-expression names by the expressions they denote. If r_i used d_j for some $j \geq i$, then r_i might be recursively defined, and this substitution process would not terminate.

To distinguish names from symbols, we print the names in regular definitions in boldface.

Example 3.4. As we have stated, the set of Pascal identifiers is the set of strings of letters and digits beginning with a letter. Here is a regular definition for this set.

$$\textbf{letter} \rightarrow \text{A} \mid \text{B} \mid \cdots \mid \text{Z} \mid \text{a} \mid \text{b} \mid \cdots \mid \text{z}$$
$$\textbf{digit} \rightarrow 0 \mid 1 \mid \cdots \mid 9$$
$$\textbf{id} \rightarrow \textbf{letter} \; (\; \textbf{letter} \mid \textbf{digit} \;)* \qquad \qquad \Box$$

Example 3.5. Unsigned numbers in Pascal are strings such as 5280, 39.37,

6.336E4, or 1.894E-4. The following regular definition provides a precise specification for this class of strings:

$$\begin{aligned}
\textbf{digit} &\rightarrow 0 \mid 1 \mid \cdots \mid 9 \\
\textbf{digits} &\rightarrow \textbf{digit digit*} \\
\textbf{optional\_fraction} &\rightarrow \textbf{.}\ \textbf{digits} \mid \epsilon \\
\textbf{optional\_exponent} &\rightarrow (\ \text{E}\ (\ \textbf{+} \mid \textbf{-} \mid \epsilon\ )\ \textbf{digits}\ ) \mid \epsilon \\
\textbf{num} &\rightarrow \textbf{digits optional\_fraction optional\_exponent}
\end{aligned}$$

This definition says that an **optional_fraction** is either a decimal point followed by one or more digits, or it is missing (the empty string). An **optional_exponent**, if it is not missing, is an E followed by an optional + or − sign, followed by one or more digits. Note that at least one digit must follow the period, so **num** does not match 1. but it does match 1.0. □

Notational Shorthands

Certain constructs occur so frequently in regular expressions that it is convenient to introduce notational shorthands for them.

1. *One or more instances.* The unary postfix operator $^+$ means "one or more instances of." If r is a regular expression that denotes the language $L(r)$, then $(r)^+$ is a regular expression that denotes the language $(L(r))^+$. Thus, the regular expression a^+ denotes the set of all strings of one or more a's. The operator $^+$ has the same precedence and associativity as the operator $*$. The two algebraic identities $r* = r^+ \mid \epsilon$ and $r^+ = rr*$ relate the Kleene and positive closure operators.

2. *Zero or one instance.* The unary postfix operator ? means "zero or one instance of." The notation r? is a shorthand for $r \mid \epsilon$. If r is a regular expression, then (r)? is a regular expression that denotes the language $L(r) \cup \{\epsilon\}$. For example, using the $^+$ and ? operators, we can rewrite the regular definition for **num** in Example 3.5 as

$$\begin{aligned}
\textbf{digit} &\rightarrow 0 \mid 1 \mid \cdots \mid 9 \\
\textbf{digits} &\rightarrow \textbf{digit}^+ \\
\textbf{optional\_fraction} &\rightarrow (\ \textbf{.}\ \textbf{digits}\ )? \\
\textbf{optional\_exponent} &\rightarrow (\ \text{E}\ (\ \textbf{+} \mid \textbf{-}\ )?\ \textbf{digits}\ )? \\
\textbf{num} &\rightarrow \textbf{digits optional\_fraction optional\_exponent}
\end{aligned}$$

3. *Character classes.* The notation [abc] where a, b, and c are alphabet symbols denotes the regular expression a | b | c. An abbreviated character class such as [a−z] denotes the regular expression a | b | ⋯ | z. Using character classes, we can describe identifiers as being strings generated by the regular expression

[A−Za−z][A−Za−z0−9]*

Nonregular Sets

Some languages cannot be described by any regular expression. To illustrate the limits of the descriptive power of regular expressions, here we give examples of programming language constructs that cannot be described by regular expressions. Proofs of these assertions can be found in the references.

Regular expressions cannot be used to describe balanced or nested constructs. For example, the set of all strings of balanced parentheses cannot be described by a regular expression. On the other hand, this set can be specified by a context-free grammar.

Repeating strings cannot be described by regular expressions. The set

$$\{wcw \,|\, w \text{ is a string of } a\text{'s and } b\text{'s }\}$$

cannot be denoted by any regular expression, nor can it be described by a context-free grammar.

Regular expressions can be used to denote only a fixed number of repetitions or an unspecified number of repetitions of a given construct. Two arbitrary numbers cannot be compared to see whether they are the same. Thus, we cannot describe Hollerith strings of the form $n H a_1 a_2 \cdots a_n$ from early versions of Fortran with a regular expression, because the number of characters following H must match the decimal number before H.

3.4 RECOGNITION OF TOKENS

In the previous section, we considered the problem of how to specify tokens. In this section, we address the question of how to recognize them. Throughout this section, we use the language generated by the following grammar as a running example.

Example 3.6. Consider the following grammar fragment:

$$
\begin{aligned}
stmt \;\rightarrow\; &\textbf{if } expr \textbf{ then } stmt \\
\mid\; &\textbf{if } expr \textbf{ then } stmt \textbf{ else } stmt \\
\mid\; &\epsilon \\
expr \;\rightarrow\; &term \textbf{ relop } term \\
\mid\; &term \\
term \;\rightarrow\; &\textbf{id} \\
\mid\; &\textbf{num}
\end{aligned}
$$

where the terminals **if**, **then**, **else**, **relop**, **id**, and **num** generate sets of strings given by the following regular definitions:

$$
\begin{aligned}
\textbf{if} \;\rightarrow\; &\texttt{if} \\
\textbf{then} \;\rightarrow\; &\texttt{then} \\
\textbf{else} \;\rightarrow\; &\texttt{else} \\
\textbf{relop} \;\rightarrow\; &\texttt{<} \;|\; \texttt{<=} \;|\; \texttt{=} \;|\; \texttt{<>} \;|\; \texttt{>} \;|\; \texttt{>=} \\
\textbf{id} \;\rightarrow\; &\textbf{letter (letter } | \textbf{ digit)*} \\
\textbf{num} \;\rightarrow\; &\textbf{digit}^{+} \;(\; . \; \textbf{digit}^{+} \;)? \;(\; \text{E}(\;+\,|-\;)? \; \textbf{digit}^{+} \;)?
\end{aligned}
$$

where **letter** and **digit** are as defined previously.

For this language fragment the lexical analyzer will recognize the keywords if, then, else, as well as the lexemes denoted by **relop**, **id**, and **num**. To simplify matters, we assume keywords are reserved; that is, they cannot be used as identifiers. As in Example 3.5, **num** represents the unsigned integer and real numbers of Pascal.

In addition, we assume lexemes are separated by white space, consisting of nonnull sequences of blanks, tabs, and newlines. Our lexical analyzer will strip out white space. It will do so by comparing a string against the regular definition **ws**, below.

> **delim** → **blank** | **tab** | **newline**
> **ws** → **delim**$^+$

If a match for **ws** is found, the lexical analyzer does not return a token to the parser. Rather, it proceeds to find a token following the white space and returns that to the parser.

Our goal is to construct a lexical analyzer that will isolate the lexeme for the next token in the input buffer and produce as output a pair consisting of the appropriate token and attribute-value, using the translation table given in Fig. 3.10. The attribute-values for the relational operators are given by the symbolic constants LT, LE, EQ, NE, GT, GE.   □

REGULAR EXPRESSION	TOKEN	ATTRIBUTE-VALUE
ws	-	-
if	**if**	-
then	**then**	-
else	**else**	-
id	**id**	pointer to table entry
num	**num**	pointer to table entry
<	**relop**	LT
<=	**relop**	LE
=	**relop**	EQ
<>	**relop**	NE
>	**relop**	GT
>=	**relop**	GE

Fig. 3.10. Regular-expression patterns for tokens.

Transition Diagrams

As an intermediate step in the construction of a lexical analyzer, we first produce a stylized flowchart, called a *transition diagram*. Transition diagrams depict the actions that take place when a lexical analyzer is called by the parser to get the next token, as suggested by Fig. 3.1. Suppose the input buffer is as in Fig. 3.3 and the lexeme-beginning pointer points to the character following the last lexeme found. We use a transition diagram to keep track of information about characters that are seen as the forward pointer scans the input. We do so by moving from position to position in the diagram as characters are read.

Positions in a transition diagram are drawn as circles and are called *states*. The states are connected by arrows, called *edges*. Edges leaving state *s* have labels indicating the input characters that can next appear after the transition diagram has reached state *s*. The label **other** refers to any character that is not indicated by any of the other edges leaving *s*.

We assume the transition diagrams of this section are *deterministic*; that is, no symbol can match the labels of two edges leaving one state. Starting in Section 3.5, we shall relax this condition, making life much simpler for the designer of the lexical analyzer and, with proper tools, no harder for the implementor.

One state is labeled the *start* state; it is the initial state of the transition diagram where control resides when we begin to recognize a token. Certain states may have actions that are executed when the flow of control reaches that state. On entering a state we read the next input character. If there is an edge from the current state whose label matches this input character, we then go to the state pointed to by the edge. Otherwise, we indicate failure.

Figure 3.11 shows a transition diagram for the patterns >= and >. The transition diagram works as follows. Its start state is state 0. In state 0, we read the next input character. The edge labeled > from state 0 is to be followed to state 6 if this input character is >. Otherwise, we have failed to recognize either > or >=.

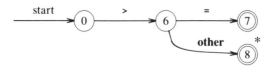

Fig. 3.11. Transition diagram for >=.

On reaching state 6 we read the next input character. The edge labeled = from state 6 is to be followed to state 7 if this input character is an =. Otherwise, the edge labeled **other** indicates that we are to go to state 8. The double circle on state 7 indicates that it is an accepting state, a state in which the token >= has been found.

Notice that the character > and another extra character are read as we follow the sequence of edges from the start state to the accepting state 8. Since the extra character is not a part of the relational operator >, we must retract the forward pointer one character. We use a * to indicate states on which this input retraction must take place.

In general, there may be several transition diagrams, each specifying a group of tokens. If failure occurs while we are following one transition diagram, then we retract the forward pointer to where it was in the start state of this diagram, and activate the next transition diagram. Since the lexeme-beginning and forward pointers marked the same position in the start state of the diagram, the forward pointer is retracted to the position marked by the lexeme-beginning pointer. If failure occurs in all transition diagrams, then a lexical error has been detected and we invoke an error-recovery routine.

Example 3.7. A transition diagram for the token **relop** is shown in Fig. 3.12. Notice that Fig. 3.11 is a part of this more complex transition diagram.   □

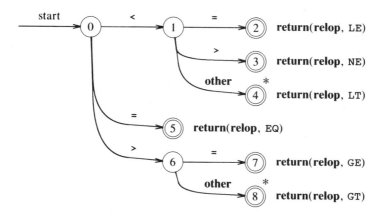

Fig. 3.12. Transition diagram for relational operators.

Example 3.8. Since keywords are sequences of letters, they are exceptions to the rule that a sequence of letters and digits starting with a letter is an identi-fier. Rather than encode the exceptions into a transition diagram, a useful trick is to treat keywords as special identifiers, as in Section 2.7. When the accepting state in Fig. 3.13 is reached, we execute some code to determine if the lexeme leading to the accepting state is a keyword or an identifier.

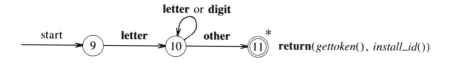

Fig. 3.13. Transition diagram for identifiers and keywords.

A simple technique for separating keywords from identifiers is to initialize appropriately the symbol table in which information about identifiers is saved. For the tokens of Fig. 3.10 we need to enter the strings if, then, and else into the symbol table before any characters in the input are seen. We also make a note in the symbol table of the token to be returned when one of these strings is recognized. The return statement next to the accepting state in Fig. 3.13 uses *gettoken*() and *install_id*() to obtain the token and attribute-value, respectively, to be returned. The procedure *install_id*() has access to the buffer, where the identifier lexeme has been located. The symbol table is examined and if the lexeme is found there marked as a keyword, *install_id*() returns 0. If the lexeme is found and is a program variable, *install_id*() returns a pointer to the symbol table entry. If the lexeme is not found in the symbol table, it is installed as a variable and a pointer to the newly created entry is returned.

The procedure *gettoken*() similarly looks for the lexeme in the symbol table. If the lexeme is a keyword, the corresponding token is returned; otherwise, the token **id** is returned.

Note that the transition diagram does not change if additional keywords are to be recognized; we simply initialize the symbol table with the strings and tokens of the additional keywords.   □

The technique of placing keywords in the symbol table is almost essential if the lexical analyzer is coded by hand. Without doing so, the number of states in a lexical analyzer for a typical programming language is several hundred, while using the trick, fewer than a hundred states will probably suffice.

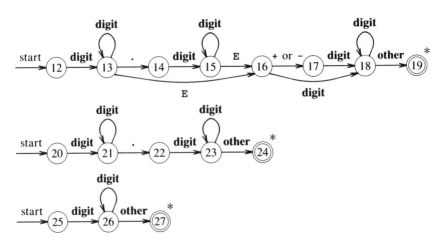

Fig. 3.14. Transition diagrams for unsigned numbers in Pascal.

Example 3.9. A number of issues arise when we construct a recognizer for unsigned numbers given by the regular definition

num → **digit**$^+$ (.**digit**$^+$)? ($E(+|-)$? **digit**$^+$)?

Note that the definition is of the form **digits fraction**? **exponent**? in which **fraction** and **exponent** are optional.

The lexeme for a given token must be the longest possible. For example, the lexical analyzer must not stop after seeing 12 or even 12.3 when the input is 12.3E4. Starting at states 25, 20, and 12 in Fig. 3.14, accepting states will be reached after 12, 12.3, and 12.3E4 are seen, respectively, provided 12.3E4 is followed by a non-digit in the input. The transition diagrams with start states 25, 20, and 12 are for **digits**, **digits fraction**, and **digits fraction**? **exponent**, respectively, so the start states must be tried in the reverse order 12, 20, 25.

The action when any of the accepting states 19, 24, or 27 is reached is to call a procedure *install_num* that enters the lexeme into a table of numbers and returns a pointer to the created entry. The lexical analyzer returns the token **num** with this pointer as the lexical value.   □

Information about the language that is not in the regular definitions of the tokens can be used to pinpoint errors in the input. For example, on input 1.<x, we fail in states 14 and 22 in Fig. 3.14 with next input character <. Rather than returning the number 1, we may wish to report an error and continue as if the input were 1.0<x. Such knowledge can also be used to simplify the transition diagrams, because error-handling may be used to recover from some situations that would otherwise lead to failure.

There are several ways in which the redundant matching in the transition diagrams of Fig. 3.14 can be avoided. One approach is to rewrite the transition diagrams by combining them into one, a nontrivial task in general. Another is to change the response to failure during the process of following a diagram. An approach explored later in this chapter allows us to pass through several accepting states; we revert back to the last accepting state that we passed through when failure occurs.

Example 3.10. A sequence of transition diagrams for all tokens of Example 3.6 is obtained if we put together the transition diagrams of Fig. 3.12, 3.13, and 3.14. Lower-numbered start states are to be attempted before higher numbered states.

The only remaining issue concerns white space. The treatment of **ws**, representing white space, is different from that of the patterns discussed above because nothing is returned to the parser when white space is found in the input. A transition diagram recognizing **ws** by itself is

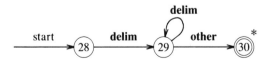

Nothing is returned when the accepting state is reached; we merely go back to the start state of the first transition diagram to look for another pattern.

Whenever possible, it is better to look for frequently occurring tokens before less frequently occurring ones, because a transition diagram is reached only after we fail on all earlier diagrams. Since white space is expected to occur frequently, putting the transition diagram for white space near the beginning should be an improvement over testing for white space at the end. □

Implementing a Transition Diagram

A sequence of transition diagrams can be converted into a program to look for the tokens specified by the diagrams. We adopt a systematic approach that works for all transition diagrams and constructs programs whose size is proportional to the number of states and edges in the diagrams.

Each state gets a segment of code. If there are edges leaving a state, then its code reads a character and selects an edge to follow, if possible. A function nextchar() is used to read the next character from the input buffer, advance the forward pointer at each call, and return the character read.[3] If there is an edge labeled by the character read, or labeled by a character class containing the character read, then control is transferred to the code for the state pointed to by that edge. If there is no such edge, and the current state is not one that indicates a token has been found, then a routine fail() is invoked to retract the forward pointer to the position of the beginning pointer and to initiate a search for a token specified by the next transition diagram. If there are no other transition diagrams to try, fail() calls an error-recovery routine.

To return tokens we use a global variable lexical_value, which is assigned the pointers returned by functions install_id() and install_num() when an identifier or number, respectively, is found. The token class is returned by the main procedure of the lexical analyzer, called nexttoken().

We use a case statement to find the start state of the next transition diagram. In the C implementation in Fig. 3.15, two variables state and start keep track of the present state and the starting state of the current transition diagram. The state numbers in the code are for the transition diagrams of Figures 3.12 – 3.14.

Edges in transition diagrams are traced by repeatedly selecting the code fragment for a state and executing the code fragment to determine the next state as shown in Fig. 3.16. We show the code for state 0, as modified in Example 3.10 to handle white space, and the code for two of the transition diagrams from Fig. 3.13 and 3.14. Note that the C construct

        while(1) *stmt*

repeats *stmt* "forever," i.e., until a return occurs.

---

[3] A more efficient implementation would use an in-line macro in place of the function nextchar().

```
int state = 0, start = 0;
int lexical_value;
    /* to "return" second component of token */
int fail()
{
    forward = token_beginning;
    switch (start) {
        case 0:    start = 9; break;
        case 9:    start = 12; break;
        case 12:   start = 20; break;
        case 20:   start = 25; break;
        case 25:   recover(); break;
        default:   /* compiler error */
    }
    return start;
}
```

Fig. 3.15. C code to find next start state.

Since C does not allow both a token and an attribute-value to be returned, install_id() and install_num() appropriately set some global variable to the attribute-value corresponding to the table entry for the **id** or **num** in question.

If the implementation language does not have a case statement, we can create an array for each state, indexed by characters. If *state* 1 is such an array, then *state* 1[*c*] is a pointer to a piece of code that must be executed whenever the lookahead character is *c*. This code would normally end with a goto to code for the next state. The array for state *s* is referred to as the indirect transfer table for *s*.

3.5 A LANGUAGE FOR SPECIFYING LEXICAL ANALYZERS

Several tools have been built for constructing lexical analyzers from special-purpose notations based on regular expressions. We have already seen the use of regular expressions for specifying token patterns. Before we consider algorithms for compiling regular expressions into pattern-matching programs, we give an example of a tool that might use such an algorithm.

In this section, we describe a particular tool, called Lex, that has been widely used to specify lexical analyzers for a variety of languages. We refer to the tool as the *Lex compiler*, and to its input specification as the *Lex language*. Discussion of an existing tool will allow us to show how the specification of patterns using regular expressions can be combined with actions, e.g., making entries into a symbol table, that a lexical analyzer may be required to perform. Lex-like specifications can be used even if a Lex

```
token nexttoken( )
{   while( 1 ) {
        switch (state) {
        case 0:   c = nextchar( );
            /* c is lookahead character */
            if (c==blank !! c==tab !! c==newline) {
                state = 0;
                lexeme_beginning++;
                    /* advance beginning of lexeme */
            }
            else if (c == '<') state = 1;
            else if (c == '=') state = 5;
            else if (c == '>') state = 6;
            else state = fail( );
            break;

            ... /* cases 1-8 here */

        case 9:   c = nextchar( );
            if (isletter(c)) state = 10;
            else state = fail( );
            break;
        case 10:  c = nextchar( );
            if (isletter(c)) state = 10;
            else if (isdigit(c)) state = 10;
            else state = 11;
            break;
        case 11:  retract(1); install_id( );
            return ( gettoken( ) );

            ... /* cases 12-24 here */

        case 25:  c = nextchar( );
            if  (isdigit(c)) state = 26;
            else state = fail( );
            break;
        case 26:  c = nextchar( );
            if (isdigit(c)) state = 26;
            else state = 27;
            break;
        case 27:  retract(1); install_num( );
            return ( NUM );
        }
    }
}
```

Fig. 3.16. C code for lexical analyzer.

compiler is not available; the specifications can be manually transcribed into a working program using the transition diagram techniques of the previous section.

Lex is generally used in the manner depicted in Fig. 3.17. First, a specification of a lexical analyzer is prepared by creating a program lex.l in the Lex language. Then, lex.l is run through the Lex compiler to produce a C program lex.yy.c. The program lex.yy.c consists of a tabular representation of a transition diagram constructed from the regular expressions of lex.l, together with a standard routine that uses the table to recognize lexemes. The actions associated with regular expressions in lex.l are pieces of C code and are carried over directly to lex.yy.c. Finally, lex.yy.c is run through the C compiler to produce an object program a.out, which is the lexical analyzer that transforms an input stream into a sequence of tokens.

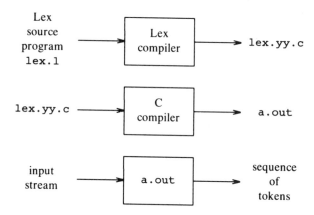

Fig. 3.17. Creating a lexical analyzer with Lex.

Lex Specifications

A Lex program consists of three parts:

    declarations
    %%
    translation rules
    %%
    auxiliary procedures

The declarations section includes declarations of variables, manifest constants, and regular definitions. (A manifest constant is an identifier that is declared to represent a constant.) The regular definitions are statements similar to those given in Section 3.3 and are used as components of the regular expressions appearing in the translation rules.

The translation rules of a Lex program are statements of the form

$$p_1 \quad \{ action_1 \}$$
$$p_2 \quad \{ action_2 \}$$
$$\ldots \qquad \ldots$$
$$p_n \quad \{ action_n \}$$

where each p_i is a regular expression and each $action_i$ is a program fragment describing what action the lexical analyzer should take when pattern p_i matches a lexeme. In Lex, the actions are written in C; in general, however, they can be in any implementation language.

The third section holds whatever auxiliary procedures are needed by the actions. Alternatively, these procedures can be compiled separately and loaded with the lexical analyzer.

A lexical analyzer created by Lex behaves in concert with a parser in the following manner. When activated by the parser, the lexical analyzer begins reading its remaining input, one character at a time, until it has found the longest prefix of the input that is matched by one of the regular expressions p_i. Then, it executes $action_i$. Typically, $action_i$ will return control to the parser. However, if it does not, then the lexical analyzer proceeds to find more lexemes, until an action causes control to return to the parser. The repeated search for lexemes until an explicit return allows the lexical analyzer to process white space and comments conveniently.

The lexical analyzer returns a single quantity, the token, to the parser. To pass an attribute value with information about the lexeme, we can set a global variable called `yylval`.

Example 3.11. Figure 3.18 is a Lex program that recognizes the tokens of Fig. 3.10 and returns the token found. A few observations about the code will introduce us to many of the important features of Lex.

In the declarations section, we see (a place for) the declaration of certain manifest constants used by the translation rules.[4] These declarations are surrounded by the special brackets %{ and %}. Anything appearing between these brackets is copied directly into the lexical analyzer `lex.yy.c`, and is not treated as part of the regular definitions or the translation rules. Exactly the same treatment is accorded the auxiliary procedures in the third section. In Fig. 3.18, there are two procedures, `install_id` and `install_num`, that are used by the translation rules; these procedures will be copied into `lex.yy.c` verbatim.

Also included in the definitions section are some regular definitions. Each such definition consists of a name and a regular expression denoted by that name. For example, the first name defined is `delim`; it stands for the

---

[4] It is common for the program `lex.yy.c` to be used as a subroutine of a parser generated by Yacc, a parser generator to be discussed in Chapter 4. In this case, the declaration of the manifest constants would be provided by the parser, when it is compiled with the program `lex.yy.c`.

```
%{
    /* definitions of manifest constants
    LT, LE, EQ, NE, GT, GE,
    IF, THEN, ELSE, ID, NUMBER, RELOP */
%}

/* regular definitions */
delim       [ \t\n]
ws          {delim}+
letter      [A-Za-z]
digit       [0-9]
id          {letter}({letter}|{digit})*
number      {digit}+(\.{digit}+)?(E[+\-]?{digit}+)?

%%

{ws}        {/* no action and no return */}
if          {return(IF);}
then        {return(THEN);}
else        {return(ELSE);}
{id}        {yylval = install_id(); return(ID);}
{number}    {yylval = install_num(); return(NUMBER);}
"<"         {yylval = LT; return(RELOP);}
"<="        {yylval = LE; return(RELOP);}
"="         {yylval = EQ; return(RELOP);}
"<>"        {yylval = NE; return(RELOP);}
">"         {yylval = GT; return(RELOP);}
">="        {yylval = GE; return(RELOP);}

%%

install_id() {
    /* procedure to install the lexeme, whose
    first character is pointed to by yytext and
    whose length is yyleng, into the symbol table
    and return a pointer thereto */
}

install_num() {
    /* similar procedure to install a lexeme that
    is a number */
}
```

Fig. 3.18. Lex program for the tokens of Fig. 3.10.

character class [\t\n], that is, any of the three symbols blank, tab (represented by \t), or newline (represented by \n). The second definition is of white space, denoted by the name ws. White space is any sequence of one or more delimiter characters. Notice that the word delim must be surrounded by braces in Lex, to distinguish it from the pattern consisting of the five letters delim.

In the definition of letter, we see the use of a character class. The shorthand [A-Za-z] means any of the capital letters A through Z or the lowercase letters a through z. The fifth definition, of id, uses parentheses, which are metasymbols in Lex, with their natural meaning as groupers. Similarly, the vertical bar is a Lex metasymbol representing union.

In the last regular definition, of number, we observe a few more details. We see ? used as a metasymbol, with its customary meaning of "zero or one occurrences of." We also note the backslash used as an escape, to let a character that is a Lex metasymbol have its natural meaning. In particular, the decimal point in the definition of number is expressed by \. because a dot by itself represents the character class of all characters except the newline, in Lex as in many UNIX system programs that deal with regular expressions. In the character class [+\-], we placed a backslash before the minus sign because the minus sign standing for itself could be confused with its use to denote a range, as in [A-Z].[5]

There is another way to cause characters to have their natural meaning, even if they are metasymbols of Lex: surround them with quotes. We have shown an example of this convention in the translation rules section, where the six relational operators are surrounded by quotes.[6]

Now, let us consider the translation rules in the section following the first %%. The first rule says that if we see ws, that is, any maximal sequence of blanks, tabs, and newlines, we take no action. In particular, we do not return to the parser. Recall that the structure of the lexical analyzer is such that it keeps trying to recognize tokens, until the action associated with one found causes a return.

The second rule says that if the letters if are seen, return the token IF, which is a manifest constant representing some integer understood by the parser to be the token **if**. The next two rules handle keywords then and else similarly.

In the rule for **id**, we see two statements in the associated action. First, the variable yylval is set to the value returned by procedure install_id; the definition of that procedure is in the third section. yylval is a variable

---

[5] Actually, Lex handles the character class [+-] correctly without the backslash, because the minus sign appearing at the end cannot represent a range.

[6] We did so because < and > are Lex metasymbols; they surround the names of "states," enabling Lex to change state when encountering certain tokens, such as comments or quoted strings, that must be treated differently from the usual text. There is no need to surround the equal sign by quotes, but neither is it forbidden.

whose definition appears in the Lex output `lex.yy.c`, and which is also available to the parser. The purpose of `yylval` is to hold the lexical value returned, since the second statement of the action, `return(ID)`, can only return a code for the token class.

We do not show the details of the code for `install_id`. However, we may suppose that it looks in the symbol table for the lexeme matched by the pattern **id**. Lex makes the lexeme available to routines appearing in the third section through two variables `yytext` and `yyleng`. The variable `yytext` corresponds to the variable that we have been calling *lexeme_beginning*, that is, a pointer to the first character of the lexeme; `yyleng` is an integer telling how long the lexeme is. For example, if `install_id` fails to find the identifier in the symbol table, it might create a new entry for it. The `yyleng` characters of the input, starting at `yytext`, might be copied into a character array and delimited by an end-of-string marker as in Section 2.7. The new symbol-table entry would point to the beginning of this copy.

Numbers are treated similarly by the next rule, and for the last six rules, `yylval` is used to return a code for the particular relational operator found, while the actual return value is the code for token **relop** in each case.

Suppose the lexical analyzer resulting from the program of Fig. 3.18 is given an input consisting of two tabs, the letters `if`, and a blank. The two tabs are the longest initial prefix of the input matched by a pattern, namely the pattern **ws**. The action for **ws** is to do nothing, so the lexical analyzer moves the lexeme-beginning pointer, `yytext`, to the `i` and begins to search for another token.

The next lexeme to be matched is `if`. Note that the patterns `if` and `{id}` both match this lexeme, and no pattern matches a longer string. Since the pattern for keyword `if` precedes the pattern for identifiers in the list of Fig. 3.18, the conflict is resolved in favor of the keyword. In general, this ambiguity-resolving strategy makes it easy to reserve keywords by listing them ahead of the pattern for identifiers.

For another example, suppose `<=` are the first two characters read. While pattern `<` matches the first character, it is not the longest pattern matching a prefix of the input. Thus Lex's strategy of selecting the longest prefix matched by a pattern makes it easy to resolve the conflict between `<` and `<=` in the expected manner – by choosing `<=` as the next token.   □

The Lookahead Operator

As we saw in Section 3.1, lexical analyzers for certain programming language constructs need to look ahead beyond the end of a lexeme before they can determine a token with certainty. Recall the example from Fortran of the pair of statements

```
DO 5 I = 1.25
DO 5 I = 1,25
```

In Fortran, blanks are not significant outside of comments and Hollerith strings, so suppose that all removable blanks are stripped before lexical analysis begins. The above statements then appear to the lexical analyzer as

```
DO5I=1.25
DO5I=1,25
```

In the first statement, we cannot tell until we see the decimal point that the string DO is part of the identifier DO5I. In the second statement, DO is a keyword by itself.

In Lex, we can write a pattern of the form r_1/r_2, where r_1 and r_2 are regular expressions, meaning match a string in r_1, but only if followed by a string in r_2. The regular expression r_2 after the lookahead operator / indicates the right context for a match; it is used only to restrict a match, not to be part of the match. For example, a Lex specification that recognizes the keyword DO in the context above is

```
DO/({letter} ¦ {digit})* = ({letter} ¦ {digit})*,
```

With this specification, the lexical analyzer will look ahead in its input buffer for a sequence of letters and digits followed by an equal sign followed by letters and digits followed by a comma to be sure that it did not have an assignment statement. Then only the characters D and O, preceding the lookahead operator / would be part of the lexeme that was matched. After a successful match, yytext points to the D and yyleng = 2. Note that this simple lookahead pattern allows DO to be recognized when followed by garbage, like Z4=6Q, but it will never recognize DO that is part of an identifier.

Example 3.12. The lookahead operator can be used to cope with another difficult lexical analysis problem in Fortran: distinguishing keywords from identifiers. For example, the input

```
IF(I, J) = 3
```

is a perfectly good Fortran assignment statement, not a logical if-statement. One way to specify the keyword IF using Lex is to define its possible right contexts using the lookahead operator. The simple form of the logical if-statement is

IF (*condition*) *statement*

Fortran 77 introduced another form of the logical if-statement:

```
IF ( condition ) THEN
      then_block
ELSE
      else_block
END IF
```

We note that every unlabeled Fortran statement begins with a letter and that every right parenthesis used for subscripting or operand grouping must be followed by an operator symbol such as =, +, or comma, another right parenthesis, or the end of the statement. Such a right parenthesis cannot be followed by a letter. In this situation, to confirm that IF is a keyword rather than an array name we scan forward looking for a right parenthesis followed by a letter before seeing a newline character (we assume continuation cards "cancel" the previous newline character). This pattern for the keyword IF can be written as

```
IF / \( .* \) {letter}
```

The dot stands for "any character but newline" and the backslashes in front of the parentheses tell Lex to treat them literally, not as metasymbols for grouping in regular expressions (see Exercise 3.10).   □

Another way to attack the problem posed by if-statements in Fortran is, after seeing IF(, to determine whether IF has been declared an array. We scan for the full pattern indicated above only if it has been so declared. Such tests make the automatic implementation of a lexical analyzer from a Lex specification harder, and they may even cost time in the long run, since frequent checks must be made by the program simulating a transition diagram to determine whether any such tests must be made. It should be noted that tokenizing Fortran is such an irregular task that it is frequently easier to write an ad hoc lexical analyzer for Fortran in a conventional programming language than it is to use an automatic lexical analyzer generator.

3.6 FINITE AUTOMATA

A *recognizer* for a language is a program that takes as input a string x and answers "yes" if x is a sentence of the language and "no" otherwise. We compile a regular expression into a recognizer by constructing a generalized transition diagram called a finite automaton. A finite automaton can be deterministic or nondeterministic, where "nondeterministic" means that more than one transition out of a state may be possible on the same input symbol.

Both deterministic and nondeterministic finite automata are capable of recognizing precisely the regular sets. Thus they both can recognize exactly what regular expressions can denote. However, there is a time-space tradeoff; while deterministic finite automata can lead to faster recognizers than nondeterministic automata, a deterministic finite automaton can be much bigger than an equivalent nondeterministic automaton. In the next section, we present methods for converting regular expressions into both kinds of finite automata. The conversion into a nondeterministic automaton is more direct so we discuss these automata first.

The examples in this section and the next deal primarily with the language denoted by the regular expression $(a|b)*abb$, consisting of the set of all strings of a's and b's ending in abb. Similar languages arise in practice. For example, a regular expression for the names of all files that end in .o is of the form $(.|o|c)*.o$, with c representing any character other than a dot or an o. As another example, after the opening /*, comments in C consist of

any sequence of characters ending in */, with the added requirement that no
proper prefix ends in */.

Nondeterministic Finite Automata

A *nondeterministic finite automaton* (NFA, for short) is a mathematical model
that consists of

1. a set of *states S*
2. a set of input symbols Σ (the *input symbol alphabet*)
3. a transition function *move* that maps state-symbol pairs to sets of states
4. a state s_0 that is distinguished as the *start* (or *initial*) *state*
5. a set of states *F* distinguished as *accepting* (or *final*) *states*

An NFA can be represented diagrammatically by a labeled directed graph,
called a *transition graph*, in which the nodes are the states and the labeled
edges represent the transition function. This graph looks like a transition
diagram, but the same character can label two or more transitions out of one
state, and edges can be labeled by the special symbol ϵ as well as by input
symbols.

The transition graph for an NFA that recognizes the language $(a|b)^*abb$ is
shown in Fig. 3.19. The set of states of the NFA is $\{0, 1, 2, 3\}$ and the input
symbol alphabet is $\{a, b\}$. State 0 in Fig. 3.19 is distinguished as the start
state, and the accepting state 3 is indicated by a double circle.

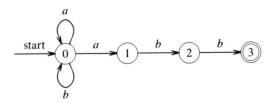

Fig. 3.19. A nondeterministic finite automaton.

When describing an NFA, we use the transition graph representation. In a
computer, the transition function of an NFA can be implemented in several
different ways, as we shall see. The easiest implementation is a *transition
table* in which there is a row for each state and a column for each input symbol and ϵ, if necessary. The entry for row *i* and symbol *a* in the table is the
set of states (or more likely in practice, a pointer to the set of states) that can
be reached by a transition from state *i* on input *a*. The transition table for the
NFA of Fig. 3.19 is shown in Fig. 3.20.

The transition table representation has the advantage that it provides fast
access to the transitions of a given state on a given character; its disadvantage
is that it can take up a lot of space when the input alphabet is large and most
transitions are to the empty set. Adjacency list representations of the

STATE	INPUT SYMBOL	
	a	b
0	{0, 1}	{0}
1	–	{2}
2	–	{3}

Fig. 3.20. Transition table for the finite automaton of Fig. 3.19.

transition function provide more compact implementations, but access to a given transition is slower. It should be clear that we can easily convert any one of these implementations of a finite automaton into another.

An NFA *accepts* an input string x if and only if there is some path in the transition graph from the start state to some accepting state, such that the edge labels along this path spell out x. The NFA of Fig. 3.19 accepts the input strings *abb, aabb, babb, aaabb,* · · · . For example, *aabb* is accepted by the path from 0, following the edge labeled a to state 0 again, then to states 1, 2, and 3 via edges labeled a, b, and b, respectively.

A path can be represented by a sequence of state transitions called *moves*. The following diagram shows the moves made in accepting the input string *aabb*:

$$0 \xrightarrow{\ a\ } 0 \xrightarrow{\ a\ } 1 \xrightarrow{\ b\ } 2 \xrightarrow{\ b\ } 3$$

In general, more than one sequence of moves can lead to an accepting state. Notice that several other sequences of moves may be made on the input string *aabb*, but none of the others happen to end in an accepting state. For example, another sequence of moves on input *aabb* keeps re-entering the non-accepting state 0:

$$0 \xrightarrow{\ a\ } 0 \xrightarrow{\ a\ } 0 \xrightarrow{\ b\ } 0 \xrightarrow{\ b\ } 0$$

The *language defined by* an NFA is the set of input strings it accepts. It is not hard to show that the NFA of Fig. 3.19 accepts $(a|b)^*abb$.

Example 3.13. In Fig. 3.21, we see an NFA to recognize $aa^*|bb^*$. String *aaa* is accepted by moving through states 0, 1, 2, 2, and 2. The labels of these edges are ϵ, a, a, and a, whose concatenation is *aaa*. Note that ϵ's "disappear" in a concatenation.   □

Deterministic Finite Automata

A *deterministic finite automaton* (DFA, for short) is a special case of a non-deterministic finite automaton in which

1.   no state has an ϵ-transition, i.e., a transition on input ϵ, and

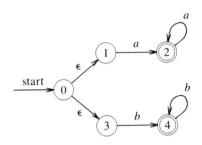

Fig. 3.21. NFA accepting $aa^* | bb^*$.

2.   for each state s and input symbol a, there is at most one edge labeled a leaving s.

A deterministic finite automaton has at most one transition from each state on any input. If we are using a transition table to represent the transition function of a DFA, then each entry in the transition table is a single state. As a consequence, it is very easy to determine whether a deterministic finite automaton accepts an input string, since there is at most one path from the start state labeled by that string. The following algorithm shows how to simulate the behavior of a DFA on an input string.

Algorithm 3.1. Simulating a DFA.

Input. An input string x terminated by an end-of-file character **eof**. A DFA D with start state s_0 and set of accepting states F.

Output. The answer "yes" if D accepts x; "no" otherwise.

Method. Apply the algorithm in Fig. 3.22 to the input string x. The function $move(s, c)$ gives the state to which there is a transition from state s on input character c. The function *nextchar* returns the next character of the input string x.   □

```
s := s_0;
c := nextchar;
while c ≠ eof do
        s := move(s, c);
        c := nextchar
end;
if s is in F then
        return "yes"
else return "no";
```

Fig. 3.22. Simulating a DFA.

Example 3.14. In Fig. 3.23, we see the transition graph of a deterministic finite automaton accepting the same language $(a\,|\,b)*abb$ as that accepted by the NFA of Fig. 3.19. With this DFA and the input string *ababb*, Algorithm 3.1 follows the sequence of states 0, 1, 2, 1, 2, 3 and returns "yes".   □

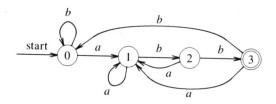

Fig. 3.23. DFA accepting $(a\,|\,b)*abb$.

Conversion of an NFA into a DFA

Note that the NFA of Fig. 3.19 has two transitions from state 0 on input *a*; that is, it may go to state 0 or 1. Similarly, the NFA of Fig. 3.21 has two transitions on ϵ from state 0. While we have not shown an example of it, a situation where we could choose a transition on ϵ or on a real input symbol also causes ambiguity. These situations, in which the transition function is multivalued, make it hard to simulate an NFA with a computer program. The definition of acceptance merely asserts that there must be some path labeled by the input string in question leading from the start state to an accepting state. But if there are many paths that spell out the same input string, we may have to consider them all before we find one that leads to acceptance or discover that no path leads to an accepting state.

We now present an algorithm for constructing from an NFA a DFA that recognizes the same language. This algorithm, often called the *subset construction*, is useful for simulating an NFA by a computer program. A closely related algorithm plays a fundamental role in the construction of LR parsers in the next chapter.

In the transition table of an NFA, each entry is a set of states; in the transition table of a DFA, each entry is just a single state. The general idea behind the NFA-to-DFA construction is that each DFA state corresponds to a set of NFA states. The DFA uses its state to keep track of all possible states the NFA can be in after reading each input symbol. That is to say, after reading input $a_1 a_2 \cdots a_n$, the DFA is in a state that represents the subset T of the states of the NFA that are reachable from the NFA's start state along some path labeled $a_1 a_2 \cdots a_n$. The number of states of the DFA can be exponential in the number of states of the NFA, but in practice this worst case occurs rarely.

Algorithm 3.2. (*Subset construction.*) Constructing a DFA from an NFA.

Input. An NFA N.

Output. A DFA D accepting the same language.

Method. Our algorithm constructs a transition table *Dtran* for D. Each DFA state is a set of NFA states and we construct *Dtran* so that D will simulate "in parallel" all possible moves N can make on a given input string.

We use the operations in Fig. 3.24 to keep track of sets of NFA states (s represents an NFA state and T a set of NFA states).

OPERATION	DESCRIPTION
ϵ-*closure*(s)	Set of NFA states reachable from NFA state s on ϵ-transitions alone.
ϵ-*closure*(T)	Set of NFA states reachable from some NFA state s in T on ϵ-transitions alone.
move(T, a)	Set of NFA states to which there is a transition on input symbol a from some NFA state s in T.

Fig. 3.24. Operations on NFA states.

Before it sees the first input symbol, N can be in any of the states in the set ϵ-*closure*(s_0), where s_0 is the start state of N. Suppose that exactly the states in set T are reachable from s_0 on a given sequence of input symbols, and let a be the next input symbol. On seeing a, N can move to any of the states in the set *move*(T, a). When we allow for ϵ-transitions, N can be in any of the states in ϵ-*closure*(*move*(T, a)), after seeing the a.

```
initially, ε-closure(s₀) is the only state in Dstates and it is unmarked;
while there is an unmarked state T in Dstates do begin
        mark T;
        for each input symbol a do begin
            U := ε-closure(move(T, a));
            if U is not in Dstates then
                    add U as an unmarked state to Dstates;
            Dtran[T, a] := U
        end
end
```

Fig. 3.25. The subset construction.

We construct *Dstates*, the set of states of D, and *Dtran*, the transition table for D, in the following manner. Each state of D corresponds to a set of NFA states that N could be in after reading some sequence of input symbols including all possible ϵ-transitions before or after symbols are read. The start state of D is ϵ-closure(s_0). States and transitions are added to D using the algorithm of Fig. 3.25. A state of D is an accepting state if it is a set of NFA states containing at least one accepting state of N.

```
push all states in T onto stack;
initialize ε-closure(T) to T;
while stack is not empty do begin
        pop t, the top element, off of stack;
        for each state u with an edge from t to u labeled ε do
            if u is not in ε-closure(T) do begin
                add u to ε-closure(T);
                push u onto stack
            end
end
```

Fig. 3.26. Computation of ϵ-closure.

The computation of ϵ-closure(T) is a typical process of searching a graph for nodes reachable from a given set of nodes. In this case the states of T are the given set of nodes, and the graph consists of just the ϵ-labeled edges of the NFA. A simple algorithm to compute ϵ-closure(T) uses a stack to hold states whose edges have not been checked for ϵ-labeled transitions. Such a procedure is shown in Fig. 3.26.   □

Example 3.15. Figure 3.27 shows another NFA N accepting the language $(a\,|\,b)^*abb$. (It happens to be the one in the next section, which will be mechanically constructed from the regular expression.) Let us apply Algorithm 3.2 to N. The start state of the equivalent DFA is ϵ-closure(0), which is $A = \{0, 1, 2, 4, 7\}$, since these are exactly the states reachable from state 0 via a path in which every edge is labeled ϵ. Note that a path can have no edges, so 0 is reached from itself by such a path.

The input symbol alphabet here is $\{a, b\}$. The algorithm of Fig. 3.25 tells us to mark A and then to compute

ϵ-closure(move(A, a)).

We first compute move(A, a), the set of states of N having transitions on a from members of A. Among the states 0, 1, 2, 4 and 7, only 2 and 7 have such transitions, to 3 and 8, so

ϵ-closure(move($\{0, 1, 2, 4, 7\}$, a)) = ϵ-closure($\{3, 8\}$) = $\{1, 2, 3, 4, 6, 7, 8\}$

Let us call this set B. Thus, Dtran[A, a] = B.

Among the states in A, only 4 has a transition on b to 5, so the DFA has a transition on b from A to

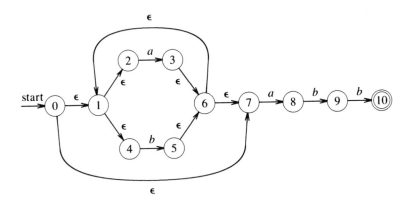

Fig. 3.27. NFA N for $(a\,|\,b)*abb$.

$C = \epsilon\text{-}closure(\{5\}) = \{1, 2, 4, 5, 6, 7\}$

Thus, $Dtran[A, b] = C$.

   If we continue this process with the now unmarked sets B and C, we eventually reach the point where all sets that are states of the DFA are marked. This is certain since there are "only" 2^{11} different subsets of a set of eleven states, and a set, once marked, is marked forever. The five different sets of states we actually construct are:

$A = \{0, 1, 2, 4, 7\}$ $D = \{1, 2, 4, 5, 6, 7, 9\}$
$B = \{1, 2, 3, 4, 6, 7, 8\}$ $E = \{1, 2, 4, 5, 6, 7, 10\}$
$C = \{1, 2, 4, 5, 6, 7\}$

State A is the start state, and state E is the only accepting state. The complete transition table $Dtran$ is shown in Fig. 3.28.

	INPUT SYMBOL	
STATE	a	b
A	B	C
B	B	D
C	B	C
D	B	E
E	B	C

Fig. 3.28. Transition table $Dtran$ for DFA.

   Also, a transition graph for the resulting DFA is shown in Fig. 3.29. It should be noted that the DFA of Fig. 3.23 also accepts $(a\,|\,b)*abb$ and has one

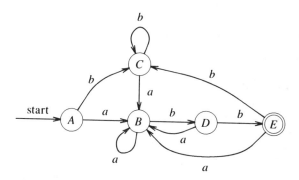

Fig. 3.29. Result of applying the subset construction to Fig. 3.27.

fewer state. We discuss the question of minimization of the number of states of a DFA in Section 3.9.

□

3.7 FROM A REGULAR EXPRESSION TO AN NFA

There are many strategies for building a recognizer from a regular expression, each with its own strengths and weaknesses. One strategy that has been used in a number of text-editing programs is to construct an NFA from a regular expression and then to simulate the behavior of the NFA on an input string using Algorithms 3.3 and 3.4 of this section. If run-time speed is essential, we can convert the NFA into a DFA using the subset construction of the previous section. In Section 3.9, we see an alternative implementation of a DFA from a regular expression in which an intervening NFA is not explicitly constructed. This section concludes with a discussion of time-space tradeoffs in the implementation of recognizers based on NFA and DFA.

Construction of an NFA from a Regular Expression

We now give an algorithm to construct an NFA from a regular expression. There are many variants of this algorithm, but here we present a simple version that is easy to implement. The algorithm is syntax-directed in that it uses the syntactic structure of the regular expression to guide the construction process. The cases in the algorithm follow the cases in the definition of a regular expression. We first show how to construct automata to recognize ϵ and any symbol in the alphabet. Then, we show how to construct automata for expressions containing an alternation, concatenation, or Kleene closure operator. For example, for the expression $r|s$, we construct an NFA inductively from the NFA's for r and s.

As the construction proceeds, each step introduces at most two new states, so the resulting NFA constructed for a regular expression has at most twice as many states as there are symbols and operators in the regular expression.

Algorithm 3.3. (*Thompson's construction.*) An NFA from a regular expression.

Input. A regular expression r over an alphabet Σ.

Output. An NFA N accepting $L(r)$.

Method. We first parse r into its constituent subexpressions. Then, using rules (1) and (2) below, we construct NFA's for each of the basic symbols in r (those that are either ϵ or an alphabet symbol). The basic symbols correspond to parts (1) and (2) in the definition of a regular expression. It is important to understand that if a symbol a occurs several times in r, a separate NFA is constructed for each occurrence.

Then, guided by the syntactic structure of the regular expression r, we combine these NFA's inductively using rule (3) below until we obtain the NFA for the entire expression. Each intermediate NFA produced during the course of the construction corresponds to a subexpression of r and has several important properties: it has exactly one final state, no edge enters the start state, and no edge leaves the final state.

1.   For ϵ, construct the NFA

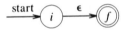

Here i is a new start state and f a new accepting state. Clearly, this NFA recognizes $\{\epsilon\}$.

2.   For a in Σ, construct the NFA

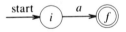

Again i is a new start state and f a new accepting state. This machine recognizes $\{a\}$.

3.   Suppose $N(s)$ and $N(t)$ are NFA's for regular expressions s and t.

a)   For the regular expression $s|t$, construct the following composite NFA $N(s|t)$:

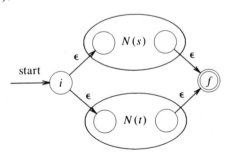

Here i is a new start state and f a new accepting state. There is a transition on ϵ from i to the start states of $N(s)$ and $N(t)$. There is a transition on ϵ from the accepting states of $N(s)$ and $N(t)$ to the new accepting state f. The start and accepting states of $N(s)$ and $N(t)$ are not start or accepting states of $N(s|t)$. Note that any path from i to f must pass through either $N(s)$ or $N(t)$ exclusively. Thus, we see that the composite NFA recognizes $L(s) \cup L(t)$.

b) For the regular expression st, construct the composite NFA $N(st)$:

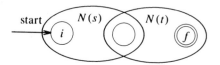

The start state of $N(s)$ becomes the start state of the composite NFA and the accepting state of $N(t)$ becomes the accepting state of the composite NFA. The accepting state of $N(s)$ is merged with the start state of $N(t)$; that is, all transitions from the start state of $N(t)$ become transitions from the accepting state of $N(s)$. The new merged state loses its status as a start or accepting state in the composite NFA. A path from i to f must go first through $N(s)$ and then through $N(t)$, so the label of that path will be a string in $L(s)L(t)$. Since no edge enters the start state of $N(t)$ or leaves the accepting state of $N(s)$, there can be no path from i to f that travels from $N(t)$ back to $N(s)$. Thus, the composite NFA recognizes $L(s)L(t)$.

c) For the regular expression $s*$, construct the composite NFA $N(s*)$:

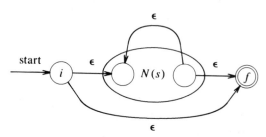

Here i is a new start state and f a new accepting state. In the composite NFA, we can go from i to f directly, along an edge labeled ϵ, representing the fact that ϵ is in $(L(s))*$, or we can go from i to f passing through $N(s)$ one or more times. Clearly, the composite NFA recognizes $(L(s))*$.

d) For the parenthesized regular expression (s), use $N(s)$ itself as the NFA.

Every time we construct a new state, we give it a distinct name. In this way, no two states of any component NFA can have the same name. Even if the same symbol appears several times in r, we create for each instance of that symbol a separate NFA with its own states.   □

We can verify that each step of the construction of Algorithm 3.3 produces an NFA that recognizes the correct language. In addition, the construction produces an NFA $N(r)$ with the following properties.

1. $N(r)$ has at most twice as many states as the number of symbols and operators in r. This follows from the fact each step of the construction creates at most two new states.

2. $N(r)$ has exactly one start state and one accepting state. The accepting state has no outgoing transitions. This property holds for each of the constituent automata as well.

3.   Each state of $N(r)$ has either one outgoing transition on a symbol in Σ or at most two outgoing ϵ-transitions.

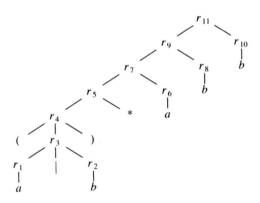

Fig. 3.30. Decomposition of $(a|b)*abb$.

Example 3.16. Let us use Algorithm 3.3 to construct $N(r)$ for the regular expression $r = (a|b)*abb$. Figure 3.30 shows a parse tree for r that is analogous to the parse trees constructed for arithmetic expressions in Section 2.2. For the constituent r_1, the first a, we construct the NFA

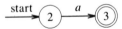

For r_2 we construct

We can now combine $N(r_1)$ and $N(r_2)$ using the union rule to obtain the

NFA for $r_3 = r_1|r_2$

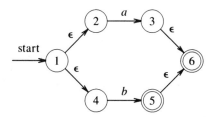

The NFA for (r_3) is the same as that for r_3. The NFA for $(r_3)*$ is then:

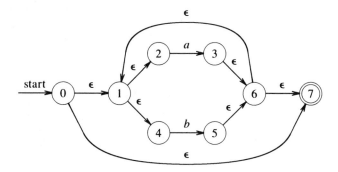

The NFA for $r_6 = a$ is

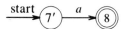

To obtain the automaton for $r_5 r_6$, we merge states 7 and 7', calling the resulting state 7, to obtain

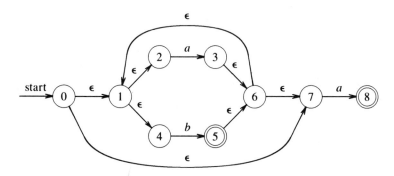

Continuing in this fashion we obtain the NFA for $r_{11} = (a|b)*abb$ that was first exhibited in Fig. 3.27.   □

Two-Stack Simulation of an NFA

We now present an algorithm that, given an NFA N constructed by Algorithm 3.3 and an input string x, determines whether N accepts x. The algorithm works by reading the input one character at a time and computing the complete set of states that N could be in after having read each prefix of the input. The algorithm takes advantage of the special properties of the NFA produced by Algorithm 3.3 to compute each set of nondeterministic states efficiently. It can be implemented to run in time proportional to $|N| \times |x|$, where $|N|$ is the number of states in N and $|x|$ is the length of x.

Algorithm 3.4. Simulating an NFA.

Input. An NFA N constructed by Algorithm 3.3 and an input string x. We assume x is terminated by an end-of-file character **eof**. N has start state s_0 and set of accepting states F.

Output. The answer "yes" if N accepts x; "no" otherwise.

Method. Apply the algorithm sketched in Fig. 3.31 to the input string x. The algorithm in effect performs the subset construction at run time. It computes a transition from the current set of states S to the next set of states in two stages. First, it determines *move*(S, a), all states that can be reached from a state in S by a transition on a, the current input character. Then, it computes the ϵ-*closure* of *move*(S, a), that is, all states that can be reached from *move*(S, a) by zero or more ϵ-transitions. The algorithm uses the function *nextchar* to read the characters of x, one at a time. When all characters of x have been seen, the algorithm returns "yes" if an accepting state is in the set S of current states; "no", otherwise.   □

```
S := ε-closure({s₀});
a := nextchar;
while a ≠ eof do begin
        S := ε-closure(move(S, a));
        a := nextchar
end
if S ∩ F ≠ ∅ then
        return "yes";
else return "no";
```

Fig. 3.31. Simulating the NFA of Algorithm 3.3.

Algorithm 3.4 can be efficiently implemented using two stacks and a bit vector indexed by NFA states. We use one stack to keep track of the current set of nondeterministic states and the other stack to compute the next set of nondeterministic states. We can use the algorithm in Fig. 3.26 to compute the ϵ-*closure*. The bit vector can be used to determine in constant time whether a nondeterministic state is already on a stack so that we do not add it twice. Once we have computed the next state on the second stack, we can interchange the roles of the two stacks. Since each nondeterministic state has at most two out-transitions, each state can give rise to at most two new states in a transition. Let us write $|N|$ for the number of states of N. Since there can be at most $|N|$ states on a stack, the computation of the next set of states from the current set of states can be done in time proportional to $|N|$. Thus, the total time needed to simulate the behavior of N on input x is proportional to $|N| \times |x|$.

Example 3.17. Let N be the NFA of Fig. 3.27 and let x be the string consisting of the single character a. The start state is $\epsilon\text{-}closure(\{0\}) = \{0, 1, 2, 4, 7\}$. On input symbol a there is a transition from 2 to 3 and from 7 to 8. Thus, T is $\{3, 8\}$. Taking the $\epsilon\text{-}closure$ of T gives us the next state $\{1, 2, 3, 4, 6, 7, 8\}$. Since none of these nondeterministic states is accepting, the algorithm returns "no."

Notice that Algorithm 3.4 does the subset construction at run-time. For example, compare the above transitions with the states of the DFA in Fig. 3.29 constructed from the NFA of Fig. 3.27. The start and next state sets on input a correspond to states A and B of the DFA.   □

Time-Space Tradeoffs

Given a regular expression r and an input string x, we now have two methods for determining whether x is in $L(r)$. One approach is to use Algorithm 3.3 to construct an NFA N from r. This construction can be done in $O(|r|)$ time, where $|r|$ is the length of r. N has at most twice as many states as $|r|$, and at most two transitions from each state, so a transition table for N can be stored in $O(|r|)$ space. We can then use Algorithm 3.4 to determine whether N accepts x in $O(|r| \times |x|)$ time. Thus, using this approach, we can determine whether x is in $L(r)$ in total time proportional to the length of r times the length of x. This approach has been used in a number of text editors to search for regular expression patterns when the target string x is generally not very long.

A second approach is to construct a DFA from the regular expression r by applying Thompson's construction to r and then the subset construction, Algorithm 3.2, to the resulting NFA. (An implementation that avoids constructing the intermediate NFA explicitly is given in Section 3.9.) Implementing the transition function with a transition table, we can use Algorithm 3.1 to simulate the DFA on input x in time proportional to the length of x, independent of the number of states in the DFA. This approach has often been used in pattern-matching programs that search text files for regular expression patterns. Once the finite automaton has been constructed, the searching can proceed very rapidly, so this approach is advantageous when the target string x is very long.

There are, however, certain regular expressions whose smallest DFA has a number of states that is exponential in the size of the regular expression. For example, the regular expression $(a|b)*a(a|b)(a|b) \cdots (a|b)$, where there are $n-1$ $(a|b)$'s at the end, has no DFA with fewer than 2^n states. This regular expression denotes any string of a's and b's in which the nth character from the right end is an a. It is not hard to prove that any DFA for this expression must keep track of the last n characters it sees on the input; otherwise, it may give an erroneous answer. Clearly, at least 2^n states are required to keep track of all possible sequences of n a's and b's. Fortunately, expressions such as this do not occur frequently in lexical analysis applications, but there are applications where similar expressions do arise.

A third approach is to use a DFA, but avoid constructing all of the transition table by using a technique called "lazy transition evaluation." Here, transitions are computed at run time but a transition from a given state on a given character is not determined until it is actually needed. The computed transitions are stored in a cache. Each time a transition is about to be made, the cache is consulted. If the transition is not there, it is computed and stored in the cache. If the cache becomes full, we can erase some previously computed transition to make room for the new transition.

Figure 3.32 summarizes the worst-case space and time requirements for determining whether an input string x is in the language denoted by a regular expression r using recognizers constructed from nondeterministic and deterministic finite automata. The "lazy" technique combines the space requirement of the NFA method with the time requirement of the DFA approach. Its space requirement is the size of the regular expression plus the size of the cache; its observed running time is almost as fast as that of a deterministic recognizer. In some applications, the "lazy" technique is considerably faster than the DFA approach, because no time is wasted computing state transitions that are never used.

Automaton	Space	Time
NFA	$O(|r|)$	$O(|r| \times |x|)$
DFA	$O(2^{|r|})$	$O(|x|)$

Fig. 3.32. Space and time taken to recognize regular expressions.

3.8 DESIGN OF A LEXICAL ANALYZER GENERATOR

In this section, we consider the design of a software tool that automatically constructs a lexical analyzer from a program in the Lex language. Although we discuss several methods, and none is precisely identical to that used by the UNIX system Lex command, we refer to these programs for constructing lexical analyzers as Lex compilers.

We assume that we have a specification of a lexical analyzer of the form

$$p_1 \quad \{ action_1 \}$$
$$p_2 \quad \{ action_2 \}$$
$$\cdots \qquad \cdots$$
$$p_n \quad \{ action_n \}$$

where, as in Section 3.5, each pattern p_i is a regular expression and each action $action_i$ is a program fragment that is to be executed whenever a lexeme matched by p_i is found in the input.

Our problem is to construct a recognizer that looks for lexemes in the input buffer. If more than one pattern matches, the recognizer is to choose the longest lexeme matched. If there are two or more patterns that match the longest lexeme, the first-listed matching pattern is chosen.

A finite automaton is a natural model around which to build a lexical analyzer, and the one constructed by our Lex compiler has the form shown in Fig. 3.33(b). There is an input buffer with two pointers to it, a lexeme-beginning and a forward pointer, as discussed in Section 3.2. The Lex compiler constructs a transition table for a finite automaton from the regular expression patterns in the Lex specification. The lexical analyzer itself consists of a finite automaton simulator that uses this transition table to look for the regular expression patterns in the input buffer.

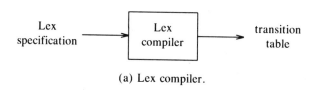

(a) Lex compiler.

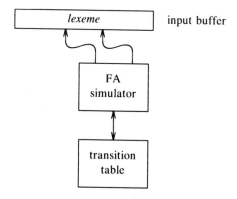

(b) Schematic lexical analyzer.

Fig. 3.33. Model of Lex compiler.

The remainder of this section shows that the implementation of a Lex compiler can be based on either nondeterministic or deterministic automata. At the end of the last section we saw that the transition table of an NFA for a regular expression pattern can be considerably smaller than that of a DFA, but the DFA has the decided advantage of being able to recognize patterns faster than the NFA.

Pattern Matching Based on NFA's

One method is to construct the transition table of a nondeterministic finite automaton N for the composite pattern $p_1|p_2|\cdots|p_n$. This can be done by first creating an NFA $N(p_i)$ for each pattern p_i using Algorithm 3.3, then adding a new start state s_0, and finally linking s_0 to the start state of each $N(p_i)$ with an ϵ-transition, as shown in Fig. 3.34.

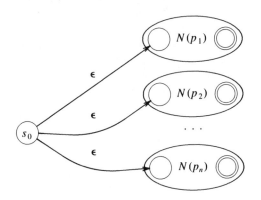

Fig. 3.34. NFA constructed from Lex specification.

To simulate this NFA we can use a modification of Algorithm 3.4. The modification ensures that the combined NFA recognizes the longest prefix of the input that is matched by a pattern. In the combined NFA, there is an accepting state for each pattern p_i. When we simulate the NFA using Algorithm 3.4, we construct the sequence of sets of states that the combined NFA can be in after seeing each input character. Even if we find a set of states that contains an accepting state, to find the longest match we must continue to simulate the NFA until it reaches *termination*, that is, a set of states from which there are no transitions on the current input symbol.

We presume that the Lex specification is designed so that a valid source program cannot entirely fill the input buffer without having the NFA reach termination. For example, each compiler puts some restriction on the length of an identifier, and violations of this limit will be detected when the input buffer overflows, if not sooner.

To find the correct match, we make two modifications to Algorithm 3.4. First, whenever we add an accepting state to the current set of states, we record the current input position and the pattern p_i corresponding to this accepting state. If the current set of states already contains an accepting state, then only the pattern that appears first in the Lex specification is recorded. Second, we continue making transitions until we reach termination. Upon termination, we retract the forward pointer to the position at which the last match occurred. The pattern making this match identifies the token found, and the lexeme matched is the string between the lexeme-beginning and forward pointers.

Usually, the Lex specification is such that some pattern, possibly an error pattern, will always match. If no pattern matches, however, we have an error condition for which no provision was made, and the lexical analyzer should transfer control to some default error recovery routine.

Example 3.18. A simple example illustrates the above ideas. Suppose we have the following Lex program consisting of three regular expressions and no regular definitions.

$$
\begin{array}{ll}
a & \{\ \}\ /*\ \text{actions are omitted here}\ */ \\
abb & \{\ \} \\
a*b^+ & \{\ \}
\end{array}
$$

The three tokens above are recognized by the automata of Fig. 3.35(a). We have simplified the third automaton somewhat from what would be produced by Algorithm 3.3. As indicated above, we can convert the NFA's of Fig. 3.35(a) into one combined NFA N shown in 3.35(b).

Let us now consider the behavior of N on the input string *aaba* using our modification of Algorithm 3.4. Figure 3.36 shows the sets of states and patterns that match as each character of the input *aaba* is processed. This figure shows that the initial set of states is $\{0, 1, 3, 7\}$. States 1, 3, and 7 each have a transition on a, to states 2, 4, and 7, respectively. Since state 2 is the accepting state for the first pattern, we record the fact that the first pattern matches after reading the first a.

However, there is a transition from state 7 to state 7 on the second input character, so we must continue making transitions. There is a transition from state 7 to state 8 on the input character b. State 8 is the accepting state for the third pattern. Once we reach state 8, there are no transitions possible on the next input character a so we have reached termination. Since the last match occurred after we read the third input character, we report that the third pattern has matched the lexeme *aab*.   □

The role of $action_i$ associated with the pattern p_i in the Lex specification is as follows. When an instance of p_i is recognized, the lexical analyzer executes the associated program $action_i$. Note that $action_i$ is not executed just because the NFA enters a state that includes the accepting state for p_i; $action_i$ is only executed if p_i turns out to be the pattern yielding the longest match.

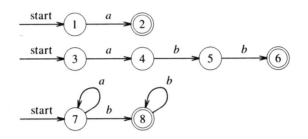

(a) NFA for *a*, *abb*, and $a*b^+$.

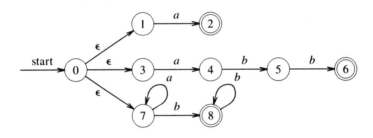

(b) Combined NFA.

Fig. 3.35. NFA recognizing three different patterns.

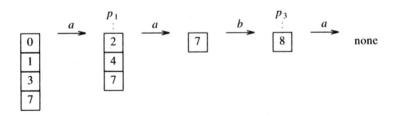

Fig. 3.36. Sequence of sets of states entered in processing input *aaba*.

DFA for Lexical Analyzers

Another approach to the construction of a lexical analyzer from a Lex specification is to use a DFA to perform the pattern matching. The only nuance is
to make sure we find the proper pattern matches. The situation is completely
analogous to the modified simulation of an NFA just described. When we
convert an NFA to a DFA using the subset construction Algorithm 3.2, there

may be several accepting states in a given subset of nondeterministic states. In such a situation, the accepting state corresponding to the pattern listed first in the Lex specification has priority. As in the NFA simulation, the only other modification we need to perform is to continue making state transitions until we reach a state with no next state (i.e., the state $\emptyset$) for the current input symbol. To find the lexeme matched, we return to the last input position at which the DFA entered an accepting state.

STATE	INPUT SYMBOL		PATTERN ANNOUNCED
	a	b	
0137	247	8	none
247	7	58	a
8	-	8	$a*b^+$
7	7	8	none
58	-	68	$a*b^+$
68	-	8	abb

Fig. 3.37. Transition table for a DFA.

Example 3.19. If we convert the NFA in Figure 3.35 to a DFA, we obtain the transition table in Fig. 3.37, where the states of the DFA have been named by lists of the states of the NFA. The last column in Fig. 3.37 indicates one of the patterns recognized upon entering that DFA state. For example, among NFA states 2, 4, and 7, only 2 is accepting, and it is the accepting state of the automaton for regular expression a in Fig. 3.35(a). Thus, DFA state 247 recognizes pattern a.

Note that the string abb is matched by two patterns, abb and $a*b^+$, recognized at NFA states 6 and 8. DFA state 68, in the last line of the transition table, therefore includes two accepting states of the NFA. We note that abb appears before $a*b^+$ in the translation rules of our Lex specification, so we announce that abb has been found in DFA state 68.

On input string aaba, the DFA enters the states suggested by the NFA simulation shown in Fig. 3.36. Consider a second example, the input string aba. The DFA of Fig. 3.37 starts off in state 0137. On input a it goes to state 247. Then on input b it progresses to state 58, and on input a it has no next state. We have thus reached termination, progressing through the DFA states 0137, then 247, then 58. The last of these includes the accepting NFA state 8 from Fig. 3.35(a). Thus in state 58 the DFA announces that the pattern $a*b^+$ has been recognized, and selects ab, the prefix of the input that led to state 58, as the lexeme.   □

Implementing the Lookahead Operator

Recall from Section 3.4 that the lookahead operator / is necessary in some situations, since the pattern that denotes a particular token may need to describe some trailing context for the actual lexeme. When converting a pattern with / to an NFA, we can treat the / as if it were ε, so that we do not actually look for / on the input. However, if a string denoted by this regular expression is recognized in the input buffer, the end of the lexeme is not the position of the NFA's accepting state. Rather it is at the last occurrence of the state of this NFA having a transition on the (imaginary) /.

Example 3.20. The NFA recognizing the pattern for IF given in Example 3.12 is shown in Fig. 3.38. State 6 indicates the presence of keyword IF; however, we find the token IF by scanning backwards to the last occurrence of state 2.   □

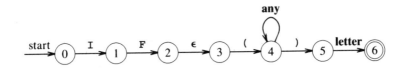

Fig. 3.38. NFA recognizing Fortran keyword IF.

3.9 OPTIMIZATION OF DFA-BASED PATTERN MATCHERS

In this section, we present three algorithms that have been used to implement and optimize pattern matchers constructed from regular expressions. The first algorithm is suitable for inclusion in a Lex compiler because it constructs a DFA directly from a regular expression, without constructing an intermediate NFA along the way.

The second algorithm minimizes the number of states of any DFA, so it can be used to reduce the size of a DFA-based pattern matcher. The algorithm is efficient; its running time is $O(n \log n)$, where n is the number of states in the DFA. The third algorithm can be used to produce fast but more compact representations for the transition table of a DFA than a straightforward two-dimensional table.

Important States of an NFA

Let us call a state of an NFA *important* if it has a non-ε out-transition. The subset construction in Fig. 3.25 uses only the important states in a subset T when it determines ε-*closure*(*move*(T, a)), the set of states that is reachable from T on input a. The set *move*(s, a) is nonempty only if state s is important. During the construction, two subsets can be identified if they have the same important states, and either both or neither include accepting states of the NFA.

When the subset construction is applied to an NFA obtained from a regular expression by Algorithm 3.3, we can exploit the special properties of the NFA to combine the two constructions. The combined construction relates the important states of the NFA with the symbols in the regular expression. Thompson's construction builds an important state exactly when a symbol in the alphabet appears in a regular expression. For example, important states will be constructed for each a and b in $(a|b)*abb$.

Moreover, the resulting NFA has exactly one accepting state, but the accepting state is not important because it has no transitions leaving it. By concatenating a unique right-end marker # to a regular expression r, we give the accepting state of r a transition on #, making it an important state of the NFA for r#. In other words, by using the augmented regular expression (r)# we can forget about accepting states as the subset construction proceeds; when the construction is complete, any DFA state with a transition on # must be an accepting state.

We represent an augmented regular expression by a syntax tree with basic symbols at the leaves and operators at the interior nodes. We refer to an interior node as a *cat-node*, *or-node*, or *star-node* if it is labeled by a concatenation, $|$, or * operator, respectively. Figure 3.39(a) shows a syntax tree for an augmented regular expression with cat-nodes marked by dots. The syntax tree for a regular expression can be constructed in the same manner as a syntax tree for an arithmetic expression (see Chapter 2).

Leaves in the syntax tree for a regular expression are labeled by alphabet symbols or by ϵ. To each leaf not labeled by ϵ we attach a unique integer and refer to this integer as the *position* of the leaf and also as a position of its symbol. A repeated symbol therefore has several positions. Positions are shown below the symbols in the syntax tree of Fig. 3.39(a). The numbered states in the NFA of Fig. 3.39(c) correspond to the positions of the leaves in the syntax tree in Fig. 3.39(a). It is no coincidence that these states are the important states of the NFA. Non-important states are named by upper case letters in Fig. 3.39(c).

The DFA in Fig. 3.39(b) can be obtained from the NFA in Fig. 3.39(c) if we apply the subset construction and identify subsets containing the same important states. The identification results in one fewer state being constructed, as a comparison with Fig. 3.29 shows.

From a Regular Expression to a DFA

In this section, we show how to construct a DFA directly from an augmented regular expression (r)#. We begin by constructing a syntax tree T for (r)# and then computing four functions: *nullable*, *firstpos*, *lastpos*, and *followpos*, by making traversals over T. Finally, we construct the DFA from *followpos*. The functions *nullable*, *firstpos*, and *lastpos* are defined on the nodes of the syntax tree and are used to compute *followpos*, which is defined on the set of positions.

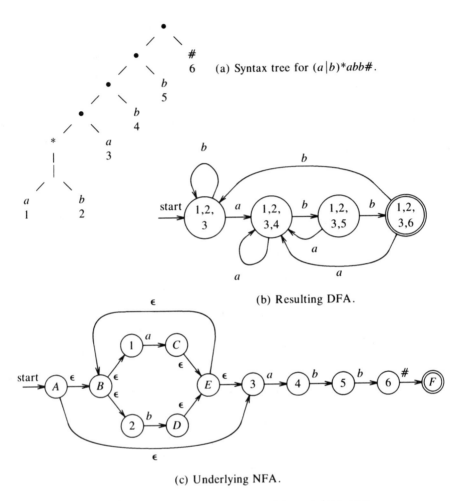

(a) Syntax tree for $(a|b)^*abb\#$.

(b) Resulting DFA.

(c) Underlying NFA.

Fig. 3.39. DFA and NFA constructed from $(a|b)^*abb\#$.

Remembering the equivalence between the important NFA states and the positions of the leaves in the syntax tree of the regular expression, we can short-circuit the construction of the NFA by building the DFA whose states correspond to sets of positions in the tree. The ϵ-transitions of the NFA represent some fairly complicated structure of the positions; in particular, they encode the information regarding when one position can follow another. That is, each symbol in an input string to a DFA can be matched by certain positions. An input symbol c can only be matched by positions at which there is a c, but not every position with a c can necessarily match a particular occurrence of c in the input stream.

The notion of a position matching an input symbol will be defined in terms of the function *followpos* on positions of the syntax tree. If i is a position, then *followpos*(i) is the set of positions j such that there is some input string $\cdots cd \cdots$ such that i corresponds to this occurrence of c and j to this occurrence of d.

Example 3.21. In Fig. 3.39(a), *followpos*$(1) = \{1, 2, 3\}$. The reasoning is that if we see an a corresponding to position 1, then we have just seen an occurrence of $a|b$ in the closure $(a|b)^*$. We could next see the first position of another occurrence of $a|b$, which explains why 1 and 2 are in *followpos*(1). We could also next see the first position of what follows $(a|b)^*$, that is, position 3. □

In order to compute the function *followpos*, we need to know what positions can match the first or last symbol of a string generated by a given subexpression of a regular expression. (Such information was used informally in Example 3.21.) If r^* is such a subexpression, then every position that can be first in r follows every position that can be last in r. Similarly, if rs is a subexpression, then every first position of s follows every last position of r.

At each node n of the syntax tree of a regular expression, we define a function *firstpos*(n) that gives the set of positions that can match the first symbol of a string generated by the subexpression rooted at n. Likewise, we define a function *lastpos*(n) that gives the set of positions that can match the last symbol in such a string. For example, if n is the root of the whole tree in Fig. 3.39(a), then *firstpos*$(n) = \{1, 2, 3\}$ and *lastpos*$(n) = \{6\}$. We give an algorithm for computing these functions momentarily.

In order to compute *firstpos* and *lastpos*, we need to know which nodes are the roots of subexpressions that generate languages that include the empty string. Such nodes are called *nullable*, and we define *nullable*(n) to be true if node n is nullable, false otherwise.

We can now give the rules to compute the functions *nullable*, *firstpos*, *lastpos*, and *followpos*. For the first three functions, we have a basis rule that tells about expressions of a basic symbol, and then three inductive rules that allow us to determine the value of the functions working up the syntax tree from the bottom; in each case the inductive rules correspond to the three operators, union, concatenation, and closure. The rules for *nullable* and *firstpos* are given in Fig. 3.40. The rules for *lastpos*(n) are the same as those for *firstpos*(n), but with c_1 and c_2 reversed, and are not shown.

The first rule for *nullable* states that if n is a leaf labeled ϵ, then *nullable*(n) is surely true. The second rule states that if n is a leaf labeled by an alphabet symbol, then *nullable*(n) is false. In this case, each leaf corresponds to a single input symbol, and therefore cannot generate ϵ. The last rule for *nullable* states that if n is a star-node with child c_1, then *nullable*(n) is true, because the closure of an expression generates a language that includes ϵ.

As another example, the fourth rule for *firstpos* states that if n is a cat-node with left child c_1 and right child c_2, and if *nullable*(c_1) is true, then

$$firstpos(n) = firstpos(c_1) \cup firstpos(c_2)$$

NODE n	$nullable(n)$	$firstpos(n)$
n is a leaf labeled ϵ	**true**	$\varnothing$
n is a leaf labeled with position i	**false**	$\{i\}$
n | c_1 c_2	$nullable(c_1)$ **or** $nullable(c_2)$	$firstpos(c_1) \cup firstpos(c_2)$
n $\cdot$ c_1 c_2	$nullable(c_1)$ **and** $nullable(c_2)$	**if** $nullable(c_1)$ **then** $firstpos(c_1) \cup firstpos(c_2)$ **else** $firstpos(c_1)$
n $*$ c_1	**true**	$firstpos(c_1)$

Fig. 3.40. Rules for computing *nullable* and *firstpos*.

otherwise, $firstpos(n) = firstpos(c_1)$. What this rule says is that if in an expression rs, r generates ϵ, then the first positions of s "show through" r and are also first positions of rs; otherwise, only the first positions of r are first positions of rs. The reasoning behind the remaining rules for *nullable* and *firstpos* are similar.

The function *followpos(i)* tells us what positions can follow position i in the syntax tree. Two rules define all the ways one position can follow another.

1. If n is a cat-node with left child c_1 and right child c_2, and i is a position in *lastpos*(c_1), then all positions in *firstpos*(c_2) are in *followpos*(i).

2. If n is a star-node, and i is a position in *lastpos*(n), then all positions in *firstpos*(n) are in *followpos*(i).

If *firstpos* and *lastpos* have been computed for each node, *followpos* of each position can be computed by making one depth-first traversal of the syntax tree.

Example 3.22. Figure 3.41 shows the values of *firstpos* and *lastpos* at all nodes in the tree of Fig. 3.39(a); *firstpos*(n) appears to the left of node n and *lastpos*(n) to the right. For example, *firstpos* at the leftmost leaf labeled a is $\{1\}$, since this leaf is labeled with position 1. Similarly, *firstpos* of the second leaf is $\{2\}$, since this leaf is labeled with position 2. By the third rule in Fig. 3.40, *firstpos* of their parent is $\{1, 2\}$.

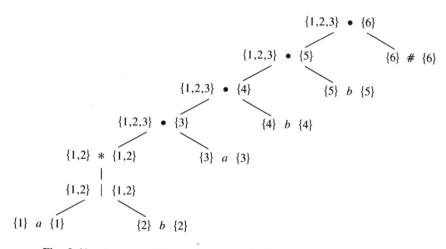

Fig. 3.41. *firstpos* and *lastpos* for nodes in syntax tree for $(a|b)*abb\#$.

The node labeled * is the only nullable node. Thus, by the if-condition of the fourth rule, *firstpos* for the parent of this node (the one representing expression $(a|b)*a$) is the union of $\{1, 2\}$ and $\{3\}$, which are the *firstpos*'s of its left and right children. On the other hand, the else-condition applies for *lastpos* of this node, since the leaf at position 3 is not nullable. Thus, the parent of the star-node has *lastpos* containing only 3.

Let us now compute *followpos* bottom up for each node of the syntax tree of Fig. 3.41. At the star-node, we add both 1 and 2 to *followpos*(1) and to *followpos*(2) using rule (2). At the parent of the star-node, we add 3 to *followpos*(1) and *followpos*(2) using rule (1). At the next cat-node, we add 4 to *followpos*(3) using rule (1). At the next two cat-nodes we add 5 to *followpos*(4) and 6 to *followpos*(5) using the same rule. This completes the construction of *followpos*. Figure 3.42 summarizes *followpos*.

NODE	*followpos*
1	$\{1, 2, 3\}$
2	$\{1, 2, 3\}$
3	$\{4\}$
4	$\{5\}$
5	$\{6\}$
6	-

Fig. 3.42. The function *followpos*.

We can illustrate the function *followpos* by creating a directed graph with a node for each position and directed edge from node i to node j if j is in *followpos*(i). Figure 3.43 shows this directed graph for *followpos* of Fig.

3.42.

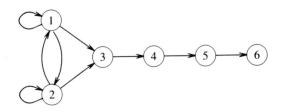

Fig. 3.43. Directed graph for the function *followpos*.

It is interesting to note that this diagram would become an NFA without ε-transitions for the regular expression in question if we:

1.   make all positions in *firstpos* of the root be start states,
2.   label each directed edge (*i*, *j*) by the symbol at position *j*, and
3.   make the position associated with # be the only accepting state.

It should therefore come as no surprise that we can convert the *followpos* graph into a DFA using the subset construction. The entire construction can be carried out on the positions, using the following algorithm.   □

Algorithm 3.5. Construction of a DFA from a regular expression *r*.

Input. A regular expression *r*.

Output. A DFA *D* that recognizes $L(r)$.

Method.

1.   Construct a syntax tree for the augmented regular expression (*r*)#, where # is a unique endmarker appended to (*r*).

2.   Construct the functions *nullable*, *firstpos*, *lastpos*, and *followpos* by making depth-first traversals of *T*.

3.   Construct *Dstates*, the set of states of *D*, and *Dtran*, the transition table for *D* by the procedure in Fig. 3.44. The states in *Dstates* are sets of positions; initially, each state is "unmarked," and a state becomes "marked" just before we consider its out-transitions. The start state of *D* is *firstpos*(*root*), and the accepting states are all those containing the position associated with the endmarker #.   □

Example 3.23. Let us construct a DFA for the regular expression (*a*|*b*)*abb. The syntax tree for ((*a*|*b*)*abb)# is shown in Fig. 3.39(a). *nullable* is true only for the node labeled *. The functions *firstpos* and *lastpos* are shown in Fig. 3.41, and *followpos* is shown in Fig. 3.42.

From Fig. 3.41, *firstpos* of the root is {1, 2, 3}. Let this set be *A* and

initially, the only unmarked state in *Dstates* is *firstpos* (*root*),
 where *root* is the root of the syntax tree for (*r*)#;
while there is an unmarked state *T* in *Dstates* **do begin**
  mark *T*;
  for each input symbol *a* **do begin**
   let *U* be the set of positions that are in *followpos* (*p*)
    for some position *p* in *T*,
     such that the symbol at position *p* is *a*;
   if *U* is not empty and is not in *Dstates* **then**
    add *U* as an unmarked state to *Dstates*;
   Dtran [*T*, *a*] := *U*
  end
 end

Fig. 3.44. Construction of DFA.

consider input symbol *a*. Positions 1 and 3 are for *a*, so let *B* = *followpos* (1) ∪ *followpos* (3) = {1, 2, 3, 4}. Since this set has not yet been seen, we set *Dtran* [*A*, *a*] := *B*.

When we consider input *b*, we note that of the positions in *A*, only 2 is associated with *b*, so we must consider the set *followpos* (2) = {1, 2, 3}. Since this set has already been seen, we do not add it to *Dstates*, but we add the transition *Dtran* [*A*, *b*] := *A*.

We now continue with *B* = {1, 2, 3, 4}. The states and transitions we finally obtain are the same as those that were shown in Fig. 3.39(b).   □

Minimizing the Number of States of a DFA

An important theoretical result is that every regular set is recognized by a minimum-state DFA that is unique up to state names. In this section, we show how to construct this minimum-state DFA by reducing the number of states in a given DFA to the bare minimum without affecting the language that is being recognized. Suppose that we have a DFA *M* with set of states *S* and input symbol alphabet Σ. We assume that every state has a transition on every input symbol. If that were not the case, we can introduce a new "dead state" *d*, with transitions from *d* to *d* on all inputs, and add a transition from state *s* to *d* on input *a* if there was no transition from *s* on *a*.

We say that string *w* *distinguishes* state *s* from state *t* if, by starting with the DFA *M* in state *s* and feeding it input *w*, we end up in an accepting state, but starting in state *t* and feeding it input *w*, we end up in a nonaccepting state, or vice versa. For example, ε distinguishes any accepting state from any nonaccepting state, and in the DFA of Fig. 3.29, states *A* and *B* are distinguished by the input *bb*, since *A* goes to the nonaccepting state *C* on input *bb*, while *B* goes to the accepting state *E* on that same input.

Our algorithm for minimizing the number of states of a DFA works by finding all groups of states that can be distinguished by some input string. Each group of states that cannot be distinguished is then merged into a single state. The algorithm works by maintaining and refining a partition of the set of states. Each group of states within the partition consists of states that have not yet been distinguished from one another, and any pair of states chosen from different groups have been found distinguishable by some input.

Initially, the partition consists of two groups: the accepting states and the nonaccepting states. The fundamental step is to take some group of states, say $A = \{s_1, s_2, \ldots, s_k\}$ and some input symbol a, and look at what transitions states $s_1, \ldots, s_k$ have on input a. If these transitions are to states that fall into two or more different groups of the current partition, then we must split A so that the transitions from the subsets of A are all confined to a single group of the current partition. Suppose, for example, that s_1 and s_2 go to states t_1 and t_2 on input a, and t_1 and t_2 are in different groups of the partition. Then we must split A into at least two subsets so that one subset contains s_1 and the other s_2. Note that t_1 and t_2 are distinguished by some string w, so s_1 and s_2 are distinguished by string aw.

We repeat this process of splitting groups in the current partition until no more groups need to be split. While we have justified why states that have been split into different groups really can be distinguished, we have not indicated why states that are not split into different groups are certain not to be distinguishable by any input string. Such is the case, however, and we leave a proof of that fact to the reader interested in the theory (see, for example, Hopcroft and Ullman [1979]). Also left to the interested reader is a proof that the DFA constructed by taking one state for each group of the final partition and then throwing away the dead state and states not reachable from the start state has as few states as any DFA accepting the same language.

Algorithm 3.6. Minimizing the number of states of a DFA.

Input. A DFA M with set of states S, set of inputs Σ, transitions defined for all states and inputs, start state s_0, and set of accepting states F.

Output. A DFA M' accepting the same language as M and having as few states as possible.

Method.

1. Construct an initial partition Π of the set of states with two groups: the accepting states F and the nonaccepting states $S - F$.

2. Apply the procedure of Fig. 3.45 to Π to construct a new partition Π_{new}.

3. If $\Pi_{new} = \Pi$, let $\Pi_{final} = \Pi$ and continue with step (4). Otherwise, repeat step (2) with $\Pi := \Pi_{new}$.

4. Choose one state in each group of the partition Π_{final} as the *representative*

for that group. The representatives will be the states of the reduced DFA
M'. Let s be a representative state, and suppose on input a there is a
transition of M from s to t. Let r be the representative of t's group (r
may be t). Then M' has a transition from s to r on a. Let the start state
of M' be the representative of the group containing the start state s_0 of
M, and let the accepting states of M' be the representatives that are in F.
Note that each group of Π_{final} either consists only of states in F or has no
states in F.

5.   If M' has a dead state, that is, a state d that is not accepting and that has
transitions to itself on all input symbols, then remove d from M'. Also
remove any states not reachable from the start state. Any transitions to d
from other states become undefined.   □

> **for** each group G of Π **do begin**
>   partition G into subgroups such that two states s and t
>   of G are in the same subgroup if and only if for all
>   input symbols a, states s and t have transitions on a
>   to states in the same group of Π;
>   /* at worst, a state will be in a subgroup by itself */
>   replace G in Π_{new} by the set of all subgroups formed
> **end**

Fig. 3.45.   Construction of Π_{new}.

Example 3.24. Let us reconsider the DFA represented in Fig. 3.29. The initial partition Π consists of two groups: (E), the accepting state, and $(ABCD)$,
the nonaccepting states. To construct Π_{new}, the algorithm of Fig. 3.45 first
considers (E). Since this group consists of a single state, it cannot be split
further, so (E) is placed in Π_{new}. The algorithm then considers the group
$(ABCD)$. On input a, each of these states has a transition to B, so they could
all remain in one group as far as input a is concerned. On input b, however,
A, B, and C go to members of the group $(ABCD)$ of Π, while D goes to E, a
member of another group. Thus, in Π_{new} the group $(ABCD)$ must be split into
two new groups (ABC) and (D); Π_{new} is thus $(ABC)(D)(E)$.

In the next pass through the algorithm of Fig. 3.45, we again have no splitting on input a, but (ABC) must be split into two new groups $(AC)(B)$, since
on input b, A and C each have a transition to C, while B has a transition to D,
a member of a group of the partition different from that of C. Thus the next
value of Π is $(AC)(B)(D)(E)$.

In the next pass through the algorithm of Fig. 3.45, we cannot split any of
the groups consisting of a single state. The only possibility is to try to split
(AC). But A and C go the same state B on input a, and they go to the same
state C on input b. Hence, after this pass, $\Pi_{new} = \Pi$. Π_{final} is thus
$(AC)(B)(D)(E)$.

If we choose A as the representative for the group (AC), and choose B, D, and E for the singleton groups, then we obtain the reduced automaton whose transition table is shown in Fig. 3.46. State A is the start state and state E is the only accepting state.

STATE	INPUT SYMBOL	
	a	b
A	B	A
B	B	D
D	B	E
E	B	A

Fig. 3.46. Transition table of reduced DFA.

For example, in the reduced automaton, state E has a transition to state A on input b, since A is the representative of the group for C and there is a transition from E to C on input b in the original automaton. A similar change has taken place in the entry for A and input b; otherwise, all other transitions are copied from Fig. 3.29. There is no dead state in Fig. 3.46, and all states are reachable from the start state A.   □

State Minimization in Lexical Analyzers

To apply the state minimization procedure to the DFA's constructed in Section 3.7, we must begin Algorithm 3.5 with an initial partition that places in different groups all states indicating different tokens.

Example 3.25. In the case of the DFA of Fig. 3.37, the initial partition would group 0137 with 7, since they each gave no indication of a token recognized; 8 and 58 would also be grouped, since they each indicated token $a*b^+$. Other states would be in groups by themselves. Then we immediately discover that 0137 and 7 belong in different groups since they go to different groups on input a. Likewise, 8 and 58 do not belong together because of their transitions on input b. Thus the DFA of Fig. 3.37 is the minimum-state automaton doing its job.   □

Table-Compression Methods

As we have indicated, there are many ways to implement the transition function of a finite automaton. The process of lexical analysis occupies a reasonable portion of the compiler's time, since it is the only process that must look at the input one character at a time. Therefore the lexical analyzer should minimize the number of operations it performs per input character. If a DFA is used to help implement the lexical analyzer, then an efficient representation of the transition function is desirable. A two-dimensional array, indexed by states and characters, provides the fastest access, but it can take up too much space (say several hundred states by 128 characters). A more compact but slower scheme is to use a linked list to store the transitions out of each state, with a "default" transition at the end of the list. The most frequently occurring transition is one obvious choice for the default.

There is a more subtle implementation that combines the fast access of the array representation with the compactness of the list structures. Here we use a data structure consisting of four arrays indexed by state numbers as depicted in Fig. 3.47.[7] The *base* array is used to determine the base location of the entries for each state stored in the *next* and *check* arrays. The *default* array is used to determine an alternative base location in case the current base location is invalid.

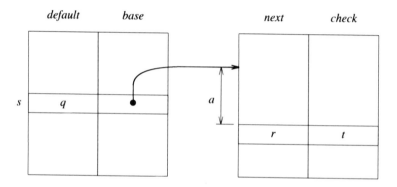

Fig. 3.47. Data structure for representing transition tables.

To compute *nextstate* (s, a), the transition for state s on input symbol a, we first consult the pair of arrays *next* and *check*. In particular, we find their entries for state s in location $l = base[s]+a$, where character a is treated as an integer. We take *next*$[l]$ to be the next state for s on input a if *check*$[l] = s$. If *check*$[l] \neq s$, we determine $q = default[s]$ and repeat the entire procedure recursively, using q in place of s. The procedure is the following:

> **procedure** *nextstate* (s, a);
>   **if** *check*$[base[s]+a] = s$ **then**
>   **return** *next*$[base[s]+a]$
>   **else**
>   **return** *nextstate* $(default[s], a)$

The intended use of the structure of Fig. 3.47 is to make the *next-check* arrays short, by taking advantage of the similarities among states. For

---

[7] There would be in practice another array indexed by s, giving the pattern that matches, if any, when state s is entered. This information is derived from the NFA states making up DFA state s.

example, state q, the default for state s, might be the state that says we are "working on an identifier," such as state 10 in Fig. 3.13. Perhaps s is entered after seeing th a prefix of the keyword then as well as a prefix of an identifier. On input character e we must go to a special state that remembers we have seen the, but otherwise state s behaves as state q does. Thus, we set $check[base[s]+e]$ to s and $next[base[s]+e]$ to the state for the.

While we may not be able to choose *base* values so that no *next-check* entries remain unused, experience shows that the simple strategy of setting the *base* to the lowest number such that the special entries can be filled in without conflicting with existing entries is fairly good and utilizes little more space than the minimum possible.

We can shorten *check* into an array indexed by states if the DFA has the property that the incoming edges to each state t all have the same label a. To implement this scheme, we set $check[t] = a$ and replace the test on line 2 of procedure *nextstate* by

$$\textbf{if } check[next[base[s]+a]] = a \textbf{ then}$$

EXERCISES

3.1 What is the input alphabet of each of the following languages?
  a) Pascal
  b) C
  c) Fortran 77
  d) Ada
  e) Lisp

3.2 What are the conventions regarding the use of blanks in each of the languages of Exercise 3.1?

3.3 Identify the lexemes that make up the tokens in the following programs. Give reasonable attribute values for the tokens.
  a) Pascal

```
function max ( i, j : integer ) : integer ;
{ return maximum of integers i and j }
begin
    if i > j then max := i
    else max := j
end;
```

  b) C

```
int max ( i, j ) int i, j;
/* return maximum of integers i and j */
{
    return i>j?i:j;
}
```

c) Fortran 77

```
        FUNCTION MAX ( I, J )
C       RETURN MAXIMUM OF INTEGERS I AND J
        IF (I .GT. J) THEN
            MAX = I
        ELSE
            MAX = J
        END IF
        RETURN
```

3.4 Write a program for the function nextchar( ) of Section 3.4 using the buffering scheme with sentinels described in Section 3.2.

3.5 In a string of length n, how many of the following are there?
a) prefixes
b) suffixes
c) substrings
d) proper prefixes
e) subsequences

*3.6 Describe the languages denoted by the following regular expressions:
a) $0(0|1)^*0$
b) $((\epsilon|0)1^*)^*$
c) $(0|1)^*0(0|1)(0|1)$
d) $0^*10^*10^*10^*$
e) $(00|11)^*((01|10)(00|11)^*(01|10)(00|11)^*)^*$

*3.7 Write regular definitions for the following languages.
a) All strings of letters that contain the five vowels in order.
b) All strings of letters in which the letters are in ascending lexicographic order.
c) Comments consisting of a string surrounded by /* and */ without an intervening */ unless it appears inside the quotes " and ".
*d) All strings of digits with no repeated digit.
e) All strings of digits with at most one repeated digit.
f) All strings of 0's and 1's with an even number of 0's and an odd number of 1's.
g) The set of chess moves, such as $p-k4$ or $kbp \times qn$.
h) All strings of 0's and 1's that do not contain the substring 011.
i) All strings of 0's and 1's that do not contain the subsequence 011.

3.8 Specify the lexical form of numeric constants in the languages of Exercise 3.1.

3.9 Specify the lexical form of identifiers and keywords in the languages of Exercise 3.1.

3.10 The regular expression constructs permitted by Lex are listed in Fig.
3.48 in decreasing order of precedence. In this table, *c* stands for any
single character, *r* for a regular expression, and *s* for a string.

EXPRESSION	MATCHES	EXAMPLE
c	any non-operator character *c*	a
\c	character *c* literally	*
"*s*"	string *s* literally	"**"
.	any character but newline	a.*b
^	beginning of line	^abc
$	end of line	abc$
[*s*]	any character in *s*	[abc]
[^*s*]	any character not in *s*	[^abc]
*r**	zero or more *r*'s	a*
r+	one or more *r*'s	a+
r?	zero or one *r*	a?
r{*m,n*}	*m* to *n* occurrences of *r*	a{1,5}
$r_1 r_2$	r_1 then r_2	ab
$r_1 \mid r_2$	r_1 or r_2	a¦b
(*r*)	*r*	(a¦b)
r_1 / r_2	r_1 when followed by r_2	abc/123

Fig. 3.48. Lex regular expressions.

a) The special meaning of the operator symbols

$$\backslash \quad " \quad . \quad \char`^ \quad \$ \quad [\quad] \quad * \quad + \quad ? \quad \{ \quad \} \quad \mid \quad /$$

must be turned off if the operator symbol is to be used as a matching character. This can be done by quoting the character, using
one of two styles of quotation. The expression "*s*" matches the
string *s* literally, provided no " appears in *s*. For example, "**"
matches the string **. We could also have matched this string
with the expression **. Note that an unquoted * is an instance
of the Kleene closure operator. Write a Lex regular expression
that matches the string "\.

b) In Lex, a *complemented* character class is a character class in which
the first symbol is ^. A complemented character class matches
any character not in the class. Thus, [^a] matches any character
that is not an a, [^A-Za-z] matches any character that is not an
upper or lower case letter, and so on. Show that for every regular
definition with complemented character classes there is an
equivalent regular expression without complemented character
classes.

c) The regular expression $r\{m,n\}$ matches from m to n occurrences of the pattern r. For example, $a\{1,5\}$ matches a string of one to five a's. Show that for every regular expression containing repetition operators there is an equivalent regular expression without repetition operators.

d) The operator $\hat{}$ matches the leftmost end of a line. This is the same operator that introduces a complemented character class, but the context in which $\hat{}$ appears will always determine a unique meaning for this operator. The operator $\$$ matches the rightmost end of a line. For example, $\hat{}[\hat{}aeiou]*\$$ matches any line that does not contain a lower case vowel. For every regular expression containing the $\hat{}$ and $\$$ operators is there an equivalent regular expression without these operators?

3.11 Write a Lex program that copies a file, replacing each nonnull sequence of white space by a single blank.

3.12 Write a Lex program that copies a Fortran program, replacing all instances of DOUBLE PRECISION by REAL.

3.13 Use your specification for keywords and identifiers for Fortran 77 from Exercise 3.9 to identify the tokens in the following statements:

```
IF(I) = TOKEN
IF(I) ASSIGN5TOKEN
IF(I) 10,20,30
IF(I) GOTO15
IF(I) THEN
```

Can you write your specification for keywords and identifiers in Lex?

3.14 In the UNIX system, the shell command sh uses the operators in Fig. 3.49 in filename expressions to describe sets of filenames. For example, the filename expression *.o matches all filenames ending in .o; sort.? matches all filenames that are of the form sort.c where c is any character. Character classes may be abbreviated as in [a-z]. Show how shell filename expressions can be represented by regular expressions.

3.15 Modify Algorithm 3.1 to find the longest prefix of the input that is accepted by the DFA.

3.16 Construct nondeterministic finite automata for the following regular expressions using Algorithm 3.3. Show the sequence of moves made by each in processing the input string *ababbab*.
a) $(a|b)*$
b) $(a*|b*)*$

EXPRESSION	MATCHES	EXAMPLE
$'s'$	string s literally	$'\backslash'$
$\backslash c$	character c literally	$\backslash'$
*	any string	*.o
?	any character	sort1.?
[s]	any character in s	sort.[cso]

Fig. 3.49. Filename expressions in the program sh.

    c) $((\epsilon | a)b^*)^*$
    d) $(a|b)^*abb(a|b)^*$

3.17 Convert the NFA's in Exercise 3.16 into DFA's using Algorithm 3.2. Show the sequence of moves made by each in processing the input string $ababbab$.

3.18 Construct DFA's for the regular expressions in Exercise 3.16 using Algorithm 3.5. Compare the size of the DFA's with those constructed in Exercise 3.17.

3.19 Construct a deterministic finite automaton from the transition diagrams for the tokens in Fig. 3.10.

3.20 Extend the table of Fig. 3.40 to include the regular expression operators ? and $^+$.

3.21 Minimize the states in the DFA's of Exercise 3.18 using Algorithm 3.6.

3.22 We can prove that two regular expressions are equivalent by showing that their minimum-state DFA's are the same, except for state names. Using this technique, show that the following regular expressions are all equivalent.
    a) $(a|b)^*$
    b) $(a^* | b^*)^*$
    c) $((\epsilon | a)b^*)^*$

3.23 Construct minimum-state DFA's for the following regular expressions.
    a) $(a|b)^*a(a|b)$
    b) $(a|b)^*a(a|b)(a|b)$
    c) $(a|b)^*a(a|b)(a|b)(a|b)$
  **d) Prove that any deterministic finite automaton for the regular expression $(a|b)^*a(a|b)(a|b) \cdots (a|b)$, where there are $n-1$ $(a|b)$'s at the end, must have at least 2^n states.

3.24 Construct the representation of Fig. 3.47 for the transition table of Exercise 3.19. Pick default states and try the following two methods of constructing the *next* array and compare the amounts of space used:

a) Starting with the densest states (those with the largest number of entries differing from their default states) first, place the entries for the states in the *next* array.

b) Place the entries for the states in the *next* array in a random order.

3.25 A variant of the table compression scheme of Section 3.9 would be to avoid a recursive *nextstate* procedure by using a fixed default location for each state. Construct the representation of Fig. 3.47 for the transition table of Exercise 3.19 using this nonrecursive technique. Compare the space requirements with those of Exercise 3.24.

3.26 Let $b_1 b_2 \cdots b_m$ be a pattern string, called a *keyword*. A *trie* for a keyword is a transition diagram with $m+1$ states in which each state corresponds to a prefix of the keyword. For $1 \le s \le m$, there is a transition from state $s-1$ to state s on symbol b_s. The start and final states correspond to the empty string and the complete keyword, respectively. The trie for the keyword *ababaa* is:

We now define a *failure function* f on each state of the transition diagram, except the start state. Suppose states s and t represent prefixes u and v of the keyword. Then, we define $f(s) = t$ if and only if v is the longest proper suffix of u that is also the prefix of the keyword. The failure function f for the above trie is

s	1	2	3	4	5	6
$f(s)$	0	0	1	2	3	1

For example, states 3 and 1 represent prefixes *aba* and *a* of the keyword *ababaa*. $f(3) = 1$ because *a* is the longest proper suffix of *aba* that is prefix of the keyword.

a) Construct the failure function for the keyword *abababaab*.

*b) Let the states in the trie be 0, 1, . . . , m, with 0 the start state. Show that the algorithm in Fig. 3.50 correctly computes the failure function.

*c) Show that in the overall execution of the algorithm in Fig. 3.50 the assignment statement $t := f(t)$ in the inner loop is executed at most m times.

*d) Show that the algorithm runs in $O(m)$ time.

```
/* compute failure function f for b₁ · · · bₘ */
t := 0; f (1) := 0;
for s := 1 to m − 1 do begin
      while t > 0 and b_{s+1} ≠ b_{t+1} do t := f (t);
      if b_{s+1} = b_{t+1} then begin t := t+1; f (s+1) := t end;
      else f (s+1) := 0
end
```

Fig. 3.50. Algorithm to compute failure function for Exercise 3.26.

3.27 Algorithm KMP in Fig. 3.51 uses the failure function f constructed as in Exercise 3.26 to determine whether keyword $b_1 \cdots b_m$ is a substring of a target string $a_1 \cdots a_n$. States in the trie for $b_1 \cdots b_m$ are numbered from 0 to m as in Exercise 3.26(b).

```
/* does a₁ · · · aₙ contain b₁ · · · bₘ as a substring */
s := 0;
for i := 1 to n do begin
      while s > 0 and a_i ≠ b_{s+1} do s := f (s);
      if a_i = b_{s+1} then s := s+1
      if s = m then return "yes"
end;
return "no"
```

Fig. 3.51. Algorithm KMP.

a) Apply Algorithm KMP to determine whether *ababaa* is a substring of *abababaab*.

*b) Prove that Algorithm KMP returns "yes" if and only if $b_1 \cdots b_m$ is a substring of $a_1 \cdots a_n$.

*c) Show that Algorithm KMP runs in $O(m+n)$ time.

*d) Given a keyword y, show that the failure function can be used to construct, in $O(|y|)$ time, a DFA with $|y| + 1$ states for the regular expression $.*y.*$, where $.$ stands for any input character.

3.28 Define the *period* of a string s to be an integer p such that s can be expressed as $(uv)^k u$, for some $k \geq 0$, where $|uv| = p$ and v is not the empty string. For example, 2 and 4 are periods of the string *abababa*.

a) Show that p is a period of a string s if and only if $st = us$ for some strings t and u of length p.

b) Show that if p and q are periods of a string s and if $p+q \leq |s| + \gcd(p,q)$, then $\gcd(p,q)$ is a period of s, where $\gcd(p,q)$ is the greatest common divisor of p and q.

c) Let $sp(s_i)$ be the smallest period of the prefix of length i of a string s. Show that the failure function f has the property that $f(j) = j - sp(s_{j-1})$.

*3.29 Let the *shortest repeating prefix* of a string s be the shortest prefix u of s such that $s = u^k$, for some $k \geq 1$. For example, ab is the shortest repeating prefix of $abababab$ and aba is the shortest repeating prefix of aba. Construct an algorithm that finds the shortest repeating prefix of a string s in $O(|s|)$ time. *Hint.* Use the failure function of Exercise 3.26.

3.30 A *Fibonacci string* is defined as follows:

$$s_1 = b$$
$$s_2 = a$$
$$s_k = s_{k-1}s_{k-2}, \text{ for } k > 2.$$

For example, $s_3 = ab$, $s_4 = aba$, and $s_5 = abaab$.

a) What is the length of s_n?

**b) What is the smallest period of s_n?

c) Construct the failure function for s_6.

*d) Using induction, show that the failure function for s_n can be expressed by $f(j) = j - |s_{k-1}|$, where k is such that $|s_k| \leq j+1 < |s_{k+1}|$ for $1 \leq j \leq |s_n|$.

e) Apply Algorithm KMP to determine whether s_6 is a substring of the target string s_7.

f) Construct a DFA for the regular expression $.*s_6.*$.

**g) In Algorithm KMP, what is the maximum number of consecutive applications of the failure function executed in determining whether s_k is a substring of the target string s_{k+1}?

3.31 We can extend the trie and failure function concepts of Exercise 3.26 from a single keyword to a set of keywords as follows. Each state in the trie corresponds to a prefix of one or more keywords. The start state corresponds to the empty string, and a state that corresponds to a complete keyword is a final state. Additional states may be made final during the computation of the failure function. The transition diagram for the set of keywords {he, she, his, hers} is shown in Fig. 3.52.

For the trie we define a *transition function* g that maps state-symbol pairs to states such that $g(s, b_{j+1}) = s'$ if state s corresponds to a prefix $b_1 \cdots b_j$ of some keyword and s' corresponds to a prefix $b_1 \cdots b_j b_{j+1}$. If s_0 is the start state, we define $g(s_0, a) = s_0$ for all input symbols a that are not the initial symbol of any keyword. We then set $g(s, a) = fail$ for any transition not defined. Note that there are no *fail* transitions for the start state.

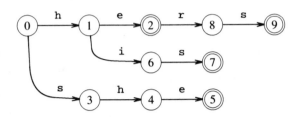

Fig. 3.52. Trie for keywords {he, she, his, hers}.

Suppose states s and t represent prefixes u and v of some keywords. Then, we define $f(s) = t$ if and only if v is the longest proper suffix of u that is also the prefix of some keyword. The failure function f for the transition diagram above is

s	1	2	3	4	5	6	7	8	9
$f(s)$	0	0	0	1	2	0	3	0	3

For example, states 4 and 1 represent prefixes sh and h. $f(4) = 1$ because h is the longest proper suffix of sh that is a prefix of some keyword. The failure function f can be computed for states of increasing depth using the algorithm in Fig. 3.53. The depth of a state is its distance from the start state.

```
for each state s of depth 1 do
    f(s) := s₀;
for each depth d ≥ 1 do
    for each state s_d of depth d and character a
        such that g(s_d, a) = s' do begin
            s := f(s_d);
            while g(s, a) = fail do s := f(s);
            f(s') := g(s, a);
end
```

Fig. 3.53. Algorithm to compute failure function for trie of keywords.

Note that since $g(s_0, c) \neq fail$ for any character c, the while-loop in Fig. 3.53 is guaranteed to terminate. After setting $f(s')$ to $g(t, a)$, if $g(t, a)$ is a final state, we also make s' a final state, if it is not already.

a) Construct the failure function for the set of keywords {*aaa, abaaa, ababaaa*}.

*b) Show that the algorithm in Fig. 3.53 correctly computes the failure function.

*c) Show that the failure function can be computed in time proportional to the sum of the lengths of the keywords.

3.32 Let g be the transition function and f the failure function of Exercise 3.31 for a set of keywords $K = \{y_1, y_2, \ldots, y_k\}$. Algorithm AC in Fig. 3.54 uses g and f to determine whether a target string $a_1 \cdots a_n$ contains a substring that is a keyword. State s_0 is the start state of the transition diagram for K, and F is the set of final states.

```
/* does a₁ · · · aₙ contain a keyword as a substring */
s := s₀;
for i := 1 to n do begin
      while g(s, aᵢ) = fail do s = f(s);
      s := g(s, aᵢ);
      if s is in F then return "yes"
end;
return "no"
```

Fig. 3.54. Algorithm AC.

a) Apply Algorithm AC to the input string ushers using the transition and failure functions of Exercise 3.31.

*b) Prove that Algorithm AC returns "yes" if and only if some keyword y_i is a substring of $a_1 \cdots a_n$.

*c) Show that Algorithm AC makes at most $2n$ state transitions in processing an input string of length n.

*d) Show that from the transition diagram and failure function for a set of keywords $\{y_1, y_2, \ldots, y_k\}$ a DFA with at most $\sum_{i=1}^{k} |y_i| + 1$ states can be constructed in linear time for the regular expression $.*(y_1|y_2| \cdots |y_k).*$.

e) Modify Algorithm AC to print out each keyword found in the target string.

3.33 Use the algorithm in Exercise 3.32 to construct a lexical analyzer for the keywords in Pascal.

3.34 Define $lcs(x, y)$, a *longest common subsequence* of two strings x and y, to be a string that is a subsequence of both x and y and is as long as any such subsequence. For example, tie is a longest common subsequence of striped and tiger. Define $d(x, y)$, the *distance* between x and y, to be the minimum number of insertions and deletions required to transform x into y. For example, $d($striped, tiger$) = 6$.

a) Show that for any two strings x and y, the distance between x and y and the length of their longest common subsequence are related by $d(x, y) = |x| + |y| - |lcs(x, y)|$.

*b) Write an algorithm that takes two strings x and y as input and produces a longest common subsequence of x and y as output.

3.35 Define $e(x, y)$, the *edit distance* between two strings x and y, to be the minimum number of character insertions, deletions, and replacements that are required to transform x into y. Let $x = a_1 \cdots a_m$ and $y = b_1 \cdots b_n$. $e(x, y)$ can be computed by a dynamic programming algorithm using a distance array $d[0..m, 0..n]$ in which $d[i, j]$ is the edit distance between $a_1 \cdots a_i$ and $b_1 \cdots b_j$. The algorithm in Fig. 3.55 can be used to compute the d matrix. The function $repl$ is just the cost of a character replacement: $repl(a_i, b_j) = 0$ if $a_i = b_j$, 1 otherwise.

```
for i := 0 to m do d[i, 0] := i;
for j := 1 to n do d[0, j] := j;
for i := 1 to m do
    for j := 1 to n do
        D[i, j] := min(d[i-1, j-1] + repl(a_i, b_j),
                       d[i-1, j] + 1,
                       d[i, j-1] + 1)
```

Fig. 3.55. Algorithm to compute edit distance between two strings.

a) What is the relation between the distance metric of Exercise 3.34 and edit distance?

b) Use the algorithm in Fig. 3.55 to compute the edit distance between *ababb* and *babaaa*.

c) Construct an algorithm that prints out the minimal sequence of editing transformations required to transform x into y.

3.36 Give an algorithm that takes as input a string x and a regular expression r, and produces as output a string y in $L(r)$ such that $d(x, y)$ is as small as possible, where d is the distance function in Exercise 3.34.

PROGRAMMING EXERCISES

P3.1 Write a lexical analyzer in Pascal or C for the tokens shown in Fig. 3.10.

P3.2 Write a specification for the tokens of Pascal and from this specification construct transition diagrams. Use the transition diagrams to implement a lexical analyzer for Pascal in a language like C or Pascal.

P3.3 Complete the Lex program in Fig. 3.18. Compare the size and speed of the resulting lexical analyzer produced by Lex with the program written in Exercise P3.1.

P3.4 Write a Lex specification for the tokens of Pascal and use the Lex compiler to construct a lexical analyzer for Pascal.

P3.5 Write a program that takes as input a regular expression and the name of a file, and produces as output all lines of the file that contain a substring denoted by the regular expression.

P3.6 Add an error recovery scheme to the Lex program in Fig. 3.18 to enable it to continue to look for tokens in the presence of errors.

P3.7 Program a lexical analyzer from the DFA constructed in Exercise 3.18 and compare this lexical analyzer with that constructed in Exercises P3.1 and P3.3.

P3.8 Construct a tool that produces a lexical analyzer from a regular expression description of a set of tokens.

BIBLIOGRAPHIC NOTES

The restrictions imposed on the lexical aspects of a language are often determined by the environment in which the language was created. When Fortran was designed in 1954, punched cards were a common input medium. Blanks were ignored in Fortran partially because keypunchers, who prepared cards from handwritten notes, tended to miscount blanks (Backus [1981]). Algol 58's separation of the hardware representation from the reference language was a compromise reached after a member of the design committee insisted, "No! I will never use a period for a decimal point." (Wegstein [1981]).

Knuth [1973a] presents additional techniques for buffering input. Feldman [1979b] discusses the practical difficulties of token recognition in Fortran 77.

Regular expressions were first studied by Kleene [1956], who was interested in describing the events that could be represented by McCulloch and Pitts [1943] finite automaton model of nervous activity. The minimization of finite automata was first studied by Huffman [1954] and Moore [1956]. The equivalence of deterministic and nondeterministic automata as far as their ability to recognize languages was shown by Rabin and Scott [1959]. McNaughton and Yamada [1960] describe an algorithm to construct a DFA directly from a regular expression. More of the theory of regular expressions can be found in Hopcroft and Ullman [1979].

It was quickly appreciated that tools to build lexical analyzers from regular expression specifications would be useful in the implementation of compilers. Johnson et al. [1968] discuss an early such system. Lex, the language discussed in this chapter, is due to Lesk [1975], and has been used to construct lexical analyzers for many compilers using the UNIX system. The compact implementation scheme in Section 3.9 for transition tables is due to S. C.

Johnson, who first used it in the implementation of the Yacc parser generator (Johnson [1975]). Other table-compression schemes are discussed and evaluated in Dencker, Dürre, and Heuft [1984].

The problem of compact implementation of transition tables has been theoretically studied in a general setting by Tarjan and Yao [1979] and by Fredman, Komlós, and Szemerédi [1984]. Cormack, Horspool, and Kaiserswerth [1985] present a perfect hashing algorithm based on this work.

Regular expressions and finite automata have been used in many applications other than compiling. Many text editors use regular expressions for context searches. Thompson [1968], for example, describes the construction of an NFA from a regular expression (Algorithm 3.3) in the context of the QED text editor. The UNIX system has three general purpose regular expression searching programs: grep, egrep, and fgrep. grep does not allow union or parentheses for grouping in its regular expressions, but it does allow a limited form of backreferencing as in Snobol. grep employs Algorithms 3.3 and 3.4 to search for its regular expression patterns. The regular expressions in egrep are similar to those in Lex, except for iteration and lookahead. egrep uses a DFA with lazy state construction to look for its regular expression patterns, as outlined in Section 3.7. fgrep looks for patterns consisting of sets of keywords using the algorithm in Aho and Corasick [1975], which is discussed in Exercises 3.31 and 3.32. Aho [1980] discusses the relative performance of these programs.

Regular expressions have been widely used in text retrieval systems, in database query languages, and in file processing languages like AWK (Aho, Kernighan, and Weinberger [1979]). Jarvis [1976] used regular expressions to describe imperfections in printed circuits. Cherry [1982] used the keyword-matching algorithm in Exercise 3.32 to look for poor diction in manuscripts.

The string pattern matching algorithm in Exercises 3.26 and 3.27 is from Knuth, Morris, and Pratt [1977]. This paper also contains a good discussion of periods in strings. Another efficient algorithm for string matching was invented by Boyer and Moore [1977] who showed that a substring match can usually be determined without having to examine all characters of the target string. Hashing has also been proven as an effective technique for string pattern matching (Harrison [1971]).

The notion of a longest common subsequence discussed in Exercise 3.34 has been used in the design of the UNIX system file comparison program diff (Hunt and McIlroy [1976]). An efficient practical algorithm for computing longest common subsequences is described in Hunt and Szymanski [1977]. The algorithm for computing minimum edit distances in Exercise 3.35 is from Wagner and Fischer [1974]. Wagner [1974] contains a solution to Exercise 3.36. Sankoff and Kruskal [1983] contains a fascinating discussion of the broad range of applications of minimum distance recognition algorithms from the study of patterns in genetic sequences to problems in speech processing.

CHAPTER 4

Syntax
Analysis

Every programming language has rules that prescribe the syntactic structure of well-formed programs. In Pascal, for example, a program is made out of blocks, a block out of statements, a statement out of expressions, an expression out of tokens, and so on. The syntax of programming language constructs can be described by context-free grammars or BNF (Backus-Naur Form) notation, introduced in Section 2.2. Grammars offer significant advantages to both language designers and compiler writers.

- A grammar gives a precise, yet easy-to-understand, syntactic specification of a programming language.

- From certain classes of grammars we can automatically construct an efficient parser that determines if a source program is syntactically well formed. As an additional benefit, the parser construction process can reveal syntactic ambiguities and other difficult-to-parse constructs that might otherwise go undetected in the initial design phase of a language and its compiler.

- A properly designed grammar imparts a structure to a programming language that is useful for the translation of source programs into correct object code and for the detection of errors. Tools are available for converting grammar-based descriptions of translations into working programs.

- Languages evolve over a period of time, acquiring new constructs and performing additional tasks. These new constructs can be added to a language more easily when there is an existing implementation based on a grammatical description of the language.

The bulk of this chapter is devoted to parsing methods that are typically used in compilers. We first present the basic concepts, then techniques that are suitable for hand implementation, and finally algorithms that have been used in automated tools. Since programs may contain syntactic errors, we extend the parsing methods so they recover from commonly occurring errors.

4.1 THE ROLE OF THE PARSER

In our compiler model, the parser obtains a string of tokens from the lexical analyzer, as shown in Fig. 4.1, and verifies that the string can be generated by the grammar for the source language. We expect the parser to report any syntax errors in an intelligible fashion. It should also recover from commonly occurring errors so that it can continue processing the remainder of its input.

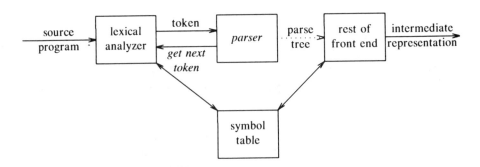

Fig. 4.1. Position of parser in compiler model.

There are three general types of parsers for grammars. Universal parsing methods such as the Cocke-Younger-Kasami algorithm and Earley's algorithm can parse any grammar (see the bibliographic notes). These methods, however, are too inefficient to use in production compilers. The methods commonly used in compilers are classified as being either top-down or bottom-up. As indicated by their names, top-down parsers build parse trees from the top (root) to the bottom (leaves), while bottom-up parsers start from the leaves and work up to the root. In both cases, the input to the parser is scanned from left to right, one symbol at a time.

The most efficient top-down and bottom-up methods work only on subclasses of grammars, but several of these subclasses, such as the LL and LR grammars, are expressive enough to describe most syntactic constructs in programming languages. Parsers implemented by hand often work with LL grammars; e.g., the approach of Section 2.4 constructs parsers for LL grammars. Parsers for the larger class of LR grammars are usually constructed by automated tools.

In this chapter, we assume the output of the parser is some representation of the parse tree for the stream of tokens produced by the lexical analyzer. In practice, there are a number of tasks that might be conducted during parsing, such as collecting information about various tokens into the symbol table, performing type checking and other kinds of semantic analysis, and generating intermediate code as in Chapter 2. We have lumped all of these activities into the "rest of front end" box in Fig. 4.1. We shall discuss these activities in detail in the next three chapters.

In the remainder of this section, we consider the nature of syntactic errors and general strategies for error recovery. Two of these strategies, called panic-mode and phrase-level recovery, are discussed in more detail together with the individual parsing methods. The implementation of each strategy calls upon the compiler writer's judgment, but we shall give some hints regarding approach.

Syntax Error Handling

If a compiler had to process only correct programs, its design and implementation would be greatly simplified. But programmers frequently write incorrect programs, and a good compiler should assist the programmer in identifying and locating errors. It is striking that although errors are so commonplace, few languages have been designed with error handling in mind. Our civilization would be radically different if spoken languages had the same requirement for syntactic accuracy as computer languages. Most programming language specifications do not describe how a compiler should respond to errors; the response is left to the compiler designer. Planning the error handling right from the start can both simplify the structure of a compiler and improve its response to errors.

We know that programs can contain errors at many different levels. For example, errors can be

- lexical, such as misspelling an identifier, keyword, or operator
- syntactic, such as an arithmetic expression with unbalanced parentheses
- semantic, such as an operator applied to an incompatible operand
- logical, such as an infinitely recursive call

Often much of the error detection and recovery in a compiler is centered around the syntax analysis phase. One reason for this is that many errors are syntactic in nature or are exposed when the stream of tokens coming from the lexical analyzer disobeys the grammatical rules defining the programming language. Another is the precision of modern parsing methods; they can detect the presence of syntactic errors in programs very efficiently. Accurately detecting the presence of semantic and logical errors at compile time is a much more difficult task. In this section, we present a few basic techniques for recovering from syntax errors; their implementation is discussed in conjunction with the parsing methods in this chapter.

The error handler in a parser has simple-to-state goals:

- It should report the presence of errors clearly and accurately.

- It should recover from each error quickly enough to be able to detect subsequent errors.

- It should not significantly slow down the processing of correct programs.

The effective realization of these goals presents difficult challenges.

Fortunately, common errors are simple ones and a relatively straightforward error-handling mechanism often suffices. In some cases, however, an error may have occurred long before the position at which its presence is detected, and the precise nature of the error may be very difficult to deduce. In difficult cases, the error handler may have to guess what the programmer had in mind when the program was written.

Several parsing methods, such as the LL and LR methods, detect an error as soon as possible. More precisely, they have the *viable-prefix property*, meaning they detect that an error has occurred as soon as they see a prefix of the input that is not a prefix of any string in the language.

Example 4.1. To gain an appreciation of the kinds of errors that occur in practice, let us examine the errors Ripley and Druseikis [1978] found in a sample of student Pascal programs.

They discovered that errors do not occur that frequently; 60% of the programs compiled were syntactically and semantically correct. Even when errors did occur, they were quite sparse; 80% of the statements having errors had only one error, 13% had two. Finally, most errors were trivial; 90% were single token errors.

Many of the errors could be classified simply: 60% were punctuation errors, 20% operator and operand errors, 15% keyword errors, and the remaining five per cent other kinds. The bulk of the punctuation errors revolved around the incorrect use of semicolons.

For some concrete examples, consider the following Pascal program.

```
(1)      program prmax(input, output);
(2)      var
(3)          x, y: integer;
(4)      function max(i:integer; j:integer) : integer;
(5)      { return maximum of integers i and j }
(6)      begin
(7)          if i > j then max := i
(8)          else max := j
(9)      end;

(10)     begin
(11)         readln (x,y);
(12)         writeln (max(x,y))
(13)     end.
```

A common punctuation error is to use a comma in place of the semicolon in the argument list of a function declaration (e.g., using a comma in place of the first semicolon on line (4)); another is to leave out a mandatory semicolon at the end of a line (e.g., the semicolon at the end of line (4)); another is to put in an extraneous semicolon at the end of a line before an else (e.g., putting a semicolon at the end of line (7)).

Perhaps one reason why semicolon errors are so common is that the use of semicolons varies greatly from one language to another. In Pascal, a semicolon is a statement separator; in PL/1 and C, it is a statement terminator. Some studies have suggested that the latter usage is less error prone (Gannon and Horning [1975]).

A typical example of an operator error is to leave out the colon from `:=`. Misspellings of keywords are usually rare, but leaving out the `i` from `writeln` would be a representative example.

Many Pascal compilers have no difficulty handling common insertion, deletion, and mutation errors. In fact, several Pascal compilers will correctly compile the above program with a common punctuation or operator error; they will issue only a warning diagnostic, pinpointing the offending construct.

However, another common type of error is much more difficult to repair correctly. This is a missing `begin` or `end` (e.g., line (9) missing). Most compilers would not try to repair this kind of error.   □

How should an error handler report the presence of an error? At the very least, it should report the place in the source program where an error is detected because there is a good chance that the actual error occurred within the previous few tokens. A common strategy employed by many compilers is to print the offending line with a pointer to the position at which an error is detected. If there is a reasonable likelihood of what the error actually is, an informative, understandable diagnostic message is also included; e.g., "semicolon missing at this position."

Once an error is detected, how should the parser recover? As we shall see, there are a number of general strategies, but no one method clearly dominates. In most cases, it is not adequate for the parser to quit after detecting the first error, because subsequent processing of the input may reveal additional errors. Usually, there is some form of error recovery in which the parser attempts to restore itself to a state where processing of the input can continue with a reasonable hope that correct input will be parsed and otherwise handled correctly by the compiler.

An inadequate job of recovery may introduce an annoying avalanche of "spurious" errors, those that were not made by the programmer, but were introduced by the changes made to the parser state during error recovery. In a similar vein, syntactic error recovery may introduce spurious semantic errors that will later be detected by the semantic analysis or code generation phases. For example, in recovering from an error, the parser may skip a declaration of some variable, say `zap`. When `zap` is later encountered in expressions, there is nothing syntactically wrong, but since there is no symbol-table entry for `zap`, a message "`zap` undefined" is generated.

A conservative strategy for a compiler is to inhibit error messages that stem from errors uncovered too close together in the input stream. After discovering one syntax error, the compiler should require several tokens to be parsed successfully before permitting another error message. In some cases, there may be too many errors for the compiler to continue sensible processing. (For example, how should a Pascal compiler respond to a Fortran program as input?) It seems that an error-recovery strategy has to be a carefully considered compromise, taking into account the kinds of errors that are likely to occur and reasonable to process.

As we have mentioned, some compilers attempt error repair, a process in which the compiler attempts to guess what the programmer intended to write. The PL/C compiler (Conway and Wilcox [1973]) is an example of this type of compiler. Except possibly in an environment of short programs written by beginning students, extensive error repair is not likely to be cost effective. In fact, with the increasing emphasis on interactive computing and good programming environments, the trend seems to be toward simple error-recovery mechanisms.

Error-Recovery Strategies

There are many different general strategies that a parser can employ to recover from a syntactic error. Although no one strategy has proven itself to be universally acceptable, a few methods have broad applicability. Here we introduce the following strategies:

- panic mode
- phrase level
- error productions
- global correction

Panic-mode recovery. This is the simplest method to implement and can be used by most parsing methods. On discovering an error, the parser discards input symbols one at a time until one of a designated set of synchronizing tokens is found. The synchronizing tokens are usually delimiters, such as semicolon or **end**, whose role in the source program is clear. The compiler designer must select the synchronizing tokens appropriate for the source language, of course. While panic-mode correction often skips a considerable amount of input without checking it for additional errors, it has the advantage of simplicity and, unlike some other methods to be considered later, it is guaranteed not to go into an infinite loop. In situations where multiple errors in the same statement are rare, this method may be quite adequate.

Phrase-level recovery. On discovering an error, a parser may perform local correction on the remaining input; that is, it may replace a prefix of the remaining input by some string that allows the parser to continue. A typical local correction would be to replace a comma by a semicolon, delete an extraneous semicolon, or insert a missing semicolon. The choice of the local correction is left to the compiler designer. Of course, we must be careful to choose replacements that do not lead to infinite loops, as would be the case, for example, if we always inserted something on the input ahead of the current input symbol.

This type of replacement can correct any input string and has been used in several error-repairing compilers. The method was first used with top-down parsing. Its major drawback is the difficulty it has in coping with situations in which the actual error has occurred before the point of detection.

Error productions. If we have a good idea of the common errors that might be encountered, we can augment the grammar for the language at hand with productions that generate the erroneous constructs. We then use the grammar augmented by these error productions to construct a parser. If an error production is used by the parser, we can generate appropriate error diagnostics to indicate the erroneous construct that has been recognized in the input.

Global correction. Ideally, we would like a compiler to make as few changes as possible in processing an incorrect input string. There are algorithms for choosing a minimal sequence of changes to obtain a globally least-cost correction. Given an incorrect input string x and grammar G, these algorithms will find a parse tree for a related string y, such that the number of insertions, deletions, and changes of tokens required to transform x into y is as small as possible. Unfortunately, these methods are in general too costly to implement in terms of time and space, so these techniques are currently only of theoretical interest.

We should point out that a closest correct program may not be what the programmer had in mind. Nevertheless, the notion of least-cost correction does provide a yardstick for evaluating error-recovery techniques, and it has been used for finding optimal replacement strings for phrase-level recovery.

4.2 CONTEXT-FREE GRAMMARS

Many programming language constructs have an inherently recursive structure that can be defined by context-free grammars. For example, we might have a conditional statement defined by a rule such as

> If S_1 and S_2 are statements and E is an expression, then
>
> "**if** E **then** S_1 **else** S_2" is a statement. (4.1)

This form of conditional statement cannot be specified using the notation of regular expressions; in Chapter 3, we saw that regular expressions can specify the lexical structure of tokens. On the other hand, using the syntactic variable *stmt* to denote the class of statements and *expr* the class of expressions, we can readily express (4.1) using the grammar production

$$stmt \;\rightarrow\; \textbf{if}\; expr\; \textbf{then}\; stmt\; \textbf{else}\; stmt \qquad (4.2)$$

In this section, we review the definition of a context-free grammar and introduce terminology for talking about parsing. From Section 2.2, a context-free grammar (grammar for short) consists of terminals, nonterminals, a start symbol, and productions.

1. Terminals are the basic symbols from which strings are formed. The word "token" is a synonym for "terminal" when we are talking about grammars for programming languages. In (4.2), each of the keywords **if**, **then**, and **else** is a terminal.

2. Nonterminals are syntactic variables that denote sets of strings. In (4.2), *stmt* and *expr* are nonterminals. The nonterminals define sets of strings that help define the language generated by the grammar. They also impose a hierarchical structure on the language that is useful for both syntax analysis and translation.

3. In a grammar, one nonterminal is distinguished as the start symbol, and the set of strings it denotes is the language defined by the grammar.

4. The productions of a grammar specify the manner in which the terminals and nonterminals can be combined to form strings. Each production consists of a nonterminal, followed by an arrow (sometimes the symbol ::= is used in place of the arrow), followed by a string of nonterminals and terminals.

Example 4.2. The grammar with the following productions defines simple arithmetic expressions.

$$expr \rightarrow expr \; op \; expr$$
$$expr \rightarrow (\; expr \;)$$
$$expr \rightarrow - \; expr$$
$$expr \rightarrow \textbf{id}$$
$$op \rightarrow +$$
$$op \rightarrow -$$
$$op \rightarrow *$$
$$op \rightarrow /$$
$$op \rightarrow \uparrow$$

In this grammar, the terminal symbols are

  id $+ \; - \; * / \uparrow ( )$

The nonterminal symbols are *expr* and *op*, and *expr* is the start symbol.   □

Notational Conventions

To avoid always having to state that "these are the terminals," "these are the nonterminals," and so on, we shall employ the following notational conventions with regard to grammars throughout the remainder of this book.

1. These symbols are terminals:

   i)   Lower-case letters early in the alphabet such as a, b, c.
   ii) Operator symbols such as $+, -$, etc.
   iii) Punctuation symbols such as parentheses, comma, etc.
   iv) The digits $0, 1, \ldots, 9$.
   v)   Boldface strings such as **id** or **if**.

2. These symbols are nonterminals:

   i)   Upper-case letters early in the alphabet such as A, B, C.

ii)   The letter S, which, when it appears, is usually the start symbol.

iii)   Lower-case italic names such as *expr* or *stmt*.

3.   Upper-case letters late in the alphabet, such as X, Y, Z, represent *grammar symbols*, that is, either nonterminals or terminals.

4.   Lower-case letters late in the alphabet, chiefly u, v, . . . , z, represent strings of terminals.

5.   Lower-case Greek letters, α, β, γ, for example, represent strings of grammar symbols. Thus, a generic production could be written as $A \rightarrow \alpha$, indicating that there is a single nonterminal A on the left of the arrow (the *left side* of the production) and a string of grammar symbols α to the right of the arrow (the *right side* of the production).

6.   If $A \rightarrow \alpha_1$, $A \rightarrow \alpha_2$, . . . , $A \rightarrow \alpha_k$ are all productions with A on the left (we call them *A-productions*), we may write $A \rightarrow \alpha_1 |\alpha_2| \cdots |\alpha_k$. We call α_1, α_2, . . . , α_k the *alternatives* for A.

7.   Unless otherwise stated, the left side of the first production is the start symbol.

Example 4.3. Using these shorthands, we could write the grammar of Example 4.2 concisely as

$$E \rightarrow E \ A \ E \ | \ (\ E \ ) \ | \ - E \ | \ \mathbf{id}$$
$$A \rightarrow + \ | \ - \ | \ * \ | \ / \ | \ \uparrow$$

Our notational conventions tell us that E and A are nonterminals, with E the start symbol. The remaining symbols are terminals.   □

Derivations

There are several ways to view the process by which a grammar defines a language. In Section 2.2, we viewed this process as one of building parse trees, but there is also a related derivational view that we frequently find useful. In fact, this derivational view gives a precise description of the top-down construction of a parse tree. The central idea here is that a production is treated as a rewriting rule in which the nonterminal on the left is replaced by the string on the right side of the production.

For example, consider the following grammar for arithmetic expressions, with the nonterminal E representing an expression.

$$E \rightarrow E + E \ | \ E * E \ | \ (\ E \ ) \ | \ - E \ | \ \mathbf{id} \qquad (4.3)$$

The production $E \rightarrow - E$ signifies that an expression preceded by a minus sign is also an expression. This production can be used to generate more complex expressions from simpler expressions by allowing us to replace any instance of an E by $- E$. In the simplest case, we can replace a single E by $- E$. We can describe this action by writing

$$E \Rightarrow -E$$

which is read "E derives $-E$." The production $E \rightarrow (E)$ tells us that we could also replace one instance of an E in any string of grammar symbols by (E); e.g., $E*E \Rightarrow (E)*E$ or $E*E \Rightarrow E*(E)$.

We can take a single E and repeatedly apply productions in any order to obtain a sequence of replacements. For example,

$$E \Rightarrow -E \Rightarrow -(E) \Rightarrow -(\mathbf{id})$$

We call such a sequence of replacements a *derivation* of $-(\mathbf{id})$ from E. This derivation provides a proof that one particular instance of an expression is the string $-(\mathbf{id})$.

In a more abstract setting, we say that $\alpha A \beta \Rightarrow \alpha \gamma \beta$ if $A \rightarrow \gamma$ is a production and α and β are arbitrary strings of grammar symbols. If $\alpha_1 \Rightarrow \alpha_2 \Rightarrow \cdots \Rightarrow \alpha_n$, we say α_1 *derives* α_n. The symbol $\Rightarrow$ means "derives in one step." Often we wish to say "derives in zero or more steps." For this purpose we can use the symbol $\overset{*}{\Rightarrow}$. Thus,

1. $\alpha \overset{*}{\Rightarrow} \alpha$ for any string α, and
2. If $\alpha \overset{*}{\Rightarrow} \beta$ and $\beta \Rightarrow \gamma$, then $\alpha \overset{*}{\Rightarrow} \gamma$.

Likewise, we use $\overset{+}{\Rightarrow}$ to mean "derives in one or more steps."

Given a grammar G with start symbol S, we can use the $\overset{+}{\Rightarrow}$ relation to define $L(G)$, the *language generated by* G. Strings in $L(G)$ may contain only terminal symbols of G. We say a string of terminals w is in $L(G)$ if and only if $S \overset{+}{\Rightarrow} w$. The string w is called a *sentence* of G. A language that can be generated by a grammar is said to be a *context-free language*. If two grammars generate the same language, the grammars are said to be *equivalent*.

If $S \overset{*}{\Rightarrow} \alpha$, where α may contain nonterminals, then we say that α is a *sentential form* of G. A sentence is a sentential form with no nonterminals.

Example 4.4. The string $-(\mathbf{id}+\mathbf{id})$ is a sentence of grammar (4.3) because there is the derivation

$$E \Rightarrow -E \Rightarrow -(E) \Rightarrow -(E+E) \Rightarrow -(\mathbf{id}+E) \Rightarrow -(\mathbf{id}+\mathbf{id}) \qquad (4.4)$$

The strings E, $-E$, $-(E)$, ..., $-(\mathbf{id}+\mathbf{id})$ appearing in this derivation are all sentential forms of this grammar. We write $E \overset{*}{\Rightarrow} -(\mathbf{id}+\mathbf{id})$ to indicate that $-(\mathbf{id}+\mathbf{id})$ can be derived from E.

We can show by induction on the length of a derivation that every sentence in the language of grammar (4.3) is an arithmetic expression involving the binary operators $+$ and $*$, the unary operator $-$, parentheses, and the operand $\mathbf{id}$. Similarly, we can show by induction on the length of an arithmetic expression that all such expressions can be generated by this grammar. Thus, grammar (4.3) generates precisely the set of all arithmetic expressions involving binary $+$ and $*$, unary $-$, parentheses, and the operand $\mathbf{id}$. □

At each step in a derivation, there are two choices to be made. We need to choose which nonterminal to replace, and having made this choice, which alternative to use for that nonterminal. For example, derivation (4.4) of Example 4.4 could continue from $-(E+E)$ as follows

$$-(E+E) \Rightarrow -(E+\mathbf{id}) \Rightarrow -(\mathbf{id}+\mathbf{id}) \tag{4.5}$$

Each nonterminal in (4.5) is replaced by the same right side as in Example 4.4, but the order of replacements is different.

To understand how certain parsers work we need to consider derivations in which only the leftmost nonterminal in any sentential form is replaced at each step. Such derivations are termed *leftmost*. If $\alpha \Rightarrow \beta$ by a step in which the leftmost nonterminal in α is replaced, we write $\alpha \underset{lm}{\Rightarrow} \beta$. Since derivation (4.4) is leftmost, we can rewrite it as:

$$E \underset{lm}{\Rightarrow} -E \underset{lm}{\Rightarrow} -(E) \underset{lm}{\Rightarrow} -(E+E) \underset{lm}{\Rightarrow} -(\mathbf{id}+E) \underset{lm}{\Rightarrow} -(\mathbf{id}+\mathbf{id})$$

Using our notational conventions, every leftmost step can be written $wA\gamma \underset{lm}{\Rightarrow} w\delta\gamma$ where w consists of terminals only, $A \to \delta$ is the production applied, and γ is a string of grammar symbols. To emphasize the fact that α derives β by a leftmost derivation, we write $\alpha \underset{lm}{\overset{*}{\Rightarrow}} \beta$. If $S \underset{lm}{\overset{*}{\Rightarrow}} \alpha$, then we say α is a *left-sentential form* of the grammar at hand.

Analogous definitions hold for *rightmost* derivations in which the rightmost nonterminal is replaced at each step. Rightmost derivations are sometimes called *canonical* derivations.

Parse Trees and Derivations

A parse tree may be viewed as a graphical representation for a derivation that filters out the choice regarding replacement order. Recall from Section 2.2 that each interior node of a parse tree is labeled by some nonterminal A, and that the children of the node are labeled, from left to right, by the symbols in the right side of the production by which this A was replaced in the derivation. The leaves of the parse tree are labeled by nonterminals or terminals and, read from left to right, they constitute a sentential form, called the yield or frontier of the tree. For example, the parse tree for $-(\mathbf{id}+\mathbf{id})$ implied by derivation (4.4) is shown in Fig. 4.2.

To see the relationship between derivations and parse trees, consider any derivation $\alpha_1 \Rightarrow \alpha_2 \Rightarrow \cdots \Rightarrow \alpha_n$, where α_1 is a single nonterminal A. For each sentential form α_i in the derivation, we construct a parse tree whose yield is α_i. The process is an induction on i. For the basis, the tree for $\alpha_1 = A$ is a single node labeled A. To do the induction, suppose we have already constructed a parse tree whose yield is $\alpha_{i-1} = X_1 X_2 \cdots X_k$. (Recalling our conventions, each X_i is either a nonterminal or a terminal.) Suppose α_i is derived from α_{i-1} by replacing X_j, a nonterminal, by $\beta = Y_1 Y_2 \cdots Y_r$. That is, at the ith step of the derivation, production $X_j \to \beta$ is applied to α_{i-1} to derive $\alpha_i = X_1 X_2 \cdots X_{j-1} \beta X_{j+1} \cdots X_k$.

To model this step of the derivation, we find the jth leaf from the left in the current parse tree. This leaf is labeled X_j. We give this leaf r children, labeled $Y_1, Y_2, \ldots, Y_r$, from the left. As a special case, if $r = 0$, i.e.,

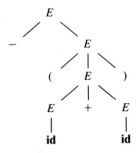

Fig. 4.2. Parse tree for $-(\text{id} + \text{id})$.

$\beta = \epsilon$, then we give the jth leaf one child labeled ϵ.

Example 4.5. Consider derivation (4.4). The sequence of parse trees constructed from this derivation is shown in Fig. 4.3. In the first step of the derivation, $E \Rightarrow -E$. To model this step, we add two children, labeled $-$ and E, to the root E of the initial tree to create the second tree.

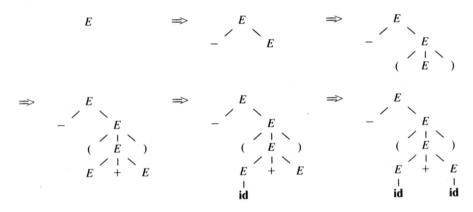

Fig. 4.3. Building the parse tree from derivation (4.4).

In the second step of the derivation, $-E \Rightarrow -(E)$. Consequently, we add three children, labeled (, E, and), to the leaf labeled E of the second tree to obtain the third tree with yield $-(E)$. Continuing in this fashion we obtain the complete parse tree as the sixth tree.   □

As we have mentioned, a parse tree ignores variations in the order in which symbols in sentential forms are replaced. For example, if derivation (4.4) were continued as in line (4.5), the same final parse tree of Fig. 4.3 would result. These variations in the order in which productions are applied can also be eliminated by considering only leftmost (or rightmost) derivations. It is not hard to see that every parse tree has associated with it a unique leftmost and a unique rightmost derivation. In what follows, we shall frequently parse by producing a leftmost or rightmost derivation, understanding that instead of this derivation we could produce the parse tree itself. However, we should not assume that every sentence necessarily has only one parse tree or only one leftmost or rightmost derivation.

Example 4.6. Let us again consider the arithmetic expression grammar (4.3). The sentence **id**+**id**∗**id** has the two distinct leftmost derivations:

$$
\begin{aligned}
E &\Rightarrow E+E \\
  &\Rightarrow \mathbf{id}+E \\
  &\Rightarrow \mathbf{id}+E*E \\
  &\Rightarrow \mathbf{id}+\mathbf{id}*E \\
  &\Rightarrow \mathbf{id}+\mathbf{id}*\mathbf{id}
\end{aligned}
\qquad
\begin{aligned}
E &\Rightarrow E*E \\
  &\Rightarrow E+E*E \\
  &\Rightarrow \mathbf{id}+E*E \\
  &\Rightarrow \mathbf{id}+\mathbf{id}*E \\
  &\Rightarrow \mathbf{id}+\mathbf{id}*\mathbf{id}
\end{aligned}
$$

with the two corresponding parse trees shown in Fig. 4.4.   □

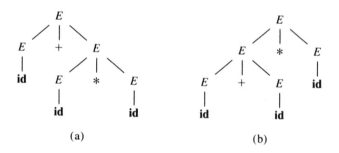

Fig. 4.4. Two parse trees for **id**+**id**∗**id**.

Note that the parse tree of Fig. 4.4(a) reflects the commonly assumed precedence of + and ∗, while the tree of Fig. 4.4(b) does not. That is, it is customary to treat operator ∗ as having higher precedence than +, corresponding to the fact that we would normally evaluate an expression like $a+b*c$ as $a+(b*c)$, rather than as $(a+b)*c$.

Ambiguity

A grammar that produces more than one parse tree for some sentence is said to be *ambiguous*. Put another way, an ambiguous grammar is one that produces more than one leftmost or more than one rightmost derivation for the same sentence. For certain types of parsers, it is desirable that the grammar be made unambiguous, for if it is not, we cannot uniquely determine which parse tree to select for a sentence. For some applications we shall also consider methods whereby we can use certain ambiguous grammars, together with *disambiguating rules* that "throw away" undesirable parse trees, leaving us with only one tree for each sentence.

4.3 WRITING A GRAMMAR

Grammars are capable of describing most, but not all, of the syntax of programming languages. A limited amount of syntax analysis is done by a lexical analyzer as it produces the sequence of tokens from the input characters. Certain constraints on the input, such as the requirement that identifiers be declared before they are used, cannot be described by a context-free grammar. Therefore, the sequences of tokens accepted by a parser form a superset of a programming language; subsequent phases must analyze the output of the parser to ensure compliance with rules that are not checked by the parser (see Chapter 6).

We begin this section by considering the division of work between a lexical analyzer and a parser. Because each parsing method can handle grammars only of a certain form, the initial grammar may have to be rewritten to make it parsable by the method chosen. Suitable grammars for expressions can often be constructed using associativity and precedence information, as in Section 2.2. In this section, we consider transformations that are useful for rewriting grammars so they become suitable for top-down parsing. We conclude this section by considering some programming language constructs that cannot be described by any grammar.

Regular Expressions vs. Context-Free Grammars

Every construct that can be described by a regular expression can also be described by a grammar. For example, the regular expression $(a|b)*abb$ and the grammar

$$A_0 \rightarrow aA_0 \mid bA_0 \mid aA_1$$
$$A_1 \rightarrow bA_2$$
$$A_2 \rightarrow bA_3$$
$$A_3 \rightarrow \epsilon$$

describe the same language, the set of strings of a's and b's ending in abb.

We can mechanically convert a nondeterministic finite automaton (NFA) into a grammar that generates the same language as recognized by the NFA. The grammar above was constructed from the NFA of Fig. 3.23 using the following construction: For each state i of the NFA, create a nonterminal symbol A_i. If state i has a transition to state j on symbol a, introduce the production $A_i \rightarrow aA_j$. If state i goes to state j on input ϵ, introduce the production $A_i \rightarrow A_j$. If i is an accepting state, introduce $A_i \rightarrow \epsilon$. If i is the start state, make A_i be the start symbol of the grammar.

Since every regular set is a context-free language, we may reasonably ask, "Why use regular expressions to define the lexical syntax of a language?" There are several reasons.

1. The lexical rules of a language are frequently quite simple, and to describe them we do not need a notation as powerful as grammars.

2. Regular expressions generally provide a more concise and easier to understand notation for tokens than grammars.

3. More efficient lexical analyzers can be constructed automatically from regular expressions than from arbitrary grammars.

4. Separating the syntactic structure of a language into lexical and nonlexical parts provides a convenient way of modularizing the front end of a compiler into two manageable-sized components.

There are no firm guidelines as to what to put into the lexical rules, as opposed to the syntactic rules. Regular expressions are most useful for describing the structure of lexical constructs such as identifiers, constants, keywords, and so forth. Grammars, on the other hand, are most useful in describing nested structures such as balanced parentheses, matching begin-end's, corresponding if-then-else's, and so on. As we have noted, these nested structures cannot be described by regular expressions.

Verifying the Language Generated by a Grammar

Although compiler designers rarely do it for a complete programming language grammar, it is important to be able to reason that a given set of productions generates a particular language. Troublesome constructs can be studied by writing a concise, abstract grammar and studying the language that it generates. We shall construct such a grammar for conditionals below.

A proof that a grammar G generates a language L has two parts: we must show that every string generated by G is in L, and conversely that every string in L can indeed be generated by G.

Example 4.7. Consider the grammar (4.6)

$$S \rightarrow (S)S \mid \epsilon \tag{4.6}$$

It may not be initially apparent, but this simple grammar generates all strings of balanced parentheses, and only such strings. To see this, we shall show first that every sentence derivable from S is balanced, and then that every balanced string is derivable from S. To show that every sentence derivable from S is balanced, we use an inductive proof on the number of steps in a derivation. For the basis step, we note that the only string of terminals derivable from S in one step is the empty string, which surely is balanced.

Now assume that all derivations of fewer than n steps produce balanced sentences, and consider a leftmost derivation of exactly n steps. Such a derivation must be of the form

$$S \Rightarrow (S)S \overset{*}{\Rightarrow} (x)S \overset{*}{\Rightarrow} (x)y$$

The derivations of x and y from S take fewer than n steps so, by the inductive hypothesis, x and y are balanced. Therefore, the string $(x)y$ must be balanced.

We have thus shown that any string derivable from S is balanced. We must next show that every balanced string is derivable from S. To do this we use induction on the length of a string. For the basis step, the empty string is derivable from S.

Now assume that every balanced string of length less than $2n$ is derivable from S, and consider a balanced string w of length $2n$, $n \geq 1$. Surely w begins with a left parenthesis. Let (x) be the shortest prefix of w having an equal number of left and right parentheses. Then w can be written as $(x)y$ where both x and y are balanced. Since x and y are of length less than $2n$, they are derivable from S by the inductive hypothesis. Thus, we can find a derivation of the form

$$S \Rightarrow (S)S \overset{*}{\Rightarrow} (x)S \overset{*}{\Rightarrow} (x)y$$

proving that $w = (x)y$ is also derivable from S.   □

Eliminating Ambiguity

Sometimes an ambiguous grammar can be rewritten to eliminate the ambiguity. As an example, we shall eliminate the ambiguity from the following "dangling-else" grammar:

$$\begin{aligned}
stmt \rightarrow \; & \textbf{if } expr \textbf{ then } stmt \\
| \; & \textbf{if } expr \textbf{ then } stmt \textbf{ else } stmt \\
| \; & \textbf{other}
\end{aligned} \qquad (4.7)$$

Here "**other**" stands for any other statement. According to this grammar, the compound conditional statement

$$\textbf{if } E_1 \textbf{ then } S_1 \textbf{ else if } E_2 \textbf{ then } S_2 \textbf{ else } S_3$$

has the parse tree shown in Fig. 4.5. Grammar (4.7) is ambiguous since the string

$$\textbf{if } E_1 \textbf{ then if } E_2 \textbf{ then } S_1 \textbf{ else } S_2 \qquad (4.8)$$

has the two parse trees shown in Fig. 4.6.

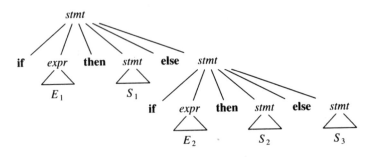

Fig. 4.5. Parse tree for conditional statement.

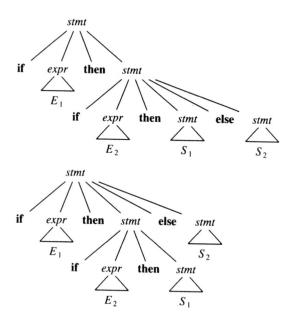

Fig. 4.6. Two parse trees for an ambiguous sentence.

In all programming languages with conditional statements of this form, the first parse tree is preferred. The general rule is, "Match each **else** with the closest previous unmatched **then**." This disambiguating rule can be incorporated directly into the grammar. For example, we can rewrite grammar (4.7) as the following unambiguous grammar. The idea is that a statement appearing between a **then** and an **else** must be "matched;" i.e., it must not end with an unmatched **then** followed by any statement, for the **else** would then be forced to match this unmatched **then**. A matched statement is either an **if-then-else** statement containing no unmatched statements or it is any other kind of unconditional statement. Thus, we may use the grammar

$$
\begin{aligned}
stmt \;\rightarrow\; & matched\_stmt \\
& |\; unmatched\_stmt \\
matched\_stmt \;\rightarrow\; & \textbf{if } expr \textbf{ then } matched\_stmt \textbf{ else } matched\_stmt \\
& |\; \textbf{other} \\
unmatched\_stmt \;\rightarrow\; & \textbf{if } expr \textbf{ then } stmt \\
& |\; \textbf{if } expr \textbf{ then } matched\_stmt \textbf{ else } unmatched\_stmt
\end{aligned}
\tag{4.9}
$$

This grammar generates the same set of strings as (4.7), but it allows only one parsing for string (4.8), namely the one that associates each **else** with the closest previous unmatched **then**.

Elimination of Left Recursion

A grammar is *left recursive* if it has a nonterminal A such that there is a derivation $A \stackrel{+}{\Rightarrow} A\alpha$ for some string α. Top-down parsing methods cannot handle left-recursive grammars, so a transformation that eliminates left recursion is needed. In Section 2.4, we discussed simple left recursion, where there was one production of the form $A \rightarrow A\alpha$. Here we study the general case. In Section 2.4, we showed how the left-recursive pair of productions $A \rightarrow A\alpha \mid \beta$ could be replaced by the non-left-recursive productions

$$A \rightarrow \beta A'$$
$$A' \rightarrow \alpha A' \mid \epsilon$$

without changing the set of strings derivable from A. This rule by itself suffices in many grammars.

Example 4.8. Consider the following grammar for arithmetic expressions.

$$
\begin{aligned}
E &\rightarrow E + T \mid T \\
T &\rightarrow T * F \mid F \\
F &\rightarrow (E) \mid \textbf{id}
\end{aligned}
\qquad (4.10)
$$

Eliminating the *immediate left recursion* (productions of the form $A \rightarrow A\alpha$) to the productions for E and then for T, we obtain

$$
\begin{aligned}
E &\rightarrow TE' \\
E' &\rightarrow +TE' \mid \epsilon \\
T &\rightarrow FT' \\
T' &\rightarrow *FT' \mid \epsilon \\
F &\rightarrow (E) \mid \textbf{id}
\end{aligned}
\qquad (4.11)
$$

□

No matter how many A-productions there are, we can eliminate immediate left recursion from them by the following technique. First, we group the A-productions as

$$A \rightarrow A\alpha_1 \mid A\alpha_2 \mid \cdots \mid A\alpha_m \mid \beta_1 \mid \beta_2 \mid \cdots \mid \beta_n$$

where no β_i begins with an A. Then, we replace the A-productions by

$$
\begin{aligned}
A &\rightarrow \beta_1 A' \mid \beta_2 A' \mid \cdots \mid \beta_n A' \\
A' &\rightarrow \alpha_1 A' \mid \alpha_2 A' \mid \cdots \mid \alpha_m A' \mid \epsilon
\end{aligned}
$$

The nonterminal A generates the same strings as before but is no longer left recursive. This procedure eliminates all immediate left recursion from the A and A' productions (provided no α_i is ϵ), but it does not eliminate left recursion involving derivations of two or more steps. For example, consider the grammar

$$
\begin{aligned}
S &\rightarrow Aa \mid b \\
A &\rightarrow Ac \mid Sd \mid \epsilon
\end{aligned}
\qquad (4.12)
$$

The nonterminal S is left-recursive because $S \Rightarrow Aa \Rightarrow Sda$, but it is not immediately left recursive.

Algorithm 4.1, below, will systematically eliminate left recursion from a grammar. It is guaranteed to work if the grammar has no cycles (derivations of the form $A \overset{+}{\Rightarrow} A$) or ϵ-productions (productions of the form $A \rightarrow \epsilon$). Cycles can be systematically eliminated from a grammar as can ϵ-productions (see Exercises 4.20 and 4.22).

Algorithm 4.1. Eliminating left recursion.

Input. Grammar G with no cycles or ϵ-productions.

Output. An equivalent grammar with no left recursion.

Method. Apply the algorithm in Fig. 4.7 to G. Note that the resulting non-left-recursive grammar may have ϵ-productions.   □

1.   Arrange the nonterminals in some order $A_1, A_2, \ldots, A_n$.

2.   **for** $i := 1$ **to** n **do**
       for $j := 1$ **to** $i-1$ **do begin**
           replace each production of the form $A_i \rightarrow A_j\gamma$ by
               the productions $A_i \rightarrow \delta_1\gamma \mid \delta_2\gamma \mid \cdots \mid \delta_k\gamma$,
               where $A_j \rightarrow \delta_1 \mid \delta_2 \mid \cdots \mid \delta_k$ are all the
               current A_j-productions;
           eliminate the immediate left recursion among the A_i-productions
       end

Fig. 4.7. Algorithm to eliminate left recursion from a grammar.

The reason the procedure in Fig. 4.7 works is that after the $i-1^{\text{st}}$ iteration of the outer **for** loop in step (2), any production of the form $A_k \rightarrow A_l\alpha$, where $k < i$, must have $l > k$. As a result, on the next iteration, the inner loop (on j) progressively raises the lower limit on m in any production $A_i \rightarrow A_m\alpha$, until we must have $m \geq i$. Then, eliminating immediate left recursion for the A_i-productions forces m to be greater than i.

Example 4.9. Let us apply this procedure to grammar (4.12). Technically, Algorithm 4.1 is not guaranteed to work, because of the ϵ-production, but in this case the production $A \rightarrow \epsilon$ turns out to be harmless.

We order the nonterminals S, A. There is no immediate left recursion among the S-productions, so nothing happens during step (2) for the case $i = 1$. For $i = 2$, we substitute the S-productions in $A \rightarrow Sd$ to obtain the following A-productions.

$A \rightarrow Ac \mid Aad \mid bd \mid \epsilon$

Eliminating the immediate left recursion among the A-productions yields the following grammar.

$$S \rightarrow Aa \mid b$$
$$A \rightarrow bdA' \mid A'$$
$$A' \rightarrow cA' \mid adA' \mid \epsilon$$ □

Left Factoring

Left factoring is a grammar transformation that is useful for producing a grammar suitable for predictive parsing. The basic idea is that when it is not clear which of two alternative productions to use to expand a nonterminal A, we may be able to rewrite the A-productions to defer the decision until we have seen enough of the input to make the right choice.

For example, if we have the two productions

$$stmt \rightarrow \textbf{if } expr \textbf{ then } stmt \textbf{ else } stmt$$
$$\mid \textbf{ if } expr \textbf{ then } stmt$$

on seeing the input token **if**, we cannot immediately tell which production to choose to expand $stmt$. In general, if $A \rightarrow \alpha\beta_1 \mid \alpha\beta_2$ are two A-productions, and the input begins with a nonempty string derived from α, we do not know whether to expand A to $\alpha\beta_1$ or to $\alpha\beta_2$. However, we may defer the decision by expanding A to $\alpha A'$. Then, after seeing the input derived from α, we expand A' to β_1 or to β_2. That is, left-factored, the original productions become

$$A \rightarrow \alpha A'$$
$$A' \rightarrow \beta_1 \mid \beta_2$$

Algorithm 4.2. Left factoring a grammar.

Input. Grammar G.

Output. An equivalent left-factored grammar.

Method. For each nonterminal A find the longest prefix α common to two or more of its alternatives. If $\alpha \neq \epsilon$, i.e., there is a nontrivial common prefix, replace all the A productions $A \rightarrow \alpha\beta_1 \mid \alpha\beta_2 \mid \cdots \mid \alpha\beta_n \mid \gamma$ where γ represents all alternatives that do not begin with α by

$$A \rightarrow \alpha A' \mid \gamma$$
$$A' \rightarrow \beta_1 \mid \beta_2 \mid \cdots \mid \beta_n$$

Here A' is a new nonterminal. Repeatedly apply this transformation until no two alternatives for a nonterminal have a common prefix.   □

Example 4.10. The following grammar abstracts the dangling-else problem:

$$S \rightarrow iEtS \mid iEtSeS \mid a \qquad\qquad\qquad (4.13)$$
$$E \rightarrow b$$

Here i, t, and e stand for **if, then** and **else**, E and S for "expression" and "statement." Left-factored, this grammar becomes:

$$S \rightarrow iEtSS' \mid a$$
$$S' \rightarrow eS \mid \epsilon$$
$$E \rightarrow b \qquad (4.14)$$

Thus, we may expand S to $iEtSS'$ on input i, and wait until $iEtS$ has been seen to decide whether to expand S' to eS or to ϵ. Of course, grammars (4.13) and (4.14) are both ambiguous, and on input e, it will not be clear which alternative for S' should be chosen. Example 4.19 discusses a way out of this dilemma. □

Non-Context-Free Language Constructs

It should come as no surprise that some languages cannot be generated by any grammar. In fact, a few syntactic constructs found in many programming languages cannot be specified using grammars alone. In this section, we shall present several of these constructs, using simple abstract languages to illustrate the difficulties.

Example 4.11. Consider the abstract language $L_1 = \{wcw \mid w$ is in $(a \mid b)*\}$. L_1 consists of all words composed of a repeated string of a's and b's separated by a c, such as $aabcaab$. It can be proven this language is not context free. This language abstracts the problem of checking that identifiers are declared before their use in a program. That is, the first w in wcw represents the declaration of an identifier w. The second w represents its use. While it is beyond the scope of this book to prove it, the non-context-freedom of L_1 directly implies the non-context-freedom of programming languages like Algol and Pascal, which require declaration of identifiers before their use, and which allow identifiers of arbitrary length.

For this reason, a grammar for the syntax of Algol or Pascal does not specify the characters in an identifier. Instead, all identifiers are represented by a token such as **id** in the grammar. In a compiler for such a language, the semantic analysis phase checks that identifiers have been declared before their use. □

Example 4.12. The language $L_2 = \{a^n b^m c^n d^m \mid n \geq 1$ and $m \geq 1\}$ is not context free. That is, L_2 consists of strings in the language generated by the regular expression $a*b*c*d*$ such that the number of a's and c's are equal and the number of b's and d's are equal. (Recall a^n means a written n times.) L_2 abstracts the problem of checking that the number of formal parameters in the declaration of a procedure agrees with the number of actual parameters in a use of the procedure. That is, a^n and b^m could represent the formal parameter lists in two procedures declared to have n and m arguments, respectively. Then c^n and d^m represent the actual parameter lists in calls to these two procedures.

Again note that the typical syntax of procedure definitions and uses does not concern itself with counting the number of parameters. For example, the CALL statement in a Fortran-like language might be described

$$stmt \rightarrow \textbf{call id} \ (\ expr\_list \ )$$
$$expr\_list \rightarrow expr\_list \ , \ expr$$
$$| \ expr$$

with suitable productions for *expr*. Checking that the number of actual parameters in the call is correct is usually done during the semantic analysis phase.   □

Example 4.13. The language $L_3 = \{a^n b^n c^n \mid n \geq 0\}$, that is, strings in $L(a*b*c*)$ with equal numbers of a's, b's and c's, is not context free. An example of a problem that embeds L_3 is the following. Typeset text uses italics where ordinary typed text uses underlining. In converting a file of text destined to be printed on a line printer to text suitable for a phototypesetter, one has to replace underlined words by italics. An underlined word is a string of letters followed by an equal number of backspaces and an equal number of underscores. If we regard a as any letter, b as backspace, and c as underscore, the language L_3 represents underlined words. The conclusion is that we cannot use a grammar to describe underlined words in this fashion. On the other hand, if we represent an underlined word as a sequence of letter-backspace-underscore triples then we can represent underlined words with the regular expression $(abc)*$.   □

It is interesting to note that languages very similar to L_1, L_2, and L_3 are context free. For example, $L'_1 = \{wcw^R \mid w$ is in $(a \mid b)*\}$, where w^R stands for w reversed, is context free. It is generated by the grammar

$$S \rightarrow aSa \mid bSb \mid c$$

The language $L'_2 = \{a^n b^m c^m d^n \mid n \geq 1$ and $m \geq 1\}$ is context free, with grammar

$$S \rightarrow aSd \mid aAd$$
$$A \rightarrow bAc \mid bc$$

Also, $L''_2 = \{a^n b^n c^m d^m \mid n \geq 1$ and $m \geq 1\}$ is context free, with grammar

$$S \rightarrow AB$$
$$A \rightarrow aAb \mid ab$$
$$B \rightarrow cBd \mid cd$$

Finally, $L'_3 = \{a^n b^n \mid n \geq 1\}$ is context free, with grammar

$$S \rightarrow aSb \mid ab$$

It is worth noting that L'_3 is the prototypical example of a language not definable by any regular expression. To see this, suppose L'_3 were the language defined by some regular expression. Equivalently, suppose we could construct a DFA D accepting L'_3. D must have some finite number of states, say k. Consider the sequence of states $s_0, s_1, s_2, \ldots, s_k$ entered by D having read $\epsilon, a, aa, \ldots, a^k$. That is, s_i is the state entered by D having read i a's.

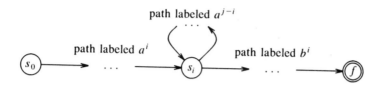

Fig. 4.8. DFA D accepting $a^i b^i$ and $a^j b^i$.

Since D has only k different states, at least two states in the sequence $s_0, s_1, \ldots, s_k$ must be the same, say s_i and s_j. From state s_i a sequence of i b's takes D to an accepting state f, since $a^i b^i$ is in L'_3. But then there is also a path from the initial state s_0 to s_i to f labeled $a^j b^i$, as shown in Fig. 4.8. Thus, D also accepts $a^j b^i$, which is not in L'_3, contradicting the assumption that L'_3 is the language accepted by D.

Colloquially, we say that "a finite automaton cannot keep count," meaning that a finite automaton cannot accept a language like L'_3 which would require it to keep count of the number of a's before it sees the b's. Similarly, we say "a grammar can keep count of two items but not three," since with a grammar we can define L'_3 but not L_3.

4.4 TOP-DOWN PARSING

In this section, we introduce the basic ideas behind top-down parsing and show how to construct an efficient non-backtracking form of top-down parser called a predictive parser. We define the class of LL(1) grammars from which predictive parsers can be constructed automatically. Besides formalizing the discussion of predictive parsers in Section 2.4, we consider nonrecursive predictive parsers. This section concludes with a discussion of error recovery. Bottom-up parsers are discussed in Sections 4.5 – 4.7.

Recursive-Descent Parsing

Top-down parsing can be viewed as an attempt to find a leftmost derivation for an input string. Equivalently, it can be viewed as an attempt to construct a parse tree for the input starting from the root and creating the nodes of the parse tree in preorder. In Section 2.4, we discussed the special case of recursive-descent parsing, called predictive parsing, where no backtracking is required. We now consider a general form of top-down parsing, called recursive descent, that may involve backtracking, that is, making repeated scans of the input. However, backtracking parsers are not seen frequently. One reason is that backtracking is rarely needed to parse programming language constructs. In situations like natural language parsing, backtracking is still not very efficient, and tabular methods such as the dynamic programming algorithm of Exercise 4.63 or the method of Earley [1970] are preferred. See Aho and Ullman [1972b] for a description of general parsing methods.

Backtracking is required in the next example, and we shall suggest a way of keeping track of the input when backtracking takes place.

Example 4.14. Consider the grammar

$$S \rightarrow cAd \hspace{5cm} (4.15)$$
$$A \rightarrow ab \mid a$$

and the input string $w = cad$. To construct a parse tree for this string top-down, we initially create a tree consisting of a single node labeled S. An input pointer points to c, the first symbol of w. We then use the first production for S to expand the tree and obtain the tree of Fig. 4.9(a).

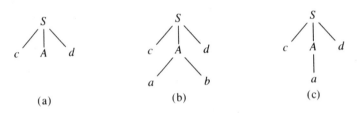

Fig. 4.9. Steps in top-down parse.

The leftmost leaf, labeled c, matches the first symbol of w, so we now advance the input pointer to a, the second symbol of w, and consider the next leaf, labeled A. We can then expand A using the first alternative for A to obtain the tree of Fig. 4.9(b). We now have a match for the second input symbol so we advance the input pointer to d, the third input symbol, and compare d against the next leaf, labeled b. Since b does not match d, we report failure and go back to A to see whether there is another alternative for A that we have not tried but that might produce a match.

In going back to A, we must reset the input pointer to position 2, the position it had when we first came to A, which means that the procedure for A (analogous to the procedure for nonterminals in Fig. 2.17) must store the input pointer in a local variable. We now try the second alternative for A to obtain the tree of Fig. 4.9(c). The leaf a matches the second symbol of w and the leaf d matches the third symbol. Since we have produced a parse tree for w, we halt and announce successful completion of parsing. □

A left-recursive grammar can cause a recursive-descent parser, even one with backtracking, to go into an infinite loop. That is, when we try to expand A, we may eventually find ourselves again trying to expand A without having consumed any input.

Predictive Parsers

In many cases, by carefully writing a grammar, eliminating left recursion from it, and left factoring the resulting grammar, we can obtain a grammar that can be parsed by a recursive-descent parser that needs no backtracking, i.e., a predictive parser, as discussed in Section 2.4. To construct a predictive parser, we must know, given the current input symbol a and the nonterminal A to be expanded, which one of the alternatives of production $A \rightarrow \alpha_1 | \alpha_2 | \cdots | \alpha_n$ is the unique alternative that derives a string beginning with a. That is, the proper alternative must be detectable by looking at only the first symbol it derives. Flow-of-control constructs in most programming languages, with their distinguishing keywords, are usually detectable in this way. For example, if we have the productions

> *stmt* → **if** *expr* **then** *stmt* **else** *stmt*
> | **while** *expr* **do** *stmt*
> | **begin** *stmt_list* **end**

then the keywords **if**, **while**, and **begin** tell us which alternative is the only one that could possibly succeed if we are to find a statement.

Transition Diagrams for Predictive Parsers

In Section 2.4, we discussed the implementation of predictive parsers by recursive procedures, e.g., those of Fig. 2.17. Just as a transition diagram was seen in Section 3.4 to be a useful plan or flowchart for a lexical analyzer, we can create a transition diagram as a plan for a predictive parser.

Several differences between the transition diagrams for a lexical analyzer and a predictive parser are immediately apparent. In the case of the parser, there is one diagram for each nonterminal. The labels of edges are tokens and nonterminals. A transition on a token (terminal) means we should take that transition if that token is the next input symbol. A transition on a nonterminal A is a call of the procedure for A.

To construct the transition diagram of a predictive parser from a grammar, first eliminate left recursion from the grammar, and then left factor the grammar. Then for each nonterminal A do the following:

1. Create an initial and final (return) state.

2. For each production $A \rightarrow X_1 X_2 \cdots X_n$, create a path from the initial to the final state, with edges labeled $X_1, X_2, \ldots, X_n$.

The predictive parser working off the transition diagrams behaves as follows. It begins in the start state for the start symbol. If after some actions it is in state s with an edge labeled by terminal a to state t, and if the next input symbol is a, then the parser moves the input cursor one position right and goes to state t. If, on the other hand, the edge is labeled by a nonterminal A, the parser instead goes to the start state for A, without moving the input cursor. If it ever reaches the final state for A, it immediately goes to state t, in effect having "read" A from the input during the time it moved from state s to t. Finally, if there is an edge from s to t labeled ϵ, then from state s the parser immediately goes to state t, without advancing the input.

A predictive parsing program based on a transition diagram attempts to match terminal symbols against the input, and makes a potentially recursive procedure call whenever it has to follow an edge labeled by a nonterminal. A nonrecursive implementation can be obtained by stacking the states s when there is a transition on a nonterminal out of s, and popping the stack when the final state for a nonterminal is reached. We shall discuss the implementation of transition diagrams in more detail shortly.

The above approach works if the given transition diagram does not have nondeterminism, in the sense that there is more than one transition from a state on the same input. If ambiguity occurs, we may be able to resolve it in an ad-hoc way, as in the next example. If the nondeterminism cannot be eliminated, we cannot build a predictive parser, but we could build a recursive-descent parser using backtracking to systematically try all possibilities, if that were the best parsing strategy we could find.

Example 4.15. Figure 4.10 contains a collection of transition diagrams for grammar (4.11). The only ambiguities concern whether or not to take an ϵ-edge. If we interpret the edges out of the initial state for E' as saying take the transition on $+$ whenever that is the next input and take the transition on ϵ otherwise, and make the analogous assumption for T', then the ambiguity is removed, and we can write a predictive parsing program for grammar (4.11).□

Transition diagrams can be simplified by substituting diagrams in one another; these substitutions are similar to the transformations on grammars used in Section 2.5. For example, in Fig. 4.11(a), the call of E' on itself has been replaced by a jump to the beginning of the diagram for E'.

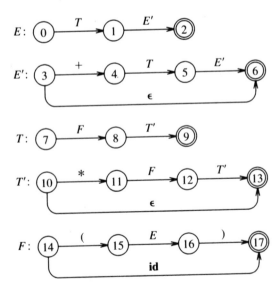

Fig. 4.10. Transition diagrams for grammar (4.11).

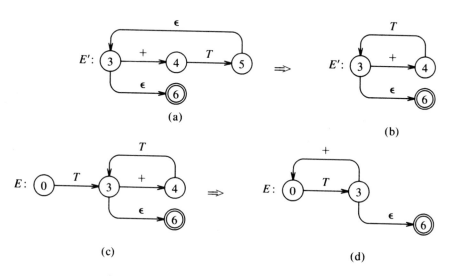

Fig. 4.11. Simplified transition diagrams.

Figure 4.11(b) shows an equivalent transition diagram for E'. We may then substitute the diagram of Fig. 4.11(b) for the transition on E' in the diagram for E in Fig. 4.10, yielding the diagram of Fig. 4.11(c). Lastly, we observe that the first and third nodes in Fig. 4.11(c) are equivalent and we merge them. The result, Fig. 4.11(d), is repeated as the first diagram in Fig. 4.12. The same techniques apply to the diagrams for T and T'. The complete set of resulting diagrams is shown in Fig. 4.12. A C implementation of this predictive parser runs 20-25% faster than a C implementation of Fig. 4.10.

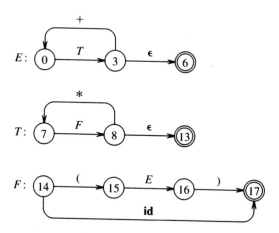

Fig. 4.12. Simplified transition diagrams for arithmetic expressions.

Nonrecursive Predictive Parsing

It is possible to build a nonrecursive predictive parser by maintaining a stack explicitly, rather than implicitly via recursive calls. The key problem during predictive parsing is that of determining the production to be applied for a nonterminal. The nonrecursive parser in Fig. 4.13 looks up the production to be applied in a parsing table. In what follows, we shall see how the table can be constructed directly from certain grammars.

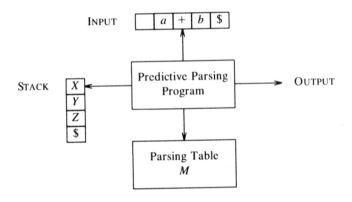

Fig. 4.13. Model of a nonrecursive predictive parser.

A table-driven predictive parser has an input buffer, a stack, a parsing table, and an output stream. The input buffer contains the string to be parsed, followed by $, a symbol used as a right endmarker to indicate the end of the input string. The stack contains a sequence of grammar symbols with $ on the bottom, indicating the bottom of the stack. Initially, the stack contains the start symbol of the grammar on top of $. The parsing table is a two-dimensional array $M[A, a]$, where A is a nonterminal, and a is a terminal or the symbol $.

The parser is controlled by a program that behaves as follows. The program considers X, the symbol on top of the stack, and a, the current input symbol. These two symbols determine the action of the parser. There are three possibilities.

1. If $X = a = \$$, the parser halts and announces successful completion of parsing.

2. If $X = a \neq \$$, the parser pops X off the stack and advances the input pointer to the next input symbol.

3. If X is a nonterminal, the program consults entry $M[X, a]$ of the parsing table M. This entry will be either an X-production of the grammar or an error entry. If, for example, $M[X, a] = \{X \rightarrow UVW\}$, the parser replaces X on top of the stack by WVU (with U on top). As output, we shall

assume that the parser just prints the production used; any other code could be executed here. If $M[X, a]$ = **error**, the parser calls an error recovery routine.

The behavior of the parser can be described in terms of its *configurations*, which give the stack contents and the remaining input.

Algorithm 4.3. Nonrecursive predictive parsing.

Input. A string w and a parsing table M for grammar G.

Output. If w is in $L(G)$, a leftmost derivation of w; otherwise, an error indication.

Method. Initially, the parser is in a configuration in which it has $\$S$ on the stack with S, the start symbol of G on top, and $w\$$ in the input buffer. The program that utilizes the predictive parsing table M to produce a parse for the input is shown in Fig. 4.14.   □

```
set ip to point to the first symbol of w$;
repeat
        let X be the top stack symbol and a the symbol pointed to by ip;
        if X is a terminal or $ then
            if X = a then
                pop X from the stack and advance ip
            else error()
        else        /* X is a nonterminal */
            if M[X, a] = X → Y₁Y₂ · · · Yₖ then begin
                pop X from the stack;
                push Yₖ, Yₖ₋₁, . . . , Y₁ onto the stack, with Y₁ on top;
                output the production X → Y₁Y₂ · · · Yₖ
            end
            else error()
until X = $   /* stack is empty */
```

Fig. 4.14. Predictive parsing program.

Example 4.16. Consider the grammar (4.11) from Example 4.8. A predictive parsing table for this grammar is shown in Fig. 4.15. Blanks are error entries; non-blanks indicate a production with which to expand the top nonterminal on the stack. Note that we have not yet indicated how these entries could be selected, but we shall do so shortly.

With input **id** + **id** * **id** the predictive parser makes the sequence of moves in Fig. 4.16. The input pointer points to the leftmost symbol of the string in the INPUT column. If we observe the actions of this parser carefully, we see that it is tracing out a leftmost derivation for the input, that is, the productions output are those of a leftmost derivation. The input symbols that have

NONTER-	INPUT SYMBOL					
MINAL	**id**	**+**	*****	**(**	**)**	**$**
E	$E \rightarrow TE'$			$E \rightarrow TE'$		
E'		$E' \rightarrow +TE'$			$E' \rightarrow \epsilon$	$E' \rightarrow \epsilon$
T	$T \rightarrow FT'$			$T \rightarrow FT'$		
T'		$T' \rightarrow \epsilon$	$T' \rightarrow *FT'$		$T' \rightarrow \epsilon$	$T' \rightarrow \epsilon$
F	$F \rightarrow \mathbf{id}$			$F \rightarrow (E)$		

Fig. 4.15. Parsing table M for grammar (4.11).

already been scanned, followed by the grammar symbols on the stack (from the top to bottom), make up the left-sentential forms in the derivation. □

STACK	INPUT	OUTPUT
$\$E$	**id + id * id$**	
$\$E'T$	**id + id * id$**	$E \rightarrow TE'$
$\$E'T'F$	**id + id * id$**	$T \rightarrow FT'$
$\$E'T'\mathbf{id}$	**id + id * id$**	$F \rightarrow \mathbf{id}$
$\$E'T'$	**+ id * id$**	
$\$E'$	**+ id * id$**	$T' \rightarrow \epsilon$
$\$E'T+$	**+ id * id$**	$E' \rightarrow +TE'$
$\$E'T$	**id * id$**	
$\$E'T'F$	**id * id$**	$T \rightarrow FT'$
$\$E'T'\mathbf{id}$	**id * id$**	$F \rightarrow \mathbf{id}$
$\$E'T'$	*** id$**	
$\$E'T'F*$	*** id$**	$T' \rightarrow *FT'$
$\$E'T'F$	**id$**	
$\$E'T'\mathbf{id}$	**id$**	$F \rightarrow \mathbf{id}$
$\$E'T'$	**$**	
$\$E'$	**$**	$T' \rightarrow \epsilon$
$\$$	**$**	$E' \rightarrow \epsilon$

Fig. 4.16. Moves made by predictive parser on input **id+id*id**.

FIRST and FOLLOW

The construction of a predictive parser is aided by two functions associated with a grammar G. These functions, FIRST and FOLLOW, allow us to fill in the entries of a predictive parsing table for G, whenever possible. Sets of tokens yielded by the FOLLOW function can also be used as synchronizing tokens during panic-mode error recovery.

If α is any string of grammar symbols, let $FIRST(\alpha)$ be the set of terminals that begin the strings derived from α. If $\alpha \stackrel{*}{\Rightarrow} \epsilon$, then ϵ is also in FIRST(α).

Define *FOLLOW*(*A*), for nonterminal *A*, to be the set of terminals *a* that can appear immediately to the right of *A* in some sentential form, that is, the set of terminals *a* such that there exists a derivation of the form $S \stackrel{*}{\Rightarrow} \alpha A a \beta$ for some α and β. Note that there may be, at some time during the derivation, have been symbols between *A* and *a*, but if so, they derived ϵ and disappeared. If *A* can be the rightmost symbol in some sentential form, then $ is in FOLLOW(*A*).

To compute FIRST(*X*) for all grammar symbols *X*, apply the following rules until no more terminals or ϵ can be added to any FIRST set.

1. If *X* is terminal, then FIRST(*X*) is {*X*}.

2. If $X \rightarrow \epsilon$ is a production, then add ϵ to FIRST(*X*).

3. If *X* is nonterminal and $X \rightarrow Y_1 Y_2 \cdots Y_k$ is a production, then place *a* in FIRST(*X*) if for some *i*, *a* is in FIRST(Y_i), and ϵ is in all of FIRST(Y_1), ..., FIRST(Y_{i-1}); that is, $Y_1 \cdots Y_{i-1} \stackrel{*}{\Rightarrow} \epsilon$. If ϵ is in FIRST(Y_j) for all $j = 1, 2, \ldots, k$, then add ϵ to FIRST(*X*). For example, everything in FIRST(Y_1) is surely in FIRST(*X*). If Y_1 does not derive ϵ, then we add nothing more to FIRST(*X*), but if $Y_1 \stackrel{*}{\Rightarrow} \epsilon$, then we add FIRST($Y_2$) and so on.

Now, we can compute FIRST for any string $X_1 X_2 \cdots X_n$ as follows. Add to FIRST($X_1 X_2 \cdots X_n$) all the non-ϵ symbols of FIRST(X_1). Also add the non-ϵ symbols of FIRST(X_2) if ϵ is in FIRST(X_1), the non-ϵ symbols of FIRST(X_3) if ϵ is in both FIRST(X_1) and FIRST(X_2), and so on. Finally, add ϵ to FIRST($X_1 X_2 \cdots X_n$) if, for all *i*, FIRST(X_i) contains ϵ.

To compute FOLLOW(*A*) for all nonterminals *A*, apply the following rules until nothing can be added to any FOLLOW set.

1. Place $ in FOLLOW(*S*), where *S* is the start symbol and $ is the input right endmarker.

2. If there is a production $A \rightarrow \alpha B \beta$, then everything in FIRST(β) except for ϵ is placed in FOLLOW(*B*).

3. If there is a production $A \rightarrow \alpha B$, or a production $A \rightarrow \alpha B \beta$ where FIRST(β) contains ϵ (i.e., $\beta \stackrel{*}{\Rightarrow} \epsilon$), then everything in FOLLOW(*A*) is in FOLLOW(*B*).

Example 4.17. Consider again grammar (4.11), repeated below:

$$E \rightarrow TE'$$
$$E' \rightarrow +TE' \mid \epsilon$$
$$T \rightarrow FT'$$
$$T' \rightarrow *FT' \mid \epsilon$$
$$F \rightarrow (E) \mid \textbf{id}$$

Then:

$FIRST(E) = FIRST(T) = FIRST(F) = \{(, \mathbf{id}\}.$

$FIRST(E') = \{+, \epsilon\}$

$FIRST(T') = \{*, \epsilon\}$

$FOLLOW(E) = FOLLOW(E') = \{), \$\}$

$FOLLOW(T) = FOLLOW(T') = \{+,), \$\}$

$FOLLOW(F) = \{+, *,), \$\}$

For example, **id** and left parenthesis are added to $FIRST(F)$ by rule (3) in the definition of FIRST with $i = 1$ in each case, since $FIRST(\mathbf{id}) = \{\mathbf{id}\}$ and $FIRST('(') = \{ (\}$ by rule (1). Then by rule (3) with $i = 1$, the production $T \rightarrow FT'$ implies that **id** and left parenthesis are in $FIRST(T)$ as well. As another example, ϵ is in $FIRST(E')$ by rule (2).

To compute FOLLOW sets, we put $\$$ in $FOLLOW(E)$ by rule (1) for FOLLOW. By rule (2) applied to production $F \rightarrow (E)$, the right parenthesis is also in $FOLLOW(E)$. By rule (3) applied to production $E \rightarrow TE'$, $\$$ and right parenthesis are in $FOLLOW(E')$. Since $E' \stackrel{*}{\Rightarrow} \epsilon$, they are also in $FOLLOW(T)$. For a last example of how the FOLLOW rules are applied, the production $E \rightarrow TE'$ implies, by rule (2), that everything other than ϵ in $FIRST(E')$ must be placed in $FOLLOW(T)$. We have already seen that $\$$ is in $FOLLOW(T)$.   □

Construction of Predictive Parsing Tables

The following algorithm can be used to construct a predictive parsing table for a grammar G. The idea behind the algorithm is the following. Suppose $A \rightarrow \alpha$ is a production with a in $FIRST(\alpha)$. Then, the parser will expand A by α when the current input symbol is a. The only complication occurs when $\alpha = \epsilon$ or $\alpha \stackrel{*}{\Rightarrow} \epsilon$. In this case, we should again expand A by α if the current input symbol is in $FOLLOW(A)$, or if the $\$$ on the input has been reached and $\$$ is in $FOLLOW(A)$.

Algorithm 4.4. Construction of a predictive parsing table.

Input. Grammar G.

Output. Parsing table M.

Method.

1.   For each production $A \rightarrow \alpha$ of the grammar, do steps 2 and 3.

2.   For each terminal a in $FIRST(\alpha)$, add $A \rightarrow \alpha$ to $M[A, a]$.

3.   If ϵ is in $FIRST(\alpha)$, add $A \rightarrow \alpha$ to $M[A, b]$ for each terminal b in $FOLLOW(A)$. If ϵ is in $FIRST(\alpha)$ and $\$$ is in $FOLLOW(A)$, add $A \rightarrow \alpha$ to $M[A, \$]$.

4.   Make each undefined entry of M be **error**.

Example 4.18. Let us apply Algorithm 4.4 to grammar (4.11). Since FIRST(TE') = FIRST(T) = {(, **id**}, production $E \rightarrow TE'$ causes $M[E, ($] and $M[E,$ **id**] to acquire the entry $E \rightarrow TE'$.

Production $E' \rightarrow +TE'$ causes $M[E', +]$ to acquire $E' \rightarrow +TE'$. Production $E' \rightarrow \epsilon$ causes $M[E',)]$ and $M[E', \$]$ to acquire $E' \rightarrow \epsilon$ since FOLLOW(E') = {), \$}.

The parsing table produced by Algorithm 4.4 for grammar (4.11) was shown in Fig. 4.15.   □

LL(1) Grammars

Algorithm 4.4 can be applied to any grammar G to produce a parsing table M. For some grammars, however, M may have some entries that are multiply-defined. For example, if G is left recursive or ambiguous, then M will have at least one multiply-defined entry.

Example 4.19. Let us consider grammar (4.13) from Example 4.10 again; it is repeated here for convenience.

$$S \rightarrow iEtSS' \mid a$$
$$S' \rightarrow eS \mid \epsilon$$
$$E \rightarrow b$$

The parsing table for this grammar is shown in Fig. 4.17.

NONTER-MINAL	INPUT SYMBOL					
	a	b	e	i	t	$\$$
S	$S \rightarrow a$			$S \rightarrow iEtSS'$		
S'			$S' \rightarrow \epsilon$ $S' \rightarrow eS$			$S' \rightarrow \epsilon$
E		$E \rightarrow b$				

Fig. 4.17. Parsing table M for grammar (4.13).

The entry for $M[S', e]$ contains both $S' \rightarrow eS$ and $S' \rightarrow \epsilon$, since FOLLOW(S') = {e, \$}. The grammar is ambiguous and the ambiguity is manifested by a choice in what production to use when an e (**else**) is seen. We can resolve the ambiguity if we choose $S' \rightarrow eS$. This choice corresponds to associating **else**'s with the closest previous **then**'s. Note that the choice $S' \rightarrow \epsilon$ would prevent e from ever being put on the stack or removed from the input, and is therefore surely wrong.   □

A grammar whose parsing table has no multiply-defined entries is said to be $LL(1)$. The first "L" in LL(1) stands for scanning the input from left to right, the second "L" for producing a leftmost derivation, and the "1" for using one input symbol of lookahead at each step to make parsing action decisions. It can be shown that Algorithm 4.4 produces for every LL(1) grammar G a parsing table that parses all and only the sentences of G.

LL(1) grammars have several distinctive properties. No ambiguous or left-recursive grammar can be LL(1). It can also be shown that a grammar G is LL(1) if and only if whenever $A \rightarrow \alpha \mid \beta$ are two distinct productions of G the following conditions hold:

1. For no terminal a do both α and β derive strings beginning with a.

2. At most one of α and β can derive the empty string.

3. If $\beta \overset{*}{\Rightarrow} \epsilon$, then α does not derive any string beginning with a terminal in FOLLOW(A).

Clearly, grammar (4.11) for arithmetic expressions is LL(1). Grammar (4.13), modeling if-then-else statements, is not.

There remains the question of what should be done when a parsing table has multiply-defined entries. One recourse is to transform the grammar by eliminating all left recursion and then left factoring whenever possible, hoping to produce a grammar for which the parsing table has no multiply-defined entries. Unfortunately, there are some grammars for which no amount of alteration will yield an LL(1) grammar. Grammar (4.13) is one such example; its language has no LL(1) grammar at all. As we saw, we can still parse (4.13) with a predictive parser by arbitrarily making $M[S', e] = \{S' \rightarrow eS\}$. In general, there are no universal rules by which multiply-defined entries can be made single-valued without affecting the language recognized by the parser.

The main difficulty in using predictive parsing is in writing a grammar for the source language such that a predictive parser can be constructed from the grammar. Although left-recursion elimination and left factoring are easy to do, they make the resulting grammar hard to read and difficult to use for translation purposes. To alleviate some of this difficulty, a common organization for a parser in a compiler is to use a predictive parser for control constructs and to use operator precedence (discussed in Section 4.6) for expressions. However, if an LR parser generator, as discussed in Section 4.9, is available, one can get all the benefits of predictive parsing and operator precedence automatically.

Error Recovery in Predictive Parsing

The stack of a nonrecursive predictive parser makes explicit the terminals and nonterminals that the parser hopes to match with the remainder of the input. We shall therefore refer to symbols on the parser stack in the following discussion. An error is detected during predictive parsing when the terminal on top of the stack does not match the next input symbol or when nonterminal A is on top of the stack, a is the next input symbol, and the parsing table entry $M[A, a]$ is empty.

Panic-mode error recovery is based on the idea of skipping symbols on the the input until a token in a selected set of synchronizing tokens appears. Its effectiveness depends on the choice of synchronizing set. The sets should be chosen so that the parser recovers quickly from errors that are likely to occur in practice. Some heuristics are as follows:

1. As a starting point, we can place all symbols in FOLLOW(A) into the synchronizing set for nonterminal A. If we skip tokens until an element of FOLLOW(A) is seen and pop A from the stack, it is likely that parsing can continue.

2. It is not enough to use FOLLOW(A) as the synchronizing set for A. For example, if semicolons terminate statements, as in C, then keywords that begin statements may not appear in the FOLLOW set of the nonterminal generating expressions. A missing semicolon after an assignment may therefore result in the keyword beginning the next statement being skipped. Often, there is a hierarchical structure on constructs in a language; e.g., expressions appear within statements, which appear within blocks, and so on. We can add to the synchronizing set of a lower construct the symbols that begin higher constructs. For example, we might add keywords that begin statements to the synchronizing sets for the nonterminals generating expressions.

3. If we add symbols in FIRST(A) to the synchronizing set for nonterminal A, then it may be possible to resume parsing according to A if a symbol in FIRST(A) appears in the input.

4. If a nonterminal can generate the empty string, then the production deriving ϵ can be used as a default. Doing so may postpone some error detection, but cannot cause an error to be missed. This approach reduces the number of nonterminals that have to be considered during error recovery.

5. If a terminal on top of the stack cannot be matched, a simple idea is to pop the terminal, issue a message saying that the terminal was inserted, and continue parsing. In effect, this approach takes the synchronizing set of a token to consist of all other tokens.

Example 4.20. Using FOLLOW and FIRST symbols as synchronizing tokens works reasonably well when expressions are parsed according to grammar (4.11). The parsing table for this grammar in Fig. 4.15 is repeated in Fig. 4.18, with "synch" indicating synchronizing tokens obtained from the FOLLOW set of the nonterminal in question. The FOLLOW sets for the nonterminal are obtained from Example 4.17.

The table in Fig. 4.18 is to be used as follows. If the parser looks up entry $M[A, a]$ and finds that it is blank, then the input symbol a is skipped. If the entry is synch, then the nonterminal on top of the stack is popped in an attempt to resume parsing. If a token on top of the stack does not match the input symbol, then we pop the token from the stack, as mentioned above.

On the erroneous input) **id** * + **id** the parser and error recovery mechanism of Fig. 4.18 behave as in Fig. 4.19.   □

NONTER-	INPUT SYMBOL					
MINAL	**id**	**+**	**∗**	**(**	**)**	**$**
E	$E \rightarrow TE'$			$E \rightarrow TE'$	synch	synch
E'		$E' \rightarrow +TE'$			$E' \rightarrow \epsilon$	$E' \rightarrow \epsilon$
T	$T \rightarrow FT'$	synch		$T \rightarrow FT'$	synch	synch
T'		$T' \rightarrow \epsilon$	$T' \rightarrow *FT'$		$T' \rightarrow \epsilon$	$T' \rightarrow \epsilon$
F	$F \rightarrow \mathbf{id}$	synch	synch	$F \rightarrow (E)$	synch	synch

Fig. 4.18. Synchronizing tokens added to parsing table of Fig. 4.15.

STACK	INPUT	REMARK
$\$E$	$)\,\mathbf{id} * + \mathbf{id}\,\$$	error, skip)
$\$E$	$\mathbf{id} * + \mathbf{id}\,\$$	**id** is in FIRST(E)
$\$E'T$	$\mathbf{id} * + \mathbf{id}\,\$$	
$\$E'T'F$	$\mathbf{id} * + \mathbf{id}\,\$$	
$\$E'T'\mathbf{id}$	$\mathbf{id} * + \mathbf{id}\,\$$	
$\$E'T'$	$* + \mathbf{id}\,\$$	
$\$E'T'F*$	$* + \mathbf{id}\,\$$	
$\$E'T'F$	$+ \mathbf{id}\,\$$	error, $M[F, +]$ = synch
$\$E'T'$	$+ \mathbf{id}\,\$$	F has been popped
$\$E'$	$+ \mathbf{id}\,\$$	
$\$E'T +$	$+ \mathbf{id}\,\$$	
$\$E'T$	$\mathbf{id}\,\$$	
$\$E'T'F$	$\mathbf{id}\,\$$	
$\$E'T'\mathbf{id}$	$\mathbf{id}\,\$$	
$\$E'T'$	$\$$	
$\$E'$	$\$$	
$\$$	$\$$	

Fig. 4.19. Parsing and error recovery moves made by predictive parser.

The above discussion of panic-mode recovery does not address the important issue of error messages. In general, informative error messages have to be supplied by the compiler designer.

Phrase-level recovery. Phrase-level recovery is implemented by filling in the blank entries in the predictive parsing table with pointers to error routines. These routines may change, insert, or delete symbols on the input and issue appropriate error messages. They may also pop from the stack. It is questionable whether we should permit alteration of stack symbols or the pushing of new symbols onto the stack, since then the steps carried out by the parser might not correspond to the derivation of any word in the language at all. In any event, we must be sure that there is no possibility of an infinite loop. Checking that any recovery action eventually results in an input symbol being consumed (or the stack being shortened if the end of the input has been reached) is a good way to protect against such loops.

4.5 BOTTOM-UP PARSING

In this section, we introduce a general style of bottom-up syntax analysis, known as shift-reduce parsing. An easy-to-implement form of shift-reduce parsing, called operator-precedence parsing, is presented in Section 4.6. A much more general method of shift-reduce parsing, called LR parsing, is discussed in Section 4.7. LR parsing is used in a number of automatic parser generators.

Shift-reduce parsing attempts to construct a parse tree for an input string beginning at the leaves (the bottom) and working up towards the root (the top). We can think of this process as one of "reducing" a string w to the start symbol of a grammar. At each *reduction* step a particular substring matching the right side of a production is replaced by the symbol on the left of that production, and if the substring is chosen correctly at each step, a rightmost derivation is traced out in reverse.

Example 4.21. Consider the grammar

$$S \rightarrow aABe$$
$$A \rightarrow Abc \mid b$$
$$B \rightarrow d$$

The sentence *abbcde* can be reduced to S by the following steps:

abbcde
aAbcde
aAde
aABe
S

We scan *abbcde* looking for a substring that matches the right side of some production. The substrings *b* and *d* qualify. Let us choose the leftmost *b* and replace it by A, the left side of the production $A \rightarrow b$; we thus obtain the string *aAbcde*. Now the substrings *Abc*, *b*, and *d* match the right side of some production. Although *b* is the leftmost substring that matches the right side of some production, we choose to replace the substring *Abc* by A, the left side of the production $A \rightarrow Abc$. We now obtain *aAde*. Then replacing *d* by B, the left side of the production $B \rightarrow d$, we obtain *aABe*. We can now replace this entire string by S. Thus, by a sequence of four reductions we are able to reduce *abbcde* to S. These reductions, in fact, trace out the following rightmost derivation in reverse:

$$S \underset{rm}{\Rightarrow} aABe \underset{rm}{\Rightarrow} aAde \underset{rm}{\Rightarrow} aAbcde \underset{rm}{\Rightarrow} abbcde \qquad \Box$$

Handles

Informally, a "handle" of a string is a substring that matches the right side of a production, and whose reduction to the nonterminal on the left side of the production represents one step along the reverse of a rightmost derivation. In many cases the leftmost substring β that matches the right side of some production $A \to \beta$ is not a handle, because a reduction by the production $A \to \beta$ yields a string that cannot be reduced to the start symbol. In Example 4.21, if we replaced b by A in the second string $aAbcde$ we would obtain the string $aAAcde$ that cannot be subsequently reduced to S. For this reason, we must give a more precise definition of a handle.

Formally, a *handle* of a right-sentential form γ is a production $A \to \beta$ and a position of γ where the string β may be found and replaced by A to produce the previous right-sentential form in a rightmost derivation of γ. That is, if $S \underset{rm}{\overset{*}{\Rightarrow}} \alpha A w \underset{rm}{\Rightarrow} \alpha \beta w$, then $A \to \beta$ in the position following α is a handle of $\alpha \beta w$. The string w to the right of the handle contains only terminal symbols. Note we say "a handle" rather than "the handle" because the grammar could be ambiguous, with more than one rightmost derivation of $\alpha \beta w$. If a grammar is unambiguous, then every right-sentential form of the grammar has exactly one handle.

In the example above, $abbcde$ is a right-sentential form whose handle is $A \to b$ at position 2. Likewise, $aAbcde$ is a right-sentential form whose handle is $A \to Abc$ at position 2. Sometimes we say "the substring β is a handle of $\alpha \beta w$" if the position of β and the production $A \to \beta$ we have in mind are clear.

Figure 4.20 portrays the handle $A \to \beta$ in the parse tree of a right-sentential form $\alpha \beta w$. The handle represents the leftmost complete subtree consisting of a node and all its children. In Fig. 4.20, A is the bottommost leftmost interior node with all its children in the tree. Reducing β to A in $\alpha \beta w$ can be thought of as "pruning the handle," that is, removing the children of A from the parse tree.

Example 4.22. Consider the following grammar

(1) $E \to E + E$
(2) $E \to E * E$ (4.16)
(3) $E \to (E)$
(4) $E \to \mathbf{id}$

and the rightmost derivation

$$E \underset{rm}{\Rightarrow} \underline{E + E}$$
$$\underset{rm}{\Rightarrow} E + \underline{E * E}$$
$$\underset{rm}{\Rightarrow} E + E * \underline{\mathbf{id}_3}$$
$$\underset{rm}{\Rightarrow} E + \underline{\mathbf{id}_2} * \mathbf{id}_3$$
$$\underset{rm}{\Rightarrow} \underline{\mathbf{id}_1} + \mathbf{id}_2 * \mathbf{id}_3$$

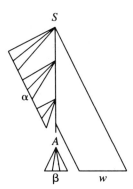

Fig. 4.20. The handle $A \to \beta$ in the parse tree for $\alpha\beta w$.

We have subscripted the **id**'s for notational convenience and underlined a handle of each right-sentential form. For example, $\mathbf{id}_1$ is a handle of the right-sentential form $\mathbf{id}_1 + \mathbf{id}_2 * \mathbf{id}_3$ because **id** is the right side of the production $E \to \mathbf{id}$, and replacing $\mathbf{id}_1$ by E produces the previous right-sentential form $E + \mathbf{id}_2 * \mathbf{id}_3$. Note that the string appearing to the right of a handle contains only terminal symbols.

Because grammar (4.16) is ambiguous, there is another rightmost derivation of the same string:

$$E \underset{rm}{\Rightarrow} \underline{E * E}$$
$$\underset{rm}{\Rightarrow} E * \underline{\mathbf{id}_3}$$
$$\underset{rm}{\Rightarrow} \underline{E + E} * \mathbf{id}_3$$
$$\underset{rm}{\Rightarrow} E + \underline{\mathbf{id}_2} * \mathbf{id}_3$$
$$\underset{rm}{\Rightarrow} \underline{\mathbf{id}_1} + \mathbf{id}_2 * \mathbf{id}_3$$

Consider the right sentential form $E + E * \mathbf{id}_3$. In this derivation, $E + E$ is a handle of $E + E * \mathbf{id}_3$ whereas $\mathbf{id}_3$ by itself is a handle of this same right-sentential form according to the derivation above.

The two rightmost derivations in this example are analogs of the two leftmost derivations in Example 4.6. The first derivation gives $*$ a higher precedence than $+$, whereas the second gives $+$ the higher precedence.   □

Handle Pruning

A rightmost derivation in reverse can be obtained by "handle pruning." That is, we start with a string of terminals w that we wish to parse. If w is a sentence of the grammar at hand, then $w = \gamma_n$, where γ_n is the nth right-sentential form of some as yet unknown rightmost derivation

$$S = \gamma_0 \underset{rm}{\Rightarrow} \gamma_1 \underset{rm}{\Rightarrow} \gamma_2 \underset{rm}{\Rightarrow} \cdots \underset{rm}{\Rightarrow} \gamma_{n-1} \underset{rm}{\Rightarrow} \gamma_n = w.$$

To reconstruct this derivation in reverse order, we locate the handle β_n in γ_n and replace β_n by the left side of some production $A_n \rightarrow \beta_n$ to obtain the $(n-1)$st right-sentential form γ_{n-1}. Note that we do not yet know how handles are to be found, but we shall see methods of doing so shortly.

We then repeat this process. That is, we locate the handle β_{n-1} in γ_{n-1} and reduce this handle to obtain the right-sentential form γ_{n-2}. If by continuing this process we produce a right-sentential form consisting only of the start symbol S, then we halt and announce successful completion of parsing. The reverse of the sequence of productions used in the reductions is a rightmost derivation for the input string.

Example 4.23. Consider the grammar (4.16) of Example 4.22 and the input string $\mathbf{id}_1 + \mathbf{id}_2 * \mathbf{id}_3$. The sequence of reductions shown in Fig. 4.21 reduces $\mathbf{id}_1 + \mathbf{id}_2 * \mathbf{id}_3$ to the start symbol E. The reader should observe that the sequence of right-sentential forms in this example is just the reverse of the sequence in the first rightmost derivation in Example 4.22.   □

RIGHT-SENTENTIAL FORM	HANDLE	REDUCING PRODUCTION
$\mathbf{id}_1 + \mathbf{id}_2 * \mathbf{id}_3$	$\mathbf{id}_1$	$E \rightarrow \mathbf{id}$
$E + \mathbf{id}_2 * \mathbf{id}_3$	$\mathbf{id}_2$	$E \rightarrow \mathbf{id}$
$E + E * \mathbf{id}_3$	$\mathbf{id}_3$	$E \rightarrow \mathbf{id}$
$E + E * E$	$E * E$	$E \rightarrow E * E$
$E + E$	$E + E$	$E \rightarrow E + E$
E		

Fig. 4.21. Reductions made by shift-reduce parser.

Stack Implementation of Shift-Reduce Parsing

There are two problems that must be solved if we are to parse by handle pruning. The first is to locate the substring to be reduced in a right-sentential form, and the second is to determine what production to choose in case there is more than one production with that substring on the right side. Before we get to these questions, let us first consider the type of data structures to use in a shift-reduce parser.

A convenient way to implement a shift-reduce parser is to use a stack to hold grammar symbols and an input buffer to hold the string w to be parsed. We use $\$$ to mark the bottom of the stack and also the right end of the input. Initially, the stack is empty, and the string w is on the input, as follows:

STACK	INPUT
$\$$	$w\ \$$

The parser operates by shifting zero or more input symbols onto the stack until a handle β is on top of the stack. The parser then reduces β to the left side of the appropriate production. The parser repeats this cycle until it has detected an error or until the stack contains the start symbol and the input is empty:

STACK	INPUT
$S	$

After entering this configuration, the parser halts and announces successful completion of parsing.

Example 4.24. Let us step through the actions a shift-reduce parser might make in parsing the input string $id_1 + id_2 * id_3$ according to grammar (4.16), using the first derivation of Example 4.22. The sequence is shown in Fig. 4.22. Note that because grammar (4.16) has two rightmost derivations for this input there is another sequence of steps a shift-reduce parser might take. □

	STACK	INPUT	ACTION
(1)	$	$id_1 + id_2 * id_3$\$	shift
(2)	$id_1	$+ id_2 * id_3$\$	reduce by $E \rightarrow id$
(3)	$E	$+ id_2 * id_3$\$	shift
(4)	$E +	$id_2 * id_3$\$	shift
(5)	$E + id_2	$* id_3$\$	reduce by $E \rightarrow id$
(6)	$E + E	$* id_3$\$	shift
(7)	$E + E *	id_3\$	shift
(8)	$E + E * id_3	$	reduce by $E \rightarrow id$
(9)	$E + E * E	$	reduce by $E \rightarrow E * E$
(10)	$E + E	$	reduce by $E \rightarrow E + E$
(11)	$E	$	accept

Fig. 4.22. Configurations of shift-reduce parser on input $id_1 + id_2 * id_3$.

While the primary operations of the parser are shift and reduce, there are actually four possible actions a shift-reduce parser can make: (1) shift, (2) reduce, (3) accept, and (4) error.

1. In a *shift* action, the next input symbol is shifted onto the top of the stack.

2. In a *reduce* action, the parser knows the right end of the handle is at the top of the stack. It must then locate the left end of the handle within the stack and decide with what nonterminal to replace the handle.

3. In an *accept* action, the parser announces successful completion of parsing.

4. In an *error* action, the parser discovers that a syntax error has occurred and calls an error recovery routine.

There is an important fact that justifies the use of a stack in shift-reduce parsing: the handle will always eventually appear on top of the stack, never inside. This fact becomes obvious when we consider the possible forms of two successive steps in any rightmost derivation. These two steps can be of the form

$$(1) \quad S \underset{rm}{\overset{*}{\Rightarrow}} \alpha A z \underset{rm}{\overset{*}{\Rightarrow}} \alpha \beta B y z \underset{rm}{\overset{*}{\Rightarrow}} \alpha \beta \gamma y z$$

$$(2) \quad S \underset{rm}{\overset{*}{\Rightarrow}} \alpha B x A z \underset{rm}{\overset{*}{\Rightarrow}} \alpha B x y z \underset{rm}{\overset{*}{\Rightarrow}} \alpha \gamma x y z$$

In case (1), A is replaced by $\beta B y$, and then the rightmost nonterminal B in that right side is replaced by γ. In case (2), A is again replaced first, but this time the right side is a string y of terminals only. The next rightmost nonterminal B will be somewhere to the left of y.

Let us consider case (1) in reverse, where a shift-reduce parser has just reached the configuration

STACK	INPUT
$\$\alpha\beta\gamma$	$yz\$$

The parser now reduces the handle γ to B to reach the configuration

STACK	INPUT
$\$\alpha\beta B$	$yz\$$

Since B is the rightmost nonterminal in $\alpha\beta Byz$, the right end of the handle of $\alpha\beta Byz$ cannot occur inside the stack. The parser can therefore shift the string y onto the stack to reach the configuration

STACK	INPUT
$\$\alpha\beta By$	$z\$$

in which βBy is the handle, and it gets reduced to A.

In case (2), in configuration

STACK	INPUT
$\$\alpha\gamma$	$xyz\$$

the handle γ is on top of the stack. After reducing the handle γ to B, the parser can shift the string xy to get the next handle y on top of the stack:

STACK	INPUT
$\$\alpha Bxy$	$z\$$

Now the parser reduces y to A.

In both cases, after making a reduction the parser had to shift zero or more symbols to get the next handle onto the stack. It never had to go into the stack to find the handle. It is this aspect of handle pruning that makes a stack a particularly convenient data structure for implementing a shift-reduce parser. We still must explain how choices of action are to be made so the shift-reduce parser works correctly. Operator precedence and LR parsers are two such techniques that we shall discuss shortly.

Viable Prefixes

The set of prefixes of right sentential forms that can appear on the stack of a shift-reduce parser are called *viable prefixes*. An equivalent definition of a viable prefix is that it is a prefix of a right-sentential form that does not continue past the right end of the rightmost handle of that sentential form. By this definition, it is always possible to add terminal symbols to the end of a viable prefix to obtain a right-sentential form. Therefore, there is apparently no error as long as the portion of the input seen to a given point can be reduced to a viable prefix.

Conflicts During Shift-Reduce Parsing

There are context-free grammars for which shift-reduce parsing cannot be used. Every shift-reduce parser for such a grammar can reach a configuration in which the parser, knowing the entire stack contents and the next input symbol, cannot decide whether to shift or to reduce (a *shift/reduce conflict*), or cannot decide which of several reductions to make (a *reduce/reduce conflict*). We now give some examples of syntactic constructs that give rise to such grammars. Technically, these grammars are not in the LR(k) class of grammars defined in Section 4.7; we refer to them as non-LR grammars. The k in LR(k) refers to the number of symbols of lookahead on the input. Grammars used in compiling usually fall in the LR(1) class, with one symbol lookahead.

Example 4.25. An ambiguous grammar can never be LR. For example, consider the dangling-else grammar (4.7) of Section 4.3:

> *stmt* → **if** *expr* **then** *stmt*
> | **if** *expr* **then** *stmt* **else** *stmt*
> | **other**

If we have a shift-reduce parser in configuration

STACK	INPUT
· · · **if** *expr* **then** *stmt*	**else** · · · **$**

we cannot tell whether **if** *expr* **then** *stmt* is the handle, no matter what appears below it on the stack. Here there is a shift/reduce conflict. Depending on what follows the **else** on the input, it might be correct to reduce **if** *expr* **then** *stmt* to *stmt*, or it might be correct to shift **else** and then to look for another *stmt* to complete the alternative **if** *expr* **then** *stmt* **else** *stmt*. Thus, we cannot tell whether to shift or reduce in this case, so the grammar is not LR(1). More generally, no ambiguous grammar, as this one certainly is, can be LR(k) for any k.

We should mention, however, that shift-reduce parsing can be easily adapted to parse certain ambiguous grammars, such as the if-then-else grammar above. When we construct such a parser for a grammar containing the two productions above, there will be a shift/reduce conflict: on **else**, either shift, or reduce by *stmt* → **if** *expr* **then** *stmt*. If we resolve the conflict in favor of shifting, the parser will behave naturally. We discuss parsers for such ambiguous grammars in Section 4.8.   □

Another common cause of non-LR-ness occurs when we know we have a handle, but the stack contents and the next input symbol are not sufficient to determine which production should be used in a reduction. The next example illustrates this situation.

Example 4.26. Suppose we have a lexical analyzer that returns token **id** for all identifiers, regardless of usage. Suppose also that our language invokes procedures by giving their names, with parameters surrounded by parentheses, and that arrays are referenced by the same syntax. Since the translation of indices in array references and parameters in procedure calls are different, we want to use different productions to generate lists of actual parameters and indices. Our grammar might therefore have (among others) productions such as:

(1)	$stmt \rightarrow$ **id** (*parameter_list*)
(2)	$stmt \rightarrow expr := expr$
(3)	*parameter_list* $\rightarrow$ *parameter_list* , *parameter*
(4)	*parameter_list* $\rightarrow$ *parameter*
(5)	*parameter* $\rightarrow$ **id**
(6)	*expr* $\rightarrow$ **id** (*expr_list*)
(7)	*expr* $\rightarrow$ **id**
(8)	*expr_list* $\rightarrow$ *expr_list* , *expr*
(9)	*expr_list* $\rightarrow$ *expr*

A statement beginning with A(I,J) would appear as the token stream **id**(**id**, **id**) to the parser. After shifting the first three tokens onto the stack, a shift-reduce parser would be in configuration

STACK	INPUT
$\cdots$ **id** (**id**	, **id**) $\cdots$

It is evident that the **id** on top of the stack must be reduced, but by which production? The correct choice is production (5) if A is a procedure and production (7) if A is an array. The stack does not tell which; information in the symbol table obtained from the declaration of A has to be used.

One solution is to change the token **id** in production (1) to **procid** and to use a more sophisticated lexical analyzer that returns token **procid** when it recognizes an identifier which is the name of a procedure. Doing this would require the lexical analyzer to consult the symbol table before returning a token.

If we made this modification, then on processing A(I,J) the parser would be either in the configuration

STACK	INPUT
$\cdots$ **procid** (**id**	, **id**) $\cdots$

or in the configuration above. In the former case, we choose reduction by production (5); in the latter case by production (7). Notice how the symbol third from the top of the stack determines the reduction to be made, even though it is not involved in the reduction. Shift-reduce parsing can utilize information far down in the stack to guide the parse.   □

4.6 OPERATOR-PRECEDENCE PARSING

The largest class of grammars for which shift-reduce parsers can be built successfully – the LR grammars – will be discussed in Section 4.7. However, for a small but important class of grammars we can easily construct efficient shift-reduce parsers by hand. These grammars have the property (among other essential requirements) that no production right side is ϵ or has two adjacent nonterminals. A grammar with the latter property is called an *operator grammar*.

Example 4.27. The following grammar for expressions

$$E \rightarrow EAE \mid (E) \mid -E \mid \textbf{id}$$
$$A \rightarrow + \mid - \mid * \mid / \mid \uparrow$$

is not an operator grammar, because the right side *EAE* has two (in fact three) consecutive nonterminals. However, if we substitute for *A* each of its alternatives, we obtain the following operator grammar:

$$E \rightarrow E+E \mid E-E \mid E*E \mid E/E \mid E \uparrow E \mid (E) \mid -E \mid \textbf{id} \qquad (4.17)$$

We now describe an easy-to-implement parsing technique called operator-precedence parsing. Historically, the technique was first described as a manipulation on tokens without any reference to an underlying grammar. In fact, once we finish building an operator-precedence parser from a grammar, we may effectively ignore the grammar, using the nonterminals on the stack only as placeholders for attributes associated with the nonterminals.

As a general parsing technique, operator-precedence parsing has a number of disadvantages. For example, it is hard to handle tokens like the minus sign, which has two different precedences (depending on whether it is unary or binary). Worse, since the relationship between a grammar for the language being parsed and the operator-precedence parser itself is tenuous, one cannot always be sure the parser accepts exactly the desired language. Finally, only a small class of grammars can be parsed using operator-precedence techniques.

Nevertheless, because of its simplicity, numerous compilers using operator-precedence parsing techniques for expressions have been built successfully. Often these parsers use recursive descent, described in Section 4.4, for statements and higher-level constructs. Operator-precedence parsers have even been built for entire languages.

In operator-precedence parsing, we define three disjoint *precedence relations*, $<\cdot$, $\doteq$, and $\cdot>$, between certain pairs of terminals. These precedence relations guide the selection of handles and have the following meanings:

RELATION	MEANING
$a \lessdot b$	a "yields precedence to" b
$a \doteq b$	a "has the same precedence as" b
$a \gtrdot b$	a "takes precedence over" b

We should caution the reader that while these relations may appear similar to the arithmetic relations "less than," "equal to," and "greater than," the precedence relations have quite different properties. For example, we could have $a \lessdot b$ and $a \gtrdot b$ for the same language, or we might have none of $a \lessdot b$, $a \doteq b$, and $a \gtrdot b$ holding for some terminals a and b.

There are two common ways of determining what precedence relations should hold between a pair of terminals. The first method we discuss is intuitive and is based on the traditional notions of associativity and precedence of operators. For example, if $*$ is to have higher precedence than $+$, we make $+ \lessdot *$ and $* \gtrdot +$. This approach will be seen to resolve the ambiguities of grammar (4.17), and it enables us to write an operator-precedence parser for it (although the unary minus sign causes problems).

The second method of selecting operator-precedence relations is first to construct an unambiguous grammar for the language, a grammar that reflects the correct associativity and precedence in its parse trees. This job is not difficult for expressions; the syntax of expressions in Section 2.2 provides the paradigm. For the other common source of ambiguity, the dangling **else**, grammar (4.9) is a useful model. Having obtained an unambiguous grammar, there is a mechanical method for constructing operator-precedence relations from it. These relations may not be disjoint, and they may parse a language other than that generated by the grammar, but with the standard sorts of arithmetic expressions, few problems are encountered in practice. We shall not discuss this construction here; see Aho and Ullman [1972b].

Using Operator-Precedence Relations

The intention of the precedence relations is to delimit the handle of a right-sentential form, with $\lessdot$ marking the left end, $\doteq$ appearing in the interior of the handle, and $\gtrdot$ marking the right end. To be more precise, suppose we have a right-sentential form of an operator grammar. The fact that no adjacent nonterminals appear on the right sides of productions implies that no right-sentential form will have two adjacent nonterminals either. Thus, we may write the right-sentential form as $\beta_0 a_1 \beta_1 \cdots a_n \beta_n$, where each β_i is either ϵ (the empty string) or a single nonterminal, and each a_i is a single terminal.

Suppose that between a_i and a_{i+1} exactly one of the relations $\lessdot$, $\doteq$, and $\gtrdot$ holds. Further, let us use $\$$ to mark each end of the string, and define $\$ \lessdot b$ and $b \gtrdot \$$ for all terminals b. Now suppose we remove the nonterminals from the string and place the correct relation $\lessdot$, $\doteq$, or $\gtrdot$, between each pair of terminals and between the endmost terminals and the $'s marking the ends of the string. For example, suppose we initially have the right-sentential form **id** + **id** * **id** and the precedence relations are those given in Fig. 4.23. These relations are some of those that we would choose to parse according to grammar (4.17).

	id	+	*	$
id		$\cdot>$	$\cdot>$	$\cdot>$
+	$<\cdot$	$\cdot>$	$<\cdot$	$\cdot>$
*	$<\cdot$	$\cdot>$	$\cdot>$	$\cdot>$
$	$<\cdot$	$<\cdot$	$<\cdot$	

Fig. 4.23. Operator-precedence relations.

Then the string with the precedence relations inserted is:

$$\$ <\cdot \ \textbf{id} \ \cdot> \ + \ <\cdot \ \textbf{id} \ \cdot> \ * \ <\cdot \ \textbf{id} \ \cdot> \ \$ \qquad (4.18)$$

For example, $<\cdot$ is inserted between the leftmost $ and **id** since $<\cdot$ is the entry in row $ and column **id**. The handle can be found by the following process.

1. Scan the string from the left end until the first $\cdot>$ is encountered. In (4.18) above, this occurs between the first **id** and +.

2. Then scan backwards (to the left) over any $\doteq$'s until a $<\cdot$ is encountered. In (4.18), we scan backwards to $.

3. The handle contains everything to the left of the first $\cdot>$ and to the right of the $<\cdot$ encountered in step (2), including any intervening or surrounding nonterminals. (The inclusion of surrounding nonterminals is necessary so that two adjacent nonterminals do not appear in a right-sentential form.) In (4.18), the handle is the first **id**.

If we are dealing with grammar (4.17), we then reduce **id** to E. At this point we have the right-sentential form $E + \textbf{id}*\textbf{id}$. After reducing the two remaining **id**'s to E by the same steps, we obtain the right-sentential form $E + E*E$. Consider now the string $+*$ obtained by deleting the nonterminals. Inserting the precedence relations, we get

$$\$ <\cdot \ + \ <\cdot \ * \ \cdot> \ \$$$

indicating that the left end of the handle lies between + and * and the right end between * and $. These precedence relations indicate that, in the right-sentential form $E + E*E$, the handle is $E*E$. Note how the E's surrounding the * become part of the handle.

Since the nonterminals do not influence the parse, we need not worry about distinguishing among them. A single marker "nonterminal" can be kept on the stack of a shift-reduce parser to indicate placeholders for attribute values.

It may appear from the discussion above that the entire right-sentential form must be scanned at each step to find the handle. Such is not the case if we use a stack to store the input symbols already seen and if the precedence relations are used to guide the actions of a shift-reduce parser. If the precedence relation $<\cdot$ or $\doteq$ holds between the topmost terminal symbol on the stack and the next input symbol, the parser shifts; it has not yet found the right end of the handle. If the relation $\cdot>$ holds, a reduction is called for. At this point the parser has found the right end of the handle, and the precedence relations can be used to find the left end of the handle in the stack.

If no precedence relation holds between a pair of terminals (indicated by a blank entry in Fig. 4.23), then a syntactic error has been detected and an error recovery routine must be invoked, as discussed later in this section. The above ideas can be formalized by the following algorithm.

Algorithm 4.5. Operator-precedence parsing algorithm.

Input. An input string w and a table of precedence relations.

Output. If w is well formed, a *skeletal* parse tree, with a placeholder nonterminal E labeling all interior nodes; otherwise, an error indication.

Method. Initially, the stack contains \$ and the input buffer the string $w\$$. To parse, we execute the program of Fig. 4.24.   □

```
(1)    set ip to point to the first symbol of w$;
(2)    repeat forever
(3)        if $ is on top of the stack and ip points to $ then
(4)            return
           else begin
(5)            let a be the topmost terminal symbol on the stack
                   and let b be the symbol pointed to by ip;
(6)            if a <· b or a ≐ b then begin
(7)                push b onto the stack;
(8)                advance ip to the next input symbol;
               end;
(9)            else if a ·> b then          /* reduce */
(10)               repeat
(11)                   pop the stack
(12)               until the top stack terminal is related by <·
                       to the terminal most recently popped
(13)            else error()
           end
```

Fig. 4.24. Operator-precedence parsing algorithm.

Operator-Precedence Relations from Associativity and Precedence

We are always free to create operator-precedence relations any way we see fit and hope that the operator-precedence parsing algorithm will work correctly when guided by them. For a language of arithmetic expressions such as that generated by grammar (4.17) we can use the following heuristic to produce a proper set of precedence relations. Note that grammar (4.17) is ambiguous, and right-sentential forms could have many handles. Our rules are designed to select the "proper" handles to reflect a given set of associativity and precedence rules for binary operators.

1. If operator θ_1 has higher precedence than operator θ_2, make $\theta_1 \cdot > \theta_2$ and $\theta_2 < \cdot \theta_1$. For example, if $*$ has higher precedence than $+$, make $* \cdot > +$ and $+ < \cdot *$. These relations ensure that, in an expression of the form $E+E*E+E$, the central $E*E$ is the handle that will be reduced first.

2. If θ_1 and θ_2 are operators of equal precedence (they may in fact be the same operator), then make $\theta_1 \cdot > \theta_2$ and $\theta_2 \cdot > \theta_1$ if the operators are left-associative, or make $\theta_1 < \cdot \theta_2$ and $\theta_2 < \cdot \theta_1$ if they are right-associative. For example, if $+$ and $-$ are left-associative, then make $+ \cdot > +$, $+ \cdot > -$, $- \cdot > -$, and $- \cdot > +$. If $\uparrow$ is right associative, then make $\uparrow < \cdot \uparrow$. These relations ensure that $E-E+E$ will have handle $E-E$ selected and $E \uparrow E \uparrow E$ will have the last $E \uparrow E$ selected.

3. Make $\theta < \cdot$ **id**, **id** $\cdot > \theta$, $\theta < \cdot$ (, ($< \cdot \theta$,) $\cdot > \theta$, $\theta \cdot >$), $\theta \cdot > \$$, and $\$ < \cdot \theta$ for all operators θ. Also, let

($\doteq$)	$\$ < \cdot$ (	$\$ < \cdot$ **id**
($< \cdot$ (	**id** $\cdot > \$$	) $\cdot > \$$
($< \cdot$ **id**	**id** $\cdot >$)	) $\cdot >$)

These rules ensure that both **id** and (E) will be reduced to E. Also, $\$$ serves as both the left and right endmarker, causing handles to be found between $\$$'s wherever possible.

Example 4.28. Figure 4.25 contains the operator-precedence relations for grammar (4.17), assuming

1. $\uparrow$ is of highest precedence and right-associative,

2. $*$ and $/$ are of next highest precedence and left-associative, and

3. $+$ and $-$ are of lowest precedence and left-associative,

(Blanks denote error entries.) The reader should try out the table to see that it works correctly, ignoring problems with unary minus for the moment. Try the table on the input **id** $*$ (**id** $\uparrow$ **id**)$-$**id**$/$**id**, for example.   □

	+	−	*	/	↑	id	(	)	$
+	·>	·>	<·	<·	<·	<·	<·	·>	·>
−	·>	·>	<·	<·	<·	<·	<·	·>	·>
*	·>	·>	·>	·>	<·	<·	<·	·>	·>
/	·>	·>	·>	·>	<·	<·	<·	·>	·>
↑	·>	·>	·>	·>	<·	<·	<·	·>	·>
id	·>	·>	·>	·>	·>			·>	·>
(	<·	<·	<·	<·	<·	<·	<·	≐	
)	·>	·>	·>	·>	·>			·>	·>
$	<·	<·	<·	<·	<·	<·	<·		

Fig. 4.25. Operator-precedence relations.

Handling Unary Operators

If we have a unary operator such as ¬ (logical negation), which is not also a binary operator, we can incorporate it into the above scheme for creating operator-precedence relations. Supposing ¬ to be a unary prefix operator, we make $\theta <\cdot$ ¬ for any operator θ, whether unary or binary. We make ¬ $\cdot> \theta$ if ¬ has higher precedence than θ and ¬ $<\cdot \theta$ if not. For example, if ¬ has higher precedence than &, and & is left-associative, we would group $E\&¬E\&E$ as $(E\&(¬E))\&E$, by these rules. The rule for unary postfix operators is analogous.

The situation changes when we have an operator like the minus sign − that is both unary prefix and binary infix. Even if we give unary and binary minus the same precedence, the table of Fig. 4.25 will fail to parse strings like **id**∗−**id** correctly. The best approach in this case is to use the lexical analyzer to distinguish between unary and binary minus, by having it return a different token when it sees unary minus. Unfortunately, the lexical analyzer cannot use lookahead to distinguish the two; it must remember the previous token. In Fortran, for example, a minus sign is unary if the previous token was an operator, a left parenthesis, a comma, or an assignment symbol.

Precedence Functions

Compilers using operator-precedence parsers need not store the table of precedence relations. In most cases, the table can be encoded by two *precedence functions* f and g that map terminal symbols to integers. We attempt to select f and g so that, for symbols a and b,

1. $f(a) < g(b)$ whenever $a <\cdot b$,
2. $f(a) = g(b)$ whenever $a \doteq b$, and
3. $f(a) > g(b)$ whenever $a \cdot> b$.

Thus the precedence relation between a and b can be determined by a numerical comparison between $f(a)$ and $g(b)$. Note, however, that error entries in the precedence matrix are obscured, since one of (1), (2), or (3) holds no matter what $f(a)$ and $g(b)$ are. The loss of error detection capability is generally not considered serious enough to prevent the using of precedence functions where possible; errors can still be caught when a reduction is called for and no handle can be found.

Not every table of precedence relations has precedence functions to encode it, but in practical cases the functions usually exist.

Example 4.29. The precedence table of Fig. 4.25 has the following pair of precedence functions,

	+	−	*	/	↑	(	)	id	$
f	2	2	4	4	4	0	6	6	0
g	1	1	3	3	5	5	0	5	0

For example, $* <\!\cdot\ \textbf{id}$, and $f(*) < g(\textbf{id})$. Note that $f(\textbf{id}) > g(\textbf{id})$ suggests that $\textbf{id} \cdot\!> \textbf{id}$; but, in fact, no precedence relation holds between **id** and **id**. Other error entries in Fig. 4.25 are similarly replaced by one or another precedence relation.   □

A simple method for finding precedence functions for a table, if such functions exist, is the following.

Algorithm 4.6. Constructing precedence functions.

Input. An operator precedence matrix.

Output. Precedence functions representing the input matrix, or an indication that none exist.

Method.

1. Create symbols f_a and g_a for each a that is a terminal or $.

2. Partition the created symbols into as many groups as possible, in such a way that if $a \doteq b$, then f_a and g_b are in the same group. Note that we may have to put symbols in the same group even if they are not related by $\doteq$. For example, if $a \doteq b$ and $c \doteq b$, then f_a and f_c must be in the same group, since they are both in the same group as g_b. If, in addition, $c \doteq d$, then f_a and g_d are in the same group even though $a \doteq d$ may not hold.

3. Create a directed graph whose nodes are the groups found in (2). For any a and b, if $a <\!\cdot\ b$, place an edge from the group of g_b to the group of f_a. If $a \cdot\!> b$, place an edge from the group of f_a to that of g_b. Note that an edge or path from f_a to g_b means that $f(a)$ must exceed $g(b)$; a path from g_b to f_a means that $g(b)$ must exceed $f(a)$.

4. If the graph constructed in (3) has a cycle, then no precedence functions exist. If there are no cycles, let $f(a)$ be the length of the longest path

beginning at the group of f_a; let $g(a)$ be the length of the longest path from the group of g_a.   □

Example 4.30. Consider the matrix of Fig. 4.23. There are no $\doteq$ relationships, so each symbol is in a group by itself. Figure 4.26 shows the graph constructed using Algorithm 4.6.

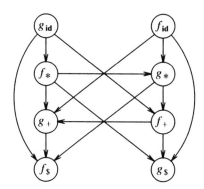

Fig. 4.26. Graph representing precedence functions.

There are no cycles, so precedence functions exist. As $f_\$$ and $g_\$$ have no out-edges, $f(\$) = g(\$) = 0$. The longest path from g_+ has length 1, so $g(+) = 1$. There is a path from g_{id} to f_* to g_* to f_+ to g_+ to $f_\$$, so $g(\mathbf{id}) = 5$. The resulting precedence functions are:

	+	*	**id**	$
f	2	4	4	0
g	1	3	5	0

□

Error Recovery in Operator-Precedence Parsing

There are two points in the parsing process at which an operator-precedence parser can discover syntactic errors:

1. If no precedence relation holds between the terminal on top of the stack and the current input.[1]
2. If a handle has been found, but there is no production with this handle as a right side.

Recall that the operator-precedence parsing algorithm (Algorithm 4.5) appears to reduce handles composed of terminals only. However, while nonterminals

---

[1] In compilers using precedence functions to represent the precedence tables, this source of error detection may be unavailable.

are treated anonymously, they still have places held for them on the parsing stack. Thus when we talk in (2) above about a handle matching a production's right side, we mean that the terminals are the same and the positions occupied by nonterminals are the same.

We should observe that, besides (1) and (2) above, there are no other points at which errors could be detected. When scanning down the stack to find the left end of the handle in steps (10-12) of Fig. 4.24, the operator-precedence parsing algorithm, we are sure to find a $<\cdot$ relation, since $ marks the bottom of stack and is related by $<\cdot$ to any symbol that could appear immediately above it on the stack. Note also that we never allow adjacent symbols on the stack in Fig. 4.24 unless they are related by $<\cdot$ or $\doteq$. Thus steps (10-12) must succeed in making a reduction.

Just because we find a sequence of symbols $a <\cdot b_1 \doteq b_2 \doteq \cdots \doteq b_k$ on the stack, however, does not mean that $b_1 b_2 \cdots b_k$ is the string of terminal symbols on the right side of some production. We did not check for this condition in Fig. 4.24, but we clearly can do so, and in fact we must do so if we wish to associate semantic rules with reductions. Thus we have an opportunity to detect errors in Fig. 4.24, modified at steps (10-12) to determine what production is the handle in a reduction.

Handling Errors During Reductions

We may divide the error detection and recovery routine into several pieces. One piece handles errors of type (2). For example, this routine might pop symbols off the stack just as in steps (10-12) of Fig. 4.24. However, as there is no production to reduce by, no semantic actions are taken; a diagnostic message is printed instead. To determine what the diagnostic should say, the routine handling case (2) must decide what production the right side being popped "looks like." For example, suppose abc is popped, and there is no production right side consisting of a, b and c together with zero or more nonterminals. Then we might consider if deletion of one of a, b, and c yields a legal right side (nonterminals omitted). For example, if there were a right side $aEcE$, we might issue the diagnostic

```
illegal b on line (line containing b)
```

We might also consider changing or inserting a terminal. Thus if $abEdc$ were a right side, we might issue a diagnostic

```
missing d on line (line containing c)
```

We may also find that there is a right side with the proper sequence of terminals, but the wrong pattern of nonterminals. For example, if abc is popped off the stack with no intervening or surrounding nonterminals, and abc is not a right side but $aEbc$ is, we might issue a diagnostic

```
missing E on line (line containing b)
```

Here E stands for an appropriate syntactic category represented by nonterminal E. For example, if a, b, or c is an operator, we might say "expression;" if a is a keyword like **if**, we might say "conditional."

In general, the difficulty of determining appropriate diagnostics when no legal right side is found depends upon whether there are a finite or infinite number of possible strings that could be popped in lines (10-12) of Fig. 4.24. Any such string $b_1 b_2 \cdots b_k$ must have $\doteq$ relations holding between adjacent symbols, so $b_1 \doteq b_2 \doteq \cdots \doteq b_k$. If an operator precedence table tells us that there are only a finite number of sequences of terminals related by $\doteq$, then we can handle these strings on a case-by-case basis. For each such string x we can determine in advance a minimum-distance legal right side y and issue a diagnostic implying that x was found when y was intended.

It is easy to determine all strings that could be popped from the stack in steps (10-12) of Fig. 4.24. These are evident in the directed graph whose nodes represent the terminals, with an edge from a to b if and only if $a \doteq b$. Then the possible strings are the labels of the nodes along paths in this graph. Paths consisting of a single node are possible. However, in order for a path $b_1 b_2 \cdots b_k$ to be "poppable" on some input, there must be a symbol a (possibly \$) such that $a <\!\cdot\, b_1$. Call such a b_1 *initial*. Also, there must be a symbol c (possibly \$) such that $b_k \cdot\!> c$. Call b_k *final*. Only then could a reduction be called for and $b_1 b_2 \cdots b_k$ be the sequence of symbols popped. If the graph has a path from an initial to a final node containing a cycle, then there are an infinity of strings that might be popped; otherwise, there are only a finite number.

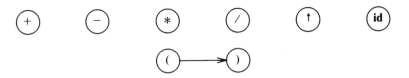

Fig. 4.27. Graph for precedence matrix of Fig. 4.25.

Example 4.31. Let us reconsider grammar (4.17):

$$E \rightarrow E+E \mid E-E \mid E*E \mid E/E \mid E \uparrow E \mid (E) \mid -E \mid \textbf{id}$$

The precedence matrix for this grammar was shown in Fig. 4.25, and its graph is given in Fig. 4.27. There is only one edge, because the only pair related by $\doteq$ is the left and right parenthesis. All but the right parenthesis are initial, and all but the left parenthesis are final. Thus the only paths from an initial to a final node are the paths $+$, $-$, $*$, $/$, **id**, and $\uparrow$ of length one, and the path from (to) of length two. There are but a finite number, and each corresponds to the terminals of some production's right side in the grammar. Thus the error checker for reductions need only check that the proper set of nonterminal markers appears among the terminal strings being reduced. Specifically, the checker does the following:

1. If $+$, $-$, $*$, $/$, or $\uparrow$ is reduced, it checks that nonterminals appear on both sides. If not, it issues the diagnostic

`missing operand`

2. If **id** is reduced, it checks that there is no nonterminal to the right or left. If there is, it can warn

`missing operator`

3. If ( ) is reduced, it checks that there is a nonterminal between the parentheses. If not, it can say

`no expression between parentheses`

Also it must check that no nonterminal appears on either side of the parentheses. If one does, it issues the same diagnostic as in (2).   □

If there are an infinity of strings that may be popped, error messages cannot be tabulated on a case-by-case basis. We might use a general routine to determine whether some production right side is close (say distance 1 or 2, where distance is measured in terms of tokens, rather than characters, inserted, deleted, or changed) to the popped string and if so, issue a specific diagnostic on the assumption that that production was intended. If no production is close to the popped string, we can issue a general diagnostic to the effect that "something is wrong in the current line."

Handling Shift/Reduce Errors

We must now discuss the other way in which the operator-precedence parser detects errors. When consulting the precedence matrix to decide whether to shift or reduce (lines (6) and (9) of Fig. 4.24), we may find that no relation holds between the top stack symbol and the first input symbol. For example, suppose a and b are the two top stack symbols (b is at the top), c and d are the next two input symbols, and there is no precedence relation between b and c. To recover, we must modify the stack, input or both. We may change symbols, insert symbols onto the input or stack, or delete symbols from the input or stack. If we insert or change, we must be careful that we do not get into an infinite loop, where, for example, we perpetually insert symbols at the beginning of the input without being able to reduce or to shift any of the inserted symbols.

One approach that will assure us no infinite loops is to guarantee that after recovery the current input symbol can be shifted (if the current input is $\$$, guarantee that no symbol is placed on the input, and the stack is eventually shortened). For example, given ab on the stack and cd on the input, if $a \lessdot\!\cdot c^2$

---

[2] We use $\leqslant\!\cdot$ to mean $\lessdot$ or $\doteq$.

we might pop b from the stack. Another choice is to delete c from the input if $b \leq \cdot d$. A third choice is to find a symbol e such that $b \leq \cdot e \leq \cdot c$ and insert e in front of c on the input. More generally, we might insert a string of symbols such that

$$b \leq \cdot e_1 \leq \cdot e_2 \leq \cdots \leq \cdot e_n \leq \cdot c$$

if a single symbol for insertion could not be found. The exact action chosen should reflect the compiler designer's intuition regarding what error is likely in each case.

For each blank entry in the precedence matrix we must specify an error-recovery routine; the same routine could be used in several places. Then when the parser consults the entry for a and b in step (6) of Fig. 4.24, and no precedence relation holds between a and b, it finds a pointer to the error-recovery routine for this error.

Example 4.32. Consider the precedence matrix of Fig. 4.25 again. In Fig. 4.28, we show the rows and columns of this matrix that have one or more blank entries, and we have filled in these blanks with the names of error handling routines.

	id	(	)	$
id	e3	e3	$\cdot >$	$\cdot >$
(	$< \cdot$	$< \cdot$	$\doteq$	e4
)	e3	e3	$\cdot >$	$\cdot >$
$	$< \cdot$	$< \cdot$	e2	e1

Fig. 4.28. Operator-precedence matrix with error entries.

The substance of these error handling routines is as follows:

e1: /* called when whole expression is missing */
    insert **id** onto the input
    issue diagnostic: "missing operand"

e2: /* called when expression begins with a right parenthesis */
    delete) from the input
    issue diagnostic: "unbalanced right parenthesis"

e3: /* called when **id** or) is followed by **id** or (*/
    insert + onto the input
    issue diagnostic: "missing operator"

e4: /* called when expression ends with a left parenthesis */
    pop (from the stack
    issue diagnostic: "missing right parenthesis"

Let us consider how this error-handling mechanism would treat the erroneous input **id** +). The first actions taken by the parser are to shift **id**, reduce it to E (we again use E for anonymous nonterminals on the stack), and then to shift the +. We now have configuration

STACK	INPUT
$\$E+$	)$\$$

Since + ·>) a reduction is called for, and the handle is +. The error checker for reductions is required to inspect for E's to left and right. Finding one missing, it issues the diagnostic

```
missing operand
```

and does the reduction anyway.

Our configuration is now

$$\$E \qquad\qquad)\$$$

There is no precedence relation between $\$$ and), and the entry in Fig. 4.28 for this pair of symbols is e2. Routine e2 causes diagnostic

```
unbalanced right parenthesis
```

to be printed and removes the right parenthesis from the input. We are now left with the final configuration for the parser.

$$\$E \qquad\qquad \$ \qquad\qquad \Box$$

4.7 LR PARSERS

This section presents an efficient, bottom-up syntax analysis technique that can be used to parse a large class of context-free grammars. The technique is called LR(k) parsing; the "L" is for left-to-right scanning of the input, the "R" for constructing a rightmost derivation in reverse, and the k for the number of input symbols of lookahead that are used in making parsing decisions. When (k) is omitted, k is assumed to be 1. LR parsing is attractive for a variety of reasons.

- LR parsers can be constructed to recognize virtually all programming-language constructs for which context-free grammars can be written.

- The LR parsing method is the most general nonbacktracking shift-reduce parsing method known, yet it can be implemented as efficiently as other shift-reduce methods.

- The class of grammars that can be parsed using LR methods is a proper superset of the class of grammars that can be parsed with predictive parsers.

- An LR parser can detect a syntactic error as soon as it is possible to do so on a left-to-right scan of the input.

The principal drawback of the method is that it is too much work to construct an LR parser by hand for a typical programming-language grammar. One needs a specialized tool – an LR parser generator. Fortunately, many such generators are available, and we shall discuss the design and use of one, Yacc, in Section 4.9. With such a generator, one can write a context-free grammar and have the generator automatically produce a parser for that grammar. If the grammar contains ambiguities or other constructs that are difficult to parse in a left-to-right scan of the input, then the parser generator can locate these constructs and inform the compiler designer of their presence.

After discussing the operation of an LR parser, we present three techniques for constructing an LR parsing table for a grammar. The first method, called simple LR (SLR for short), is the easiest to implement, but the least powerful of the three. It may fail to produce a parsing table for certain grammars on which the other methods succeed. The second method, called canonical LR, is the most powerful, and the most expensive. The third method, called lookahead LR (LALR for short), is intermediate in power and cost between the other two. The LALR method will work on most programming-language grammars and, with some effort, can be implemented efficiently. Some techniques for compressing the size of an LR parsing table are considered later in this section.

The LR Parsing Algorithm

The schematic form of an LR parser is shown in Fig. 4.29. It consists of an input, an output, a stack, a driver program, and a parsing table that has two parts (*action* and *goto*). The driver program is the same for all LR parsers; only the parsing table changes from one parser to another. The parsing program reads characters from an input buffer one at a time. The program uses a stack to store a string of the form $s_0X_1s_1X_2s_2 \cdots X_ms_m$, where s_m is on top. Each X_i is a grammar symbol and each s_i is a symbol called a *state*. Each state symbol summarizes the information contained in the stack below it, and the combination of the state symbol on top of the stack and the current input symbol are used to index the parsing table and determine the shift-reduce parsing decision. In an implementation, the grammar symbols need not appear on the stack; however, we shall always include them in our discussions to help explain the behavior of an LR parser.

The parsing table consists of two parts, a parsing action function *action* and a goto function *goto*. The program driving the LR parser behaves as follows. It determines s_m, the state currently on top of the stack, and a_i, the current input symbol. It then consults $action[s_m, a_i]$, the parsing action table entry for state s_m and input a_i, which can have one of four values:

1. shift s, where s is a state,
2. reduce by a grammar production $A \rightarrow \beta$,
3. accept, and
4. error.

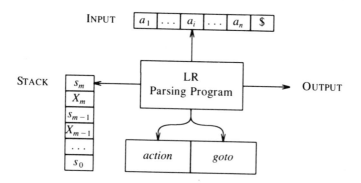

Fig. 4.29. Model of an LR parser.

The function *goto* takes a state and grammar symbol as arguments and produces a state. We shall see that the *goto* function of a parsing table constructed from a grammar G using the SLR, canonical LR, or LALR method is the transition function of a deterministic finite automaton that recognizes the viable prefixes of G. Recall that the viable prefixes of G are those prefixes of right-sentential forms that can appear on the stack of a shift-reduce parser, because they do not extend past the rightmost handle. The initial state of this DFA is the state initially put on top of the LR parser stack.

A *configuration* of an LR parser is a pair whose first component is the stack contents and whose second component is the unexpended input:

$$(s_0 X_1 s_1 X_2 s_2 \cdots X_m s_m, \quad a_i a_{i+1} \cdots a_n \$)$$

This configuration represents the right-sentential form

$$X_1 X_2 \cdots X_m a_i a_{i+1} \cdots a_n$$

in essentially the same way as a shift-reduce parser would; only the presence of states on the stack is new.

The next move of the parser is determined by reading a_i, the current input symbol, and s_m, the state on top of the stack, and then consulting the parsing action table entry $action[s_m, a_i]$. The configurations resulting after each of the four types of move are as follows:

1. If $action[s_m, a_i] = $ shift s, the parser executes a shift move, entering the configuration

$$(s_0 X_1 s_1 X_2 s_2 \cdots X_m s_m a_i s, \quad a_{i+1} \cdots a_n \$)$$

Here the parser has shifted both the current input symbol a_i and the next state s, which is given in $action[s_m, a_i]$, onto the stack; a_{i+1} becomes the current input symbol.

2.   If $action[s_m, a_i]$ = reduce $A \rightarrow \beta$, then the parser executes a reduce move, entering the configuration

$$(s_0 \; X_1 \; s_1 \; X_2 \; s_2 \; \cdots \; X_{m-r} \; s_{m-r} \; A \; s, \quad a_i \; a_{i+1} \; \cdots \; a_n\$)$$

where $s = goto[s_{m-r}, A]$ and r is the length of β, the right side of the production. Here the parser first popped $2r$ symbols off the stack (r state symbols and r grammar symbols), exposing state s_{m-r}. The parser then pushed both A, the left side of the production, and s, the entry for $goto[s_{m-r}, A]$, onto the stack. The current input symbol is not changed in a reduce move. For the LR parsers we shall construct, $X_{m-r+1} \; \cdots \; X_m$, the sequence of grammar symbols popped off the stack, will always match β, the right side of the reducing production.

The output of an LR parser is generated after a reduce move by executing the semantic action associated with the reducing production. For the time being, we shall assume the output consists of just printing the reducing production.

3.   If $action[s_m, a_i]$ = accept, parsing is completed.

4.   If $action[s_m, a_i]$ = error, the parser has discovered an error and calls an error recovery routine.

The LR parsing algorithm is summarized below. All LR parsers behave in this fashion; the only difference between one LR parser and another is the information in the parsing action and goto fields of the parsing table.

Algorithm 4.7. LR parsing algorithm.

Input. An input string w and an LR parsing table with functions *action* and *goto* for a grammar G.

Output. If w is in $L(G)$, a bottom-up parse for w; otherwise, an error indication.

Method. Initially, the parser has s_0 on its stack, where s_0 is the initial state, and $w\$$ in the input buffer. The parser then executes the program in Fig. 4.30 until an accept or error action is encountered.   □

Example 4.33. Figure 4.31 shows the parsing action and goto functions of an LR parsing table for the following grammar for arithmetic expressions with binary operators + and *:

(1) $E \rightarrow E + T$
(2) $E \rightarrow T$
(3) $T \rightarrow T * F$
(4) $T \rightarrow F$
(5) $F \rightarrow (E)$
(6) $F \rightarrow \mathbf{id}$

The codes for the actions are:

set *ip* to point to the first symbol of *w*$;
repeat forever begin
    let *s* be the state on top of the stack and
        a the symbol pointed to by *ip*;
    if *action* [*s*, *a*] = shift *s'* **then begin**
        push *a* then *s'* on top of the stack;
        advance *ip* to the next input symbol
    end
    else if *action* [*s*, *a*] = reduce *A* → β **then begin**
        pop 2∗|β| symbols off the stack;
        let *s'* be the state now on top of the stack;
        push *A* then *goto* [*s'*, *A*] on top of the stack;
        output the production *A* → β
    end
    else if *action* [*s*, *a*] = accept **then**
        return
    else *error* ()
end

Fig. 4.30. LR parsing program.

STATE	action						goto		
	id	**+**	**∗**	**(**	**)**	**$**	**E**	**T**	**F**
0	s5			s4			1	2	3
1		s6				acc			
2		r2	s7		r2	r2			
3		r4	r4		r4	r4			
4	s5			s4			8	2	3
5		r6	r6		r6	r6			
6	s5			s4				9	3
7	s5			s4					10
8		s6			s11				
9		r1	s7		r1	r1			
10		r3	r3		r3	r3			
11		r5	r5		r5	r5			

Fig. 4.31. Parsing table for expression grammar.

1. *si* means shift and stack state *i*,
2. r*j* means reduce by production numbered *j*,
3. acc means accept,
4. blank means error.

Note that the value of *goto*[*s*, *a*] for terminal *a* is found in the action field connected with the shift action on input *a* for state *s*. The goto field gives *goto*[*s*, *A*] for nonterminals *A*. Also, bear in mind that we have not yet explained how the entries for Fig. 4.31 were selected; we shall deal with this issue shortly.

On input **id** * **id** + **id**, the sequence of stack and input contents is shown in Fig. 4.32. For example, at line (1) the LR parser is in state 0 with **id** the first input symbol. The action in row 0 and column **id** of the action field of Fig. 4.31 is s5, meaning shift and cover the stack with state 5. That is what has happened at line (2): the first token **id** and the state symbol 5 have both been pushed onto the stack, and **id** has been removed from the input.

Then, * becomes the current input symbol, and the action of state 5 on input * is to reduce by *F* → **id**. Two symbols are popped off the stack (one state symbol and one grammar symbol). State 0 is then exposed. Since the goto of state 0 on *F* is 3, *F* and 3 are pushed onto the stack. We now have the configuration in line (3). Each of the remaining moves is determined similarly.   □

	STACK	INPUT	ACTION
(1)	0	**id** * **id** + **id** $	shift
(2)	0 **id** 5	* **id** + **id** $	reduce by *F* → **id**
(3)	0 *F* 3	* **id** + **id** $	reduce by *T* → *F*
(4)	0 *T* 2	* **id** + **id** $	shift
(5)	0 *T* 2 * 7	**id** + **id** $	shift
(6)	0 *T* 2 * 7 **id** 5	+ **id** $	reduce by *F* → **id**
(7)	0 *T* 2 * 7 *F* 10	+ **id** $	reduce by *T* → *T* ∗ *F*
(8)	0 *T* 2	+ **id** $	reduce by *E* → *T*
(9)	0 *E* 1	+ **id** $	shift
(10)	0 *E* 1 + 6	**id** $	shift
(11)	0 *E* 1 + 6 **id** 5	$	reduce by *F* → **id**
(12)	0 *E* 1 + 6 *F* 3	$	reduce by *T* → *F*
(13)	0 *E* 1 + 6 *T* 9	$	*E* → *E* + *T*
(14)	0 *E* 1	$	accept

Fig. 4.32. Moves of LR parser on **id** * **id** + **id**.

LR Grammars

How do we construct an LR parsing table for a given grammar? A grammar for which we can construct a parsing table is said to be an *LR grammar*. There are context-free grammars that are not LR, but these can generally be avoided for typical programming-language constructs. Intuitively, in order for a grammar to be LR it is sufficient that a left-to-right shift-reduce parser be able to recognize handles when they appear on top of the stack.

An LR parser does not have to scan the entire stack to know when the handle appears on top. Rather, the state symbol on top of the stack contains all the information it needs. It is a remarkable fact that if it is possible to recognize a handle knowing only the grammar symbols on the stack, then there is a finite automaton that can, by reading the grammar symbols on the stack from top to bottom, determine what handle, if any, is on top of the stack. The goto function of an LR parsing table is essentially such a finite automaton. The automaton need not, however, read the stack on every move. The state symbol stored on top of the stack is the state the handle-recognizing finite automaton would be in if it had read the grammar symbols of the stack from bottom to top. Thus, the LR parser can determine from the state on top of the stack everything that it needs to know about what is in the stack.

Another source of information that an LR parser can use to help make its shift-reduce decisions is the next k input symbols. The cases $k=0$ or $k=1$ are of practical interest, and we shall only consider LR parsers with $k \leq 1$ here. For example, the action table in Fig. 4.31 uses one symbol of lookahead. A grammar that can be parsed by an LR parser examining up to k input symbols on each move is called an *LR(k) grammar*.

There is a significant difference between LL and LR grammars. For a grammar to be LR(k), we must be able to recognize the occurrence of the right side of a production, having seen all of what is derived from that right side with k input symbols of lookahead. This requirement is far less stringent than that for LL(k) grammars where we must be able to recognize the use of a production seeing only the first k symbols of what its right side derives. Thus, LR grammars can describe more languages than LL grammars.

Constructing SLR Parsing Tables

We now show how to construct from a grammar an LR parsing table. We shall give three methods, varying in their power and ease of implementation. The first, called "simple LR" or *SLR* for short, is the weakest of the three in terms of the number of grammars for which it succeeds, but is the easiest to implement. We shall refer to the parsing table constructed by this method as an SLR table, and to an LR parser using an SLR parsing table as an SLR parser. A grammar for which an SLR parser can be constructed is said to be an SLR grammar. The other two methods augment the SLR method with lookahead information, so the SLR method is a good starting point for studying LR parsing.

An *LR(0) item* (*item* for short) of a grammar G is a production of G with a dot at some position of the right side. Thus, production $A \rightarrow XYZ$ yields the four items

$$A \rightarrow \cdot XYZ$$
$$A \rightarrow X \cdot YZ$$
$$A \rightarrow XY \cdot Z$$
$$A \rightarrow XYZ \cdot$$

The production $A \to \epsilon$ generates only one item, $A \to \cdot$. An item can be represented by a pair of integers, the first giving the number of the production and the second the position of the dot. Intuitively, an item indicates how much of a production we have seen at a given point in the parsing process. For example, the first item above indicates that we hope to see a string derivable from XYZ next on the input. The second item indicates that we have just seen on the input a string derivable from X and that we hope next to see a string derivable from YZ.

The central idea in the SLR method is first to construct from the grammar a deterministic finite automaton to recognize viable prefixes. We group items together into sets, which give rise to the states of the SLR parser. The items can be viewed as the states of an NFA recognizing viable prefixes, and the "grouping together" is really the subset construction discussed in Section 3.6.

One collection of sets of LR(0) items, which we call the *canonical* LR(0) collection, provides the basis for constructing SLR parsers. To construct the canonical LR(0) collection for a grammar, we define an augmented grammar and two functions, *closure* and *goto*.

If G is a grammar with start symbol S, then G', the *augmented grammar* for G, is G with a new start symbol S' and production $S' \to S$. The purpose of this new starting production is to indicate to the parser when it should stop parsing and announce acceptance of the input. That is, acceptance occurs when and only when the parser is about to reduce by $S' \to S$.

The Closure Operation

If I is a set of items for a grammar G, then *closure*(I) is the set of items constructed from I by the two rules:

1. Initially, every item in I is added to *closure*(I).

2. If $A \to \alpha \cdot B \beta$ is in *closure*(I) and $B \to \gamma$ is a production, then add the item $B \to \cdot \gamma$ to I, if it is not already there. We apply this rule until no more new items can be added to *closure*(I).

Intuitively, $A \to \alpha \cdot B \beta$ in *closure*(I) indicates that, at some point in the parsing process, we think we might next see a substring derivable from $B\beta$ as input. If $B \to \gamma$ is a production, we also expect we might see a substring derivable from γ at this point. For this reason we also include $B \to \cdot \gamma$ in *closure*(I).

Example 4.34. Consider the augmented expression grammar:

$$\begin{aligned}
E' &\to E \\
E &\to E + T \mid T \\
T &\to T * F \mid F \\
F &\to (E) \mid \mathbf{id}
\end{aligned} \qquad (4.19)$$

If I is the set of one item $\{[E' \to \cdot E]\}$, then *closure*(I) contains the items

$$E' \rightarrow \cdot E$$
$$E \rightarrow \cdot E + T$$
$$E \rightarrow \cdot T$$
$$T \rightarrow \cdot T * F$$
$$T \rightarrow \cdot F$$
$$F \rightarrow \cdot (E)$$
$$F \rightarrow \cdot \mathbf{id}$$

Here, $E' \rightarrow \cdot E$ is put in *closure(I)* by rule (1). Since there is an E immediately to the right of a dot, by rule (2) we add the E-productions with dots at the left end, that is, $E \rightarrow \cdot E + T$ and $E \rightarrow \cdot T$. Now there is a T immediately to the right of a dot, so we add $T \rightarrow \cdot T * F$ and $T \rightarrow \cdot F$. Next, the F to the right of a dot forces $F \rightarrow \cdot (E)$ and $F \rightarrow \cdot \mathbf{id}$ to be added. No other items are put into *closure (I)* by rule (2).   □

The function *closure* can be computed as in Fig. 4.33. A convenient way to implement the function *closure* is to keep a boolean array *added*, indexed by the nonterminals of G, such that *added[B]* is set to **true** if and when we add the items $B \rightarrow \cdot \gamma$ for each B-production $B \rightarrow \gamma$.

function *closure* (*I*);
begin
    $J := I$;
    repeat
        for each item $A \rightarrow \alpha \cdot B \beta$ in J and each production
            $B \rightarrow \gamma$ of G such that $B \rightarrow \cdot \gamma$ is not in J **do**
                add $B \rightarrow \cdot \gamma$ to J
        until no more items can be added to J;
        return J
end

Fig. 4.33. Computation of *closure*.

Note that if one B-production is added to the closure of I with the dot at the left end, then all B-productions will be similarly added to the closure. In fact, it is not necessary in some circumstances actually to list the items $B \rightarrow \cdot \gamma$ added to I by *closure*. A list of the nonterminals B whose productions were so added will suffice. In fact, it turns out that we can divide all the sets of items we are interested in into two classes of items.

1. *Kernel items*, which include the initial item, $S' \rightarrow \cdot S$, and all items whose dots are not at the left end.

2. *Nonkernel items*, which have their dots at the left end.

Moreover, each set of items we are interested in is formed by taking the closure of a set of kernel items; the items added in the closure can never be kernel items, of course. Thus, we can represent the sets of items we are really interested in with very little storage if we throw away all nonkernel items, knowing that they could be regenerated by the closure process.

The Goto Operation

The second useful function is $goto(I, X)$ where I is a set of items and X is a grammar symbol. $goto(I, X)$ is defined to be the closure of the set of all items $[A \rightarrow \alpha X \cdot \beta]$ such that $[A \rightarrow \alpha \cdot X \beta]$ is in I. Intuitively, if I is the set of items that are valid for some viable prefix γ, then $goto(I, X)$ is the set of items that are valid for the viable prefix γX.

Example 4.35. If I is the set of two items $\{[E' \rightarrow E \cdot], [E \rightarrow E \cdot + T]\}$, then $goto(I, +)$ consists of

$$E \rightarrow E + \cdot T$$
$$T \rightarrow \cdot T * F$$
$$T \rightarrow \cdot F$$
$$F \rightarrow \cdot (E)$$
$$F \rightarrow \cdot \mathbf{id}$$

We computed $goto(I, +)$ by examining I for items with $+$ immediately to the right of the dot. $E' \rightarrow E \cdot$ is not such an item, but $E \rightarrow E \cdot + T$ is. We moved the dot over the $+$ to get $\{E \rightarrow E + \cdot T\}$ and then took the closure of this set. □

The Sets-of-Items Construction

We are now ready to give the algorithm to construct C, the canonical collection of sets of LR(0) items for an augmented grammar G'; the algorithm is shown in Fig. 4.34.

```
procedure items(G');
begin
        C := {closure({[S' → ·S]})};
        repeat
              for each set of items I in C and each grammar symbol X
                        such that goto(I, X) is not empty and not in C do
                        add goto(I, X) to C
              until no more sets of items can be added to C
        end
```

Fig. 4.34. The sets-of-items construction.

Example 4.36. The canonical collection of sets of LR(0) items for grammar (4.19) of Example 4.34 is shown in Fig. 4.35. The *goto* function for this set of items is shown as the transition diagram of a deterministic finite automaton D in Fig. 4.36.   □

I_0: $E' \rightarrow \cdot E$
$E \rightarrow \cdot E + T$
$E \rightarrow \cdot T$
$T \rightarrow \cdot T * F$
$T \rightarrow \cdot F$
$F \rightarrow \cdot (E)$
$F \rightarrow \cdot \mathbf{id}$

I_1: $E' \rightarrow E \cdot$
$E \rightarrow E \cdot + T$

I_2: $E \rightarrow T \cdot$
$T \rightarrow T \cdot * F$

I_3: $T \rightarrow F \cdot$

I_4: $F \rightarrow (\cdot E)$
$E \rightarrow \cdot E + T$
$E \rightarrow \cdot T$
$T \rightarrow \cdot T * F$
$T \rightarrow \cdot F$
$F \rightarrow \cdot (E)$
$F \rightarrow \cdot \mathbf{id}$

I_5: $F \rightarrow \mathbf{id} \cdot$

I_6: $E \rightarrow E + \cdot T$
$T \rightarrow \cdot T * F$
$T \rightarrow \cdot F$
$F \rightarrow \cdot (E)$
$F \rightarrow \cdot \mathbf{id}$

I_7: $T \rightarrow T * \cdot F$
$F \rightarrow \cdot (E)$
$F \rightarrow \cdot \mathbf{id}$

I_8: $F \rightarrow (E \cdot)$
$E \rightarrow E \cdot + T$

I_9: $E \rightarrow E + T \cdot$
$T \rightarrow T \cdot * F$

I_{10}: $T \rightarrow T * F \cdot$

I_{11}: $F \rightarrow (E) \cdot$

Fig. 4.35. Canonical LR(0) collection for grammar (4.19).

If each state of D in Fig. 4.36 is a final state and I_0 is the initial state, then D recognizes exactly the viable prefixes of grammar (4.19). This is no accident. For every grammar G, the *goto* function of the canonical collection of sets of items defines a deterministic finite automaton that recognizes the viable prefixes of G. In fact, one can visualize a nondeterministic finite automaton N whose states are the items themselves. There is a transition from $A \rightarrow \alpha \cdot X \beta$ to $A \rightarrow \alpha X \cdot \beta$ labeled X, and there is a transition from $A \rightarrow \alpha \cdot B \beta$ to $B \rightarrow \cdot \gamma$ labeled ϵ. Then *closure*(I) for set of items (states of N) I is exactly the ϵ-*closure* of a set of NFA states defined in Section 3.6. Thus, *goto*(I, X) gives the transition from I on symbol X in the DFA constructed from N by the subset construction. Viewed in this way, the procedure *items* (G') in Fig. 4.34 is just the subset construction itself applied to the NFA N constructed from G' as we have described.

Valid items. We say item $A \rightarrow \beta_1 \cdot \beta_2$ is *valid* for a viable prefix $\alpha \beta_1$ if there is a derivation $S' \underset{rm}{\overset{*}{\Rightarrow}} \alpha A w \underset{rm}{\overset{*}{\Rightarrow}} \alpha \beta_1 \beta_2 w$. In general, an item will be valid for many viable prefixes. The fact that $A \rightarrow \beta_1 \cdot \beta_2$ is valid for $\alpha \beta_1$ tells us a lot about whether to shift or reduce when we find $\alpha \beta_1$ on the parsing stack. In

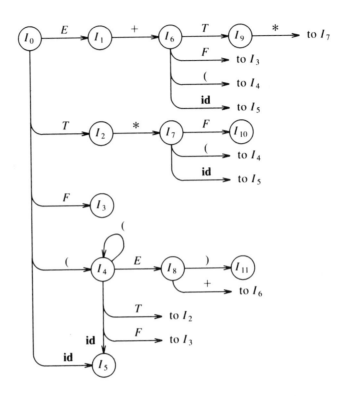

Fig. 4.36. Transition diagram of DFA D for viable prefixes.

particular, if $\beta_2 \neq \epsilon$, then it suggests that we have not yet shifted the handle onto the stack, so shift is our move. If $\beta_2 = \epsilon$, then it looks as if $A \rightarrow \beta_1$ is the handle, and we should reduce by this production. Of course, two valid items may tell us to do different things for the same viable prefix. Some of these conflicts can be resolved by looking at the next input symbol, and others can be resolved by the methods of the next section, but we should not suppose that all parsing action conflicts can be resolved if the LR method is used to construct a parsing table for an arbitrary grammar.

We can easily compute the set of valid items for each viable prefix that can appear on the stack of an LR parser. In fact, it is a central theorem of LR parsing theory that the set of valid items for a viable prefix γ is exactly the set of items reached from the initial state along a path labeled γ in the DFA constructed from the canonical collection of sets of items with transitions given by *goto*. In essence, the set of valid items embodies all the useful information that can be gleaned from the stack. While we shall not prove this theorem here, we shall give an example.

Example 4.37. Let us consider the grammar (4.19) again, whose sets of items and *goto* function are exhibited in Fig. 4.35 and 4.36. Clearly, the string $E + T *$ is a viable prefix of (4.19). The automaton of Fig. 4.36 will be in state I_7 after having read $E + T *$. State I_7 contains the items

$$T \rightarrow T * \cdot F$$
$$F \rightarrow \cdot(E)$$
$$F \rightarrow \cdot\mathbf{id}$$

which are precisely the items valid for $E + T *$. To see this, consider the following three rightmost derivations

$E' \Rightarrow E$	$E' \Rightarrow E$	$E' \Rightarrow E$
$\Rightarrow E + T$	$\Rightarrow E + T$	$\Rightarrow E + T$
$\Rightarrow E + T*F$	$\Rightarrow E + T*F$	$\Rightarrow E + T*F$
	$\Rightarrow E + T*(E)$	$\Rightarrow E + T*\mathbf{id}$

The first derivation shows the validity of $T \rightarrow T * \cdot F$, the second the validity of $F \rightarrow \cdot(E)$, and the third the validity of $F \rightarrow \cdot\mathbf{id}$ for the viable prefix $E + T *$. It can be shown that there are no other valid items for $E + T *$, and we leave a proof to the interested reader.   □

SLR Parsing Tables

Now we shall show how to construct the SLR parsing action and goto functions from the deterministic finite automaton that recognizes viable prefixes. Our algorithm will not produce uniquely defined parsing action tables for all grammars, but it does succeed on many grammars for programming languages. Given a grammar, G, we augment G to produce G', and from G' we construct C, the canonical collection of sets of items for G'. We construct *action*, the parsing action function, and *goto*, the goto function, from C using the following algorithm. It requires us to know FOLLOW(A) for each nonterminal A of a grammar (see Section 4.4).

Algorithm 4.8. Constructing an SLR parsing table.

Input. An augmented grammar G'.

Output. The SLR parsing table functions *action* and *goto* for G'.

Method.

1. Construct $C = \{I_0, I_1, \ldots, I_n\}$, the collection of sets of LR(0) items for G'.

2. State i is constructed from I_i. The parsing actions for state i are determined as follows:

   a) If $[A \rightarrow \alpha \cdot a\beta]$ is in I_i and $goto(I_i, a) = I_j$, then set *action*$[i, a]$ to "shift j." Here a must be a terminal.

   b) If $[A \rightarrow \alpha \cdot]$ is in I_i, then set *action*$[i, a]$ to "reduce $A \rightarrow \alpha$" for all a

in FOLLOW(A); here A may not be S'.

c)   If $[S' \rightarrow S\cdot]$ is in I_i, then set $action[i, \$]$ to "accept."

If any conflicting actions are generated by the above rules, we say the grammar is not SLR(1). The algorithm fails to produce a parser in this case.

3.   The goto transitions for state i are constructed for all nonterminals A using the rule: If $goto(I_i, A) = I_j$, then $goto[i, A] = j$.

4.   All entries not defined by rules (2) and (3) are made "error."

5.   The initial state of the parser is the one constructed from the set of items containing $[S' \rightarrow \cdot S]$.   □

The parsing table consisting of the parsing action and goto functions determined by Algorithm 4.8 is called the *SLR(1) table for G*. An LR parser using the SLR(1) table for G is called the SLR(1) parser for G, and a grammar having an SLR(1) parsing table is said to be *SLR(1)*. We usually omit the "(1)" after the "SLR," since we shall not deal here with parsers having more than one symbol of lookahead.

Example 4.38. Let us construct the SLR table for grammar (4.19). The canonical collection of sets of LR(0) items for (4.19) was shown in Fig. 4.35. First consider the set of items I_0:

$$E' \rightarrow \cdot E$$
$$E \rightarrow \cdot E + T$$
$$E \rightarrow \cdot T$$
$$T \rightarrow \cdot T * F$$
$$T \rightarrow \cdot F$$
$$F \rightarrow \cdot (E)$$
$$F \rightarrow \cdot \mathbf{id}$$

The item $F \rightarrow \cdot (E)$ gives rise to the entry $action[0, (] = $ shift 4, the item $F \rightarrow \cdot \mathbf{id}$ to the entry $action[0, \mathbf{id}] = $ shift 5. Other items in I_0 yield no actions. Now consider I_1:

$$E' \rightarrow E\cdot$$
$$E \rightarrow E\cdot + T$$

The first item yields $action[1, \$] = $ accept, the second yields $action[1, +] = $ shift 6. Next consider I_2:

$$E \rightarrow T\cdot$$
$$T \rightarrow T\cdot * F$$

Since FOLLOW(E) $= \{\$, +,)\}$, the first item makes $action[2, \$] = action[2, +] = action[2,)] = $ reduce $E \rightarrow T$. The second item makes $action[2, *] = $ shift 7. Continuing in this fashion we obtain the parsing action and goto tables that were shown in Fig. 4.31. In that figure, the numbers of productions in reduce actions are the same as the order in which they appear

in the original grammar (4.18). That is, $E \rightarrow E+T$ is number 1, $E \rightarrow T$ is 2, and so on.
□

Example 4.39. Every SLR(1) grammar is unambiguous, but there are many unambiguous grammars that are not SLR(1). Consider the grammar with productions

$$
\begin{align}
S &\rightarrow L = R \\
S &\rightarrow R \\
L &\rightarrow *R \\
L &\rightarrow \textbf{id} \\
R &\rightarrow L
\end{align}
$$
(4.20)

We may think of L and R as standing for l-value and r-value, respectively, and $*$ as an operator indicating "contents of."[3] The canonical collection of sets of LR(0) items for grammar (4.20) is shown in Fig. 4.37.

I_0: $S' \rightarrow \cdot S$
$S \rightarrow \cdot L = R$
$S \rightarrow \cdot R$
$L \rightarrow \cdot *R$
$L \rightarrow \cdot \textbf{id}$
$R \rightarrow \cdot L$

I_1: $S' \rightarrow S \cdot$

I_2: $S \rightarrow L \cdot = R$
$R \rightarrow L \cdot$

I_3: $S \rightarrow R \cdot$

I_4: $L \rightarrow * \cdot R$
$R \rightarrow \cdot L$
$L \rightarrow \cdot *R$
$L \rightarrow \cdot \textbf{id}$

I_5: $L \rightarrow \textbf{id} \cdot$

I_6: $S \rightarrow L = \cdot R$
$R \rightarrow \cdot L$
$L \rightarrow \cdot *R$
$L \rightarrow \cdot \textbf{id}$

I_7: $L \rightarrow *R \cdot$

I_8: $R \rightarrow L \cdot$

I_9: $S \rightarrow L = R \cdot$

Fig. 4.37. Canonical LR(0) collection for grammar (4.20).

Consider the set of items I_2. The first item in this set makes $action[2, =]$ be "shift 6." Since FOLLOW(R) contains $=$, (to see why, consider $S \Rightarrow L = R \Rightarrow *R = R$), the second item sets $action[2, =]$ to "reduce $R \rightarrow L$." Thus entry $action[2, =]$ is multiply defined. Since there is both a shift and a reduce entry in $action[2, =]$, state 2 has a shift/reduce conflict on

---

[3] As in Section 2.8, an l-value designates a location and an r-value is a value that can be stored in a location.

input symbol $=$.

Grammar (4.20) is not ambiguous. This shift/reduce conflict arises from the fact that the SLR parser construction method is not powerful enough to remember enough left context to decide what action the parser should take on input $=$ having seen a string reducible to L. The canonical and LALR methods, to be discussed next, will succeed on a larger collection of grammars, including grammar (4.20). It should be pointed out, however, that there are unambiguous grammars for which every LR parser construction method will produce a parsing action table with parsing action conflicts. Fortunately, such grammars can generally be avoided in programming language applications.   □

Constructing Canonical LR Parsing Tables

We shall now present the most general technique for constructing an LR parsing table from a grammar. Recall that in the SLR method, state i calls for reduction by $A \rightarrow \alpha$ if the set of items I_i contains item $[A \rightarrow \alpha \cdot]$ and a is in FOLLOW(A). In some situations, however, when state i appears on top of the stack, the viable prefix $\beta\alpha$ on the stack is such that βA cannot be followed by a in a right-sentential form. Thus, the reduction by $A \rightarrow \alpha$ would be invalid on input a.

Example 4.40. Let us reconsider Example 4.39, where in state 2 we had item $R \rightarrow L\cdot$, which could correspond to $A \rightarrow \alpha$ above, and a could be the $=$ sign, which is in FOLLOW(R). Thus, the SLR parser calls for reduction by $R \rightarrow L$ in state 2 with $=$ as the next input (the shift action is also called for because of item $S \rightarrow L\cdot = R$ in state 2). However, there is no right-sentential form of the grammar in Example 4.39 that begins $R = \cdots$. Thus state 2, which is the state corresponding to viable prefix L only, should not really call for reduction of that L to R.   □

It is possible to carry more information in the state that will allow us to rule out some of these invalid reductions by $A \rightarrow \alpha$. By splitting states when necessary, we can arrange to have each state of an LR parser indicate exactly which input symbols can follow a handle α for which there is a possible reduction to A.

The extra information is incorporated into the state by redefining items to include a terminal symbol as a second component. The general form of an item becomes $[A \rightarrow \alpha \cdot \beta, a]$, where $A \rightarrow \alpha\beta$ is a production and a is a terminal or the right endmarker $. We call such an object an *LR(1) item*. The 1 refers to the length of the second component, called the *lookahead* of the item.[4] The lookahead has no effect in an item of the form $[A \rightarrow \alpha \cdot \beta, a]$, where β is not ϵ, but an item of the form $[A \rightarrow \alpha \cdot, a]$ calls for a reduction by $A \rightarrow \alpha$ only if

---

[4] Lookaheads that are strings of length greater than one are possible, of course, but we shall not consider such lookaheads here.

the next input symbol is a. Thus, we are compelled to reduce by $A \rightarrow \alpha$ only on those input symbols a for which $[A \rightarrow \alpha\cdot, a]$ is an LR(1) item in the state on top of the stack. The set of such a's will always be a subset of FOLLOW(A), but it could be a proper subset, as in Example 4.40.

Formally, we say LR(1) item $[A \rightarrow \alpha \cdot \beta, a]$ is *valid* for a viable prefix γ if there is a derivation $S \overset{*}{\underset{rm}{\Rightarrow}} \delta A w \underset{rm}{\Rightarrow} \delta \alpha \beta w$, where

1. $\gamma = \delta \alpha$, and
2. either a is the first symbol of w, or w is ϵ and a is \$.

Example 4.41. Let us consider the grammar

$$S \rightarrow BB$$
$$B \rightarrow aB \mid b$$

There is a rightmost derivation $S \overset{*}{\underset{rm}{\Rightarrow}} aaBab \underset{rm}{\Rightarrow} aaaBab$. We see that item $[B \rightarrow a \cdot B, a]$ is valid for a viable prefix $\gamma = aaa$ by letting $\delta = aa$, $A = B$, $w = ab$, $\alpha = a$, and $\beta = B$ in the above definition.

There is also a rightmost derivation $S \overset{*}{\underset{rm}{\Rightarrow}} BaB \underset{rm}{\Rightarrow} BaaB$. From this derivation we see that item $[B \rightarrow a \cdot B, \$]$ is valid for viable prefix Baa.   □

The method for constructing the collection of sets of valid LR(1) items is essentially the same as the way we built the canonical collection of sets of LR(0) items. We only need to modify the two procedures *closure* and *goto*.

To appreciate the new definition of the *closure* operation, consider an item of the form $[A \rightarrow \alpha \cdot B\beta, a]$ in the set of items valid for some viable prefix γ. Then there is a rightmost derivation $S \overset{*}{\underset{rm}{\Rightarrow}} \delta A a x \underset{rm}{\Rightarrow} \delta \alpha B \beta a x$, where $\gamma = \delta \alpha$. Suppose $\beta a x$ derives terminal string by. Then for each production of the form $B \rightarrow \eta$ for some η, we have derivation $S \overset{*}{\underset{rm}{\Rightarrow}} \gamma B b y \underset{rm}{\Rightarrow} \gamma \eta b y$. Thus, $[B \rightarrow \cdot \eta, b]$ is valid for γ. Note that b can be the first terminal derived from β, or it is possible that β derives ϵ in the derivation $\beta a x \overset{*}{\Rightarrow} by$, and b can therefore be a. To summarize both possibilities we say that b can be any terminal in FIRST($\beta a x$), where FIRST is the function from Section 4.4. Note that x cannot contain the first terminal of by, so FIRST($\beta a x$) = FIRST(βa). We now give the LR(1) sets of items construction.

Algorithm 4.9. Construction of the sets of LR(1) items.

Input. An augmented grammar G'.

Output. The sets of LR(1) items that are the set of items valid for one or more viable prefixes of G'.

Method. The procedures *closure* and *goto* and the main routine *items* for constructing the sets of items are shown in Fig. 4.38.   □

Example 4.42. Consider the following augmented grammar.

$$S' \rightarrow S$$
$$S \rightarrow CC$$
$$C \rightarrow cC \mid d$$ (4.21)

function *closure* (*I*);
begin
    repeat
        for each item [*A* → α·*B*β, *a*] in *I*,
            each production *B* → γ in *G'*,
            and each terminal *b* in FIRST(β*a*)
            such that [*B* → ·γ, *b*] is not in *I* **do**
                add [*B* → ·γ, *b*] to *I*;
    until no more items can be added to *I*;
    return I
end;

function *goto* (*I*, *X*);
begin
    let *J* be the set of items [*A* → α*X*·β, *a*] such that
    [*A* → α·*X*β, *a*] is in *I*;
    return *closure* (*J*)
end;

procedure *items* (*G'*);
begin
    C := {*closure* ({[*S'* → ·*S*, $]})};
    repeat
        for each set of items *I* in *C* and each grammar symbol *X*
            such that *goto* (*I*, *X*) is not empty and not in *C* **do**
                add *goto* (*I*, *X*) to *C*
    until no more sets of items can be added to *C*
end

Fig. 4.38. Sets of LR(1) items construction for grammar *G'*.

We begin by computing the closure of {[*S'* → ·*S*, $]}. To close, we match the item [*S'* → ·*S*, $] with the item [*A* → α·*B*β, *a*] in the procedure *closure*. That is, *A* = *S'*, α = ε, *B* = *S*, β = ε, and *a* = $. Function *closure* tells us to add [*B* → ·γ, *b*] for each production *B* → γ and terminal *b* in FIRST(β*a*). In terms of the present grammar, *B* → γ must be *S* → *CC*, and since β is ε and *a* is $, *b* may only be $. Thus we add [*S* → ·*CC*, $].

We continue to compute the closure by adding all items [*C* → ·γ, *b*] for *b* in FIRST(*C*$). That is, matching [*S* → ·*CC*, $] against [*A* → α·*B*β, *a*] we have *A* = *S*, α = ε, *B* = *C*, β = *C*, and *a* = $. Since *C* does not derive the empty string, FIRST(*C*$) = FIRST(*C*). Since FIRST(*C*) contains terminals *c* and *d*, we add items [*C* → ·*cC*, *c*], [*C* → ·*cC*, *d*], [*C* → ·*d*, *c*] and [*C* → ·*d*, *d*]. None of the new items has a nonterminal immediately to the right of the dot, so we have completed our first set of LR(1) items. The initial set of items is:

I_0: $S' \rightarrow \cdot S, \$$
         $S \rightarrow \cdot CC, \$$
         $C \rightarrow \cdot cC, c/d$
         $C \rightarrow \cdot d, c/d$

The brackets have been omitted for notational convenience, and we use the notation $[C \rightarrow \cdot cC, c/d]$ as a shorthand for the two items $[C \rightarrow \cdot cC, c]$ and $[C \rightarrow \cdot cC, d]$.

Now we compute $goto(I_0, X)$ for the various values of X. For $X = S$ we must close the item $[S' \rightarrow S\cdot, \$]$. No additional closure is possible, since the dot is at the right end. Thus we have the next set of items:

I_1: $S' \rightarrow S\cdot, \$$

For $X = C$ we close $[S \rightarrow C\cdot C, \$]$. We add the C-productions with second component $\$$ and then can add no more, yielding:

I_2: $S \rightarrow C\cdot C, \$$
         $C \rightarrow \cdot cC, \$$
         $C \rightarrow \cdot d, \$$

Next, let $X = c$. We must close $\{[C \rightarrow c\cdot C, c/d]\}$. We add the C-productions with second component c/d, yielding:

I_3: $C \rightarrow c\cdot C, c/d$
         $C \rightarrow \cdot cC, c/d$
         $C \rightarrow \cdot d, c/d$

Finally, let $X = d$, and we wind up with the set of items:

I_4: $C \rightarrow d\cdot, c/d$

We have finished considering $goto$ on I_0. We get no new sets from I_1, but I_2 has $goto$'s on C, c, and d. On C we get:

I_5: $S \rightarrow CC\cdot, \$$

no closure being needed. On c we take the closure of $\{[C \rightarrow c\cdot C, \$]\}$, to obtain:

I_6: $C \rightarrow c\cdot C, \$$
         $C \rightarrow \cdot cC, \$$
         $C \rightarrow \cdot d, \$$

Note that I_6 differs from I_3 only in second components. We shall see that it is common for several sets of LR(1) items for a grammar to have the same first components and differ in their second components. When we construct the collection of sets of LR(0) items for the same grammar, each set of LR(0) items will coincide with the set of first components of one or more sets of LR(1) items. We shall have more to say about this phenomenon when we discuss LALR parsing.

Continuing with the $goto$ function for I_2, $goto(I_2, d)$ is seen to be:

I_7: $C \rightarrow d\cdot$, \$

Turning now to I_3, the *goto*'s of I_3 on c and d are I_3 and I_4, respectively, and *goto* (I_3, C) is:

I_8: $C \rightarrow cC\cdot$, c/d

I_4 and I_5 have no *goto*'s. The *goto*'s of I_6 on c and d are I_6 and I_7, respectively, and *goto* (I_6, C) is:

I_9: $C \rightarrow cC\cdot$, \$

The remaining sets of items yield no *goto*'s, so we are done. Figure 4.39 shows the ten sets of items with their *goto*'s.   □

We now give the rules whereby the LR(1) parsing action and goto functions are constructed from the sets of LR(1) items. The action and goto functions are represented by a table as before. The only difference is in the values of the entries.

Algorithm 4.10. Construction of the canonical LR parsing table.

Input. An augmented grammar G'.

Output. The canonical LR parsing table functions *action* and *goto* for G'.

Method.

1.   Construct $C = \{I_0, I_1, \ldots, I_n\}$, the collection of sets of LR(1) items for G'.

2.   State i of the parser is constructed from I_i. The parsing actions for state i are determined as follows:

   a)   If $[A \rightarrow \alpha\cdot a\beta, b]$ is in I_i and *goto* $(I_i, a) = I_j$, then set *action* $[i, a]$ to "shift j." Here, a is required to be a terminal.

   b)   If $[A \rightarrow \alpha\cdot, a]$ is in I_i, $A \neq S'$, then set *action* $[i, a]$ to "reduce $A \rightarrow \alpha$."

   c)   If $[S' \rightarrow S\cdot, \$]$ is in I_i, then set *action* $[i, \$]$ to "accept."

If a conflict results from the above rules, the grammar is said not to be LR(1), and the algorithm is said to fail.

3.   The goto transitions for state i are determined as follows: If *goto* $(I_i, A) = I_j$, then *goto* $[i, A] = j$.

4.   All entries not defined by rules (2) and (3) are made "error."

5.   The initial state of the parser is the one constructed from the set containing item $[S' \rightarrow \cdot S, \$]$.   □

The table formed from the parsing action and goto functions produced by Algorithm 4.10 is called the *canonical* LR(1) parsing table. An LR parser using this table is called a canonical LR(1) parser. If the parsing action

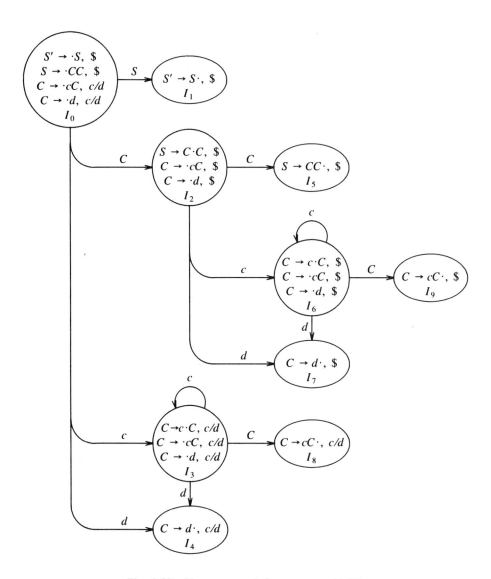

Fig. 4.39. The *goto* graph for grammar (4.21).

function has no multiply-defined entries, then the given grammar is called an *LR(1) grammar*. As before, we omit the "(1)" if it is understood.

Example 4.43. The canonical parsing table for the grammar (4.21) is shown in Fig. 4.40. Productions 1, 2, and 3 are $S \rightarrow CC$, $C \rightarrow cC$, and $C \rightarrow d$.   □

Every SLR(1) grammar is an LR(1) grammar, but for an SLR(1) grammar the canonical LR parser may have more states than the SLR parser for the

	action			*goto*	
STATE	c	d	$	S	C
0	s3	s4		1	2
1			acc		
2	s6	s7			5
3	s3	s4			8
4	r3	r3			
5			r1		
6	s6	s7			9
7			r3		
8	r2	r2			
9			r2		

Fig. 4.40. Canonical parsing table for grammar (4.21).

same grammar. The grammar of the previous examples is SLR and has an SLR parser with seven states, compared with the ten of Fig. 4.40.

Constructing LALR Parsing Tables

We now introduce our last parser construction method, the LALR (*lookahead*-LR) technique. This method is often used in practice because the tables obtained by it are considerably smaller than the canonical LR tables, yet most common syntactic constructs of programming languages can be expressed conveniently by an LALR grammar. The same is almost true for SLR grammars, but there are a few constructs that cannot be conveniently handled by SLR techniques (see Example 4.39, for example).

For a comparison of parser size, the SLR and LALR tables for a grammar always have the same number of states, and this number is typically several hundred states for a language like Pascal. The canonical LR table would typically have several thousand states for the same size language. Thus, it is much easier and more economical to construct SLR and LALR tables than the canonical LR tables.

By way of introduction, let us again consider the grammar (4.21), whose sets of LR(1) items were shown in Fig. 4.39. Take a pair of similar looking states, such as I_4 and I_7. Each of these states has only items with first component $C \rightarrow d\cdot$. In I_4, the lookaheads are c or d; in I_7, $ is the only lookahead.

To see the difference between the roles of I_4 and I_7 in the parser, note that grammar (4.21) generates the regular set c^*dc^*d. When reading an input $cc \cdots cdcc \cdots cd$, the parser shifts the first group of c's and their following d onto the stack, entering state 4 after reading the d. The parser then calls for a reduction by $C \rightarrow d$, provided the next input symbol is c or d. The requirement that c or d follow makes sense, since these are the symbols that could begin strings in c^*d. If $ follows the first d, we have an input like ccd, which is not in the language, and state 4 correctly declares an error if $ is the next input.

The parser enters state 7 after reading the second d. Then, the parser must see $ on the input, or it started with a string not of the form c^*dc^*d. It thus makes sense that state 7 should reduce by $C \rightarrow d$ on input $ and declare error on inputs c or d.

Let us now replace I_4 and I_7 by I_{47}, the union of I_4 and I_7, consisting of the set of three items represented by $[C \rightarrow d\cdot, c/d/\$]$. The goto's on d to I_4 or I_7 from $I_0, I_2, I_3,$ and I_6 now enter I_{47}. The action of state 47 is to reduce on any input. The revised parser behaves essentially like the original, although it might reduce d to C in circumstances where the original would declare error, for example, on input like ccd or $cdcdc$. The error will eventually be caught; in fact, it will be caught before any more input symbols are shifted.

More generally, we can look for sets of LR(1) items having the same *core*, that is, set of first components, and we may merge these sets with common cores into one set of items. For example, in Fig. 4.39, I_4 and I_7 form such a pair, with core $\{C \rightarrow d\cdot\}$. Similarly, I_3 and I_6 form another pair, with core $\{C \rightarrow c\cdot C, C \rightarrow \cdot cC, C \rightarrow \cdot d\}$. There is one more pair, I_8 and I_9, with core $\{C \rightarrow cC\cdot\}$. Note that, in general, a core is a set of LR(0) items for the grammar at hand, and that an LR(1) grammar may produce more than two sets of items with the same core.

Since the core of $goto(I, X)$ depends only on the core of I, the goto's of merged sets can themselves be merged. Thus, there is no problem revising the goto function as we merge sets of items. The action functions are modified to reflect the non-error actions of all sets of items in the merger.

Suppose we have an LR(1) grammar, that is, one whose sets of LR(1) items produce no parsing action conflicts. If we replace all states having the same core with their union, it is possible that the resulting union will have a conflict, but it is unlikely for the following reason: Suppose in the union there is a conflict on lookahead a because there is an item $[A \rightarrow \alpha\cdot, a]$ calling for a reduction by $A \rightarrow \alpha$, and there is another item $[B \rightarrow \beta\cdot a\gamma, b]$ calling for a shift. Then some set of items from which the union was formed has item $[A \rightarrow \alpha\cdot, a]$, and since the cores of all these states are the same, it must have an item $[B \rightarrow \beta\cdot a\gamma, c]$ for some c. But then this state has the same shift/reduce conflict on a, and the grammar was not LR(1) as we assumed. Thus, the merging of states with common cores can never produce a shift/reduce conflict that was not present in one of the original states, because shift actions depend only on the core, not the lookahead.

It is possible, however, that a merger will produce a reduce/reduce conflict, as the following example shows.

Example 4.44. Consider the grammar

$$S' \rightarrow S$$
$$S \rightarrow aAd \mid bBd \mid aBe \mid bAe$$
$$A \rightarrow c$$
$$B \rightarrow c$$

which generates the four strings *acd*, *ace*, *bcd*, and *bce*. The reader can check that the grammar is LR(1) by constructing the sets of items. Upon doing so, we find the set of items $\{[A \rightarrow c\cdot, d], [B \rightarrow c\cdot, e]\}$ valid for viable prefix *ac* and $\{[A \rightarrow c\cdot, e], [B \rightarrow c\cdot, d]\}$ valid for *bc*. Neither of these sets generates a conflict, and their cores are the same. However, their union, which is

$$A \rightarrow c\cdot, d/e$$
$$B \rightarrow c\cdot, d/e$$

generates a reduce/reduce conflict, since reductions by both $A \rightarrow c$ and $B \rightarrow c$ are called for on inputs *d* and *e*.   □

We are now prepared to give the first of two LALR table construction algorithms. The general idea is to construct the sets of LR(1) items, and if no conflicts arise, merge sets with common cores. We then construct the parsing table from the collection of merged sets of items. The method we are about to describe serves primarily as a definition of LALR(1) grammars. Constructing the entire collection of LR(1) sets of items requires too much space and time to be useful in practice.

Algorithm 4.11. An easy, but space-consuming LALR table construction.

Input. An augmented grammar G'.

Output. The LALR parsing table functions *action* and *goto* for G'.

Method.

1. Construct $C = \{I_0, I_1, \ldots, I_n\}$, the collection of sets of LR(1) items.

2. For each core present among the set of LR(1) items, find all sets having that core, and replace these sets by their union.

3. Let $C' = \{J_0, J_1, \ldots, J_m\}$ be the resulting sets of LR(1) items. The parsing actions for state *i* are constructed from J_i in the same manner as in Algorithm 4.10. If there is a parsing action conflict, the algorithm fails to produce a parser, and the grammar is said not to be LALR(1).

4. The *goto* table is constructed as follows. If *J* is the union of one or more sets of LR(1) items, that is, $J = I_1 \cup I_2 \cup \cdots \cup I_k$, then the cores of $goto(I_1, X)$, $goto(I_2, X)$, $\ldots$, $goto(I_k, X)$ are the same, since $I_1, I_2, \ldots, I_k$ all have the same core. Let *K* be the union of all sets of items having the same core as $goto(I_1, X)$. Then $goto(J, X) = K$.   □

The table produced by Algorithm 4.11 is called the *LALR parsing table* for G. If there are no parsing action conflicts, then the given grammar is said to

be an *LALR* (1) *grammar*. The collection of sets of items constructed in step
(3) is called the *LALR* (1) *collection*.

Example 4.45. Again consider the grammar (4.21) whose *goto* graph was
shown in Fig. 4.39. As we mentioned, there are three pairs of sets of items
that can be merged. I_3 and I_6 are replaced by their union:

I_{36}: $C \rightarrow c \cdot C$, $c/d/\$$
$\phantom{I_{36}:}$ $C \rightarrow \cdot cC$, $c/d/\$$
$\phantom{I_{36}:}$ $C \rightarrow \cdot d$, $c/d/\$$

I_4 and I_7 are replaced by their union:

I_{47}: $C \rightarrow d \cdot$, $c/d/\$$

and I_8 and I_9 are replaced by their union:

I_{89}: $C \rightarrow cC \cdot$, $c/d/\$$

The LALR action and goto functions for the condensed sets of items are
shown in Fig. 4.41.

STATE	action			goto	
	c	d	$\$$	S	C
0	s36	s47		1	2
1			acc		
2	s36	s47			5
36	s36	s47			89
47	r3	r3	r3		
5			r1		
89	r2	r2	r2		

Fig. 4.41. LALR parsing table for grammar (4.21).

To see how the goto's are computed, consider $goto(I_{36}, C)$. In the original
set of LR(1) items, $goto(I_3, C) = I_8$, and I_8 is now part of I_{89}, so we make
$goto(I_{36}, C)$ be I_{89}. We could have arrived at the same conclusion if we considered I_6, the other part of I_{36}. That is, $goto(I_6, C) = I_9$, and I_9 is now
part of I_{89}. For another example, consider $goto(I_2, c)$, an entry that is exercised after the shift action of I_2 on input c. In the original sets of LR(1)
items, $goto(I_2, c) = I_6$. Since I_6 is now part of I_{36}, $goto(I_2, c)$ becomes I_{36}.
Thus, the entry in Fig. 4.41 for state 2 and input c is made s36, meaning shift
and push state 36 onto the stack. □

When presented with a string from the language $c*dc*d$, both the LR parser
of Fig. 4.40 and the LALR parser of Fig. 4.41 make exactly the same
sequence of shifts and reductions, although the names of the states on the
stack may differ; i.e., if the LR parser puts I_3 or I_6 on the stack, the LALR

parser will put I_{36} on the stack. This relationship holds in general for an LALR grammar. The LR and LALR parsers will mimic one another on correct inputs.

However, when presented with erroneous input, the LALR parser may proceed to do some reductions after the LR parser has declared an error, although the LALR parser will never shift another symbol after the LR parser declares an error. For example, on input ccd followed by $, the LR parser of Fig. 4.34 will put

$$0 \; c \; 3 \; c \; 3 \; d \; 4$$

on the stack, and in state 4 will discover an error, because $ is the next input symbol and state 4 has action error on $. In contrast, the LALR parser of Fig. 4.41 will make the corresponding moves, putting

$$0 \; c \; 36 \; c \; 36 \; d \; 47$$

on the stack. But state 47 on input $ has action reduce $C \rightarrow d$. The LALR parser will thus change its stack to

$$0 \; c \; 36 \; c \; 36 \; C \; 89$$

Now the action of state 89 on input $ is reduce $C \rightarrow cC$. The stack becomes

$$0 \; c \; 36 \; C \; 89$$

whereupon a similar reduction is called for, obtaining stack

$$0 \; C \; 2$$

Finally, state 2 has action error on input $, so the error is now discovered.   □

Efficient Construction of LALR Parsing Tables

There are several modifications we can make to Algorithm 4.11 to avoid constructing the full collection of sets of LR(1) items in the process of creating an LALR(1) parsing table. The first observation is that we can represent a set of items I by its kernel, that is, by those items that are either the initial item $[S' \rightarrow \cdot S, \$]$, or that have the dot somewhere other than at the beginning of the right side.

Second, we can compute the parsing actions generated by I from the kernel alone. Any item calling for a reduction by $A \rightarrow \alpha$ will be in the kernel unless $\alpha = \epsilon$. Reduction by $A \rightarrow \epsilon$ is called for on input a if and only if there is a kernel item $[B \rightarrow \gamma \cdot C\delta, b]$ such that $C \underset{rm}{\overset{*}{\Rightarrow}} A\eta$ for some η, and a is in FIRST($\eta\delta b$). The set of nonterminals A such that $C \underset{rm}{\overset{*}{\Rightarrow}} A\eta$ can be precomputed for each nonterminal C.

The shift actions generated by I can be determined from the kernel of I as follows. We shift on input a if there is a kernel item $[B \rightarrow \gamma \cdot C\delta, b]$ where $C \underset{rm}{\overset{*}{\Rightarrow}} ax$ in a derivation in which the last step does not use an ϵ-production. The set of such a's can also be precomputed for each C.

Here is how the goto transitions for I can be computed from the kernel. If

$[B \rightarrow \gamma \cdot X\delta, b]$ is in the kernel of I, then $[B \rightarrow \gamma X \cdot \delta, b]$ is in the kernel of $goto(I, X)$. Item $[A \rightarrow X \cdot \beta, a]$ is also in the kernel of $goto(I, X)$ if there is an item $[B \rightarrow \gamma \cdot C\delta, b]$ in the kernel of I, and $C \underset{rm}{\overset{*}{\Rightarrow}} A\eta$ for some η. If we precompute for each pair of nonterminals C and A whether $C \underset{rm}{\overset{*}{\Rightarrow}} A\eta$ for some η, then computing sets of items from kernels only is just slightly less efficient than doing so with closed sets of items.

To compute the LALR(1) sets of items for an augmented grammar G', we start with the kernel $S' \rightarrow \cdot S$ of the initial set of items I_0. Then, we compute the kernels of the goto transitions from I_0 as outlined above. We continue computing the goto transitions for each new kernel generated until we have the kernels of the entire collection of sets of LR(0) items.

Example 4.46. Let us again consider the augmented grammar

$$S' \rightarrow S$$
$$S \rightarrow L = R \mid R$$
$$L \rightarrow * R \mid \textbf{id}$$
$$R \rightarrow L$$

The kernels of the sets of LR(0) items for this grammar are shown in Fig. 4.42. □

I_0:	$S' \rightarrow \cdot S$	I_5:	$L \rightarrow \textbf{id} \cdot$
I_1:	$S' \rightarrow S \cdot$	I_6:	$S \rightarrow L = \cdot R$
I_2:	$S \rightarrow L \cdot = R$	I_7:	$L \rightarrow *R \cdot$
	$R \rightarrow L \cdot$	I_8:	$R \rightarrow L \cdot$
I_3:	$S \rightarrow R \cdot$	I_9:	$S \rightarrow L = R \cdot$
I_4:	$L \rightarrow * \cdot R$		

Fig. 4.42. Kernels of the sets of LR(0) items for grammar (4.20).

Now we expand the kernels by attaching to each LR(0) item the proper lookahead symbols (second components). To see how lookahead symbols propagate from a set of items I to $goto(I, X)$, consider an LR(0) item $B \rightarrow \gamma \cdot C\delta$ in the kernel of I. Suppose $C \underset{rm}{\overset{*}{\Rightarrow}} A\eta$ for some η (perhaps $C = A$ and $\eta = \epsilon$), and $A \rightarrow X\beta$ is a production. Then LR(0) item $A \rightarrow X \cdot \beta$ is in $goto(I, X)$.

Suppose now that we are computing not LR(0) items, but LR(1) items, and $[B \rightarrow \gamma \cdot C\delta, b]$ is in the set I. Then for what values of a will $[A \rightarrow X \cdot \beta, a]$ be in $goto(I, X)$? Certainly if some a is in FIRST($\eta\delta$), then the derivation $C \underset{rm}{\overset{*}{\Rightarrow}} A\eta$ tells us that $[A \rightarrow X \cdot \beta, a]$ must be in $goto(I, X)$. In this case, the value of b is irrelevant, and we say that a, as a lookahead for $A \rightarrow X \cdot \beta$, is generated *spontaneously*. By definition, \$ is generated spontaneously as a lookahead for the item $S' \rightarrow \cdot S$ in the initial set of items.

But there is another source of lookaheads for item $A \rightarrow X \cdot \beta$. If $\eta\delta \overset{*}{\Rightarrow} \epsilon$, then $[A \rightarrow X \cdot \beta, \, b]$ will also be in $goto(I, X)$. We say, in this case, that look-aheads *propagate* from $B \rightarrow \gamma \cdot C \delta$ to $A \rightarrow X \cdot \beta$. A simple method to determine when an LR(1) item in I generates a lookahead in $goto(I, X)$ spontaneously, and when lookaheads propagate, is contained in the next algorithm.

Algorithm 4.12. Determining lookaheads.

Input. The kernel K of a set of LR(0) items I and a grammar symbol X.

Output. The lookaheads spontaneously generated by items in I for kernel items in $goto(I, X)$ and the items in I from which lookaheads are propagated to kernel items in $goto(I, X)$.

Method. The algorithm is given in Fig. 4.43. It uses a dummy lookahead symbol # to detect situations in which lookaheads propagate.   □

```
for each item B → γ·δ in K do begin
        J' := closure({[B → γ·δ, #]});
        if [A → α·Xβ, a] is in J' where a is not # then
                lookahead a is generated spontaneously for item
                        A → αX·β in goto(I, X);
        if [A → α·Xβ, #] is in J' then
                lookaheads propagate from B → γ·δ in I to
                        A → αX·β in goto(I, X)
end
```

Fig. 4.43. Discovering propagated and spontaneous lookaheads.

Now let us consider how we go about finding the lookaheads associated with the items in the kernels of the sets of LR(0) items. First, we know that $\$$ is a lookahead for $S' \rightarrow \cdot S$ in the initial set of LR(0) items. Algorithm 4.12 gives us all the lookaheads generated spontaneously. After listing all those lookaheads, we must allow them to propagate until no further propagation is possible. There are many different approaches, all of which in some sense keep track of "new" lookaheads that have propagated to an item but which have not yet propagated out. The next algorithm describes one technique to propagate lookaheads to all items.

Algorithm 4.13. Efficient computation of the kernels of the LALR(1) collection of sets of items.

Input. An augmented grammar G'.

Output. The kernels of the LALR(1) collection of sets of items for G'.

Method.

1. Using the method outlined above, construct the kernels of the sets of LR(0) items for G.

2. Apply Algorithm 4.12 to the kernel of each set of LR(0) items and gram-
    mar symbol X to determine which lookaheads are spontaneously gen-
    erated for kernel items in $goto(I, X)$, and from which items in I look-
    aheads are propagated to kernel items in $goto(I, X)$.

3. Initialize a table that gives, for each kernel item in each set of items, the
    associated lookaheads. Initially, each item has associated with it only
    those lookaheads that we determined in (2) were generated spontane-
    ously.

4. Make repeated passes over the kernel items in all sets. When we visit an
    item i, we look up the kernel items to which i propagates its lookaheads,
    using information tabulated in (2). The current set of lookaheads for i is
    added to those already associated with each of the items to which i pro-
    pagates its lookaheads. We continue making passes over the kernel items
    until no more new lookaheads are propagated.   □

Example 4.47. Let us construct the kernels of the LALR(1) items for the
grammar in the previous example. The kernels of the LR(0) items were
shown in Fig. 4.42. When we apply Algorithm 4.12 to the kernel of set of
items I_0, we compute $closure(\{[S' \rightarrow \cdot S, \#]\})$, which is

$$S' \rightarrow \cdot S, \#$$
$$S \rightarrow \cdot L = R, \#$$
$$S \rightarrow \cdot R, \#$$
$$L \rightarrow \cdot *R, \#/=$$
$$L \rightarrow \cdot id, \#/=$$
$$R \rightarrow \cdot L, \#$$

Two items in this closure cause lookaheads to be generated spontaneously.
Item $[L \rightarrow \cdot *R, =]$ causes lookahead $=$ to be spontaneously generated for
kernel item $L \rightarrow *\cdot R$ in I_4 and item $[L \rightarrow \cdot id, =]$ causes $=$ to be spontaneously generated for kernel item $L \rightarrow id\cdot$ in I_5.

The pattern of propagation of lookaheads among the kernel items determined in step (2) of Algorithm 4.13 is summarized in Fig. 4.44. For example,
the gotos of I_0 on symbols S, L, R, $*$, and **id** are respectively I_1, I_2, I_3, I_4,
and I_5. For I_0 we computed only the closure of the lone kernel item
$[S' \rightarrow \cdot S, \#]$. Thus, $S' \rightarrow \cdot S$ propagates its lookahead to each kernel item in
I_1 through I_5.

In Fig. 4.45, we show steps (3) and (4) of Algorithm 4.13. The column
labeled INIT shows the spontaneously generated lookaheads for each kernel
item. On the first pass, the lookahead $ propagates from $S' \rightarrow S$ in I_0 to the
six items listed in Fig. 4.44. The lookahead $=$ propagates from $L \rightarrow *\cdot R$ in I_4
to items $L \rightarrow *R\cdot$ in I_7 and $R \rightarrow L\cdot$ in I_8. It also propagates to itself and to
$L \rightarrow id\cdot$ in I_5, but these lookaheads are already present. In the second and
third passes, the only new lookahead propagated is $, discovered for the suc-
cessors of I_2 and I_4 on pass 2 and for the successor of I_6 on pass 3. No new
lookaheads are propagated on pass 4, so the final set of lookaheads is shown

From		To	
I_0:	$S' \rightarrow \cdot S$	I_1:	$S' \rightarrow S\cdot$
		I_2:	$S \rightarrow L\cdot = R$
		I_2:	$R \rightarrow L\cdot$
		I_3:	$S \rightarrow R\cdot$
		I_4:	$L \rightarrow *\cdot R$
		I_5:	$L \rightarrow \mathbf{id}\cdot$
I_2:	$S \rightarrow L\cdot = R$	I_6:	$S \rightarrow L = \cdot R$
I_4:	$L \rightarrow *\cdot R$	I_4:	$L \rightarrow *\cdot R$
		I_5:	$L \rightarrow \mathbf{id}\cdot$
		I_7:	$L \rightarrow *R\cdot$
		I_8:	$R \rightarrow L\cdot$
I_6:	$S \rightarrow L = \cdot R$	I_4:	$L \rightarrow *\cdot R$
		I_5:	$L \rightarrow *\cdot R$
		I_8:	$R \rightarrow L\cdot$
		I_9:	$S \rightarrow L = R\cdot$

Fig. 4.44. Propagation of lookaheads.

in the rightmost column of Fig. 4.45.

Note that the shift/reduce conflict found in Example 4.39 using the SLR method has disappeared with the LALR technique. The reason is that only lookahead $ is associated with $R \rightarrow L\cdot$ in I_2, so there is no conflict with the parsing action of shift on = generated by item $S \rightarrow L\cdot = R$ in I_2.   □

Compaction of LR Parsing Tables

A typical programming language grammar with 50 to 100 terminals and 100 productions may have an LALR parsing table with several hundred states. The action function may easily have 20,000 entries, each requiring at least 8 bits to encode. Clearly a more efficient encoding than a two-dimensional array may be important. We shall briefly mention a few techniques that have been used to compress the action and goto fields of an LR parsing table.

One useful technique for compacting the action field is to recognize that usually many rows of the action table are identical. For example, in Fig. 4.40, states 0 and 3 have identical action entries, and so do 2 and 6. We can therefore save considerable space, at little cost in time, if we create a pointer for each state into a one-dimensional array. Pointers for states with the same actions point to the same location. To access information from this array, we assign each terminal a number from zero to one less than the number of terminals, and we use this integer as an offset from the pointer value for each state. In a given state, the parsing action for the ith terminal will be found i locations past the pointer value for that state.

SET	ITEM	LOOKAHEADS			
		INIT	PASS 1	PASS 2	PASS 3
I_0:	$S' \to \cdot S$	\$	\$	\$	\$
I_1:	$S' \to S\cdot$		\$	\$	\$
I_2:	$S \to L\cdot = R$		\$	\$	\$
I_2:	$R \to L\cdot$		\$	\$	\$
I_3:	$S \to R\cdot$		\$	\$	\$
I_4:	$L \to * \cdot R$	=	=/\$	=/\$	=/\$
I_5:	$L \to \mathbf{id}\cdot$	=	=/\$	=/\$	=/\$
I_6:	$S \to L = \cdot R$			\$	\$
I_7:	$L \to *R\cdot$		=	=/\$	=/\$
I_8:	$R \to L\cdot$		=	=/\$	=/\$
I_9:	$S \to L = R\cdot$				\$

Fig. 4.45. Computation of lookaheads.

Further space efficiency can be achieved at the expense of a somewhat slower parser (generally considered a reasonable trade, since an LR-like parser consumes only a small fraction of the total compilation time) by creating a list for the actions of each state. The list consists of (terminal-symbol, action) pairs. The most frequent action for a state can be placed at the end of the list, and in place of a terminal we may use the notation "any," meaning that if the current input symbol has not been found so far on the list, we should do that action no matter what the input is. Moreover, error entries can safely be replaced by reduce actions, for further uniformity along a row. The errors will be detected later, before a shift move.

Example 4.48. Consider the parsing table of Fig. 4.31. First, note that the actions for states 0, 4, 6, and 7 agree. We can represent them all by the list:

SYMBOL	ACTION
id	s5
(	s4
any	error

State 1 has a similar list:

+	s6
\$	acc
any	error

In state 2, we can replace the error entries by r2, so reduction by production 2 will occur on any input but *. Thus the list for state 2 is:

*	s7
any	r2

State 3 has only error and r4 entries. We can replace the former by the latter, so the list for state 3 consists of only the pair (any, r4). States 5, 10, and 11 can be treated similarly. The list for state 8 is:

+	s6
)	s11
any	error

and for state 9:

*	s7
any	r1	□

We can also encode the *goto* table by a list, but here it appears more efficient to make a list of pairs for each nonterminal A. Each pair on the list for A is of the form (*current_state, next_state*), indicating

$$goto\,[current\_state,\ A\,] = next\_state$$

This technique is useful because there tend to be rather few states in any one column of the *goto* table. The reason is that the goto on nonterminal A can only be a state derivable from a set of items in which some items have A immediately to the left of a dot. No set has items with X and Y immediately to the left of a dot if $X \neq Y$. Thus, each state appears in at most one *goto* column.

For more space reduction, we note that the error entries in the goto table are never consulted. We can therefore replace each error entry by the most common non-error entry in its column. This entry becomes the default; it is represented in the list for each column by one pair with "any" in place of current-state.

Example 4.49. Consider Fig. 4.31 again. The column for F has entry 10 for state 7, and all other entries are either 3 or error. We may replace error by 3 and create for column F the list:

current_state	next_state
7	10
any	3

Similarly, a suitable list for column T is:

6	9
any	2

For column E we may choose either 1 or 8 to be the default; two entries are necessary in either case. For example, we might create for column E the list:

	4	8
	any	1	□

If the reader totals up the number of entries in the lists created in this example and the previous one, and then adds the pointers from states to action lists and from nonterminals to next-state lists, he will not be impressed with the space savings over the matrix implementation of Fig. 4.31. We should not be misled by this small example, however. For practical grammars, the space needed for the list representation is typically less than ten percent of that needed for the matrix representation.

We should also point out that the table-compression methods for finite automata that were discussed in Section 3.9 can also be used to represent LR parsing tables. Application of these methods is discussed in the exercises.

4.8 USING AMBIGUOUS GRAMMARS

It is a theorem that every ambiguous grammar fails to be LR, and thus is not in any of the classes of grammars discussed in the previous section. Certain types of ambiguous grammars, however, are useful in the specification and implementation of languages, as we shall see in this section. For language constructs like expressions an ambiguous grammar provides a shorter, more natural specification than any equivalent unambiguous grammar. Another use of ambiguous grammars is in isolating commonly occurring syntactic constructs for special case optimization. With an ambiguous grammar, we can specify the special case constructs by carefully adding new productions to the grammar.

We should emphasize that although the grammars we use are ambiguous, in all cases we specify disambiguating rules that allow only one parse tree for each sentence. In this way, the overall language specification still remains unambiguous. We also stress that ambiguous constructs should be used sparingly and in a strictly controlled fashion; otherwise, there can be no guarantee as to what language is recognized by a parser.

Using Precedence and Associativity to Resolve Parsing Action Conflicts

Consider expressions in programming languages. The following grammar for arithmetic expressions with operators + and *

$$E \rightarrow E + E \mid E * E \mid (E) \mid \mathbf{id} \tag{4.22}$$

is ambiguous because it does not specify the associativity or precedence of the operators + and *. The unambiguous grammar

$$
\begin{aligned}
E &\rightarrow E + T \mid T \\
T &\rightarrow T * F \mid F \\
F &\rightarrow (E) \mid \mathbf{id}
\end{aligned}
\tag{4.23}
$$

generates the same language, but gives + a lower precedence than *, and makes both operators left-associative. There are two reasons why we might want to use grammar (4.22) instead of (4.23). First, as we shall see, we can easily change the associativities and precedence levels of the operators + and * without disturbing the productions of (4.22) or the number of states in the resulting parser. Second, the parser for (4.23) will spend a substantial fraction of its time reducing by the productions $E \rightarrow T$ and $T \rightarrow F$, whose sole function is to enforce associativity and precedence. The parser for (4.22) will not waste time reducing by these *single* productions, as they are called.

I_0: $E' \rightarrow \cdot E$
       $E \rightarrow \cdot E + E$
       $E \rightarrow \cdot E * E$
       $E \rightarrow \cdot (E)$
       $E \rightarrow \cdot \mathbf{id}$

I_1: $E' \rightarrow E \cdot$
       $E \rightarrow E \cdot + E$
       $E \rightarrow E \cdot * E$

I_2: $E \rightarrow (\cdot E)$
       $E \rightarrow \cdot E + E$
       $E \rightarrow \cdot E * E$
       $E \rightarrow \cdot (E)$
       $E \rightarrow \cdot \mathbf{id}$

I_3: $E \rightarrow \mathbf{id} \cdot$

I_4: $E \rightarrow E + \cdot E$
       $E \rightarrow \cdot E + E$
       $E \rightarrow \cdot E * E$
       $E \rightarrow \cdot (E)$
       $E \rightarrow \cdot \mathbf{id}$

I_5: $E \rightarrow E * \cdot E$
       $E \rightarrow \cdot E + E$
       $E \rightarrow \cdot E * E$
       $F \rightarrow \cdot (E)$
       $E \rightarrow \cdot \mathbf{id}$

I_6: $E \rightarrow (E \cdot)$
       $E \rightarrow E \cdot + E$
       $E \rightarrow E \cdot * E$

I_7: $E \rightarrow E + E \cdot$
       $E \rightarrow E \cdot + E$
       $E \rightarrow E \cdot * E$

I_8: $E \rightarrow E * E \cdot$
       $E \rightarrow E \cdot + E$
       $E \rightarrow E \cdot * E$

I_9: $E \rightarrow (E) \cdot$

Fig. 4.46. Sets of LR(0) items for augmented grammar (4.22).

The sets of LR(0) items for (4.22) augmented by $E' \rightarrow E$ are shown in Fig. 4.46. Since grammar (4.22) is ambiguous, parsing action conflicts will be generated when we try to produce an LR parsing table from the sets of items. The states corresponding to sets of items I_7 and I_8 generate these conflicts. Suppose we use the SLR approach to constructing the parsing action table. The conflict generated by I_7 between reduction by $E \rightarrow E + E$ and shift on + and * cannot be resolved because + and * are each in FOLLOW(E). Thus both actions would be called for on inputs + and *. A similar conflict is generated by I_8, between reduction by $E \rightarrow E * E$ and shift on inputs + and *. In fact, each of our LR parsing table construction methods will generate these conflicts.

However, these problems can be resolved using the precedence and associativity information for + and ∗. Consider the input **id** + **id** ∗ **id**, which
causes a parser based on Fig. 4.46 to enter state 7 after processing **id** + **id**; in
particular the parser reaches a configuration

STACK	INPUT
$0 E 1 + 4 E 7$	∗ **id** $

Assuming that ∗ takes precedence over +, we know the parser should shift
∗ onto the stack, preparing to reduce the ∗ and its surrounding **id**'s to an
expression. This is what the SLR parser of Fig. 4.31 for the same language
would do, and it is what an operator-precedence parser would do. On the
other hand, if + takes precedence over ∗, we know the parser should reduce
$E + E$ to E. Thus the relative precedence of + followed by ∗ uniquely determines how the parsing action conflict between reducing $E \rightarrow E + E$ and shifting
on ∗ in state 7 should be resolved.

If the input had been **id** + **id** + **id**, instead, the parser would still reach a
configuration in which it had stack $0E1+4E7$ after processing input **id** + **id**.
On input + there is again a shift/reduce conflict in state 7. Now, however,
the associativity of the + operator determines how this conflict should be
resolved. If + is left-associative, the correct action is to reduce by $E \rightarrow E + E$.
That is, the **id**'s surrounding the first + must be grouped first. Again this
choice coincides with what the SLR or operator-precedence parsers would do
for the grammar of Example 4.34.

In summary, assuming + is left-associative, the action of state 7 on input +
should be to reduce by $E \rightarrow E + E$, and assuming that ∗ takes precedence over
+, the action of state 7 on input ∗ should be to shift. Similarly, assuming
that ∗ is left-associative and takes precedence over +, we can argue that state
8, which can appear on top of the stack only when $E ∗ E$ are the top three
grammar symbols, should have action reduce $E \rightarrow E ∗ E$ on both + and ∗
inputs. In the case of input +, the reason is that ∗ takes precedence over +,
while in the case of input ∗, the rationale is that ∗ is left-associative.

Proceeding in this way, we obtain the LR parsing table shown in Fig. 4.47.
Productions 1−4 are $E \rightarrow E + E$, $E \rightarrow E ∗ E$, $E \rightarrow (E)$, and $E \rightarrow$ **id**, respectively. It is interesting that a similar parsing action table would be produced
by eliminating the reductions by the single productions $E \rightarrow T$ and $T \rightarrow F$ from
the SLR table for grammar (4.23) shown in Fig. 4.31. Ambiguous grammars
like (4.22) can be handled in a similar way in the context of LALR and
canonical LR parsing.

The "Dangling-else" Ambiguity

Consider again the following grammar for conditional statements:

$stmt \rightarrow$ **if** *expr* **then** *stmt* **else** *stmt*
    | **if** *expr* **then** *stmt*
    | **other**

STATE	action						goto
	id	+	*	(	)	$	E
0	s3			s2			1
1		s4	s5			acc	
2	s3			s2			6
3		r4	r4		r4	r4	
4	s3			s2			8
5	s3			s2			8
6		s4	s5		s9		
7		r1	s5		r1	r1	
8		r2	r2		r2	r2	
9		r3	r3		r3	r3	

Fig. 4.47. Parsing table for grammar (4.22).

As we noted in Section 4.3, this grammar is ambiguous because it does not resolve the dangling-else ambiguity. To simplify the discussion, let us consider an abstraction of the above grammar, where i stands for **if** $expr$ **then**, e stands for **else**, and a stands for "all other productions." We can then write the grammar, with augmenting production $S' \rightarrow S$, as:

$$S' \rightarrow S \qquad\qquad\qquad\qquad (4.24)$$
$$S \rightarrow iSeS \mid iS \mid a$$

The sets of LR(0) items for grammar (4.24) are shown in Fig. 4.48. The ambiguity in (4.24) gives rise to a shift/reduce conflict in I_4. There, $S \rightarrow iS \cdot eS$ calls for a shift of e and, since $\text{FOLLOW}(S) = \{e, \$\}$, item $S \rightarrow iS \cdot$ calls for reduction by $S \rightarrow iS$ on input e.

Translating back to the **if** $\cdots$ **then** $\cdots$ **else** terminology, given

    if $expr$ **then** $stmt$

on the stack and **else** as the first input symbol, should we shift **else** onto the stack (i.e., shift e) or reduce **if** $expr$ **then** $stmt$ to $stmt$ (i.e., reduce by $S \rightarrow iS$)? The answer is that we should shift **else**, because it is "associated" with the previous **then**. In the terminology of grammar (4.24), the e on the input, standing for **else**, can only form part of the right side beginning with the iS on the top of the stack. If what follows e on the input cannot be parsed as an S, completing right side $iSeS$, then it can be shown that there is no other parse possible.

We are drawn to the conclusion that the shift/reduce conflict in I_4 should be resolved in favor of shift on input e. The SLR parsing table constructed from the sets of items of Fig. 4.48, using this resolution of the parsing action conflict in I_4 on input e, is shown in Fig. 4.49. Productions 1 through 3 are $S \rightarrow iSeS$, $S \rightarrow iS$, and $S \rightarrow a$, respectively.

I_0: $S' \rightarrow \cdot S$
$S \rightarrow \cdot iSeS$
$S \rightarrow \cdot iS$
$S \rightarrow \cdot a$

I_1: $S' \rightarrow S\cdot$

I_2: $S \rightarrow i\cdot SeS$
$S \rightarrow i\cdot S$
$S \rightarrow \cdot iSeS$
$S \rightarrow \cdot iS$
$S \rightarrow \cdot a$

I_3: $S \rightarrow a\cdot$

I_4: $S \rightarrow iS\cdot eS$
$S \rightarrow iS\cdot$

I_5: $S \rightarrow iSe\cdot S$
$S \rightarrow \cdot iSeS$
$S \rightarrow \cdot iS$
$S \rightarrow \cdot a$

I_6: $S \rightarrow iSeS\cdot$

Fig. 4.48. LR(0) states for augmented grammar (4.24).

STATE	action				goto
	i	e	a	$\$$	S
0	s2		s3		1
1				acc	
2	s2		s3		4
3		r3		r3	
4		s5		r2	
5	s2		s3		6
6		r1		r1	

Fig. 4.49. LR parsing table for abstract "dangling-else" grammar.

For example, on input *iiaea*, the parser makes the moves shown in Fig. 4.50, corresponding to the correct resolution of the "dangling-else." At line (5), state 4 selects the shift action on input *e*, whereas at line (9), state 4 calls for reduction by $S \rightarrow iS$ on $\$$ input.

By way of comparison, if we are unable to use an ambiguous grammar to specify conditional statements, then we would have to use a bulkier grammar along the lines of (4.9).

Ambiguities from Special-Case Productions

Our final example suggesting the usefulness of ambiguous grammars occurs if we introduce an additional production to specify a special case of a syntactic construct generated in a more general fashion by the rest of the grammar. When we add the extra production, we generate a parsing action conflict. We can often resolve the conflict satisfactorily by a disambiguating rule that says

	STACK	INPUT
(1)	0	*iiaea*$
(2)	0*i* 2	*iaea*$
(3)	0*i* 2*i* 2	*aea*$
(4)	0*i* 2*i* 2*a* 3	*ea*$
(5)	0*i* 2*i* 2*S* 4	*ea*$
(6)	0*i* 2*i* 2*S* 4*e* 5	*a*$
(7)	0*i* 2*i* 2*S* 4*e* 5*a* 3	$
(8)	0*i* 2*i* 2*S* 4*e* 5*S* 6	$
(9)	0*i* 2*S* 4	$
(10)	0*S* 1	$

Fig. 4.50. Parsing actions taken on input *iiaea*.

reduce by the special-case production. The semantic action associated with the additional production then allows the special case to be handled by a more specific mechanism.

An interesting use of special-case productions was made by Kernighan and Cherry [1975] in their equation-typesetting preprocessor EQN, which was used to help typeset this book. In EQN, the syntax of a mathematical expression is described by a grammar that uses a subscript operator **sub** and a superscript operator **sup**, as shown in the grammar fragment (4.25). Braces are used by the preprocessor to bracket compound expressions, and *c* is used as a token representing any string of text.

$$
\begin{aligned}
&(1) \quad E \rightarrow E \text{ sub } E \text{ sup } E \\
&(2) \quad E \rightarrow E \text{ sub } E \\
&(3) \quad E \rightarrow E \text{ sup } E \\
&(4) \quad E \rightarrow \{\, E \,\} \\
&(5) \quad E \rightarrow c
\end{aligned}
\qquad (4.25)
$$

Grammar (4.25) is ambiguous for several reasons. The grammar does not specify the associativity and precedence of the operators **sub** and **sup**. Even if we resolve the ambiguities arising from the associativity and precedence of the **sub** and **sup**, say by making these two operators of equal precedence and right associative, the grammar will still be ambiguous. This is because production (1) isolates a special case of expressions generated by productions (2) and (3), namely expressions of the form E **sub** E **sup** E. The reason for treating expressions of this form specially is that many typesetters would prefer to typeset an expression like a **sub** i **sup** 2 as a_i^2 rather than as $a_i{}^2$. By merely adding a special case production, Kernighan and Cherry were able to get EQN to produce this special case output.

To see how this kind of ambiguity can be treated in the LR setting, let us construct an SLR parser for grammar (4.25). The sets of LR(0) items for this

I_0: $E' \rightarrow \cdot E$
     $E \rightarrow \cdot E$ **sub** E **sup** E
     $E \rightarrow \cdot E$ **sub** E
     $E \rightarrow \cdot E$ **sup** E
     $E \rightarrow \cdot\{ E \}$
     $E \rightarrow \cdot c$

I_1: $E' \rightarrow E \cdot$
     $E \rightarrow E \cdot$ **sub** E **sup** E
     $E \rightarrow E \cdot$ **sub** E
     $E \rightarrow E \cdot$ **sup** E

I_2: $E \rightarrow \{\cdot E \}$
     $E \rightarrow \cdot E$ **sub** E **sup** E
     $E \rightarrow \cdot E$ **sub** E
     $E \rightarrow \cdot E$ **sup** E
     $E \rightarrow \cdot\{ E \}$
     $E \rightarrow \cdot c$

I_3: $E \rightarrow c \cdot$

I_4: $E \rightarrow E$ **sub** $\cdot E$ **sup** E
     $E \rightarrow E$ **sub** $\cdot E$
     $E \rightarrow \cdot E$ **sub** E **sup** E
     $E \rightarrow \cdot E$ **sub** E
     $E \rightarrow \cdot E$ **sup** E
     $E \rightarrow \cdot\{ E \}$
     $E \rightarrow \cdot c$

I_5: $E \rightarrow E$ **sup** $\cdot E$
     $E \rightarrow \cdot E$ **sub** E **sup** E
     $E \rightarrow \cdot E$ **sub** E
     $E \rightarrow \cdot E$ **sup** E
     $E \rightarrow \cdot\{ E \}$
     $E \rightarrow \cdot c$

I_6: $E \rightarrow E \cdot$ **sub** E **sup** E
     $E \rightarrow E \cdot$ **sub** E
     $E \rightarrow E \cdot$ **sup** E
     $E \rightarrow \{ E \cdot\}$

I_7: $E \rightarrow E \cdot$ **sub** E **sup** E
     $E \rightarrow E$ **sub** $E \cdot$ **sup** E
     $E \rightarrow E \cdot$ **sub** E
     $E \rightarrow E$ **sub** $E \cdot$
     $E \rightarrow E \cdot$ **sup** E

I_8: $E \rightarrow E \cdot$ **sub** E **sup** E
     $E \rightarrow E \cdot$ **sub** E
     $E \rightarrow E \cdot$ **sup** E
     $E \rightarrow E$ **sup** $E \cdot$

I_9: $E \rightarrow \{ E \} \cdot$

I_{10}: $E \rightarrow E$ **sub** E **sup** $\cdot E$
     $E \rightarrow E$ **sup** $\cdot E$
     $E \rightarrow \cdot E$ **sub** E **sup** E
     $E \rightarrow \cdot E$ **sub** E
     $E \rightarrow \cdot E$ **sup** E
     $E \rightarrow \cdot\{ E \}$
     $E \rightarrow \cdot c$

I_{11}: $E \rightarrow E \cdot$ **sub** E **sup** E
     $E \rightarrow E$ **sub** E **sup** $E \cdot$
     $E \rightarrow E \cdot$ **sub** E
     $E \rightarrow E \cdot$ **sup** E
     $E \rightarrow E$ **sup** $E \cdot$

Fig. 4.51. LR(0) sets of items for grammar (4.25).

grammar are shown in Fig. 4.51. In this collection, three sets of items yield parsing action conflicts. I_7, I_8, and I_{11} generate shift/reduce conflicts on the tokens **sub** and **sup** because the associativity and precedence of these operators have not been specified. We resolve these parsing action conflicts when we make **sub** and **sup** of equal precedence and right-associative. Thus, shift is preferred in each case.

I_{11} also generates a reduce/reduce conflict on inputs } and $ between the two productions

$E \rightarrow E$ **sub** E **sup** E
$E \rightarrow E$ **sup** E

State I_{11} will be on top of the stack when we have seen an input that has been reduced to E **sub** E **sup** E on the stack. If we resolve the reduce/reduce conflict in favor of production (1), we shall treat an equation of the form form E **sub** E **sup** E as a special case. Using these disambiguating rules, we obtain the SLR parsing table show in Fig. 4.52.

STATE	action						goto
	sub	**sup**	{	}	c	$	E
0			s2		s3		1
1	s4	s5				acc	
2			s2		s3		6
3	r5	r5		r5		r5	
4			s2		s3		7
5			s2		s3		8
6	s4	s5		s9			
7	s4	s10		r2		r2	
8	s4	s5		r3		r3	
9	r4	r4		r4		r4	
10			s2		s3		11
11	s4	s5		r1		r1	

Fig. 4.52. Parsing table for grammar (4.25).

Writing unambiguous grammars that factor out special case syntactic constructs is very difficult. To appreciate how difficult this is, the reader is invited to construct an equivalent unambiguous grammar for (4.25) that isolates expressions of the form E **sub** E **sup** E.

Error Recovery in LR Parsing

An LR parser will detect an error when it consults the parsing action table and finds an error entry. Errors are never detected by consulting the goto table. Unlike an operator-precedence parser, an LR parser will announce error as soon as there is no valid continuation for the portion of the input thus far scanned. A canonical LR parsing will never make even a single reduction before announcing an error. The SLR and LALR parsers may make several reductions before announcing an error, but they will never shift an erroneous input symbol onto the stack.

In LR parsing, we can implement panic-mode error recovery as follows.

We scan down the stack until a state s with a goto on a particular nonterminal A is found. Zero or more input symbols are then discarded until a symbol a is found that can legitimately follow A. The parser then stacks the state $goto[s, A]$ and resumes normal parsing. There might be more than one choice for the nonterminal A. Normally these would be nonterminals representing major program pieces, such as an expression, statement, or block. For example, if A is the nonterminal *stmt*, a might be semicolon or **end**.

This method of recovery attempts to isolate the phrase containing the syntactic error. The parser determines that a string derivable from A contains an error. Part of that string has already been processed, and the result of this processing is a sequence of states on top of the stack. The remainder of the string is still on the input, and the parser attempts to skip over the remainder of this string by looking for a symbol on the input that can legitimately follow A. By removing states from the stack, skipping over the input, and pushing $goto[s, A]$ on the stack, the parser pretends that it has found an instance of A and resumes normal parsing.

Phrase-level recovery is implemented by examining each error entry in the LR parsing table and deciding on the basis of language usage the most likely programmer error that would give rise to that error. An appropriate recovery procedure can then be constructed; presumably the top of the stack and/or first input symbols would be modified in a way deemed appropriate for each error entry.

Compared with operator-precedence parsers, the design of specific error-handling routines for an LR parser is relatively easy. In particular, we do not have to worry about faulty reductions; any reduction called for by an LR parser is surely correct. Thus we may fill in each blank entry in the action field with a pointer to an error routine that will take an appropriate action selected by the compiler designer. The actions may include insertion or deletion of symbols from the stack or the input or both, or alteration and transposition of input symbols, just as for the operator-precedence parser. Like that parser, we must make our choices without allowing the possibility that the LR parser will get into an infinite loop. A strategy that assures at least one input symbol will be removed or eventually shifted, or that the stack will eventually shrink if the end of the input has been reached, is sufficient in this regard. Popping a stack state that covers a nonterminal should be avoided, because this modification eliminates from the stack a construct that has already been successfully parsed.

Example 4.50. Consider again the expression grammar

$$E \rightarrow E + E \mid E * E \mid (E) \mid \textbf{id}$$

Figure 4.53 shows the LR parsing table from Fig. 4.47 for this grammar, modified for error detection and recovery. We have changed each state that calls for a particular reduction on some input symbols by replacing error entries in that state by the reduction. This change has the effect of postponing the error detection until one or more reductions are made, but the error will still be caught before any shift move takes place. The remaining blank entries from Fig. 4.47 have been replaced by calls to error routines.

STATE	action						goto
	id	+	*	(	)	$	E
0	s3	e1	e1	s2	e2	e1	1
1	e3	s4	s5	e3	e2	acc	
2	s3	e1	e1	s2	e2	e1	6
3	r4	r4	r4	r4	r4	r4	
4	s3	e1	e1	s2	e2	e1	7
5	s3	e1	e1	s2	e2	e1	8
6	e3	s4	s5	e3	s9	e4	
7	r1	r1	s5	r1	r1	r1	
8	r2	r2	r2	r2	r2	r2	
9	r3	r3	r3	r3	r3	r3	

Fig. 4.53. LR parsing table with error routines.

The error routines are as follows. The similarity of these actions and the errors they represent to the error actions in Example 4.32 (operator precedence) should be noted. However, case e1 in the LR parser is frequently handled by the reduction processor of the operator-precedence parser.

e1: /* This routine is called from states 0, 2, 4 and 5, all of which expect the beginning of an operand, either an **id** or a left parenthesis. Instead, an operator, + or *, or the end of the input was found. */
push an imaginary **id** onto the stack and cover it with state 3 (the goto of states 0, 2, 4 and 5 on **id**)[5]
issue diagnostic "missing operand"

e2: /* This routine is called from states 0, 1, 2, 4 and 5 on finding a right parenthesis. */
remove the right parenthesis from the input
issue diagnostic "unbalanced right parenthesis"

e3: /* This routine is called from states 1 or 6 when expecting an operator, and an **id** or right parenthesis is found. */
push + onto the stack and cover it with state 4.
issue diagnostic "missing operator"

e4: /* This routine is called from state 6 when the end of the input is found.

---

[5] Note that in practice grammar symbols are not placed on the stack. It is useful to imagine them there to remind us of the symbols which the states "represent."

State 6 expects an operator or a right parenthesis. */
push a right parenthesis onto the stack and cover it with state 9.
issue diagnostic "missing right parenthesis"

On the erroneous input **id** +) discussed in Example 4.32, the sequence of
configurations entered by the parser is shown in Fig. 4.54.   □

Stack	Input	Error Message and Action
0	**id**+)$	
0**id**3	+)$	
0E1	+)$	
0E1+4	)$	
0E1+4	$	"unbalanced right parenthesis"
		e2 removes right parenthesis
0E1+4**id**3	$	"missing operand"
		e1 pushes **id** 3 on stack
0E1+4E7	$	
0E1	$	

Fig. 4.54. Parsing and error recovery moves made by LR parser.

4.9 PARSER GENERATORS

This section shows how a parser generator can be used to facilitate the construction of the front end of a compiler. We shall use the LALR parser generator Yacc as the basis of our discussion, since it implements many of the
concepts discussed in the previous two sections and it is widely available.
Yacc stands for "yet another compiler-compiler," reflecting the popularity of
parser generators in the early 1970's when the first version of Yacc was
created by S. C. Johnson. Yacc is available as a command on the UNIX system, and has been used to help implement hundreds of compilers.

The Parser Generator Yacc

A translator can be constructed using Yacc in the manner illustrated in Fig.
4.55. First, a file, say `translate.y`, containing a Yacc specification of the
translator is prepared. The UNIX system command

```
yacc translate.y
```

transforms the file `translate.y` into a C program called `y.tab.c` using the
LALR method outlined in Algorithm 4.13. The program `y.tab.c` is a
representation of an LALR parser written in C, along with other C routines
that the user may have prepared. The LALR parsing table is compacted as
described in Section 4.7. By compiling `y.tab.c` along with the `ly` library

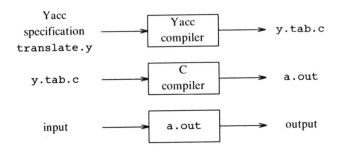

Fig. 4.55. Creating an input/output translator with Yacc.

that contains the LR parsing program using the command

```
cc y.tab.c -ly
```

we obtain the desired object program a.out that performs the translation specified by the original Yacc program.[6] If other procedures are needed, they can be compiled or loaded with y.tab.c, just as with any C program.

A Yacc source program has three parts:

```
declarations
%%
translation rules
%%
supporting C-routines
```

Example 4.51. To illustrate how to prepare a Yacc source program, let us construct a simple desk calculator that reads an arithmetic expression, evaluates it, and then prints its numeric value. We shall build the desk calculator starting with the following grammar for arithmetic expressions:

$$E \rightarrow E + T \mid T$$
$$T \rightarrow T * F \mid F$$
$$F \rightarrow (E) \mid \textbf{digit}$$

The token **digit** is a single digit between 0 and 9. A Yacc desk calculator program derived from this grammar is shown in Fig. 4.56.   □

The declarations part. There are two optional sections in the declarations part of a Yacc program. In the first section, we put ordinary C declarations, delimited by %{ and %}. Here we place declarations of any temporaries used by the translation rules or procedures of the second and third sections. In

---

[6] The name **ly** is system dependent.

```
%{
#include <ctype.h>
%}

%token DIGIT

%%
line    :   expr '\n'              { printf("%d\n", $1); }
        ;
expr    :   expr '+' term         { $$ = $1 + $3; }
        |   term
        ;
term    :   term '*' factor       { $$ = $1 * $3; }
        |   factor
        ;
factor  :   '(' expr ')'          { $$ = $2; }
        |   DIGIT
        ;
%%
yylex() {
    int c;
    c = getchar();
    if (isdigit(c)) {
        yylval = c-'0';
        return DIGIT;
    }
    return c;
}
```

Fig. 4.56. Yacc specification of a simple desk calculator.

Fig. 4.56, this section contains only the include-statement

```
#include <ctype.h>
```

that causes the C preprocessor to include the standard header file `<ctype.h>` that contains the predicate `isdigit`.

Also in the declarations part are declarations of grammar tokens. In Fig. 4.56, the statement

```
%token DIGIT
```

declares `DIGIT` to be a token. Tokens declared in this section can then be used in the second and third parts of the Yacc specification.

The translation rules part. In the part of the Yacc specification after the first %% pair, we put the translation rules. Each rule consists of a grammar

production and the associated semantic action. A set of productions that we
have been writing

$$<\text{left side}> \rightarrow <\text{alt 1}> \mid <\text{alt 2}> \mid \cdots \mid <\text{alt } n>$$

would be written in Yacc as

```
<left side>    :   <alt 1>     { semantic action 1 }
               |   <alt 2>     { semantic action 2 }
             . . .
               |   <alt n>     { semantic action n }
               ;
```

In a Yacc production, a quoted single character 'c' is taken to be the terminal symbol c, and unquoted strings of letters and digits not declared to be
tokens are taken to be nonterminals. Alternative right sides can be separated
by a vertical bar, and a semicolon follows each left side with its alternatives
and their semantic actions. The first left side is taken to be the start symbol.

A Yacc semantic action is a sequence of C statements. In a semantic
action, the symbol $$ refers to the attribute value associated with the nonter-
minal on the left, while $i refers to the value associated with the ith grammar
symbol (terminal or nonterminal) on the right. The semantic action is per-
formed whenever we reduce by the associated production, so normally the
semantic action computes a value for $$ in terms of the $i's. In the Yacc
specification, we have written the two E-productions

$$E \rightarrow E + T \mid T$$

and their associated semantic actions as

```
expr    :   expr '+' term    { $$ = $1 + $3; }
        |   term
        ;
```

Note that the nonterminal term in the first production is the third grammar
symbol on the right, while '+' is the second. The semantic action associated
with the first production adds the value of the expr and the term on the
right and assigns the result as the value for the nonterminal expr on the left.
We have omitted the semantic action for the second production altogether,
since copying the value is the default action for productions with a single
grammar symbol on the right. In general, { $$ = $1; } is the default
semantic action.

Notice that we have added a new starting production

```
line    :   expr '\n'        { printf("%d\n", $1); }
```

to the Yacc specification. This production says that an input to the desk cal-
culator is to be an expression followed by a newline character. The semantic
action associated with this production prints the decimal value of the expres-
sion followed by a newline character.

The supporting C-routines part. The third part of a Yacc specification consists of supporting C-routines. A lexical analyzer by the name `yylex()` must be provided. Other procedures such as error recovery routines may be added as necessary.

The lexical analyzer `yylex()` produces pairs consisting of a token and its associated attribute value. If a token such as `DIGIT` is returned, the token must be declared in the first section of the Yacc specification. The attribute value associated with a token is communicated to the parser through a Yacc-defined variable `yylval`.

The lexical analyzer in Fig. 4.56 is very crude. It reads input characters one at a time using the C-function `getchar()`. If the character is a digit, the value of the digit is stored in the variable `yylval`, and the token `DIGIT` is returned. Otherwise, the character itself is returned as the token.

Using Yacc with Ambiguous Grammars

Let us now modify the Yacc specification so that the resulting desk calculator becomes more useful. First, we shall allow the desk calculator to evaluate a sequence of expressions, one to a line. We shall also allow blank lines between expressions. We do this by changing the first rule to

```
lines   :   lines expr '\n'   { printf("%g\n", $2); }
        |   lines '\n'
        |
        ;
```

In Yacc, an empty alternative, as the third line is, denotes ϵ.

Second, we shall enlarge the class of expressions to include numbers instead of single digits and to include the arithmetic operators $+$, $-$ (both binary and unary), $*$, and $/$. The easiest way to specify this class of expressions is to use the ambiguous grammar

$$E \rightarrow E+E \mid E-E \mid E*E \mid E/E \mid (E) \mid -E \mid \textbf{number}$$

The resulting Yacc specification is shown in Fig. 4.57.

Since the grammar in the Yacc specification in Fig. 4.57 is ambiguous, the LALR algorithm will generate parsing action conflicts. Yacc will report the number of parsing action conflicts that are generated. A description of the sets of items and the parsing action conflicts can be obtained by invoking Yacc with a `-v` option. This option generates an additional file `y.output` that contains the kernels of the sets of items found by the parsing, a description of the parsing action conflicts generated by the LALR algorithm, and a readable representation of the LR parsing table showing how the parsing action conflicts were resolved. Whenever Yacc reports that it has found parsing action conflicts, it is wise to create and consult the file `y.output` to see why the parsing action conflicts were generated and to see whether they were resolved correctly.

```
%{
#include <ctype.h>
#include <stdio.h>
#define YYSTYPE double  /* double type for Yacc stack */
%}

%token NUMBER
%left '+' '-'
%left '*' '/'
%right UMINUS

%%
lines      :  lines expr '\n'   { printf("%g\n", $2); }
           |  lines '\n'
           |  /* ε */
           ;
expr       :  expr '+' expr      { $$ = $1 + $3; }
           |  expr '-' expr      { $$ = $1 - $3; }
           |  expr '*' expr      { $$ = $1 * $3; }
           |  expr '/' expr      { $$ = $1 / $3; }
           |  '(' expr ')'       { $$ = $2; }
           |  '-' expr  %prec UMINUS { $$ = - $2; }
           |  NUMBER
           ;
%%
yylex() {
    int c;
    while ( ( c = getchar() ) == ' ' );
    if ( (c == '.') || (isdigit(c)) ) {
        ungetc(c, stdin);
        scanf("%lf", &yylval);
        return NUMBER;
    }
    return c;
}
```

Fig. 4.57. Yacc specification for a more advanced desk calculator.

Unless otherwise instructed Yacc will resolve all parsing action conflicts using the following two rules:

1. A reduce/reduce conflict is resolved by choosing the conflicting production listed first in the Yacc specification. Thus, in order to make the correct resolution in the typesetting grammar (4.25), it is sufficient to list production (1) ahead of production (3).

2. A shift/reduce conflict is resolved in favor of shift. This rule resolves the shift/reduce conflict arising from the dangling-else ambiguity correctly.

Since these default rules may not always be what the compiler writer wants, Yacc provides a general mechanism for resolving shift/reduce conflicts. In the declarations portion, we can assign precedences and associativities to terminals. The declaration

```
%left '+' '-'
```

makes + and − be of the same precedence and be left associative. We can declare an operator to be right associative by saying

```
%right '^'
```

and we can force an operator to be a nonassociative binary operator (i.e., two occurrences of the operator cannot be combined at all) by saying

```
%nonassoc '<'
```

The tokens are given precedences in the order in which they appear in the declarations part, lowest first. Tokens in the same declaration have the same precedence. Thus, the declaration

```
%right UMINUS
```

in Fig. 4.57 gives the token UMINUS a precedence level higher than that of the five preceding terminals.

Yacc resolves shift/reduce conflicts by attaching a precedence and associativity to each production involved in a conflict, as well as to each terminal involved in a conflict. If it must choose between shifting input symbol a and reducing by production $A \rightarrow \alpha$, Yacc reduces if the precedence of the production is greater than that of a, or if the precedences are the same and the associativity of the production is left. Otherwise, shift is the chosen action.

Normally, the precedence of a production is taken to be the same as that of its rightmost terminal. This is the sensible decision in most cases. For example, given productions

$$E \rightarrow E + E \mid E * E$$

we would prefer to reduce by $E \rightarrow E + E$ with lookahead +, because the + in the right side has the same precedence as the lookahead, but is left associative. With lookahead *, we would prefer to shift, because the lookahead has higher precedence than the + in the production.

In those situations where the rightmost terminal does not supply the proper precedence to a production, we can force a precedence by appending to a production the tag

```
%prec <terminal>
```

The precedence and associativity of the production will then be the same as that of the terminal, which presumably is defined in the declaration section.

Yacc does not report shift/reduce conflicts that are resolved using this precedence and associativity mechanism.

This "terminal" can be a placeholder, like UMINUS in Fig. 4.57; this terminal is not returned by the lexical analyzer, but is declared solely to define a precedence for a production. In Fig. 4.57, the declaration

```
%right UMINUS
```

assigns to the token UMINUS a precedence that is higher than that of * and /. In the translation rules part, the tag

```
%prec UMINUS
```

at the end of the production

```
expr    :    '-' expr
```

makes the unary minus operator in this production have a higher precedence than any other operator.

Creating Yacc Lexical Analyzers with Lex

Lex was designed to produce lexical analyzers that could be used with Yacc. The Lex library ll will provide a driver program named yylex( ), the name required by Yacc for its lexical analyzer. If Lex is used to produce the lexical analyzer, we replace the routine yylex( ) in the third part of the Yacc specification by the statement

```
#include "lex.yy.c"
```

and we have each Lex action return a terminal known to Yacc. By using the #include "lex.yy.c" statement, the program yylex has access to Yacc's names for tokens, since the Lex output file is compiled as part of the Yacc output file y.tab.c.

Under the UNIX system, if the Lex specification is in the file first.l and the Yacc specification in second.y, we can say

```
lex first.l
yacc second.y
cc y.tab.c -ly -ll
```

to obtain the desired translator.

The Lex specification in Fig. 4.58 can be used in place of the lexical analyzer in Fig. 4.57. The last pattern is \n. since . in Lex matches any character but a newline.

Error Recovery in Yacc

In Yacc, error recovery can be performed using a form of error productions. First, the user decides what "major" nonterminals will have error recovery associated with them. Typical choices are some subset of the nonterminals

```
number          [0-9]+\.?¦[0-9]*\.[0-9]+
%%
[ ]             { /* skip blanks */ }
{number}        { sscanf(yytext, "%lf", &yylval);
                  return NUMBER; }
\n¦.            { return yytext[0]; }
```

Fig. 4.58. Lex specification for `yylex()` in Fig. 4.57.

generating expressions, statements, blocks, and procedures. The user then adds to the grammar error productions of the form $A \to$ **error** α, where A is a major nonterminal and α is a string of grammar symbols, perhaps the empty string; **error** is a Yacc reserved word. Yacc will generate a parser from such a specification, treating the error productions as ordinary productions.

However, when the parser generated by Yacc encounters an error, it treats the states whose sets of items contain error productions in a special way. On encountering an error, Yacc pops symbols from its stack until it finds the topmost state on its stack whose underlying set of items includes an item of the form $A \to \cdot$ **error** α. The parser then "shifts" a fictitious token **error** onto the stack, as though it saw the token **error** on its input.

When α is ϵ, a reduction to A occurs immediately and the semantic action associated with the production $A \to$ **error** (which might be a user-specified error-recovery routine) is invoked. The parser then discards input symbols until it finds an input symbol on which normal parsing can proceed.

If α is not empty, Yacc skips ahead on the input looking for a substring that can be reduced to α. If α consists entirely of terminals, then it looks for this string of terminals on the input, and "reduces" them by shifting them onto the stack. At this point, the parser will have **error** α on top of its stack. The parser will then reduce **error** α to A, and resume normal parsing.

For example, an error production of the form

$\qquad stmt \to$ **error** ;·

would specify to the parser that it should skip just beyond the next semicolon on seeing an error, and assume that a statement had been found. The semantic routine for this error production would not need to manipulate the input, but could generate a diagnostic message and set a flag to inhibit generation of object code, for example.

Example 4.52. Figure 4.59 shows the Yacc desk calculator of Fig. 4.57 with the error production

```
lines : error '\n'
```

This error production causes the desk calculator to suspend normal parsing when a syntax error is found on an input line. On encountering the error, the

```
%{
#include <ctype.h>
#include <stdio.h>
#define YYSTYPE double /* double type for Yacc stack */
%}

%token NUMBER
%left '+' '-'
%left '*' '/'
%right UMINUS

%%
lines   :  lines expr '\n'   { printf("%g\n", $2); }
        |  lines '\n'
        |  /* empty */
        |  error '\n'{ yyerror("reenter last line:");
                       yyerrok; }
        ;
expr    :  expr '+' expr     { $$ = $1 + $3; }
        |  expr '-' expr     { $$ = $1 - $3; }
        |  expr '*' expr     { $$ = $1 * $3; }
        |  expr '/' expr     { $$ = $1 / $3; }
        |  '(' expr ')'      { $$ = $2; }
        |  '-' expr  %prec UMINUS { $$ = - $2; }
        |  NUMBER
        ;
%%
#include "lex.yy.c"
```

Fig. 4.59. Desk calculator with error recovery.

parser in the desk calculator starts popping symbols from its stack until it encounters a state that has a shift action on the token **error**. State 0 is such a state (in this example, it's the only such state), since its items include

lines → · **error** '\n'

Also, state 0 is always on the bottom of the stack. The parser shifts the token **error** onto the stack, and then proceeds to skip ahead in the input until it has found a newline character. At this point the parser shifts the newline onto the stack, reduces **error** '\n' to *lines*, and emits the diagnostic message "reenter last line:". The special Yacc routine **yyerrok** resets the parser to its normal mode of operation.   □

EXERCISES

4.1 Consider the grammar

$$S \rightarrow (L) \mid a$$
$$L \rightarrow L , S \mid S$$

a) What are the terminals, nonterminals, and start symbol?
b) Find parse trees for the following sentences:
   i) (a, a)
   ii) $(a, (a, a))$
   iii) $(a, ((a, a), (a, a)))$
c) Construct a leftmost derivation for each of the sentences in (b).
d) Construct a rightmost derivation for each of the sentences in (b).
*e) What language does this grammar generate?

4.2 Consider the grammar

$$S \rightarrow aSbS \mid bSaS \mid \epsilon$$

a) Show that this grammar is ambiguous by constructing two different leftmost derivations for the sentence *abab*.
b) Construct the corresponding rightmost derivations for *abab*.
c) Construct the corresponding parse trees for *abab*.
*d) What language does this grammar generate?

4.3 Consider the grammar

$$bexpr \rightarrow bexpr \textbf{ or } bterm \mid bterm$$
$$bterm \rightarrow bterm \textbf{ and } bfactor \mid bfactor$$
$$bfactor \rightarrow \textbf{not } bfactor \mid (\, bexpr \,) \mid \textbf{true} \mid \textbf{false}$$

a) Construct a parse tree for the sentence **not (true or false)**.
b) Show that this grammar generates all boolean expressions.
*c) Is this grammar ambiguous? Why?

4.4 Consider the grammar

$$R \rightarrow R \,'|' \, R \mid RR \mid R* \mid (R) \mid a \mid b$$

Note that the first vertical bar is the "or" symbol, not a separator between alternatives.
a) Show that this grammar generates all regular expressions over the symbols *a* and *b*.
b) Show that this grammar is ambiguous.
*c) Construct an equivalent unambiguous grammar that gives the operators *, concatenation, and | the precedences and associativities defined in Section 3.3.
d) Construct a parse tree in both grammars for the sentence $a|b*c$.

4.5 The following grammar for **if-then-else** statements is proposed to remedy the dangling-else ambiguity:

$$
\begin{aligned}
stmt \;\rightarrow\; & \textbf{if } expr \textbf{ then } stmt \\
& |\; matched\_stmt \\
matched\_stmt \;\rightarrow\; & \textbf{if } expr \textbf{ then } matched\_stmt \textbf{ else } stmt \\
& |\; \textbf{other}
\end{aligned}
$$

Show that this grammar is still ambiguous.

*4.6 Try to design a grammar for each of the following languages. Which languages are regular?
  a) The set of all strings of 0's and 1's such that every 0 is immediately followed by at least one 1.
  b) Strings of 0's and 1's with an equal number of 0's and 1's.
  c) Strings of 0's and 1's with an unequal number of 0's and 1's.
  d) Strings of 0's and 1's in which 011 does not appear as a substring.
  e) Strings of 0's and 1's of the form xy where $x \neq y$.
  f) Strings of 0's and 1's of the form xx.

4.7 Construct a grammar for the expressions of each of the following languages.
  a) Pascal
  b) C
  c) Fortran 77
  d) Ada
  e) Lisp

4.8 Construct unambiguous grammars for the statements in each of the languages of Exercise 4.7.

4.9 We can use regular-expression-like operators in the right sides of grammar productions. Square brackets can be used to denote an optional part of a production. For example, we might write

$$stmt \;\rightarrow\; \textbf{if } expr \textbf{ then } stmt \,[\, \textbf{else } stmt \,]$$

to denote an optional else-statement. In general, $A \rightarrow \alpha \,[\, \beta \,]\, \gamma$ is equivalent to the two productions $A \rightarrow \alpha\beta\gamma$ and $A \rightarrow \alpha\gamma$.

Curly brackets can be used to denote a phrase that can be repeated zero or more times. For example,

$$stmt \;\rightarrow\; \textbf{begin } stmt \,\{\, ; stmt \,\}\, \textbf{end}$$

denotes a list of semicolon-separated $stmt$'s enclosed between **begin** and **end**. In general, $A \rightarrow \alpha \,\{\, \beta \,\}\, \gamma$ is equivalent to $A \rightarrow \alpha B\gamma$ and $B \rightarrow \beta B \mid \epsilon$.

In a sense, $[\, \beta \,]$ stands for the regular expression $\beta \mid \epsilon$, and $\{\, \beta \,\}$ stands for β^*. We may generalize these notations to allow any

regular expression of grammar symbols on the right side of productions.

a) Modify the above *stmt*-production so that a semicolon-terminated
list of *stmt*'s appears on the right side.

b) Give a set of context-free productions generating the same set of
strings as $A \rightarrow B^*a(C|D)$.

c) Show how to replace any production $A \rightarrow r$, where r is a regular
expression, by a finite collection of context-free productions.

4.10 The following grammar generates declarations for a single identifier:

$$
\begin{aligned}
stmt &\rightarrow \textbf{declare id } option\_list \\
option\_list &\rightarrow option\_list\ option \mid \epsilon \\
option &\rightarrow mode \mid scale \mid precision \mid base \\
mode &\rightarrow \textbf{real} \mid \textbf{complex} \\
scale &\rightarrow \textbf{fixed} \mid \textbf{floating} \\
precision &\rightarrow \textbf{single} \mid \textbf{double} \\
base &\rightarrow \textbf{binary} \mid \textbf{decimal}
\end{aligned}
$$

a) Show how this grammar can be generalized to permit n options A_i,
$1 \le i \le n$, each of which can be either a_i or b_i.

b) The above grammar permits redundant or contradictory declarations such as

```
declare zap real fixed real floating
```

We could insist that the syntax of the language forbid such
declarations. We are thus left with a finite number of token
sequences that are syntactically correct. Obviously these legal
declarations form a context-free language, indeed a regular set.
Write a grammar for declarations with n options, each option
appearing at most once.

**c) Show that a grammar for part (b) must have at least 2^n symbols.

d) What does (c) say about the feasibility of enforcing nonredun-
dancy and noncontradiction among options in declarations via the
syntactic definition of a language?

4.11 a) Eliminate the left-recursion from the grammar in Exercise 4.1.

b) Construct a predictive parser for the grammar in (a). Show the
behavior of the parser on the sentences in Exercise 4.1(b).

4.12 Construct a recursive-descent parser with backtracking for the grammar in Exercise 4.2. Can you construct a predictive parser for this
grammar?

4.13 The grammar

$$S \rightarrow aSa \mid aa$$

generates all even length strings of a's except for the empty string.

   a) Construct a recursive-descent parser with backtracking for this grammar that tries the alternative *aSa* before *aa*. Show that the procedure for *S* succeeds on 2, 4, or 8 *a*'s, but fails on 6 *a*'s.

  *b) What language does your parser recognize?

4.14 Construct a predictive parser for the grammar in Exercise 4.3.

4.15 Construct a predictive parser from the unambiguous grammar for regular expressions in Exercise 4.4.

*4.16 Show that no left-recursive grammar can be LL(1).

*4.17 Show that no LL(1) grammar can be ambiguous.

4.18 Show that a grammar with no ϵ-productions in which each alternative begins with a distinct terminal is always LL(1).

4.19 A grammar symbol *X* is *useless* if there is no derivation of the form $S \overset{*}{\Rightarrow} wXy \overset{*}{\Rightarrow} wxy$. That is, *X* can never appear in the derivation of some sentence.

  *a) Write an algorithm to eliminate all productions containing useless symbols from a grammar.

  b) Apply your algorithm to the grammar

$$S \rightarrow 0 \mid A$$
$$A \rightarrow AB$$
$$B \rightarrow 1$$

4.20 We say a grammar is ϵ-*free* if either it has no ϵ-productions or there is exactly one ϵ-production $S \rightarrow \epsilon$ and then the start symbol *S* does not appear on the right side of any production.

  a) Write an algorithm to convert a given grammar into an equivalent ϵ-free grammar. *Hint.* First determine all nonterminals that can generate the empty string.

  b) Apply your algorithm to the grammar in Exercise 4.2.

4.21 A *single* production is one with a single nonterminal as its right side.

  a) Write an algorithm to convert a grammar into an equivalent grammar with no single productions.

  b) Apply your algorithm to the expression grammar (4.10).

4.22 A *cycle-free* grammar has no derivations of the form $A \overset{+}{\Rightarrow} A$ for any nonterminal *A*.

  a) Write an algorithm to convert a grammar into an equivalent cycle-free grammar.

  b) Apply your algorithm to the grammar $S \rightarrow SS \mid (S) \mid \epsilon$.

4.23 a) Using the grammar in Exercise 4.1 construct a rightmost derivation for $(a, (a, a))$ and show the handle of each right-sentential form.

b) Show the steps of a shift-reduce parser corresponding to the right-most derivation of (a).

c) Show the steps in the bottom-up construction of a parse tree during the shift-reduce parse of (b).

4.24 Figure 4.60 shows operator-precedence relations for the grammar of Exercise 4.1. Using these precedence relations, parse the sentences in Exercise 4.1(b).

	a	(	)	,	$
a			$\cdot>$	$\cdot>$	$\cdot>$
(	$<\cdot$	$<\cdot$	$\doteq$	$<\cdot$	
)			$\cdot>$	$\cdot>$	$\cdot>$
,	$<\cdot$	$<\cdot$	$\cdot>$	$\cdot>$	
$	$<\cdot$	$<\cdot$			

Fig. 4.60. Operator-precedence relations for the grammar of Exercise 4.1.

4.25 Find operator-precedence functions for the table of Fig. 4.60.

4.26 There is a mechanical way to produce operator-precedence relations from an operator grammar, including those with many different nonterminals. Define *leading*(A) for nonterminal A to be the set of terminals a such that a is the leftmost terminal in some string derived from A, and define *trailing*(A) to be the set of terminals that can be the rightmost in a string derived from A. Then for terminals a and b, we say $a \doteq b$ if there is a right side of the form $\alpha a \beta b \gamma$, where β is either empty or a single nonterminal, and α and γ are arbitrary. We say $a <\cdot b$ if there is a right side of the form $\alpha a A \beta$, and b is in *leading*(A); we say $a \cdot> b$ if there is a right side of the form $\alpha A b \beta$, and a is in *trailing*(A). In both cases, α and β are arbitrary strings. Also, $\$ <\cdot b$ whenever b is in *leading*(S), where S is the start symbol, and $a \cdot> \$$ whenever a is in *trailing*(S).

a) For the grammar of Exercise 4.1 compute *leading* and *trailing* for S and T.

b) Verify that the precedence relations of Figure 4.60 are the ones derived from this grammar.

4.27 Generate operator-precedence relations for the following grammars.

a) The grammar of Exercise 4.2.

b) The grammar of Exercise 4.3.

c) The expression grammar (4.10).

4.28 Construct an operator-precedence parser for regular expressions.

4.29 A grammar is said to be a (uniquely invertible) *operator-precedence grammar* if it is an operator grammar with no two right sides that have the same pattern of terminals, and the method of Exercise 4.26 yields at most one precedence relation between any pair of terminals. Which of the grammars of Exercise 4.27 are operator-precedence grammars?

4.30 A grammar is said to be in *Greibach normal form* (GNF) is it is ϵ-free and each production (except $S \to \epsilon$ if it exists) is of the form $A \to a\alpha$, where a is a terminal and α is a string of nonterminals, possibly empty.

  **a) Write an algorithm to convert a grammar into an equivalent Greibach normal form grammar.

  b) Apply your algorithm to the expression grammar (4.10).

*4.31 Show that every grammar can be converted into an equivalent operator grammar. *Hint.* First transform the grammar into Greibach normal form.

*4.32 Show that every grammar can be converted into an operator grammar in which each production is of one of the forms

$$A \to aBcC \quad A \to aBb \quad A \to aB \quad A \to a$$

If ϵ is in the language, then $S \to \epsilon$ is also a production.

4.33 Consider the ambiguous grammar

$$S \to AS \mid b$$
$$A \to SA \mid a$$

  a) Construct the collection of sets of LR(0) items for this grammar.

  b) Construct an NFA in which each state is an LR(0) item from (a). Show that the goto graph of the canonical collection of LR(0) items for this grammar is the same as the DFA constructed from the NFA using the subset construction.

  c) Construct the parsing table using the SLR Algorithm 4.8.

  d) Show all moves allowed by the table from (c) on the input *abab*.

  e) Construct the canonical parsing table.

  f) Construct the parsing table using the LALR Algorithm 4.11.

  g) Construct the parsing table using the LALR Algorithm 4.13.

4.34 Construct an SLR parsing table for the grammar in Exercise 4.3.

4.35 Consider the following grammar

$$E \to E + T \mid T$$
$$T \to T F \mid F$$
$$F \to F^* \mid a \mid b$$

a) Construct the SLR parsing table for this grammar.

b) Construct the LALR parsing table.

4.36 Compact the parsing tables constructed in Exercises 4.33, 4.34, and 4.35, according to the method of Section 4.7.

4.37 a) Show that the following grammar

$$S \rightarrow AaAb \mid BbBa$$
$$A \rightarrow \epsilon$$
$$B \rightarrow \epsilon$$

is LL(1) but not SLR(1).

  **b) Show that every LL(1) grammar is an LR(1) grammar.

*4.38** Show that no LR(1) grammar can be ambiguous.

4.39 Show that the following grammar

$$S \rightarrow Aa \mid bAc \mid dc \mid bda$$
$$A \rightarrow d$$

is LALR(1) but not SLR(1).

4.40 Show that the following grammar

$$S \rightarrow Aa \mid bAc \mid Bc \mid bBa$$
$$A \rightarrow d$$
$$B \rightarrow d$$

is LR(1) but not LALR(1).

*4.41** Consider the family of grammars G_n defined by:

$$S \rightarrow A_i b_i \qquad 1 \le i \le n$$
$$A_i \rightarrow a_j A_i \mid a_j \qquad 1 \le i, j \le n \text{ and } j \ne i$$

a) Show that G_n has $2n^2 - n$ productions and $2^n + n^2 + n$ sets of LR(0) items. What does this result say about how big an LR parser can get compared to the size of the grammar?

b) Is G_n SLR(1)?

c) Is G_n LALR(1)?

4.42 Write an algorithm to compute for each nonterminal A in a grammar the set of nonterminals B such that $A \stackrel{*}{\Rightarrow} B\alpha$ for some string of grammar symbols α.

4.43 Write an algorithm to compute for each nonterminal A in a grammar the set of terminals a such that $A \stackrel{*}{\Rightarrow} aw$ for some string of terminals w, where the last step of the derivation does not use an ϵ-production.

4.44 Construct an SLR parsing table for the grammar of Exercise 4.4. Resolve the parsing action conflicts in such a way that regular expressions will be parsed normally.

4.45 Construct an SLR parser for the dangling-else grammar (4.7), treating *expr* as a terminal. Resolve the parsing action conflict in the usual way.

4.46 a) Construct an SLR parsing table for the grammar

$$E \rightarrow E \text{ sub } R \mid E \text{ sup } E \mid \{ E \} \mid c$$
$$R \rightarrow E \text{ sup } E \mid E$$

Resolve the parsing action conflict so that expressions will be parsed in the same way as by the LR parser in Fig. 4.52.

b) Can every reduce/reduce conflict generated in the LR parsing table construction process be converted into a shift/reduce conflict by transforming the grammar?

*4.47 Construct an equivalent LR grammar for the typesetting grammar (4.25) that factors out expressions of the form $E \text{ sub } E \text{ sup } E$ as a special case.

*4.48 Consider the following ambiguous grammar for n binary infix operators:

$$E \rightarrow E \theta_1 E \mid E \theta_2 E \mid \cdots \mid E \theta_n E \mid (E) \mid \mathbf{id}$$

Assume that all operators are left-associative and that θ_i takes precedence over θ_j if $i > j$.

a) Construct the SLR sets of items for this grammar. How many sets of items are there, as a function of n?

b) Construct the SLR parsing table for this grammar and compact it using the list representation in Section 4.7. What is the total length of all the lists used in the representation, as a function of n?

c) How many steps does it take to parse $\mathbf{id} \; \theta_i \; \mathbf{id} \; \theta_j \; \mathbf{id}$?

*4.49 Repeat Exercise 4.48 for the unambiguous grammar

$$
\begin{aligned}
E_1 \quad &\rightarrow \quad E_1 \, \theta_1 \, E_2 \mid E_2 \\
E_2 \quad &\rightarrow \quad E_2 \, \theta_2 \, E_3 \mid E_3 \\
&\quad \cdots \\
E_n \quad &\rightarrow \quad E_n \, \theta_n \, E_{n+1} \mid E_{n+1} \\
E_{n+1} \quad &\rightarrow \quad (E_1) \mid \mathbf{id}
\end{aligned}
$$

What do your answers to Exercises 4.48 and 4.49 say about the relative efficiency of parsers for equivalent ambiguous and unambiguous grammars? What about the relative efficiency of constructing the parser?

4.50 Write a Yacc program that will take arithmetic expressions as input and produce the corresponding postfix expression as output.

4.51 Write a Yacc "desk calculator" program that will evaluate boolean expressions.

4.52 Write a Yacc program that will take a regular expression as input and produce its parse tree as output.

4.53 Trace out the moves that would be made by the predictive, operator-precedence, and LR parsers of Examples 4.20, 4.32, and 4.50 on the following erroneous inputs:
a) (**id** + (* **id**)
b) * + **id**) + (**id** *

*4.54 Construct error-correcting operator-precedence and LR parsers for the following grammar:

$$
\begin{aligned}
stmt \;\rightarrow\; & \textbf{if } e \textbf{ then } stmt \\
\mid\; & \textbf{if } e \textbf{ then } stmt \textbf{ else } stmt \\
\mid\; & \textbf{while } e \textbf{ do } stmt \\
\mid\; & \textbf{begin } list \textbf{ end} \\
\mid\; & s \\
list \;\rightarrow\; & list \; ; \; stmt \\
\mid\; & stmt
\end{aligned}
$$

*4.55 The grammar in Exercise 4.54 can be made LL by replacing the productions for *list* by

$$
\begin{aligned}
list \;\rightarrow\; & stmt \; list' \\
list' \;\rightarrow\; & ; \; stmt \mid \epsilon
\end{aligned}
$$

Construct an error-correcting predictive parser for the revised grammar.

4.56 Show the behavior of your parsers of Exercises 4.54 and 4.55 on the erroneous inputs
a) **if** *e* **then** *s* ; **if** *e* **then** *s* **end**
b) **while** *e* **do begin** *s* ; **if** *e* **then** *s* ; **end**

4.57 Write predictive, operator-precedence, and LR parsers with panic-mode error recovery for the grammars of Exercises 4.54 and 4.55, using semicolon and **end** as synchronizing tokens. Show the behavior of your parsers on the erroneous inputs of Exercise 4.56.

4.58 In Section 4.6, we proposed a graph-oriented method for determining the set of strings that could be popped from the stack in a reduce move of an operator-precedence parser.
   *a) Give an algorithm for finding a regular expression denoting all such strings.
   b) Give an algorithm to determine whether the set of such strings is finite or infinite, listing them if finite.

c) Apply your algorithms from (a) and (b) to the grammar of Exercise 4.54.

**4.59 We made the claim for the error-correcting parsers of Figs. 4.18, 4.28, and 4.53 that any error correction eventually resulted in at least one more symbol being removed from the input or the stack being shortened if the end of the input has been reached. The corrections chosen, however, did not all cause an input symbol to be consumed immediately. Can you prove that no infinite loops are possible for the parsers of Figs. 4.18, 4.28, and 4.53? *Hint.* It helps to observe that for the operator-precedence parser, consecutive terminals on the stack are related by $\le\!\cdot$, even if there have been errors. For the LR parser, the stack will still contain a viable prefix, even in the presence of errors.

**4.60 Give an algorithm for detecting unreachable entries in predictive, operator-precedence, and LR parsing tables.

4.61 The LR parser of Fig. 4.53 handles the four situations in which the top state is 4 or 5 (which occur when + and * are on top of the stack, respectively) and the next input is + or * in exactly the same way: by calling the routine e1, which inserts an **id** between them. We could easily envision an LR parser for expressions involving the full set of arithmetic operators behaving in the same fashion: insert **id** between the adjacent operators. In certain languages (such as PL/1 or C but not Fortran or Pascal), it would be wise to treat, in a special way, the case in which / is on top of the stack and * is the next input. Why? What would be a reasonable course of action for the error corrector to take?

4.62 A grammar is said to be in *Chomsky normal form* (CNF) if it is ϵ-free and each non-ϵ-production is of the form $A \to BC$ or of the form $A \to a$.
   *a) Give an algorithm to convert a grammar into an equivalent Chomsky normal form grammar.
   b) Apply your algorithm to the expression grammar (4.10).

4.63 Given a grammar G in Chomsky normal form and an input string $w = a_1 a_2 \cdots a_n$, write an algorithm to determine whether w is in $L(G)$. *Hint.* Using dynamic programming fill in an $n \times n$ table T in which $T[i, j] = \{A \mid A \overset{*}{\Rightarrow} a_i a_{i+1} \cdots a_j\}$. The input string w is in $L(G)$ if and only if S is in $T[1, n]$.

*4.64 a) Given a Chomsky normal form grammar G, show how to add productions for single insertion, deletion, and mutation errors to the grammar so that the enlarged grammar generates all possible token strings.

b) Modify the parsing algorithm in Exercise 4.63 so that, given any string w, it will find a parse for w that uses the fewest number of error productions.

4.65 Write a Yacc parser for arithmetic expressions that uses the error-recovery mechanism in Example 4.50.

BIBLIOGRAPHIC NOTES

The highly influential Algol 60 report (Naur [1963]) used Backus-Naur Form (BNF) to define the syntax of a major programming language. The equivalence of BNF and context-free grammars was quickly noted, and the theory of formal languages received a great deal of attention in the 1960's. Hopcroft and Ullman [1979] cover the basics of the field.

Parsing methods became much more systematic after the development of context-free grammars. Several general techniques for parsing any context-free grammar were invented. One of the earliest is the dynamic programming technique suggested in Exercise 4.63, which was independently discovered by J. Cocke, Younger [1967], and Kasami [1965]. As his Ph. D. thesis, Earley [1970] also developed a universal parsing algorithm for all context-free grammars. Aho and Ullman [1972b and 1973a] discuss these and other parsing methods in detail.

Many different parsing methods have been employed in compilers. Sheridan [1959] describes the parsing method used in the original Fortran compiler that introduced additional parentheses around operands in order to be able to parse expressions. The idea of operator precedence and the use of precedence functions is from Floyd [1963]. In the 1960's, a large number of bottom-up parsing strategies were proposed. These include simple precedence (Wirth and Weber [1966]), bounded-context (Floyd [1964], Graham [1964]), mixed-strategy precedence (McKeeman, Horning, and Wortman [1970]), and weak precedence (Ichbiah and Morse [1970]).

Recursive-descent and predictive parsing are widely used in practice. Because of its flexibility, recursive-descent parsing was used in many early compiler-writing systems such as META (Schorre [1964]) and TMG (McClure [1965]). A solution to Exercise 4.13 can be found in Birman and Ullman [1973], along with some of the theory of this parsing method. Pratt [1973] proposes a top-down operator-precedence parsing method.

LL grammars were studied by Lewis and Stearns [1968] and their properties were developed in Rosenkrantz and Stearns [1970]. Predictive parsers were studied extensively by Knuth [1971a]. Lewis, Rosenkrantz, and Stearns [1976] describe the use of predictive parsers in compilers. Algorithms for transforming grammars into LL(1) form are presented in Foster [1968], Wood [1969], Stearns [1971], and Soisalon-Soininen and Ukkonen [1979].

LR grammars and parsers were first introduced by Knuth [1965] who described the construction of canonical LR parsing tables. The LR method was not deemed practical until Korenjak [1969] showed that with it reasonable-sized parsers could be produced for programming language grammars. When DeRemer [1969, 1971] devised the SLR and LALR methods, which are simpler than Korenjak's, the LR technique became the method of choice for automatic parser generators. Today, LR parser generators are common in compiler-construction environments.

A great deal of research went into the engineering of LR parsers. The use of ambiguous grammars in LR parsing is due to Aho, Johnson, and Ullman [1975] and Earley [1975a]. The elimination of reductions by single productions has been discussed in Anderson, Eve, and Horning [1973], Aho and Ullman [1973b], Demers [1975], Backhouse [1976], Joliat [1976], Pager [1977b], Soisalon-Soininen [1980], and Tokuda [1981].

Techniques for computing LALR(1) lookahead sets have been proposed by LaLonde [1971], Anderson, Eve, and Horning [1973], Pager [1977a], Kristensen and Madsen [1981], DeRemer and Pennello [1982], and Park, Choe, and Chang [1985] who also provide some experimental comparisons.

Aho and Johnson [1974] give a general survey of LR parsing and discuss some of the algorithms underlying the Yacc parser generator, including the use of error productions for error recovery. Aho and Ullman [1972b and 1973a] give an extensive treatment of LR parsing and its theoretical underpinnings.

Many error-recovery techniques for parsers have been proposed. Error-recovery techniques are surveyed by Ciesinger [1979] and by Sippu [1981]. Irons [1963] proposed a grammar-based approach to syntactic error recovery. Error productions were employed by Wirth [1968] for handling errors in a PL360 compiler. Leinius [1970] proposed the strategy of phrase-level recovery. Aho and Peterson [1972] show how global least-cost error recovery can be achieved using error productions in conjunction with general parsing algorithms for context-free grammars. Mauney and Fischer [1982] extend these ideas to local least-cost repair for LL and LR parsers using the parsing technique of Graham, Harrison, and Ruzzo [1980]. Graham and Rhodes [1975] discuss error recovery in the context of precedence parsing.

Horning [1976] discusses qualities good error messages should have. Sippu and Soisalon-Soininen [1983] compare the performance of the error-recovery technique in the Helsinki Language Processor (Räihä et al. [1983]) with the "forward move" recovery technique of Pennello and DeRemer [1978], the LR error-recovery technique of Graham, Haley, and Joy [1979], and the "global context" recovery technique of Pai and Kieburtz [1980].

Error correction during parsing is discussed by Conway and Maxwell [1963], Moulton and Muller [1967], Conway and Wilcox [1973], Levy 1975], Tai [1978], and Röhrich [1980]. Aho and Peterson [1972] contains a solution to Exercise 4.63.

CHAPTER 5

Syntax-Directed
Translation

This chapter develops the theme of Section 2.3, the translation of languages guided by context-free grammars. We associate information with a programming language construct by attaching attributes to the grammar symbols representing the construct. Values for attributes are computed by "semantic rules" associated with the grammar productions.

There are two notations for associating semantic rules with productions, syntax-directed definitions and translation schemes. Syntax-directed definitions are high-level specifications for translations. They hide many implementation details and free the user from having to specify explicitly the order in which translation takes place. Translation schemes indicate the order in which semantic rules are to be evaluated, so they allow some implementation details to be shown. We use both notations in Chapter 6 for specifying semantic checking, particularly the determination of types, and in Chapter 8 for generating intermediate code.

Conceptually, with both syntax-directed definitions and translation schemes, we parse the input token stream, build the parse tree, and then traverse the tree as needed to evaluate the semantic rules at the parse-tree nodes (see Fig. 5.1). Evaluation of the semantic rules may generate code, save information in a symbol table, issue error messages, or perform any other activities. The translation of the token stream is the result obtained by evaluating the semantic rules.

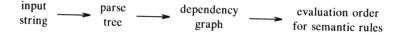

Fig. 5.1. Conceptual view of syntax-directed translation.

An implementation does not have to follow the outline in Fig. 5.1 literally. Special cases of syntax-directed definitions can be implemented in a single pass by evaluating semantic rules during parsing, without explicitly constructing a parse tree or a graph showing dependencies between attributes. Since single-pass implementation is important for compile-time efficiency, much of this chapter is devoted to studying such special cases. One important subclass, called the "L-attributed" definitions, encompasses virtually all translations that can be performed without explicit construction of a parse tree.

5.1 SYNTAX-DIRECTED DEFINITIONS

A syntax-directed definition is a generalization of a context-free grammar in which each grammar symbol has an associated set of attributes, partitioned into two subsets called the synthesized and inherited attributes of that grammar symbol. If we think of a node for the grammar symbol in a parse tree as a record with fields for holding information, then an attribute corresponds to the name of a field.

An attribute can represent anything we choose: a string, a number, a type, a memory location, or whatever. The value of an attribute at a parse-tree node is defined by a semantic rule associated with the production used at that node. The value of a synthesized attribute at a node is computed from the values of attributes at the children of that node in the parse tree; the value of an inherited attribute is computed from the values of attributes at the siblings and parent of that node.

Semantic rules set up dependencies between attributes that will be represented by a graph. From the dependency graph, we derive an evaluation order for the semantic rules. Evaluation of the semantic rules defines the values of the attributes at the nodes in the parse tree for the input string. A semantic rule may also have side effects, e.g., printing a value or updating a global variable. Of course, an implementation need not explicitly construct a parse tree or a dependency graph; it just has to produce the same output for each input string.

A parse tree showing the values of attributes at each node is called an annotated parse tree. The process of computing the attribute values at the nodes is called *annotating* or *decorating* the parse tree.

Form of a Syntax-Directed Definition

In a syntax-directed definition, each grammar production $A \rightarrow \alpha$ has associated with it a set of semantic rules of the form $b := f(c_1, c_2, \ldots, c_k)$ where f is a function, and either

1. b is a synthesized attribute of A and $c_1, c_2, \ldots, c_k$ are attributes belonging to the grammar symbols of the production, or

2. b is an inherited attribute of one of the grammar symbols on the right side of the production, and $c_1, c_2, \ldots, c_k$ are attributes belonging to the grammar symbols of the production.

In either case, we say that attribute b *depends* on attributes $c_1, c_2, \ldots, c_k$. An *attribute grammar* is a syntax-directed definition in which the functions in semantic rules cannot have side effects.

Functions in semantic rules will often be written as expressions. Occasionally, the only purpose of a semantic rule in a syntax-directed definition is to create a side effect. Such semantic rules are written as procedure calls or program fragments. They can be thought of as rules defining the values of dummy synthesized attributes of the nonterminal on the left side of the associated production; the dummy attribute and the := sign in the semantic rule are not shown.

Example 5.1. The syntax-directed definition in Fig. 5.2 is for a desk-calculator program. This definition associates an integer-valued synthesized attribute called *val* with each of the nonterminals E, T, and F. For each E, T, and F-production, the semantic rule computes the value of attribute *val* for the nonterminal on the left side from the values of *val* for the nonterminals on the right side.

PRODUCTION	SEMANTIC RULES
$L \rightarrow E$ **n**	$print(E.val)$
$E \rightarrow E_1 + T$	$E.val := E_1.val + T.val$
$E \rightarrow T$	$E.val := T.val$
$T \rightarrow T_1 * F$	$T.val := T_1.val \times F.val$
$T \rightarrow F$	$T.val := F.val$
$F \rightarrow (E)$	$F.val := E.val$
$F \rightarrow$ **digit**	$F.val :=$ **digit**.$lexval$

Fig. 5.2. Syntax-directed definition of a simple desk calculator.

The token **digit** has a synthesized attribute *lexval* whose value is assumed to be supplied by the lexical analyzer. The rule associated with the production $L \rightarrow E$ **n** for the starting nonterminal L is just a procedure that prints as output the value of the arithmetic expression generated by E; we can think of this rule as defining a dummy attribute for the nonterminal L. A Yacc specification for this desk calculator was presented in Fig. 4.56 to illustrate translation during LR parsing.   □

In a syntax-directed definition, terminals are assumed to have synthesized attributes only, as the definition does not provide any semantic rules for terminals. Values for attributes of terminals are usually supplied by the lexical analyzer, as discussed in Section 3.1. Furthermore, the start symbol is assumed not to have any inherited attributes, unless otherwise stated.

Synthesized Attributes

Synthesized attributes are used extensively in practice. A syntax-directed definition that uses synthesized attributes exclusively is said to be an *S-attributed definition*. A parse tree for an S-attributed definition can always be annotated by evaluating the semantic rules for the attributes at each node bottom up, from the leaves to the root. Section 5.3 describes how an LR-parser generator can be adapted to mechanically implement an S-attributed definition based on an LR grammar.

Example 5.2. The S-attributed definition in Example 5.1 specifies a desk calculator that reads an input line containing an arithmetic expression involving digits, parentheses, the operators + and *, followed by a newline character **n**, and prints the value of the expression. For example, given the expression 3*5+4 followed by a newline, the program prints the value 19. Figure 5.3 contains an annotated parse tree for the input **3*5+4n**. The output, printed at the root of the tree, is the value of $E.val$ at the first child of the root.

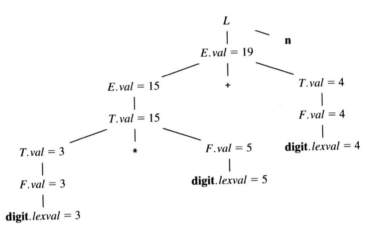

Fig. 5.3. Annotated parse tree for **3*5+4 n**.

To see how attribute values are computed, consider the leftmost bottommost interior node, which corresponds to the use of the production $F \rightarrow$ **digit**. The corresponding semantic rule, $F.val := $ **digit**.$lexval$, defines the attribute $F.val$ at that node to have the value 3 because the value of **digit**.$lexval$ at the child of this node is 3. Similarly, at the parent of this F-node, the attribute $T.val$ has the value 3.

Now consider the node for the production $T \rightarrow T * F$. The value of the attribute $T.val$ at this node is defined by

PRODUCTION	SEMANTIC RULE
$T \rightarrow T_1 * F$	$T.val := T_1.val \times F.val$

When we apply the semantic rule at this node, $T_1.val$ has the value 3 from the left child and $F.val$ the value 5 from the right child. Thus, $T.val$ acquires the value 15 at this node.

The rule associated with the production for the starting nonterminal $L \rightarrow E$ **n** prints the value of the expression generated by E. □

Inherited Attributes

An inherited attribute is one whose value at a node in a parse tree is defined in terms of attributes at the parent and/or siblings of that node. Inherited attributes are convenient for expressing the dependence of a programming language construct on the context in which it appears. For example, we can use an inherited attribute to keep track of whether an identifier appears on the left or right side of an assignment in order to decide whether the address or the value of the identifier is needed. Although it is always possible to rewrite a syntax-directed definition to use only synthesized attributes, it is often more natural to use syntax-directed definitions with inherited attributes.

In the following example, an inherited attribute distributes type information to the various identifiers in a declaration.

Example 5.3. A declaration generated by the nonterminal D in the syntax-directed definition in Fig. 5.4 consists of the keyword **int** or **real**, followed by a list of identifiers. The nonterminal T has a synthesized attribute *type*, whose value is determined by the keyword in the declaration. The semantic rule $L.in := T.type$, associated with production $D \rightarrow TL$, sets inherited attribute $L.in$ to the type in the declaration. The rules then pass this type down the parse tree using the inherited attribute $L.in$. Rules associated with the productions for L call procedure *addtype* to add the type of each identifier to its entry in the symbol table (pointed to by attribute *entry*).

PRODUCTION	SEMANTIC RULES
$D \rightarrow T L$	$L.in := T.type$
$T \rightarrow$ **int**	$T.type := integer$
$T \rightarrow$ **real**	$T.type := real$
$L \rightarrow L_1$, **id**	$L_1.in := L.in$ $addtype(\mathbf{id}.entry, L.in)$
$L \rightarrow$ **id**	$addtype(\mathbf{id}.entry, L.in)$

Fig. 5.4. Syntax-directed definition with inherited attribute $L.in$.

Figure 5.5 shows an annotated parse tree for the sentence **real id$_1$, id$_2$, id$_3$**. The value of $L.in$ at the three L-nodes gives the type of the identifiers **id$_1$**, **id$_2$**, and **id$_3$**. These values are determined by computing the value of the attribute $T.type$ at the left child of the root and then evaluating $L.in$ top-down at the three L-nodes in the right subtree of the root. At each L-node we also call the procedure *addtype* to insert into the symbol table the fact that the identifier at the right child of this node has type real.   □

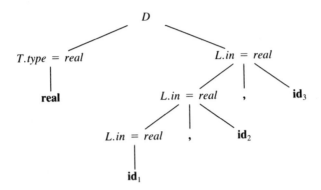

Fig. 5.5. Parse tree with inherited attribute *in* at each node labeled *L*.

Dependency Graphs

If an attribute b at a node in a parse tree depends on an attribute c, then the semantic rule for b at that node must be evaluated after the semantic rule that defines c. The interdependencies among the inherited and synthesized attributes at the nodes in a parse tree can be depicted by a directed graph called a *dependency graph*.

Before constructing a dependency graph for a parse tree, we put each semantic rule into the form $b := f(c_1, c_2, \ldots, c_k)$, by introducing a dummy synthesized attribute b for each semantic rule that consists of a procedure call. The graph has a node for each attribute and an edge to the node for b from the node for c if attribute b depends on attribute c. In more detail, the dependency graph for a given parse tree is constructed as follows.

> **for** each node n in the parse tree **do**
>> **for** each attribute a of the grammar symbol at n **do**
>>> construct a node in the dependency graph for a;
>
> **for** each node n in the parse tree **do**
>> **for** each semantic rule $b := f(c_1, c_2, \ldots, c_k)$
>>> associated with the production used at n **do**
>> **for** $i := 1$ **to** k **do**
>>> construct an edge from the node for c_i to the node for b;

For example, suppose $A.a := f(X.x, Y.y)$ is a semantic rule for the production $A \rightarrow XY$. This rule defines a synthesized attribute $A.a$ that depends on the attributes $X.x$ and $Y.y$. If this production is used in the parse tree, then there will be three nodes $A.a$, $X.x$, and $Y.y$ in the dependency graph with an edge to $A.a$ from $X.x$ since $A.a$ depends on $X.x$, and an edge to $A.a$ from $Y.y$ since $A.a$ also depends on $Y.y$.

If the production $A \rightarrow XY$ has the semantic rule $X.i := g(A.a, Y.y)$ associated with it, then there will be an edge to $X.i$ from $A.a$ and also an edge to $X.i$ from $Y.y$, since $X.i$ depends on both $A.a$ and $Y.y$.

Example 5.4. Whenever the following production is used in a parse tree, we add the edges shown in Fig. 5.6 to the dependency graph.

PRODUCTION	SEMANTIC RULE
$E \rightarrow E_1 + E_2$	$E.val := E_1.val + E_2.val$

The three nodes of the dependency graph marked by • represent the synthesized attributes $E.val$, $E_1.val$, and $E_2.val$ at the corresponding nodes in the parse tree. The edge to $E.val$ from $E_1.val$ shows that $E.val$ depends on $E_1.val$ and the edge to $E.val$ from $E_2.val$ shows that $E.val$ also depends on $E_2.val$. The dotted lines represent the parse tree and are not part of the dependency graph.   □

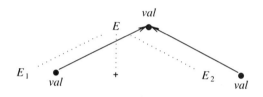

Fig. 5.6. *E.val* is synthesized from $E_1.val$ and $E_2.val$.

Example 5.5. Figure 5.7 shows the dependency graph for the parse tree in Fig. 5.5. Nodes in the dependency graphs are marked by numbers; these numbers will be used below. There is an edge to node 5 for $L.in$ from node 4 for $T.type$ because the inherited attribute $L.in$ depends on the attribute $T.type$ according to the semantic rule $L.in := T.type$ for the production $D \rightarrow TL$. The two downward edges into nodes 7 and 9 arise because $L_1.in$ depends on $L.in$ according to the semantic rule $L_1.in := L.in$ for the production $L \rightarrow L_1$, **id**. Each of the semantic rules *addtype* (**id**.*entry*, $L.in$) associated with the L-productions leads to the creation of a dummy attribute. Nodes 6, 8, and 10 are constructed for these dummy attributes.   □

Evaluation Order

A *topological sort* of a directed acyclic graph is any ordering $m_1, m_2, \ldots, m_k$ of the nodes of the graph such that edges go from nodes earlier in the ordering to later nodes; that is, if $m_i \rightarrow m_j$ is an edge from m_i to m_j, then m_i appears before m_j in the ordering.

Any topological sort of a dependency graph gives a valid order in which the semantic rules associated with the nodes in a parse tree can be evaluated. That is, in the topological sort, the dependent attributes $c_1, c_2, \ldots, c_k$ in a semantic rule $b := f(c_1, c_2, \ldots, c_k)$ are available at a node before f is evaluated.

The translation specified by a syntax-directed definition can be made precise

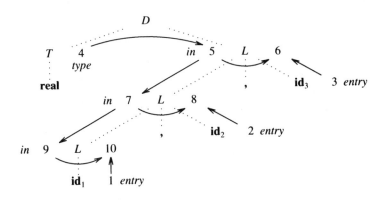

Fig. 5.7. Dependency graph for parse tree of Fig. 5.5.

as follows. The underlying grammar is used to construct a parse tree for the input. The dependency graph is constructed as discussed above. From a topological sort of the dependency graph, we obtain an evaluation order for the semantic rules. Evaluation of the semantic rules in this order yields the translation of the input string.

Example 5.6. Each of the edges in the dependency graph in Fig. 5.7 goes from a lower-numbered node to a higher-numbered node. Hence, a topological sort of the dependency graph is obtained by writing down the nodes in the order of their numbers. From this topological sort, we obtain the following program. We write a_n for the attribute associated with the node numbered n in the dependency graph.

$$a_4 := real;$$
$$a_5 := a_4;$$
$$addtype(\textbf{id}_3.entry, a_5);$$
$$a_7 := a_5;$$
$$addtype(\textbf{id}_2.entry, a_7);$$
$$a_9 := a_7;$$
$$addtype(\textbf{id}_1.entry, a_9);$$

Evaluating these semantic rules stores the type *real* in the symbol-table entry for each identifier.   □

Several methods have been proposed for evaluating semantic rules:

1.   *Parse-tree methods.* At compile time, these methods obtain an evaluation order from a topological sort of the dependency graph constructed from the parse tree for each input. These methods will fail to find an evaluation order only if the dependency graph for the particular parse tree under consideration has a cycle.

2. *Rule-based methods*. At compiler-construction time, the semantic rules associated with productions are analyzed, either by hand, or by a specialized tool. For each production, the order in which the attributes associated with that production are evaluated is predetermined at compiler-construction time.

3. *Oblivious methods*. An evaluation order is chosen without considering the semantic rules. For example, if translation takes place during parsing, then the order of evaluation is forced by the parsing method, independent of the semantic rules. An oblivious evaluation order restricts the class of syntax-directed definitions that can be implemented.

Rule-based and oblivious methods need not explicitly construct the dependency graph at compile time, so they can be more efficient in their use of compile time and space.

A syntax-directed definition is said to be *circular* if the dependency graph for some parse tree generated by its grammar has a cycle. Section 5.10 discusses how to test a syntax-directed definition for circularity.

5.2 CONSTRUCTION OF SYNTAX TREES

In this section, we show how syntax-directed definitions can be used to specify the construction of syntax trees and other graphical representations of language constructs.

The use of syntax trees as an intermediate representation allows translation to be decoupled from parsing. Translation routines that are invoked during parsing must live with two kinds of restrictions. First, a grammar that is suitable for parsing may not reflect the natural hierarchical structure of the constructs in the language. For example, a grammar for Fortran may view a subroutine as consisting simply of a list of statements. However, analysis of the subroutine may be easier if we use a tree representation that reflects the nesting of DO loops. Second, the parsing method constrains the order in which nodes in a parse tree are considered. This order may not match the order in which information about a construct becomes available. For this reason, compilers for C usually construct syntax trees for declarations.

Syntax Trees

An (abstract) syntax tree is a condensed form of parse tree useful for representing language constructs. The production $S \rightarrow$ **if** B **then** S_1 **else** S_2 might appear in a syntax tree as

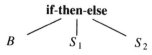

In a syntax tree, operators and keywords do not appear as leaves, but rather are associated with the interior node that would be the parent of those leaves

in the parse tree. Another simplification found in syntax trees is that chains
of single productions may be collapsed; the parse tree of Fig. 5.3 becomes the
syntax tree

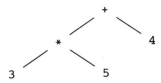

Syntax-directed translation can be based on syntax trees as well as parse
trees. The approach is the same in each case; we attach attributes to the
nodes as in a parse tree.

Constructing Syntax Trees for Expressions

The construction of a syntax tree for an expression is similar to the translation
of the expression into postfix form. We construct subtrees for the subexpressions by creating a node for each operator and operand. The children of an
operator node are the roots of the nodes representing the subexpressions constituting the operands of that operator.

Each node in a syntax tree can be implemented as a record with several
fields. In the node for an operator, one field identifies the operator and the
remaining fields contain pointers to the nodes for the operands. The operator
is often called the *label* of the node. When used for translation, the nodes in
a syntax tree may have additional fields to hold the values (or pointers to
values) of attributes attached to the node. In this section, we use the following functions to create the nodes of syntax trees for expressions with binary
operators. Each function returns a pointer to a newly created node.

1. *mknode*(*op, left, right*) creates an operator node with label *op* and two
    fields containing pointers to *left* and *right*.

2. *mkleaf* (**id**, *entry*) creates an identifier node with label **id** and a field con-
    taining *entry*, a pointer to the symbol-table entry for the identifier.

3. *mkleaf* (**num**, *val*) creates a number node with label **num** and a field con-
    taining *val*, the value of the number.

Example 5.7. The following sequence of functions calls creates the syntax
tree for the expression a – 4 + c in Fig. 5.8. In this sequence,
$p_1, p_2, \ldots, p_5$ are pointers to nodes, and *entrya* and *entryc* are pointers to
the symbol-table entries for identifiers a and c, respectively.

(1) p_1 := *mkleaf* (**id**, *entrya*);   (4) p_4 := *mkleaf* (**id**, *entryc*);
(2) p_2 := *mkleaf* (**num**, 4);   (5) p_5 := *mknode* ('+', p_3, p_4);
(3) p_3 := *mknode* ('–', p_1, p_2);

The tree is constructed bottom up. The function calls *mkleaf* (**id**, *entrya*)
and *mkleaf* (**num**, 4) construct the leaves for a and 4; the pointers to these

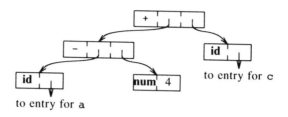

Fig. 5.8. Syntax tree for `a-4+c`.

nodes are saved using p_1 and p_2. The call *mknode* $('-',p_1,p_2)$ then constructs the interior node with the leaves for a and 4 as children. After two more steps, p_5 is left pointing to the root.   □

A Syntax-Directed Definition for Constructing Syntax Trees

Figure 5.9 contains an S-attributed definition for constructing a syntax tree for an expression containing the operators + and −. It uses the underlying productions of the grammar to schedule the calls of the functions *mknode* and *mkleaf* to construct the tree. The synthesized attribute *nptr* for E and T keeps track of the pointers returned by the function calls.

PRODUCTION	SEMANTIC RULES
$E \rightarrow E_1 + T$	$E.nptr := mknode('+', E_1.nptr, T.nptr)$
$E \rightarrow E_1 - T$	$E.nptr := mknode('-', E_1.nptr, T.nptr)$
$E \rightarrow T$	$E.nptr := T.nptr$
$T \rightarrow (E)$	$T.nptr := E.nptr$
$T \rightarrow$ **id**	$T.nptr := mkleaf(\textbf{id}, \textbf{id}.entry)$
$T \rightarrow$ **num**	$T.nptr := mkleaf(\textbf{num}, \textbf{num}.val)$

Fig. 5.9. Syntax-directed definition for constructing a syntax tree for an expression.

Example 5.8. An annotated parse tree depicting the construction of a syntax tree for the expression `a-4+c` is shown in Fig. 5.10. The parse tree is shown dotted. The parse-tree nodes labeled by the nonterminals E and T use the synthesized attribute *nptr* to hold a pointer to the syntax-tree node for the expression represented by the nonterminal.

The semantic rules associated with the productions $T \rightarrow$ **id** and $T \rightarrow$ **num** define attribute *T.nptr* to be a pointer to a new leaf for an identifier and a number, respectively. Attributes **id**.*entry* and **num**.*val* are the lexical values assumed to be returned by the lexical analyzer with the tokens **id** and **num**.

In Fig. 5.10, when an expression E is a single term, corresponding to a use

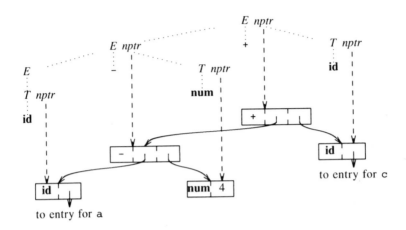

Fig. 5.10. Construction of a syntax-tree for a–4+c.

of the production $E \rightarrow T$, the attribute $E.nptr$ gets the value of $T.nptr$. When the semantic rule $E.nptr := mknode(\,'-', E_1.nptr, T.nptr)$ associated with the production $E \rightarrow E_1 - T$ is invoked, previous rules have set $E_1.nptr$ and $T.nptr$ to be pointers to the leaves for a and 4, respectively.

In interpreting Fig. 5.10, it is important to realize that the lower tree, formed from records is a "real" syntax tree that constitutes the output, while the dotted tree above is the parse tree, which may exist only in a figurative sense. In the next section, we show how an S-attributed definition can be simply implemented using the stack of a bottom-up parser to keep track of attribute values. In fact, with this implementation, the node-building functions are invoked in the same order as in Example 5.7.   □

Directed Acyclic Graphs for Expressions

A directed acyclic graph (hereafter called a *dag*) for an expression identifies the common subexpressions in the expression. Like a syntax tree, a dag has a node for every subexpression of the expression; an interior node represents an operator and its children represent its operands. The difference is that a node in a dag representing a common subexpression has more than one "parent;" in a syntax tree, the common subexpression would be represented as a duplicated subtree.

Figure 5.11 contains a dag for the expression

        a + a * (b - c) + (b - c) * d

The leaf for a has two parents because a is common to the two subexpressions a and a * (b–c). Likewise, both occurrences of the common subexpression b–c are represented by the same node, which also has two parents.

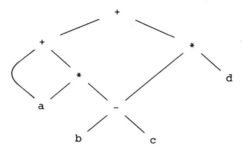

Fig. 5.11. Dag for the expression `a+a*(b-c)+(b-c)*d`.

The syntax-directed definition of Fig. 5.9 will construct a dag instead of a syntax tree if we modify the operations for constructing nodes. A dag is obtained if the function constructing a node first checks to see whether an identical node already exists. For example, before constructing a new node with label *op* and fields with pointers to *left* and *right*, *mknode* (*op, left, right*) can check whether such a node has already been constructed. If so, *mknode* (*op, left, right*) can return a pointer to the previously constructed node. The leaf-constructing functions *mkleaf* can behave similarly.

Example 5.9. The sequence of instructions in Fig. 5.12 constructs the dag in Fig. 5.11, provided *mknode* and *mkleaf* create new nodes only when necessary, returning pointers to existing nodes with the correct label and children whenever possible. In Fig. 5.12, *a, b, c,* and *d* point to the symbol-table entries for identifiers a, b, c, and d.

(1)	$p_1 := mkleaf(\textbf{id}, a);$		(8)	$p_8 := mkleaf(\textbf{id}, b);$
(2)	$p_2 := mkleaf(\textbf{id}, a);$		(9)	$p_9 := mkleaf(\textbf{id}, c);$
(3)	$p_3 := mkleaf(\textbf{id}, b);$		(10)	$p_{10} := mknode('-', p_8, p_9);$
(4)	$p_4 := mkleaf(\textbf{id}, c);$		(11)	$p_{11} := mkleaf(\textbf{id}, d);$
(5)	$p_5 := mknode('-', p_3, p_4);$		(12)	$p_{12} := mknode('*', p_{10}, p_{11});$
(6)	$p_6 := mknode('*', p_2, p_5);$		(13)	$p_{13} := mknode('+', p_7, p_{12});$
(7)	$p_7 := mknode('+', p_1, p_6);$			

Fig. 5.12. Instructions for constructing the dag of Fig. 5.11.

When the call *mkleaf* (**id**, *a*) is repeated on line 2, the node constructed by the previous call *mkleaf* (**id**, *a*) is returned, so $p_1 = p_2$. Similarly, the nodes returned on lines 8 and 9 are the same as those returned on lines 3 and 4, respectively. Hence, the node returned on line 10 must be the same one constructed by the call of *mknode* on line 5.   □

In many applications, nodes are implemented as records stored in an array, as in Fig. 5.13. In the figure, each record has a label field that determines the nature of the node. We can refer to a node by its index or position in the array. The integer index of a node is often called a *value number* for historical reasons. For example, using value numbers, we can say node 3 has label +, its left child is node 1, and its right child is node 2. The following algorithm can be used to create nodes for a dag representation of an expression.

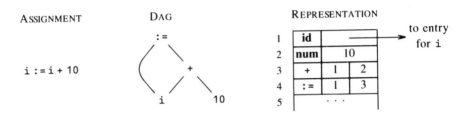

Fig. 5.13. Nodes in a dag for i := i + 10 allocated from an array.

Algorithm 5.1. Value-number method for constructing a node in a dag.

Suppose that nodes are stored in an array, as in Fig. 5.13, and that each node is referred to by its value number. Let the *signature* of an operator node be a triple $<op, l, r>$ consisting of its label *op*, left child *l*, and right child *r*.

Input. Label *op*, node *l*, and node *r*.

Output. A node with signature $<op, l, r>$.

Method. Search the array for a node *m* with label *op*, left child *l*, and right child *r*. If there is such a node, return *m*; otherwise, create a new node *n* with label *op*, left child *l*, right child *r*, and return *n*.

An obvious way to determine if node *m* is already in the array is to keep all previously created nodes on a list and to check each node on the list to see if it has the desired signature. The search for *m* can be made more efficient by using *k* lists, called buckets, and using a hashing function *h* to determine which bucket to search.[1]

The hash function *h* computes the number of a bucket from the value of *op*, *l*, and *r*. It will always return the same bucket number, given the same arguments. If *m* is not in the bucket $h(op, l, r)$, then a new node *n* is created and added to this bucket, so subsequent searches will find it there. Several signatures may hash into the same bucket number, but in practice we expect each bucket to contain a small number of nodes.

Each bucket can be implemented as a linked list as shown in Fig. 5.14.

---

[1] Any data structure that implements dictionaries in the sense of Aho, Hopcroft, and Ullman [1983] suffices. The important property of the structure is that given a key, i.e., a label *op* and two nodes *l* and *r*, we can rapidly obtain a node *m* with signature $<op, l, r>$, or determine that none exists.

Each cell in a linked list represents a node. The bucket headers, consisting of pointers to the first cell in a list, are stored in an array. The bucket number returned by $h(op, l, r)$ is an index into this array of bucket headers.

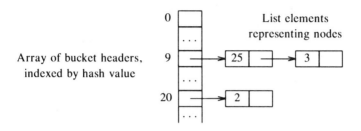

Fig. 5.14. Data structure for searching buckets.

This algorithm can be adapted to apply to nodes that are not allocated sequentially from an array. In many compilers, nodes are allocated as they are needed, to avoid preallocating an array that may hold too many nodes most of the time and not enough nodes some of the time. In this case, we cannot assume that nodes are in sequential storage, so we have to use pointers to refer to nodes. If the hash function can be made to compute the bucket number from a label and pointers to children, then we can use pointers to nodes instead of value numbers. Otherwise, we can number the nodes in any way and use this number as the value number of the node.   □

Dags can also be used to represent sets of expressions, since a dag can have more than one root. In Chapters 9 and 10, the computations performed by a sequence of assignment statements will be represented as a dag.

5.3 BOTTOM-UP EVALUATION OF S-ATTRIBUTED DEFINITIONS

Now that we have seen how to use syntax-directed definitions to specify translations, we can begin to study how to implement translators for them. A translator for an arbitrary syntax-directed definition can be difficult to build. However, there are large classes of useful syntax-directed definitions for which it is easy to construct translators. In this section, we examine one such class: the S-attributed definitions, that is, the syntax-directed definitions with only synthesized attributes. The following sections consider the implementation of definitions that have inherited attributes as well.

Synthesized attributes can be evaluated by a bottom-up parser as the input is being parsed. The parser can keep the values of the synthesized attributes associated with the grammar symbols on its stack. Whenever a reduction is made, the values of the new synthesized attributes are computed from the attributes appearing on the stack for the grammar symbols on the right side of the reducing production. This section shows how the parser stack can be extended to hold the values of these synthesized attributes. We shall see in

Section 5.6 that this implementation also supports some inherited attributes.

Only synthesized attributes appear in the syntax-directed definition in Fig. 5.9 for constructing the syntax tree for an expression. The approach of this section can therefore be applied to construct syntax trees during bottom-up parsing. As we shall see in Section 5.5, the translation of expressions during top-down parsing often uses inherited attributes. We therefore defer translation during top-down parsing until after "left-to-right" dependencies are examined in the next section.

Synthesized Attributes on the Parser Stack

A translator for an S-attributed definition can often be implemented with the help of an LR-parser generator, such as the one discussed in Section 4.9. From an S-attributed definition, the parser generator can construct a translator that evaluates attributes as it parses the input.

A bottom-up parser uses a stack to hold information about subtrees that have been parsed. We can use extra fields in the parser stack to hold the values of synthesized attributes. Figure 5.15 shows an example of a parser stack with space for one attribute value. Let us suppose, as in the figure, that the stack is implemented by a pair of arrays *state* and *val*. Each *state* entry is a pointer (or index) to an LR(1) parsing table. (Note that the grammar symbol is implicit in the state and need not be stored in the stack.) It is convenient, however, to refer to the state by the unique grammar symbol that it covers when placed on the parsing stack as described in Section 4.7. If the *i*th *state* symbol is A, then $val[i]$ will hold the value of the attribute associated with the parse tree node corresponding to this A.

	state	val
	$\cdots$	$\cdots$
	X	$X.x$
	Y	$Y.y$
$top \rightarrow$	Z	$Z.z$
	$\cdots$	$\cdots$

Fig. 5.15. Parser stack with a field for synthesized attributes.

The current top of the stack is indicated by the pointer *top*. We assume that synthesized attributes are evaluated just before each reduction. Suppose the semantic rule $A.a := f(X.x, Y.y, Z.z)$ is associated with the production $A \rightarrow XYZ$. Before XYZ is reduced to A, the value of the attribute $Z.z$ is in $val[top]$, that of $Y.y$ in $val[top-1]$, and that of $X.x$ in $val[top-2]$. If a symbol has no attribute, then the corresponding entry in the *val* array is undefined. After the reduction, *top* is decremented by 2, the state covering A is put in *state* [*top*] (i.e., where X was), and the value of the synthesized attribute $A.a$ is put in *val* [*top*].

Example 5.10. Consider again the syntax-directed definition of the desk calculator in Fig. 5.2. The synthesized attributes in the annotated parse tree of Fig. 5.3 can be evaluated by an LR parser during a bottom-up parse of the input line **3∗5+4n**. As before, we assume that the lexical analyzer supplies the value of attribute **digit**.*lexval*, which is the numeric value of each token representing a digit. When the parser shifts a **digit** onto the stack, the token **digit** is placed in *state* [*top*] and its attribute value is placed in *val* [*top*].

We can use the techniques of Section 4.7 to construct an LR parser for the underlying grammar. To evaluate attributes, we modify the parser to execute the code fragments shown in Fig. 5.16 just before making the appropriate reduction. Note that we can associate attribute evaluation with reductions, because each reduction determines the production to be applied. The code fragments have been obtained from the semantic rules in Fig. 5.2 by replacing each attribute by a position in the *val* array.

PRODUCTION	CODE FRAGMENT
$L \rightarrow E$ **n**	*print* (*val* [*top*])
$E \rightarrow E_1 + T$	*val* [*ntop*] := *val* [*top* −2] + *val* [*top*]
$E \rightarrow T$	
$T \rightarrow T_1 * F$	*val* [*ntop*] := *val* [*top* −2] × *val* [*top*]
$T \rightarrow F$	
$F \rightarrow (E)$	*val* [*ntop*] := *val* [*top* −1]
$F \rightarrow$ **digit**	

Fig. 5.16. Implementation of a desk calculator with an LR parser.

The code fragments do not show how the variables *top* and *ntop* are managed. When a production with r symbols on the right side is reduced, the value of *ntop* is set to *top* −r +1. After each code fragment is executed, *top* is set to *ntop*.

Figure 5.17 shows the sequence of moves made by the parser on input **3∗5+4 n**. The contents of the *state* and *val* fields of the parsing stack are shown after each move. We again take the liberty of replacing stack states by their corresponding grammar symbols. We take the further liberty of showing, instead of token **digit**, the actual input digit.

Consider the sequence of events on seeing the input symbol 3. In the first move, the parser shifts the state corresponding to the token **digit** (whose attribute value is 3) onto the stack. (The state is represented by 3 and the value 3 is in the *val* field.) On the second move, the parser reduces by the production $F \rightarrow$ **digit** and implements the semantic rule $F.val$:= **digit**.*lexval*. On the third move the parser reduces by $T \rightarrow F$. No code fragment is associated with

INPUT	state			val			PRODUCTION USED		
3*5+4 **n**	–			–					
*5+4 **n**	3			3					
*5+4 **n**	F			3			F	→	**digit**
*5+4 **n**	T			3			T	→	F
5+4 **n**	T	*		3	_				
+4 **n**	T	*	5	3	_	5			
+4 **n**	T	*	F	3	_	5	F	→	**digit**
+4 **n**	T			15			T	→	T * F
+4 **n**	E			15			E	→	T
4 **n**	E	+		15	_				
n	E	+	4	15	_	4			
n	E	+	F	15	_	4	F	→	**digit**
n	E	+	T	15	_	4	T	→	F
n	E			19			E	→	E + T
	E	**n**		19	_				
	L			19			L	→	E **n**

Fig. 5.17.   Moves made by translator on input 3*5+4 **n**.

this production, so the *val* array is left unchanged. Note that after each reduction the top of the *val* stack contains the attribute value associated with the left side of the reducing production.   □

In the implementation sketched above, code fragments are executed just before a reduction takes place. Reductions provide a "hook" on which actions consisting of arbitrary code fragments can be hung. That is, we can allow the user to associate an action with a production that is executed when a reduction according to that production takes place. Translation schemes considered in the next section provide a notation for interleaving actions with parsing. In Section 5.6, we shall see how a larger class of syntax-directed definitions can be implemented during bottom-up parsing.

5.4 L-ATTRIBUTED DEFINITIONS

When translation takes place during parsing, the order of evaluation of attributes is linked to the order in which nodes of a parse tree are "created" by the parsing method. A natural order that characterizes many top-down and bottom-up translation methods is the one obtained by applying the procedure *dfvisit* in Fig. 5.18 to the root of a parse tree. We call this evaluation order the *depth-first order*. Even if the parse tree is not actually constructed, it is useful to study translation during parsing by considering depth-first evaluation of attributes at the nodes of a parse tree.

procedure *dfvisit* (*n* : node);
begin
      for each child *m* of *n*, from left to right **do begin**
          evaluate inherited attributes of *m*;
          dfvisit (*m*)
      end;
      evaluate synthesized attributes of *n*
end

Fig. 5.18. Depth-first evaluation order for attributes in a parse tree.

We now introduce a class of syntax-directed definitions, called L-attributed definitions, whose attributes can always be evaluated in depth-first order. (The L is for "left," because attribute information appears to flow from left to right.) Implementation of progressively larger classes of L-attributed definitions is covered in the next three sections of this chapter. L-attributed definitions include all syntax-directed definitions based on LL(1) grammars; Section 5.5 gives a method for implementing such definitions in a single pass using predictive parsing methods. A larger class of L-attributed definitions is implemented in Section 5.6 during bottom-up parsing, by extending the translation methods of Section 5.3. A general method for implementing all L-attributed definitions is outlined in Section 5.7.

L-Attributed Definitions

A syntax-directed definition is *L-attributed* if each inherited attribute of X_j, $1 \leq j \leq n$, on the right side of $A \rightarrow X_1 X_2 \cdots X_n$, depends only on

1. the attributes of the symbols $X_1, X_2, \ldots, X_{j-1}$ to the left of X_j in the production and

2. the inherited attributes of A.

Note that every S-attributed definition is L-attributed, because the restrictions (1) and (2) apply only to inherited attributes.

Example 5.11. The syntax-directed definition in Fig. 5.19 is not L-attributed because the inherited attribute $Q.i$ of the grammar symbol Q depends on the attribute $R.s$ of the grammar symbol to its right. Other examples of definitions that are not L-attributed can be found in Sections 5.8 and 5.9. □

Translation Schemes

A translation scheme is a context-free grammar in which attributes are associated with the grammar symbols and semantic actions enclosed between braces {} are inserted within the right sides of productions, as in Section 2.3. We

PRODUCTION	SEMANTIC RULES
$A \rightarrow L\ M$	$L.i := l(A.i)$ $M.i := m(L.s)$ $A.s := f(M.s)$
$A \rightarrow Q\ R$	$R.i := r(A.i)$ $Q.i := q(R.s)$ $A.s := f(Q.s)$

Fig. 5.19. A non-L-attributed syntax-directed definition.

shall use translation schemes in this chapter as a useful notation for specifying translation during parsing.

The translation schemes considered in this chapter can have both synthesized and inherited attributes. In the simple translation schemes considered in Chapter 2, the attributes were of string type, one for each symbol, and for every production $A \rightarrow X_1 \cdots X_n$, the semantic rule formed the string for A by concatenating the strings for $X_1, \ldots, X_n$, in order, with some optional additional strings in between. We saw that we could perform the translation by simply printing the literal strings in the order they appeared in the semantic rules.

Example 5.12. Here is a simple translation scheme that maps infix expressions with addition and subtraction into corresponding postfix expressions. It is a slight reworking of the translation scheme (2.14) from Chapter 2.

$$
\begin{aligned}
E &\rightarrow T\ R \\
R &\rightarrow \textbf{addop}\ T\ \{print(\textbf{addop}.lexeme)\}\ R_1 \mid \epsilon \\
T &\rightarrow \textbf{num}\ \{print(\textbf{num}.val)\}
\end{aligned}
\qquad (5.1)
$$

Figure 5.20 shows the parse tree for the input 9−5+2 with each semantic action attached as the appropriate child of the node corresponding to the left side of their production. In effect, we treat actions as though they are terminal symbols, a viewpoint that is a convenient mnemonic for establishing when the actions are to be executed. We have taken the liberty of showing the actual numbers and additive operator in place of the tokens **num** and **addop**. When performed in depth-first order, the actions in Fig. 5.20 print the output 95−2+.   □

When designing a translation scheme, we must observe some restrictions to ensure that an attribute value is available when an action refers to it. These restrictions, motivated by L-attributed definitions, ensure that an action does not refer to an attribute that has not yet been computed.

The easiest case occurs when only synthesized attributes are needed. For this case, we can construct the translation scheme by creating an action

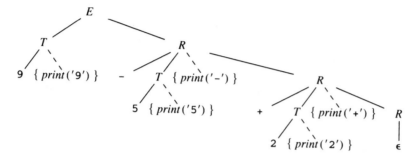

Fig. 5.20. Parse tree for 9-5+2 showing actions.

consisting of an assignment for each semantic rule, and placing this action at the end of the right side of the associated production. For example, the production and semantic rule

$$\text{PRODUCTION} \qquad \text{SEMANTIC RULE}$$
$$T \rightarrow T_1 * F \qquad T.val := T_1.val \times F.val$$

yield the following production and semantic action

$$T \rightarrow T_1 * F \ \{ T.val := T_1.val \times F.val \}$$

If we have both inherited and synthesized attributes, we must be more careful:

1. An inherited attribute for a symbol on the right side of a production must be computed in an action before that symbol.

2. An action must not refer to a synthesized attribute of a symbol to the right of the action.

3. A synthesized attribute for the nonterminal on the left can only be computed after all attributes it references have been computed. The action computing such attributes can usually be placed at the end of the right side of the production.

In the next two sections, we show how a translation scheme satisfying these three requirements can be implemented by generalizations of top-down and bottom-up parsers.

The following translation scheme does not satisfy the first of these three requirements.

$$S \rightarrow A_1 \ A_2 \quad \{ A_1.in := 1; A_2.in := 2 \}$$
$$A \rightarrow a \qquad \{ print(A.in) \}$$

We find that the inherited attribute $A.in$ in the second production is not defined when an attempt is made to print its value during a depth-first traversal of the parse tree for the input string aa. That is, a depth-first traversal starts at S and visits the subtrees for A_1 and A_2 before the values of $A_1.in$ and $A_2.in$ are set. If the action defining the values of $A_1.in$ and $A_2.in$ is embedded before the A's on the right side of $S \rightarrow A_1 A_2$, instead of after, then $A.in$ will be defined each time $print(A.in)$ occurs.

It is always possible to start with an L-attributed syntax-directed definition and construct a translation scheme that satisfies the three requirements above. The next example illustrates this construction. It is based on the mathematics-formatting language EQN, described briefly in Section 1.2. Given the input

    E sub 1 .val

EQN places E, 1, and *.val* in the relative positions and sizes shown in Fig. 5.21. Notice that the subscript 1 is printed in a smaller size and font, and is moved down relative to E and *.val*.

$$\boxed{E}\boxed{{}_1}\boxed{.val}$$

Fig. 5.21. Syntax-directed placement of boxes.

Example 5.13. From the L-attributed definition in Fig. 5.22 we shall construct the translation scheme in Fig. 5.23. In the figures, the nonterminal B (for box) represents a formula. The production $B \rightarrow B B$ represents the juxtaposition of two boxes, and $B \rightarrow B$ **sub** B represents the placement of the second subscript box in a smaller size than the first box in the proper relative position for a subscript.

The inherited attribute *ps* (for point size) affects the height of a formula. The rule for production $B \rightarrow$ **text** causes the normalized height of the text to be multiplied by the point size to get the actual height of the text. The attribute h of **text** is obtained by table lookup, given the character represented by the token **text**. When production $B \rightarrow B_1 B_2$ is applied, B_1 and B_2 inherit the point size from B by copy rules. The height of B, represented by the synthesized attribute ht, is the maximum of the heights of B_1 and B_2.

When production $B \rightarrow B_1$ **sub** B_2 is used, the function *shrink* lowers the point size of B_2 by 30%. The function *disp* allows for the downward displacement of the box B_2 as it computes the height of B. The rules that generate the actual typesetter commands as output are not shown.

The definition in Fig. 5.22 is L-attributed. The only inherited attribute is *ps* of the nonterminal B. Each semantic rule defines *ps* only in terms of the inherited attribute of the nonterminal on the left of the production. Hence, the definition is L-attributed.

The translation scheme in Fig. 5.23 is obtained by inserting assignments corresponding to the semantic rules in Fig. 5.22 into the productions,

PRODUCTION	SEMANTIC RULES
$S \rightarrow B$	$B.ps := 10$ $S.ht := B.ht$
$B \rightarrow B_1 \, B_2$	$B_1.ps := B.ps$ $B_2.ps := B.ps$ $B.ht := max(B_1.ht, \, B_2.ht)$
$B \rightarrow B_1 \, \mathbf{sub} \, B_2$	$B_1.ps := B.ps$ $B_2.ps := shrink(B.ps)$ $B.ht := disp(B_1.ht, \, B_2.ht)$
$B \rightarrow \mathbf{text}$	$B.ht := \mathbf{text}.h \times B.ps$

Fig. 5.22. Syntax-directed definition for size and height of boxes.

$$
\begin{aligned}
S \rightarrow \quad & \{ B.ps := 10 \} \\
B \quad & \{ S.ht := B.ht \}
\end{aligned}
$$

$$
\begin{aligned}
B \rightarrow \quad & \{ B_1.ps := B.ps \} \\
B_1 \quad & \{ B_2.ps := B.ps \} \\
B_2 \quad & \{ B.ht := max(B_1.ht, \, B_2.ht) \}
\end{aligned}
$$

$$
\begin{aligned}
B \rightarrow \quad & \{ B_1.ps := B.ps \} \\
B_1 \quad & \\
\mathbf{sub} \quad & \{ B_2.ps := shrink(B.ps) \} \\
B_2 \quad & \{ B.ht := disp(B_1.ht, \, B_2.ht) \}
\end{aligned}
$$

$$
B \rightarrow \mathbf{text} \quad \{ B.ht := \mathbf{text}.h \times B.ps \}
$$

Fig. 5.23. Translation scheme constructed from Fig. 5.22.

following the three requirements given above. For readability, each grammar symbol in a production is written on a separate line and actions are shown to the right. Thus,

$$
S \rightarrow \{ B.ps := 10 \} \, B \, \{ S.ht := B.ht \}
$$

is written as

$$
\begin{aligned}
S \rightarrow \quad & \{ B.ps := 10 \} \\
B \quad & \{ S.ht := B.ht \}
\end{aligned}
$$

Note that actions setting inherited attributes $B_1.ps$ and $B_2.ps$ appear just before B_1 and B_2 on the right sides of productions.   □

5.5 TOP-DOWN TRANSLATION

In this section, L-attributed definitions will be implemented during predictive parsing. We work with translation schemes rather than syntax-directed definitions so we can be explicit about the order in which actions and attribute evaluations take place. We also extend the algorithm for left-recursion elimination to translation schemes with synthesized attributes.

Eliminating Left Recursion from a Translation Scheme

Since most arithmetic operators associate to the left, it is natural to use left-recursive grammars for expressions. We now extend the algorithm for eliminating left recursion in Sections 2.4 and 4.3 to allow for attributes when the underlying grammar of a translation scheme is transformed. The transformation applies to translation schemes with synthesized attributes. It allows many of the syntax-directed definitions of Sections 5.1 and 5.2 to be implemented using predictive parsing. The next example motivates the transformation.

Example 5.14. The translation scheme in Fig. 5.24 is transformed below into the translation scheme in Fig. 5.25. The new scheme produces the annotated parse tree of Fig. 5.26 for the expression 9−5+2. The arrows in the figure suggest a way of determining the value of the expression.

$$
\begin{aligned}
E &\rightarrow E_1 + T & \{ E.val := E_1.val + T.val \} \\
E &\rightarrow E_1 - T & \{ E.val := E_1.val - T.val \} \\
E &\rightarrow T & \{ E.val := T.val \} \\
T &\rightarrow (E) & \{ T.val := E.val \} \\
T &\rightarrow \mathbf{num} & \{ T.val := \mathbf{num}.val \}
\end{aligned}
$$

Fig. 5.24. Translation scheme with left-recursive grammar.

In Fig. 5.26, the individual numbers are generated by T, and $T.val$ takes its value from the lexical value of the number, given by attribute $\mathbf{num}.val$. The 9 in the subexpression 9−5 is generated by the leftmost T, but the minus operator and 5 are generated by the R at the right child of the root. The inherited attribute $R.i$ obtains the value 9 from $T.val$. The subtraction 9−5 and the passing of the result 4 down to the middle node for R are done by embedding the following action between T and R_1 in $R \rightarrow -T R_1$:

$$\{ R_1.i := R.i - T.val \}$$

A similar action adds 2 to the value of 9−5, yielding the result $R.i = 6$ at the bottom node for R. The result is needed at the root as the value of $E.val$; the synthesized attribute s for R, not shown in Fig. 5.26, is used to copy the result up to the root.   □

For top-down parsing, we can assume that an action is executed at the time that a symbol in the same position would be expanded. Thus, in the second

$$E \rightarrow T \qquad \{ \quad R.i := T.val \}$$
$$\qquad R \qquad \{ E.val := R.s \}$$

$$R \rightarrow +$$
$$\qquad T \qquad \{ \quad R_1.i := R.i + T.val \}$$
$$\qquad R_1 \qquad \{ \quad R.s := R_1.s \}$$

$$R \rightarrow -$$
$$\qquad T \qquad \{ \quad R_1.i := R.i - T.val \}$$
$$\qquad R_1 \qquad \{ \quad R.s := R_1.s \}$$

$$R \rightarrow \epsilon \qquad \{ \quad R.s := R.i \}$$

$$T \rightarrow ($$
$$\qquad E$$
$$\qquad) \qquad \{ T.val := E.val \}$$

$$T \rightarrow \textbf{num} \quad \{ T.val := \textbf{num}.val \}$$

Fig. 5.25. Transformed translation scheme with right-recursive grammar.

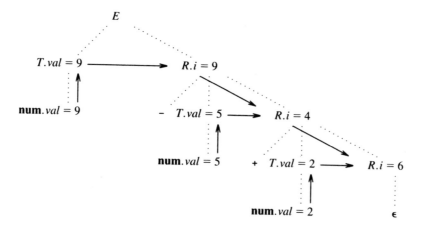

Fig. 5.26. Evaluation of the expression 9–5+2.

production in Fig. 5.25, the first action (assignment to $R_1.i$) is done after T has been fully expanded to terminals, and the second action is done after R_1 has been fully expanded. As noted in the discussion of L-attributed definitions in Section 5.4, an inherited attribute of a symbol must be computed by an action appearing before the symbol and a synthesized attribute of the nonterminal on the left must be computed after all the attributes it depends on have been computed.

In order to adapt other left-recursive translation schemes for predictive parsing, we shall express the use of attributes $R.i$ and $R.s$ in Fig. 5.25 more abstractly. Suppose we have the following translation scheme

$$A \rightarrow A_1 Y \quad \{ A.a := g(A_1.a, Y.y) \}$$
$$A \rightarrow X \qquad \{ A.a := f(X.x) \} \tag{5.2}$$

Each grammar symbol has a synthesized attribute written using the corresponding lower case letter, and f and g are arbitrary functions. The generalization to additional A-productions and to productions with strings in place of symbols X and Y can be done as in Example 5.15, below.

The algorithm for eliminating left recursion in Section 2.4 constructs the following grammar from (5.2):

$$A \rightarrow X R$$
$$R \rightarrow Y R \mid \epsilon \tag{5.3}$$

Taking the semantic actions into account, the transformed scheme becomes

$$A \rightarrow X \quad \{ R.i := f(X.x) \}$$
$$R \quad \{ A.a := R.s \}$$
$$R \rightarrow Y \quad \{ R_1.i := g(R.i, Y.y) \} \tag{5.4}$$
$$R_1 \quad \{ R.s := R_1.s \}$$
$$R \rightarrow \epsilon \quad \{ R.s := R.i \}$$

The transformed scheme uses attributes i and s for R, as in Fig. 5.25. To see why the results of (5.2) and (5.4) are the same, consider the two annotated parse trees in Fig. 5.27. The value of $A.a$ is computed according to (5.2) in Fig. 5.27(a). Figure 5.27(b) contains the computation of $R.i$ down the tree according to (5.4). The value of $R.i$ at the bottom is passed up unchanged as $R.s$, and it becomes the correct value of $A.a$ at the root ($R.s$ is not shown in Fig. 5.27(b)).

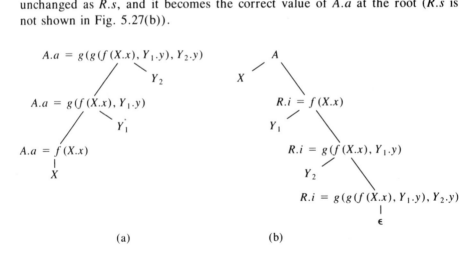

Fig. 5.27. Two ways of computing an attribute value.

Example 5.15. If the syntax-directed definition in Fig. 5.9 for constructing syntax trees is converted into a translation scheme, then the productions and semantic actions for E become:

$$E \to E_1 + T \quad \{ \ E.nptr := mknode('+', E_1.nptr, T.nptr) \ \}$$
$$E \to E_1 - T \quad \{ \ E.nptr := mknode('-', E_1.nptr, T.nptr) \ \}$$
$$E \to T \qquad\quad \{ \ E.nptr := T.nptr \ \}$$

When left recursion is eliminated from this translation scheme, nonterminal E corresponds to A in (5.2) and the strings $+T$ and $-T$ in the first two productions correspond to Y; nonterminal T in the third production corresponds to X. The transformed translation scheme is shown in Fig. 5.28. The productions and semantic actions for T are similar to those in the original definition in Fig. 5.9.

$$
\begin{aligned}
E \to \ &T \qquad \{ \quad R.i := T.nptr \ \} \\
       &R \qquad \{ \ E.nptr := R.s \ \} \\[6pt]
R \to \ &+ \\
       &T \qquad \{ \quad R_1.i := mknode('+', R.i, T.nptr) \ \} \\
       &R_1 \quad\ \ \{ \quad R.s := R_1.s \ \} \\[6pt]
R \to \ &- \\
       &T \qquad \{ \quad R_1.i := mknode('-', R.i, T.nptr) \ \} \\
       &R_1 \quad\ \ \{ \quad R.s := R_1.s \ \} \\[6pt]
R \to \ &\epsilon \qquad\ \{ \quad R.s := R.i \ \} \\[6pt]
T \to \ &(\\
       &E \\
       &) \qquad\ \{ \ T.nptr := E.nptr \ \} \\[6pt]
T \to \ &\mathbf{id} \quad\ \ \{ \ T.nptr := mkleaf(\mathbf{id}, \mathbf{id}.entry) \ \} \\[6pt]
T \to \ &\mathbf{num} \ \{ \ T.nptr := mkleaf(\mathbf{num}, \mathbf{num}.val) \ \}
\end{aligned}
$$

Fig. 5.28. Transformed translation scheme for constructing syntax trees.

Figure 5.29 shows how the actions in Fig. 5.28 construct a syntax tree for a−4+c. Synthesized attributes are shown to the right of the node for a grammar symbol, and inherited attributes are shown to the left. A leaf in the syntax tree is constructed by actions associated with the productions $T \to \mathbf{id}$ and $T \to \mathbf{num}$, as in Example 5.8. At the leftmost T, attribute $T.nptr$ points to the leaf for a. A pointer to the node for a is inherited as attribute $R.i$ on the right side of $E \to TR$.

When the production $R \to -TR_1$ is applied at the right child of the root, $R.i$ points to the node for a, and $T.nptr$ to the node for 4. The node for a−4 is constructed by applying $mknode$ to the minus operator and these pointers.

Finally, when production $R \to \epsilon$ is applied, $R.i$ points to the root of the entire syntax tree. The entire tree is returned through the s attributes of the nodes for R (not shown in Fig. 5.29) until it becomes the value of $E.nptr$. ☐

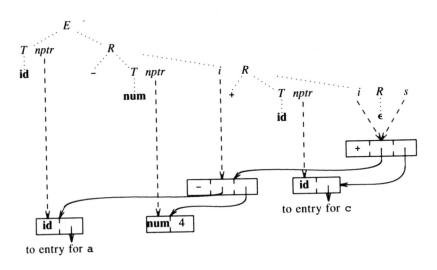

Fig. 5.29. Use of inherited attributes to construct syntax trees.

Design of a Predictive Translator

The next algorithm generalizes the construction of predictive parsers to implement a translation scheme based on a grammar suitable for top-down parsing.

Algorithm 5.2. Construction of a predictive syntax-directed translator.

Input. A syntax-directed translation scheme with an underlying grammar suitable for predictive parsing.

Output. Code for a syntax-directed translator.

Method. The technique is a modification of the predictive-parser construction in Section 2.4.

1. For each nonterminal A, construct a function that has a formal parameter for each inherited attribute of A and that returns the values of the synthesized attributes of A (possibly as a record, as a pointer to a record with a field for each attribute, or using the call-by-reference mechanism for passing parameters, discussed in Section 7.5). For simplicity, we assume that each nonterminal has just one synthesized attribute. The function for A has a local variable for each attribute of each grammar symbol that appears in a production for A.

2. As in Section 2.4, the code for nonterminal A decides what production to use based on the current input symbol.

3. The code associated with each production does the following. We consider the tokens, nonterminals, and actions on the right side of the production from left to right.

i)   For token X with synthesized attribute x, save the value of x in the variable declared for $X.x$. Then generate a call to match token X and advance the input.

ii) For nonterminal B, generate an assignment $c := B(b_1, b_2, \ldots, b_k)$ with a function call on the right side, where $b_1, b_2, \ldots, b_k$ are the variables for the inherited attributes of B and c is the variable for the synthesized attribute of B.

iii) For an action, copy the code into the parser, replacing each reference to an attribute by the variable for that attribute.   □

Algorithm 5.2 is extended in Section 5.7 to implement any L-attributed definition, provided a parse tree has already been constructed. In Section 5.8, we consider ways of improving the translators constructed by Algorithm 5.2. For example, it may be possible to eliminate copy statements of the form $x := y$ or to use a single variable to hold the values of several attributes. Some such improvements can also be done automatically using the methods of Chapter 10.

Example 5.16. The grammar in Fig. 5.28 is LL(1), and hence suitable for top-down parsing. From the attributes of the nonterminals in the grammar, we obtain the following types for the arguments and results of the functions for E, R, and T. Since E and T do not have inherited attributes, they have no arguments.

> **function** E : ↑ syntax_tree_node;
> **function** $R(i$: ↑ syntax_tree_node): ↑ syntax_tree_node;
> **function** T : ↑ syntax_tree_node;

We combine two of the R-productions in Fig. 5.28 to make the translator smaller. The new productions use token **addop** to represent + and −:

$$
\begin{array}{lll}
R \rightarrow \textbf{addop} & & \\
\quad T & \{\ R_1.i := mknode(\textbf{addop}.lexeme, R.i, T.nptr)\ \} & \\
\quad R_1 & \{\ R.s := R_1.s\ \} & \text{(5.5)} \\
R \rightarrow \epsilon & \{\ R.s := R.i\ \} &
\end{array}
$$

The code for R is based on the parsing procedure in Fig. 5.30. If the lookahead symbol is **addop**, then the production $R \rightarrow \textbf{addop}\,T\,R$ is applied by using the procedure *match* to read the next input token after **addop**, and then calling the procedures for T and R. Otherwise, the procedure does nothing, to mimic the production $R \rightarrow \epsilon$.

The procedure for R in Fig. 5.31 contains code for evaluating attributes. The lexical value *lexval* of the token **addop** is saved in *addoplexeme*, **addop** is matched, T is called, and its result is saved using *nptr*. Variable *i1* corresponds to the inherited attribute $R_1.i$, and *s1* to the synthesized attribute $R_1.s$. The **return** statement returns the value of s just before control leaves the function. The functions for E and T are constructed similarly.   □

```
procedure R;
begin
    if lookahead = addop then begin
        match (addop); T ; R
    end
    else begin /* do nothing */
    end
end;
```

Fig. 5.30. Parsing procedure for the productions $R \rightarrow$ **addop** $T\ R\ |\ \epsilon$.

```
function R (i : ↑ syntax_tree_node): ↑ syntax_tree_node;
    var nptr, i1, s1, s : ↑ syntax_tree_node;
        addoplexeme : char;
begin
    if lookahead = addop then begin
        /* production R → addop T R */
        addoplexeme := lexval;
        match (addop);
        nptr := T ;
        i1 := mknode (addoplexeme, i, nptr);
        s1 := R (i1);
        s := s1
    end
    else s := i;    /* production R → ε */
    return s
end;
```

Fig. 5.31. Recursive-descent construction of syntax trees.

5.6 BOTTOM-UP EVALUATION OF INHERITED ATTRIBUTES

In this section, we present a method to implement L-attributed definitions in the framework of bottom-up parsing. The method is capable of handling all L-attributed definitions considered in the previous section in that it can implement any L-attributed definition based on an LL(1) grammar. It can also implement many (but not all) L-attributed definitions based on LR(1) grammars. The method is a generalization of the bottom-up translation technique introduced in Section 5.3.

Removing Embedding Actions from Translation Schemes

In the bottom-up translation method of Section 5.3, we relied upon all translation actions being at the right end of the production, while in the predictive-parsing method of Section 5.5 we needed to embed actions at various places within the right side. To begin our discussion of how inherited attributes can be handled bottom up, we introduce a transformation that makes all embedded actions in a translation scheme occur at the right ends of their productions.

The transformation inserts new *marker* nonterminals generating ϵ into the base grammar. We replace each embedded action by a distinct marker nonterminal M and attach the action to the end of the production $M \rightarrow \epsilon$. For example, the translation scheme

$$
\begin{aligned}
E &\rightarrow T \ R \\
R &\rightarrow + \ T \ \{print('+')\} \ R \ | \ - \ T \ \{print('-')\} \ R \ | \ \epsilon \\
T &\rightarrow \mathbf{num} \ \{print(\mathbf{num}.val)\}
\end{aligned}
$$

is transformed using marker nonterminals M and N into

$$
\begin{aligned}
E &\rightarrow T \ R \\
R &\rightarrow + \ T \ M \ R \ | \ - \ T \ N \ R \ | \ \epsilon \\
T &\rightarrow \mathbf{num} \ \{print(\mathbf{num}.val)\} \\
M &\rightarrow \epsilon \ \{print('+')\} \\
N &\rightarrow \epsilon \ \{print('-')\}
\end{aligned}
$$

The grammars in the two translation schemes accept exactly the same language and, by drawing a parse tree with extra nodes for the actions, we can show that the actions are performed in the same order. Actions in the transformed translation scheme terminate productions, so they can be performed just before the right side is reduced during bottom-up parsing.

Inheriting Attributes on the Parser Stack

A bottom-up parser reduces the right side of production $A \rightarrow XY$ by removing X and Y from the top of the parser stack and replacing them by A. Suppose X has a synthesized attribute $X.s$, which the implementation of Section 5.3 kept along with X on the parser stack.

Since the value of $X.s$ is already on the parser stack before any reductions take place in the subtree below Y, this value can be inherited by Y. That is, if inherited attribute $Y.i$ is defined by the copy rule $Y.i := X.s$, then the value $X.s$ can be used where $Y.i$ is called for. As we shall see, copy rules play an important role in the evaluation of inherited attributes during bottom-up parsing.

Example 5.17. The type of an identifier can be passed by copy rules using inherited attributes as shown in Fig. 5.32 (adapted from Fig. 5.7). We shall first examine the moves made by a bottom-up parser on the input

```
real p, q, r
```

Then we show how the value of attribute $T.type$ can be accessed when the productions for L are applied. The translation scheme we wish to implement is

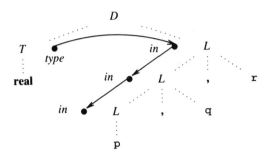

Fig. 5.32. At each node for L, $L.in = T.type$.

$$
\begin{array}{ll}
D \rightarrow T & \{\ L.in := T.type\ \} \\
\quad\ \ L & \\
T \rightarrow \textbf{int} & \{\ T.type := integer\ \} \\
T \rightarrow \textbf{real} & \{\ T.type := real\ \} \\
L \rightarrow & \{\ L_1.in := L.in\ \} \\
\quad\ \ L_1\ \textbf{,\ id} & \{\ addtype\,(\textbf{id}.entry,\ L.in)\ \} \\
L \rightarrow \textbf{id} & \{\ addtype\,(\textbf{id}.entry,\ L.in)\ \}
\end{array}
$$

If we ignore the actions in the above translation scheme, the sequence of moves made by the parser on the input of Fig. 5.32 is as in Fig. 5.33. For clarity, we show the corresponding grammar symbol instead of a stack state and the actual identifier instead of the token **id**.

INPUT	state	PRODUCTION USED
real p,q,r	–	
p,q,r	**real**	
p,q,r	T	$T \rightarrow$ **real**
,q,r	T p	
,q,r	$T\ L$	$L \rightarrow$ **id**
q,r	$T\ L$,	
,r	$T\ L$, q	
,r	$T\ L$	$L \rightarrow L$, **id**
r	$T\ L$,	
	$T\ L$, r	
	$T\ L$	$L \rightarrow L$, **id**
	D	$D \rightarrow T\ L$

Fig. 5.33. Whenever a right side for L is reduced, T is just below the right side.

Suppose as in Section 5.3 that the parser stack is implemented as a pair of arrays *state* and *val*. If *state*[*i*] is for grammar symbol X, then *val*[*i*] holds a synthesized attribute $X.s$. The contents of the *state* array are shown in Fig. 5.33. Note that every time the right side of a production for L is reduced in Fig. 5.33, T is in the stack just below the right side. We can use this fact to access the attribute value $T.type$.

The implementation in Fig. 5.34 uses the fact that attribute $T.type$ is at a known place in the *val* stack, relative to the top. Let *top* and *ntop* be the indices of the top entry in the stack just before and after a reduction takes place, respectively. From the copy rules defining $L.in$, we know that $T.type$ can be used in place of $L.in$.

When the production $L \rightarrow \mathbf{id}$ is applied, **id**.*entry* is on top of the *val* stack and $T.type$ is just below it. Hence, *addtype*(*val*[*top*], *val*[*top* − 1]) is equivalent to *addtype*(**id**.*entry*, $T.type$). Similarly, since the right side of the production $L \rightarrow L$, **id** has three symbols, $T.type$ appears in *val*[*top* − 3] when this reduction takes place. The copy rules involving $L.in$ are eliminated because the value of $T.type$ in the stack is used instead.   □

PRODUCTION	CODE FRAGMENT
$D \rightarrow T L$;	
$T \rightarrow \mathbf{int}$	*val*[*ntop*] := *integer*
$T \rightarrow \mathbf{real}$	*val*[*ntop*] := *real*
$L \rightarrow L$, **id**	*addtype*(*val*[*top*], *val*[*top* − 3])
$L \rightarrow \mathbf{id}$	*addtype*(*val*[*top*], *val*[*top* − 1])

Fig. 5.34. The value of $T.type$ is used in place of $L.in$.

Simulating the Evaluation of Inherited Attributes

Reaching into the parser stack for an attribute value works only if the grammar allows the position of the attribute value to be predicted.

Example 5.18. As an instance where we cannot predict the position, consider the following translation scheme:

PRODUCTION	SEMANTIC RULES	
$S \rightarrow aAC$	$C.i := A.s$	
$S \rightarrow bABC$	$C.i := A.s$	(5.6)
$C \rightarrow c$	$C.s := g(C.i)$	

C inherits the synthesized attribute $A.s$ by a copy rule. Note that there may or may not be a B between A and C in the stack. When reduction by $C \rightarrow c$ is performed, the value of $C.i$ is either in *val*[*top* − 1] or in *val*[*top* − 2], but it is not clear which case applies.

In Fig. 5.35, a fresh marker nonterminal M is inserted just before C on the right side of the second production in (5.6). If we are parsing according to production $S \rightarrow bABMC$, then $C.i$ inherits the value of $A.s$ indirectly through $M.i$ and $M.s$. When the production $M \rightarrow \epsilon$ is applied, a copy rule $M.s := M.i$ ensures that the value $M.s = M.i = A.s$ appears just before the part of the stack used for parsing the subtree for C. Thus, the value of $C.i$ can be found in $val[top-1]$ when $C \rightarrow c$ is applied, independent of whether the first or second productions in the following modification of (5.6) are used.

PRODUCTION	SEMANTIC RULES
$S \rightarrow aAC$	$C.i := A.s$
$S \rightarrow bABMC$	$M.i := A.s;\ C.i := M.s$
$C \rightarrow c$	$C.s := g(C.i)$
$M \rightarrow \epsilon$	$M.s := M.i$

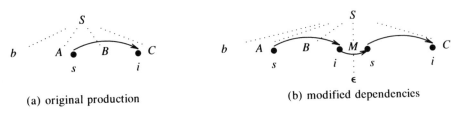

(a) original production   (b) modified dependencies

Fig. 5.35. Copying an attribute value through a marker M.

Marker nonterminals can also be used to simulate semantic rules that are not copy rules. For example, consider

PRODUCTION	SEMANTIC RULES	
$S \rightarrow aAC$	$C.i := f(A.s)$	(5.7)

This time the rule defining $C.i$ is not a copy rule, so the value of $C.i$ is not already in the val stack. This problem can also be solved using a marker.

PRODUCTION	SEMANTIC RULES	
$S \rightarrow aANC$	$N.i := A.s;\ C.i := N.s$	(5.8)
$N \rightarrow \epsilon$	$N.s := f(N.i)$	

The distinct nonterminal N inherits $A.s$ by a copy rule. Its synthesized attribute $N.s$ is set to $f(A.s)$; then $C.i$ inherits this value using a copy rule. When we reduce by $N \rightarrow \epsilon$, we find the value of $N.i$ in the place for $A.s$, that is, in $val[top-1]$. When we reduce by $S \rightarrow aANC$, the value of $C.i$ is also found in $val[top-1]$, because it is $N.s$. Actually, we do not need $C.i$ at this time; we needed it during the reduction of a terminal string to C, when its value was safely stored on the stack with N.

Example 5.19. Three marker nonterminals L, M, and N are used in Fig. 5.36 to ensure that the value of inherited attribute $B.ps$ appears at a known position in the parser stack while the subtree for B is being reduced. The original attribute grammar appears in Fig. 5.22 and its relevance to text formatting is explained in Example 5.13.

PRODUCTION	SEMANTIC RULES
$S \rightarrow L\ B$	$B.ps := L.s$ $S.ht := B.ht$
$L \rightarrow \epsilon$	$L.s := 10$
$B \rightarrow B_1\ M\ B_2$	$B_1.ps := B.ps$ $M.i := B.ps$ $B_2.ps := M.s$ $B.ht := max(B_1.ht,\ B_2.ht)$
$B \rightarrow B_1\ \mathbf{sub}\ N\ B_2$	$B_1.ps := B.ps$ $N.i := B.ps$ $B_2.ps := N.s$ $B.ht := disp(B_1.ht,\ B_2.ht)$
$B \rightarrow \mathbf{text}$	$B.ht := \mathbf{text}.h \times B.ps$
$M \rightarrow \epsilon$	$M.s := M.i$
$N \rightarrow \epsilon$	$N.s := shrink(N.i)$

Fig. 5.36. All inherited attributes are set by copy rules.

Initialization is done using L. The production for S is $S \rightarrow L\,B$ in Fig. 5.36, so L will remain on the stack while the subtree below B is reduced. The value 10 of the inherited attribute $B.ps = L.s$ is entered into the parser stack by the rule $L.s := 10$ associated with $L \rightarrow \epsilon$.

Marker M in $B \rightarrow B_1 M B_2$ plays a role similar to that of M in Fig. 5.35; it ensures that the value of $B.ps$ appears just below B_2 in the parser stack. In production $B \rightarrow B_1 \mathbf{sub} N B_2$, the nonterminal N is used as it is in (5.8). N inherits, via the copy rule $N.i := B.ps$, the attribute value that $B_2.ps$ depends on, and synthesizes the value of $B_2.ps$ by the rule $N.s := shrink(N.i)$. The consequence, which we leave as an exercise, is that the value of $B.ps$ is always immediately below the right side when we reduce to B.

Code fragments implementing the syntax-directed definition of Fig. 5.36 are shown in Fig. 5.37. All inherited attributes are set by copy rules in Fig. 5.36, so the implementation obtains their values by keeping track of their position in the *val* stack. As in previous examples, *top* and *ntop* give the indices of the top of the stack before and after a reduction, respectively. □

Systematic introduction of markers, as in the modification of (5.6) and (5.7), can make it possible to evaluate L-attributed definitions during LR parsing. Since there is only one production for each marker, a grammar

PRODUCTION	CODE FRAGMENT
$S \rightarrow L\ B$	$val\,[ntop\,] := val\,[top\,]$
$L \rightarrow \epsilon$	$val\,[ntop\,] := 10$
$B \rightarrow B_1\ M\ B_2$	$val\,[ntop\,] := max\,(val\,[top-2],\ val\,[top\,])$
$B \rightarrow B_1\ \mathbf{sub}\ N\ B_2$	$val\,[ntop\,] := disp\,(val\,[top-3],\ val\,[top\,])$
$B \rightarrow \mathbf{text}$	$val\,[ntop\,] := val\,[top\,] \times val\,[top-1]$
$M \rightarrow \epsilon$	$val\,[ntop\,] := val\,[top-1]$
$N \rightarrow \epsilon$	$val\,[ntop\,] := shrink\,(val\,[top-2])$

Fig. 5.37. Implementation of the syntax-directed definition in Fig. 5.36.

remains LL(1) when markers are added. Any LL(1) grammar is also an LR(1) grammar so no parsing conflicts arise when markers are added to an LL(1) grammar. Unfortunately, the same cannot be said of all LR(1) grammars; that is, parsing conflicts can arise if markers are introduced in certain LR(1) grammars.

The ideas of the previous examples can be formalized in the following algorithm.

Algorithm 5.3. Bottom-up parsing and translation with inherited attributes.

Input. An L-attributed definition with an underlying LL(1) grammar.

Output. A parser that computes the values of all attributes on its parsing stack.

Method. Let us assume for simplicity that every nonterminal A has one inherited attribute $A.i$, and every grammar symbol X has a synthesized attribute $X.s$. If X is a terminal, then its synthesized attribute is really the lexical value returned with X by the lexical analyzer; that lexical value appears on the stack, in an array *val*, as in the previous examples.

For every production $A \rightarrow X_1 \cdots X_n$, introduce n new marker nonterminals, $M_1, \ldots, M_n$, and replace the production by $A \rightarrow M_1 X_1 \cdots M_n X_n$.[2] The synthesized attribute $X_j.s$ will go on the parser stack in the *val* array entry associated with X_j. The inherited attribute $X_j.i$, if there is one, appears in the same array, but associated with M_j.

An important invariant is that as we parse, the inherited attribute $A.i$, if it exists, is found in the position of the *val* array immediately below the position for M_1. As we assume the start symbol has no inherited attribute, there is no problem with the case when the start symbol is A, but even if there were such

---

[2] Although inserting M_1 before X_1 simplifies the discussion of marker nonterminals, it has the unfortunate side effect of introducing parsing conflicts into a left-recursive grammar. See Exercise 5.21. As noted below, M_1 can be eliminated.

an inherited attribute, it could be placed below the bottom of the stack. We may prove the invariant by an easy induction on the number of steps in the bottom-up parse, noting the fact that inherited attributes are associated with the marker nonterminals M_j, and that the attribute $X_j.i$ is computed at M_j before we begin the reduction to X_j.

To see that the attributes can be computed as intended during a bottom-up parse, consider two cases. First, if we reduce to a marker nonterminal M_j, we know which production $A \rightarrow M_1X_1 \cdots M_nX_n$ that marker belongs to. We therefore know the positions of any attributes that the inherited attribute $X_j.i$ needs for its computation. $A.i$ is in $val[top-2j+2]$, $X_1.i$ is in $val[top-2j+3]$, $X_1.s$ is in $val[top-2j+4]$, $X_2.i$ is in $val[top-2j+5]$, and so on. Therefore, we may compute $X_j.i$ and store it in $val[top+1]$, which becomes the new top of stack after the reduction. Notice how the fact that the grammar is LL(1) is important, or else we might not be sure that we were reducing ϵ to one particular marker nonterminal, and thus could not locate the proper attributes, or even know what formula to apply in general. We ask the reader to take on faith, or derive a proof of the fact that every LL(1) grammar with markers is still LR(1).

The second case occurs when we reduce to a nonmarker symbol, say by production $A \rightarrow M_1X_1 \cdots M_nX_n$. Then, we have only to compute the synthesized attribute $A.s$; note that $A.i$ was already computed, and lives at the position on the stack just below the position into which we insert A itself. The attributes needed to compute $A.s$ are clearly available at known positions on the stack, the positions of the X_j's, during the reduction.

The following simplifications reduce the number of markers; the second avoids parsing conflicts in left-recursive grammars.

1. If X_j has no inherited attribute, we need not use marker M_j. Of course, the expected positions for attributes on the stack will change if M_j is omitted, but this change can be incorporated easily into the parser.

2. If $X_1.i$ exists, but is computed by a copy rule $X_1.i = A.i$, then we can omit M_1, since we know by our invariant that $A.i$ will already be located where we want it, just below X_1 on the stack, and this value can therefore serve for $X_1.i$ as well.   □

Replacing Inherited by Synthesized Attributes

It is sometimes possible to avoid the use of inherited attributes by changing the underlying grammar. For example, a declaration in Pascal can consist of a list of identifiers followed by a type, e.g., m, n : integer. A grammar for such declarations may include productions of the form

$D \rightarrow L : T$
$T \rightarrow$ **integer** | **char**
$L \rightarrow L$, **id** | **id**

Since identifiers are generated by L but the type is not in the subtree for L, we cannot associate the type with an identifier using synthesized attributes alone. In fact, if nonterminal L inherits a type from T to its right in the first production, we get a syntax-directed definition that is not L-attributed, so translations based on it cannot be done during parsing.

A solution to this problem is to restructure the grammar to include the type as the last element of the list of identifiers:

$D \rightarrow$ **id** L
$L \rightarrow$ **,** **id** L | **:** T
$T \rightarrow$ **integer** | **char**

Now, the type can be carried along as a synthesized attribute $L.type$. As each identifier is generated by L, its type can be entered into the symbol table.

A Difficult Syntax-Directed Definition

Algorithm 5.3, for implementing inherited attributes during bottom-up parsing, extends to some, but not all, LR grammars. The L-attributed definition in Fig. 5.38 is based on a simple LR(1) grammar, but it cannot be implemented, as is, during LR parsing. Nonterminal L in $L \rightarrow \epsilon$ inherits the count of the number of 1's generated by S. Since the production $L \rightarrow \epsilon$ is the first that a bottom-up parser would reduce by, the translator at that time cannot know the number of 1's in the input.

PRODUCTION	SEMANTIC RULES
$S \rightarrow L$	$L.count := 0$
$L \rightarrow L_1$ **1**	$L_1.count := L.count + 1$
$L \rightarrow \epsilon$	$print(L.count)$

Fig. 5.38. Difficult syntax-directed definition.

5.7 RECURSIVE EVALUATORS

Recursive functions that evaluate attributes as they traverse a parse tree can be constructed from a syntax-directed definition using a generalization of the techniques for predictive translation in Section 5.5. Such functions allow us to implement syntax-directed definitions that cannot be implemented simultaneously with parsing. In this section, we associate a single translation function with each nonterminal. The function visits the children of a node for the nonterminal in some order determined by the production at the node; it is not necessary that the children be visited in a left-to-right order. In Section 5.10, we shall see how the effect of translation during more than one pass can be achieved by associating multiple procedures with nonterminals.

Left-to Right Traversals

In Algorithm 5.2, we showed how an L-attributed definition based on an LL(1) grammar can be implemented by constructing a recursive function that parses and translates each nonterminal. All L-attributed syntax-directed definitions can be implemented if a similar recursive function is invoked on a node for that nonterminal in a previously constructed parse tree. By looking at the production at the node, the function can determine what its children are. The function for a nonterminal A takes a node and the values of the inherited attributes for A as arguments, and returns the values of the synthesized attributes for A as results.

The details of the construction are exactly as in Algorithm 5.2, except for step 2 where the function for a nonterminal decides what production to use based on the current input symbol. The function here employs a case statement to determine the production used at a node. We give an example to illustrate the method.

Example 5.20. Consider the syntax-directed definition for determining the size and height of formulas in Fig. 5.22. The nonterminal B has an inherited attribute ps and a synthesized attribute ht. Using Algorithm 5.2, modified as mentioned above, we construct the function for B shown in Fig. 5.39.

Function B takes a node n and a value corresponding to $B.ps$ at the node as arguments, and returns a value corresponding to $B.ht$ at node n. The function has a case for each production with B on the left. The code corresponding to each production simulates the semantic rules associated with the production. The order in which the rules are applied must be such that inherited attributes of a nonterminal are computed before the function for the nonterminal is called.

In the code corresponding to the production $B \rightarrow B$ **sub** B, variables ps, $ps1$, and $ps2$ hold the values of the inherited attributes $B.ps$, $B_1.ps$, and $B_2.ps$. Similarly ht, $ht1$, and $ht2$ hold the values of $B.ht$, $B_1.ht$, and $B_2.ht$. We use the function $child(m, i)$ to refer to the ith child of node m. Since B_2 is the label of the third child of node n, the value of $B_2.ht$ is determined by the function call $B(child(n, 3), ps2)$. □

Other Traversals

Once an explicit parse tree is available, we are free to visit the children of a node in any order. Consider the non-L-attributed definition of Example 5.21. In a translation specified by this definition, the children of a node for one production need to be visited from left to right, while the children of a node for the other production need to be visited from right to left.

This abstract example illustrates the power of using mutually recursive functions for evaluating the attributes at the nodes of a parse tree. The functions need not depend on the order in which the parse tree nodes are created. The main consideration for evaluation during a traversal is that the inherited attributes at a node be computed before the node is first visited and that the

```
function B (n, ps);
       var ps1, ps2, ht1, ht2;
begin
       case production at node n of
       'B → B₁ B₂':
           ps1 := ps;
           ht1 := B (child (n, 1), ps1);
           ps2 := ps;
           ht2 := B (child (n, 2), ps2);
           return max (ht1, ht2);
       'B → B₁ sub B₂':
           ps1 := ps;
           ht1 := B (child (n, 1), ps1);
           ps2 := shrink (ps);
           ht2 := B (child (n, 3), ps2);
           return disp (ht1, ht2);
       'B → text':
           return ps × text.h;
       default:
           error
       end
end;
```

Fig. 5.39. Function for nonterminal B in Fig. 5.22.

synthesized attributes be computed before we leave the node for the last time.

Example 5.21. Each of the nonterminals in Fig. 5.40 has an inherited attribute i and a synthesized attribute s. The dependency graphs for the two productions are also shown. The rules associated with $A \rightarrow L M$ set up left-to-right dependencies and the rules associated with $A \rightarrow Q R$ set up right-to-left dependencies.

The function for nonterminal A is shown in Fig. 5.41; we assume that functions for L, M, Q, and R can be constructed. Variables in Fig. 5.41 are named after the nonterminal and its attribute; e.g, li and ls are the variables corresponding to $L.i$ and $L.s$.

The code corresponding to the production $A \rightarrow L M$ is constructed as in Example 5.20. That is, we determine the inherited attribute of L, call the function for L to determine the synthesized attribute of L, and repeat the process for M. The code corresponding to $A \rightarrow Q R$ visits the subtree for R before it visits the subtree for Q. Otherwise, the code for the two productions is very similar.   □

PRODUCTION	SEMANTIC RULES
$A \to L\ M$	$L.i := l(A.i)$
	$M.i := m(L.s)$
	$A.s := f(M.s)$
$A \to Q\ R$	$R.i := r(A.i)$
	$Q.i := q(R.s)$
	$A.s := f(Q.s)$

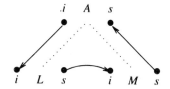 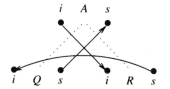

Fig. 5.40. Productions and semantic rules for nonterminal A.

```
function A (n, ai);
begin
     case production at node n of
     'A → L M':          /* left-to-right order */
          li := l(ai);
          ls := L(child(n, 1), li);
          mi := m(ls);
          ms := M(child(n, 2), mi)
          return f(ms);
     'A → Q R':          /* right-to-left order */
          ri := r(ai);
          rs := R(child(n, 2), ri);
          qi := q(rs);
          qs := Q(child(n, 1), qi);
          return f(qs);
     default:
          error
     end
end;
```

Fig. 5.41. Dependencies in Fig. 5.40 determine the order children are visited in.

5.8 SPACE FOR ATTRIBUTE VALUES AT COMPILE TIME

In this section we consider the compile-time assignment of space for attribute values. We shall use information from the dependency graph for a parse tree, so the approach of this section is suitable for parse-tree methods that determine the evaluation order from the dependency graph. In the next section we consider the case in which the evaluation order can be predicted in advance, so we can decide on the space for attributes once and for all when the compiler is constructed.

Given a not necessarily depth-first order of evaluation for attributes, the *lifetime* of an attribute begins when the attribute is first computed and ends when all attributes that depend on it have been computed. We can conserve space by holding an attribute value only during its lifetime.

In order to emphasize that the techniques in this section apply to any evaluation order, we shall consider the following syntax-directed definition that is not L-attributed, for passing type information to identifiers in a declaration.

Example 5.22. The syntax-directed definition in Fig. 5.42 is an extension of that in Fig. 5.4 to allow declarations of the form

        real c[12][31];   (5.9)
        int   x[3], y[5];   (5.10)

A parse tree for (5.10) is shown by the dotted lines in Fig. 5.43(a). The numbers at the nodes are discussed in the next example. As in Example 5.3, the type obtained from T is inherited by L and passed down towards the identifiers in the declaration. An edge from $T.type$ to $L.in$ shows that $L.in$ depends on $T.type$. The syntax-directed definition in Fig. 5.42 is not L-attributed because $I_1.in$ depends on **num**.*val* and **num** is to the right of I_1 in $I \rightarrow I_1$ [**num**].   □

Assigning Space for Attributes at Compile Time

Suppose we are given a sequence of registers to hold attribute values. For convenience, we assume that each register can hold any attribute value. If attributes represent different types, then we can form groups of attributes that take the same amount of storage and consider each group separately. We rely on information about the lifetimes of attributes to determine the registers into which they are evaluated.

Example 5.23. Suppose that attributes are evaluated in the order given by the node numbers in the dependency graph of Fig. 5.43,[3] constructed in the last example. The lifetime of each node begins when its attribute is evaluated and

---

[3] The dependency graph in Fig. 5.43 does not show nodes corresponding to the semantic rule *addtype* (**id**.*entry*, *I.in*) because no space is allocated for dummy attributes. Note, however, that this semantic rule must not be evaluated until after the value of *I.in* is available. An algorithm to determine this fact must work with a dependency graph containing nodes for this semantic rule.

PRODUCTION	RULES
$D \rightarrow T\,L$	$L.in := T.type$
$T \rightarrow$ **int**	$T.type := integer$
$T \rightarrow$ **real**	$T.type := real$
$L \rightarrow L_1\,,\,I$	$L_1.in := L.in$ $I.in := L.in$
$L \rightarrow I$	$I.in := L.in$
$I \rightarrow I_1\,[\,$ **num** $\,]$	$I_1.in := array(\textbf{num}.val,\ I.in)$
$I \rightarrow$ **id**	$addtype(\textbf{id}.entry,\ I.in)$

Fig. 5.42. Passing the type to identifiers in a declaration.

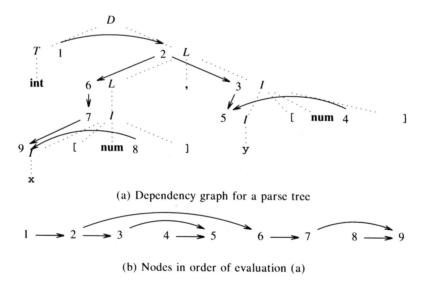

(a) Dependency graph for a parse tree

(b) Nodes in order of evaluation (a)

Fig. 5.43. Determining lifetimes of attribute values.

ends when its attribute is used for the last time. For example, the lifetime of node 1 ends when 2 is evaluated because 2 is the only node that depends on 1. The lifetime of 2 ends when 6 is evaluated.   □

A method for evaluating attributes that uses as few registers as possible is given in Fig. 5.44. We consider the nodes of dependency graph D for a parse

tree in the order they are to be evaluated. Initially, we have a pool of registers $r_1, r_2, \ldots$. If attribute b is defined by the semantic rule
$b := f(c_1, c_2, \ldots, c_k)$, then the lifetime of one or more of $c_1, c_2, \ldots, c_k$
might end with the evaluation of b; registers holding such attributes are
returned after b is evaluated. Whenever possible, b is evaluated into a register that held one of $c_1, c_2, \ldots, c_k$.

```
for each node m in m₁, m₂, . . . , mₙ do begin
        for each node n whose lifetime ends with the evaluation of m do
            mark n's register;
        if some register r is marked then begin
            unmark r;
            evaluate m into register r;
            return marked registers to the pool
        end
        else /* no registers were marked */
            evaluate m into a register from the pool;
        /* actions using the value of m can be inserted here */
        if the lifetime of m has ended then
            return m's register to the pool
end
```

Fig. 5.44. Assigning attribute values to registers.

Registers used during an evaluation of the dependency graph of Fig. 5.43
are shown in Fig. 5.45. We start by evaluating node 1 to register r_1. The
lifetime of node 1 ends when 2 is evaluated, so 2 is evaluated into r_1. Node 3
gets a fresh register r_2, because node 6 will need the value of 2.

$$
\begin{array}{ccccccccc}
1 & \longrightarrow & 2 & \longrightarrow & 3 & & 4 & \longrightarrow & 5 & & 6 & \longrightarrow & 7 & & 8 & \longrightarrow & 9 \\
r_1 & & r_1 & & r_2 & & r_3 & & r_2 & & r_1 & & r_1 & & r_2 & & r_1
\end{array}
$$

Fig. 5.45. Registers used for attribute values in Fig. 5.43.

Avoiding Copies

We can improve the method of Fig. 5.44 by treating copy rules as a special
case. A copy rule has the form $b := c$, so if the value of c is in register r,
then the value of b already appears in register r. The number of attributes
defined by copy rules can be significant, so we wish to avoid making explicit
copies.

A set of nodes having the same value forms an equivalence class. The method of Fig. 5.44 can be modified as follows to hold the value of an equivalence class in a register. When node m is considered, we first check if it is defined by a copy rule. If it is, then its value must already be in a register, and m joins the equivalence class with values in that register. Furthermore, a register is returned to the pool only at the end of the lifetimes of all nodes with values in the register.

Example 5.24. The dependency graph in Fig. 5.43 is redrawn in Fig. 5.46, with an equal sign before each node defined by a copy rule. From the syntax-directed definition in Fig. 5.42, we find that the type determined at node 1 is copied to each element in the list of identifiers, resulting in nodes 2, 3, 6, and 7 of Fig. 5.43 being copies of 1.

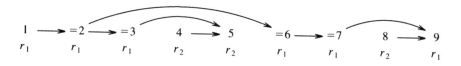

Fig. 5.46. Registers used, taking copy rules into account.

Since 2 and 3 are copies of 1, their values are taken from register r_1 in Fig. 5.46. Note that the lifetime of 3 ends when 5 is evaluated, but register r_1 holding the value of 3 is not returned to the pool because the lifetime of 2 in its equivalence class has not ended.

The following code shows how the declaration (5.10) of Example 5.22 might be processed by a compiler:

```
r₁ := integer;        /* evaluates nodes 1, 2, 3, 6, 7 */
r₂ := 5;              /* evaluates node 4 */
r₂ := array(r₂, r₁);  /* type of y */
addtype(y, r₂);
r₂ := 3;              /* evaluates node 8 */
r₂ := array(r₂, r₁);  /* type of x */
addtype(x, r₂);
```

In the above, x and y point to the symbol-table entries for **x** and **y**, and procedure *addtype* must be called at the appropriate times to add the types of **x** and **y** to their symbol-table entries. □

5.9 ASSIGNING SPACE AT COMPILER-CONSTRUCTION TIME

Although it is possible to hold all attribute values on a single stack during a traversal, we can sometimes avoid making copies by using multiple stacks. In general, if dependencies between attributes make it inconvenient to place certain attribute values on a stack, we can save them at nodes in an explicitly constructed syntax tree.

We have already seen the use of a stack to hold attribute values during bottom-up parsing in Sections 5.3 and 5.6. A stack is also used implicitly by a recursive-descent parser to keep track of procedure calls; this issue will be discussed in Chapter 7.

The use of a stack can be combined with other techniques for saving space. The print actions used extensively in the translation schemes in Chapter 2 emit string-valued attributes to an output file whenever possible. While constructing syntax trees in Section 5.2, we passed pointers to nodes instead of complete subtrees. In general, rather than passing large objects, we can save space by passing pointers to them. These techniques will be applied in Examples 5.27 and 5.28.

Predicting Lifetimes from the Grammar

When the evaluation order for attributes is obtained from a particular traversal of the parse tree, we can predict the lifetimes of attributes at compiler-construction time. For example, suppose children are visited from left to right during a depth-first traversal, as in Section 5.4. Starting at a node for production $A \rightarrow B C$, the subtree for B is visited, the subtree for C is visited, and then we return to the node for A. The parent of A cannot refer to the attributes of B and C, so their lifetimes must end when we return to A. Note that these observations are based on the production $A \rightarrow B C$ and the order in which the nodes for these nonterminals are visited. We do not need to know about the subtrees at B and C.

With any evaluation order, if the lifetime of attribute c is contained in that of b, then the value of c can be held in a stack above the value of b. Here b and c do not have to be attributes of the same nonterminal. For the production $A \rightarrow B C$, we can use a stack during a depth-first traversal in the following way.

Start at the node for A with the inherited attributes of A already on the stack. Then evaluate and push the values of the inherited attributes of B. These attributes remain on the stack as we traverse the subtree of B, returning with the synthesized attributes of B above them. This process is repeated with C; that is, we push its inherited attributes, traverse its subtree and return with its synthesized attributes on top. Writing $\mathbf{I}(X)$ and $\mathbf{S}(X)$ for the inherited and synthesized attributes of X, respectively, the stack now contains

$$\mathbf{I}(A), \mathbf{I}(B), \mathbf{S}(B), \mathbf{I}(C), \mathbf{S}(C) \tag{5.11}$$

All of the attribute values needed to compute the synthesized attributes of A are now on the stack, so we can return to A with the stack containing

$$\mathbf{I}(A), \mathbf{S}(A)$$

Notice that the number (and presumably the size) of inherited and synthesized attributes of a grammar symbol is fixed. Thus, at each step of the above process we know how far down into the stack we have to reach to find an attribute.

Example 5.25. Suppose that attribute values for the typesetting translation of Fig. 5.22 are held in a stack as discussed above. Starting at a node for production $B \rightarrow B_1 B_2$ with $B.ps$ on top of the stack, the stack contents before and after visiting a node are shown in Fig. 5.47 to the left and right of the node, respectively. As usual stacks grow downwards.

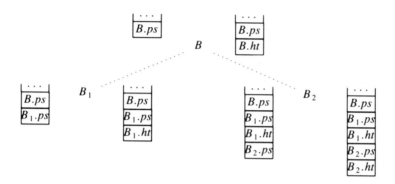

Fig. 5.47. Stack contents before and after visiting a node.

Note that just before a node for nonterminal B is visited for the first time, its ps attribute is on top of the stack. Just after the last visit, i.e., when the traversal moves up from that node, its ht and ps attributes are in the top two positions of the stack.   □

When an attribute b is defined by a copy rule $b := c$ and the value of c is on top of the stack of attribute values, it may not be necessary to push a copy of c onto the stack. There may be more opportunities for eliminating copy rules if more than one stack is used to hold attribute values. In the next example, we use separate stacks for synthesized and inherited attributes. A comparison with Example 5.25 shows that more copy rules can be eliminated if separate stacks are used.

Example 5.26. With the syntax-directed definition of Fig. 5.22, suppose we use separate stacks for the inherited attribute ps and the synthesized attribute ht. We maintain the stacks so that $B.ps$ is on top of the ps stack just before B is first visited and just after B is last visited. $B.ht$ will be on top of the ht stack just after B is visited.

With separate stacks we can take advantage of both the copy rules $B_1.ps := B.ps$ and $B_2.ps := B.ps$ associated with $B \rightarrow B_1 B_2$. As shown in Fig. 5.48, we do not need to push $B_1.ps$ because its value is already on top of the stack as $B.ps$.

A translation scheme based on the syntax-directed definition of Fig. 5.22 is shown in Fig. 5.49. Operation $push(v, s)$ pushes the value v onto stack s and

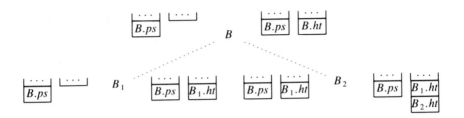

Fig. 5.48. Using separate stacks for attributes *ps* and *ht*

pop (*s*) pops the value on top of stack *s*. We use *top* (*s*) to refer to the top element of stack *s*.   □

$S \rightarrow$ { *push* (10, *ps*) }
    B

$B \rightarrow B_1$
    B_2 { *h*2 := *top* (*ht*); *pop* (*ht*);
        *h*1 := *top* (*ht*); *pop* (*ht*);
        push (*max* (*h*1, *h*2), *ht*) }

$B \rightarrow B_1$
    sub { *push* (*shrink* (*top* (*ps*)), *ps*) }
    B_2 { *pop* (*ps*);
        *h*2 := *top* (*ht*); *pop* (*ht*);
        *h*1 := *top* (*ht*); *pop* (*ht*);
        push (*disp* (*h*1, *h*2), *ht*) }

$B \rightarrow$ **text** { *push* (**text**.*h* × *top* (*ps*), *ht*) }

Fig. 5.49. Translation scheme maintaining stacks *ps* and *ht*.

The next example combines the use of a stack for attribute values with actions to emit code.

Example 5.27. Here, we consider techniques for implementing a syntax-directed definition specifying the generation of intermediate code. The value of a boolean expression *E* **and** *F* is false if *E* is false. In C, subexpression *F* must not be evaluated if *E* is false. The evaluation of such boolean expressions is considered in Section 8.4.

Boolean expressions in the syntax-directed definition in Fig. 5.50 are constructed from identifiers and the **and** operator. Each expression *E* inherits two labels *E.true* and *E.false* marking the points control must jump to if *E* is true and false, respectively.

PRODUCTION	SEMANTIC RULES
$E \rightarrow E_1$ **and** E_2	$E_1.true := newlabel$
	$E_1.false := E.false$
	$E_2.true := E.true$
	$E_2.false := E.false$
	$E.code := E_1.code \parallel gen('\textbf{label}' E_1.true) \parallel E_2.code$
$E \rightarrow$ **id**	$E.code := gen('\textbf{if}' \text{ id}.place \text{ '}\textbf{goto}' E.true) \parallel$
	$gen('\textbf{goto}' E.false)$

Fig. 5.50. Short-circuit evaluation of boolean expressions.

Suppose $E \rightarrow E_1$ **and** E_2. If E_1 evaluates to false, then control flows to the inherited label $E.false$; otherwise, E_1 evaluates to true so control flows to the code for evaluating E_2. A new label generated by function *newlabel* marks the beginning of the code for E_2. Individual instructions are formed using *gen*. For further discussion of the relevance of Fig. 5.50 to intermediate code generation see Section 8.4.

The syntax-directed definition in Fig. 5.50 is L-attributed, so we can construct a translation scheme for it. The translation scheme in Fig. 5.51 uses a procedure *emit* to generate and emit instructions incrementally. Also shown in the figure are actions for setting the values of the inherited attributes, inserted before the appropriate grammar symbol as discussed in Section 5.4.

$$E \rightarrow \quad \{ E_1.true := newlabel;$$
$$\qquad\qquad E_1.false := E.false \}$$
$$\quad E_1$$
$$\textbf{and} \quad \{ emit('\textbf{label}' E_1.true) \};$$
$$\qquad\qquad E_2.true := E.true;$$
$$\qquad\qquad E_2.false := E.false \}$$
$$\quad E_2$$

$$E \rightarrow \textbf{id} \quad \{ emit('\textbf{if}' \text{ id}.place \text{ '}\textbf{goto}' E.true);$$
$$\qquad\qquad emit('\textbf{goto}' E.false) \}$$

Fig. 5.51. Emitting code for boolean expressions.

The translation scheme in Fig. 5.52 goes further; it uses separate stacks to hold the values of the inherited attributes $E.true$ and $E.false$. As in Example 5.26, copy rules have no effect on the stacks. To implement the rule $E_1.true := newlabel$, a new label is pushed onto the true stack before E_1 is visited. The lifetime of this label ends with the action $emit('\textbf{label}' \text{ } top(true))$, corresponding to $emit('\textbf{label}' E_1.true)$, so the true stack is popped after the action. The *false* stack does not change in this example, but it is needed when the **or** operator is allowed in addition to the **and** operator.   □

$$E \rightarrow \qquad \{ push(newlabel, \ true) \}$$
$$\qquad E_1$$
$$\qquad \textbf{and} \quad \{ \ emit('\textbf{label}' \ top(true)); $$
$$\qquad\qquad\qquad pop(true) \ \}$$
$$\qquad E_2$$
$$E \rightarrow \textbf{id} \quad \{ \ emit('\textbf{if}' \ id.place \ '\textbf{goto}' \ top(true)); $$
$$\qquad\qquad\qquad emit('\textbf{goto}' \ top(false)) \ \}$$

Fig. 5.52. Emitting code for boolean expressions.

Nonoverlapping Lifetimes

A single register is a special case of a stack. If each *push* operation is followed by a *pop*, then there can be at most one element in the stack at a time. In this case, we can use a register instead of a stack. In terms of lifetimes, if the lifetimes of two attributes do not overlap, their values can be held in the same register.

Example 5.28. The syntax-directed definition in Fig. 5.53 constructs syntax trees for list-like expressions with operators at just one precedence level. It is taken from the translation scheme in Fig. 5.28.

PRODUCTION	SEMANTIC RULES
$E \rightarrow T \ R$	$R.i := T.nptr$ $E.nptr := R.s$
$R \rightarrow \textbf{addop} \ T \ R_1$	$R_1.i := mknode(\textbf{addop}.lexeme, R.i, T.nptr)$ $R.s := R_1.s$
$R \rightarrow \epsilon$	$R.s := R.i$
$T \rightarrow \textbf{num}$	$T.nptr := mkleaf(\textbf{num}, \textbf{num}.val)$

Fig. 5.53. A syntax-directed definition adapted from Fig. 5.28.

We claim that the lifetime of each attribute of R ends when the attribute that depends on it is evaluated. We can show that, for any parse tree, the R attributes can be evaluated into the same register r. The following reasoning is typical of that needed to analyze grammars. The induction is on the size of the subtree attached at R in the parse tree fragment in Fig. 5.54.

The smallest subtree is obtained if $R \rightarrow \epsilon$ is applied, in which case $R.s$ is a copy of $R.i$, so both their values are in register r. For a larger subtree, the production at the root of the subtree must be for $R \rightarrow \textbf{addop} \ T \ R_1$. The

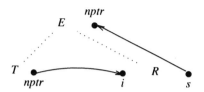

Fig. 5.54. Dependency graph for $E \rightarrow T R$.

lifetime of $R.i$ ends when $R_1.i$ is evaluated, so $R_1.i$ can be evaluated into register r. From the inductive hypothesis, all the attributes for instances of nonterminal R in the subtree for R_1 can be assigned the same register. Finally, $R.s$ is a copy of $R_1.s$, so its value is already in r.

The translation scheme in Fig. 5.55 evaluates the attributes in the attribute grammar of Fig. 5.53, using register r to hold the values of the attributes $R.i$ and $R.s$ for all instances of nonterminal R.

$$
\begin{aligned}
E \rightarrow T \quad & \{ \; r := T.nptr \quad \text{/* } r \text{ now holds } R.i \text{ */} \} \\
R \quad & \{ \; E.nptr := r \quad \text{/* } r \text{ has returned with } R.s \text{ */} \} \\
R \rightarrow \textbf{addop} & \\
T \quad & \{ \; r := mknode\,(\textbf{addop}.lexeme, \; r, \; T.nptr) \} \\
R & \\
R \rightarrow \epsilon & \\
T \rightarrow \textbf{num} \quad & \{ \; T.nptr := mkleaf\,(\textbf{num}, \; \textbf{num}.val) \}
\end{aligned}
$$

Fig. 5.55. Transformed translation scheme for constructing syntax trees.

For completeness, we show in Fig. 5.56 the code for implementing the translation scheme above; it is constructed according to Algorithm 5.2. Nonterminal R no longer has attributes, so R becomes a procedure rather than a function. Variable r was made local to function E, so it is possible for E to be called recursively, although we do not need to do so in the scheme of Fig. 5.55. This code can be improved further by eliminating tail recursion and then replacing the remaining call of R by the body of the resulting procedure, as in Section 2.5.   □

5.10 ANALYSIS OF SYNTAX-DIRECTED DEFINITIONS

In Section 5.7, attributes were evaluated during a traversal of a tree using a set of mutually recursive functions. The function for a nonterminal mapped the values of the inherited attributes at a node to the values of the synthesized attributes at that node.

```
function E : ↑ syntax_tree_node;
      var  r : ↑ syntax_tree_node;
           addoplexeme : char;

      procedure R;
      begin
          if lookahead = addop then begin
              addoplexeme := lexval;
              match (addop);
              r := mknode (addoplexeme, r, T);
              R
          end
      end;

begin
      r := T; R
      return r
end;
```

Fig. 5.56. Compare procedure R with the code in Fig. 5.31.

The approach of Section 5.7 extends to translations that cannot be performed during a single depth-first traversal. Here, we shall use a separate function for each synthesized attribute of each nonterminal, although groups of synthesized attributes can be evaluated by a single function. The construction in Section 5.7 deals with the special case in which all synthesized attributes form one group. The grouping of attributes is determined from the dependencies set up by the semantic rules in a syntax-directed definition. The following abstract example illustrates the construction of a recursive evaluator.

Example 5.29. The syntax-directed definition in Fig. 5.57 is motivated by a problem we shall consider in Chapter 6. Briefly, the problem is as follows. An "overloaded" identifier can have a set of possible types; as a result, an expression can have a set of possible types. Context information is used to select one of the possible types for each subexpression. The problem can be solved by making a bottom-up pass to synthesize the set of possible types, followed by a top-down pass to narrow down the set to a single type.

The semantic rules in Fig. 5.57 are an abstraction of this problem. Synthesized attribute s represents the set of possible types and inherited attribute i represents the context information. An additional synthesized attribute t that cannot be evaluated in the same pass as s might represent the generated code or the type selected for a subexpression. Dependency graphs for the productions in Fig. 5.57 are shown in Fig. 5.58.   □

PRODUCTION	SEMANTIC RULES
$S \rightarrow E$	$E.i := g(E.s)$ $S.r := E.t$
$E \rightarrow E_1 E_2$	$E.s := fs(E_1.s, E_2.s)$ $E_1.i := fi1(E.i)$ $E_2.i := fi2(E.i)$ $E.t := ft(E_1.t, E_2.t)$
$E \rightarrow \mathbf{id}$	$E.s := \mathbf{id}.s$ $E.t := h(E.i)$

Fig. 5.57. Synthesized attributes s and t cannot be evaluated together.

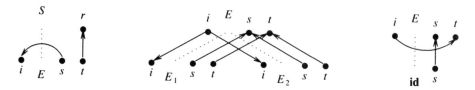

Fig. 5.58. Dependency graphs for productions in Fig. 5.57.

Recursive Evaluation of Attributes

The dependency graph for a parse tree is formed by pasting together smaller graphs corresponding to the semantic rules for a production. The dependency graph D_p for production p is based only on the semantic rules for a single production, i.e., on the semantic rules for the synthesized attributes of the left side and the inherited attributes of the grammar symbols on the right side of the production. That is, the graph D_p shows local dependencies only. For example, all edges in the dependency graph for $E \rightarrow E_1 E_2$ in Fig. 5.58 are between instances of the same attribute. From this dependency graph, we cannot tell that the s attributes must be computed before the other attributes.

A close look at the dependency graph for the parse tree in Fig. 5.59 shows that the attributes of each instance of nonterminal E must be evaluated in the order $E.s$, $E.i$, $E.t$. Note that all attributes in Fig. 5.59 can be evaluated in three passes: a bottom-up pass to evaluate the s attributes, a top-down pass to evaluate the i attributes, and a final bottom-up pass to evaluate the t attributes.

In a recursive evaluator, the function for a synthesized attribute takes the values of some of the inherited attributes as parameters. In general, if synthesized attribute $A.a$ can depend on inherited attribute $A.b$, then the function

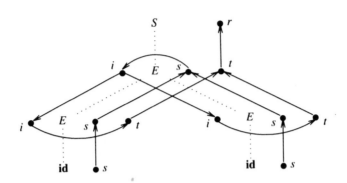

Fig. 5.59. Dependency graph for a parse tree.

for $A.a$ takes $A.b$ as a parameter. Before analyzing dependencies, we consider an example showing their use.

Example 5.30. The functions Es and Et in Fig. 5.60 return the values of the synthesized attributes s and t at a node n labeled E. As in Section 5.7, there is a case for each production in the function for a nonterminal. The code executed in each case simulates the semantic rules associated with the production in Fig. 5.57.

From the above discussion of the dependency graph in Fig. 5.59 we know that attribute $E.t$ at a node in a parse tree may depend on $E.i$. We therefore pass inherited attribute i as a parameter to the function Et for attribute t. Since attribute $E.s$ does not depend on any inherited attributes, function Es has no parameters corresponding to attribute values. □

Strongly Noncircular Syntax-Directed Definitions

Recursive evaluators can be constructed for a class of syntax-directed definitions, called "strongly noncircular" definitions. For a definition in this class, the attributes at each node for a nonterminal can be evaluated according to the same (partial) order. When we construct the function for a synthesized attribute of the nonterminal, this order is used to select the inherited attributes that become the parameters of the function.

We give a definition of this class and show that the syntax-directed definition in Fig. 5.57 falls in the class. We then give an algorithm for testing circularity and strong noncircularity, and show how the implementation of Example 5.30 extends to all strongly noncircular definitions.

Consider nonterminal A at a node n in a parse tree. The dependency graph for the parse tree may in general have paths that start at an attribute of node n, go through attributes of other nodes in the parse tree, and end at another attribute of n. For our purposes, it is enough to look at paths that stay within the part of the parse tree below A. A little thought reveals that such paths go

function $Es(n)$;
begin
    case production at node n **of**
    $'E \rightarrow E_1 E_2'$:
        $s1 := Es(child(n, 1))$;
        $s2 := Es(child(n, 2))$;
        return $fs(s1, s2)$;
    $'E \rightarrow \text{id}'$:
        return id.s;
    default:
        error
    end
end;

function $Et(n, i)$;
begin
    case production at node n **of**
    $'E \rightarrow E_1 E_2'$:
        $i1 := fi1(i)$;
        $t1 := Et(child(n, 1), i1)$;
        $i2 := fi2(i)$;
        $t2 := Et(child(n, 2), i2)$;
        return $ft(t1, t2)$;
    $'E \rightarrow \text{id}'$:
        return $h(i)$;
    default:
        error
    end
end;

function $Sr(n)$;
begin
    $s := Es(child(n, 1))$;
    $i := g(s)$;
    $t := Et(child(n, 1), i)$;
    return t
end;

Fig. 5.60. Functions for synthesized attributes in Fig. 5.57.

from some inherited attribute of A to some synthesized attribute of A. We shall make an estimate (possibly too pessimistic) of the set of such paths by considering partial orders on the attributes of A.

Let production p have nonterminals $A_1, A_2, \ldots, A_n$ occurring on the right side. Let RA_j be a partial order on the attributes of A_j, for $1 \leq j \leq n$. We write $D_p[RA_1, RA_2, \ldots, RA_n]$ for the graph obtained by adding edges to D_p as follows: if RA_j orders attribute $A_j.b$ before $A_j.c$ then add an edge from $A_j.b$ to $A_j.c$.

A syntax-directed definition is said to be *strongly noncircular* if for each nonterminal A we can find a partial order RA on the attributes of A such that for each production p with left side A and nonterminals $A_1, A_2, \ldots, A_n$ occurring on the right side

1. $D_p[RA_1, RA_2, \ldots, RA_n]$ is acyclic, and

2. if there is an edge from attribute $A.b$ to $A.c$ in $D_p[RA_1, RA_2, \ldots, RA_n]$, then RA orders $A.b$ before $A.c$.

Example 5.31. Let p be the production $E \rightarrow E_1 E_2$ from Fig. 5.57, whose dependency graph D_p is in the center of Fig. 5.58. Let RE be the partial order (total order in this case) $s \rightarrow i \rightarrow t$. There are two occurrences of nonterminals on the right side of p, written E_1 and E_2, as usual. Thus, RE_1 and RE_2 are the same as RE, and the graph $D_p[RE_1, RE_2]$ is as shown in Fig. 5.61.

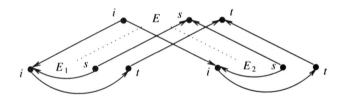

Fig. 5.61. Augmented dependency graph for a production.

Among the attributes associated with the root E in Fig. 5.61, the only paths are from i to t. Since RE makes i precede t, there is no violation of condition (2).   □

Given a strongly noncircular definition and partial order RA for each nonterminal A, the function for synthesized attribute s of A takes arguments as follows: if RA orders inherited attribute i before s, then i is an argument of the function, otherwise not.

A Circularity Test

A syntax-directed definition is said to be *circular* if the dependency graph for some parse tree has a cycle; circular definitions are ill-formed and meaningless. There is no way we can begin to compute any of the attribute values on the cycle. Computing the partial orders that ensure that a definition is strongly noncircular is closely related to testing if a definition is circular. We shall therefore first consider a test for circularity.

Example 5.32. In the following syntax-directed definition, paths between the attributes of A depend on which production is applied. If $A \rightarrow 1$ is applied, then $A.s$ depends on $A.i$; otherwise, it does not. For complete information about the possible dependencies we therefore have to keep track of sets of partial orders on the attributes of a nonterminal.

PRODUCTION	SEMANTIC RULES
$S \rightarrow A$	$A.i := c$
$A \rightarrow 1$	$A.s := f(A.i)$
$A \rightarrow 2$	$A.s := d$

□

The idea behind the algorithm in Fig. 5.62 is as follows. We represent partial orders by directed acyclic graphs. Given dags on the attributes of symbols on the right side of a production, we can determine a dag for the attributes of the left side as follows.

```
for grammar symbol X do
    ℱ(X) has a single graph with the attributes of X and no edges;
repeat
    change := false;
    for production p given by A → X₁X₂ · · · Xₖ do begin
        for dags G₁ ∈ ℱ(X₁), . . . , Gₖ ∈ ℱ(Xₖ) do begin
            D := Dₚ;
            for edge b → c in Gⱼ, 1≤j≤k do
                add an edge in D between attributes b and c of Xⱼ;
            if D has a cycle then
                fail the circularity test
            else begin
                G := a new graph with nodes for the attributes
                    of A and no edges;
                for each pair of attributes b and c of A do
                    if there is a path in D from b to c then
                        add b → c to G;
                if G is not already in ℱ(A) then begin
                    add G to ℱ(A);
                    change := true
                end
            end
        end
    end
until change = false
```

Fig. 5.62. A circularity test.

Let production p be $A \rightarrow X_1X_2 \cdots X_k$ with dependency graph D_p. Let D_j be a dag for X_j, $1 \leq j \leq k$. Each edge $b \rightarrow a$ in D_j is temporarily added in to the dependency graph D_p for the production. If the resulting graph has a cycle, then the syntax-directed definition is circular. Otherwise, paths in the resulting graph determine a new dag on the attributes of the left side of the production, and the resulting dag is added to $\mathcal{F}(A)$.

The circularity test in Fig. 5.62 takes time exponential in the number of graphs in the sets $\mathcal{F}(X)$ for any grammar symbol X. There are syntax-directed definitions that cannot be tested for circularity in polynomial time.

We can convert the algorithm in Fig. 5.62 into a more efficient test if a syntax-directed definition is strongly noncircular, as follows. Instead of maintaining a family of graphs $\mathcal{F}(X)$ for each X, we summarize the information in the family by keeping a single graph $F(X)$. Note that each graph in $\mathcal{F}(X)$ has the same nodes for the attributes of X, but may have different edges. $F(X)$ is the graph on the nodes for the attributes of X that has an edge between $X.b$ and $X.c$ if any graph in $\mathcal{F}(X)$ does. $F(X)$ represents a "worst-case estimate" of dependencies between attributes of X. In particular, if $F(X)$ is acyclic, then the syntax-directed definition is guaranteed to be noncircular. However, the converse need not be true; i.e., if $F(X)$ has a cycle, it is not necessarily true that the syntax-directed definition is circular.

The modified circularity test constructs acyclic graphs $F(X)$ for each X if it succeeds. From these graphs we can construct an evaluator for the syntax-directed definition. The method is a straightforward generalization of Example 5.30. The function for synthesized attribute $X.s$ takes as arguments all and only the inherited attributes that precede s in $F(X)$. The function, called at node n, calls other functions that compute the needed synthesized attributes at the children of n. The routines to compute these attributes are passed values for the inherited attributes they need. The fact that the strong noncircularity test succeeded guarantees that these inherited attributes can be computed.

EXERCISES

5.1 For the input expression $(4*7+1)*2$, construct an annotated parse tree according to the syntax-directed definition of Fig. 5.2

5.2 Construct the parse tree and syntax tree for the expression $((a)+(b))$ according to
a) the syntax-directed definition of Fig. 5.9, and
b) the translation scheme of Fig. 5.28.

5.3 Construct the dag and identify the value numbers for the subexpressions of the following expression, assuming + associates from the left:
$a+a+(a+a+a+(a+a+a+a))$.

*5.4 Give a syntax-directed definition to translate infix expressions into infix expressions without redundant parentheses. For example, since + and * associate to the left, $((a*(b+c))*(d))$ can be rewritten as $a*(b+c)*d$.

5.5 Give a syntax-directed definition to differentiate expressions formed by applying the arithmetic operators + and * to the variable **x** and constants; e.g., **x*(3*x+x*x)**. Assume that no simplification takes place, so **3*x** translates into **3*1+0*x**.

5.6 The following grammar generates expressions formed by applying an arithmetic operator + to integer and real constants. When two integers are added, the resulting type is integer, otherwise, it is real.

$$E \rightarrow E + T \mid T$$
$$T \rightarrow \textbf{num . num} \mid \textbf{num}$$

a) Give a syntax-directed definition to determine the type of each subexpression.

b) Extend the syntax-directed definition of (a) to translate expressions into postfix notation as well as determining types. Use the unary operator **inttoreal** to convert an integer value into an equivalent real value, so that both operands of + in the postfix form have the same type.

5.7 Extend the syntax-directed definition of Fig. 5.22 to keep track of the widths of boxes in addition to keeping track of their heights. Assume that terminal **text** has synthesized attribute w giving the normalized width of the text.

5.8 Let synthesized attribute *val* give the value of the binary number generated by S in the following grammar. For example, on input 101.101, $S.val = 5.625$

$$S \rightarrow L . L \mid L$$
$$L \rightarrow L B \mid B$$
$$B \rightarrow 0 \mid 1$$

a) Use synthesized attributes to determine $S.val$.

b) Determine $S.val$ with a syntax-directed definition in which the only synthesized attribute of B is c, giving the contribution of the bit generated by B to the final value. For example, the contribution of the first and last bits in 101.101 to the value 5.625 is 4 and 0.125, respectively.

5.9 Rewrite the underlying grammar in the syntax-directed definition of Example 5.3 so that type information can be propagated using synthesized attributes alone.

*5.10 When statements generated by the following grammar are translated into abstract machine code, a break statement translates into a jump to the instruction following the nearest enclosing while statement. For simplicity, expressions are represented by the terminal **expr** and other kinds of statements by the terminal **other**. These terminals have a synthesized attribute *code* giving their translation.

$S \rightarrow$ **while expr do begin** S **end**
$| \quad S ; S$
$| \quad$ **break**
$| \quad$ **other**

Give a syntax-directed definition translating statements into code for the stack machine of Section 2.8. Make sure that break statements within nested while statements are translated correctly.

5.11 Eliminate left recursion from the syntax-directed definitions in Exercise 5.6(a) and (b).

5.12 Expressions generated by the following grammar can have assignments within them.

$S \rightarrow E$
$E \rightarrow E := E \quad | \quad E + E \quad | \quad (E) \quad | \quad$ **id**

The semantics of expressions are as in C. That is, b:=c is an expression that assigns the value of c to b; the r-value of this expression is the same as that of c. Furthermore, a:=(b:=c) assigns the value of c to b and then to a.

a) Construct a syntax-directed definition for checking that the left side of an expression is an l-value. Use an inherited attribute *side* of nonterminal E to indicate whether the expression generated by E appears on the left or right side of an assignment.

b) Extend the syntax-directed definition in (a) to generate intermediate code for the stack machine of Section 2.8 as it checks the input.

5.13 Rewrite the underlying grammar of Exercise 5.12 so that it groups the subexpressions of := to the right and the subexpressions of + to the left.

a) Construct a translation scheme that simulates the syntax-directed definition of Exercise 5.12(b).

b) Modify the translation scheme of (a) to emit code incrementally to an output file.

5.14 Give a translation scheme for checking that the same identifier does not appear twice in a list of identifiers.

5.15 Suppose declarations are generated by the following grammar.

$D \rightarrow$ **id** L
$L \rightarrow$, **id** $L \quad | \quad : T$
$T \rightarrow$ **integer** $| \quad$ **real**

a) Construct a translation scheme to enter the type of each identifier into the symbol table, as in Example 5.3.

    b) Construct a predictive translator from the translation scheme in (a).

5.16 The following grammar is an unambiguous version of the underlying grammar in Fig. 5.22. The braces { } are used only for grouping boxes, and are eliminated during translation.

$$S \rightarrow L$$
$$L \rightarrow L\ B \mid B$$
$$B \rightarrow B\ \text{sub}\ F \mid F$$
$$F \rightarrow \{\ L\ \} \mid \textbf{text}$$

    a) Adapt the syntax-directed definition in Fig. 5.22 to use the above grammar.

    b) Convert the syntax-directed definition of (a) into a translation scheme.

*5.17 Extend the transformation for eliminating left recursion in Section 5.5 to allow the following for nonterminal A in (5.2).

    a) Inherited attributes defined by copy rules.

    b) Inherited attributes.

5.18 Eliminate left recursion from the translation scheme of Exercise 5.16(b).

*5.19 Suppose we have an L-attributed definition whose underlying grammar is either LL(1), or one for which we can resolve ambiguities and construct a predictive parser. Show that we may keep inherited and synthesized attributes on the parser stack of a top-down parser driven by the predictive parsing table.

*5.20 Prove that adding unique marker nonterminals anywhere in an LL(1) grammar results in a grammar that is LR(1).

5.21 Consider the following modification of the LR(1) grammar $L \rightarrow L\,b \mid a$:

$$L \rightarrow M\,L\,b \mid a$$
$$M \rightarrow \epsilon$$

    a) What order would a bottom-up parser apply the productions in the parse tree for the input string *abbb*?

    *b) Show that the modified grammar is not LR(1).

*5.22 Show that in a translation scheme based on Fig. 5.36, the value of inherited attribute $B.ps$ is always immediately below the right side, whenever we reduce a right side to B.

5.23 Algorithm 5.3 for bottom-up parsing and translation with inherited attributes uses marker nonterminals to hold the values of inherited attributes at predictable positions in the parser stack. Fewer markers may be needed if the values are placed on a stack separate from the parsing stack.

    a) Convert the syntax-directed definition in Fig. 5.36 into a translation scheme.

    b) Modify the translation scheme constructed in (a) so that the value of inherited attribute *ps* appears on a separate stack. Eliminate marker nonterminal *M* in the process.

*5.24 Consider translation during parsing as in Exercise 5.23. S. C. Johnson suggests the following method for simulating a separate stack for inherited attributes, using markers and a global variable for each inherited attribute. In the following production, the value *v* is pushed onto stack *i* by the first action and is popped by the second action:

$$A \rightarrow \alpha \ \{ \ push(v, i) \ \} \ \beta \ \{ \ pop(i) \ \}$$

Stack *i* can be simulated by the following productions that use a global variable *g* and a marker nonterminal *M* with synthesized attribute *s*:

$$A \rightarrow \alpha \ M \ \beta \ \{ \ g := M.s \ \}$$
$$M \rightarrow \epsilon \ \{ \ M.s := g; \ g := v \ \}$$

    a) Apply this transformation to the translation scheme of Exercise 5.23(b). Replace all references to the top of the separate stack by references to the global variable.

    b) Show that the translation scheme constructed in (a) computes the same values for the synthesized attribute of the start symbol as that in Exercise 5.23(b).

5.25 Use the approach of Section 5.8 to implement all the *E.side* attributes in the translation scheme of Exercise 5.12(b) by a single boolean variable.

5.26 Modify the use of the stack during the depth-first traversal in Example 5.26 so that the values on the stack correspond to those kept on the parser stack in Example 5.19.

BIBLIOGRAPHIC NOTES

The use of synthesized attributes to specify the translation of a language appears in Irons [1961]. The idea of a parser calling for semantic actions is discussed by Samelson and Bauer [1960] and Brooker and Morris [1962]. Along with inherited attributes, dependency graphs and a test for strong noncircularity appear in Knuth [1968] — a test for circularity appears in a correction to the paper. The extended example in the paper uses disciplined side effects to global attributes attached to the root of a parse tree. If attributes can be functions, inherited attributes can be eliminated; as done in denotational semantics, we can associate a function from inherited to synthesized attributes with a nonterminal. Such observations appear in Mayoh [1981].

One application in which side effects in semantic rules are undesirable is syntax-directed editing. Suppose an editor is generated from an attribute grammar for the source language, as in Reps [1984], and consider an editing change to the source program that results in a portion of the parse tree for the program being deleted. As long as there are no side effects, attribute values for the changed program can be recomputed incrementally.

Ershov [1958] uses hashing to keep track of common subexpressions.

The definition of L-attributed grammars in Lewis, Rosenkrantz, and Stearns [1974] is motivated by translation during parsing. Similar restrictions on attribute dependencies apply to each of the left-to-right depth-first traversals in Bochmann [1976]. Affix grammars, as introduced by Koster [1971], are related to L-attributed grammars. Restrictions on L-attributed grammars are proposed in Koskimies and Räihä [1983] to control access to global attributes.

The mechanical construction of a predictive translator, similar to those constructed by Algorithm 5.2, is described by Bochmann and Ward [1978]. The impression that top-down parsing allows more flexibility for translation is shown to be false by a proof in Brosgol [1974] that a translation scheme based on an LL(1) grammar can be simulated during LR(1) parsing. Independently, Watt [1977] used marker nonterminals to ensure that the values of inherited attributes appear on a stack during bottom-up parsing. Positions on the right sides of productions where marker nonterminals can safely be inserted without losing the LR(1) property are considered in Purdom and Brown [1980] (see Exercise 5.21). Simply requiring inherited attributes to be defined by copy rules is not enough to ensure that attributes can be evaluated during bottom-up parsing; sufficient conditions on semantic rules are given in Tarhio [1982]. A characterization, in terms of parser states, of attributes that can be evaluated during LR(1) parsing, is given by Jones and Madsen [1980]. As an example of a translation that cannot be done during parsing, Giegerich and Wilhelm [1978] consider code generation for boolean expressions. We shall see in Section 8.6 that backpatching can be used for this problem, so a complete second pass is not necessary.

A number of tools for implementing syntax-directed definitions have been developed, starting with FOLDS by Fang [1972], but few have seen widespread use. DELTA by Lorho [1977] constructed a dependency graph at compile time. It saved space by keeping track of the lifetimes of attributes and eliminating copy rules. Parse-tree based attribute evaluation methods are discussed by Kennedy and Ramanathan [1979] and Cohen and Harry [1979].

Attribute evaluation methods are surveyed by Engelfriet [1984]. A companion paper by Courcelle [1984] surveys the theoretical foundations. HLP, described by Räihä et al. [1983], makes alternating depth-first traversals, as suggested by Jazayeri and Walter [1975]. LINGUIST by Farrow [1984] also makes alternating passes. Ganzinger et al. [1982] report that MUG allows the order in which children of a node are visited to be determined by the production at the node. GAG, due to Kastens, Hutt, and Zimmerman [1982] allows repeated visits to children of a node. GAG implements the class of ordered attribute grammars defined by Kastens [1980]. The idea of repeated visits appears in the earlier paper by Kennedy and Warren [1976], where evaluators for the larger class of strongly noncircular grammars are constructed. Saarinen [1978] describes a modification of Kennedy and Warren's method that saves space by keeping attribute values on a stack if they are not needed during a later visit. An implementation described by Jourdan [1984] constructs recursive evaluators for this class. Recursive evaluators are also constructed by Katayama [1984]. A quite different approach is taken in NEATS by Madsen [1980], where a dag is constructed for expressions representing attribute values.

Analysis of dependencies at compiler-construction time can save time and space at compile time. Testing for circularity is a typical analysis problem. Jazayeri, Ogden, and Rounds [1975] prove that a circularity test requires an exponential amount of time as a function of grammar size. Techniques for improving the implementation of a circularity test are considered by Lorho and Pair [1975], Räihä and Saarinen [1982], and Deransart, Jourdan, and Lorho [1984].

The space used by naive evaluators has led to the development of techniques for conserving space. The algorithm for assigning attribute values to registers in Section 5.8 was described in a quite different context by Marill [1962]. The problem of finding a topological sort of the dependency graph that minimizes the number of registers used is shown to be NP-complete in Sethi [1975]. Compile-time analysis of lifetimes in a multi-pass evaluator appears in Räihä [1981] and Jazayeri and Pozefsky [1981]. Branquart et al. [1976] mention the use of separate stacks for holding synthesized and inherited attributes during a traversal. GAG performs lifetime analysis and places attribute values in global variables, stacks, and parse tree nodes as needed. A comparison of the space-saving techniques used by GAG and LINGUIST is made by Farrow and Yellin [1984].

CHAPTER 6

Type
Checking

A compiler must check that the source program follows both the syntactic and semantic conventions of the source language. This checking, called *static checking* (to distinguish it from *dynamic* checking during execution of the target program), ensures that certain kinds of programming errors will be detected and reported. Examples of static checks include:

1. *Type checks.* A compiler should report an error if an operator is applied to an incompatible operand; for example, if an array variable and a function variable are added together.

2. *Flow-of-control checks.* Statements that cause flow of control to leave a construct must have some place to which to transfer the flow of control. For example, a break statement in C causes control to leave the smallest enclosing while, for, or switch statement; an error occurs if such an enclosing statement does not exist.

3. *Uniqueness checks.* There are situations in which an object must be defined exactly once. For example, in Pascal, an identifier must be declared uniquely, labels in a case statement must be distinct, and elements in a scalar type may not be repeated.

4. *Name-related checks.* Sometimes, the same name must appear two or more times. For example, in Ada, a loop or block may have a name that appears at the beginning and end of the construct. The compiler must check that the same name is used at both places.

In this chapter, we focus on type checking. As the above examples indicate, most of the other static checks are routine and can be implemented using the techniques of the last chapter. Some of them can be folded into other activities. For example, as we enter information about a name into a symbol table, we can check that the name is declared uniquely. Many Pascal compilers combine static checking and intermediate code generation with parsing. With more complex constructs, like those of Ada, it may be convenient to have a separate type-checking pass between parsing and intermediate code generation, as indicated in Fig. 6.1.

A type checker verifies that the type of a construct matches that expected by

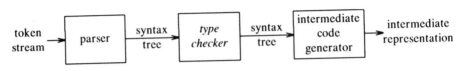

Fig. 6.1. Position of type checker.

its context. For example, the built-in arithmetic operator mod in Pascal requires integer operands, so a type checker must verify that the operands of mod have type integer. Similarly, the type checker must verify that dereferencing is applied only to a pointer, that indexing is done only on an array, that a user-defined function is applied to the correct number and type of arguments, and so forth. A specification of a simple type checker appears in Section 6.2. The representation of types and the question of when two types match are discussed in Section 6.3.

Type information gathered by a type checker may be needed when code is generated. For example, arithmetic operators like + usually apply to either integers or reals, perhaps to other types, and we have to look at the context of + to determine the sense that is intended. A symbol that can represent different operations in different contexts is said to be "overloaded." Overloading may be accompanied by coercion of types, where a compiler supplies an operator to convert an operand into the type expected by the context.

A distinct notion from overloading is that of "polymorphism." The body of a polymorphic function can be executed with arguments of several types. A unification algorithm for inferring types of polymorphic functions concludes this chapter.

6.1 TYPE SYSTEMS

The design of a type checker for a language is based on information about the syntactic constructs in the language, the notion of types, and the rules for assigning types to language constructs. The following excerpts from the Pascal report and the C reference manual, respectively, are examples of information that a compiler writer might have to start with.

- "If both operands of the arithmetic operators of addition, subtraction and multiplication are of type integer, then the result is of type integer."

- "The result of the unary & operator is a pointer to the object referred to by the operand. If the type of the operand is '...', the type of the result is 'pointer to ...'."

Implicit in the above excerpts is the idea that each expression has a type

associated with it. Furthermore, types have structure; the type "pointer to
..." is constructed from the type that "..." refers to.

In both Pascal and C, types are either basic or constructed. Basic types are
the atomic types with no internal structure as far as the programmer is concerned. In Pascal, the basic types are boolean, character, integer, and real.
Subrange types, like 1..10, and enumerated types, like

```
(violet, indigo, blue, green, yellow, orange, red)
```

can be treated as basic types. Pascal allows a programmer to construct types
from basic types and other constructed types, with arrays, records, and sets
being examples. In addition, pointers and functions can also be treated as
constructed types.

Type Expressions

The type of a language construct will be denoted by a "type expression."
Informally, a type expression is either a basic type or is formed by applying an
operator called a *type constructor* to other type expressions. The sets of basic
types and constructors depend on the language to be checked.

This chapter uses the following definition of *type expressions*:

1. A basic type is a type expression. Among the basic types are *boolean*,
    char, *integer*, and *real*. A special basic type, *type_error*, will signal an
    error during type checking. Finally, a basic type *void* denoting "the
    absence of a value" allows statements to be checked.

2. Since type expressions may be named, a type name is a type expression.
    An example of the use of type names appears in 3(c) below; type expres-
    sions containing names are discussed in Section 6.3.

3. A type constructor applied to type expressions is a type expression. Con-
    structors include:

    a) *Arrays.* If T is a type expression, then $array(I, T)$ is a type expres-
        sion denoting the type of an array with elements of type T and index
        set I. I is often a range of integers. For example, the Pascal
        declaration

        ```
        var A: array[1..10] of integer;
        ```

        associates the type expression $array(1..10, integer)$ with A.

    b) *Products.* If T_1 and T_2 are type expressions, then their Cartesian
        product $T_1 \times T_2$ is a type expression. We assume that $\times$ associates
        to the left.

    c) *Records.* The difference between a record and a product is that the
        fields of a record have names. The *record* type constructor will be
        applied to a tuple formed from field names and field types. (Techni-
        cally, the field names should be part of the type constructor, but it is

convenient to keep field names together with their associated types. In Chapter 8, the type constructor *record* is applied to a pointer to a symbol table containing entries for the field names.) For example, the Pascal program fragment

```
type row = record
                address: integer;
                lexeme: array [1..15] of char
            end;
     var  table: array [1..101] of row;
```

declares the type name `row` representing the type expression

$$record((\text{address} \times integer) \times (\text{lexeme} \times array(1..15, char)))$$

and the variable `table` to be an array of records of this type.

d) *Pointers.* If T is a type expression, then *pointer*(T) is a type expression denoting the type "pointer to an object of type T." For example, in Pascal, the declaration

```
var p: ↑ row
```

declares variable p to have type *pointer*(`row`).

e) *Functions.* Mathematically, a function maps elements of one set, the *domain*, to another set, the *range*. We may treat functions in programming languages as mapping a *domain type D* to a *range type R*. The type of such a function will be denoted by the type expression $D \to R$. For example, the built-in function mod of Pascal has domain type $int \times int$, i.e., a pair of integers, and range type int. Thus, we say mod has the type[1]

$$int \times int \to int$$

As another example, the Pascal declaration

```
function f(a, b: char) : ↑ integer;  · · ·
```

says that the domain type of f is denoted by $char \times char$ and range type by *pointer*(*integer*). The type of f is thus denoted by the type expression

$$char \times char \to pointer(integer)$$

Often, for implementation reasons discussed in the next chapter, there are limitations on the type that a function may return; e.g., no arrays or functions may be returned. However, there are languages, of which Lisp is the most prominent example, that allow functions to

---

[1] We assume that $\times$ has higher precedence than $\to$, so $int \times int \to int$ is the same as $(int \times int) \to int$. Also, $\to$ associates to the right.

return objects of arbitrary types, so, for example, we can define a function g of type

$$(integer \rightarrow integer) \rightarrow (integer \rightarrow integer)$$

That is, g takes as argument a function that maps an integer to an integer and g produces as a result another function of the same type.

4.   Type expressions may contain variables whose values are type expressions. Type variables will be introduced in Section 6.6.

A convenient way to represent a type expressions is to use a graph. Using the syntax-directed approach of Section 5.2, we can construct a tree or a dag for a type expression, with interior nodes for type constructors and leaves for basic types, type names, and type variables (see Fig. 6.2). Examples of representations of type expressions that have been used in compilers are given in Section 6.3.

Fig. 6.2. Tree and dag, respectively, for *char × char → pointer (integer)*.

Type Systems

A *type system* is a collection of rules for assigning type expressions to the various parts of a program. A type checker implements a type system. The type systems in this chapter are specified in a syntax-directed manner, so they can be readily implemented using the techniques of the previous chapter.

Different type systems may be used by different compilers or processors of the same language. For example, in Pascal, the type of an array includes the index set of the array, so a function with an array argument can only be applied to arrays with that index set. Many Pascal compilers, however, allow the index set to be left unspecified when an array is passed as an argument. Thus these compilers use a different type system than that in the Pascal language definition. Similarly, in the UNIX system, the `lint` command examines C programs for possible bugs using a more detailed type system than the C compiler itself uses.

Static and Dynamic Checking of Types

Checking done by a compiler is said to be static, while checking done when the target program runs is termed dynamic. In principle, any check can be done dynamically, if the target code carries the type of an element along with the value of that element.

A *sound* type system eliminates the need for dynamic checking for type errors because it allows us to determine statically that these errors cannot occur when the target program runs. That is, if a sound type system assigns a type other than *type_error* to a program part, then type errors cannot occur when the target code for the program part is run. A language is *strongly typed* if its compiler can guarantee that the programs it accepts will execute without type errors.

In practice, some checks can be done only dynamically. For example, if we first declare

```
table: array[0..255] of char;
i: integer
```

and then compute `table[i]`, a compiler cannot in general guarantee that during execution, the value of `i` will lie in the range 0 to 255.[2]

Error Recovery

Since type checking has the potential for catching errors in programs, it is important for a type checker to do something reasonable when an error is discovered. At the very least, the compiler must report the nature and location of the error. It is desirable for the type checker to recover from errors, so it can check the rest of the input. Since error handling affects the type-checking rules, it has to be designed into the type system right from the start; the rules must be prepared to cope with errors.

The inclusion of error handling may result in a type system that goes beyond the one needed to specify correct programs. For example, once an error has occurred, we may not know the type of the incorrectly formed program fragment. Coping with missing information requires techniques similar to those needed for languages that do not require identifiers to be declared before they are used. Type variables, discussed in Section 6.6, can be used to to ensure consistent usage of undeclared or apparently misdeclared identifiers.

6.2 SPECIFICATION OF A SIMPLE TYPE CHECKER

In this section, we specify a type checker for a simple language in which the type of each identifier must be declared before the identifier is used. The type checker is a translation scheme that synthesizes the type of each expression from the types of its subexpressions. The type checker can handle arrays, pointers, statements, and functions.

---

[2] Data-flow analysis techniques similar to those in Chapter 10 can be used to infer if i is within bounds in some programs. However, no technique can make the decision correctly in all cases.

A Simple Language

The grammar in Fig. 6.3 generates programs, represented by the nonterminal
P, consisting of a sequence of declarations D followed by a single expression
E.

$$P \rightarrow D \; ; \; E$$
$$D \rightarrow D \; ; \; D \quad | \quad \textbf{id} : T$$
$$T \rightarrow \textbf{char} \quad | \quad \textbf{integer} \quad | \quad \textbf{array} \; [\; \textbf{num} \;] \; \textbf{of} \; T \quad | \quad \uparrow T$$
$$E \rightarrow \textbf{literal} \quad | \quad \textbf{num} \quad | \quad \textbf{id} \quad | \quad E \; \textbf{mod} \; E \quad | \quad E \; [\; E \;] \quad | \quad E \uparrow$$

Fig. 6.3. Grammar for source language.

One program generated by the grammar in Fig. 6.3 is:

```
key: integer;
key mod 1999
```

Before discussing expressions, consider the types in the language. The
language itself has two basic types, *char* and *integer*; a third basic type
type_error is used to signal errors. For simplicity, we assume that all arrays
start at 1. For example,

```
array [256] of char
```

leads to the type expression *array*(1..256, *char*) consisting of the constructor
array applied to the subrange 1..256 and the type *char*. As in Pascal, the prefix operator $\uparrow$ in declarations builds a pointer type, so

```
↑ integer
```

leads to the type expression *pointer*(*integer*), consisting of the constructor
pointer applied to the type *integer*.

In the translation scheme of Fig. 6.4, the action associated with the production $D \rightarrow \textbf{id} : T$ saves a type in a symbol-table entry for an identifier. The
action *addtype*(**id**.*entry*, *T.type*) is applied to synthesized attribute *entry* pointing to the symbol-table entry for **id** and a type expression represented by synthesized attribute *type* of nonterminal T.

If T generates **char** or **integer**, then *T.type* is defined to be *char* or *integer*,
respectively. The upper bound of an array is obtained from the attribute *val*
of token **num** that gives the integer represented by **num**. Arrays are assumed
to start at 1, so the type constructor *array* is applied to the subrange
1..**num**.*val* and the element type.

Since D appears before E on the right side of $P \rightarrow D \; ; \; E$, we can be sure
that the types of all declared identifiers will be saved before the expression
generated by E is checked. (See Chapter 5.) In fact, by suitably modifying
the grammar in Fig. 6.3, we can implement the translation schemes in this
section during either top-down or bottom-up parsing, if desired.

$$P \rightarrow D \; ; \; E$$
$$D \rightarrow D \; ; \; D$$
$$D \rightarrow \textbf{id} : T \qquad\qquad\qquad \{ \; addtype \, (\textbf{id}.entry, \; T.type) \; \}$$
$$T \rightarrow \textbf{char} \qquad\qquad\qquad \{ \; T.type := char \; \}$$
$$T \rightarrow \textbf{integer} \qquad\qquad\quad \{ \; T.type := integer \; \}$$
$$T \rightarrow \uparrow T_1 \qquad\qquad\qquad\; \{ \; T.type := pointer \, (T_1.type) \; \}$$
$$T \rightarrow \textbf{array} \; [\; \textbf{num} \;] \; \textbf{of} \; T_1 \quad \{ \; T.type := array \, (1 .. \textbf{num}.val, \; T_1.type) \; \}$$

Fig. 6.4. The part of a translation scheme that saves the type of an identifier.

Type Checking of Expressions

In the following rules, the synthesized attribute *type* for E gives the type expression assigned by the type system to the expression generated by E. The following semantic rules say that constants represented by the tokens **literal** and **num** have type *char* and *integer*, respectively:

$$E \rightarrow \textbf{literal} \qquad\qquad \{ \; E.type := char \; \}$$
$$E \rightarrow \textbf{num} \qquad\qquad\quad\; \{ \; E.type := integer \; \}$$

We use a function *lookup* (e) to fetch the type saved in the symbol-table entry pointed to by e. When an identifier appears in an expression, its declared type is fetched and assigned to the attribute *type*:

$$E \rightarrow \textbf{id} \qquad\qquad\qquad \{ \; E.type := lookup \, (\textbf{id}.entry) \; \}$$

The expression formed by applying the mod operator to two subexpressions of type *integer* has type *integer*; otherwise, its type is *type_error*. The rule is

$$E \rightarrow E_1 \; \textbf{mod} \; E_2 \qquad \{ \; E.type := \textbf{if} \; E_1.type = integer \; \textbf{and}$$
$$E_2.type = integer \; \textbf{then} \; integer$$
$$\textbf{else} \; type\_error \; \}$$

In an array reference $E_1 [E_2]$, the index expression E_2 must have type integer, in which case the result is the element type t obtained from the type *array* (s, t) of E_1; we make no use of the index set s of the array.

$$E \rightarrow E_1 \; [\; E_2 \;] \qquad\quad \{ \; E.type := \textbf{if} \; E_2.type = integer \; \textbf{and}$$
$$E_1.type = array \, (s, \; t) \; \textbf{then} \; t$$
$$\textbf{else} \; type\_error \; \}$$

Within expressions, the postfix operator $\uparrow$ yields the object pointed to by its operand. The type of $E \uparrow$ is the type t of the object pointed to by the pointer E:

$$E \rightarrow E_1 \uparrow \qquad\qquad\quad \{ \; E.type := \textbf{if} \; E_1.type = pointer \, (t) \; \textbf{then} \; t$$
$$\textbf{else} \; type\_error \; \}$$

We leave it to the reader to add productions and semantic rules to permit additional types and operations within expressions. For example, to allow identifiers to have the type *boolean*, we can introduce the production $T \rightarrow$ **boolean** to the grammar of Fig. 6.3. The introduction of comparison operators like < and logical connectives like **and** into the productions for E would allow the construction of expressions of type *boolean*.

Type Checking of Statements

Since language constructs like statements typically do not have values, the special basic type *void* can be assigned to them. If an error is detected within a statement, the type assigned to the statement is *type_error*.

The statements we consider are assignment, conditional, and while statements. Sequences of statements are separated by semicolons. The productions in Fig. 6.5 can be combined with those of Fig. 6.3 if we change the production for a complete program to $P \rightarrow D ; S$. A program now consists of declarations followed by statements; the above rules for checking expressions are still needed because statements can have expressions within them.

$$
\begin{array}{ll}
S \rightarrow \textbf{id} := E & \{ \ S.type := \textbf{if } id.type = E.type \textbf{ then } void \\
& \qquad\qquad\quad \textbf{else } type\_error \ \} \\[4pt]
S \rightarrow \textbf{if } E \textbf{ then } S_1 & \{ \ S.type := \textbf{if } E.type = boolean \textbf{ then } S_1.type \\
& \qquad\qquad\quad \textbf{else } type\_error \ \} \\[4pt]
S \rightarrow \textbf{while } E \textbf{ do } S_1 & \{ \ S.type := \textbf{if } E.type = boolean \textbf{ then } S_1.type \\
& \qquad\qquad\quad \textbf{else } type\_error \ \} \\[4pt]
S \rightarrow S_1 ; S_2 & \{ \ S.type := \textbf{if } S_1.type = void \textbf{ and} \\
& \qquad\qquad\qquad\qquad S_2.type = void \textbf{ then } void \\
& \qquad\qquad\quad \textbf{else } type\_error \ \}
\end{array}
$$

Fig. 6.5. Translation scheme for checking the type of statements.

Rules for checking statements are given in Fig. 6.5. The first rule checks that the left and right sides of an assignment statement have the same type.[3] The second and third rules specify that expressions in conditional and while statements must have type *boolean*. Errors are propagated by the last rule in Fig. 6.5 because a sequence of statements has type *void* only if each substatement has type *void*. In these rules, a mismatch of types produces the type *type_error*; a friendly type checker would, of course, report the nature and location of the type mismatch as well.

---

[3] If an expression is allowed on the left side of an assignment, then we also have to distinguish between *l*-values and *r*-values. For example, 1 := 2 is incorrect because the constant 1 cannot be assigned to.

Type Checking of Functions

The application of a function to an argument can be captured by the production

$$E \rightarrow E \ (\ E \ )$$

in which an expression is the application of one expression to another. The rules for associating type expressions with nonterminal T can be augmented by the following production and action to permit function types in declarations.

$$T \rightarrow T_1 \ '\rightarrow' \ T_2 \qquad \{ \ T.type := T_1.type \rightarrow T_2.type \ \}$$

Quotes around the arrow used as a function constructor distinguish it from the arrow used as the metasymbol in a production.

The rule for checking the type of a function application is

$$E \rightarrow E_1 \ (\ E_2 \ ) \qquad \{ \ E.type := \textbf{if} \ E_2.type = s \ \textbf{and}$$
$$E_1.type = s \rightarrow t \ \textbf{then} \ t$$
$$\textbf{else} \ type\_error \ \}$$

This rule says that in an expression formed by applying E_1 to E_2, the type of E_1 must be a function $s \rightarrow t$ from the type s of E_2 to some range type t; the type of $E_1(E_2)$ is t.

Many issues related to type checking in the presence of functions can be discussed with respect to the simple syntax above. The generalization to functions with more than one argument is done by constructing a product type consisting of the arguments. Note that n arguments of type $T_1, \ldots, T_n$ can be viewed as a single argument of type $T_1 \times \cdots \times T_n$. For example, we might write

```
root : (real → real) × real  →  real            (6.1)
```

to declare a function root that takes a function from reals to reals and a real as arguments and returns a real. Pascal-like syntax for this declaration is

```
function root (function f (real): real; x: real): real
```

The syntax in (6.1) separates the declaration of the type of a function from the names of its parameters.

6.3 EQUIVALENCE OF TYPE EXPRESSIONS

The checking rules in the last section have the form, "**if** two type expressions are equal **then** return a certain type **else** return *type_error*." It is therefore important to have a precise definition of when two type expressions are equivalent. Potential ambiguities arise when names are given to type expressions and the names are then used in subsequent type expressions. The key issue is whether a name in a type expression stands for itself or whether it is an abbreviation for another type expression.

Since there is interaction between the notion of equivalence of types and the representation of types, we shall talk about both together. For efficiency, compilers use representations that allow type equivalence to be determined quickly. The notion of type equivalence implemented by a specific compiler can often be explained using the concepts of structural and name equivalence discussed in this section. The discussion is in terms of a graph representation of type expressions with leaves for basic types and type names, and interior nodes for type constructors, as in Fig. 6.2. As we shall see, recursively defined types lead to cycles in the type graph if a name is treated as an abbreviation for a type expression.

Structural Equivalence of Type Expressions

As long as type expressions are built from basic types and constructors, a natural notion of equivalence between two type expressions is *structural equivalence*; i.e., two expressions are either the same basic type, or are formed by applying the same constructor to structurally equivalent types. That is, two type expressions are structurally equivalent if and only if they are identical. For example, the type expression *integer* is equivalent only to *integer* because they are the same basic type. Similarly, *pointer(integer)* is equivalent only to *pointer(integer)* because the two are formed by applying the same constructor *pointer* to equivalent types. If we use the value-number method of Algorithm 5.1 to construct a dag representation of type expressions, then identical type expressions will be represented by the same node.

Modifications of the notion of structural equivalence are often needed in practice to reflect the actual type-checking rules of the source language. For example, when arrays are passed as parameters, we may not wish to include the array bounds as part of the type.

The algorithm for testing structural equivalence in Fig. 6.6 can be adapted to test modified notions of equivalence. It assumes that the only type constructors are for arrays, products, pointers, and functions. The algorithm recursively compares the structure of type expressions without checking for cycles so it can be applied to a tree or a dag representation. Identical type expressions do not need to be represented by the same node in the dag. Structural equivalence of nodes in type graphs with cycles can be tested using an algorithm in Section 6.7.

The array bounds s_1 and t_1 in

$$s = array(s_1, s_2)$$
$$t = array(t_1, t_2)$$

are ignored if the test for array equivalence in lines 4 and 5 of Fig. 6.6 is reformulated as

> **else if** $s = array(s_1, s_2)$ **and** $t = array(t_1, t_2)$ **then**
> **return** $sequiv(s_2, t_2)$

In certain situations, we can find a representation for type expressions that is significantly more compact than the type graph notation. In the next

(1) **function** *sequiv* (*s*, *t*): boolean;
      begin
(2)   **if** *s* and *t* are the same basic type **then**
(3)   **return true**
(4)   **else if** *s* = *array* (*s*₁, *s*₂) **and** *t* = *array* (*t*₁, *t*₂) **then**
(5)   **return** *sequiv* (*s*₁, *t*₁) **and** *sequiv* (*s*₂, *t*₂)
(6)   **else if** *s* = *s*₁ × *s*₂ **and** *t* = *t*₁ × *t*₂ **then**
(7)   **return** *sequiv* (*s*₁, *t*₁) **and** *sequiv* (*s*₂, *t*₂)
(8)   **else if** *s* = *pointer* (*s*₁) **and** *t* = *pointer* (*t*₁) **then**
(9)   **return** *sequiv* (*s*₁, *t*₁)
(10)   **else if** *s* = *s*₁ → *s*₂ **and** *t* = *t*₁ → *t*₂ **then**
(11)   **return** *sequiv* (*s*₁, *t*₁) **and** *sequiv* (*s*₂, *t*₂)
      else
(12)   **return false**
      end

Fig. 6.6. Testing the structural equivalence of two type expressions *s* and *t*.

example, some of the information from a type expression is encoded as a sequence of bits, which can then be interpreted as a single integer. The encoding is such that distinct integers represent structurally inequivalent type expressions. The test for structural equivalence can be accelerated by first testing for structural inequivalence by comparing the integer representations of the types, and then applying the algorithm of Fig. 6.6 only if the integers are the same.

Example 6.1. The encoding of type expressions in this example is from a C compiler written by D. M. Ritchie. It is also used by the C compiler described in Johnson [1979].

Consider type expressions with the following type constructors for pointers, functions, and arrays: *pointer* (*t*) denotes a pointer to type *t*, *freturns* (*t*) denotes a function of some arguments that returns an object of type *t*, and *array* (*t*) denotes an array (of some indeterminate length) of elements of type *t*. Notice that we have simplified the array and function type constructors. We shall keep track of the number of elements in an array, but the number will be kept elsewhere, so it is not part of the type constructor *array*. Similarly, the only operand of the constructor *freturns* is the type of the result of a function; the types of the function arguments will be stored elsewhere. Thus, objects with structurally equivalent expressions of this type system might still fail to meet the test of Fig. 6.6 applied to the more detailed type system used there.

Since each of these constructors is a unary operator, type expressions formed by applying these constructors to basic types have a very uniform structure. Examples of such type expressions are:

char

freturns (*char*)

pointer (*freturns* (*char*))

array (*pointer* (*freturns* (*char*)))

Each of the above expressions can be represented by a sequence of bits using a simple encoding scheme. Since there are only three type constructors, we can use two bits to encode a constructor, as follows:

TYPE CONSTRUCTOR	ENCODING
pointer	01
array	10
freturns	11

The basic types of C are encoded using four bits in Johnson [1979]; our four basic types might be encoded as:

BASIC TYPE	ENCODING
boolean	0000
char	0001
integer	0010
real	0011

Restricted type expressions can now be encoded as sequences of bits. The rightmost four bits encode the basic type in a type expression. Moving from right to left, the next two bits indicate the constructor applied to the basic type, the next two bits describe the constructor applied to that, and so on. For example,

TYPE EXPRESSION	ENCODING
char	000000 0001
freturns (*char*)	000011 0001
pointer (*freturns* (*char*))	000111 0001
array (*pointer* (*freturns* (*char*)))	100111 0001

See Exercise 6.12 for more details.

Besides saving space, such a representation keeps track of the constructors that appear in any type expression. Two different bit sequences cannot represent the same type because either the basic type or the constructors in the type expressions are different. Of course, different types could have the same bit sequence since array size and function arguments are not represented.

The encoding in this example can be extended to include record types. The idea is to treat each record as a basic type in the encoding; a separate sequence of bits encodes the type of each field of the record. Type equivalence in C is examined further in Example 6.4.   □

Names for Type Expressions

In some languages, types can be given names. For example, in the Pascal program fragment

```
type link = ↑ cell;
var  next : link;
     last : link;
     p    : ↑ cell;
     q, r : ↑ cell;
```
(6.2)

the identifier `link` is declared to be a name for the type ↑`cell`. The question arises, do the variables `next`, `last`, `p`, `q`, `r` all have identical types? Surprisingly, the answer depends on the implementation. The problem arose because the Pascal Report did not define the term "identical type."

To model this situation, we allow type expressions to be named and allow these names to appear in type expressions where we previously had only basic types. For example, if `cell` is the name of a type expression, then *pointer*(`cell`) is a type expression. For the time being, suppose there are no circular type expression definitions such as defining `cell` to be the name of a type expression containing `cell`.

When names are allowed in type expressions, two notions of equivalence of type expressions arise, depending on the treatment of names. *Name equivalence* views each type name as a distinct type, so two type expressions are name equivalent if and only if they are identical. Under *structural equivalence*, names are replaced by the type expressions they define, so two type expressions are structurally equivalent if they represent two structurally equivalent type expressions when all names have been substituted out.

Example 6.2. The type expressions that might be associated with the variables in the declarations (6.2) are given in the following table.

VARIABLE	TYPE EXPRESSION
next	link
last	link
p	*pointer*(cell)
q	*pointer*(cell)
r	*pointer*(cell)

Under name equivalence, the variables `next` and `last` have the same type because they have the same associated type expressions. The variables `p`, `q`, and `r` also have the same type, but `p` and `next` do not, since their associated type expressions are different. Under structural equivalence, all five variables have the same type because `link` is a name for the type expression *pointer*(cell).   □

The concepts of structural and name equivalence are useful in explaining the rules used by various languages to associate types with identifiers through declarations.

Example 6.3. Confusion arises in Pascal from the fact that many implementations associate an implicit type name with each declared identifier. If the declaration contains a type expression that is not a name, an implicit name is created. A fresh implicit name is created every time a type expression appears in a variable declaration.

Thus, implicit names are created for the type expressions in the two declarations containing p, q, and r, in (6.2). That is, the declarations are treated as if they were

```
type link = ↑ cell;
     np   = ↑ cell;
     nqr  = ↑ cell;
var  next : link;
     last : link;
     p    : np;
     q    : nqr;
     r    : nqr;
```

Here, new type names np and nqr have been introduced. Under name equivalence, since next and last are declared with the same type name, they are treated as having equivalent types. Similarly, q and r are treated as having equivalent types because the same implicit type name is associated with them. However, p, q, and next do not have equivalent types, since they all have types with different names.

The typical implementation is to construct a type graph to represent the types. Every time a type constructor or basic type is seen, a new node is created. Every time a new type name is seen, a leaf is created, however, we keep track of the type expression to which the name refers. With this representation, two type expressions are equivalent if they are represented by the same node in the type graph. Figure 6.7 shows a type graph for the declarations (6.2). Dotted lines show the association between variables and nodes in the type graph. Note that type name cell has three parents, all labeled *pointer*. An equal sign appears between the type name link and the node in the type graph to which it refers.   □

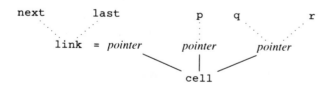

Fig. 6.7. Association of variables and nodes in the type graph.

Cycles in Representations of Types

Basic data structures like linked lists and trees are often defined recursively; e.g., a linked list is either empty or consists of a cell with a pointer to a linked list. Such data structures are usually implemented using records that contain pointers to similar records, and type names play an essential role in defining the types of such records.

Consider a linked list of cells, each containing some integer information and a pointer to the next cell in the list. Pascal declarations of type names corresponding to links and cells are:

```
type   link = ↑ cell;
       cell = record
                    info : integer;
                    next : link
              end;
```

Note that the type name `link` is defined in terms of `cell` and that `cell` is defined in terms of `link`, so their definitions are recursive.

Recursively defined type names can be substituted out if we are willing to introduce cycles into the type graph. If *pointer*(`cell`) is substituted for `link`, the type expression shown in Fig. 6.8(a) is obtained for `cell`. Using cycles as in Fig. 6.8(b), we can eliminate mention of `cell` from the part of the type graph below the node labeled *record*.

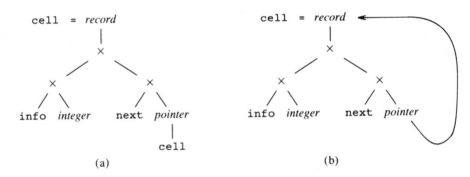

Fig. 6.8. Recursively defined type name `cell`.

Example 6.4. C avoids cycles in type graphs by using structural equivalence for all types except records. In C, the declaration of `cell` would look like

```
struct cell {
      int info;
      struct cell *next;
};
```

C uses the keyword `struct` rather than `record`, and the name `cell` becomes part of the type of the record. In effect, C uses the acyclic representation in Fig. 6.8(a).

C requires type names to be declared before they are used, with the exception of allowing pointers to undeclared record types. All potential cycles, therefore, are due to pointers to records. Since the name of a record is part of its type, testing for structural equivalence stops when a record constructor is reached — either the types being compared are equivalent because they are the same named record type or they are inequivalent. □

6.4 TYPE CONVERSIONS

Consider expressions like $x + i$ where x is of type real and i is of type integer. Since the representation of integers and reals is different within a computer, and different machine instructions are used for operations on integers and reals, the compiler may have to first convert one of the operands of + to ensure that both operands are of the same type when the addition takes place.

The language definition specifies what conversions are necessary. When an integer is assigned to a real, or vice versa, the conversion is to the type of the left side of the assignment. In expressions, the usual transformation is to convert the integer into a real number and then perform a real operation on the resulting pair of real operands. The type checker in a compiler can be used to insert these conversion operations into the intermediate representation of the source program. For example, postfix notation for $x + i$, might be

  x i inttoreal real+

Here, the **inttoreal** operator converts i from integer to real and then **real+** performs real addition on its operands.

Type conversion often arises in another context. A symbol having different meanings depending on its context is said to be overloaded. Overloading will be discussed in the next section, but it is mentioned because type conversions often accompany overloading.

Coercions

Conversion from one type to another is said to be *implicit* if it is to be done automatically by the compiler. Implicit type conversions, also called *coercions*, are limited in many languages to situations where no information is lost in principle; e.g., an integer may be converted to a real but not vice-versa. In practice, however, loss is possible when a real number must fit into the same number of bits as an integer.

Conversion is said to be *explicit* if the programmer must write something to cause the conversion. For all practical purposes, all conversions in Ada are explicit. Explicit conversions look just like function applications to a type checker, so they present no new problems.

For example, in Pascal, a built-in function ord maps a character to an integer, and chr does the inverse mapping from an integer to a character, so these conversions are explicit. C, on the other hand, coerces (i.e., implicitly converts) ASCII characters to integers between 0 and 127 in arithmetic expressions.

Example 6.5. Consider expressions formed by applying an arithmetic operator **op** to constants and identifiers, as in the grammar of Fig. 6.9. Suppose there are two types — real and integer, with integers converted to reals when necessary. Attribute *type* of nonterminal E can be either integer or real, and the type-checking rules are shown in Fig. 6.9. As in Section 6.2, function *lookup*(e) returns the type saved in the symbol-table entry pointed to by e.   □

PRODUCTION	SEMANTIC RULE
$E \rightarrow$ **num**	$E.type := integer$
$E \rightarrow$ **num . num**	$E.type := real$
$E \rightarrow$ **id**	$E.type := lookup(\textbf{id}.entry)$
$E \rightarrow E_1$ **op** E_2	$E.type :=$ **if** $E_1.type = integer$ **and** $E_2.type = integer$
	then *integer*
	else if $E_1.type = integer$ **and** $E_2.type = real$
	then *real*
	else if $E_1.type = real$ **and** $E_2.type = integer$
	then *real*
	else if $E_1.type = real$ **and** $E_2.type = real$
	then *real*
	else *type_error*

Fig. 6.9. Type-checking rules for coercion from integer to real.

Implicit conversion of constants can usually be done at compile time, often with a great improvement to the running time of the object program. In the following code fragments, X is an array of reals that is being initialized to all 1's. Using one Pascal compiler, Bentley [1982] found that the code fragment

    for I := 1 to N do X[I] := 1

took 48.4N microseconds, while the fragment

    for I := 1 to N do X[I] := 1.0

took 5.4N microseconds. Both fragments assign the value one to elements of an array of reals. However, the code generated (by this compiler) for the first fragment contained a call to a run-time routine to convert the integer representation of 1 into the real-number representation. Since it is known at compile time that X is an array of reals, a more thorough compiler would convert 1 to 1.0 at compile time.

6.5 OVERLOADING OF FUNCTIONS AND OPERATORS

An *overloaded* symbol is one that has different meanings depending on its context. In mathematics, the addition operator + is overloaded, because + in $A + B$ has different meanings when A and B are integers, reals, complex numbers, or matrices. In Ada, parentheses ( ) are overloaded; the expression A(I) can be the Ith element of the array A, a call to function A with argument I, or an explicit conversion of expression I to type A.

Overloading is *resolved* when a unique meaning for an occurrence of an overloaded symbol is determined. For example, if + can denote either integer addition or real addition, then the two occurrences of + in x + (i + j) can denote different forms of addition, depending on the types of x, i, and j. The resolution of overloading is sometimes referred to as *operator identification*, because it determines which operation an operator symbol denotes.

The arithmetic operators are overloaded in most languages. However, overloading involving arithmetic operators like + can be resolved by looking only at the arguments of the operator. The case analysis for determining whether to use the integer or real version of + is similar to that in the semantic rule for $E \rightarrow E_1$ **op** E_2 in Fig. 6.9, where the type of E is determined by looking at the possible types of E_1 and E_2.

Set of Possible Types for a Subexpression

It is not always possible to resolve overloading by looking only at the arguments of a function, as the next example shows. Instead of a single type, a subexpression standing alone may have a set of possible types. In Ada, the context must provide sufficient information to narrow the choice down to a single type.

Example 6.6. In Ada, one of the standard (i.e., built-in) interpretations of the operator * is that of a function from a pair of integers to an integer. The operator can be overloaded by adding declarations like the following:

```
function "*" ( i, j : integer ) return complex;
function "*" ( x, y : complex ) return complex;
```

After the above declarations, the possible types for * include:

$$integer \times integer \rightarrow integer$$
$$integer \times integer \rightarrow complex$$
$$complex \times complex \rightarrow complex$$

Suppose that the only possible type for 2, 3, and 5 is integer. With the above declarations, the subexpression 3*5 either has type integer or complex, depending on its context. If the complete expression is 2*(3*5), then 3*5 must have type integer because * takes either a pair of integers or a pair of complex numbers as arguments. On the other hand, 3*5 must have type complex if the complete expression is (3*5)*z and z is declared to be complex. □

In Section 6.2, we assumed that each expression had a unique type, so the type-checking rule for function application was:

$$E \rightarrow E_1 \ (E_2) \qquad \{ \ E.type := \textbf{if} \ E_2.type = s \ \textbf{and}$$
$$E_1.type = s \rightarrow t \ \textbf{then} \ t$$
$$\textbf{else} \ type\_error \ \}$$

The natural generalization of this rule to sets of types appears in Fig. 6.10. The only operation in Fig. 6.10 is that of function application; the rules for checking other operators in expressions are similar. There may be several declarations of an overloaded identifier, so we assume that a symbol-table entry may contain a set of possible types; this set is returned by the *lookup* function. The starting nonterminal E' generates a complete expression. Its role is clarified below.

PRODUCTION	SEMANTIC RULE
$E' \rightarrow E$	$E'.types := E.types$
$E \rightarrow \textbf{id}$	$E.types := lookup(\textbf{id}.entry)$
$E \rightarrow E_1 \ (E_2)$	$E.types := \{ \ t \mid \text{there exists an } s \text{ in } E_2.types$
	$\text{such that } s \rightarrow t \text{ is in } E_1.types\}$

Fig. 6.10. Determining the set of possible types of an expression.

In words, the third rule of Fig. 6.10 says that if s is one of the types of E_2 and one of the types of E_1 can map s to t, then t is one of the types of $E_1(E_2)$. A type mismatch during function application results in the set $E.types$ becoming empty, a condition we temporarily use to signal a type error.

Example 6.7. Besides illustrating the specification in Fig. 6.10, this example suggests how the approach carries over to other constructs. In particular, we consider the expression 3∗5. Let the declarations of operator ∗ be as in Example 6.6. That is, ∗ can map a pair of integers to either an integer or a complex number depending on the context. The set of possible types for the subexpressions of 3∗5 is shown in Fig. 6.11, where i and c abbreviate *integer* and *complex*, respectively.

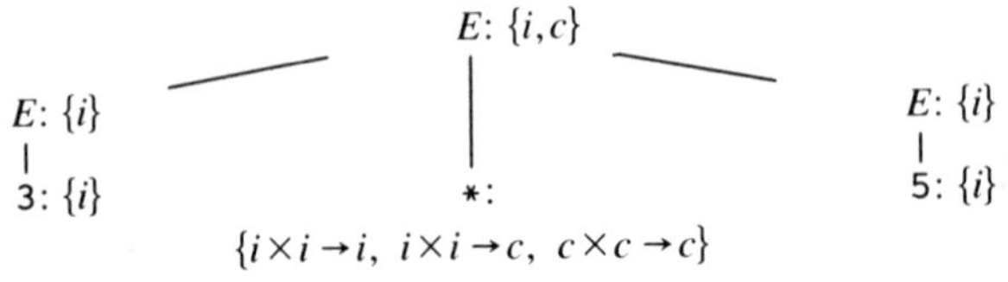

Fig. 6.11. Set of possible types for the expression 3∗5.

Again, suppose that the only possible type for 3 and 5 is *integer*. The operator ∗ is therefore applied to a pair of integers. If we treat this pair of integers as a unit, its type is given by *integer* × *integer*. There are two functions in the set of types for * that apply to pairs of integers; one returns an integer, while the other returns a complex number, so the root can have either type *integer* or type *complex*.   □

Narrowing the Set of Possible Types

Ada requires a complete expression to have a unique type. Given a unique type from the context, we can narrow down the type choices for each subexpression. If this process does not result in a unique type for each subexpression, then a type error is declared for the expression.

Before working top down from an expression to its subexpressions, we take a close look at the sets *E.types* constructed by the rules in Fig. 6.10. We show that every type t in *E.types* is a *feasible* type; i.e., it is possible to choose from among the overloaded types of the identifiers in E in such a way that E gets type t. The property holds for identifiers by declaration, since each element of **id**.*types* is feasible. For the inductive step, consider type t in *E.types*, where E is $E_1(E_2)$. From the rule for function application in Fig. 6.10, for some type s, s must be in E_2.*types* and a type $s \rightarrow t$ must be in E_1.*types*. By induction, s and $s \rightarrow t$ are feasible types for E_2 and E_1, respectively. It follows that t is a feasible type for E.

There may be several ways of arriving at a feasible type. For example, consider the expression f(x) where f can have the types $a \rightarrow c$ and $b \rightarrow c$, and x can have the types a and b. Then, f(x) has type c but x can have either type a or b.

The syntax-directed definition in Fig. 6.12 is obtained from that in Fig. 6.10 by adding semantic rules to determine inherited attribute *unique* of E. Synthesized attribute *code* of E is discussed below.

Since the entire expression is generated by E', we want E'.*types* to be a set containing a single type t. This single type is inherited as the value of *E.unique*. Again, the basic type *type_error* signals an error.

If a function $E_1(E_2)$ returns type t, then we can find a type s that is feasible for the argument E_2; at the same time, $s \rightarrow t$ is feasible for the function. The set S in the corresponding semantic rule in Fig. 6.12 is used to check that there is a unique type s with this property.

The syntax-directed definition in Fig. 6.12 can be implemented by making two depth-first traversals of a syntax tree for an expression. During the first traversal, the attribute *types* is synthesized bottom up. During the second traversal, the attribute *unique* is propagated top down, and as we return from a node, the *code* attribute can be synthesized. In practice, the type checker may simply attach a unique type to each node of the syntax tree. In Fig. 6.12, we generate postfix notation to suggest how intermediate code might be generated. In the postfix notation, each identifier and instance of the **apply** operator has a type attached to it by the function *gen*.

PRODUCTION	SEMANTIC RULES
$E' \rightarrow E$	$E'.types := E.types$ $E.unique := $ **if** $E'.types = \{t\}$ **then** t **else** $type\_error$ $E'.code := E.code$
$E \rightarrow \textbf{id}$	$E.types := lookup(\textbf{id}.entry)$ $E.code := gen(\textbf{id}.lexeme\ ' : '\ E.unique)$
$E \rightarrow E_1\ (\ E_2\ )$	$E.types := \{\ s'\ \|$ there exists an s in $E_2.types$ such that $s \rightarrow s'$ is in $E_1.types\}$ $t := E.unique$ $S := \{\ s\ \|\ s \in E_2.types$ **and** $s \rightarrow t \in E_1.types\ \}$ $E_2.unique := $ **if** $S = \{s\}$ **then** s **else** $type\_error$ $E_1.unique := $ **if** $S = \{s\}$ **then** $s \rightarrow t$ **else** $type\_error$ $E.code := E_1.code \parallel E_2.code \parallel gen('\textbf{apply}'\ ' : '\ E.unique)$

Fig. 6.12. Narrowing down the set of types for an expression.

6.6 POLYMORPHIC FUNCTIONS

An ordinary procedure allows the statements in its body to be executed with arguments of fixed types; each time a polymorphic procedure is called, the statements in its body can be executed with arguments of different types. The term "polymorphic" can also be applied to any piece of code that can be executed with arguments of different types, so we can talk of polymorphic functions and operators as well.

Built-in operators for indexing arrays, applying functions, and manipulating pointers are usually polymorphic because they are not restricted to a particular kind of array, function, or pointer. For example, the C reference manual states about the pointer operator &: "If the type of the operand is '...', the type of the result is 'pointer to ...'." Since any type can be substituted for "..." the operator & in C is polymorphic.

In Ada, "generic" functions are polymorphic, but polymorphism in Ada is restricted. Since the term "generic" has also been used to refer to overloaded functions and to the coercion of the arguments of functions, we shall avoid using that term.

This section addresses the problems that arise in designing a type checker for a language with polymorphic functions. To deal with polymorphism, we extend our set of type expressions to include expressions with type variables. The inclusion of type variables raises some algorithmic issues concerning the equivalence of type expressions.

Why Polymorphic Functions?

Polymorphic functions are attractive because they facilitate the implementation of algorithms that manipulate data structures, regardless of the types of the elements in the data structure. For example, it is convenient to have a program that determines the length of a list without having to know the types of the elements on the list.

```
type link = ↑ cell;
     cell = record
                  info: integer;
                  next: link
     end;
function length ( lptr : link ) : integer;
var  len : integer;
begin
     len := 0;
     while lptr <> nil do begin
         len := len + 1;
         lptr := lptr↑.next
     end;
     length := len
end;
```

Fig. 6.13. Pascal program for the length of a list.

Languages like Pascal require full specification of the types of function parameters, so a function for determining the length of a linked list of integers cannot be applied to a list of reals. The Pascal code in Fig. 6.13 is for lists of integers. The function length follows the next links in the list until a nil link is reached. Although the function does not in any way depend on the type of the information in a cell, Pascal requires the type of the info field to be declared when the length function is written.

```
fun length(lptr) =
        if null(lptr) then 0
        else length(tl(lptr)) + 1;
```

Fig. 6.14. ML program for the length of a list.

In a language with polymorphic functions, like ML (Milner[1984]), a function length can be written so it applies to any kind of list, as shown in Fig. 6.14. The keyword fun indicates that length is a recursive function. The functions null and tl are predefined; null tests if a list is empty, and tl returns the remainder of the list after the first element is removed. With the definition shown in Fig. 6.14, both the following applications of the function length yield 3:

```
length(["sun","mon","tue"]);
length([10,9,8]);
```

In the first, length is applied to a list of strings; in the second, it is applied to a list of integers.

Type Variables

Variables representing type expressions allow us to talk about unknown types. In the remainder of this section, we shall use Greek letters α, β, $\cdots$ for type variables in type expressions.

An important application of type variables is checking consistent usage of identifiers in a language that does not require identifiers to be declared before they are used. A variable represents the type of an undeclared identifier. We can tell by looking at the program whether the undeclared identifier is used, say, as an integer in one statement and as an array in another. Such inconsistent usage can be reported as an error. On the other hand, if the variable is always used as an integer, then we have not only ensured consistent usage; in the process, we have inferred what its type must be.

Type inference is the problem of determining the type of a language construct from the way it is used. The term is often applied to the problem of inferring the type of a function from its body.

Example 6.8. Type-inference techniques can be applied to programs in languages like C and Pascal to fill in missing type information at compile time. The code fragment in Fig. 6.15 shows a procedure mlist, which has a parameter p that is itself a procedure. All we know by looking at the first line of the procedure mlist is that p is a procedure; in particular, we do not know the number or types of the arguments taken by p. Such incomplete specifications of the type of p are allowed by C and by the Pascal reference manual.

The procedure mlist applies parameter p to every cell in a linked list. For example, p may be used to initialize or print the integer held in a cell. Despite the fact that the types of the arguments of p are not specified, we can infer from the use of p in the expression p(lptr) that the type of p must be:

link → *void*

Any call of mlist with a procedure parameter that does not have this type is an error. A procedure can be thought of as a function that does not return a value, so its result type is *void*.   □

Techniques for type inference and type checking have a lot in common. In each case, we have to deal with type expressions containing variables. Reasoning similar to that in the following example is used later in this section by

```
type link ↑cell;

procedure mlist ( lptr : link; procedure p ) ;
begin
    while lptr <> nil do begin
        p(lptr);
        lptr := lptr↑.next
    end
end;
```

Fig. 6.15. Procedure `mlist` with procedure parameter `p`.

a type checker to infer the types represented by variables.

Example 6.9. A type can be inferred for the polymorphic function `deref` in the following pseudo-program. Function `deref` has the same effect as the Pascal operator ↑ for dereferencing pointers.

```
function deref(p);
begin
    return p↑
end;
```

When the first line

```
function deref(p);
```

is seen, we know nothing about the type of `p`, so let us represent it by a type variable β. By definition, the postfix operator ↑ takes a pointer to an object, and returns the object. Since the ↑ operator is applied to `p` in expression `p↑`, it follows that `p` must be a pointer to an object of unknown type α, so we learn that

$$\beta = pointer(\alpha)$$

where α is another type variable. Furthermore, the expression `p↑` has type α, so we can write the type expression

for any type α, $pointer(\alpha) \rightarrow \alpha$ \hfill (6.3)

for the type of the function `deref`. □

A Language with Polymorphic Functions

All we have said so far about polymorphic functions is that they can be executed with arguments of "different types." Precise statements about the set of types to which a polymorphic function can be applied are made using the symbol ∀, meaning "for any type." Thus,

$\forall \alpha.\ pointer(\alpha) \rightarrow \alpha$ \hfill (6.4)

is how we write the type expression (6.3) for the type of the function `deref` in Example 6.9. The polymorphic function `length` in Fig. 6.14 takes a list of elements of any type and returns an integer, so its type can be written as:

$$\forall \alpha. \; list(\alpha) \rightarrow integer \tag{6.5}$$

Here, *list* is a type constructor. Without the $\forall$ symbol, we can only give examples of possible domain and range types for `length`:

$$list(integer) \rightarrow integer$$
$$list(list(char)) \rightarrow integer$$

Type expressions like (6.5) are the most general statements that we can make about the type of a polymorphic function.

The $\forall$ symbol is the *universal quantifier*, and the type variable to which it is applied is said to be *bound* by it. Bound variables can be renamed at will, provided all occurrences of the variable are renamed. Thus, the type expression

$$\forall \gamma. \; pointer(\gamma) \rightarrow \gamma$$

is equivalent to (6.4). A type expression with a $\forall$ symbol in it will be referred to informally as a "polymorphic type."

The language we shall use for checking polymorphic functions is generated by the grammar in Fig. 6.16.

$$
\begin{aligned}
P &\rightarrow D \; ; \; E \\
D &\rightarrow D \; ; \; D \;\; | \;\; \textbf{id} : Q \\
Q &\rightarrow \forall \; \textbf{type\_variable} \; . \; Q \;\; | \;\; T \\
T &\rightarrow T \; '{\rightarrow}' \; T \\
&\quad | \;\; T \times T \\
&\quad | \;\; \textbf{unary\_constructor} \; (\; T \;) \\
&\quad | \;\; \textbf{basic\_type} \\
&\quad | \;\; \textbf{type\_variable} \\
&\quad | \;\; (\; T \;) \\
E &\rightarrow E \, (\, E \,) \;\; | \;\; E \, , \, E \;\; | \;\; \textbf{id}
\end{aligned}
$$

Fig. 6.16. Grammar for language with polymorphic functions.

Programs generated by this grammar consist of a sequence of declarations followed by the expression E to be checked, for example,

$$
\begin{aligned}
\texttt{deref} \; &: \; \forall \alpha. \; pointer(\alpha) \rightarrow \alpha; \\
\texttt{q} \; &: \; pointer(pointer(integer)); \\
\texttt{deref(deref(q))}&
\end{aligned}
\tag{6.6}
$$

We minimize notation by having nonterminal T generate type expressions directly. The constructors $\rightarrow$ and $\times$ form function and product types. Unary constructors, represented by **unary_constructor**, allow types like *pointer*(*integer*) and *list*(*integer*) to be written. Parentheses are used simply for grouping types. Expressions whose types are to be checked have a very simple syntax: they can be identifiers, sequences of expressions forming a tuple, or the application of a function to an argument.

The type-checking rules for polymorphic functions differ in three ways from those for ordinary functions in Section 6.2. Before presenting the rules, we illustrate these differences by considering the expression `deref(deref(q))` in the program (6.6). A syntax tree for this expression is shown in Fig. 6.17. Attached to each node are two labels. The first tells us the subexpression represented by the node and the second is a type expression assigned to the subexpression. Subscripts *o* and *i* distinguish between the outer and inner occurrences of `deref`, respectively.

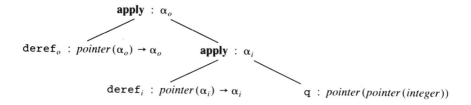

Fig. 6.17. Labeled syntax tree for `deref(deref(q))`.

The differences from the rules for ordinary functions are:

1. Distinct occurrences of a polymorphic function in the same expression need not have arguments of the same type. In the expression $deref_o(deref_i(q))$, $deref_i$ removes one level of pointer indirection, so $deref_o$ is applied to an argument of a different type. The implementation of this property is based on the interpretation of $\forall \alpha$ as "for any type α." Each occurrence of `deref` has its own view of what the bound variable α in (6.4) stands for. We therefore assign to each occurrence of `deref` a type expression formed by replacing α in (6.4) by a fresh variable and removing the $\forall$ quantifier in the process. In Fig. 6.17, the fresh variables α_o and α_i are used in the type expressions assigned to the outer and inner occurrences of `deref`, respectively.

2. Since variables can appear in type expressions, we have to reexamine the notion of equivalence of types. Suppose E_1 of type $s \rightarrow s'$ is applied to E_2 of type t. Instead of simply determining the equivalence of s and t, we must "unify" them. Unification is defined below; informally, we determine if s and t can be made structurally equivalent by replacing the type variables in s and t by type expressions. For example, at the inner node labeled **apply** in Fig. 6.17, the equality

$$pointer(\alpha_i) = pointer(pointer(integer))$$

is true if α_i is replaced by *pointer* (*integer*).

3. We need a mechanism for recording the effect of unifying two expressions. In general, a type variable may appear in several type expressions. If unification of s and s' results in variable α representing type t, then α must continue to represent t as type checking proceeds. For example, in Fig. 6.17, α_i is the range type of deref$_i$, so we can use it for the type of deref$_i$(q). Unifying the domain type of deref$_i$ with the type of q therefore affects the type expression at the inner node labeled **apply**. The other type variable α_o in Fig. 6.17 represents *integer*.

Substitutions, Instances, and Unification

Information about the types represented by variables is formalized by defining a mapping from type variables to type expressions called a *substitution*. The following recursive function *subst* (*t*) makes precise the notion of applying a substitution S to replace all type variables in an expression t. As usual, we take the function type constructor to be the "typical" constructor.

> **function** *subst* (*t* : *type_expression*) : *type_expression*;
> **begin**
>   **if** *t* is a basic type **then return** *t*
>   **else if** *t* is a variable **then return** $S(t)$
>   **else if** *t* is $t_1 \rightarrow t_2$ **then return** *subst* $(t_1) \rightarrow$ *subst* (t_2)
> **end**

For convenience, we write $S(t)$ for the type expression that results when *subst* is applied to t; the result $S(t)$ is called an *instance* of t. If substitution S does not specify an expression for variable α, we assume that $S(\alpha)$ is α; that is, S is the identity mapping on such variables.

Example 6.10. In the following, we write $s < t$ to indicate that s is an instance of t:

$$pointer \, (integer) \; < \; pointer \, (\alpha)$$
$$pointer \, (real) \; < \; pointer \, (\alpha)$$
$$integer \rightarrow integer \; < \; \alpha \rightarrow \alpha$$
$$pointer \, (\alpha) \; < \; \beta$$
$$\alpha \; < \; \beta$$

However, in the following, the type expression on the left is not an instance of the one on the right (for the reason indicated):

integer	*real*	Substitutions do not apply to basic types.
integer $\rightarrow$ *real*	$\alpha \rightarrow \alpha$	Inconsistent substitution for α.
integer $\rightarrow \alpha$	$\alpha \rightarrow \alpha$	All occurrences of α must be replaced. $\square$

Two type expressions t_1 and t_2 *unify* if there exists some substitution S such that $S(t_1) = S(t_2)$. In practice, we are interested in the *most general unifier*, which is a substitution that imposes the fewest constraints on the variables in the expressions. More precisely, the most general unifier of expressions t_1 and t_2 is a substitution S with the following properties:

1. $S(t_1) = S(t_2)$ and

2. for any other substitution S' such that $S'(t_1) = S'(t_2)$, the substitution S' is an instance of S (that is, for any t, $S'(t)$ is an instance of $S(t)$).

In what follows, when we say "unifies" we are referring to the most general unifier.

Checking Polymorphic Functions

The rules for checking expressions generated by the grammar in Fig. 6.16 will be written in terms of the following operations on a graph representation of types.

1. *fresh*(t) replaces the bound variables in type expression t by fresh variables and returns a pointer to a node representing the resulting type expression. Any $\forall$ symbols in t are removed in the process.

2. *unify*(m, n) unifies the type expressions represented by the nodes pointed to by m and n. It has the side effect of keeping track of the substitution that makes the expressions equivalent. If the expressions fail to unify, the entire type-checking process fails.[4]

Individual leaves and interior nodes in the type graph are constructed using operations *mkleaf* and *mknode* similar to those of Section 5.2. It is necessary that there be a unique leaf for each type variable, but other structurally equivalent expressions need not have unique nodes.

The *unify* operation is based on the following graph-theoretic formulation of unification and substitutions. Suppose nodes m and n of a graph represent expressions e and f, respectively. We say nodes m and n are *equivalent under* substitution S if $S(e) = S(f)$. The problem of finding the most general unifier S can be restated as the problem of grouping, into sets, nodes that must be equivalent under S. For the expressions to be equivalent, their roots must be equivalent. Also, two nodes m and n are equivalent if and only if they represent the same operator and their corresponding children are equivalent.

An algorithm for unifying a pair of expressions is deferred until the next section. The algorithm keeps track of sets of nodes that are equivalent under the substitutions that have occurred.

The type-checking rules for expressions are shown in Fig. 6.18. We do not show how declarations are processed. As type expressions generated by

---

[4] The reason for aborting the type-checking process is that the side effects of some unifications may be recorded before failure is detected. Error recovery can be implemented if the side effects of the *unify* operation are deferred until the expressions have been unified successfully.

nonterminals T and Q are examined, *mkleaf* and *mknode* add nodes to the type graph, following the dag construction in Section 5.2. When an identifier is declared, the type in the declaration is saved in the symbol table in the form of a pointer to the node representing the type. In Fig. 6.18, this pointer is referred to as the synthesized attribute **id**.*type*. As mentioned above, the *fresh* operation removes the $\forall$ symbols as it replaces bound variables by fresh variables. The action associated with production $E \to E_1 , E_2$ sets $E.type$ to the product of the types of E_1 and E_2.

$$E \to E_1 (E_2) \qquad \{ \ p := mkleaf(newtypevar);$$
$$unify(E_1.type, mknode('\to', E_2.type, p));$$
$$E.type := p \ \}$$

$$E \to E_1 , E_2 \qquad \{ \ E.type := mknode('\times', E_1.type, E_2.type) \ \}$$

$$E \to \textbf{id} \qquad \{ \ E.type := fresh(\textbf{id}.type) \ \}$$

Fig. 6.18. Translation scheme for checking polymorphic functions.

The type-checking rule for the function application $E \to E_1(E_2)$ is motivated by considering the case where $E_1.type$ and $E_2.type$ are both type variables, say, $E_1.type = \alpha$ and $E_2.type = \beta$. Here $E_1.type$ must be a function such that for some unknown type γ, we have $\alpha = \beta \to \gamma$. In Fig. 6.18, a fresh type variable corresponding to γ is created and $E_1.type$ is unified with $E_2.type \to \gamma$. A new type variable is returned by each call of *newtypevar*, a leaf for it is constructed by *mkleaf*, and a node representing the function to be unified with $E_1.type$ is constructed by *mknode*. After unification succeeds, the new leaf represents the result type.

The rules in Fig. 6.18 will be illustrated by working out a simple example in detail. We summarize the workings of the algorithm by writing down the type expression assigned to each subexpression, as in Fig. 6.19. At each function application, the *unify* operation may have the side effect of recording a type expression for some of the type variables. Such side effects are suggested by the column for a substitution in Fig. 6.19.

EXPRESSION : TYPE	SUBSTITUTION
q : *pointer(pointer(integer))*	
deref$_i$: *pointer*$(\alpha_i) \to \alpha_i$	
deref$_i$(q) : *pointer(integer)*	$\alpha_i = pointer(integer)$
deref$_o$: *pointer*$(\alpha_o) \to \alpha_o$	
deref$_o$(deref$_i$(q)) : *integer*	$\alpha_o = integer$

Fig. 6.19. Summary of bottom-up type determination.

Example 6.11. Type checking the expression `deref`$_o$`(deref`$_i$`(q))` in program (6.6) proceeds bottom up from the leaves. Once again, subscripts o and i distinguish between occurrences of `deref`. When subexpression `deref`$_o$ is considered, *fresh* constructs the following nodes using a new type variable α_o.

The number at a node indicates the equivalence class the node belongs to. The part of the type graph for the three identifiers is shown below. The dotted lines indicate that nodes numbered 3, 6, and 9 are for `deref`$_o$, `deref`$_i$, and `q`, respectively.

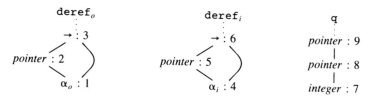

The function application `deref`$_i$`(q)` is checked by constructing a node n for a function from the type of `q` to a new type variable β. This function unifies successfully with the type of `deref`$_i$ represented by node m below. Before nodes m and n are unified, each node had a distinct number. After unification, the equivalent nodes are the ones below with the same number; the changed numbers are underlined:

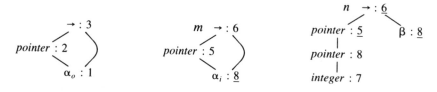

Note that the node for α_i and *pointer(integer)* are both numbered 8, that is α_i is unified with this type expression, as shown in Fig. 6.19. Subsequently, α_o is unified with *integer*.

□

The next example relates type inference of polymorphic functions in ML to the type-checking rules in Fig. 6.18. The syntax of function definitions in ML is given by

fun id$_0$ (**id**$_1$, . . . , **id**$_k$) = E ;

where **id**$_0$ represents the function name and **id**$_1$, . . . , **id**$_k$ represent its parameters. For simplicity, we assume that the syntax of expression E is as in Fig. 6.16, and that the only identifiers in E are the function name, its parameters, and built-in functions.

The approach is a formalization of that in Example 6.9, where a polymorphic type was inferred for deref. New type variables are made up for the function name and its parameters. The built-in functions have polymorphic types, in general; any type variables that appear in these types are bound by $\forall$ quantifiers. We then check that the types of the expressions $id_0(\ id_1, \ldots, id_k)$ and E match. When the match succeeds, we will have inferred a type for the function name. Finally, any variables in the inferred type are bound by $\forall$ quantifiers to give the polymorphic type for the function.

Example 6.12. Recall the ML function in Fig. 6.14 for determining the length of a list:

```
fun length(lptr) =
        if null(lptr) then 0
        else length(tl(lptr)) + 1;
```

Type variables β and γ are introduced for the types of length and lptr, respectively. We find that the type of length(lptr) matches that of the expression forming the function body and that length must have type

for any type α, $list(\alpha) \rightarrow integer$

so the type of length is

$\forall \alpha.\ list(\alpha) \rightarrow integer$

In more detail, we set up the program shown in Fig. 6.20, to which the type-checking rules of Fig. 6.18 can be applied. The declarations in the program associate the new type variables β and γ with length and lptr, and make explicit the types of the built-in operations. We write conditionals in

```
length : β;
   lptr : γ;
     if : ∀α. boolean × α × α → α;
   null : ∀α. list(α) → boolean;
     tl : ∀α. list(α) → list(α);
      0 : integer;
      1 : integer;
      + : integer × integer → integer;
  match : ∀α. α × α → α;

match(
      length(lptr),
      if( null(lptr), 0, length(tl(lptr)) + 1 )
      )
```

Fig. 6.20. Declarations followed by expression to be checked.

LINE	EXPRESSION : TYPE	SUBSTITUTION
(1)	lptr : γ	
(2)	length : β	
(3)	length(lptr) : δ	$\beta = \gamma \rightarrow \delta$
(4)	lptr : γ	
(5)	null : $list(\alpha_n) \rightarrow boolean$	
(6)	null(lptr) : $boolean$	$\gamma = list(\alpha_n)$
(7)	0 : $integer$	
(8)	lptr : $list(\alpha_n)$	
(9)	tl : $list(\alpha_t) \rightarrow list(\alpha_t)$	
(10)	tl(lptr) : $list(\alpha_n)$	$\alpha_t = \alpha_n$
(11)	length : $list(\alpha_n) \rightarrow \delta$	
(12)	length(tl(lptr)) : δ	
(13)	1 : $integer$	
(14)	+ : $integer \times integer \rightarrow integer$	
(15)	length(tl(lptr))+1 : $integer$	$\delta = integer$
(16)	if : $boolean \times \alpha_i \times \alpha_i \rightarrow \alpha_i$	
(17)	if($\cdots$) : $integer$	$\alpha_i = integer$
(18)	match : $\alpha_m \times \alpha_m \rightarrow \alpha_m$	
(19)	match($\cdots$) : $integer$	$\alpha_m = integer$

Fig. 6.21. Inferring the type $list(\alpha_n) \rightarrow integer$ for length.

the style of Fig. 6.16 by applying polymorphic operator if to three operands, representing the expression to be tested, the then part, and the else part; the declaration says that the then and else parts can be of any matching type, which is also the type of the result.

Clearly, length(lptr) must have the same type as the function body; this check is encoded using an operator match. The use of match is a technical convenience that allows all checking to be done using a program in the style of Fig. 6.16.

The effect of applying the type-checking rules in Fig. 6.18 to the program in Fig. 6.20 is summarized in Fig. 6.21. The new variables introduced by operation *fresh* applied to the polymorphic types of the built-in operations are distinguished by subscripts on α. We learn on line (3) that length must be a function from γ to some unknown type δ. Then, when the subexpression null(lptr) is checked, we find on line (6) that γ unifies with $list(\alpha_n)$, where α_n is an unknown type. At this point, we know that the type of length must be

for any type α_n, $list(\alpha_n) \rightarrow \delta$

Eventually, when the addition is checked on line (15) — we take the liberty of writing + between its arguments for clarity — δ is unified with *integer*.

When checking is complete, the type variable α_n remains in the type of length. Since no assumptions were made about α_n, any type can be substituted for it when the function is used. We therefore make it a bound variable and write

$$\forall \alpha_n. \; list(\alpha_n) \to integer$$

for the type of length.   □

6.7 AN ALGORITHM FOR UNIFICATION

Informally, unification is the problem of determining whether two expressions e and f can be made identical by substituting expressions for the variables in e and f. Testing equality of expressions is a special case of unification; if e and f have constants but no variables, then e and f unify if and only if they are identical. The unification algorithm in this section can be applied to graphs with cycles, so it can be used to test structural equivalence of circular types.[5]

Unification was defined in the last section in terms of a function S, called a substitution, mapping variables to expressions. We write $S(e)$ for the expression obtained when each variable α in e is replaced by $S(\alpha)$. S is a unifier for e and f if $S(e) = S(f)$. The algorithm in this section determines a substitution that is the most general unifier of a pair of expressions.

Example 6.13. For a perspective on most general unifiers, consider the two type expressions

$$((\alpha_1 \to \alpha_2) \times list(\alpha_3)) \to list(\alpha_2)$$
$$((\alpha_3 \to \alpha_4) \times list(\alpha_3)) \to \alpha_5$$

Two unifiers, S and S', for these expressions are:

x	$S(x)$	$S'(x)$
α_1	α_3	α_1
α_2	α_2	α_1
α_3	α_3	α_1
α_4	α_2	α_1
α_5	$list(\alpha_2)$	$list(\alpha_1)$

These substitutions map e and f as follows:

$$S(e) = S(f) = ((\alpha_3 \to \alpha_2) \times list(\alpha_3)) \to list(\alpha_2)$$
$$S'(e) = S'(f) = ((\alpha_1 \to \alpha_1) \times list(\alpha_1)) \to list(\alpha_1)$$

Substitution S is the most general unifier of e and f. Note that $S'(e)$ is an instance of $S(e)$ because we can substitute α_1 for both variables in $S(e)$.

---

[5] In some applications, it is an error to unify a variable with an expression containing that variable. Algorithm 6.1 permits such substitutions.

However, the reverse is false, because the same expression must be substituted for each occurrence of α_1 in $S'(e)$, so we cannot obtain $S(e)$ by substituting for the variable α_1 in $S'(e)$.   □

When expressions to be unified are represented by trees, the number of nodes in the tree for the substituted expression $S(e)$ can be exponential in the number of nodes in the trees for e and f, even if S is the most general unifier. However, such a size blowup need not occur if graphs rather than trees are used to represent expressions and substitutions.

We shall implement the graph-theoretic formulation of unification, also presented in the last section. The problem is that of grouping, into sets, nodes that must be equivalent under the most general unifier of two expressions. The two expressions in Example 6.13 are represented by the two nodes labeled $\rightarrow:1$ in Fig. 6.22. The integers at the nodes indicate the equivalence classes that the nodes belong to after the nodes numbered 1 are unified. These equivalence classes have the property that all interior nodes in the class are for the same operator. The corresponding children of interior nodes in an equivalence class are also equivalent.

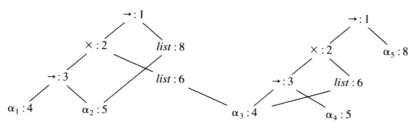

Fig. 6.22. Equivalence classes after unification.

Algorithm 6.1. Unification of a pair of nodes in a graph.

Input. A graph and a pair of nodes m and n to be unified.

Output. Boolean value true if the expressions represented by the nodes m and n unify; false, otherwise. The version of operation *unify* needed for the type-checking rules of Fig. 6.18 is obtained if the function in this algorithm is modified to fail instead of returning false.

Method. A node is represented by a record as in Fig. 6.23 with fields for a binary operator and pointers to the left and right children.

The sets of equivalent nodes are maintained using the *set* field. One node in each equivalence class is chosen the unique representative of the equivalence class by making its *set* field contain a nil pointer. The *set* fields of the remaining nodes in the equivalence class will point (possibly indirectly through other nodes in the set) to the representative. Initially, each node n is in an equivalence class by itself, with n as its own representative node.

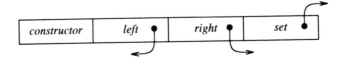

Fig. 6.23. Data structure for a node.

```
function unify (m, n : node) : boolean
begin
    s := find (m);
    t := find (n);
    if s = t then
        return true
    else if s and t are nodes that represent the same basic type then
        return true
    else if s is an op-node with children s₁ and s₂ and
                t is an op-node with children t₁ and t₂ then begin
        union(s, t);
        return unify (s₁, t₁) and unify (s₂, t₂)
    end
    else if s or t represents a variable then begin
        union(s, t);
        return true
    end
    else return false
            /* interior nodes with different operators cannot be unified */
end
```

Fig. 6.24. Unification algorithm.

The unification algorithm, shown in Fig. 6.24, uses the following two operations on nodes:

1. *find(n)* returns the representative node of the equivalence class currently containing node n.

2. *union(m, n)* merges the equivalence classes containing nodes m and n. If one of the representatives for the equivalence classes of m and n is a non-variable node, *union* makes that non-variable node be the representative for the merged equivalence class; otherwise, *union* makes one or the other of the original representatives be the new representative. This asymmetry in the specification of *union* is important because a variable cannot be used as the representative for an equivalence class for an

expression containing a type constructor or basic type. Otherwise, two inequivalent expressions may be unified through that variable.

The *union* operation on sets is implemented by simply changing the *set* field of the representative of one equivalence class so that it points to the representative of the other. To find the equivalence class that a node belongs to, we follow the *set* pointers of nodes until the representative (the node with a **nil** pointer in the set field) is reached.

Note that the algorithm in Fig. 6.24 uses $s = find(m)$ and $t = find(n)$ rather than m and n, respectively. The representative nodes s and t are equal if m and n are in the same equivalence class. If s and t represent the same basic type, the call $unify(m, n)$ returns true. If s and t are both interior nodes for a binary type constructor, we merge their equivalence classes on speculation and recursively check that their respective children are equivalent. By merging first, we decrease the number of equivalence classes before recursively checking the children, so the algorithm terminates.

The substitution of an expression for a variable is implemented by adding the leaf for the variable to the equivalence class containing the node for the expression. If either m or n is a leaf for a variable that has been put into an equivalence class that contains a node representing an expression with a type constructor or a basic type, then *find* will return a representative that reflects that type constructor or basic type, so that a variable cannot be unified with two different expressions.   □

Example 6.14. We have shown the initial graph for the two expressions of Example 6.13 in Fig. 6.25 with each node numbered and in its own equivalence class. To compute $unify(1, 9)$, the algorithm notes that nodes 1 and 9 both represent the same operator so it merges 1 and 9 into the same equivalence class and calls $unify(2, 10)$ and $unify(8, 14)$. The result of computing $unify(1, 9)$ is the graph previously shown in Fig. 6.22.   □

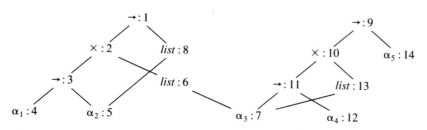

Fig. 6.25. Initial dag with each node in its own equivalence class.

If Algorithm 6.1 returns true, we can construct a substitution S that acts as the unifier, as follows. Let each node n of the resulting graph represent the expression associated with $find(n)$. Thus, for each variable α, $find(\alpha)$ gives the node n that is the representative of the equivalence class of α. The expression represented by n is $S(\alpha)$. For example, in Fig. 6.22, we see that the representative for α_3 is node 4, which represents α_1. The representative for α_5 is node 8, which represents $list(\alpha_2)$.

Example 6.15. Algorithm 6.1 can be used to test the structural equivalence of the two type expressions

$$e : real \rightarrow e$$
$$f : real \rightarrow (real \rightarrow f)$$

The type graphs for these expressions are shown in Fig. 6.26. For convenience, each node has been numbered.

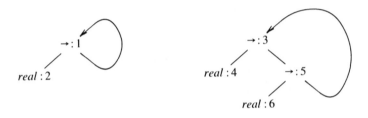

Fig. 6.26. Graph for two circular types.

We call $unify(1, 3)$ to test for the structural equivalence of these two expressions. The algorithm merges nodes 1 and 3 into one equivalence class, and recursively calls $unify(2, 4)$ and $unify(1, 5)$. Since 2 and 4 represent the same basic type, the call $unify(2, 4)$ returns true. The call $unify(1, 5)$ adds 5 to the equivalence class of 1 and 3, and recursively calls $unify(2, 6)$ and $unify(1, 3)$.

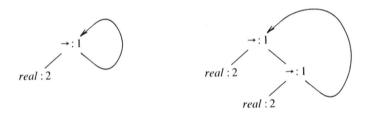

Fig. 6.27. Type graph showing equivalence classes of nodes.

The call $unify(2, 6)$ returns true because 2 and 6 also represent the same basic type. The second call of $unify(1, 3)$ terminates because we have already merged nodes 1 and 3 into the same equivalence class. The algorithm then terminates, returning true to show that the two type expressions are indeed equivalent. Figure 6.27 shows the resulting equivalence classes of nodes, where nodes with the same integer are in the same equivalence class.   □

EXERCISES

6.1 Write type expressions for the following types.

a) An array of pointers to reals, where the array index ranges from 1 to 100.

b) A two-dimensional array of integers (i.e., an array of arrays) whose rows are indexed from 0 to 9 and whose columns are indexed from −10 to 10.

c) Functions whose domains are functions from integers to pointers to integers and whose ranges are records consisting of an integer and a character.

6.2 Suppose we have the following C declarations:

```
typedef struct {
    int a, b;
    } CELL, *PCELL;
CELL foo[100];
PCELL bar(x, y) int x; CELL y {  · · ·  }
```

Write type expressions for the types of `foo` and `bar`.

6.3 The following grammar defines lists of lists of literals. The interpretation of symbols is the same as that for the grammar of Fig. 6.3 with the addition of the type **list**, which indicates a list of elements of the type T that follows.

$$
\begin{aligned}
P &\rightarrow D ; E \\
D &\rightarrow D ; D \mid \textbf{id} : T \\
T &\rightarrow \textbf{list of } T \mid \textbf{char} \mid \textbf{integer} \\
E &\rightarrow (L) \mid \textbf{literal} \mid \textbf{num} \mid \textbf{id} \\
L &\rightarrow E , L \mid E
\end{aligned}
$$

Write translation rules similar to those in Section 6.2 to determine the types of expressions (E) and lists (L).

6.4 Add to the grammar of Exercise 6.3 the production

$$E \rightarrow \textbf{nil}$$

meaning that an expression can be the null (empty) list. Revise the rules in your answer to Exercise 6.2 to take account of the fact that **nil** can stand for an empty list of elements of any type.

6.5 Using the translation scheme of Section 6.2, compute the types of the expressions in the following program fragments. Show the types at each node of the parse tree.

a) `c: char; i: integer;`
   `c mod i mod 3`

b) `p: ↑integer; a: array [10] of integer;`
   `a[p↑]`

c) `f: integer → boolean;`
   `i: integer; j: integer; k: integer;`
   `while f(i) do`
   `    k := i;`
   `    i := j mod i;`
   `    j := k`

6.6 Modify the translation scheme for checking expressions in Section 6.2 to print a descriptive message when an error is detected and to continue checking as if the expected type had been seen.

6.7 Rewrite the type-checking rules for expressions in Section 6.2 so they refer to nodes in a graph representation of type expressions. The rewritten rules should use data structures and operations supported by a language such as Pascal. Use structural equivalence of type expressions when:
a) type expressions are represented by trees, as in Fig. 6.2, and
b) the type graph is a dag with a unique node for each type expression.

6.8 Modify the translation scheme of Fig. 6.5 to handle the following.
a) Statements that have values. The value of an assignment is the value of the expression on the right of the `: =` sign. The value of a conditional or while statement is the value of the statement body; the value of a list of statements is the value of the last statement in the list.
b) Boolean expressions. Add productions for the logical operators **and**, **or**, and **not**, and for comparison operators (`<`, etc.). Then add appropriate translation rules giving the type of these expressions.

6.9 Generalize the type-checking rules for functions given at the end of Section 6.2 to handle *n*-ary functions.

6.10 Assume the type names `link` and `cell` are defined as in Section 6.3. Which among the following expressions are structurally equivalent? Which are name equivalent?
i) `link`.
ii) *pointer*(`cell`).
iii) *pointer*(`link`).
iv) *pointer*(*record*((`info` × *integer*) × (`next` × *pointer*(`cell`)))

6.11 Restate the algorithm for testing structural equivalence in Fig. 6.6 so that the arguments of *sequiv* are pointers to nodes in a dag.

6.12 Consider the encoding of restricted type expressions as sequences of bits in Example 6.1. In Johnson [1979], the two-bit fields for constructors appeared in the opposite order, with the field for the outermost constructor appearing next to the four bits for the basic type; for example,

TYPE EXPRESSION	ENCODING
char	000000 0001
freturns (char)	000011 0001
pointer (freturns (char))	001101 0001
array (pointer (freturns (char)))	110110 0001

Using the operators of C write code to construct the representation of array(t) from that of t and vice versa, assuming that the encoding is as in:

a) Johnson [1979].

b) Example 6.1.

6.13 Suppose that the type of each identifier is a subrange of integers. For expressions with the operators +, -, *, div, and mod, as in Pascal, write type-checking rules that assign to each subexpression the subrange its value must lie in.

6.14 Give an algorithm to test the equivalence of C types (see Example 6.4).

6.15 Some languages, like PL/I, will coerce a boolean value into an integer, with true identified with 1 and false with 0. For example, 3<4<5 is grouped (3<4)<5, and has the value "true" (or 1), because 3<4 has the value 1, and 1<5 is true. Write translation rules for boolean expressions that perform this coercion. Use conditional statements in the intermediate language to assign integer values to temporaries that represent the value of a boolean expression, when needed.

6.16 Generalize the algorithms of (a) Fig. 6.9 and (b) Fig. 6.12 to expressions with the type constructors array, pointer, and Cartesian product.

6.17 Which of the following recursive type expressions are equivalent?

$$e1 = integer \rightarrow e1$$
$$e2 = integer \rightarrow (integer \rightarrow e2)$$
$$e3 = integer \rightarrow (integer \rightarrow e1)$$

6.18 Using the rules of Example 6.6, determine which of the following expressions have unique types. Assume z is a complex number.

a) 1 * 2 * 3

b) 1 * (z * 2)

c) $(1*z)*z$

6.19 Suppose we allow the type conversions of Example 6.6. Under what conditions on the types of a, b, and c (integer or complex) will the expression $(a*b)*c$ have a unique type?

6.20 Express, using type variables,.the types of the following functions.
   a) The function *ref* that takes as argument an object of any type and returns a pointer to that object.
   b) A function that takes as argument an array indexed by integers, with elements of any type, and returns an array whose elements are the objects pointed to by the elements of the given array.

6.21 Find the most general unifier of the type expressions
   i) $(pointer(\alpha)) \times (\beta \to \gamma)$
   ii) $\beta \times (\gamma \to \delta)$

What if δ in (ii) were α?

6.22 Find the most general unifier for each pair of expressions from the following list, or determine that none exists.
   a) $\alpha_1 \to (\alpha_2 \to \alpha_1)$
   b) $array(\beta_1) \to (pointer(\beta_1) \to \beta_3)$
   c) $\gamma_1 \to \gamma_2$
   d) $\delta_1 \to (\delta_1 \to \delta_2)$

6.23 Extend the type-checking rules in Example 6.6 to cover records. Use the following additional syntax for type expressions and expressions:

$$T \to \textbf{record } fields \textbf{ end}$$
$$E \to E \textbf{ . id}$$
$$fields \to fields \textbf{ ; } field \mid field$$
$$field \to \textbf{id} : T$$

What restrictions does the lack of type names impose on the types that can be defined?

*6.24 The resolution of overloading in Section 6.5 proceeds in two phases: first the set of possible types for each subexpression is determined and then narrowed down in a second phase to a single type after the unique type of the entire expression is determined. What data structures would you use to resolve overloading in a single bottom-up pass?

**6.25 The resolution of overloading becomes more difficult if identifier declarations are optional. More precisely, suppose that declarations can be used to overload identifiers representing function symbols, but that all occurrences of an undeclared identifier have the same type. Show that the problem of determining if an expression in this language has a valid type is NP-complete. This problem arises during

type checking in the experimental language Hope (Burstall, Mac-
Queen, and Sannella [1980]).

6.26 Following Example 6.12, infer the following polymorphic type for
map:

$$\text{map} : \forall \alpha. \ \forall \beta. \ ((\alpha{\to}\beta){\times}list(\alpha)) \ \to \ list(\beta)$$

The ML definition of map is:

```
fun map(f, l) =
              if null(l) then nil
              else cons( f(hd(l)), map(f, tl(l)))
```

The types of built-in identifiers in the function body are:

$$
\begin{aligned}
\text{null} &: \quad \forall \alpha. \ list(\alpha) \to boolean; \\
\text{nil} &: \quad \forall \alpha. \ list(\alpha); \\
\text{cons} &: \quad \forall \alpha. \ (\alpha {\times} list(\alpha)) \to list(\alpha); \\
\text{hd} &: \quad \forall \alpha. \ list(\alpha) \to \alpha; \\
\text{tl} &: \quad \forall \alpha. \ list(\alpha) \to list(\alpha);
\end{aligned}
$$

**6.27 Show that the unification algorithm of Section 6.7 determines the
most general unifier.

*6.28 Modify the unification algorithm of Section 6.7 so that it does not
unify a variable with an expression containing that variable.

**6.29 Suppose expressions are represented by trees. Find expressions e and
f such that for any unifier S, the number of nodes in $S(e)$ is exponential in the number of nodes in e and f.

6.30 Two nodes are said to be *congruent* if they represent equivalent
expressions. Even if no two nodes in the original type graph are
congruent, after unification, it is possible for distinct nodes to be
congruent.
   a) Give an algorithm to merge a class of mutually congruent nodes
      nodes into a single node.
   **b) Extend the algorithm in (a) to merge congruent nodes until no two
      distinct nodes are congruent.

*6.31 The expression g(g) on line 9 in the complete C program in Fig.
6.28 is the application of a function to itself. The declaration on line
3 gives *integer* as the range type g, but the types of the arguments of
g is not specified. Try running the program. The compiler may issue
a warning because g is declared to be a function on line 3, instead of
a pointer to a function.
   a) What can you say about the type of g?

```
(1)  int n;
(2)  int f(g)
(3)  int g( );
(4)  {
(5)       int m;
(6)       m = n;
(7)       if( m == 0 ) return 1;
(8)       else {
(9)            n = n - 1; return m * g(g);
(10)      }
(11) }
(12) main( )
(13) {
(14)      n = 5; printf("%d factorial is %d\n", n, f(f) );
(15) }
```

Fig. 6.28. A C program containing applications of a function to itself.

b) Use the type-checking rules for polymorphic functions in Fig. 6.18
   to infer a type for g in the following program.

$$m \ : \ integer;$$
$$times \ : \ integer \times integer \ \rightarrow \ integer;$$
$$g \ : \ \alpha;$$

$$times(\ m, \ g(g) \ )$$

BIBLIOGRAPHIC NOTES

The basic types and type constructors of early languages like Fortran and
Algol 60 were limited enough that type checking was not a serious problem.
As a result, descriptions of type checking in their compilers are buried in discussions of code generation for expressions. Sheridan [1959] describes the
translation of expressions in the original Fortran compiler. The compiler kept
track of whether the type of an expression was integer or real, but coercions
were not permitted by the language. Backus [1981, p. 54] recalls, "I think
just because we didn't like the rules as to what happened with mixed mode
expressions, so we decided, 'Let's throw it out. It's easier.' " Naur [1965] is
an early paper on type checking in an Algol compiler; the techniques used by
the compiler are similar to those discussed in Section 6.2.

   Data-structuring facilities such as arrays and records were anticipated in the
1940's by Zuse in his Plankalkül that had little direct influence (Bauer and
Wössner [1972]). One of the first programming languages to allow type
expressions to be constructed systematically is Algol 68. Type expressions can

be recursively defined, and structural equivalence is used. A clear distinction between name and structural equivalence is found in EL1, the choice being left to the programmer (Wegbreit [1974]). The critique of Pascal by Welsh, Sneeringer, and Hoare [1977] drew attention to the distinction.

The combination of coercion and overloading can lead to ambiguities: coercing an argument may lead to overloading being resolved in favor of a different algorithm. Restrictions are therefore placed on one or the other. A freewheeling approach to coercions was taken in PL/I, where the first design criterion was, "*Anything goes*. If a particular combination of symbols has a reasonably sensible meaning, that meaning will be made official (Radin and Rogoway [1965])." An ordering is often placed on the set of basic types — e.g., Hext [1967] describes a lattice structure imposed on the basic types of CPL — and lower types may be coerced to higher types.

Compile-time resolution of overloading in languages such as APL (Iverson [1962]) and SETL (Schwartz [1973]) has the potential for improving the running time of programs (Bauer and Saal [1974]). Tennenbaum [1974] distinguished between "forward" resolution that determines the set of possible types of an operator from its operands and "backward" resolution based on the type expected by the context. Using a lattice of types, Jones and Muchnick [1976] and Kaplan and Ullman [1980] solve constraints on types obtained from forward and backward analysis. Overloading in Ada can be resolved by making a single forward and then a single backward pass, as in Section 6.5. This observation emerges from a number of papers: Ganzinger and Ripken [1980]; Pennello, DeRemer and Meyers [1980]; Janas [1980]; Persch et al. [1980]. Cormack [1981] offers a recursive implementation and Baker [1982] avoids an explicit backward pass by carrying along a dag of possible types.

Type inference was studied by Curry (see Curry and Feys [1958]) in connection with combinatory logic and the lambda calculus of Church [1941]. It has long been observed that the lambda calculus is at the core of a functional language. We have repeatedly used the application of a function to an argument to discuss type-checking concepts in this chapter. Functions can be defined and applied with no regard to types in the lambda calculus, and Curry was interested in their "functional character," and determining what we would now call a most general polymorphic type, consisting of a type expression with universal quantifiers as in Section 6.6. Motivated by Curry, Hindley [1969] observed that unification could be used to infer the types. Independently, in his thesis, Morris [1968a] assigned types to lambda expressions by setting up a set of equations and solving them to determine the types associated with variables. Unaware of Hindley's work, Milner [1978] also observed that unification could be used to solve the sets of equations, and applied the idea to infer types in the ML programming language.

The pragmatics of type checking in ML are described by Cardelli [1984]. This approach has been applied to a language by Meertens [1983]; Suzuki [1981] explores its application to Smalltalk 1976 (Ingalls [1978]). Mitchell

[1984] shows how coercions can be included.

Morris [1968a] observes that recursive or circular types allow types to be inferred for expressions containing the application of a function to itself. The C program in Fig. 6.28, containing an application of a function to itself, is motivated by an Algol program in Ledgard [1971]. Exercise 6.31 is from MacQueen, Plotkin, and Sethi [1984], where a semantic model for recursive polymorphic types is given. Different approaches appear in McCracken [1979] and Cartwright [1985]. Reynolds [1985] surveys the ML type system, theoretical guidelines for avoiding anomalies involving coercions and overloading, and higher order polymorphic functions.

Unification was first studied by Robinson [1965]. The unification algorithm in Section 6.7 can readily be adapted from algorithms for testing equivalence of (1) finite automata and (2) linked lists with cycles (Knuth [1973a], Section 2.3.5, Exercise 11). The almost linear algorithm for testing equivalence of finite automata due to Hopcroft and Karp [1971] can be viewed as an implementation of the sketch on p. 594 of Knuth [1973a]. Through clever use of data structures, linear algorithms for the acyclic case are presented by Paterson and Wegman [1978] and by Martelli and Montanari [1982]. An algorithm for finding congruent nodes (see Exercise 6.30) appears in Downey, Sethi, and Tarjan [1980].

Despeyroux [1984] describes a type-checker generator that uses pattern matching to create a type checker from an operational-semantic specification based on inference rules.

CHAPTER 7

Run-Time
Environments

Before considering code generation, we need to relate the static source text of a program to the actions that must occur at run time to implement the program. As execution proceeds, the same name in the source text can denote different data objects in the target machine. This chapter examines the relationship between names and data objects.

The allocation and deallocation of data objects is managed by the *run-time support* package, consisting of routines loaded with the generated target code. The design of the run-time support package is influenced by the semantics of procedures. Support packages for languages like Fortran, Pascal, and Lisp can be constructed using the techniques in this chapter.

Each execution of a procedure is referred to as an *activation* of the procedure. If the procedure is recursive, several of its activations may be alive at the same time. Each call of a procedure in Pascal leads to an activation that may manipulate data objects allocated for its use.

The representation of a data object at run time is determined by its type. Often, elementary data types, such as characters, integers, and reals, can be represented by equivalent data objects in the target machine. However, aggregates, such as arrays, strings, and structures, are usually represented by collections of primitive objects; their layout is discussed in Chapter 8.

7.1 SOURCE LANGUAGE ISSUES

For specificity, suppose that a program is made up of procedures, as in Pascal. This section distinguishes between the source text of a procedure and its activations at run time.

Procedures

A *procedure definition* is a declaration that, in its simplest form, associates an identifier with a statement. The identifier is the *procedure name*, and the statement is the *procedure body*. For example, the Pascal code in Fig. 7.1 contains the definition of the procedure named `readarray` on lines 3-7; the body of the procedure is on lines 5-7. Procedures that return values are called *functions* in many languages; however, it is convenient to refer them as

```
(1) program sort(input, output);
(2)      var a : array [0..10] of integer;

(3)      procedure readarray;
(4)          var i : integer;
(5)          begin
(6)              for i := 1 to 9 do read(a[i])
(7)          end;

(8)      function partition(y, z: integer) : integer;
(9)          var i, j, x, v: integer;
(10)         begin ...
(11)         end;

(12)     procedure quicksort(m, n: integer);
(13)         var i : integer;
(14)         begin
(15)             if ( n > m ) then begin
(16)                 i := partition(m,n);
(17)                 quicksort(m,i-1);
(18)                 quicksort(i+1,n)
(19)             end
(20)         end;

(21)     begin
(22)         a[0] := -9999; a[10] := 9999;
(23)         readarray;
(24)         quicksort(1,9)
(25)     end.
```

Fig. 7.1. A Pascal program for reading and sorting integers.

procedures. A complete program will also be treated as a procedure.

When a procedure name appears within an executable statement, we say that the procedure is *called* at that point. The basic idea is that a procedure call executes the procedure body. The main program in lines 21-25 of Fig. 7.1 calls the procedure readarray at line 23 and then calls quicksort at line 24. Note that procedure calls can also occur within expressions, as on line 16.

Some of the identifiers appearing in a procedure definition are special, and are called *formal parameters* (or just *formals*) of the procedure. (C calls them "formal arguments" and Fortran calls them "dummy arguments.") The identifiers m and n on line 12 are formal parameters of quicksort. Arguments, known as *actual parameters* (or *actuals*) may be passed to a called procedure; they are substituted for the formals in the body. Methods for setting up the correspondence between actuals and formals are discussed in Section 7.5. Line 18 of Fig. 7.1 is a call of quicksort with actual parameters i+1 and n.

Activation Trees

We make the following assumptions about the flow of control among procedures during the execution of a program:

1. Control flows sequentially; that is, the execution of a program consists of a sequence of steps, with control being at some specific point in the program at each step.

2. Each execution of a procedure starts at the beginning of the procedure body and eventually returns control to the point immediately following the place where the procedure was called. This means the flow of control between procedures can be depicted using trees, as we shall soon see.

Each execution of a procedure body is referred to as an activation of the procedure. The *lifetime* of an activation of a procedure p is the sequence of steps between the first and last steps in the execution of the procedure body, including time spent executing procedures called by p, the procedures called by them, and so on. In general, the term "lifetime" refers to a consecutive sequence of steps during the execution of a program.

In languages like Pascal, each time control enters a procedure q from procedure p, it eventually returns to p (in the absence of a fatal error). More precisely, each time control flows from an activation of a procedure p to an activation of a procedure q, it returns to the same activation of p.

If *a* and *b* are procedure activations, then their lifetimes are either nonoverlapping or are nested. That is, if *b* is entered before *a* is left, then control must leave *b* before it leaves *a*.

This nested property of activation lifetimes can be illustrated by inserting two print statements in each procedure, one before the first statement of the procedure body and the other after the last. The first statement prints enter followed by the name of the procedure and the values of the actual parameters; the last statement prints leave followed by the same information. One execution of the program in Fig. 7.1 with these print statements produced the output shown in Fig. 7.2. The lifetime of the activation quicksort(1,9) is the sequence of steps executed between printing enter quicksort(1,9) and printing leave quicksort(1,9). In Fig. 7.2, it is assumed that the value returned by partition(1,9) is 4.

A procedure is *recursive* if a new activation can begin before an earlier activation of the same procedure has ended. Figure 7.2 shows that control enters the activation of quicksort(1,9), from line 24, early in the execution of the program but leaves this activation almost at the end. In the meantime, there are several other activations of quicksort, so quicksort is recursive.

A recursive procedure p need not call itself directly; p may call another procedure q, which may then call p through some sequence of procedure calls. We can use a tree, called an *activation tree*, to depict the way control enters and leaves activations. In an activation tree,

```
Execution begins...
enter readarray
leave readarray
enter quicksort(1,9)
enter partition(1,9)
leave partition(1,9)
enter quicksort(1,3)
   . . .

leave quicksort(1,3)
enter quicksort(5,9)
   . . .

leave quicksort(5,9)
leave quicksort(1,9)
Execution terminated.
```

Fig. 7.2. Output suggesting activations of procedures in Fig. 7.1.

1.   each node represents an activation of a procedure,

2.   the root represents the activation of the main program,

3.   the node for *a* is the parent of the node for *b* if and only if control flows
     from activation *a* to *b*, and

4.   the node for *a* is to the left of the node for *b* if and only if the lifetime of
     a occurs before the lifetime of *b*.

Since each node represents a unique activation, and vice versa, it is convenient
to talk of control being at a node when it is in the activation represented by
the node.

Example 7.1.   The activation tree in Fig. 7.3 is constructed from the output in
Fig. 7.2.[1] To save space, only the first letter of each procedure is shown. The
root of the activation tree is for the entire program `sort`. During the execution of `sort`, there is an activation of `readarray`, represented by the first
child of the root, with label `r`. The next activation, represented by the second
child of the root, is for `quicksort`, with actuals 1 and 9. During this
activation, the calls of `partition` and `quicksort` on lines 16-18 of Fig. 7.1
lead to the activations p(1,9), q(1,3), and q(5,9). Note that the activations q(1,3) and q(5,9) are recursive, and that they begin and end before
q(1,9) ends.   □

---

[1] The actual calls made by `quicksort` depend on what `partition` returns (see Aho, Hopcroft,
and Ullman [1983] for details of the algorithm). Figure 7.3 represents one possible tree of calls.
It is consistent with Fig. 7.2, although certain calls low in the tree are not shown in Fig. 7.2.

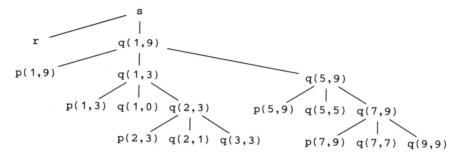

Fig. 7.3. An activation tree corresponding to the output in Fig. 7.2.

Control Stacks

The flow of control in a program corresponds to a depth-first traversal of the activation tree that starts at the root, visits a node before its children, and recursively visits children at each node in a left-to-right order. The output in Fig. 7.2 can therefore be reconstructed by traversing the activation tree in Fig. 7.3, printing enter when the node for an activation is reached for the first time and printing leave after the entire subtree of the node has been visited during the traversal.

We can use a stack, called a *control stack* to keep track of live procedure activations. The idea is to push the node for an activation onto the control stack as the activation begins and to pop the node when the activation ends. Then the contents of the control stack are related to paths to the root of the activation tree. When node *n* is at the top of the control stack, the stack contains the nodes along the path from *n* to the root.

Example 7.2. Figure 7.4 shows nodes from the activation tree of Fig. 7.3 that have been reached when control enters the activation represented by q(2,3). Activations with labels r, p(1,9), p(1,3), and q(1,0) have executed to completion, so the figure contains dashed lines to their nodes. The solid lines mark the path from q(2,3) to the root.

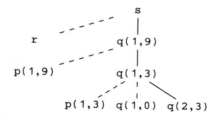

Fig. 7.4. The control stack contains nodes along a path to the root.

At this point the control stack contains the following nodes along this path to the root (the top of the stack is to the right)

　　s, q(1,9), q(1,3), q(2,3)

and no other nodes.　　　　　　　　　　　　　　　　　　　□

Control stacks extend to the stack storage-allocation technique used to implement languages such as Pascal and C. This technique is discussed in detail in Sections 7.3 and 7.4.

The Scope of a Declaration

A declaration in a language is a syntactic construct that associates information with a name. Declarations may be explicit, as in the Pascal fragment

　　var i : integer;

or they may be implicit. For example, any variable name starting with I is assumed to denote an integer in a Fortran program, unless otherwise declared.

There may be independent declarations of the same name in different parts of a program. The *scope rules* of a language determine which declaration of a name applies when the name appears in the text of a program. In the Pascal program in Fig. 7.1, i is declared thrice, on lines 4, 9, and 13, and the uses of the name i in procedures readarray, partition, and quicksort are independent of each other. The declaration on line 4 applies to the uses of i on line 6. That is, the two occurrences of i on line 6 are in the scope of the declaration on line 4. The three occurrences of i on lines 16-18 are in the scope of the declaration of i on line 13.

The portion of the program to which a declaration applies is called the *scope* of that declaration. An occurrence of a name in a procedure is said to be *local* to the procedure if it is in the scope of a declaration within the procedure; otherwise, the occurrence is said to be *nonlocal*. The distinction between local and nonlocal names carries over to any syntactic construct that can have declarations within it.

While scope is a property of the declaration of a name, it is sometimes convenient to use the abbreviation "the scope of name x" for "the scope of the declaration of name x that applies to this occurrence of x." In this sense, the scope of i on line 17 in Fig. 7.1 is the body of quicksort.[2]

At compile time, the symbol table can be used to find the declaration that applies to an occurrence of a name. When a declaration is seen, a symbol-table entry is created for it. As long as we are in the scope of the declaration, its entry is returned when the name in it is looked up. Symbol tables are discussed in Section 7.6.

---

[2] Most of the time, the terms name, identifier, variable, and lexeme can be used interchangeably without there being any confusion about the intended construct.

Bindings of Names

Even if each name is declared once in a program, the same name may denote different data objects at run time. The informal term "data object" corresponds to a storage location that can hold values.

In programming language semantics, the term *environment* refers to a function that maps a name to a storage location, and the term *state* refers to a function that maps a storage location to the value held there, as in Fig. 7.5. Using the terms *l*-value and *r*-value from Chapter 2, an environment maps a name to an *l*-value, and a state maps the *l*-value to an *r*-value.

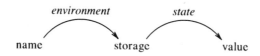

Fig. 7.5. Two-stage mapping from names to values.

Environments and states are different; an assignment changes the state, but not the environment. For example, suppose that storage address 100, associated with variable pi, holds 0. After the assignment pi := 3.14, the same storage address is associated with pi, but the value held there is 3.14.

When an environment associates storage location *s* with a name **x**, we say that **x** is *bound* to *s*; the association itself is referred to as a *binding* of **x**. The term storage "location" is to be taken figuratively. If **x** is not of a basic type, the storage *s* for **x** may be a collection of memory words.

A binding is the dynamic counterpart of a declaration, as shown in Fig. 7.6. As we have seen, more than one activation of a recursive procedure can be alive at the same time. In Pascal, a local variable name in a procedure is bound to a different storage location in each activation of a procedure. Techniques for binding local variable names are considered in Section 7.3.

STATIC NOTION	DYNAMIC COUNTERPART
definition of a procedure	activations of the procedure
declaration of a name	bindings of the name
scope of a declaration	lifetime of a binding

Fig. 7.6. Corresponding static and dynamic notions.

Questions to Ask

The way a compiler for a language must organize its storage and bind names is determined largely by answers to questions like the following:

1. May procedures be recursive?
2. What happens to the values of local names when control returns from an activation of a procedure?
3. May a procedure refer to nonlocal names?
4. How are parameters passed when a procedure is called?
5. May procedures be passed as parameters?
6. May procedures be returned as results?
7. May storage be allocated dynamically under program control?
8. Must storage be deallocated explicitly?

The effect of these issues on the run-time support needed for a given programming language is examined in the remainder of this chapter.

7.2 STORAGE ORGANIZATION

The organization of run-time storage in this section can be used for languages such as Fortran, Pascal, and C.

Subdivision of Run-Time Memory

Suppose that the compiler obtains a block of storage from the operating system for the compiled program to run in. From the discussion in the last section, this run-time storage might be subdivided to hold:

1. the generated target code,
2. data objects, and
3. a counterpart of the control stack to keep track of procedure activations.

The size of the generated target code is fixed at compile time, so the compiler can place it in a statically determined area, perhaps in the low end of memory. Similarly, the size of some of the data objects may also be known at compile time, and these too can be placed in a statically determined area, as in Fig. 7.7. One reason for statically allocating as many data objects as possible is that the addresses of these objects can be compiled into the target code. All data objects in Fortran can be allocated statically.

Implementations of languages like Pascal and C use extensions of the control stack to manage activations of procedures. When a call occurs, execution of an activation is interrupted and information about the status of the machine, such as the value of the program counter and machine registers, is saved on the stack. When control returns from the call, this activation can be restarted after restoring the values of relevant registers and setting the program counter to the point immediately after the call. Data objects whose life-

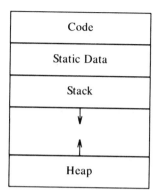

Fig. 7.7. Typical subdivision of run-time memory into code and data areas.

times are contained in that of an activation can be allocated on the stack, along with other information associated with the activation. This strategy is discussed in the next section.

A separate area of run-time memory, called a *heap*, holds all other information. Pascal allows data to be allocated under program control, as discussed in Section 7.7; the storage for such data is taken from the heap. Implementations of languages in which the lifetimes of activations cannot be represented by an activation tree might use the heap to keep information about activations. The controlled way in which data is allocated and deallocated on a stack makes it cheaper to place data on the stack than on the heap.

The sizes of the stack and the heap can change as the program executes, so we show these at opposite ends of memory in Fig. 7.7, where they can grow toward each other as needed. Pascal and C need both a run-time stack and heap, but not all languages do.

By convention, stacks grow down. That is, the "top" of the stack is drawn towards the bottom of the page. Since memory addresses increase as we go down a page, "downwards-growing" means toward higher addresses. If *top* marks the top of the stack, offsets from the top of the stack can be computed by subtracting the offset from *top*. On many machines this computation can be done efficiently by keeping the value of *top* in a register. Stack addresses can then be represented as offsets from *top*.[3]

---

[3] The organization in Fig. 7.7 assumes that the run-time memory consists of a single contiguous block of storage obtained at the start of execution. This assumption imposes a fixed limit on the combined sizes of the stack and heap. If the limit is large enough that it is rarely exceeded, then it may be wastefully large for most programs. The alternative of linking objects on the stack and heap may make it more expensive to keep track of the top of the stack. Furthermore, the target machine may favor a different placement of areas. For example, some machines allow just positive offsets from an address in a register.

Activation Records

Information needed by a single execution of a procedure is managed using a contiguous block of storage called an *activation record* or *frame*, consisting of the collection of fields shown in Fig. 7.8. Not all languages, nor all compilers use all of these fields; often registers can take the place of one or more of them. For languages like Pascal and C, it is customary to push the activation record of a procedure on the run-time stack when the procedure is called and to pop the activation record off the stack when control returns to the caller.

The purpose of the fields of an activation record is as follows, starting from the field for temporaries.

1. Temporary values, such as those arising in the evaluation of expressions, are stored in the field for temporaries.

2. The field for local data holds data that is local to an execution of a procedure. The layout of this field is discussed below.

3. The field for saved machine status holds information about the state of the machine just before the procedure is called. This information includes the values of the program counter and machine registers that have to be restored when control returns from the procedure.

4. The optional *access link* is used in Section 7.4 to refer to nonlocal data held in other activation records. For a language like Fortran access links are not needed because nonlocal data is kept in a fixed place. Access links, or the related "display" mechanism, are needed for Pascal.

5. The optional *control link* points to the activation record of the caller.

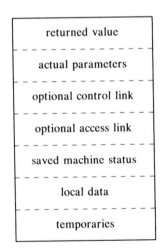

Fig. 7.8. A general activation record.

6. The field for actual parameters is used by the calling procedure to supply parameters to the called procedure. We show space for parameters in the activation record, but in practice parameters are often passed in machine registers for greater efficiency.

7. The field for the returned value is used by the called procedure to return a value to the calling procedure. Again, in practice this value is often returned in a register for greater efficiency.

The sizes of each of these fields can be determined at the time a procedure is called. In fact, the sizes of almost all fields can be determined at compile time. An exception occurs if a procedure may have a local array whose size is determined by the value of an actual parameter, available only when the procedure is called at run time. See Section 7.3 for the allocation of variable-length data in an activation record.

Compile-Time Layout of Local Data

Suppose run-time storage comes in blocks of contiguous bytes, where a byte is the smallest unit of addressable memory. On many machines, a byte is eight bits and some number of bytes form a machine word. Multibyte objects are stored in consecutive bytes and given the address of the first byte.

The amount of storage needed for a name is determined from its type. An elementary data type, such as a character, integer, or real, can usually be stored in an integral number of bytes. Storage for an aggregate, such as an array or record, must be large enough to hold all its components. For easy access to the components, storage for aggregates is typically allocated in one contiguous block of bytes. See Sections 8.2 and 8.3 for more details.

The field for local data is laid out as the declarations in a procedure are examined at compile time. Variable-length data is kept outside this field. We keep a count of the memory locations that have been allocated for previous declarations. From the count we determine a *relative* address of the storage for a local with respect to some position such as the beginning of the activation record. The relative address, or *offset*, is the difference between the addresses of the position and the data object.

The storage layout for data objects is strongly influenced by the addressing constraints of the target machine. For example, instructions to add integers may expect integers to be *aligned*, that is, placed at certain positions in memory such as an address divisible by 4. Although an array of ten characters needs only enough bytes to hold ten characters, a compiler may therefore allocate 12 bytes, leaving 2 bytes unused. Space left unused due to alignment considerations is referred to as *padding*. When space is at a premium, a compiler may *pack* data so that no padding is left; additional instructions may then need to be executed at run time to position packed data so that it can be operated on as if it were properly aligned.

Example 7.3. Figure 7.9 is a simplification of the data layout used by C compilers for two machines that we call Machine 1 and Machine 2. C provides for three sizes of integers, declared using the keywords short, int, and long. The instruction sets of the two machines are such that the compiler for Machine 1 allocates 16, 32, and 32 bits for the three sizes of integers, while the compiler for Machine 2 allocates 24, 48, and 64 bits, respectively. For comparison between machines, sizes are measured in bits in Fig. 7.9, even though neither machine allows bits to be addressed directly.

The memory of Machine 1 is organized into bytes consisting of 8 bits each. Even though every byte has an address, the instruction set favors short integers being positioned at bytes whose addresses are even, and integers being positioned at addresses that are divisible by 4. The compiler places short integers at even addresses, even if it has to skip a byte as padding in the process. Thus, four bytes, consisting of 32 bits, may be allocated for a character followed by a short integer.

In Machine 2, each word consists of 64 bits, and 24 bits are allowed for the address of a word. There are 64 possibilities for the individual bits inside a word, so 6 additional bits are needed to distinguish between them. By design, a pointer to a character on Machine 2 takes 30 bits — 24 to find the word and 6 for the position of the character inside the word.

The strong word orientation of the instruction set of Machine 2 has led the compiler to allocate a complete word at a time, even when fewer bits would suffice to represent all possible values of that type; e.g., only 8 bits are needed to represent a character. Hence, under alignment, Fig. 7.9 shows 64 bits for each type. Within each word, the bits for each basic type are in specified positions. Two words consisting of 128 bits would be allocated for a character followed by a short integer, with the character using only 8 of the bits in the first word and the short integer using only 24 of the bits in the second word. □

TYPE	SIZE (Bits)		ALIGNMENT (Bits)	
	Machine 1	Machine 2	Machine 1	Machine 2
char	8	8	8	64[a]
short	16	24	16	64
int	32	48	32	64
long	32	64	32	64
float	32	64	32	64
double	64	128	32	64
character pointer	32	30	32	64
other pointers ...	32	24	32	64
structures........	≥8	≥64	32	64

[a] Characters in an array are aligned every 8 bits.

Fig. 7.9. Data layouts used by two C compilers.

7.3 STORAGE-ALLOCATION STRATEGIES

A different storage-allocation strategy is used in each of the three data areas in the organization of Fig. 7.7.

1. Static allocation lays out storage for all data objects at compile time.

2. Stack allocation manages the run-time storage as a stack.

3. Heap allocation allocates and deallocates storage as needed at run time from a data area known as a heap.

These allocation strategies are applied in this section to activation records. We also describe how the target code of a procedure accesses the storage bound to a local name.

Static Allocation

In static allocation, names are bound to storage as the program is compiled, so there is no need for a run-time support package. Since the bindings do not change at run time, every time a procedure is activated, its names are bound to the same storage locations. This property allows the values of local names to be *retained* across activations of a procedure. That is, when control returns to a procedure, the values of the locals are the same as they were when control left the last time.

From the type of a name, the compiler determines the amount of storage to set aside for that name, as discussed in Section 7.2. The address of this storage consists of an offset from an end of the activation record for the procedure. The compiler must eventually decide where the activation records go, relative to the target code and to one another. Once this decision is made, the position of each activation record, and hence of the storage for each name in the record is fixed. At compile time we can therefore fill in the addresses at which the target code can find the data it operates on. Similarly, the addresses at which information is to be saved when a procedure call occurs are also known at compile time.

However, some limitations go along with using static allocation alone.

1. The size of a data object and constraints on its position in memory must be known at compile time.

2. Recursive procedures are restricted, because all activations of a procedure use the same bindings for local names.

3. Data structures cannot be created dynamically, since there is no mechanism for storage allocation at run time.

Fortran was designed to permit static storage allocation. A Fortran program consists of a main program, subroutines, and functions (call them all *procedures*), as in the Fortran 77 program of Fig. 7.10. Using the memory organization of Fig. 7.7, the layout of the code and the activation records for

```
(1)        PROGRAM CNSUME
(2)           CHARACTER * 50 BUF
(3)           INTEGER NEXT
(4)           CHARACTER C, PRDUCE
(5)           DATA NEXT /1/, BUF /' '/
(6)  6          C = PRDUCE( )
(7)             BUF(NEXT:NEXT) = C
(8)             NEXT = NEXT + 1
(9)             IF ( C .NE. ' ' ) GOTO 6
(10)          WRITE (*,'(A)') BUF
(11)          END

(12)       CHARACTER FUNCTION PRDUCE( )
(13)          CHARACTER * 80 BUFFER
(14)          INTEGER NEXT
(15)          SAVE BUFFER, NEXT
(16)          DATA NEXT /81/
(17)          IF ( NEXT .GT. 80 ) THEN
(18)             READ  (*,'(A)') BUFFER
(19)             NEXT = 1
(20)          END IF
(21)          PRDUCE = BUFFER(NEXT:NEXT)
(22)          NEXT = NEXT+1
(23)          END
```

Fig. 7.10. A Fortran 77 program.

this program is shown in Fig. 7.11. Within the activation record for CNSUME (read "consume" — Fortran does not like long identifiers), there is space for the locals BUF, NEXT, and C. The storage bound to BUF holds a string of fifty characters. It is followed by space for holding an integer value for NEXT and a character value for C. The fact that NEXT is also declared in PRDUCE presents no problem, because the locals of the two procedures get space in their respective activation records.

Since the sizes of the executable code and the activation records are known at compile time, memory organizations other than the one in Fig. 7.11 are possible. A Fortran compiler might place the activation record for a procedure together with the code for that procedure. On some computer systems, it is feasible to leave the relative position of the activation records unspecified and allow the link editor to link activation records and executable code.

Example 7.4. The program in Fig. 7.10 relies on the values of locals being retained across procedure activations. A SAVE statement in Fortran 77 specifies that the value of a local at the beginning of an activation must be the same as that at the end of the last activation. Initial values for these locals can be specified using a DATA statement.

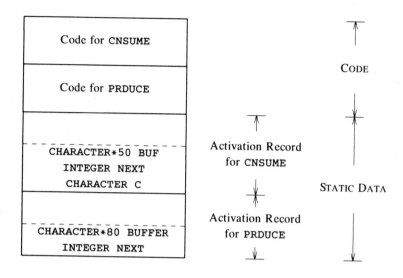

Fig. 7.11. Static storage for local identifiers of a Fortran 77 program.

The statement on line 18 of procedure PRDUCE reads one line of text at a time into a buffer. The procedure delivers successive characters each time it is activated. The main program CNSUME also has a buffer in which it accumulates characters until a blank is seen. On input

    hello world

the characters returned by the activations of PRDUCE are depicted in Fig. 7.12; the output of the program is

    hello

The buffer into which PRDUCE reads lines must retain its value between activations. The SAVE statement on line 15 ensures that when control returns to PRDUCE, locals BUFFER and NEXT have the same values as they did when control left the procedure the last time. The first time control reaches PRDUCE, the value of the local NEXT is taken from the DATA statement on line 16. In this way, NEXT is initialized to 81.   □

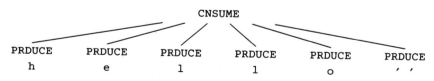

Fig. 7.12. Characters returned by activations of PRDUCE.

Stack Allocation

Stack allocation is based on the idea of a control stack; storage is organized as a stack, and activation records are pushed and popped as activations begin and end, respectively. Storage for the locals in each call of a procedure is contained in the activation record for that call. Thus locals are bound to fresh storage in each activation, because a new activation record is pushed onto the stack when a call is made. Furthermore, the values of locals are *deleted* when the activation ends; that is, the values are lost because the storage for locals disappears when the activation record is popped.

We first describe a form of stack allocation in which the sizes of all activation records are known at compile time. Situations in which incomplete information about sizes is available at compile time are considered below.

Suppose that register *top* marks the top of the stack. At run time, an activation record can be allocated and deallocated by incrementing and decrementing *top*, respectively, by the size of the record. If procedure q has an activation record of size a, then *top* is incremented by a just before the target code of q is executed. When control returns from q, *top* is decremented by a.

Example 7.5. Figure 7.13 shows the activation records that are pushed onto and popped from the run-time stack as control flows through the activation tree of Fig. 7.3. Dashed lines in the tree go to activations that have ended. Execution begins with an activation of procedure s. When control reaches the first call in the body of s, procedure r is activated and its activation record is pushed onto the stack. When control returns from this activation, the record is popped leaving just the record for s in the stack. In the activation of s, control then reaches a call of q with actuals 1 and 9, and an activation record is allocated on top of the stack for an activation of q. Whenever control is in an activation, its activation record is at the top of the stack.

Several activations occur between the last two snapshots in Fig. 7.13. In the last snapshot in Fig. 7.13, activations p(1,3) and q(1,0) have begun and ended during the lifetime of q(1,3), so their activation records have come and gone from the stack, leaving the activation record for q(1,3) on top. □

In a Pascal procedure, we can determine a relative address for local data in an activation record, as discussed in Section 7.2. At run time, suppose *top* marks the location of the end of a record. The address of a local name x in the target code for the procedure might therefore be written as $dx(top)$, to indicate that the data bound to x can be found at the location obtained by adding dx to the value in register *top*. Note that addresses can alternatively be taken as offsets from the value in any other register r pointing to a fixed position in the activation record.

Calling Sequences

Procedure calls are implemented by generating what are known as *calling sequences* in the target code. A *call sequence* allocates an activation record

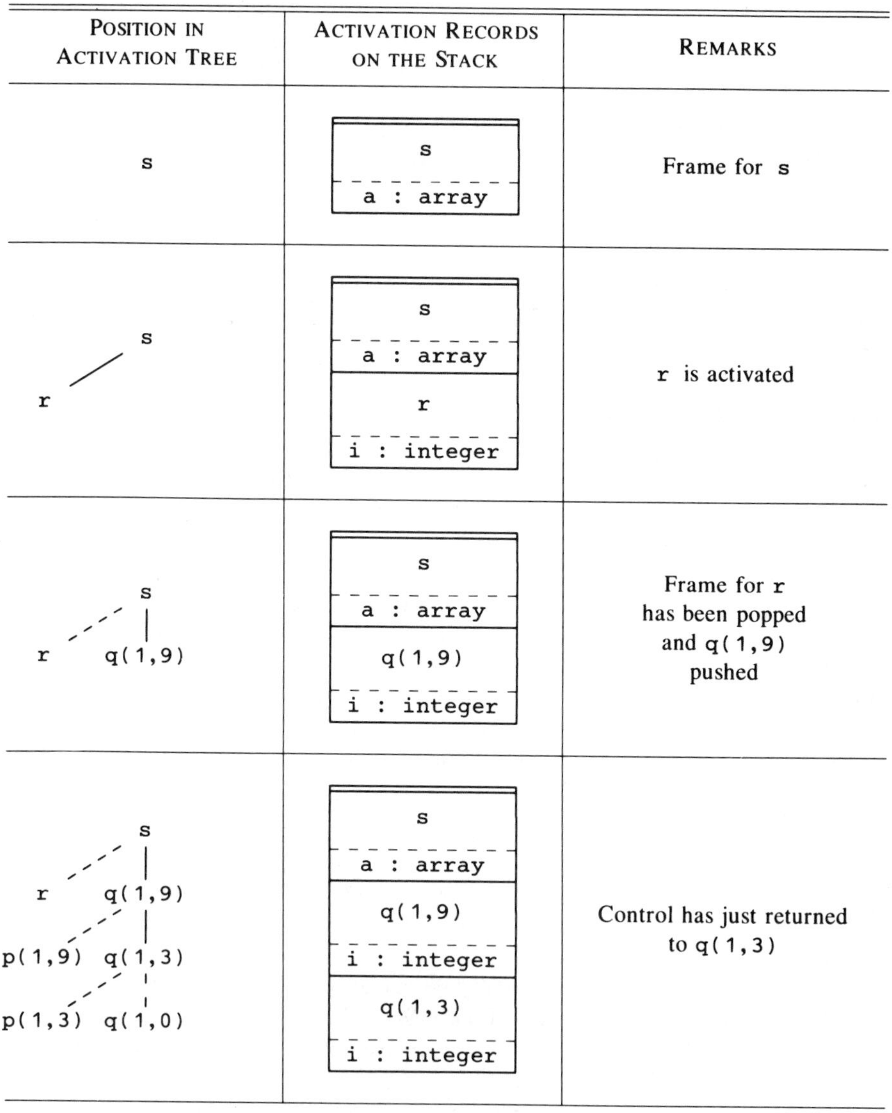

POSITION IN ACTIVATION TREE	ACTIVATION RECORDS ON THE STACK	REMARKS
s	s - - - - - - - a : array	Frame for s
s / r	s - - - - - - - a : array r - - - - - - - i : integer	r is activated
s r q(1,9)	s - - - - - - - a : array q(1,9) - - - - - - - i : integer	Frame for r has been popped and q(1,9) pushed
s r q(1,9) p(1,9) q(1,3) p(1,3) q(1,0)	s - - - - - - - a : array q(1,9) - - - - - - - i : integer q(1,3) - - - - - - - i : integer	Control has just returned to q(1,3)

Fig. 7.13. Downward-growing stack allocation of activation records.

and enters information into its fields. A *return sequence* restores the state of the machine so the calling procedure can continue execution.

Calling sequences and activation records differ, even for implementations of the same language. The code in a calling sequence is often divided between the calling procedure (the caller) and the procedure it calls (the callee). There is no exact division of run-time tasks between the caller and callee — the source language, the target machine, and the operating system impose requirements that may favor one solution over another.[4]

A principle that aids the design of calling sequences and activation records is that fields whose sizes are fixed early are placed in the middle. In the general activation record of Fig. 7.8, the control link, access link, and machine-status fields appear in the middle. The decision about whether or not to use control and access links is part of the design of the compiler, so these fields can be fixed at compiler-construction time. If exactly the same amount of machine-status information is saved for each activation, then the same code can do the saving and restoring for all activations. Moreover, programs such as debuggers will have an easier time deciphering the stack contents when an error occurs.

Even though the size of the field for temporaries is eventually fixed at compile time, this size may not be known to the front end. Careful code generation or optimization may reduce the number of temporaries needed by the procedure, so as far as the front end is concerned, the size of this field is unknown. In the general activation record, we therefore show this field after that for local data, where changes in its size will not affect the offsets of data objects relative to the fields in the middle.

Since each call has its own actual parameters, the caller usually evaluates actual parameters and communicates them to the activation record of the callee. Methods for passing parameters are discussed in Section 7.5. In the run-time stack, the activation record of the caller is just below that for the callee, as in Fig. 7.14. There is an advantage to placing the fields for parameters and a potential returned value next to the activation record of the caller. The caller can then access these fields using offsets from the end of its own activation record, without knowing the complete layout of the record for the callee. In particular, there is no reason for the caller to know about the local data or temporaries of the callee. A benefit of this information hiding is that procedures with variable numbers of arguments, such as `printf` in C, can be handled, as discussed below.

Languages like Pascal require arrays local to a procedure to have a length that can be determined at compile time. More often, the size of a local array may depend on the value of a parameter passed to the procedure. In that case, the size of all the data local to the procedure cannot be determined until the procedure is called. Techniques for handling variable-length data are discussed later in this section.

The following call sequence is motivated by the above discussion. As in Fig. 7.14, the register *top_sp* points to the end of the machine-status field in an activation record. This position is known to the caller, so it can be made responsible for setting *top_sp* before control flows to the called procedure.

---

[4] If a procedure is called *n* times, then the portion of the calling sequence in the various callers is generated *n* times. However, the portion in the callee is shared by all calls, so it is generated just once. Hence, it is desirable to put as much of the calling sequence into the callee as possible.

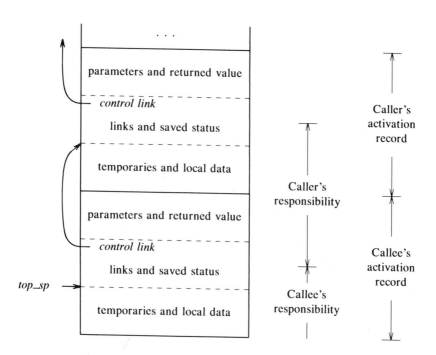

Fig. 7.14. Division of tasks between caller and callee.

The code for the callee can access its temporaries and local data using offsets from *top_sp*. The call sequence is:

1. The caller evaluates actuals.

2. The caller stores a return address and the old value of *top_sp* into the callee's activation record. The caller then increments *top_sp* to the position shown in Fig. 7.14. That is, *top_sp* is moved past the caller's local data and temporaries and the callee's parameter and status fields.

3. The callee saves register values and other status information.

4. The callee initializes its local data and begins execution.

   A possible return sequence is:

1. The callee places a return value next to the activation record of the caller.

2. Using the information in the status field, the callee restores *top_sp* and other registers and branches to a return address in the caller's code.

3. Although *top_sp* has been decremented, the caller can copy the returned value into its own activation record and use it to evaluate an expression.

   The above calling sequences allow the number of arguments of the called procedure to depend on the call. Note that, at compile time, the target code of the caller knows the number of arguments it is supplying to the callee. Hence the caller knows the size of the parameter field. However, the target code of the callee must be prepared to handle other calls as well, so it waits until it is called, and then examines the parameter field. Using the organization of Fig. 7.14, information describing the parameters must be placed next to the status field so the callee can find it. For example, consider the standard library function `printf` in C. The first argument of `printf` specifies the nature of the remaining arguments, so once `printf` can locate the first argument, it can find the remaining ones.

Variable-Length Data

A common strategy for handling variable-length data is suggested in Fig. 7.15, where procedure p has three local arrays. The storage for these arrays is not part of the activation record for p; only a pointer to the beginning of each array appears in the activation record. The relative addresses of these pointers are known at compile time, so the target code can access array elements through the pointers.

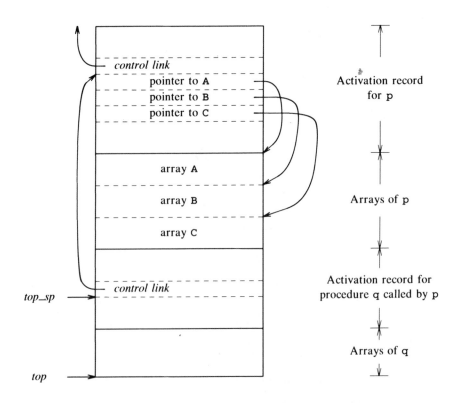

Fig. 7.15. Access to dynamically allocated arrays.

Also shown in Fig. 7.15 is a procedure q called by p. The activation record for q begins after the arrays of p, and the variable-length arrays of q begin beyond that.

Access to data on the stack is through two pointers, *top* and *top_sp*. The first of these marks the actual top of the stack; it points to the position at which the next activation record will begin. The second is used to find local data. For consistency with the organization of Fig. 7.14, suppose *top_sp* points to the end of the machine-status field. In Fig. 7.15, *top_sp* points to the end of this field in the activation record for q. Within the field is a control link to the previous value of *top_sp* when control was in the calling activation of p.

The code to reposition *top* and *top_sp* can be generated at compile time, using the sizes of the fields in the activation records. When q returns, the new value of *top* is *top_sp* minus the length of the machine-status and parameter fields in q's activation record. This length is known at compile time, at least to the caller. After adjusting *top*, the new value of *top_sp* can be copied from the control link of q.

Dangling References

Whenever storage can be deallocated, the problem of dangling references arises. A *dangling reference* occurs when there is a reference to storage that has been deallocated. It is a logical error to use dangling references, since the the value of deallocated storage is undefined according to the semantics of most languages. Worse, since that storage may later be allocated to another datum, mysterious bugs can appear in programs with dangling references.

Example 7.6. Procedure dangle in the C program of Fig. 7.16 returns a pointer to the storage bound to the local name i. The pointer is created by the operator & applied to i. When control returns to main from dangle, the storage for locals is freed and can be used for other purposes. Since p in main refers to this storage, the use of p is a dangling reference.   □

An example in Section 7.7 involves deallocation under program control.

```
main()
{
    int *p;
    p = dangle();
}
int *dangle()
{
    int i = 23;
    return &i;
}
```

Fig. 7.16. A C program that leaves p pointing to deallocated storage.

Heap Allocation

The stack allocation strategy discussed above cannot be used if either of the following is possible.

1. The values of local names must be retained when an activation ends.

2. A called activation outlives the caller. This possibility cannot occur for those languages where activation trees correctly depict the flow of control between procedures.

In each of the above cases, the deallocation of activation records need not occur in a last-in first-out fashion, so storage cannot be organized as a stack.

Heap allocation parcels out pieces of contiguous storage, as needed for activation records or other objects. Pieces may be deallocated in any order, so over time the heap will consist of alternate areas that are free and in use.

The difference between heap and stack allocation of activation records can be seen from Fig. 7.17 and 7.13. In Fig. 7.17, the record for an activation of procedure r is retained when the activation ends. The record for the new activation q(1,9) therefore cannot follow that for s physically, as it did in Fig. 7.13. Now if the retained activation record for r is deallocated, there will be free space in the heap between the activation records for s and q(1,9). It is left to the heap manager to make use of this space.

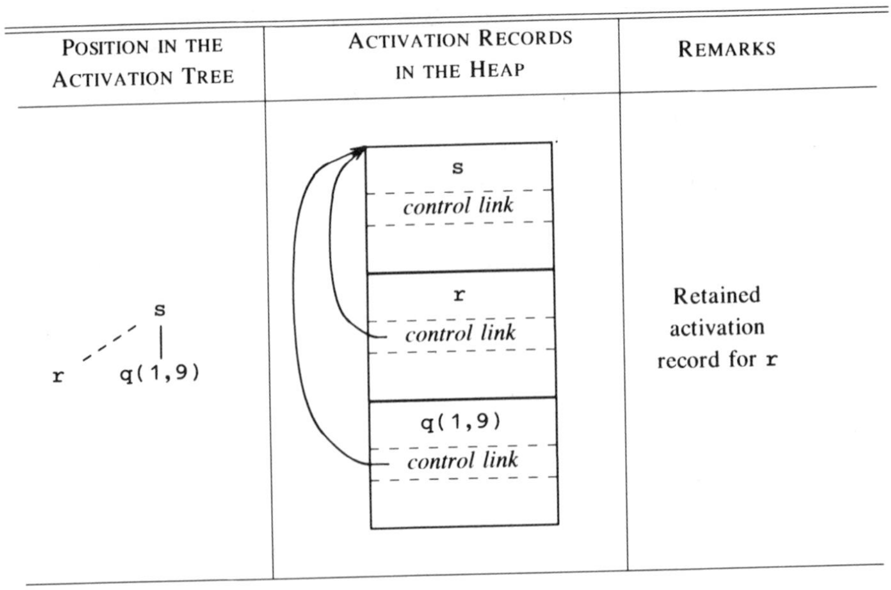

POSITION IN THE ACTIVATION TREE	ACTIVATION RECORDS IN THE HEAP	REMARKS
		Retained activation record for r

Fig. 7.17. Records for live activations need not be adjacent in a heap.

The question of efficient heap management is a somewhat specialized issue in data-structure theory; some techniques are reviewed in Section 7.8. There is generally some time and space overhead associated with using a heap manager. For efficiency reasons, it may be helpful to handle small activation records or records of a predictable size as a special case, as follows:

1. For each size of interest, keep a linked list of free blocks of that size.

2. If possible, fill a request for size s with a block of size s', where s' is the smallest size greater than or equal to s. When the block is eventually deallocated, it is returned to the linked list it came from.

3. For large blocks of storage use the heap manager.

This approach results in fast allocation and deallocation of small amounts of storage, since taking and returning a block from a linked list are efficient operations. For large amounts of storage we expect the computation to take some time to use up the storage, so the time taken by the allocator is often negligible compared with the time taken to do the computation.

7.4 ACCESS TO NONLOCAL NAMES

The storage-allocation strategies of the last section are adapted in this section to permit access to nonlocal names. Although the discussion is based on stack allocation of activation records, the same ideas apply to heap allocation.

The scope rules of a language determine the treatment of references to nonlocal names. A common rule, called the *lexical-* or *static-scope rule*, determines the declaration that applies to a name by examining the program text alone. Pascal, C, and Ada are among the many languages that use lexical scope, with an added "most closely nested" stipulation that is discussed below. An alternative rule, called the *dynamic-scope rule*, determines the declaration applicable to a name at run time, by considering the current activations. Lisp, APL, and Snobol are among the languages that use dynamic scope.

We begin with blocks and the "most closely nested" rule. Then, we consider nonlocal names in languages like C, where scopes are lexical, where all nonlocal names may be bound to statically allocated storage, and where no nested procedure declarations are allowed.

In languages like Pascal that have nested procedures and lexical scope, names belonging to different procedures may be part of the environment at a given time. We discuss two ways of finding the activation records containing the storage bound to nonlocal names: access links and displays.

A final subsection discusses the implementation of dynamic scope.

Blocks

A block is a statement containing its own local data declarations. The concept of a block originated with Algol. In C, a block has the syntax

{ *declarations statements* }

A characteristic of blocks is their nesting structure. Delimiters mark the beginning and end of a block. C uses the braces { and } as delimiters, while the Algol tradition is to use begin and end. Delimiters ensure that one block is either independent of another, or is nested inside the other. That is, it is not possible for two blocks B_1 and B_2 to overlap in such a way that first B_1 begins, then B_2, but B_1 ends before B_2. This nesting property is sometimes referred to as *block structure*.

The scope of a declaration in a block-structured language is given by the *most closely nested* rule:

1. The scope of a declaration in a block B includes B.

2. If a name x is not declared in a block B, then an occurrence of x in B is in the scope of a declaration of x in an enclosing block B' such that
   i) B' has a declaration of x, and
   ii) B' is more closely nested around B than any other block with a declaration of x.

By design, each declaration in Fig. 7.18 initializes the declared name to the number of the block that it appears in. The scope of the declaration of b in B_0 does not include B_1, because b is redeclared in B_1, indicated by $B_0 - B_1$ in the figure. Such a gap is called a *hole* in the scope of the declaration.

The most closely nested scope rule is reflected in the output of the program in Fig. 7.18. Control flows to a block from the point just before it, and flows from the block to the point just after it in the source text. The print statements are therefore executed in the order B_2, B_3, B_1, and B_0, the order in which control leaves the blocks. The values of a and b in these blocks are:

```
2  1
0  3
0  1
0  0
```

Block structure can be implemented using stack allocation. Since the scope of a declaration does not extend outside the block in which it appears, the space for the declared name can be allocated when the block is entered, and deallocated when control leaves the block. This view treats a block as a "parameterless procedure," called only from the point just before the block and returning only to the point just after the block. The nonlocal environment for a block can be maintained using the techniques for procedures later in this section. Note, however, that blocks are simpler than procedures because no parameters are passed and because the flow of control from and to a block closely follows the static program text.[5]

---

[5] A jump out of a block into an enclosing block can be implemented by popping activation records for the intervening blocks. A jump into a block is permitted by some languages. Before control is transferred in this way, activation records have to be set up for the intervening blocks. The language semantics determines how local data in these activation records is initialized.

```
main()
{
        int a = 0;
        int b = 0;
        {
            int b = 1;
            {
                int a = 2;
         B₂     printf("%d %d\n", a, b);
            }
            {
                int b = 3;
         B₃     printf("%d %d\n", a, b);
            }
            printf("%d %d\n", a, b);
        }
        printf("%d %d\n", a, b);
}
```

B_0 B_1

DECLARATION	SCOPE
int a = 0;	$B_0 - B_2$
int b = 0;	$B_0 - B_1$
int b = 1;	$B_1 - B_3$
int a = 2;	B_2
int b = 3;	B_3

Fig. 7.18. Blocks in a C program.

An alternative implementation is to allocate storage for a complete procedure body at one time. If there are blocks within the procedure, then allowance is made for the storage needed for declarations within the blocks. For block B_0 in Fig. 7.18, we can allocate storage as in Fig. 7.19. Subscripts on locals a and b identify the blocks that the locals are declared in. Note that a_2 and b_3 may be assigned the same storage because they are in blocks that are not alive at the same time.

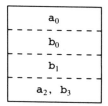

Fig. 7.19. Storage for names declared in Fig. 7.18.

In the absence of variable-length data, the maximum amount of storage needed during any execution of a block can be determined at compile time. (Variable-length data can be handled using pointers as in Section 7.3.) In making this determination, we conservatively assume that all control paths in the program can indeed be taken. That is, we assume that both the then- and else-parts of a conditional statement can be executed, and that all statements within a while loop can be reached.

Lexical Scope Without Nested Procedures

The lexical-scope rules for C are simpler than those of Pascal, discussed next, because procedure definitions cannot be nested in C. That is, a procedure definition cannot appear within another. As in Fig. 7.20, a C program consists of a sequence of declarations of variables and procedures (C calls them functions). If there is a nonlocal reference to a name a in some function, then a must be declared outside any function. The scope of a declaration outside a function consists of the function bodies that follow the declaration, with holes if the name is redeclared within a function. In Fig. 7.20, nonlocal occurrences of a in readarray, partition, and main refer to the array declared on line 1.

```
(1)  int a[11];
(2)  readarray() { ... a ... }
(3)  int partition(y,z) int y, z; { ... a ... }
(4)  quicksort(m,n) int m, n; { ... }
(5)  main() { ... a ... }
```

Fig. 7.20. C program with nonlocal occurrences of a.

In the absence of nested procedures, the stack-allocation strategy for local names in Section 7.3 can be used directly for a lexically scoped language like C. Storage for all names declared outside any procedures can be allocated statically. The position of this storage is known at compile time, so if a name is nonlocal in some procedure body, we simply use the statically determined address. Any other name must be a local of the activation at the top of the stack, accessible through the *top* pointer. Nested procedures cause this scheme to fail because a nonlocal may then refer to data deep in the stack, as discussed below.

An important benefit of static allocation for nonlocals is that declared procedures can freely be passed as parameters and returned as results (a function is passed in C by passing a pointer to it). With lexical scope and without nested procedures, any name nonlocal to one procedure is nonlocal to all procedures. Its static address can be used by all procedures, regardless of how they are activated. Similarly, if procedures are returned as results, nonlocals in the returned procedure refer to the storage statically allocated for them.

For example, consider the Pascal program in Fig. 7.21. All occurrences of name m, shown circled in Fig. 7.21, are in the scope of the declaration on line 2. Since m is nonlocal to all procedures in the program, its storage can be allocated statically. Whenever procedures f and g are executed, they can use

```
(1)  program pass(input, output);
(2)      var Ⓜ: integer;

(3)      function f(n : integer) : integer;
(4)          begin f := Ⓜ+ n end { f };

(5)      function g(n : integer) : integer;
(6)          begin g := Ⓜ* n end { g };

(7)      procedure b(function h(n : integer) : integer);
(8)          begin write(h(2)) end { b };

(9)      begin
(10)         Ⓜ:= 0;
(11)         b(f); b(g); writeln
(12)     end.
```

Fig. 7.21. Pascal program with nonlocal occurrences of m.

the static address to access the value of m. The fact that f and g are passed as parameters only affects when they are activated; it does not affect how they access the value of m.

In more detail, the call b(f) on line 11 associates the function f with the formal parameter h of the procedure b. So when the formal h is called on line 8, in write(h(2)), the function f is activated. The activation of f returns 2 because nonlocal m has value 0 and formal n has value 2. Next in the execution, the call b(g) associates g with h; this time, a call of h activates g. The output of the program is

2   0

Lexical Scope with Nested Procedures

A nonlocal occurrence of a name a in a Pascal procedure is in the scope of the most closely nested declaration of a in the static program text.

The nesting of procedure definitions in the Pascal program of Fig. 7.22 is indicated by the following indentation:

```
sort
     readarray
     exchange
     quicksort
          partition
```

The occurrence of a on line 15 in Fig. 7.22 is within function partition, which is nested within procedure quicksort. The most closely nested declaration of a is on line 2 in the procedure consisting of the entire program. The most closely nested rule applies to procedure names as well. The

```
(1)  program sort(input, output);
(2)      var a : array [0..10] of integer;
(3)          x : integer;
(4)      procedure readarray;
(5)          var i : integer;
(6)          begin ... a ... end { readarray };
(7)      procedure exchange( i, j: integer);
(8)          begin
(9)              x := a[i]; a[i] := a[j]; a[j] := x
(10)         end { exchange } ;
(11)     procedure quicksort(m, n: integer);
(12)         var k, v : integer;
(13)         function partition(y, z: integer): integer;
(14)             var  i, j : integer;
(15)             begin ... a ...
(16)                     ... v ...
(17)                     ... exchange(i,j); ...
(18)             end { partition } ;
(19)         begin ... end { quicksort };
(20)     begin ... end { sort } .
```

Fig. 7.22. A Pascal program with nested procedures.

procedure exchange, called by partition on line 17, is nonlocal to partition. Applying the rule, we first check if exchange is defined within quicksort; since it is not, we look for it in the main program sort.

Nesting Depth

The notion of *nesting depth* of a procedure is used below to implement lexical scope. Let the name of the main program be at nesting depth 1; we add 1 to the nesting depth as we go from an enclosing to an enclosed procedure. In Fig. 7.22, procedure quicksort on line 11 is at nesting depth 2, while partition on line 13 is at nesting depth 3. With each occurrence of a name, we associate the nesting depth of the procedure in which it is declared. The occurrences of a, v, and i on lines 15-17 in partition therefore have nesting depths 1, 2, and 3, respectively.

Access Links

A direct implementation of lexical scope for nested procedures is obtained by adding a pointer called an *access link* to each activation record. If procedure p is nested immediately within q in the source text, then the access link in an activation record for p points to the access link in the record for the most recent activation of q.

Snapshots of the run-time stack during an execution of the program in Fig. 7.22 are shown in Fig. 7.23. Again, to save space in the figure, only the first letter of each procedure name is shown. The access link for the activation of sort is empty, because there is no enclosing procedure. The access link for each activation of quicksort points to the record for sort. Note in Fig. 7.23(c) that the access link in the activation record for partition(1,3) points to the access link in the record of the most recent activation of quicksort, namely quicksort(1,3).

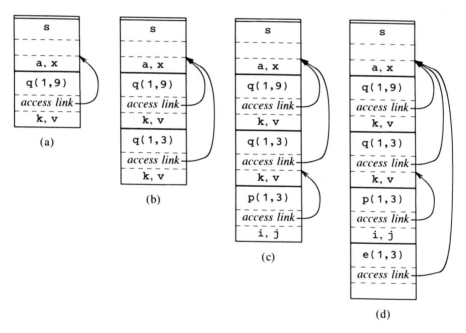

Fig. 7.23. Access links for finding storage for nonlocals.

Suppose procedure p at nesting depth n_p refers to a nonlocal a with nesting depth $n_a \leq n_p$. The storage for a can be found as follows.

1. When control is in p, an activation record for p is at the top of the stack. Follow $n_p - n_a$ access links from the record at the top of the stack. The value of $n_p - n_a$ can be precomputed at compile time. If the access link in one record points to the access link in another, then a link can be followed by performing a single indirection operation.

2. After following $n_p - n_a$ links, we reach an activation record for the procedure that a is local to. As discussed in the last section, its storage is at

a fixed offset relative to a position in the record. In particular, the offset can be relative to the access link.

Hence, the address of nonlocal a in procedure p is given by the following pair computed at compile time and stored in the symbol table:

$(n_p - n_a$, offset within activation record containing a)

The first component gives the number of access links to be traversed.

For example, on lines 15-16 in Fig. 7.22, the procedure partition at nesting depth 3 references nonlocals a and v at nesting depths 1 and 2, respectively. The activation records containing the storage for these nonlocals are found by following $3-1=2$ and $3-2=1$ access links, respectively, from the record for partition.

The code to set up access links is part of the calling sequence. Suppose procedure p at nesting depth n_p calls procedure x at nesting depth n_x. The code for setting up the access link in the called procedure depends on whether or not the called procedure is nested within the caller.

1. Case $n_p < n_x$. Since the called procedure x is nested more deeply than p, it must be declared within p, or it would not be accessible to p. This case occurs when sort calls quicksort in Fig. 7.23(a) and when quicksort calls partition in Fig. 7.23(c). In this case, the access link in the called procedure must point to the access link in the activation record of the caller just below in the stack.

2. Case $n_p \geq n_x$. From the scope rules, the enclosing procedures at nesting depths 1, 2, . . . , $n_x - 1$ of the called and calling procedures must be the same, as when quicksort calls itself in Fig. 7.23(b) and when partition calls exchange in Fig. 7.23(d). Following $n_p - n_x + 1$ access links from the caller we reach the most recent activation record of the procedure that statically encloses both the called and calling procedures most closely. The access link reached is the one to which the access link in the called procedure must point. Again, $n_p - n_x + 1$ can be computed at compile time.

Procedure Parameters

Lexical scope rules apply even when a nested procedure is passed as a parameter. The function f on lines 6-7 of the Pascal program in Fig. 7.24 has a nonlocal m; all occurrences of m are shown circled. On line 8, procedure c assigns 0 to m and then passes f as a parameter to b. Note that the scope of the declaration of m on line 5 does not include the body of b on lines 2-3.

Within the body of b, the statement writeln(h(2)) activates f because the formal h refers to f. That is, writeln prints the result of the call f(2).

How do we set up the access link for the activation of f? The answer is that a nested procedure that is passed as a parameter must take its access link along with it, as shown in Fig. 7.25. When procedure c passes f, it

```
(1)  program param(input, output);

(2)      procedure b(function h(n:integer): integer);
(3)          begin writeln(h(2)) end { b };

(4)      procedure c;
(5)          var Ⓜ: integer;

(6)          function f(n : integer) : integer;
(7)              begin f := Ⓜ+ n end { f };

(8)          begin Ⓜ:= 0; b(f) end { c };

(9)      begin
(10)         c
(11)     end.
```

Fig. 7.24. An access link must be passed with actual parameter f.

determines an access link for f, just as it would if it were calling f. This link is passed along with f to b. Subsequently, when f is activated from within b, the link is used to set up the access link in the activation record for f.

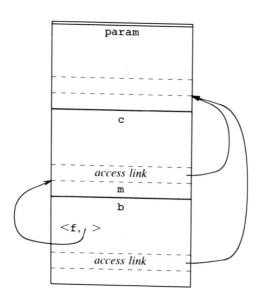

Fig. 7.25. Actual procedure parameter f carries its access link along.

Displays

Faster access to nonlocals than with access links can be obtained using an array d of pointers to activation records, called a *display*. We maintain the display so that storage for a nonlocal a at nesting depth i is in the activation record pointed to by display element $d[i]$.

Suppose control is in an activation of a procedure p at nesting depth j. Then, the first $j-1$ elements of the display point to the most recent activations of the procedures that lexically enclose procedure p, and $d[j]$ points to the activation of p. Using a display is generally faster than following access links because the activation record holding a nonlocal is found by accessing an element of d and then following just one pointer.

A simple arrangement for maintaining the display uses access links in addition to the display. As part of the call and return sequences, the display is updated by following the chain of access links. When the link to an activation record at nesting depth n is followed, display element $d[n]$ is set to point to that activation record. In effect, the display duplicates the information in the chain of access links.

The above simple arrangement can be improved upon. The method illustrated in Fig. 7.26 requires less work at procedure entry and exit in the usual case when procedures are not passed as parameters. In Fig. 7.26 the display consists of a global array, separate from the stack. The snapshots in the figure refer to an execution of the source text in Fig. 7.22. Again, only the first letter of each procedure name is shown.

Figure 7.26(a) shows the situation just before activation q(1,3) begins. Since quicksort is at nesting depth 2, display element $d[2]$ is affected when a new activation of quicksort begins. The effect of the activation q(1,3) on $d[2]$ is shown in Fig 7.26(b), where $d[2]$ now points to the new activation record; the old value of $d[2]$ is saved within the new activation record.[6] The saved value will be needed later to restore the display to its state in Fig. 7.26(a) when control returns to the activation q(1,9).

The display changes when a new activation occurs, and it must be reset when control returns from the new activation. The scope rules of Pascal and other lexically scoped languages allow the display to be maintained by the following steps. We discuss only the easier case in which procedures are not passed as parameters (see Exercise 7.8). When a new activation record for a procedure at nesting depth i is set up, we

1. save the value of $d[i]$ in the new activation record and
2. set $d[i]$ to point to the new activation record.

Just before an activation ends, $d[i]$ is reset to the saved value.

---

[6] Note that q(1,9) also saved $d[2]$, although it happens that the second display element had never before been used and does not need to be restored. It is easier for all calls of q to store $d[2]$ than to decide at run time whether such a store is necessary.

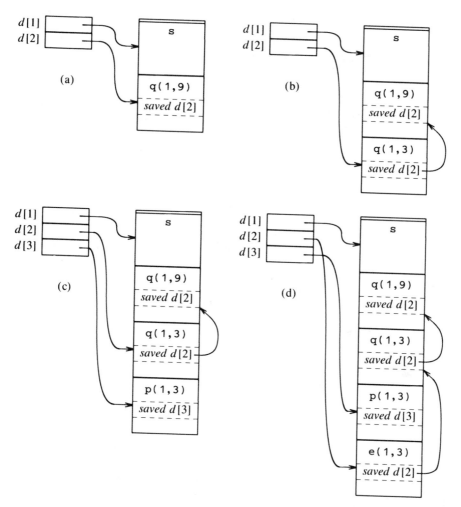

Fig. 7.26. Maintaining the display when procedures are not passed as parameters.

These steps are justified as follows. Suppose a procedure at nesting depth j calls a procedure at depth i. There are two cases, depending on whether or not the called procedure is nested within the caller in the source text, as in the discussion of access links.

1. Case $j < i$. Then $i = j + 1$ and the called procedure is nested within the caller. The first j elements of the display therefore do not need to be changed, and we set $d[i]$ to the new activation record. This case is illustrated in Fig. 7.26(a) when sort calls quicksort and also when quicksort calls partition in Fig. 7.26(c).

2. Case $j \geq i$. Again, the enclosing procedures at nesting depths $1, 2, \ldots, i-1$ of the called and calling procedure must be the same. Here, we save the old value of $d[i]$ in the new activation record, and make $d[i]$ point to the new activation record. The display is maintained correctly because the first $i-1$ elements are left as is.

An example of Case 2, with $i = j = 2$, occurs when quicksort is called recursively in Fig. 7.26(b). A more interesting example occurs when activation p(1,3) at nesting depth 3 calls e(1,3) at depth 2, and their enclosing procedure is s at depth 1, as in Fig. 7.26(d). (The program is in Fig. 7.22.) Note that when e(1,3) is called, the value of $d[3]$ belonging to p(1,3) is still in the display, although it cannot be accessed while control is in e. Should e call another procedure at depth 3, that procedure will store $d[3]$ and restore it on returning to e. We can thus show that each procedure sees the correct display for all depths up to its own depth.

There are several places where a display can be maintained. If there are enough registers, then the display, pictured as an array, can be a collection of registers. Note that the compiler can determine the maximum length of this array; it is the maximum nesting depth of procedures in the program. Otherwise, the display can be kept in statically allocated memory and all references to activation records begin by using indirect addressing through the appropriate display pointer. This approach is reasonable on a machine with indirect addressing, although each indirection costs a memory cycle. Another possibility is to store the display on the run-time stack itself, and to create a new copy at each procedure entry.

Dynamic Scope

Under dynamic scope, a new activation inherits the existing bindings of nonlocal names to storage. A nonlocal name a in the called activation refers to the same storage that it did in the calling activation. New bindings are set up for local names of the called procedure; the names refer to storage in the new activation record.

The program in Fig. 7.27 illustrates dynamic scope. Procedure show on lines 3-4 writes the value of nonlocal r. Under lexical scope in Pascal, the nonlocal r is in the scope of the declaration on line 2, so the output of the program is

```
0.250 0.250
0.250 0.250
```

However, under dynamic scope, the output is

```
0.250 0.125
0.250 0.125
```

When show is called on lines 10-11 in the main program, 0.250 is written

```
(1)  program dynamic(input,output);
(2)      var r : real;

(3)      procedure show;
(4)          begin write( r : 5:3 ) end;

(5)      procedure small;
(6)          var r : real;
(7)          begin r := 0.125; show end;

(8)      begin
(9)          r := 0.25;
(10)         show; small; writeln;
(11)         show; small; writeln
(12)     end.
```

Fig. 7.27. The output depends on whether lexical or dynamic scope is used.

because the variable r local to the main program is used. However, when show is called on line 7 from within small, 0.125 is written because the variable r local to small is used.

The following two approaches to implementing dynamic scope bear some resemblance to the use of access links and displays, respectively, in the implementation of lexical scope.

1. *Deep access.* Conceptually, dynamic scope results if access links point to the same activation records that control links do. A simple implementation is to dispense with access links and use the control link to search into the stack, looking for the first activation record containing storage for the nonlocal name. The term *deep access* comes from the fact that the search may go "deep" into the stack. The depth to which the search may go depends on the input to the program and cannot be determined at compile time.

2. *Shallow access.* Here the idea is to hold the current value of each name in statically allocated storage. When a new activation of a procedure p occurs, a local name n in p takes over the storage statically allocated for n. The previous value of n can be saved in the activation record for p and must be restored when the activation of p ends.

The tradeoff between the two approaches is that deep access takes longer to access a nonlocal, but there is no overhead associated with beginning and ending an activation. Shallow access on the other hand allows nonlocals to be looked up directly, but time is taken to maintain these values when activations begin and end. When functions are passed as parameters and returned as results, a more straightforward implementation is obtained with deep access.

7.5 PARAMETER PASSING

When one procedure calls another, the usual method of communication between them is through nonlocal names and through parameters of the called procedure. Both nonlocals and parameters are used by the procedure in Fig. 7.28 to exchange the values of a[i] and a[j]. Here the array a is nonlocal to the procedure exchange, and i and j are parameters.

```
(1)   procedure exchange(i, j: integer);
(2)        var x : integer;
(3)        begin
(4)             x := a[i]; a[i] := a[j]; a[j] := x
(5)        end
```

Fig. 7.28. The Pascal procedure swap with nonlocals and parameters.

Several common methods for associating actual and formal parameters are discussed in this section. They are: call-by-value, call-by-reference, copy-restore, call-by-name, and macro expansion. It is important to know the parameter passing method a language (or compiler) uses, because the result of a program can depend on the method used.

Why so many methods? The different methods arise from differing interpretations of what an expression represents. In an assignment like

```
a[i] := a[j]
```

expression a[j] represents a value, while a[i] represents a storage location into which the value of a[j] is placed. The decision of whether to use the location or the value represented by an expression is determined by whether the expression appears on the left or right, respectively, of the assignment symbol. As in Chapter 2, the term *l*-value refers to the storage represented by an expression, and *r*-value to the value contained in the storage. The prefixes *l*- and *r*- come from "left" and "right" side of an assignment.

Differences between parameter-passing methods are based primarily on whether an actual parameter represents an *r*-value, an *l*-value, or the text of the actual parameter itself.

Call-by-Value

This is, in a sense, the simplest possible method of passing parameters. The actual parameters are evaluated and their *r*-values are passed to the called procedure. Call-by-value is used in C, and Pascal parameters are usually passed this way. All the programs so far in this chapter have relied on this method for passing parameters. Call-by-value can be implemented as follows.

1. A formal parameter is treated just like a local name, so the storage for the formals is in the activation record of the called procedure.

2.   The caller evaluates the actual parameters and places their *r*-values in the
storage for the formals.

A distinguishing feature of call-by-value is that operations on the formal
parameters do not affect values in the activation record of the caller. If the
keyword var on line 3 in Fig. 7.29 is left out, Pascal will pass x and y by
value to the procedure swap. The call swap(a,b) on line 12 then leaves the
values of a and b undisturbed. Under call-by-value, the effect of the call
swap(a,b) is equivalent to the sequence of steps

```
   x := a
   y := b
temp := x
   x := y
   y := temp
```

where x, y, and temp are local to swap. Although these assignments change
the values of the locals x, y, and temp, the changes are lost when control
returns from the call and the activation record for swap is deallocated. The
call therefore has no effect on the activation record of the caller.

```
(1)  program reference(input,output);
(2)  var a, b: integer;
(3)  procedure swap(var x, y: integer);
(4)      var temp : integer;
(5)      begin
(6)          temp := x;
(7)             x := y;
(8)             y := temp
(9)      end;

(10) begin
(11)     a := 1; b := 2;
(12)     swap(a,b);
(13)     writeln('a =', a); writeln('b =', b)
(14) end.
```

Fig. 7.29. Pascal program with procedure swap.

A procedure called by value can affect its caller either through nonlocal
names (see exchange in Fig. 7.28) or through pointers that are explicitly
passed as values. In the C program in Fig. 7.30, x and y are declared on line
2 to be pointers to integers; the & operator in the call swap(&a, &b) on line 8
results in pointers to a and b being passed to swap. The output of this program is

```
a is now 2, b is now 1
```

```
(1)  swap(x,y)
(2)  int *x, *y;
(3)  {    int temp;
(4)       temp = *x; *x = *y; *y = temp;
(5)  }

(6)  main()
(7)  {    int a = 1, b = 2;
(8)       swap( &a, &b );
(9)       printf("a is now %d, b is now %d\n",a,b);
(10) }
```

Fig. 7.30. C program using pointers in a procedure called by value.

The use of pointers in this example suggests how a compiler using call-by-reference would exchange values.

Call-by-Reference

When parameters are passed by *reference* (also known as *call-by-address* or *call-by-location*), the caller passes to the called procedure a pointer to the storage address of each actual parameter.

1. If an actual parameter is a name or an expression having an *l*-value, then that *l*-value itself is passed.

2. However, if the actual parameter is an expression, like a + b or 2, that has no *l*-value, then the expression is evaluated in a new location, and the address of that location is passed.

A reference to a formal parameter in the called procedure becomes, in the target code, an indirect reference through the pointer passed to the called procedure.

Example 7.7. Consider the procedure swap in Fig. 7.29. A call to swap with actual parameters i and a[i], that is, swap(i, a[i]), would have the same effect as the following sequence of steps.

1. Copy the address (*l*-values) of i and a[i] into the activation record of the called procedure, say into locations arg1 and arg2 corresponding to x and y, respectively.

2. Set temp to the contents of the location pointed to by arg1 (i.e., set temp equal to I_0, where I_0 is the initial value of i). This step corresponds to temp := x on line 6 in the definition of swap.

3. Set the contents of the location pointed to by arg1 to the value of the location pointed to by arg2; that is, i := a[I_0]. This step corresponds to x := y on line 7 in swap.

4.   Set the contents of the location pointed by `arg2` equal to the value of `temp`; that is, set $a[l_0] := i$. This step corresponds to `y:=temp`.   □

Call-by-reference is used by a number of languages; `var` parameters in Pascal are passed in this way. Arrays are usually passed by reference.

Copy-Restore

A hybrid between call-by-value and call-by-reference is *copy-restore linkage*, (also known as *copy-in copy-out*, or *value-result*).

1.   Before control flows to the called procedure, the actual parameters are evaluated. The *r*-values of the actuals are passed to the called procedure as in call-by-value. In addition, however, the *l*-values of those actual parameters having *l*-values are determined before the call.

2.   When control returns, the current *r*-values of the formal parameters are copied back into the *l*-values of the actuals, using the *l*-values computed before the call. Only actuals having *l*-values are copied, of course.

The first step "copies in" the values of the actuals into the activation record of the called procedure (into the storage for the formals). The second step "copies out" the final values of the formals into the activation record of the caller (into *l*-values computed from the actuals before the call).

Note that `swap(i, a[i])` works correctly using copy-restore, since the location of `a[i]` is computed and preserved by the calling program before the call. Thus, the final value of formal parameter `y`, which will be the initial value of `i`, is copied into the correct location, even though the location of `a[i]` is changed by the call (because the value of i changes).

Copy-restore is used by some Fortran implementations. However, others use call-by-reference. Differences between the two can show up if the called procedure has more than one way of accessing a location in the activation record of the caller. The activation set up by the call `unsafe(a)` on line 6 of Fig. 7.31 can access a as a nonlocal and through formal `x`. Under call-by-reference, the assignments to both `x` and a immediately affect a, so the final value of a is 0. Under copy-restore, however, the value 1 of actual a is copied into formal `x`. The final value 2 of `x` is copied out into the *l*-value of a just before control returns, so the final value of a is 2.

```
(1)  program copyout(input,output);
(2)      var a : integer;
(3)      procedure unsafe(var x : integer);
(4)         begin x := 2; a := 0 end;
(5)      begin
(6)         a := 1; unsafe(a); writeln(a)
(7)      end.
```

Fig. 7.31. The output changes if call-by-reference is changed to copy-restore.

Call-by-Name

Call-by-name is traditionally defined by the *copy-rule* of Algol, which is:

1.   The procedure is treated as if it were a macro; that is, its body is substituted for the call in the caller, with the actual parameters literally substituted for the formals. Such a literal substitution is called *macro-expansion* or *in-line expansion*.

2.   The local names of the called procedure are kept distinct from the names of the calling procedure. We can think of each local of the called procedure being systematically renamed into a distinct new name before the macro-expansion is done.

3.   The actual parameters are surrounded by parentheses if necessary to preserve their integrity.

Example 7.8. The call `swap(i, a[i])` from Example 7.7 would be implemented as though it were

```
temp := i
   i := a[i]
a[i] := temp
```

Thus, under call-by-name, `swap` sets `i` to `a[i]`, as expected, but has the unexpected result of setting `a[a[I_0]]` — rather than `a[I_0]` — to I_0, where I_0 is the initial value of `i`. This phenomenon occurs because the location of **x** in the assignment `x := temp` of `swap` is not evaluated until needed, by which time the value of `i` has already changed. A correctly working version of `swap` apparently cannot be written if call-by-name is used (see Fleck [1976]). □

Although call-by-name is primarily of theoretical interest, the conceptually related technique of in-line expansion has been suggested for reducing the running time of a program. There is a certain cost associated with setting up an activation of a procedure — space is allocated for the activation record, the machine status is saved, links are set up, and then control is transferred. When a procedure body is small, the code devoted to the calling sequences may outweigh the code in the procedure body. It may therefore be more efficient to use in-line expansion of the body into the code for the caller, even if the size of the program grows a little. In the next example, in-line expansion is applied to a procedure called by value.

Example 7.9. Suppose that the function `f` in the assignment

$$x := f(A) + f(B)$$

is called by value. Here the actual parameters *A* and *B* are expressions. Substituting expressions *A* and *B* for each occurrence of the formal parameter in the body of `f` leads to call-by-name; recall `a[i]` in the last example.

Fresh temporary variables can be used to force the evaluation of the actual parameters before execution of the procedure body:

```
t₁ := A;
t₂ := B;
t₃ := f(t₁);
t₄ := f(t₂);
 x := t₃ + t₄;
```

Now in-line expansion will replace all occurrences of the formal by t_1 and t_2 when the first and second calls, respectively, are expanded.[7] □

The usual implementation of call-by-name is to pass to the called procedure parameterless subroutines, commonly called *thunks*, that can evaluate the *l*-value or *r*-value of the actual parameter. Like any procedure passed as a parameter in a language using lexical scope, a thunk carries an access link with it, pointing to the current activation record for the calling procedure.

7.6 SYMBOL TABLES

A compiler uses a symbol table to keep track of scope and binding information about names. The symbol table is searched every time a name is encountered in the source text. Changes to the table occur if a new name or new information about an existing name is discovered.

A symbol-table mechanism must allow us to add new entries and find existing entries efficiently. The two symbol-table mechanisms presented in this section are linear lists and hash tables. We evaluate each scheme on the basis of the time required to add n entries and make e inquiries. A linear list is the simplest to implement, but its performance is poor when e and n get large. Hashing schemes provide better performance for somewhat greater programming effort and space overhead. Both mechanisms can be adapted readily to handle the most closely nested scope rule.

It is useful for a compiler to be able to grow the symbol table dynamically, if necessary, at compile time. If the size of the symbol table is fixed when the compiler is written, then the size must be chosen large enough to handle any source program that might be presented. Such a fixed size is likely to be too large for most, and inadequate for some, programs.

Symbol-Table Entries

Each entry in the symbol table is for the declaration of a name. The format of entries does not have to be uniform, because the information saved about a name depends on the usage of the name. Each entry can be implemented as a

---

[7] There are hidden costs associated with temporary variables. They may cause extra space to be allocated in an activation record. If locals in the activation record are initialized, then extra temporaries result in time being wasted as well.

record consisting of a sequence of consecutive words of memory. To keep symbol-table records uniform, it may be convenient for some of the information about a name to be kept outside the table entry, with only a pointer to this information stored in the record.

Information is entered into the symbol table at various times. Keywords are entered into the table initially, if at all. The lexical analyzer in Section 3.4 looks up sequences of letters and digits in the symbol table to determine if a reserved keyword or a name has been collected. With this approach, keywords must be in the symbol table before lexical analysis begins. Alternatively, if the lexical analyzer intercepts reserved keywords, then they need not appear in the symbol table. If the language does not reserve keywords, then it is essential that keywords be entered into the symbol table with a warning of their possible use as a keyword.

The symbol-table entry itself can be set up when the role of a name becomes clear, with the attribute values being filled in as the information becomes available. In some cases, the entry can be initiated from the lexical analyzer as soon as a name is seen in the input. More often, one name may denote several different objects, perhaps even in the same block or procedure. For example, the C declarations

```
int    x;                                    (7.1)
struct x { float y, z; };
```

use x as both an integer and as the tag of a structure with two fields. In such cases, the lexical analyzer can only return to the parser the name itself (or a pointer to the lexeme forming that name), rather than a pointer to the symbol-table entry. The record in the symbol table is created when the syntactic role played by this name is discovered. For the declarations in (7.1), two symbol-table entries for x would be created; one with x as an integer and one as a structure.

Attributes of a name are entered in response to declarations, which may be implicit. Labels are often identifiers followed by a colon, so one action associated with recognizing such an identifier may be to enter this fact into the symbol table. Similarly, the syntax of procedure declarations specifies that certain identifiers are formal parameters.

Characters in a Name

As in Chapter 3, there is a distinction between the token **id** for an identifier or name, the lexeme consisting of the character string forming the name, and the attributes of the name. Strings of characters may be unwieldy to work with, so compilers often use some fixed-length representation of the name rather than the lexeme. The lexeme is needed when a symbol-table entry is set up for the first time, and when we look up a lexeme found in the input to determine whether it is a name that has already appeared. A common representation of a name is a pointer to a symbol-table entry for it.

If there is a modest upper bound on the length of a name, then the characters in the name can be stored in the symbol-table entry, as in Fig. 7.32(a). If
there is no limit on the length of a name, or if the limit is rarely reached, the
indirect scheme of Fig. 7.32(b) can be used. Rather than allocating in each
symbol-table entry the maximum possible amount of space to hold a lexeme,
we can utilize space more efficiently if there is only space for a pointer in a
symbol-table entry. In the record for a name, we place a pointer to a separate
array of characters (the *string table*) giving the position of the first character
of the lexeme. The indirect scheme of Fig. 7.32(b) permits the size of the
name field of the symbol-table entry itself to remain a constant.

The complete lexeme constituting a name must be stored to ensure that all
uses of the same name can be associated with the same symbol-table record.
We must, however, distinguish among occurrences of the same lexeme that
are in the scopes of different declarations.

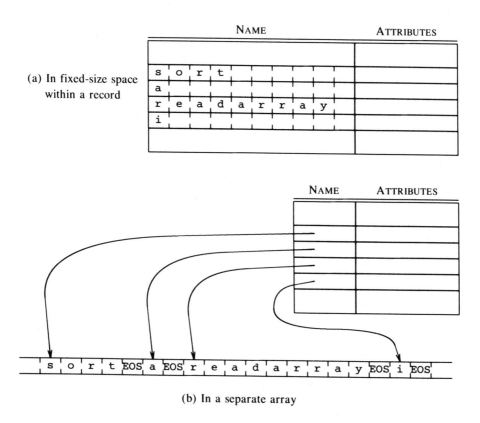

Fig. 7.32. Storing the characters of a name.

Storage Allocation Information

Information about the storage locations that will be bound to names at run time is kept in the symbol table. Consider names with static storage first. If the target code is assembly language, we can let the assembler take care of storage locations for the various names. All we have to do is to scan the symbol table, after generating assembly code for the program, and generate assembly language data definitions to be appended to the assembly language program for each name.

If machine code is to be generated by the compiler, however, then the position of each data object relative to a fixed origin, such as the beginning of an activation record must be ascertained. The same remark applies to a block of data loaded as a module separate from the program. For example, COMMON blocks in Fortran are loaded separately, and the positions of names relative to the beginning of the COMMON block in which they lie must be determined. For reasons discussed in Section 7.9, the approach of Section 7.3 has to be modified for Fortran, in that we must assign offsets for names after all declarations for a procedure have been seen and EQUIVALENCE statements have been processed.

In the case of names whose storage is allocated on a stack or heap, the compiler does not allocate storage at all — the compiler plans out the activation record for each procedure, as in Section 7.3.

The List Data Structure for Symbol Tables

The simplest and easiest to implement data structure for a symbol table is a linear list of records, shown in Fig. 7.33. We use a single array, or equivalently several arrays, to store names and their associated information. New names are added to the list in the order in which they are encountered. The position of the end of the array is marked by the pointer *available*, pointing to where the next symbol-table entry will go. The search for a name proceeds backwards from the end of the array to the beginning. When the name is located, the associated information can be found in the words following next. If we reach the beginning of the array without finding the name, a fault occurs — an expected name is not in the table.

Note that making an entry for a name and looking up the name in the symbol table are independent operations — we may wish to do one without the other. In a block-structured language, an occurrence of a name is in the scope of the most closely nested declaration of the name. We can implement this scope rule using the list data structure by making a fresh entry for a name every time it is declared. A new entry is made in the words immediately following the pointer *available*; that pointer is increased by the size of the symbol-table record. Since entries are inserted in order, starting from the beginning of the array, they appear in the order they are created in. By searching from *available* towards the beginning of the array, we are sure to find the most recently created entry.

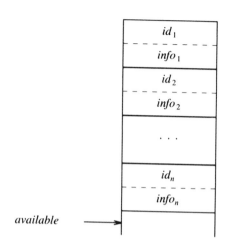

available

Fig. 7.33. A linear list of records.

If the symbol table contains n names, the work necessary to insert a new name is constant if we do the insertion without checking to see if the name is already in the table. If multiple entries for names are not allowed, then we need to look through the entire table before discovering that a name is not in the table, doing work proportional to n in the process. To find the data about a name, on the average, we search $n/2$ names, so the cost of an inquiry is also proportional to n. Thus, since insertions and inquiries take time proportional to n, the total work for inserting n names and making e inquiries is at most $cn(n+e)$, where c is a constant representing the time necessary for a few machine operations. In a medium-sized program, we might have $n = 100$ and $e = 1000$, so several hundred thousand machine operations are utilized in the bookkeeping. That may not be painful, since we are talking about less than a second of time. However, if n and e are multiplied by 10, the cost is multiplied by 100, and the bookkeeping time becomes prohibitive. Profiling yields valuable data about where a compiler spends its time and can be used to decide if too much time is being spent searching through linear lists.

Hash Tables

Variations of the searching technique known as hashing have been implemented in many compilers. Here we consider a rather simple variant known as *open hashing*, where "open" refers to the property that there need be no limit on the number of entries that can be made in the table. Even this scheme gives us the capability of performing e inquiries on n names in time proportional to $n(n+e)/m$, for any constant m of our choosing. Since m can be made as large as we like, up to n, this method is generally more efficient than linear lists and is the method of choice for symbol tables in most situations. As might be expected, the space taken by the data structure grows with m, so a time-space tradeoff is involved.

The basic hashing scheme is illustrated in Fig. 7.34. There are two parts to the data structure:

1. A *hash table* consisting of a fixed array of m pointers to table entries.

2. Table entries organized into m separate linked lists, called *buckets* (some buckets may be empty). Each record in the symbol table appears on exactly one of these lists. Storage for the records may be drawn from an array of records, as discussed in the next section. Alternatively, the dynamic storage allocation facilities of the implementation language can be used to obtain space for the records, often at some loss of efficiency.

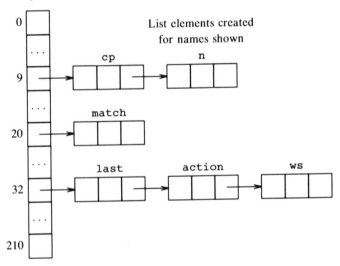

Fig. 7.34. A hash table of size 211.

To determine whether there is an entry for string s in the symbol table, we apply a *hash function* h to s, such that $h(s)$ returns an integer between 0 and $m-1$. If s is in the symbol table, then it is on the list numbered $h(s)$. If s is not yet in the symbol table, it is entered by creating a record for s that is linked at the front of the list numbered $h(s)$.

As a rule of thumb, the average list is n/m records long if there are n names in a table of size m. By choosing m so that n/m is bounded by a small constant, say 2, the time to access a table entry is essentially constant.

The space taken by the symbol table consists of m words for the hash table and cn words for table entries, where c is the number of words per table entry. Thus the space for the hash table depends only on m, and the space for table entries depends only on the number of entries.

The choice of m depends on the intended application for a symbol table. Choosing m to be a few hundred should make table lookup a negligible fraction of the total time spent by a compiler, even for moderate-sized programs. When the input to a compiler might be generated by another program, however, the number of names can greatly exceed that of most human-generated programs of the same size, and larger table sizes might be preferable.

A great deal of attention has been given to the question of how to design a hash function that is easy to compute for strings of characters and distributes strings uniformly among the m lists.

One suitable approach for computing hash functions is to proceed as follows:

1. Determine a positive integer h from the characters $c_1, c_2, \ldots, c_k$ in string s. The conversion of single characters to integers is usually supported by the implementation language. Pascal provides a function *ord* for this purpose; C automatically converts a character to an integer if an arithmetic operation is performed on it.

2. Convert the integer h determined above into the number of a list, i.e., an integer between 0 and $m-1$. Simply dividing by m and taking the remainder is a reasonable policy. Taking the remainder seems to work better if m is a prime, hence the choice 211 rather than 200 in Fig. 7.34.

Hash functions that look at all characters in a string are less easily fooled than, say, functions that look only at a few characters at the ends or in the middle of a string. Remember, the input to a compiler may have been created by a program and may therefore have a stylized form chosen to avoid conflicts with names a person or some other program might use. People tend to "cluster" names as well, with choices like `baz`, `newbaz`, `baz1`, and so on.

A simple technique for computing h is to add up the integer values of the characters in a string. A better idea is to multiply the old value of h by a constant α before adding in the next character. That is, take $h_0 = 0$, $h_i = \alpha h_{i-1} + c_i$, for $1 \leq i \leq k$, and let $h = h_k$, where k is the length of the string. (Recall, the hash value giving the number of the list is $h \bmod m$.) Simply adding up the characters is the case $\alpha = 1$. A similar strategy is to exclusive-or c_i with αh_{i-1}, instead of adding.

For 32-bit integers, if we take $\alpha = 65599$, a prime near 2^{16}, then overflow soon occurs during the computation of αh_{i-1}. Since α is a prime, ignoring overflows and keeping only the lower-order 32 bits seems to do well.

In one set of experiments, the hash function *hashpjw* in Fig. 7.35 from P. J. Weinberger's C compiler did consistently well at all table sizes tested (see Fig. 7.36). The sizes included the first primes larger than 100, 200, $\ldots$, 1500. A close second was the function that computed h by multiplying the old value by 65599, ignoring overflows, and adding in the next character. Function

```
(1)  #define PRIME 211
(2)  #define EOS '\0'
(3)  int hashpjw(s)
(4)  char    *s;
(5)  {
(6)      char *p;
(7)      unsigned h = 0, g;
(8)      for ( p = s; *p != EOS; p = p+1 ) {
(9)          h = (h << 4) + (*p);
(10)         if (g = h&0xf0000000) {
(11)             h = h ^ (g >> 24);
(12)             h = h ^ g;
(13)         }
(14)     }
(15)     return h % PRIME;
(16) }
```

Fig. 7.35. Hash function *hashpjw*, written in C.

hashpjw is computed by starting with $h = 0$. For each character c, shift the bits of h left 4 positions and add in c. If any of the four high-order bits of h is 1, shift the four bits right 24 positions, exclusive-or them into h, and reset to 0 any of the four high-order bits that was 1.

Example 7.10. For best results, the size of the hash table and the expected input must be taken into account when a hash function is designed. For example, it is desirable that the hash values for the most frequently occurring names in a language be distinct. If keywords are entered into the symbol table, then the keywords are likely to be among the most frequently occurring names, although in one sample of C programs, name i occurred over three times as often as while.

One way of testing a hash function is to look at the number of strings that fall onto the same list. Given a file F consisting of n strings, suppose b_j strings fall onto list j, for $0 \le j \le m - 1$. A measure of how uniformly the strings are distributed across lists is obtained by computing

$$\sum_{j=0}^{m-1} b_j(b_j + 1) / 2 \tag{7.2}$$

The intuitive justification for this term is that we need to look at 1 list element to find the first entry on list j, at 2 to find the second, and so on up to b_j to find the last entry. The sum of $1, 2, \ldots , b_j$ is $b_j(b_j+1) / 2$.

From Exercise 7.14, the value of (7.2) for a hash function that distributes strings randomly across buckets is

$$(n / 2m)(n + 2m - 1) \tag{7.3}$$

The ratio of the terms (7.2) and (7.3) is plotted in Fig. 7.36 for several hash functions applied to nine files. The files are:

1. The 50 most frequently occurring names and keywords in a sample of C programs.
2. Like (1), but with the 100 most frequently occurring names and keywords.
3. Like (1), but with the 500 most frequently occurring names and keywords.
4. 952 external names in the UNIX operating system kernel.
5. 627 names in a C program generated by C++ (Stroustrup [1986]).
6. 915 randomly generated character strings.
7. 614 words from Section 3.1 of this book.
8. 1201 words in English with **xxx** added as a prefix and suffix.
9. The 300 names v100, v101, ..., v399.

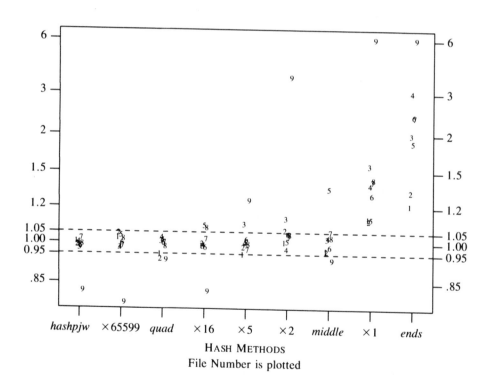

Fig. 7.36. Relative performance of hash functions for a table of size 211.

The function *hashpjw* is as in Fig. 7.35. The functions named $\times \alpha$, where α is an integer constant, compute $h \bmod m$, where h is obtained iteratively by starting with 0, multiplying the old value by α, and adding in the next

character. The function *middle* forms *h* from the middle four characters of a
string, while *ends* adds up the first three and last three characters with the
length to form *h*. Finally, *quad* groups every four consecutive characters into
an integer and then adds up the integers.   □

Representing Scope Information

The entries in the symbol table are for declarations of names. When an
occurrence of a name in the source text is looked up in the symbol table, the
entry for the appropriate declaration of that name must be returned. The
scope rules of the source language determine which declaration is appropriate.

A simple approach is to maintain a separate symbol table for each scope. In
effect, the symbol table for a procedure or scope is the compile-time
equivalent of an activation record. Information for the nonlocals of a procedure is found by scanning the symbol tables for the enclosing procedures
following the scope rules of the language. Equivalently, information about
the locals of a procedure can be attached to the node for the procedure in a
syntax tree for the program. With this approach the symbol table is
integrated into the intermediate representation of the input.

Most closely nested scope rules can be implemented by adapting the data
structures presented earlier in this section. We keep track of the local names
of a procedure by giving each procedure a unique number. Blocks must also
be numbered if the language is block-structured. The number of each procedure can be computed in a syntax-directed manner from semantic rules that
recognize the beginning and end of each procedure. The procedure number is
made a part of all locals declared in that procedure; the representation of the
local name in the symbol table is a pair consisting of the name and the procedure number. (In some arrangements, such as those described below, the
procedure number need not actually appear, as it can be deduced from the
position of the record in the symbol table.)

When we look up a newly scanned name, a match occurs only if the characters of the name match an entry character for character, and the associated
number in the symbol-table entry is the number of the procedure being processed. Most closely nested scope rules can be implemented in terms of the
following operations on a name:

> *lookup*:   find the most recently created entry
>
> *insert*:   make a new entry
>
> *delete*:   remove the most recently created entry

"Deleted" entries must be preserved; they are just removed from the active
symbol table. In a one-pass compiler, information in the symbol table about a
scope consisting of, say, a procedure body, is not needed at compile time after
the procedure body is processed. However, it may be needed at run time,
particularly if a run-time diagnostic system is implemented. In this case, the
information in the symbol table must be added to the generated code for use

by the linker or by the run-time diagnostic system. See also the treatment of field names in records in Sections 8.2 and 8.3.

Each of the data structures discussed in this section — lists and hash tables — can be maintained so as to support the above operations.

When a linear list consisting of an array of records was described earlier in this section, we mentioned how *lookup* can be implemented by inserting entries at one end so that the order of the entries in the array is the same as the order of insertion of the entries. A scan starting from the end and proceeding towards the beginning of the array finds the most recently created entry for a name. The situation is similar in a linked list, as shown in Fig. 7.37. A pointer *front* points to the most recently created entry in the list. The implementation of *insert* takes constant time because a new entry is placed at the front of the list. The implementation of *lookup* is done by scanning the list starting at the entry pointed to by *front* and following links until the desired name is found, or the end of the list is reached. In Fig. 7.37, the entry for a declared in a block B_2, nested within block B_0, appears nearer the front of the list than the entry for a declared in B_0.

front

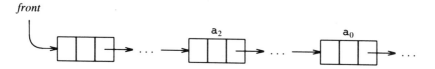

a₂ ... a₀

Fig. 7.37. The most recent entry for a is near the front.

For the *delete* operation, note that the entries for the declarations in the most deeply nested procedure appear nearest the front of the list. Thus, we do not need to keep the procedure number with every entry — if we keep track of the first entry for each procedure, then all entries up to the first can be deleted from the active symbol table when we finish processing the scope of this procedure.

A hash table consists of m lists accessed through an array. Since a name always hashes to the same list, individual lists are maintained as in Fig. 7.37. However, for implementing the *delete* operation we would rather not have to scan the entire hash table looking for lists containing entries to be deleted. The following approach can be used. Suppose each entry has two links:

1. a hash link that chains the entry to other entries whose names hash to the same value and

2. a scope link that chains all entries in the same scope.

If the scope link is left undisturbed when an entry is deleted from the hash table, then the chain formed by the scope links will constitute a separate (inactive) symbol table for the scope in question.

Deletion of entries from the hash table must be done with care, because deletion of an entry affects the previous one on its list. Recall that we delete the ith entry by making the $i-1$st entry point to the $i+1$st. Simply using the scope links to find the ith entry is therefore not enough. The $i-1$st entry can be found if the hash links form a circular linked list, in which the last entry points back to the first. Alternatively, we can use a stack to keep track of the lists containing entries to be deleted. A marker is placed in the stack when a new procedure is scanned. Above the marker are the numbers of the lists containing entries for names declared in this procedure. When we finish processing the procedure, the list numbers can be popped from the stack until the marker for the procedure is reached. Another scheme is discussed in Exercise 7.11.

7.7 LANGUAGE FACILITIES FOR DYNAMIC STORAGE ALLOCATION

In this section, we briefly describe facilities provided by some languages for the dynamic allocation of storage for data, under program control. Storage for such data is usually taken from a heap. Allocated data is often retained until it is explicitly deallocated. The allocation itself can be either *explicit* or *implicit*. In Pascal, for example, explicit allocation is performed using the standard procedure new. Execution of new(p) allocates storage for the type of object pointed to by p and p is left pointing to the newly allocated object. Deallocation is done by calling dispose in most implementations of Pascal.

Implicit allocation occurs when evaluation of an expression results in storage being obtained to hold the value of the expression. Lisp, for example, allocates a cell in a list when cons is used; cells that can no longer be reached are automatically reclaimed. Snobol allows the length of a string to vary at run time, and manages the space needed to hold the string in a heap.

Example 7.11. The Pascal program in Fig. 7.38 builds the linked list shown in Fig. 7.39 and prints the integers held in the cells; its output is

76	3
4	2
7	1

When execution of the program begins at line 15, storage for the pointer head is in the activation record for the complete program. Each time control reaches

(11)   new(p); p↑.key := k; p↑.info := i;

the call new(p) results in a cell being allocated somewhere within the heap; p↑ refers to this cell in the assignments on line 11.

Note from the output of the program that the allocated cells are accessible when control returns to the main program from insert. In other words, cells allocated using new during an activation of insert are retained when control returns to the main program from the activation.   □

```
(1) program table(input, output);
(2) type link = ↑ cell;
(3)       cell = record
(4)                  key, info : integer;
(5)                  next : link
(6)       end;
(7) var   head : link;
(8) procedure insert(k, i : integer);
(9)       var  p : link;
(10)      begin
(11)          new(p); p↑.key := k; p↑.info := i;
(12)          p↑.next := head; head := p
(13)      end;

(14) begin
(15)      head := nil;
(16)      insert(7,1); insert(4,2); insert(76,3);
(17)      writeln(head↑.key, head↑.info);
(18)      writeln(head↑.next↑.key, head↑.next↑.info);
(19)      writeln(head↑.next↑.next↑.key,
                  head↑.next↑.next↑.info)
(20) end.
```

Fig. 7.38. Dynamic allocation of cells using **new** in Pascal.

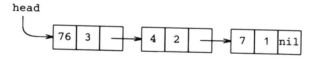

Fig. 7.39. Linked list built by program in Fig. 7.38.

Garbage

Dynamically allocated storage can become unreachable. Storage that a program allocates but cannot refer to is called *garbage*. In Fig. 7.38, suppose nil is assigned to head↑.next between lines 16 and 17:

```
(16)      insert(7,1); insert(4,2); insert(76,3);
          head↑.next := nil;
(17)      writeln(head↑.key, head↑.info);
```

The leftmost cell in Fig. 7.39 will now contain a nil pointer rather than a pointer to the middle cell. When the pointer to the middle cell is lost, the middle and rightmost cells become garbage.

Lisp performs *garbage collection*, a process discussed in the next section that reclaims inaccessible storage. Pascal and C do not have garbage collection, leaving it to the program explicitly to deallocate storage that is no longer desired. In these languages, deallocated storage can be reused, but garbage remains until the program finishes.

Dangling References

An additional complication can arise with explicit deallocation; dangling references can occur. As mentioned in Section 7.3, a dangling reference occurs when storage that has been deallocated is referred to. For example, consider the effect of executing dispose(head↑.next) between lines 16 and 17 in Fig. 7.38:

(16)	`insert(7,1); insert(4,2); insert(76,3);`
	`dispose(head↑.next);`
(17)	`writeln(head↑.key, head↑.info);`

The call to dispose deallocates the cell following the one pointed to by head as shown in Fig. 7.40. However, head↑.next has not been changed, so it is a dangling pointer to deallocated storage.

Dangling references and garbage are related concepts; dangling references occur if deallocation occurs before the last reference, whereas garbage exists if the last reference occurs before deallocation.

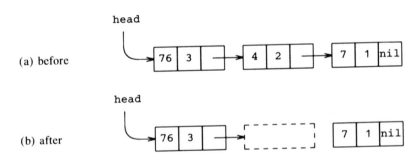

Fig. 7.40. Creation of dangling references and garbage.

7.8 DYNAMIC STORAGE ALLOCATION TECHNIQUES

The techniques needed to implement dynamic storage allocation depend on how storage is deallocated. If deallocation is implicit, then the run-time support package is responsible for determining when a storage block is no longer needed. There is less a compiler has to do if deallocation is done explicitly by the programmer. We consider explicit deallocation first.

Explicit Allocation of Fixed-Sized Blocks

The simplest form of dynamic allocation involves blocks of a fixed size. By linking the blocks in a list, as in Fig. 7.41, allocation and deallocation can be done quickly with little or no storage overhead.

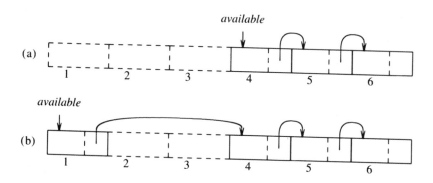

Fig. 7.41. A deallocated block is added to the list of available blocks.

Suppose that blocks are to be drawn from a contiguous area of storage. Initialization of the area is done by using a portion of each block for a link to the next block. A pointer *available* points to the first block. Allocation consists of taking a block off the list and deallocation consists of putting the block back on the list.

The compiler routines that manage blocks do not need to know the type of object that will be held in the block by the user program. We can treat each block as a variant record, with the compiler routines viewing the block as consisting of a link to the next block and the user program viewing the block as being of some other type. Thus, there is no space overhead because the user program can use the entire block for its own purposes. When the block is returned, then the compiler routines use some of the space from the block itself to link it into the list of available blocks, as shown in Fig. 7.41.

Explicit Allocation of Variable-Sized Blocks

When blocks are allocated and deallocated, storage can become *fragmented*; that is, the heap may consist of alternate blocks that are free and in use, as in Fig. 7.42.

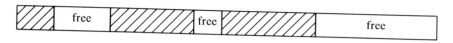

Fig. 7.42. Free and used blocks in a heap.

The situation shown in Fig. 7.42 can occur if a program allocates five blocks and then deallocates the second and fourth, for example. Fragmentation is of no consequence if blocks are of fixed size, but if they are of variable size, a situation like Fig. 7.42 is a problem, because we could not allocate a block larger than any one of the free blocks, even though the space is available in principle.

One method for allocating variable-sized blocks is called the *first-fit method*. When a block of size s is allocated, we search for the first free block that is of size $f \geq s$. This block is then subdivided into a used block of size s, and a free block of size $f - s$. Note that allocation incurs a time overhead because we must search for a free block that is large enough.

When a block is deallocated, we check to see if it is next to a free block. If possible, the deallocated block is combined with a free block next to it to create a larger free block. Combining adjacent free blocks into a larger free block prevents further fragmentation from occurring. There are a number of subtle details concerning how free blocks are allocated, deallocated, and maintained in an available list or lists. There are also several tradeoffs between time, space, and availability of large blocks. The reader is referred to Knuth [1973a] or Aho, Hopcroft, and Ullman [1983] for a discussion of these issues.

Implicit Deallocation

Implicit deallocation requires cooperation between the user program and the run-time package, because the latter needs to know when a storage block is no longer in use. This cooperation is implemented by fixing the format of storage blocks. For the present discussion, suppose that the format of a storage block is as in Fig. 7.43.

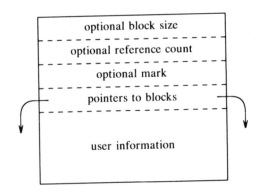

Fig. 7.43. The format of a block.

The first problem is that of recognizing block boundaries. If the size of blocks is fixed, then position information can be used. For example, if each block occupies 20 words, then a new block begins every 20 words. Otherwise, in the inaccessible storage attached to a block we keep the size of a block, so we can determine where the next block begins.

The second problem is that of recognizing if a block is in use. We assume that a block is in use if it is possible for the user program to refer to the information in the block. The reference may occur through a pointer or after following a sequence of pointers, so the compiler needs to know the position in storage of all pointers. Using the format of Fig. 7.43, pointers are kept in a fixed position in the block. Perhaps more to the point, the assumption is made that the user-information area of a block does not contain any pointers.

Two approaches can be used for implicit deallocation. We sketch them here; for more details see Aho, Hopcroft, and Ullman [1983].

1. *Reference counts.* We keep track of the number of blocks that point directly to the present block. If this count ever drops to 0, then the block can be deallocated because it cannot be referred to. In other words, the block has become garbage that can be collected. Maintaining reference counts can be costly in time; the pointer assignment p := q leads to changes in the reference counts of the blocks pointed to by both p and q. The count for the block pointed to by p goes down by one, while that for the block pointed to by q goes up by one. Reference counts are best used when pointers between blocks never appear in cycles. For example, in Fig. 7.44, neither block is accessible from any other, so they are both garbage, but each has a reference count of one.

2. *Marking techniques.* An alternative approach is to suspend temporarily execution of the user program and use the frozen pointers to determine which blocks are in use. This approach requires all the pointers into the heap to be known. Conceptually, we pour paint into the heap through these pointers. Any block that is reached by the paint is in use and the rest can be deallocated. In more detail, we go through the heap and mark all blocks *unused*. Then, we follow pointers marking as *used* any block that is reached in the process. A final sequential scan of the heap allows all blocks still marked *unused* to be collected.

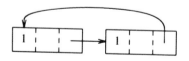

Fig. 7.44. Garbage cells with nonzero reference counts.

With variable-sized blocks, we have the additional possibility of moving used storage blocks from their current positions.[8] This process, called

---

[8] We could do so with fixed-size blocks, but no advantage results.

compaction moves all used blocks to one end of the heap, so that all the free storage can be collected into one large free block. Compaction also requires information about the pointers in blocks because when a used block is moved, all pointers to it have to be adjusted to reflect the move. Its advantage is that afterwards fragmentation of available storage is eliminated.

7.9 STORAGE ALLOCATION IN FORTRAN

Fortran was designed to permit static storage allocation, as in Section 7.3. However, there are some issues, such as the treatment of COMMON and EQUIVALENCE declarations, that are fairly special to Fortran. A Fortran compiler can create a number of *data areas*, i.e., blocks of storage in which the values of objects can be stored. In Fortran, there is one data area for each procedure and one data area for each named COMMON block and for blank COMMON, if used. The symbol table must record for each name the data area in which it belongs and its offset in that data area, that is, its position relative to the beginning of the area. The compiler must eventually decide where the data areas go relative to the executable code and to one another, but this choice is arbitrary, since the data areas are independent.

The compiler must compute the size of each data area. For the data areas of the procedures, a single counter suffices, since their sizes are known after each procedure is processed. For COMMON blocks, a record for each block must be kept during the processing of all procedures, since each procedure using a block may have its own idea of how big the block is, and the actual size is the maximum of the sizes implied by the various procedures. If procedures are separately compiled, a link editor must be used to select the size of the COMMON block to be the maximum of all such blocks with the same name among the pieces of code being linked.

For each data area the compiler creates a *memory map*, which is a description of the contents of the area. This "memory map" might simply consist of an indication, in the symbol-table entry for each name in the area, of its offset in the area. We need not necessarily have an easy way of answering the question, "What are all the names in this data area?" However, in Fortran we know the answer for the procedures' data areas, since all names declared in a procedure that are not COMMON or equivalenced to a COMMON name are in the procedure's data area. COMMON names can have their symbol-table entries linked, with one chain for each COMMON block, in the order of their appearance in the block. In fact, as the offsets of names in the data area cannot always be determined until the entire procedure is processed (Fortran arrays can be declared before their dimensions are declared), it is necessary that these chains of COMMON names be created.

A Fortran program consists of a main program, subroutines, and functions (we call them all *procedures*). Each occurrence of a name has a scope consisting of one procedure only. We can generate object code for each procedure upon reaching the end of that procedure. If we do so, it is possible that most of the information in the symbol table can be expunged. We need only preserve those names that are external to the routine just processed. These are names of other procedures and of common blocks. These names may not truly be external to the entire program being compiled, but must be preserved until the entire collection of procedures is processed.

Data in COMMON Areas

We create for each block a record giving the first and last names, belonging to the current procedure, that are declared to be in that COMMON block. When processing a declaration like

    COMMON /BLOCK1/ NAME1, NAME2

the compiler must do the following.

1. In the table for COMMON block names, create a record for BLOCK1, if one does not already exist.

2. In the symbol-table entries for NAME1 and NAME2, set a pointer to the symbol-table entry for BLOCK1, indicating that these are in COMMON and members of BLOCK1.

3. a) If the record has just now been created for BLOCK1, set a pointer in that record to the symbol-table entry for NAME1, indicating the first name in this COMMON block. Then, link the symbol-table entry for NAME1 to that for NAME2, using a field of the symbol table reserved for linking members of the same COMMON block. Finally, set a pointer in the record for BLOCK1 to the symbol-table entry for NAME2, indicating the last found member of that block.

   b) If, however, this is not the first declaration of BLOCK1, simply link NAME1 and NAME2 to the end of the list of names for BLOCK1. The pointer to the end of the list for BLOCK1, appearing in the record for BLOCK1, is updated of course.

After a procedure has been processed, we apply the equivalencing algorithm, to be discussed shortly. We may discover that some additional names belong in COMMON because they are equivalenced to names that are themselves in COMMON. We shall find that it is not actually necessary to link such a name XYZ to the chain for its COMMON block. A bit in the symbol-table entry for XYZ is set, indicating that XYZ has been equivalenced to something else. A data structure to be discussed will then give the position of XYZ relative to some name actually declared to be in COMMON.

After performing the equivalence operations, we can create a memory map for each COMMON block by scanning the list of names for that block. Initialize a counter to zero, and for each name on the list, make its offset equal to the current value of the counter. Then, add to the counter the number of memory units taken by the data object denoted by the name. The COMMON block records can then be deleted and the space reused by the next procedure.

If a name XYZ in COMMON is equivalenced to a name not in COMMON, we must determine the maximum offset from the beginning of XYZ for any word of storage needed for any name equivalenced to XYZ. For example, if XYZ is a real, equivalenced to A(5,5), where A is a 10×10 array of reals, A(1,1) appears 44 words before XYZ and A(10,10) appears 55 words after XYZ, as shown in Fig. 7.45. The existence of A does not affect the counter for the COMMON block; it is only incremented by one word when XYZ is considered, independent of what XYZ is equivalenced to. However, the end of the data area for the COMMON block must be far enough away from the beginning to accommodate the array A. We therefore record the largest offset, from the beginning of the COMMON block, of any word used by a name equivalenced to a member of that block. In Fig. 7.45, that quantity must be at least the offset of XYZ plus 55. We also check that the array A does not extend in front of the beginning of the data area; that is, the offset of XYZ must be at least 44. Otherwise, we have an error and must produce a diagnostic message.

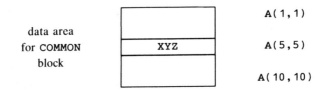

Fig. 7.45. Relation between COMMON and EQUIVALENCE statements.

A Simple Equivalence Algorithm

The first algorithms for processing equivalence statements appeared in assemblers rather than compilers. Since these algorithms can be a bit complex, especially when interactions between COMMON and EQUIVALENCE statements are considered, let us treat first a situation typical of an assembly language, where the only EQUIVALENCE statements are of the form

    EQUIVALENCE A,B+offset

where A and B are the names of locations. This statement makes A denote the location that is *offset* memory units beyond the location for B.

A sequence of EQUIVALENCE statements groups names into *equivalence sets* whose positions relative to one another are all defined by the EQUIVALENCE statements. For example, the sequence of statements

    EQUIVALENCE A, B+100
    EQUIVALENCE C, D-40
    EQUIVALENCE A, C+30
    EQUIVALENCE E, F

groups names into the sets {A, B, C, D} and {E, F}, where E and F denote the same location. C is 70 locations after B, A is 30 after C, and D is 10 after A.

To compute the equivalence sets we create a tree for each set. Each node of a tree represents a name and contains the offset of that name relative to the name at the parent of this node. The name at the root of a tree we call the *leader*. The position of any name relative to the leader can be computed by following the path from the node for that name and adding the offsets along the way.

Example 7.12. The equivalence set {A, B, C, D} mentioned above could be represented by the tree shown in Fig. 7.46. D is the leader, and we can discover that A is located 10 positions before D, since the sum of the offsets on the path from A to D is $100 + (-110) = -10$.   □

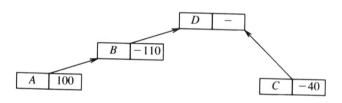

Fig. 7.46. Tree representing equivalence set.

Let us now give an algorithm for constructing trees for equivalence sets. The relevant fields in the symbol-table entries are:

1. *parent*, pointing to the symbol-table entry for the parent, null if the name is a root (or not equivalenced to anything), and

2. *offset*, giving the offset of a name relative to the parent name.

The algorithm we give assumes that any name could be the leader of an equivalence set. In practice, in an assembly language, one and only one name in the set would have an actual location defined by a pseudo-operation, and this name would be made the leader. We trust the reader can see how to modify the algorithm to make one particular name be the leader.

Algorithm 7.1. Construction of equivalence trees.

Input. A list of equivalence-defining statements of the form

    EQUIVALENCE   A, B+*dist*

Output. A collection of trees such that, for any name mentioned in the input list of equivalences, we may, by following the path from that name to the root and summing the *offset*'s found along the path, determine the position of the name relative to the leader.

Method. We repeat the steps of Fig. 7.47 for each equivalence statement EQUIVALENCE A, B+*dist*, in turn. The justification for the formula in line (12) for the offset of the leader of A relative to the leader of B is as follows. The location of A, say l_A, is equal to c plus the location of the leader of A, say m_A. The location of B, say l_B, equals d plus the location of the leader of B, say m_B. But $l_A = l_B + dist$, so $c + m_A = d + m_B + dist$. Hence $m_A - m_B$ equals $d - c + dist$. □

```
        begin
(1)         let p and q point to the nodes for A and B, respectively;
(2)         c := 0;  d := 0;   /* c and d compute the offsets of A and B
                    from the leaders of their respective sets */
(3)         while parent(p) ≠ null do begin
(4)             c := c + offset(p);
(5)             p := parent(p)
            end;     /* move p to the leader of a, accumulating
                        offsets as we go */
(6)         while parent(q) ≠ null do begin
(7)             d := d + offset(q);
(8)             q := parent(q)
            end;     /* do the same for B */
(9)         if p = q then /* A and B are already equivalenced */
(10)            if c − d ≠ dist then error;
                    /* A and B have been given two different relative positions */
            else begin     /* merge the sets of A and B */
(11)            parent(p) := q    /* make the leader of A
                        a child of B's leader */
(12)            offset(p) := d − c + dist
            end
        end
```

Fig. 7.47. Equivalence algorithm.

Example 7.13. If we process

```
EQUIVALENCE      A,  B+100
EQUIVALENCE      C,  D−40
```

we get the configuration shown in Fig. 7.46, but without the offset -110 in the node for B and with no link from B to D. When we process

```
EQUIVALENCE      A,  C+30
```

we find that p points to B after the while-loop of line (3) and q points to d after the while-loop of line (6). We also have $c = 100$ and $d = -40$. Then at line (11) we make D the parent of B and set the *offset* field for B to 100, which is $(-40) - (100) + 30$.   □

Algorithm 7.1 could take time proportional to n^2 to process n equivalences, since in the worst case the paths followed in the loops of lines (3) and (6) could include every node of their respective trees. Equivalencing requires only a tiny fraction of the time spent in compilation, so n^2 steps is not prohibitive, and an algorithm more complex than that of Fig. 7.47 is probably not justified. However, it happens that there are two easy things we can do to make Algorithm 7.1 take time that is just about linear in the number of equivalences it processes. While it is not likely that equivalence sets will be large enough, on the average, that these improvements need to be implemented, it is worth noting that equivalencing serves as a paradigm for a number of important processes involving "set merging." For example, a number of efficient algorithms for data-flow analysis depend on fast equivalence algorithms; the interested reader is referred to the bibliographic notes of Chapter 10.

The first improvement we can make is to keep a count, for each leader, of the number of nodes in its tree. Then, at lines (11) and (12), instead of arbitrarily linking the leader of A to the leader of B, link whichever has the smaller count to the other. This makes sure that the trees grow squat so paths will be short. It is left as an exercise that n equivalences performed in this manner cannot produce paths longer than $\log_2 n$ nodes.

The second idea is known as path compression. When following a path to the root in the loops of lines (3) and (6), make all nodes encountered children of the leader if they are not already so. That is, while following the path, record all the nodes $n_1, n_2, \ldots, n_k$ encountered, where n_1 is the node for A or B and n_k is the leader. Then adjust offsets and make $n_1, n_2, \ldots, n_{k-2}$ children of n_k by the steps in Fig. 7.48.

```
begin
    h := offset(n_{k-1});
    for i := k-2 downto 1 do begin
        parent(n_i) := n_k;
        h := h + offset(n_i);
        offset(n_i) := h
    end
end
```

Fig. 7.48. Adjustment of offsets.

An Equivalence Algorithm for Fortran

There are several additional features that must be added to Algorithm 7.1 to make it work for Fortran. First, we must determine whether an equivalence set is in COMMON, which we can do by recording for each leader whether any of the names in its set are in COMMON, and if so, in which block.

Second, in an assembly language, one member of an equivalence set will pin down the entire set to reality by being a label of a statement, thus allowing the addresses denoted by all names in the set to be computed relative to that one location. In Fortran, however, it is the compiler's job to determine storage locations, so an equivalence set not in COMMON may be viewed as "floating" until the compiler determines the position of the whole set in its appropriate data area. To do so correctly, the compiler needs to know the extent of the equivalence set, that is, the number of locations which the names in the set collectively occupy. To handle this problem we attach to the leader two fields, *low* and *high*, giving the offsets relative to the leader of the lowest and highest locations used by any member of the equivalence set. Third, there are minor problems introduced by the fact that names can be arrays and locations in the middle of an array can be equivalenced to locations in other arrays.

Since there are three fields (*low*, *high*, and a pointer to a COMMON block) that must be associated with each leader, we do not want to allocate space for these fields in all symbol-table entries. One course of action is to use the *parent* field from Algorithm 7.1 to point, in the case of the leader, to a record in a new table with three fields, *low*, *high*, and *comblk*. As this table and the symbol table occupy disjoint areas, we can tell to which table a pointer points. Alternatively, the symbol table can contain a bit indicating whether a name is currently a leader. If space is really at a premium, an alternative algorithm avoiding this extra table at the cost of a bit more programming effort is discussed in the exercises.

Let us consider the calculation that must replace lines (11) and (12) of Fig. 7.47. The situation in which two equivalence sets, whose leaders are pointed to by p and q, must be merged is depicted in Fig 7.49(a). The data structure representing the two sets appears in Fig. 7.49(b). First we, must check that there are not two members among the two equivalence sets that are in COMMON. Even if both are in the same block, the Fortran standard forbids their being equivalenced. If any one COMMON block contains a member of either equivalence set, then the merged set has a pointer to the record for that block in *comblk*. The code doing this check, assuming the leader pointed to by q becomes the leader of the merged set, is shown in Fig. 7.50. In place of lines (11) and (12) of Fig. 7.47 we must also compute the extent of the merged equivalence set. Figure 7.49(a) indicates the formulas for the new values of *low* and *high* relative to the leader pointed to by q.

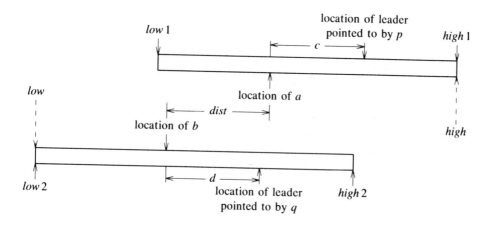

$$low = \min(low\,2,\ low\,1 - c + dist + d)$$
$$high = \max(high\,2,\ high\,1 - c + dist + d)$$

(a) relative positions of equivalence sets

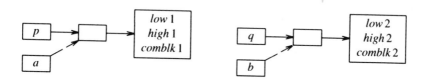

(b) data structure

Fig. 7.49. Merging equivalence sets.

```
begin
        comblk 1 := comblk (parent (p));
        comblk 2 := comblk (parent (q));
        if comblk 1 ≠ null and comblk 2 ≠ null then
            error;    /* two names in COMMON equivalent */
        else if comblk 2 = null then
            comblk (parent (q)) := comblk 1
end
```

Fig. 7.50. Computing COMMON blocks.

Thus we must do

begin
> $low(parent(q)) := \min(low(parent(q)), \; low(parent(p)) - c + dist + d);$
> $high(parent(q)) := \max(high(parent(q)), \; high(parent(p)) - c + dist + d)$

end

These statements are followed by lines (11) and (12) of Fig. 7.47 to effect the merger of the two equivalence sets.

Two last details must be covered to make Algorithm 7.1 work for Fortran. In Fortran, we may equivalence positions in the middle of arrays to other positions in other arrays or to simple names. The offset of an array A from its leader means the offset of the first location of A from the first location of the leader. If a location like A(5,7) is equivalenced to, say, B(20), we must compute the position of A(5,7) relative to A(1,1) and initialize c to the negative of this distance in line (2) of Fig. 7.47. Similarly, d must be initialized to the negative of the position of B(20) relative to B(1). The formulas in Section 8.3 together with a knowledge of the size of elements of the arrays A and B, are sufficient to calculate the initial values of c and d.

The last detail to be covered is the fact that Fortran allows an EQUIVALENCE which involves many locations, such as

        EQUIVALENCE (A(5,7), B(20), C, D(4,5,6))

These may be treated as

        EQUIVALENCE (B(20), A(5,7))
        EQUIVALENCE (C, A(5,7))
        EQUIVALENCE (D(4,5,6), A(5,7))

Note that if we do the equivalences in this order, only A becomes the leader of a set of more than one element. A record with *low*, *high*, and *comblk* can be used many times for "equivalence sets" of a single name.

Mapping Data Areas

We may now describe the rules whereby space in the various data areas is assigned for each routine's names.

1. For each COMMON block, visit all names declared to be in that block in the order of their declarations (use the chains of COMMON names created in the symbol table for this purpose). Allocate the number of words needed for each name in turn, keeping a count of the number of words allocated, so offsets can be computed for each name. If a name A is equivalenced, the extent of its equivalence set does not matter, but we must check that the *low* value for the leader of A does not extend past the beginning of the COMMON block. Consult the *high* value for the leader to put a lower limit on the last word of the block. We leave the exact formulas for these calculations to the reader.

2. Visit all names for the routine in any order.

a) If a name is in COMMON, do nothing. Space has been allocated in (1).

b) If a name is not in COMMON and not equivalenced, allocate the necessary number of words in the data area for the routine.

c) If a name A is equivalenced, find its leader, say L. If L has already been given a position in the data area for the routine, compute the position of A by adding to that position all the *offset*'s found in the path from A to L in the tree representing the equivalence set of A and L. If L has not been given a position, allocate the next *high* − *low* words in the data area for the equivalence set. The position of L in these words is −*low* words from the beginning, and the position of A can be calculated by summing *offset*'s as before.

EXERCISES

7.1 Using the scope rules of Pascal, determine the declarations that apply to each occurrence of the names a and b in Fig. 7.51. The output of the program consists of the integers 1 through 4.

```
program a(input, output);
procedure b(u, v, x, y: integer);
    var  a : record a, b : integer end;
         b : record b, a : integer end;
    begin
        with a do begin a := u; b := v end;
        with b do begin a := x; b := y end;
        writeln(a.a, a.b, b.a, b.b)
    end;
begin
    b(1, 2, 3, 4)
end.
```

Fig. 7.51. Pascal program with several declarations of a and b.

7.2 Consider a block-structured language in which a name can be declared to be an integer or a real. Suppose that expressions are represented by a terminal **expr** and that the only statements are assignments, conditionals, whiles, and sequences of statements. Assuming that integers are allocated one word and that reals are allocated two words, give a syntax-directed algorithm (based on a reasonable grammar for declarations and blocks) to determine bindings from names to words that can be used by an activation of a block. Does your allocation use the minimum number of words adequate for any execution of the block?

*7.3 In Section 7.4 we claimed that the display could be maintained correctly if each procedure at depth i stored $d[i]$ at the beginning of an activation and restored $d[i]$ at the end. Prove by induction on the number of calls that each procedure sees a correct display.

7.4 A *macro* is a form of procedure, implemented by literally substituting the body for each procedure call. Figure 7.52 shows a Pic program and its output. The first two lines define the macros show and small. The bodies of the macros are contained between the two % signs on the lines. Each of the four circles in the figure is drawn using show; the radius of the circle is given by the nonlocal name r. Blocks in Pic are delimited by [and]. Each variable assigned to within a block is implicitly declared within the block. From the output, what can you say about the scope of each occurrence of r?

```
define show  % { circle radius r at Here } %
define small % [ r = 1/12; show ] %
[
    r = 1/6;
    show; small;
    move;
    show; small;
]
```

Fig. 7.52. Circles drawn by a Pic program.

7.5 Write a procedure to insert an item into a linked list by passing a pointer to the head of the list. Under what parameter passing mechanisms does this procedure work?

7.6 What is printed by the program in Fig. 7.53, assuming (a) call-by-value, (b) call-by-reference, (c) copy-restore linkage, (d) call-by-name?

7.7 When a procedure is passed as a parameter in a lexically scoped language, its nonlocal environment can be passed using an access link. Give an algorithm to determine this link.

```
program main(input, output);
     procedure p(x, y, z);
          begin
               y := y + 1;
               z := z + x;
          end;
     begin
          a := 2;
          b := 3;
          p(a + b, a, a);
          print a
     end.
```

Fig. 7.53. Pseudo-program illustrating parameter passing.

7.8 The three kinds of environments that could be associated with a procedure passed as a parameter are illustrated by the Pascal program in Fig. 7.54. The *lexical*, *passing*, and *activation* environments of such a procedure consist of the bindings of identifiers at the point at which the procedure is defined, passed as a parameter, and activated, respectively. Consider function f, passed as a parameter on line 11.

```
(1)  program param(input, output);

(2)      procedure b(function h(n: integer): integer);
(3)          var m : integer;
(4)          begin m := 3; writeln(h(2)) end { b };

(5)      procedure c;
(6)          var m : integer;

(7)              function f(n : integer) : integer;
(8)                  begin f := m + n end { f };

(9)              procedure r;
(10)                 var m : integer;
(11)                 begin m := 7; b(f) end { r };

(12)         begin m := 0; r end { c };

(13)     begin
(14)         c
(15)     end.
```

Fig. 7.54. Example of lexical, passing, and activation environments.

Using the lexical, passing, and activation environments for f, nonlocal m on line 8 is in the scope of the declarations of m on lines 6, 10, and 3, respectively.

a) Draw the activation tree for this program.

b) What is the output of the program, using the lexical, passing, and activation environments for f?

*c) Modify the display implementation of a lexically scoped language to set up the lexical environment correctly when a procedure passed as a parameter is activated.

7.9 The statement $f := a$ on line 11 of the pseudo-program in Fig. 7.55 calls function a, which passes function $addm$ back as a result.

a) Draw the activation tree for an execution of this program.

b) Suppose that lexical scope is used for nonlocal names. Why will the program fail if stack allocation is used?

c) What is the output of the program with heap allocation?

```
(1)    program ret (input, output);
(2)    var f: function (integer) : integer;

(3)      function a : function (integer) : integer;
(4)        var m : integer;
(5)        function addm (n : integer) : integer;
(6)          begin return m + n end;
(7)        begin m := 0; return addm end;

(8)      procedure b (g : function (integer) : integer);
(9)        begin writeln (g (2)) end;

(10)   begin
(11)     f := a; b (f)
(12)   end.
```

Fig. 7.55. Pseudo-program in which function *addm* is returned as a result.

7.10 Certain languages, like Lisp, have the ability to return newly created procedures at run time. In Fig. 7.56, all functions, whether defined in the source text or created at run time, take at most one argument and return one value, either a function or a real. The operator ∘ stands for composition of functions; that is $(f \circ g)(x) = f(g(x))$.

a) What value is printed by *main*?

*b) Suppose that whenever a procedure p is created and returned, its activation record becomes a child of the activation record of the function returning p. The passing environment of p can then be maintained by keeping a tree of activation records rather than a stack. What is the tree of activation records when a is computed by *main* in Fig. 7.56?

*c) Alternatively, suppose an activation record for p is created when p is activated, and made a child of the activation record for the procedure calling p. This approach can be used to maintain the activation environment for p. Draw snapshots of the activation records and their parent-child relationships as the statements in *main* are executed. Is a stack sufficient to hold activation records when this approach is used?

```
function f (x : function);
var   y : function;
          y := x ∘ h;    /* creates y when executed */
          return y
end { f };

function h ();
      return sin
end { h };

function g (z : function);
var   w : function;
          w := arctan ∘ z;    /* creates w when executed */
          return w
end { g };

function main ();
var   a : real;
          u, v : function;
          v := f (g);
          u := v ();
          a := u (π/2);
          print a
end { main }.
```

Fig. 7.56. Pseudo-program creating functions at run time.

7.11 Another way to handle deletion from hash tables for names whose scope has been passed (as in Section 7.6) is to leave expired names on a list until that list is again searched. Assuming entries include the name of the procedure in which the declaration is made, we can in principle tell whether a name is old, and delete it if so. Give an indexing scheme for procedures that enables us to tell in $O(1)$ time whether a procedure is "old," i.e., its scope has been passed.

7.12 Many hash functions can be characterized by a sequence of integer constants $\alpha_0, \alpha_1, \ldots$. If c_i, $1 \le i \le n$, is the integer value of the ith character in string s, then the string is hashed to

$$hash(s) = (\alpha_0 + \sum_{i=1}^{n} \alpha_i c_i) \textbf{ mod } m$$

where m is the size of the hash table. For each of the following cases, determine the sequence of constants $\alpha_0, \alpha_1, \ldots$ or show that no such sequence exists. Each case determines an integer; a hash value is obtained by taking that integer mod m.

a) Take the sum of the characters.

b) Take the sum of the first and last characters.

c) Take h_n, where $h_0 = 0$ and $h_i = 2h_{i-1} + c_i$.

d) Treat the bits in the middle 4 characters as a 32-bit integer.

e) A 32-bit integer can be viewed as consisting of 4 bytes, where each byte is a digit that takes on 256 possible values. Starting with 0000, for $1 \le i \le n$, add c_i into byte i **mod** 4, with carries permitted. That is, c_1 and c_5 are added into byte 1, c_2 and c_6 into byte 2, and so on. Return the final value.

*7.13 Why do hash functions characterized by a sequence of integers $\alpha_0, \alpha_1, \ldots$ as in Exercise 7.12 sometimes perform poorly if the input consists of consecutive strings, e.g., v000, v001, ...? The symptom is that somewhere along the way, their behavior deviates from random and can be predicted.

**7.14 When n strings are hashed into m lists, the mean number of strings per list is n/m, no matter how unevenly the strings are distributed. Suppose that d is a "distribution," i.e., a random string is placed on the ith list with probability $d(i)$. Suppose that a hash function with distribution d happens to place b_j randomly selected strings in list j, $0 \le j \le m-1$. Show that the expected value $W = \sum_{j=0}^{m-1}(b_j)(b_j+1)/2$ is linearly related to the variance of the distribution d. For a uniform distribution show that the expected value of W is $(n/2m)(n+2m-1)$.

7.15 Suppose we have the following sequence of declarations in a Fortran program.

```
SUBROUTINE SUB(X,Y)
INTEGER A, B(20), C(10,15), D, E
COMPLEX F, G
COMMON /CBLK/ D, E
EQUIVALENCE (G, B(2))
EQUIVALENCE (D, F, B(1))
```

Show the contents of the data areas for SUB and CBLK (at least the portion of CBLK's area accessible from SUB). Why is there no space for X and Y?

*7.16 A useful data structure for equivalence computations is the *ring struc-ture*. We use one pointer and an offset field in each symbol-table entry to link members of an equivalence set. This structure is sug-gested in Fig. 7.57, where A, B, C, and D are equivalent, and E and F are equivalent, with the location of B being 20 words after that of A, and so on.

a) Give an algorithm to compute the offset of X relative to Y, assum-ing that X and Y are in the same equivalence set.

b) Give an algorithm to compute *low* and *high*, as defined in Section 7.9, relative to the location of some name Z.

c) Give an algorithm to process

        EQUIVALENCE U, V

Do not assume that U and V are necessarily in different equivalence sets.

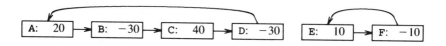

Fig. 7.57. Ring structures.

*7.17 The algorithm to map data areas given in Section 7.9 requires that we verify that *low* for the leader of A's equivalence set does not cause the space for the equivalence set of A to extend before the beginning of the COMMON block and that we calculate *high* for the leader of A to increase the upper limit of the COMMON block, if necessary. Give for-mulas in terms of *next*, the offset of A in the COMMON block, and *last*, the current last word of the block, to make the test and to update *last*, if necessary.

BIBLIOGRAPHIC NOTES

Stacks have played an essential role in the implementation of recursive func-tions. McCarthy [1981, p. 178] recalls that during a Lisp-implementation pro-ject begun in 1958 it was decided to "use a single contiguous public stack array to save the values of variables and subroutine return addresses in the implementation of recursive subroutines." The inclusion of blocks and recur-sive procedures in Algol 60 — see Naur [1981, Section 2.10] for a detailed account of their design — also stimulated development of stack allocation. The idea of a display for accessing nonlocals in a lexically scoped language is due to Dijkstra [1960, 1963]. Although Lisp uses dynamic scope, it is possible to achieve the effect of lexical scope using "funargs" consisting of a function and an access link; McCarthy [1981] describes the development of this mechanism. Successors of Lisp such as Common Lisp (Steele [1984]) have moved away from dynamic scope.

Explanations of bindings for names can be found in textbooks on programming languages, see for example Abelson and Sussman [1985], Pratt [1984], or Tennent [1981]. An alternative approach, suggested in Chapter 2, is to read the description of a compiler. The step-by-step development in Kernighan and Pike [1984] starts with a calculator for arithmetic expressions and builds an interpreter for a simple language with recursive procedures. Or see the code for Pascal-S in Wirth [1981]. A detailed description of stack allocation, the use of a display, and dynamic allocation of arrays appears in Randell and Russell [1964].

Johnson and Ritchie [1981] discuss the design of a calling sequence that allows the number of arguments of a procedure to vary from call to call. A general method for setting a global display is to follow the chain of access links, setting the display elements in the process. The approach of Section 7.4 that touches just one element, seems to have been "well known" for some time; a published reference is Rohl [1975]. Moses [1970] discusses the distinctions between the environments that apply when a function is passed as a parameter and considers the problems that arise when such environments are implemented using shallow and deep access. Stack allocation cannot be used for languages with coroutines or multiple processes. Lampson [1982] considers fast implementations using heap allocation.

In mathematical logic, quantified variables of limited scope and substitution appear with the Begriffsschrift of Frege [1879]. Substitution and parameter passing have been the subject of much debate in both the mathematical logic and programming language communities. Church [1956, p. 288] observes, "Especially difficult is the matter of correct statement of the rule of substitution for functional variables," and relates the development of such a rule for the propositional calculus. The lambda calculus of Church [1941] has been applied to environments in programming languages, for example by Landin [1964]. A pair consisting of a function and an access link is often referred to as a *closure*, following Landin [1964].

Data structures for symbol tables and algorithms for searching them are discussed in detail in Knuth [1973b] and Aho, Hopcroft, and Ullman [1974, 1983]. The lore of hashing is treated in Knuth [1973b] and Morris [1968b]. The original paper discussing hashing is Peterson [1957]. More on symbol-table organization techniques can be found in McKeeman [1976]. Example 7.10 is from Bentley, Cleveland, and Sethi [1985]. Reiss [1983] describes a symbol-table generator.

Equivalence algorithms have been described by Arden, Galler, and Graham [1961] and Galler and Fischer [1964]; we have adopted the latter approach. The efficiency of equivalence algorithms is discussed in Fischer [1972], Hopcroft and Ullman [1973], and Tarjan [1975].

CHAPTER 8

Intermediate Code
Generation

In the analysis-synthesis model of a compiler, the front end translates a source program into an intermediate representation from which the back end generates target code. Details of the target language are confined to the back end, as far as possible. Although a source program can be translated directly into the target language, some benefits of using a machine-independent intermediate form are:

1. Retargeting is facilitated; a compiler for a different machine can be created by attaching a back end for the new machine to an existing front end.

2. A machine-independent code optimizer can be applied to the intermediate representation. Such optimizers are discussed in detail in Chapter 10.

This chapter shows how the syntax-directed methods of Chapters 2 and 5 can be used to translate into an intermediate form programming language constructs such as declarations, assignments, and flow-of-control statements. For simplicity, we assume that the source program has already been parsed and statically checked, as in the organization of Fig. 8.1. Most of the syntax-directed definitions in this chapter can be implemented during either bottom-up or top-down parsing using the techniques of Chapter 5, so intermediate code generation can be folded into parsing, if desired.

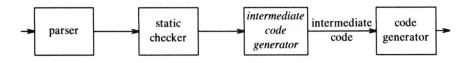

Fig. 8.1. Position of intermediate code generator.

8.1 INTERMEDIATE LANGUAGES

Syntax trees and postfix notation, introduced in Sections 5.2 and 2.3, respectively, are two kinds of intermediate representations. A third, called three-address code, will be used in this chapter. The semantic rules for generating three-address code from common programming language constructs are similar to those for constructing syntax trees or for generating postfix notation.

Graphical Representations

A syntax tree depicts the natural hierarchical structure of a source program. A dag gives the same information but in a more compact way because common subexpressions are identified. A syntax tree and dag for the assignment statement a := b * - c + b * - c appear in Fig. 8.2.

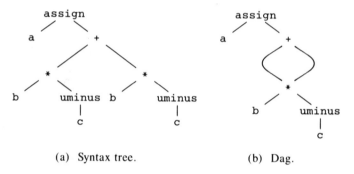

(a) Syntax tree.   (b) Dag.

Fig. 8.2. Graphical representations of a := b * - c + b * - c.

Postfix notation is a linearized representation of a syntax tree; it is a list of the nodes of the tree in which a node appears immediately after its children. The postfix notation for the syntax tree in Fig. 8.2(a) is

        a b c uminus * b c uminus * + assign   (8.1)

The edges in a syntax tree do not appear explicitly in postfix notation. They can be recovered from the order in which the nodes appear and the number of operands that the operator at a node expects. The recovery of edges is similar to the evaluation, using a stack, of an expression in postfix notation. See Section 2.8 for more details and the relationship between postfix notation and code for a stack machine.

Syntax trees for assignment statements are produced by the syntax-directed definition in Fig. 8.3; it is an extension of one in Section 5.2. Nonterminal S generates an assignment statement. The two binary operators + and * are examples of the full operator set in a typical language. Operator associativities and precedences are the usual ones, even though they have not been put into the grammar. This definition constructs the tree of Fig. 8.2(a) from the input a := b * - c + b * - c.

PRODUCTION	SEMANTIC RULE
$S \rightarrow$ **id** $:= E$	$S.nptr := mknode('\text{assign}', \ mkleaf(\textbf{id}, \textbf{id}.place), \ E.nptr)$
$E \rightarrow E_1 + E_2$	$E.nptr := mknode('\text{+}', \ E_1.nptr, \ E_2.nptr)$
$E \rightarrow E_1 * E_2$	$E.nptr := mknode('\text{*}', \ E_1.nptr, \ E_2.nptr)$
$E \rightarrow - E_1$	$E.nptr := mkunode('\text{uminus}', \ E_1.nptr)$
$E \rightarrow (\ E_1 \ )$	$E.nptr := E_1.nptr$
$E \rightarrow$ **id**	$E.nptr := mkleaf(\textbf{id}, \ \textbf{id}.place)$

Fig. 8.3. Syntax-directed definition to produce syntax trees for assignment statements.

This same syntax-directed definition will produce the dag in Fig. 8.2(b) if the functions *mkunode(op, child)* and *mknode(op, left, right)* return a pointer to an existing node whenever possible, instead of constructing new nodes. The token **id** has an attribute *place* that points to the symbol-table entry for the identifier. In Section 8.3, we show how a symbol-table entry can be found from an attribute **id**.*name*, representing the lexeme associated with that occurrence of **id**. If the lexical analyzer holds all lexemes in a single array of characters, then attribute *name* might be the index of the first character of the lexeme.

Two representations of the syntax tree in Fig. 8.2(a) appear in Fig. 8.4. Each node is represented as a record with a field for its operator and additional fields for pointers to its children. In Fig 8.4(b), nodes are allocated from an array of records and the index or position of the node serves as the pointer to the node. All the nodes in the syntax tree can be visited by following pointers, starting from the root at position 10.

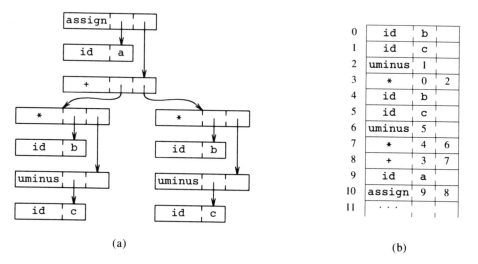

(a)   (b)

Fig. 8.4. Two representations of the syntax tree in Fig. 8.2(a).

Three-Address Code

Three-address code is a sequence of statements of the general form

    x := y *op* z

where x, y, and z are names, constants, or compiler-generated temporaries; *op* stands for any operator, such as a fixed- or floating-point arithmetic operator, or a logical operator on boolean-valued data. Note that no built-up arithmetic expressions are permitted, as there is only one operator on the right side of a statement. Thus a source language expression like x + y * z might be translated into a sequence

$$t_1 := y * z$$
$$t_2 := x + t_1$$

where t_1 and t_2 are compiler-generated temporary names. This unraveling of complicated arithmetic expressions and of nested flow-of-control statements makes three-address code desirable for target code generation and optimization. (See Chapters 10 and 12.) The use of names for the intermediate values computed by a program allows three-address code to be easily rearranged — unlike postfix notation.

Three-address code is a linearized representation of a syntax tree or a dag in which explicit names correspond to the interior nodes of the graph. The syntax tree and dag in Fig. 8.2 are represented by the three-address code sequences in Fig. 8.5. Variable names can appear directly in three-address statements, so Fig. 8.5(a) has no statements corresponding to the leaves in Fig. 8.4.

$t_1 := - c$	$t_1 := - c$
$t_2 := b * t_1$	$t_2 := b * t_1$
$t_3 := - c$	$t_5 := t_2 + t_2$
$t_4 := b * t_3$	$a := t_5$
$t_5 := t_2 + t_4$	
$a := t_5$	
(a) Code for the syntax tree.	(b) Code for the dag.

Fig. 8.5. Three-address code corresponding to the tree and dag in Fig. 8.2.

The reason for the term "three-address code" is that each statement usually contains three addresses, two for the operands and one for the result. In the implementations of three-address code given later in this section, a programmer-defined name is replaced by a pointer to a symbol-table entry for that name.

Types of Three-Address Statements

Three-address statements are akin to assembly code. Statements can have symbolic labels and there are statements for flow of control. A symbolic label represents the index of a three-address statement in the array holding intermediate code. Actual indices can be substituted for the labels either by making a separate pass, or by using "backpatching," discussed in Section 8.6.

Here are the common three-address statements used in the remainder of this book:

1. Assignment statements of the form $x := y$ *op* z, where *op* is a binary arithmetic or logical operation.

2. Assignment instructions of the form $x := op$ y, where *op* is a unary operation. Essential unary operations include unary minus, logical negation, shift operators, and conversion operators that, for example, convert a fixed-point number to a floating-point number.

3. *Copy statements* of the form $x := y$ where the value of y is assigned to x.

4. The unconditional jump goto L. The three-address statement with label L is the next to be executed.

5. Conditional jumps such as if x *relop* y goto L. This instruction applies a relational operator ($<$, $=$, $>=$, etc.) to x and y, and executes the statement with label L next if x stands in relation *relop* to y. If not, the three-address statement following if x *relop* y goto L is executed next, as in the usual sequence.

6. param x and call p, n for procedure calls and return y, where y representing a returned value is optional. Their typical use is as the sequence of three-address statements

         param x_1
         param x_2
           . . .
         param x_n
         call p, n

    generated as part of a call of the procedure $p(x_1, x_2, \ldots, x_n)$. The integer n indicating the number of actual parameters in "call p, n" is not redundant because calls can be nested. The implementation of procedure calls is outlined in Section 8.7.

7. Indexed assignments of the form $x := y[i]$ and $x[i] := y$. The first of these sets x to the value in the location i memory units beyond location y. The statement $x[i] := y$ sets the contents of the location i units beyond x to the value of y. In both these instructions, x, y, and i refer to data objects.

8. Address and pointer assignments of the form $x := \&y$, $x := *y$, and

*x := y. The first of these sets the value of x to be the location of y. Presumably y is a name, perhaps a temporary, that denotes an expression with an *l*-value such as A[i, j], and x is a pointer name or temporary. That is, the *r*-value of x is the *l*-value (location) of some object. In the statement x := *y, presumably y is a pointer or a temporary whose *r*-value is a location. The *r*-value of x is made equal to the contents of that location. Finally, *x := y sets the *r*-value of the object pointed to by x to the *r*-value of y.

The choice of allowable operators is an important issue in the design of an intermediate form. The operator set must clearly be rich enough to implement the operations in the source language. A small operator set is easier to implement on a new target machine. However, a restricted instruction set may force the front end to generate long sequences of statements for some source language operations. The optimizer and code generator may then have to work harder if good code is to be generated.

Syntax-Directed Translation into Three-Address Code

When three-address code is generated, temporary names are made up for the interior nodes of a syntax tree. The value of nonterminal E on the left side of $E \rightarrow E_1 + E_2$ will be computed into a new temporary t. In general, the three-address code for id := E consists of code to evaluate E into some temporary t, followed by the assignment id.*place* := t. If an expression is a single identifier, say y, then y itself holds the value of the expression. For the moment, we create a new name every time a temporary is needed; techniques for reusing temporaries are given in Section 8.3.

The S-attributed definition in Fig. 8.6 generates three-address code for assignment statements. Given input a := b * - c + b * - c, it produces the code in Fig. 8.5(a). The synthesized attribute $S.code$ represents the three-address code for the assignment S. The nonterminal E has two attributes:

1. $E.place$, the name that will hold the value of E, and
2. $E.code$, the sequence of three-address statements evaluating E.

The function *newtemp* returns a sequence of distinct names $t_1, t_2, \ldots$ in response to successive calls.

For convenience, we use the notation $gen(x \, ':=' \, y \, '+' \, z)$ in Fig. 8.6 to represent the three-address statement $x := y + z$. Expressions appearing instead of variables like x, y, and z are evaluated when passed to *gen*, and quoted operators or operands, like $'+'$, are taken literally. In practice, three-address statements might be sent to an output file, rather than built up into the *code* attributes.

Flow-of-control statements can be added to the language of assignments in Fig. 8.6 by productions and semantic rules like the ones for while statements in Fig. 8.7. In the figure, the code for $S \rightarrow$ **while** E **do** S_1 is generated using new attributes $S.begin$ and $S.after$ to mark the first statement in the code for E

PRODUCTION	SEMANTIC RULES
$S \to \textbf{id} := E$	$S.code := E.code \parallel gen(\textbf{id}.place \ ':=' \ E.place)$
$E \to E_1 + E_2$	$E.place := newtemp;$ $E.code := E_1.code \parallel E_2.code \parallel$ $\qquad\qquad gen(E.place \ ':=' \ E_1.place \ '+' \ E_2.place)$
$E \to E_1 * E_2$	$E.place := newtemp;$ $E.code := E_1.code \parallel E_2.code \parallel$ $\qquad\qquad gen(E.place \ ':=' \ E_1.place \ '*' \ E_2.place)$
$E \to -E_1$	$E.place := newtemp;$ $E.code := E_1.code \parallel gen(E.place \ ':=' \ 'uminus' \ E_1.place)$
$E \to (E_1)$	$E.place := E_1.place;$ $E.code := E_1.code$
$E \to \textbf{id}$	$E.place := \textbf{id}.place;$ $E.code := ''$

Fig. 8.6. Syntax-directed definition to produce three-address code for assignments.

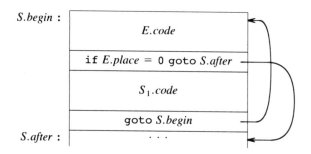

PRODUCTION	SEMANTIC RULES
$S \to \textbf{while } E \textbf{ do } S_1$	$S.begin := newlabel;$ $S.after := newlabel;$ $S.code := gen(S.begin \ ':') \parallel$ $\qquad\qquad E.code \parallel$ $\qquad\qquad gen('if' \ E.place \ '=' \ '0' \ 'goto' \ S.after) \parallel$ $\qquad\qquad S_1.code \parallel$ $\qquad\qquad gen('goto' \ S.begin) \parallel$ $\qquad\qquad gen(S.after \ ':')$

Fig. 8.7. Semantic rules generating code for a while statement.

and the statement following the code for S, respectively. These attributes represent labels created by a function *newlabel* that returns a new label every time it is called. Note that *S.after* becomes the label of the statement that comes after the code for the while statement. We assume that a non-zero expression represents true; that is, when the value of E becomes zero, control leaves the while statement.

Expressions that govern the flow of control may in general be boolean expressions containing relational and logical operators. The semantic rules for while statements in Section 8.6 differ from those in Fig. 8.7 to allow for flow of control within boolean expressions.

Postfix notation can be obtained by adapting the semantic rules in Fig. 8.6 (or see Fig. 2.5). The postfix notation for an identifier is the identifier itself. The rules for the other productions concatenate only the operator after the code for the operands. For example, associated with the production $E \rightarrow -E_1$ is the semantic rule

$E.code := E_1.code \parallel$ 'uminus'

In general, the intermediate form produced by the syntax-directed translations in this chapter can be changed by making similar modifications to the semantic rules.

Implementations of Three-Address Statements

A three-address statement is an abstract form of intermediate code. In a compiler, these statements can be implemented as records with fields for the operator and the operands. Three such representations are quadruples, triples, and indirect triples.

Quadruples

A quadruple is a record structure with four fields, which we call *op*, *arg*1, *arg*2, and *result*. The *op* field contains an internal code for the operator. The three-address statement x := y op z is represented by placing y in *arg*1, z in *arg*2, and x in *result*. Statements with unary operators like x := -y or x := y do not use *arg*2. Operators like param use neither *arg*2 nor *result*. Conditional and unconditional jumps put the target label in *result*. The quadruples in Fig. 8.8(a) are for the assignment a := b*-c + b*-c. They are obtained from the three-address code in Fig. 8.5(a).

The contents of fields *arg*1, *arg*2, and *result* are normally pointers to the symbol-table entries for the names represented by these fields. If so, temporary names must be entered into the symbol table as they are created.

Triples

To avoid entering temporary names into the symbol table, we might refer to a temporary value by the position of the statement that computes it. If we do

	op	arg 1	arg 2	result
(0)	uminus	c		t_1
(1)	*	b	t_1	t_2
(2)	uminus	c		t_3
(3)	*	b	t_3	t_4
(4)	+	t_2	t_4	t_5
(5)	:=	t_5		a

(a) Quadruples

	op	arg 1	arg 2
(0)	uminus	c	
(1)	*	b	(0)
(2)	uminus	c	
(3)	*	b	(2)
(4)	+	(1)	(3)
(5)	assign	a	(4)

(b) Triples

Fig. 8.8. Quadruple and triple representations of three-address statements.

so, three-address statements can be represented by records with only three fields: *op*, *arg*1 and *arg*2, as in Fig. 8.8(b). The fields *arg*1 and *arg*2, for the arguments of *op*, are either pointers to the symbol table (for programmer-defined names or constants) or pointers into the triple structure (for temporary values). Since three fields are used, this intermediate code format is known as triples.[1] Except for the treatment of programmer-defined names, triples correspond to the representation of a syntax tree or dag by an array of nodes, as in Fig. 8.4.

Parenthesized numbers represent pointers into the triple structure, while symbol-table pointers are represented by the names themselves. In practice, the information needed to interpret the different kinds of entries in the *arg*1 and *arg*2 fields can be encoded into the *op* field or some additional fields. The triples in Fig. 8.8(b) correspond to the quadruples in Fig. 8.8(a). Note that the copy statement a := t_5 is encoded in the triple representation by placing a in the *arg*1 field and using the operator assign.

A ternary operation like x[i] := y requires two entries in the triple structure, as shown in Fig. 8.9(a), while x := y[i] is naturally represented as two operations in Fig. 8.9(b).

	op	arg 1	arg 2
(0)	[ ]=	x	i
(1)	assign	(0)	y

(a) x[i] := y

	op	arg 1	arg 2
(0)	=[ ]	y	i
(1)	assign	x	(0)

(b) x := y[i]

Fig. 8.9. More triple representations.

---

[1] Some refer to triples as "two-address code," preferring to identify "quadruples" with the term "three-address code." We shall, however, treat "three-address code" as an abstract notion with various implementations, triples and quadruples being the principal ones.

Indirect Triples

Another implementation of three-address code that has been considered is that of listing pointers to triples, rather than listing the triples themselves. This implementation is naturally called indirect triples.

For example, let us use an array *statement* to list pointers to triples in the desired order. Then the triples in Fig. 8.8(b) might be represented as in Fig. 8.10.

	statement
(0)	(14)
(1)	(15)
(2)	(16)
(3)	(17)
(4)	(18)
(5)	(19)

	op	*arg* 1	*arg* 2
(14)	uminus	c	
(15)	*	b	(14)
(16)	uminus	c	
(17)	*	b	(16)
(18)	+	(15)	(17)
(19)	assign	a	(18)

Fig. 8.10. Indirect triples representation of three-address statements.

Comparison of Representations: The Use of Indirection

The difference between triples and quadruples may be regarded as a matter of how much indirection is present in the representation. When we ultimately produce target code, each name, temporary or programmer-defined, will be assigned some run-time memory location. This location will be placed in the symbol-table entry for the datum. Using the quadruple notation, a three-address statement defining or using a temporary can immediately access the location for that temporary via the symbol table.

A more important benefit of quadruples appears in an optimizing compiler, where statements are often moved around. Using the quadruple notation, the symbol table interposes an extra degree of indirection between the computation of a value and its use. If we move a statement computing x, the statements using x require no change. However, in the triples notation, moving a statement that defines a temporary value requires us to change all references to that statement in the *arg* 1 and *arg* 2 arrays. This problem makes triples difficult to use in an optimizing compiler.

Indirect triples present no such problem. A statement can be moved by reordering the *statement* list. Since pointers to temporary values refer to the *op-arg* 1-*arg* 2 array(s), which are not changed, none of those pointers need be changed. Thus, indirect triples look very much like quadruples as far as their utility is concerned. The two notations require about the same amount of space and they are equally efficient for reordering of code. As with ordinary triples, allocation of storage to those temporaries needing it must be deferred to the code generation phase. However, indirect triples can save some space compared with quadruples if the same temporary value is used more than once. The reason is that two or more entries in the *statement* array can point to the same line of the *op-arg* 1-*arg* 2 structure. For example, lines (14) and (16) of Fig. 8.10 could be combined and we could then combine (15) and (17).

8.2 DECLARATIONS

As the sequence of declarations in a procedure or block is examined, we can lay out storage for names local to the procedure. For each local name, we create a symbol-table entry with information like the type and the relative address of the storage for the name. The relative address consists of an offset from the base of the static data area or the field for local data in an activation record.

When the front end generates addresses, it may have a target machine in mind. Suppose that addresses of consecutive integers differ by 4 on a byte-addressable machine. The address calculations generated by the front end may therefore include multiplications by 4. The instruction set of the target machine may also favor certain layouts of data objects, and hence their addresses. We ignore alignment of data objects here; Example 7.3 shows how data objects are aligned by two compilers.

Declarations in a Procedure

The syntax of languages such as C, Pascal, and Fortran, allows all the declarations in a single procedure to be processed as a group. In this case, a global variable, say *offset*, can keep track of the next available relative address.

In the translation scheme of Fig. 8.11 nonterminal P generates a sequence of declarations of the form **id** : T. Before the first declaration is considered, *offset* is set to 0. As each new name is seen, that name is entered in the symbol table with offset equal to the current value of *offset*, and *offset* is incremented by the width of the data object denoted by that name.

The procedure *enter*(*name*, *type*, *offset*) creates a symbol-table entry for *name*, gives it type *type* and relative address *offset* in its data area. We use synthesized attributes *type* and *width* for nonterminal T to indicate the type and width, or number of memory units taken by objects of that type. Attribute *type* represents a type expression constructed from the basic types *integer* and *real* by applying the type constructors *pointer* and *array*, as in Section 6.1. If type expressions are represented by graphs, then attribute *type* might be a pointer to the node representing a type expression.

In Fig. 8.11, integers have width 4 and reals have width 8. The width of an array is obtained by multiplying the width of each element by the number of elements in the array.[2] The width of each pointer is assumed to be 4. In

---

[2] For arrays whose lower bound is not 0, the calculation of addresses for array elements is simplified if the offset entered into the symbol table is adjusted as discussed in Section 8.3.

$P \rightarrow$ $\{ \; offset := 0 \; \}$
    D

$D \rightarrow D \; ; \; D$

$D \rightarrow \textbf{id} : T$ $\{ \; enter(\textbf{id}.name, \; T.type, \; offset);$
                              $offset := offset + T.width \; \}$

$T \rightarrow \textbf{integer}$ $\{ \; T.type := integer;$
                              $T.width := 4 \; \}$

$T \rightarrow \textbf{real}$ $\{ \; T.type := real;$
                              $T.width := 8 \; \}$

$T \rightarrow \textbf{array} \; [\; \textbf{num} \;] \; \textbf{of} \; T_1$ $\{ \; T.type := array(\textbf{num}.val, \; T_1.type);$
                              $T.width := \textbf{num}.val \times T_1.width \; \}$

$T \rightarrow \uparrow T_1$ $\{ \; T.type := pointer(T_1.type);$
                              $T.width := 4 \; \}$

Fig. 8.11. Computing the types and relative addresses of declared names.

Pascal and C, a pointer may be seen before we learn the type of the object pointed to (see the discussion of recursive types in Section 6.3). Storage allocation for such types is simpler if all pointers have the same width.

The initialization of *offset* in the translation scheme of Fig. 8.11 is more evident if the first production appears on one line as:

$$P \rightarrow \{ \; offset := 0 \; \} \; D \qquad\qquad (8.2)$$

Nonterminals generating ϵ, called marker nonterminals in Section 5.6, can be used to rewrite productions so that all actions appear at the ends of right sides. Using a marker nonterminal M, (8.2) can be restated as:

$P \rightarrow M \; D$
$M \rightarrow \epsilon \qquad \{ \; offset := 0 \; \}$

Keeping Track of Scope Information

In a language with nested procedures, names local to each procedure can be assigned relative addresses using the approach of Fig. 8.11. When a nested procedure is seen, processing of declarations in the enclosing procedure is temporarily suspended. This approach will be illustrated by adding semantic rules to the following language.

$P \rightarrow D$
$D \rightarrow D \; ; \; D \; \mid \; \textbf{id} : T \; \mid \; \textbf{proc id} \; ; \; D \; ; \; S$ $\qquad\qquad (8.3)$

The productions for nonterminals S for statements and T for types are not shown because we focus on declarations. The nonterminal T has synthesized attributes *type* and *width*, as in the translation scheme of Fig. 8.11.

For simplicity, suppose that there is a separate symbol table for each procedure in the language (8.3). One possible implementation of a symbol table is a linked list of entries for names. Clever implementations can be substituted if desired.

A new symbol table is created when a procedure declaration $D \rightarrow$ **proc id** D_1 ; S is seen, and entries for the declarations in D_1 are created in the new table. The new table points back to the symbol table of the enclosing procedure; the name represented by **id** itself is local to the enclosing procedure. The only change from the treatment of variable declarations in Fig. 8.11 is that the procedure *enter* is told which symbol table to make an entry in.

For example, symbol tables for five procedures are shown in Fig. 8.12. The nesting structure of the procedures can be deduced from the links between the symbol tables; the program is in Fig. 7.22. The symbol tables for procedures `readarray`, `exchange`, and `quicksort` point back to that for the containing procedure `sort`, consisting of the entire program. Since `partition` is declared within `quicksort`, its table points to that of `quicksort`.

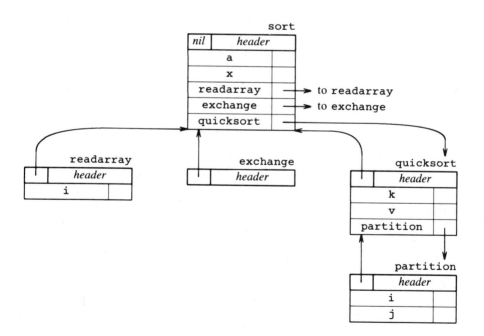

Fig. 8.12. Symbol tables for nested procedures.

The semantic rules are defined in terms of the following operations:

1. *mktable* (*previous*) creates a new symbol table and returns a pointer to the
    new table. The argument *previous* points to a previously created symbol
    table, presumably that for the enclosing procedure. The pointer *previous*
    is placed in a header for the new symbol table, along with additional
    information such as the nesting depth of a procedure. We can also
    number the procedures in the order they are declared and keep this
    number in the header.

2. *enter* (*table, name, type, offset*) creates a new entry for name *name* in the
    symbol table pointed to by *table*. Again, *enter* places type *type* and rela-
    tive address *offset* in fields within the entry.

3. *addwidth* (*table, width*) records the cumulative width of all the entries in
    table in the header associated with this symbol table.

4. *enterproc* (*table, name, newtable*) creates a new entry for procedure *name*
    in the symbol table pointed to by *table*. The argument *newtable* points to
    the symbol table for this procedure *name*.

The translation scheme in Fig. 8.13 shows how data can be laid out in one
pass, using a stack *tblptr* to hold pointers to symbol tables of the enclosing
procedures. With the symbol tables of Fig. 8.12, *tblptr* will contain pointers
to the tables for sort, quicksort, and partition when the declarations
in partition are considered. The pointer to the current symbol table is on
top. The other stack *offset* is the natural generalization to nested procedures
of attribute *offset* in Fig. 8.11. The top element of *offset* is the next available
relative address for a local of the current procedure.

All semantic actions in the subtrees for B and C in

$$A \rightarrow B\,C \ \{ \ action_A \ \}$$

are done before $action_A$ at the end of the production occurs. Hence, the
action associated with the marker M in Fig. 8.13 is the first to be done.

The action for nonterminal M initializes stack *tblptr* with a symbol table for
the outermost scope, created by operation *mktable* (*nil*). The action also
pushes relative address 0 onto stack *offset*. The nonterminal N plays a similar
role when a procedure declaration appears. Its action uses the operation
mktable (*top* (*tblptr*)) to create a new symbol table. Here, the argument
top (*tblptr*) gives the enclosing scope of the new table. A pointer to the new
table is pushed above that for the enclosing scope. Again, 0 is pushed onto
offset.

For each variable declaration **id** : T, an entry is created for **id** in the current
symbol table. This declaration leaves the stack *tblptr* unchanged; the top of
stack *offset* is incremented by $T.width$. When the action on the right side of
$D \rightarrow$ **proc id**; $N\,D_1$; S occurs, the width of all declarations generated by D_1
is on top of stack *offset*; it is recorded using *addwidth*. Stacks *tblptr* and *offset*

$P \rightarrow M D$ { $addwidth(top(tblptr), top(offset))$;
                                          $pop(tblptr)$; $pop(offset)$ }

$M \rightarrow \epsilon$ { $t := mktable(nil)$;
                                          $push(t, tblptr)$; $push(0, offset)$ }

$D \rightarrow D_1 ; D_2$

$D \rightarrow$ **proc id** ; $N D_1$; S { $t := top(tblptr)$;
                                        $addwidth(t, top(offset))$;
                                        $pop(tblptr)$; $pop(offset)$;
                                        $enterproc(top(tblptr), \mathbf{id}.name, t)$ }

$D \rightarrow$ **id** : T { $enter(top(tblptr), \mathbf{id}.name, T.type, top(offset))$;
                                        $top(offset) := top(offset) + T.width$ }

$N \rightarrow \epsilon$ { $t := mktable(top(tblptr))$;
                                          $push(t, tblptr)$; $push(0, offset)$ }

Fig. 8.13. Processing declarations in nested procedures.

are then popped, and we revert to examining the declarations in the enclosing procedure. At this point, the name of the enclosed procedure is entered into the symbol table of its enclosing procedure.

Field Names in Records

The following production allows nonterminal T to generate records in addition to basic types, pointers, and arrays:

$T \rightarrow$ **record** D **end**

The actions in the translation scheme of Fig. 8.14 emphasize the similarity between the layout of records as a language construct and activation records. Since procedure definitions do not affect the width computations in Fig. 8.13, we overlook the fact that the above production also allows procedure definitions to appear within records.

$T \rightarrow$ **record** L D **end**   { $T.type := record(top(tblptr))$;
                                        $T.width := top(offset)$;
                                        $pop(tblptr)$; $pop(offset)$ }

$L \rightarrow \epsilon$ { $t := mktable(nil)$;
                                        $push(t, tblptr)$; $push(0, offset)$ }

Fig. 8.14. Setting up a symbol table for field names in a record.

After the keyword **record** is seen, the action associated with the marker L

creates a new symbol table for the field names. A pointer to this symbol table is pushed onto stack *tblptr* and relative address 0 is pushed onto stack *offset*. The action for $D \rightarrow$ **id** : T in Fig. 8.13 therefore enters information about the field name **id** into the symbol table for the record. Furthermore, the top of stack *offset* will hold the width of all the data objects within the record after the fields have been examined. The action following **end** in Fig. 8.14 returns this width as synthesized attribute *T.width*. The type *T.type* is obtained by applying the constructor *record* to the pointer to the symbol table for this record. This pointer will be used in the next section to recover the names, types, and widths of the fields in the record from *T.type*.

8.3 ASSIGNMENT STATEMENTS

Expressions can be of type integer, real, array, and record in this section. As part of the translation of assignments into three-address code, we show how names can be looked up in the symbol table and how elements of arrays and records can be accessed.

Names in the Symbol Table

In Section 8.1, we formed three-address statements using names themselves, with the understanding that the names stood for pointers to their symbol-table entries. The translation scheme in Fig. 8.15 shows how such symbol-table entries can be found. The lexeme for the name represented by **id** is given by attribute **id**.*name*. Operation *lookup* (**id**.*name*) checks if there is an entry for this occurrence of the name in the symbol table. If so, a pointer to the entry is returned; otherwise, *lookup* returns *nil* to indicate that no entry was found.

The semantic actions in Fig. 8.15 use procedure *emit* to emit three-address statements to an output file, rather than building up *code* attributes for nonterminals, as in Fig. 8.6. From Section 2.3, translation can be done by emitting to an output file if the *code* attributes of the nonterminals on the left sides of productions are formed by concatenating the *code* attributes of the nonterminals on the right, in the same order that the nonterminals appear on the right side, perhaps with some additional strings in between.

By reinterpreting the *lookup* operation in Fig. 8.15, the translation scheme can be used even if the most closely nested scope rule applies to nonlocal names, as in Pascal. For concreteness, suppose that the context in which an assignment appears is given by the following grammar.

$$P \rightarrow M D$$
$$M \rightarrow \epsilon$$
$$D \rightarrow D \; ; \; D \; \mid \; \textbf{id} : T \; \mid \; \textbf{proc id} \; ; \; N D \; ; \; S$$
$$N \rightarrow \epsilon$$

Nonterminal P becomes the new start symbol when these productions are

$$S \rightarrow \textbf{id} := E \qquad \{ \; p := lookup\,(\textbf{id}.name); $$
$$\textbf{if } p \neq nil \textbf{ then}$$
$$emit\,(p \;':=' E.place)$$
$$\textbf{else } error \;\}$$

$$E \rightarrow E_1 + E_2 \qquad \{ \; E.place := newtemp; $$
$$emit\,(E.place \;':=' E_1.place \;'+' E_2.place) \;\}$$

$$E \rightarrow E_1 * E_2 \qquad \{ \; E.place := newtemp; $$
$$emit\,(E.place \;':=' E_1.place \;'*' E_2.place) \;\}$$

$$E \rightarrow - E_1 \qquad \{ \; E.place := newtemp; $$
$$emit\,(E.place \;':=' 'uminus' E_1.place) \;\}$$

$$E \rightarrow (\; E_1 \;) \qquad \{ \; E.place := E_1.place \;\}$$

$$E \rightarrow \textbf{id} \qquad \{ \; p := lookup\,(\textbf{id}.name); $$
$$\textbf{if } p \neq nil \textbf{ then}$$
$$E.place := p$$
$$\textbf{else } error \;\}$$

Fig. 8.15. Translation scheme to produce three-address code for assignments.

added to those in Fig. 8.15.

For each procedure generated by this grammar, the translation scheme in Fig. 8.13 sets up a separate symbol table. Each such symbol table has a header containing a pointer to the table for the enclosing procedure. (See Fig. 8.12 for an example.) When the statement forming a procedure body is examined, a pointer to the symbol table for the procedure appears on top of the stack *tblptr*. This pointer is pushed onto the stack by actions associated with the marker nonterminal N on the right side of $D \rightarrow \textbf{proc id} \; ; \; N D_1 \; ; \; S$.

Let the productions for nonterminal S be those in Fig. 8.15. Names in an assignment generated by S must have been declared in either the procedure that S appears in, or in some enclosing procedure. When applied to *name*, the modified *lookup* operation first checks if *name* appears in the current symbol table, accessible through *top(tblptr)*. If not, *lookup* uses the pointer in the header of a table to find the symbol table for the enclosing procedure and looks for the name there. If the name cannot be found in any of these scopes, then *lookup* returns *nil*.

For example, suppose that the symbol tables are as in Fig. 8.12 and that an assignment in the body of procedure `partition` is being examined. Operation *lookup*(i) will find an entry in the symbol table for `partition`. Since `v` is not in this symbol table, *lookup*(v) will use the pointer in the header in this symbol table to continue the search in the symbol table for the enclosing procedure `quicksort`.

Reusing Temporary Names

We have been going along assuming that *newtemp* generates a new temporary name each time a temporary is needed. It is useful, especially in optimizing compilers, to actually create a distinct name each time *newtemp* is called; Chapter 10 gives justification for doing so. However, the temporaries used to hold intermediate values in expression calculations tend to clutter up the symbol table, and space has to be allocated to hold their values.

Temporaries can be reused by changing *newtemp*. An alternative approach of packing distinct temporaries into the same location during code generation is explored in the next chapter.

The bulk of temporaries denoting data are generated during the syntax-directed translation of expressions, by rules such as those in Fig. 8.15. The code generated by the rules for $E \rightarrow E_1 + E_2$ has the general form:

evaluate E_1 into t_1
evaluate E_2 into t_2
$t := t_1 + t_2$

From the rules for the synthesized attribute *E.place* it follows that t_1 and t_2 are not used elsewhere in the program. The lifetimes of these temporaries are nested like matching pairs of balanced parentheses. In fact, the lifetimes of all temporaries used in the evaluation of E_2 are contained in the lifetime of t_1. It is therefore possible to modify *newtemp* so that it uses, as if it were a stack, a small array in a procedure's data area to hold temporaries.

Let us assume for simplicity that we are dealing only with integers. Keep a count c, initialized to zero. Whenever a temporary name is used as an operand, decrement c by 1. Whenever a new temporary name is generated, use $c and increase c by 1. Note that the "stack" of temporaries is not pushed or popped at run time, although it happens that stores and loads of temporary values are made by the compiler to occur at the "top."

Example 8.1. Consider the assignment

    x:= a * b + c * d - e * f

Figure 8.16 shows the sequence of three-address statements that would be generated by semantic rules in Fig. 8.15, if *newtemp* were modified. The figure also contains an indication of the "current" value of c after the generation of each statement. Note that when we compute $0 - $1, c is decremented to zero, so $0 is again available to hold the result.   □

Temporaries that may be assigned and/or used more than once, for example, in a conditional assignment, cannot be assigned names in the last-in first-out manner described above. Since they tend to be rare, all such temporary values can be assigned names of their own. The same problem of temporaries defined or used more than once occurs when we perform code optimization such as combining common subexpressions or moving a computation out of a loop (see Chapter 10). A reasonable strategy is to create a new name

STATEMENT	VALUE OF c
	0
$0 := a * b	1
$1 := c * d	2
$0 := $0 + $1	1
$1 := e * f	2
$0 := $0 - $1	1
x := $0	0

Fig. 8.16. Three-address code with stacked temporaries.

whenever we create an additional definition or use for a temporary or move its computation.

Addressing Array Elements

Elements of an array can be accessed quickly if the elements are stored in a block of consecutive locations. If the width of each array element is w, then the ith element of array A begins in location

$$base + (i - low) \times w \qquad\qquad (8.4)$$

where low is the lower bound on the subscript and $base$ is the relative address of the storage allocated for the array. That is, $base$ is the relative address of A[low].

The expression (8.4) can be partially evaluated at compile time if it is rewritten as

$$i \times w + (base - low \times w)$$

The subexpression $c = base - low \times w$ can be evaluated when the declaration of the array is seen. We assume that c is saved in the symbol table entry for A, so the relative address of A[i] is obtained by simply adding $i \times w$ to c.

Compile-time precalculation can also be applied to address calculations of elements of multi-dimensional arrays. A two-dimensional array is normally stored in one of two forms, either *row-major* (row-by-row) or *column-major* (column-by-column). Figure 8.17 shows the layout of a 2×3 array A in (a) row-major form and (b) column-major form. Fortran uses column-major form; Pascal uses row-major form, because A[i,j] is equivalent to A[i][j], and the elements of each array A[i] are stored consecutively.

In the case of a two-dimensional array stored in row-major form, the relative address of A[i_1, i_2] can be calculated by the formula

$$base + ((i_1 - low_1) \times n_2 + i_2 - low_2) \times w$$

where low_1 and low_2 are the lower bounds on the values of i_1 and i_2 and n_2 is the number of values that i_2 can take. That is, if $high_2$ is the upper bound

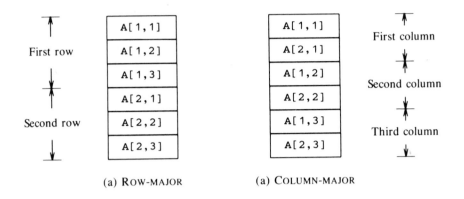

First row	A[1,1]
	A[1,2]
	A[1,3]
Second row	A[2,1]
	A[2,2]
	A[2,3]

(a) ROW-MAJOR

A[1,1]	First column
A[2,1]	
A[1,2]	Second column
A[2,2]	
A[1,3]	Third column
A[2,3]	

(a) COLUMN-MAJOR

Fig. 8.17. Layouts for a two-dimensional array.

on the value of i_2, then $n_2 = high_2 - low_2 + 1$. Assuming that i_1 and i_2 are the only values that are not known at compile time, we can rewrite the above expression as

$$((i_1 \times n_2) + i_2) \times w + (base - ((low_1 \times n_2) + low_2) \times w) \qquad (8.5)$$

The last term in this expression can be determined at compile time.

We can generalize row- or column-major form to many dimensions. The generalization of row-major form is to store the elements in such a way that, as we scan down a block of storage, the rightmost subscripts appear to vary fastest, like the numbers on an odometer. The expression (8.5) generalizes to the following expression for the relative address of $A[i_1, i_2, \ldots, i_k]$

$$((\cdots ((i_1 n_2 + i_2)n_3 + i_3) \cdots)n_k + i_k) \times w \qquad (8.6)$$
$$+ \, base - ((\cdots ((low_1 n_2 + low_2)n_3 + low_3) \cdots)n_k + low_k) \times w$$

Since for all j, $n_j = high_j - low_j + 1$ is assumed fixed, the term on the second line of (8.6) can be computed by the compiler and saved with the symbol-table entry for A.[3] Column-major form generalizes to the opposite arrangement, with the leftmost subscripts varying fastest.

Some languages permit the sizes of arrays to be specified dynamically, when a procedure is called at run-time. The allocation of such arrays on a run-time stack was considered in Section 7.3. The formulas for accessing the elements of such arrays are the same as for fixed-size arrays, but the upper and lower limits are not known at compile time.

---

[3] In C, a multi-dimensional array is simulated by defining arrays whose elements are arrays. For example, suppose x is an array of arrays of integers. Then, the language allows both $x[i]$ and $x[i][j]$ to be written, and the widths of these expressions are different. However, the lower bound of all arrays is 0, so the term on the second line of (8.6) simplifies to *base* in each case.

The chief problem in generating code for array references is to relate the computation of (8.6) to a grammar for array references. Array references can be permitted in assignments if nonterminal L with the following productions is allowed where **id** appears in Fig. 8.15:

$$L \rightarrow \textbf{id} \ [\ Elist \ ] \ | \ \textbf{id}$$
$$Elist \rightarrow Elist \ , \ E \ | \ E$$

In order that the various dimensional limits n_j of the array be available as we group index expressions into an $Elist$, it is useful to rewrite the productions as

$$L \rightarrow Elist \ ] \ | \ \textbf{id}$$
$$Elist \rightarrow Elist \ , \ E \ | \ \textbf{id} \ [\ E$$

That is, the array name is attached to the leftmost index expression rather than being joined to $Elist$ when an L is formed. These productions allow a pointer to the symbol-table entry for the array name to be passed as a synthesized attribute $array$ of $Elist$.[4]

We also use $Elist.ndim$ to record the number of dimensions (index expressions) in the $Elist$. The function $limit(array, j)$ returns n_j, the number of elements along the jth dimension of the array whose symbol-table entry is pointed to by $array$. Finally, $Elist.place$ denotes the temporary holding a value computed from index expressions in $Elist$.

An $Elist$ that produces the first m indices of a k-dimensional array reference $A[i_1, i_2, \ldots, i_k]$ will generate three-address code to compute

$$(\ \cdots \ ((i_1 n_2 + i_2)n_3 + i_3) \ \cdots \ )n_m + i_m \tag{8.7}$$

using the recurrence

$$\begin{aligned} e_1 &= i_1 \\ e_m &= e_{m-1} \times n_m + i_m \end{aligned} \tag{8.8}$$

Thus, when $m = k$, a multiplication by the width w is all that will be needed to compute the term on the first line of (8.6). Note that the i_j's here may really be values of expressions, and code to evaluate those expressions will be interspersed with code to compute (8.7).

An l-value L will have two attributes, $L.place$ and $L.offset$. In the case that L is a simple name, $L.place$ will be a pointer to the symbol-table entry for that name, and $L.offset$ will be **null**, indicating that the l-value is a simple name rather than an array reference. The nonterminal E has the same translation $E.place$, with the same meaning as in Fig 8.15.

---

[4] The transformation is similar to one mentioned at the end of Section 5.6 for eliminating inherited attributes. Here too, we could have solved the problem with inherited attributes.

The Translation Scheme for Addressing Array Elements

Semantic actions will be added to the grammar:

$$(1) \qquad S \rightarrow L := E$$
$$(2) \qquad E \rightarrow E + E$$
$$(3) \qquad E \rightarrow (E)$$
$$(4) \qquad E \rightarrow L$$
$$(5) \qquad L \rightarrow Elist\ ]$$
$$(6) \qquad L \rightarrow \mathbf{id}$$
$$(7) \quad Elist \rightarrow Elist\ ,\ E$$
$$(8) \quad Elist \rightarrow \mathbf{id}\ [\ E$$

As in the case of expressions without array references, the three-address code itself is produced by the *emit* procedure invoked in the semantic actions.

We generate a normal assignment if L is a simple name, and an indexed assignment into the location denoted by L otherwise:

(1) $S \rightarrow L := E$ { **if** $L.offset =$ **null then** /∗ L is a simple **id** ∗/
                          $emit(L.place\ ':='\ E.place)$;
          else
               $emit(L.place'['L.offset']'\ ':='\ E.place)$ }

The code for arithmetic expressions is exactly the same as in Fig. 8.15:

(2) $E \rightarrow E_1 + E_2$ { $E.place :=$ *newtemp*;
                     $emit(E.place\ ':='\ E_1.place\ '+'\ E_2.place)$ }

(3) $E \rightarrow (E_1)$ { $E.place := E_1.place$ }

When an array reference L is reduced to E, we want the *r*-value of L. Therefore we use indexing to obtain the contents of the location $L.place\,[L.offset\,]$:

(4) $E \rightarrow L$ { **if** $L.offset =$ **null then** /∗ L is a simple **id** ∗/
                          $E.place := L.place$
          else begin
               $E.place :=$ *newtemp*;
               $emit(E.place\ ':='\ L.place'['L.offset']')$
          end }

Below, $L.offset$ is a new temporary representing the first term of (8.6); function $width(Elist.array)$ returns w in (8.6). $L.place$ represents the second term of (8.6), returned by the function $c(Elist.array)$.

(5) $L \rightarrow Elist\ ]$ { $L.place :=$ *newtemp*;
                     $L.offset :=$ *newtemp*;
                     $emit(L.place\ ':='\ c(Elist.array))$;
                     $emit(L.offset\ ':='\ Elist.place\ '∗'\ width(Elist.array))$ }

A null offset indicates a simple name.

(6) $L \rightarrow$ **id**   { $L.place$:= **id**.$place$;
                                                       $L.offset$:= **null** }

When the next index expression is seen, we apply the recurrence (8.8). In the following action, $Elist_1.place$ corresponds to e_{m-1} in (8.8) and $Elist.place$ to e_m. Note that if $Elist_1$ has $m-1$ components, then $Elist$ on the left side of the production has m components.

(7) $Elist \rightarrow Elist_1$, E { $t := newtemp$;
                                               $m := Elist_1.ndim + 1$;
                                               $emit(t' := ' Elist_1.place '*' limit(Elist_1.array, m))$;
                                               $emit(t' := ' t '+' E.place)$;
                                               $Elist.array := Elist_1.array$;
                                               $Elist.place := t$;
                                               $Elist.ndim := m$ }

$E.place$ holds both the value of the expression E and the value of (8.7) for $m = 1$.

(8) $Elist \rightarrow$ **id** [E { $Elist.array :=$ **id**.$place$;
                                               $Elist.place := E.place$;
                                               $Elist.ndim := 1$ }

Example 8.2. Let A be a 10×20 array with $low_1 = low_2 = 1$. Therefore, $n_1 = 10$ and $n_2 = 20$. Take w to be 4. An annotated parse tree for the assignment x := A[y,z] is shown in Fig. 8.18. The assignment is translated into the following sequence of three-address statements:

```
t₁ := y * 20
t₁ := t₁ + z
t₂ := c           /* constant c = baseₐ - 84 */
t₃ := 4 * t₁
t₄ := t₂[t₃]
x := t₄
```

For each variable, we have used its name in place of **id**.$place$.   □

Type Conversions within Assignments

In practice, there would be many different types of variables and constants, so the compiler must either reject certain mixed-type operations or generate appropriate coercion (type conversion) instructions.

Consider the grammar for assignment statements as above, but suppose there are two types — real and integer, with integers converted to reals when

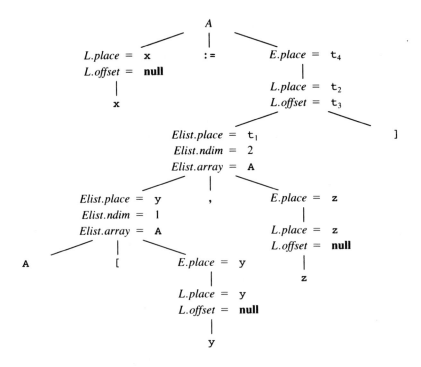

Fig. 8.18. Annotated parse tree for x := A[y, z].

necessary. We introduce another attribute *E.type*, whose value is either *real* or *integer*. The semantic rule for *E.type* associated with the production $E \rightarrow E + E$ is:

$E \rightarrow E + E$ { *E.type* :=
            if $E_1.type = integer$ **and**
                 $E_2.type = integer$ **then** *integer*
      else *real* }

This rule is in the spirit of Section 6.4; however, here and elsewhere in this chapter, we omit the checks for type errors; a discussion of type checking appears in Chapter 6.

The entire semantic rule for $E \rightarrow E + E$ and most of the other productions must be modified to generate, when necessary, three-address statements of the form x := inttoreal y, whose effect is to convert integer y to a real of equal value, called x. We must also include with the operator code an indication of whether fixed- or floating-point arithmetic is intended. The complete semantic action for a production of the form $E \rightarrow E_1 + E_2$ is listed in Fig. 8.19.

```
E.place := newtemp;
if E₁.type = integer and E₂.type = integer then begin
    emit(E.place ':=' E₁.place 'int +' E₂.place);
    E.type := integer
end
else if E₁.type = real and E₂.type = real then begin
    emit(E.place ':=' E₁.place 'real +' E₂.place);
    E.type := real
end
else if E₁.type = integer and E₂.type = real then begin
    u := newtemp;
    emit(u ':=' 'inttoreal' E₁.place);
    emit(E.place ':=' u 'real +' E₂.place);
    E.type := real
end
else if E₁.type = real and E₂.type = integer then begin
    u := newtemp;
    emit(u ':=' 'inttoreal' E₂.place);
    emit(E.place ':=' E₁.place 'real +' u);
    E.type := real
end
else
    E.type := type_error;
```

Fig. 8.19. Semantic action for $E \rightarrow E_1 + E_2$.

For example, for the input

```
x := y + i * j
```

assuming x and y have type *real*, and i and j have type *integer*, the output would look like

```
t₁ := i int* j
t₃ := inttoreal t₁
t₂ := y real+ t₃
x := t₂
```

The semantic action of Fig. 8.19 uses two attributes $E.place$ and $E.type$ for the nonterminal E. As the number of types subject to conversion increases, the number of cases that arise increases quadratically (or worse, if there are operators with more than two arguments). Therefore with large numbers of types, careful organization of the semantic actions becomes more important.

Accessing Fields in Records

The compiler must keep track of both the types and relative addresses of the
fields of a record. An advantage of keeping this information in symbol-table
entries for the field names is that the routine for looking up names in the symbol table can also be used for field names. With this in mind, a separate symbol table was created for each record type by the semantic actions in Fig. 8.14
in the last section. If t is a pointer to the symbol table for a record type, then
the type $record(t)$ formed by applying the constructor $record$ to the pointer
was returned as $T.type$.

We use the expression

```
p↑.info + 1
```

to illustrate how a pointer to the symbol table can be extracted from an attribute $E.type$. From the operations in this expression it follows that p must be a
pointer to a record with a field name info whose type is arithmetic. If types
are constructed as in Fig. 8.13 and 8.14, the type of p must be given by a type
expression

$pointer(record(t))$

The type of p↑ is then $record(t)$, from which t can be extracted. The field
name info is looked up in the symbol table pointed to by t.

8.4 BOOLEAN EXPRESSIONS

In programming languages, boolean expressions have two primary purposes.
They are used to compute logical values, but more often they are used as conditional expressions in statements that alter the flow of control, such as if-
then, if-then-else, or while-do statements.

Boolean expressions are composed of the boolean operators (**and**, **or**, and
not) applied to elements that are boolean variables or relational expressions.
In turn, relational expressions are of the form E_1 **relop** E_2, where E_1 and E_2
are arithmetic expressions. Some languages, such as PL/I, allow more general
expressions, where boolean, arithmetic, and relational operators can be
applied to expressions of any type whatever, with no distinction between
boolean and arithmetic values; a coercion is performed when necessary. In
this section, we consider boolean expressions generated by the following grammar:

$$E \rightarrow E \text{ or } E \mid E \text{ and } E \mid \text{not } E \mid (E) \mid \text{id relop id} \mid \text{true} \mid \text{false}$$

We use the attribute op to determine which of the comparison operators
$<$, $\leq$, $=$, $\neq$, $>$, or $\geq$ is represented by **relop**. As is customary, we assume
that **or** and **and** are left-associative, and that **or** has lowest precedence, then
and, then **not**.

Methods of Translating Boolean Expressions

There are two principal methods of representing the value of a boolean expression. The first method is to encode true and false numerically and to evaluate a boolean expression analogously to an arithmetic expression. Often 1 is used to denote true and 0 to denote false, although many other encodings are also possible. For example, we could let any nonzero quantity denote true and zero denote false, or we could let any nonnegative quantity denote true and any negative number denote false.

The second principal method of implementing boolean expressions is by flow of control, that is, representing the value of a boolean expression by a position reached in a program. This method is particularly convenient in implementing the boolean expressions in flow-of-control statements, such as the if-then and while-do statements. For example, given the expression $E_1 \text{ or } E_2$, if we determine that E_1 is true, then we can conclude that the entire expression is true without having to evaluate E_2.

The semantics of the programming language determines whether all parts of a boolean expression must be evaluated. If the language definition permits (or requires) portions of a boolean expression to go unevaluated, then the compiler can optimize the evaluation of boolean expressions by computing only enough of an expression to determine its value. Thus, in an expression such as $E_1 \text{ or } E_2$, neither E_1 nor E_2 is necessarily evaluated fully. If either E_1 or E_2 is an expression with side effects (e.g., contains a function that changes a global variable), then an unexpected answer may be obtained.

Neither of the above methods is uniformly superior to the other. For example, the BLISS/11 optimizing compiler (Wulf et al. 1975), among others, chooses the appropriate method for each expression individually. This section considers both methods for the translation of boolean expressions to three-address code.

Numerical Representation

Let us first consider the implementation of boolean expressions using 1 to denote true and 0 to denote false. Expressions will be evaluated completely, from left to right, in a manner similar to arithmetic expressions. For example, the translation for

```
a or b and not c
```

is the three-address sequence

```
t₁ := not c
t₂ := b and t₁
t₃ := a or t₂
```

A relational expression such as $a < b$ is equivalent to the conditional statement if $a < b$ then 1 else 0, which can be translated into the three-address code sequence (again, we arbitrarily start statement numbers at 100):

```
100:   if a < b goto 103
101:   t := 0
102:   goto 104
103:   t := 1
104:
```

A translation scheme for producing three-address code for boolean expressions is shown in Fig. 8.20. In this scheme, we assume that *emit* places three-address statements into an output file in the right format, that *nextstat* gives the index of the next three-address statement in the output sequence, and that *emit* increments *nextstat* after producing each three-address statement.

$E \rightarrow E_1$ **or** E_2 { *E.place* := *newtemp*;
                              emit(*E.place* ':=' E_1.*place* 'or' E_2.*place*) }

$E \rightarrow E_1$ **and** E_2 { *E.place* := *newtemp*;
                              emit(*E.place* ':=' E_1.*place* 'and' E_2.*place*) }

$E \rightarrow$ **not** E_1 { *E.place* := *newtemp*;
                              emit(*E.place* ':=' 'not' E_1.*place*) }

$E \rightarrow (E_1)$ { *E.place* := E_1.*place* }

$E \rightarrow$ **id**$_1$ **relop id**$_2$ { *E.place* := *newtemp*;
                              emit('if' **id**$_1$.*place* **relop**.*op* **id**$_2$.*place* 'goto' *nextstat* +3);
                              emit(*E.place* ':=' '0');
                              emit('**goto**' *nextstat* +2);
                              emit(*E.place* ':=' '1') }

$E \rightarrow$ **true**   { *E.place* := *newtemp*;
                              emit(*E.place* ':=' '1') }

$E \rightarrow$ **false**   { *E.place* := *newtemp*;
                              emit(*E.place* ':=' '0') }

Fig. 8.20. Translation scheme using a numerical representation for booleans.

Example 8.3. The scheme in Fig. 8.20 would generate the three-address code in Fig. 8.21 for the expression a < b or c < d and e < f.   □

Short-Circuit Code

We can also translate a boolean expression into three-address code without generating code for any of the boolean operators and without having the code necessarily evaluate the entire expression. This style of evaluation is sometimes called "short-circuit" or "jumping" code. It is possible to evaluate boolean expressions without generating code for the boolean operators **and**, **or**, and **not** if we represent the value of an expression by a position in the code sequence. For example, in Fig. 8.21, we can tell what value t_1 will

```
100:  if a < b goto 103        107:  t₂ := 1
101:  t₁ := 0                   108:  if e < f goto 111
102:  goto 104                  109:  t₃ := 0
103:  t₁ := 1                   110:  goto 112
104:  if c < d goto 107         111:  t₃ := 1
105:  t₂ := 0                   112:  t₄ := t₂ and t₃
106:  goto 108                  113:  t₅ := t₁ or t₄
```

Fig. 8.21. Translation of $a < b$ or $c < d$ and $e < f$.

have by whether we reach statement 101 or statement 103, so the value of t_1 is redundant. For many boolean expressions, it is possible to determine the value of the expression without having to evaluate it completely.

Flow-of-Control Statements

We now consider the translation of boolean expressions into three-address code in the context of if-then, if-then-else, and while-do statements such as those generated by the following grammar:

$$S \rightarrow \textbf{if } E \textbf{ then } S_1$$
$$| \quad \textbf{if } E \textbf{ then } S_1 \textbf{ else } S_2$$
$$| \quad \textbf{while } E \textbf{ do } S_1$$

In each of these productions, E is the boolean expression to be translated. In the translation, we assume that a three-address statement can be symbolically labeled, and that the function *newlabel* returns a new symbolic label each time it is called.

With a boolean expression E, we associate two labels: $E.true$, the label to which control flows if E is true, and $E.false$, the label to which control flows if E is false. The semantic rules for translating a flow-of-control statement S allow control to flow from the translation $S.code$ to the three-address instruction immediately following $S.code$. In some cases, the instruction immediately following $S.code$ is a jump to some label L. A jump to a jump to L from within $S.code$ is avoided using an inherited attribute $S.next$. The value of $S.next$ is a label that is attached to the first three-address instruction to be executed after the code for S.[5] The initialization of $S.next$ is not shown.

In translating the if-then statement $S \rightarrow \textbf{if } E \textbf{ then } S_1$, a new label $E.true$ is created and attached to the first three-address instruction generated for the statement S_1, as in Fig. 8.22(a). A syntax-directed definition appears in Fig. 8.23. The code for E generates a jump to $E.true$ if E is true and a jump to $S.next$ if E is false. We therefore set $E.false$ to $S.next$.

---

[5] If implemented literally, the approach of inheriting a label $S.next$ can lead to a proliferation of labels. The backpatching approach of Section 8.6 creates labels only when they are needed.

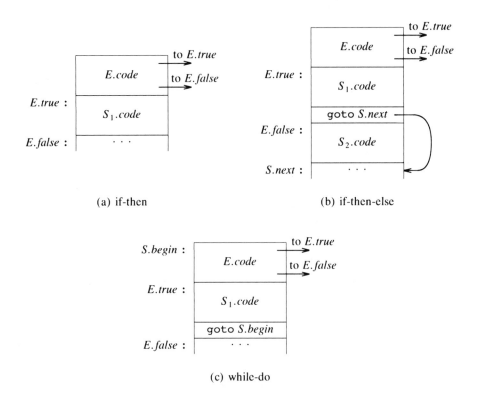

(a) if-then

(b) if-then-else

(c) while-do

Fig. 8.22. Code for if-then, if-then-else, and while-do statements.

In translating the if-then-else statement $S \rightarrow \textbf{if } E \textbf{ then } S_1 \textbf{ else } S_2$, the code for the boolean expression E has jumps out of it to the first instruction of the code for S_1 if E is true, and to the first instruction of the code for S_2 if E is false, as illustrated in Fig. 8.22(b). As with the if-then statement, an inherited attribute $S.next$ gives the label of the three-address instruction to be executed next after executing the code for S. An explicit goto $S.next$ appears after the code for S_1, but not after S_2. We leave it to the reader to show that, with these semantic rules, if $S.next$ is not the label of the instruction immediately following $S_2.code$, then an enclosing statement will supply the jump to label $S.next$ after the code for S_2.

The code for $S \rightarrow \textbf{while } E \textbf{ do } S_1$ is formed as shown in Fig. 8.22(c). A new label $S.begin$ is created and attached to the first instruction generated for E. Another new label $E.true$ is attached to the first instruction for S_1. The code for E generates a jump to this label if E is true, a jump to $S.next$ if E is false; again, we set $E.false$ to be $S.next$. After the code for S_1 we place the instruction goto $S.begin$, which causes a jump back to the beginning of the code for the boolean expression. Note that $S_1.next$ is set to this label $S.begin$, so jumps from within $S_1.code$ can go directly to $S.begin$.

PRODUCTION	SEMANTIC RULES
$S \rightarrow$ **if** E **then** S_1	$E.true := newlabel;$ $E.false := S.next;$ $S_1.next := S.next;$ $S.code := E.code \parallel$ $\qquad gen(E.true \; ':') \parallel S_1.code$
$S \rightarrow$ **if** E **then** S_1 **else** S_2	$E.true := newlabel;$ $E.false := newlabel;$ $S_1.next := S.next;$ $S_2.next := S.next;$ $S.code := E.code \parallel$ $\qquad gen(E.true \; ':') \parallel S_1.code \parallel$ $\qquad gen(\text{'goto'} \; S.next) \parallel$ $\qquad gen(E.false \; ':') \parallel S_2.code$
$S \rightarrow$ **while** E **do** S_1	$S.begin := newlabel;$ $E.true := newlabel;$ $E.false := S.next;$ $S_1.next := S.begin;$ $S.code := gen(S.begin \; ':') \parallel E.code \parallel$ $\qquad gen(E.true \; ':') \parallel S_1.code \parallel$ $\qquad gen(\text{'goto'} \; S.begin)$

Fig. 8.23. Syntax-directed definition for flow-of-control statements.

We discuss the translation of flow-of-control statements in more detail in Section 8.6 where an alternative method, called "backpatching," emits code for such statements in one pass.

Control-Flow Translation of Boolean Expressions

We now discuss $E.code$, the code produced for the boolean expressions E in Fig. 8.23. As we have indicated, E is translated into a sequence of three-address statements that evaluates E as a sequence of conditional and unconditional jumps to one of two locations: $E.true$, the place control is to reach if E is true, and $E.false$, the place control is to reach if E is false.

The basic idea behind the translation is the following. Suppose E is of the form a < b. Then the generated code is of the form

```
if a < b goto E.true
goto E.false
```

Suppose E is of the form E_1 **or** E_2. If E_1 is true, then we immediately know that E itself is true, so $E_1.true$ is the same as $E.true$. If E_1 is false, then

E_2 must be evaluated, so we make $E_1.false$ be the label of the first statement in the code for E_2. The true and false exits of E_2 can be made the same as the true and false exits of E, respectively.

Analogous considerations apply to the translation of E_1 **and** E_2. No code is needed for an expression E of the form **not** E_1: We just interchange the true and false exits of E_1 to get the true and false exits of E. A syntax-directed definition that generates three-address code for boolean expressions in this manner is shown in Fig. 8.24. Note that the *true* and *false* attributes are inherited.

PRODUCTION	SEMANTIC RULES
$E \rightarrow E_1$ **or** E_2	$E_1.true := E.true;$ $E_1.false := newlabel;$ $E_2.true := E.true;$ $E_2.false := E.false;$ $E.code := E_1.code \parallel gen(E_1.false':') \parallel E_2.code$
$E \rightarrow E_1$ **and** E_2	$E_1.true := newlabel;$ $E_1.false := E.false;$ $E_2.true := E.true;$ $E_2.false := E.false;$ $E.code := E_1.code \parallel gen(E_1.true':') \parallel E_2.code$
$E \rightarrow$ **not** E_1	$E_1.true := E.false;$ $E_1.false := E.true;$ $E.code := E_1.code$
$E \rightarrow (E_1)$	$E_1.true := E.true;$ $E_1.false := E.false;$ $E.code := E_1.code$
$E \rightarrow id_1$ **relop** id_2	$E.code := gen('if' \ id_1.place \ \textbf{relop}.op \ id_2.place \ 'goto' \ E.true) \parallel$ $gen('goto' \ E.false)$
$E \rightarrow$ **true**	$E.code := gen('goto' \ E.true)$
$E \rightarrow$ **false**	$E.code := gen('goto' \ E.false)$

Fig. 8.24. Syntax-directed definition to produce three-address code for booleans.

Example 8.4. Let us again consider the expression

```
a < b or c < d and e < f
```

Suppose the true and false exits for the entire expression have been set to Ltrue and Lfalse. Then using the definition in Fig. 8.24 we would obtain the following code:

```
        if a < b goto Ltrue
        goto L1
  L1:   if c < d goto L2
        goto Lfalse
  L2:   if e < f goto Ltrue
        goto Lfalse
```

Note that the code generated is not optimal, in that the second statement can be eliminated without changing the value of the code. Redundant instructions of this form can be subsequently removed by a simple peephole optimizer (see Chapter 9). Another approach that avoids generating these redundant jumps is to translate a relational expression of the form $id_1 < id_2$ into the statement if $id_1 \geq id_2$ goto E.*false* with the presumption that when the relation is true we fall through the code. □

Example 8.5. Consider the statement

```
while a < b do
    if c < d then
        x := y + z
    else
        x := y - z
```

The syntax-directed definition above, coupled with schemes for assignment statements and boolean expressions, would produce the following code:

```
  L1:   if a < b goto L2
        goto Lnext
  L2:   if c < d goto L3
        goto L4
  L3:   t₁ := y + z
        x := t₁
        goto L1
  L4:   t₂ := y - z
        x := t₂
        goto L1
  Lnext:
```

We note that the first two gotos can be eliminated by changing the directions of the tests. This type of local transformation can be done by peephole optimization discussed in Chapter 9. □

Mixed-Mode Boolean Expressions

It is important to realize that we have simplified the grammar for boolean expressions. In practice, boolean expressions often contain arithmetic subexpressions as in $(a+b) < c$. In languages where false has the numerical value 0 and true the value 1, $(a < b) + (b < a)$ can even be considered an arithmetic expression, with value 0 if a and b have the same value, and 1 otherwise.

The method of representing boolean expressions by jumping code can still be used, even if arithmetic expressions are represented by code to compute their value. For example, consider the representative grammar

$$E \rightarrow E + E \mid E \textbf{ and } E \mid E \textbf{ relop } E \mid \textbf{id}$$

We may suppose that $E + E$ produces an integer arithmetic result (the inclusion of real or other arithmetic types makes matters more complicated but adds nothing to the instructive value of this example), while expressions E **and** E and E **relop** E produce boolean values represented by flow of control. Expression E **and** E requires both arguments to be boolean, but the operations + and **relop** take either type of argument, including mixed ones. $E \rightarrow \textbf{id}$ is also deemed arithmetic, although we could extend this example by allowing boolean identifiers.

To generate code in this situation, we can use a synthesized attribute $E.type$, which will be either *arith* or *bool* depending on the type of E. E will have inherited attributes $E.true$ and $E.false$ for boolean expressions and synthesized attribute $E.place$ for arithmetic expressions. Part of the semantic rule for $E \rightarrow E_1 + E_2$ is shown in Fig. 8.25.

$E.type := arith$;
if $E_1.type = arith$ **and** $E_2.type = arith$ **then begin**
/∗ normal arithmetic add ∗/
$E.place := newtemp$;
$E.code := E_1.code \parallel E_2.code \parallel$
    $gen(E.place ':=' E_1.place '+' E_2.place)$
end
else if $E_1.type = arith$ **and** $E_2.type = bool$ **then begin**
$E.place := newtemp$;
$E_2.true := newlabel$;
$E_2.false := newlabel$;
$E.code := E_1.code \parallel E_2.code \parallel$
    $gen(E_2.true':' E.place ':=' E_1.place + 1) \parallel$
    $gen('goto' \; nextstat + 1) \parallel$
    $gen(E_2.false':' E.place ':=' E_1.place)$
else if · · ·

Fig. 8.25. Semantic rule for production $E \rightarrow E_1 + E_2$.

In the mixed-mode case, we generate the code for E_1, then E_2, followed by the three statements:

$E_2.true$: $E.place := E_1.place + 1$
        $goto \; nextstat + 1$
$E_2.false$: $E.place := E_1.place$

The first statement computes the value $E_1 + 1$ for E when E_2 is true, the third the value E_1 for E when E_2 is false. The second statement is a jump over the third. The semantic rules for the remaining cases and the other productions are quite similar, and we leave them as exercises.

8.5 CASE STATEMENTS

The "switch" or "case" statement is available in a variety of languages; even the Fortran computed and assigned goto's can be regarded as varieties of the switch statement. Our switch-statement syntax is shown in Fig. 8.26.

```
switch expression
      begin
            case value:    statement
            case value:    statement
                 . . .
            case value:    statement
            default:       statement
      end
```

Fig. 8.26. Switch-statement syntax.

There is a selector expression, which is to be evaluated, followed by n constant values that the expression might take, perhaps including a *default* "value," which always matches the expression if no other value does. The intended translation of a switch is code to:

1.   Evaluate the expression.

2.   Find which value in the list of cases is the same as the value of the expression. Recall that the default value matches the expression if none of the values explicitly mentioned in cases does.

3.   Execute the statement associated with the value found.

Step (2) is an n-way branch, which can be implemented in one of several ways. If the number of cases is not too great, say 10 at most, then it is reasonable to use a sequence of conditional goto's, each of which tests for an individual value and transfers to the code for the corresponding statement.

A more compact way to implement this sequence of conditional goto's is to create a table of pairs, each pair consisting of a value and a label for the code of the corresponding statement. Code is generated to place at the end of this table the value of the expression itself, paired with the label for the default statement. A simple loop can be generated by the compiler to compare the value of the expression with each value in the table, being assured that if no other match is found, the last (default) entry is sure to match.

If the number of values exceeds 10 or so, it is more efficient to construct a

hash table (see Section 7.6) for the values, with the labels of the various statements as entries. If no entry for the value possessed by the switch expression
is found, a jump to the default statement can be generated.

There is a common special case in which an even more efficient implementation of the n-way branch exists. If the values all lie in some small range,
say i_{min} to i_{max}, and the number of different values is a reasonable fraction of
$i_{max} - i_{min}$, then we can construct an array of labels, with the label of the
statement for value j in the entry of the table with offset $j - i_{min}$ and the label
for the default in entries not filled otherwise. To perform the switch, evaluate
the expression to obtain the value j, check that it is in the range i_{min} to i_{max}
and transfer indirectly to the table entry at offset $j - i_{min}$. For example, if the
expression is of type character, a table of, say, 128 entries (depending on the
character set) may be created and transferred through with no range testing.

Syntax-Directed Translation of Case Statements

Consider the following switch statement.

```
switch E
    begin
        case V₁:      S₁
        case V₂:      S₂
              . . .
        case Vₙ₋₁:    Sₙ₋₁
        default:      Sₙ
    end
```

With a syntax-directed translation scheme, it is convenient to translate this
case statement into intermediate code that has the form of Fig. 8.27.

The tests all appear at the end so that a simple code generator can recognize
the multiway branch and generate efficient code for it, using the most
appropriate implementation suggested at the beginning of this section. If we
generate the more straightforward sequence shown in Fig 8.28, the compiler
would have to do extensive analysis to find the most efficient implementation.
Note that it is inconvenient to place the branching statements at the beginning,
because the compiler could not then emit code for each of the S_i's as it saw
them.

To translate into the form of Fig. 8.27, when we see the keyword **switch**,
we generate two new labels test and next, and a new temporary t. Then
as we parse the expression E, we generate code to evaluate E into t. After
processing E, we generate the jump goto test.

Then as we see each **case** keyword, we create a new label L_i and enter it
into the symbol table. We place on a stack, used only to store cases, a pointer
to this symbol-table entry and the value V_i of the case constant. (If this
switch is embedded in one of the statements internal to another switch, we
place a marker on the stack to separate cases for the interior switch from
those for the outer switch.)

```
              code to evaluate E into t
              goto test
L₁:           code for S₁
              goto next
L₂:           code for S₂
              goto next
                  . . .
Lₙ₋₁:         code for Sₙ₋₁
              goto next
Lₙ:           code for Sₙ
              goto next
test:         if t = V₁ goto L₁
              if t = V₂ goto L₂
                  . . .
              if t = Vₙ₋₁ goto Lₙ₋₁
              goto Lₙ
next:
```

Fig. 8.27. Translation of a case statement.

```
              code to evaluate E into t
              if t ≠ V₁ goto L₁
              code for S₁
              goto next
L₁:           if t ≠ V₂ goto L₂
              code for S₂
              goto next
L₂:
                  . . .
Lₙ₋₂:         if t ≠ Vₙ₋₁ goto Lₙ₋₁
              code for Sₙ₋₁
              goto next
Lₙ₋₁:         code for Sₙ
next:
```

Fig. 8.28. Another translation of a case statement.

We process each statement **case** V_i: S_i by emitting the newly created label L_i, followed by the code for S_i, followed by the jump goto next. Then when the keyword **end** terminating the body of the switch is found, we are ready to generate the code for the n-way branch. Reading the pointer-value pairs on the case stack from the bottom to the top, we can generate a sequence of three-address statements of the form

```
case V₁ L₁
case V₂ L₂

    . . .

case Vₙ₋₁ Lₙ₋₁
case t Lₙ
label next
```

where t is the name holding the value of the selector expression E, and L_n is the label for the default statement. The case V_i L_i three-address statement is a synonym for if $t = V_i$ goto L_i in Fig. 8.27, but the case is easier for the final code generator to detect as a candidate for special treatment. At the code-generation phase, these sequences of case statements can be translated into an n-way branch of the most efficient type, depending on how many there are and whether the values fall into a small range.

8.6 BACKPATCHING

The easiest way to implement the syntax-directed definitions in Section 8.4 is to use two passes. First, construct a syntax tree for the input, and then walk the tree in depth-first order, computing the translations given in the definition. The main problem with generating code for boolean expressions and flow-of-control statements in a single pass is that during one single pass we may not know the labels that control must go to at the time the jump statements are generated. We can get around this problem by generating a series of branching statements with the targets of the jumps temporarily left unspecified. Each such statement will be put on a list of goto statements whose labels will be filled in when the proper label can be determined. We call this subsequent filling in of labels *backpatching*.

In this section, we show how backpatching can be used to generate code for boolean expressions and flow-of-control statements in one pass. The translations we generate will be of the same form as those in Section 8.4, except for the manner in which we generate labels. For specificity, we generate quadruples into a quadruple array. Labels will be indices into this array. To manipulate lists of labels, we use three functions:

1. *makelist*(i) creates a new list containing only i, an index into the array of quadruples; *makelist* returns a pointer to the list it has made.

2. *merge*(p_1, p_2) concatenates the lists pointed to by p_1 and p_2, and returns a pointer to the concatenated list.

3. *backpatch*(p, i) inserts i as the target label for each of the statements on the list pointed to by p.

Boolean Expressions

We now construct a translation scheme suitable for producing quadruples for boolean expressions during bottom-up parsing. We insert a marker nonterminal M into the grammar to cause a semantic action to pick up, at appropriate times, the index of the next quadruple to be generated. The grammar we use is the following:

(1) $E \rightarrow E_1$ **or** $M\ E_2$
(2) | E_1 **and** $M\ E_2$
(3) | **not** E_1
(4) | $(\ E_1\ )$
(5) | id_1 **relop** id_2
(6) | **true**
(7) | **false**
(8) $M \rightarrow \epsilon$

Synthesized attributes *truelist* and *falselist* of nonterminal E are used to generate jumping code for boolean expressions. As code is generated for E, jumps to the true and false exits are left incomplete, with the label field unfilled. These incomplete jumps are placed on lists pointed to by E.*truelist* and E.*falselist*, as appropriate.

The semantic actions reflect the considerations mentioned above. Consider the production $E \rightarrow E_1$ **and** $M\ E_2$. If E_1 is false, then E is also false, so the statements on E_1.*falselist* become part of E.*falselist*. If E_1 is true, however, we must next test E_2, so the target for the statements E_1.*truelist* must be the beginning of the code generated for E_2. This target is obtained using the marker nonterminal M. Attribute M.*quad* records the number of the first statement of E_2.*code*. With the production $M \rightarrow \epsilon$ we associate the semantic action

$$\{\ M.quad := nextquad\ \}$$

The variable *nextquad* holds the index of the next quadruple to follow. This value will be backpatched onto the E_1.*truelist* when we have seen the remainder of the production $E \rightarrow E_1$ **and** $M\ E_2$. The translation scheme is as follows.

(1) $E \rightarrow E_1$ **or** $M\ E_2$ { *backpatch* $(E_1.falselist, M.quad)$;
                                  $E.truelist := merge(E_1.truelist,\ E_2.truelist)$;
                                  $E.falselist := E_2.falselist$ }

(2) $E \rightarrow E_1$ **and** $M\ E_2$ { *backpatch* $(E_1.truelist, M.quad)$;
                                  $E.truelist := E_2.truelist$;
                                  $E.falselist := merge(E_1.falselist,\ E_2.falselist)$ }

(3) $E \rightarrow \textbf{not } E_1$ { $E.truelist := E_1.falselist$;
                                $E.falselist := E_1.truelist$ }

(4) $E \rightarrow (E_1)$ { $E.truelist := E_1.truelist$;
                                $E.falselist := E_1.falselist$ }

(5) $E \rightarrow \textbf{id}_1 \textbf{ relop id}_2$ { $E.truelist := makelist(nextquad)$;
                                $E.falselist := makelist(nextquad + 1)$;
                                $emit('\texttt{if}' \ \textbf{id}_1.place \ \textbf{relop}.op \ \textbf{id}_2.place \ '\texttt{goto \_}')$
                                $emit('\texttt{goto \_}')$ }

(6) $E \rightarrow \textbf{true}$ { $E.truelist := makelist(nextquad)$;
                                $emit('\texttt{goto \_}')$ }

(7) $E \rightarrow \textbf{false}$ { $E.falselist := makelist(nextquad)$;
                                $emit('\texttt{goto \_}')$ }

(8) $M \rightarrow \epsilon$ { $M.quad := nextquad$ }

For simplicity, semantic action (5) generates two statements, a conditional goto and an unconditional one. Neither has its target filled in. The index of the first generated statement is made into a list, and $E.truelist$ is given a pointer to that list. The second generated statement $\texttt{goto \_}$ is also made into a list and given to $E.falselist$.

Example 8.6. Consider again the expression $\texttt{a < b or c < d and e < f}$. An annotated parse tree is shown in Fig. 8.29. The actions are performed during a depth-first traversal of the tree. Since all actions appear at the ends of right sides, they can be performed in conjunction with reductions during a bottom-up parse. In response to the reduction of $\texttt{a < b}$ to E by production (5), the two quadruples

```
100:  if a < b goto _
101:  goto _
```

are generated. (We again arbitrarily start statement numbers at 100.) The marker nonterminal M in the production $E \rightarrow E_1 \textbf{ or } M E_2$ records the value of $nextquad$, which at this time is 102. The reduction of $\texttt{c < d}$ to E by production (5) generates the quadruples

```
102:  if c < d goto _
103:  goto _
```

We have now seen E_1 in the production $E \rightarrow E_1 \textbf{ and } M E_2$. The marker nonterminal in this production records the current value of $nextquad$, which is now 104. Reducing $\texttt{e < f}$ into E by production (5) generates

```
104:  if e < f goto _
105:  goto _
```

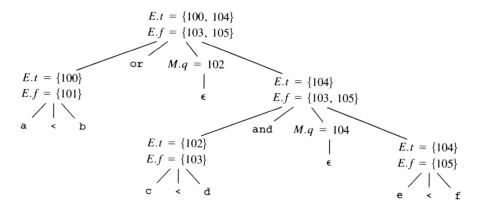

Fig. 8.29. Annotated parse tree for `a < b or c < d and e < f`.

We now reduce by $E \rightarrow E_1$ **and** $M\ E_2$. The corresponding semantic action calls *backpatch*({102},104) where {102} as argument denotes a pointer to the list containing only 102, that list being the one pointed to by $E_1.truelist$. This call to *backpatch* fills in 104 in statement 102. The six statements generated so far are thus:

```
100:  if a < b goto _
101:  goto _
102:  if c < d goto 104
103:  goto _
104:  if e < f goto _
105:  goto _
```

The semantic action associated with the final reduction by $E \rightarrow E_1$ **or** $M\ E_2$ calls *backpatch*({101},102) which leaves the statements looking like:

```
100:  if a < b goto _
101:  goto 102
102:  if c < d goto 104
103:  goto _
104:  if e < f goto _
105:  goto _
```

The entire expression is true if and only if the goto's of statements 100 or 104 are reached, and is false if and only if the goto's of statements 103 or 105 are reached. These instructions will have their targets filled in later in the compilation, when it is seen what must be done depending on the truth or falsehood of the expression.   □

Flow-of-Control Statements

We now show how backpatching can be used to translate flow-of-control state-ments in one pass. As above, we fix our attention on the generation of quad-ruples, and the notation regarding translation field names and list-handling procedures from that section carries over to this section as well. As a larger example, we develop a translation scheme for statements generated by the fol-lowing grammar:

(1) $S \rightarrow$ **if** E **then** S
(2) | **if** E **then** S **else** S
(3) | **while** E **do** S
(4) | **begin** L **end**
(5) | A
(6) $L \rightarrow L$; S
(7) | S

Here S denotes a statement, L a statement list, A an assignment statement, and E a boolean expression. Note that there must be other productions, such as those for assignment statements. The productions given, however, will be sufficient to illustrate the techniques used to translate flow-of-control state-ments.

   We use the same structure of code for if-then, if-then-else, and while-do statements as in Section 8.4. We make the tacit assumption that the code that follows a given statement in execution also follows it physically in the quad-ruple array. If that is not true, an explicit jump must be provided.

   Our general approach will be to fill in the jumps out of statements when their targets are found. Not only do boolean expressions need two lists of jumps that occur when the expression is true and when it is false, but state-ments also need lists of jumps (given by attribute *nextlist*) to the code that fol-lows them in the execution sequence.

Scheme to Implement the Translation

We now describe a syntax-directed translation scheme to generate translations for the flow-of-control constructs given above. The nonterminal E has two attributes $E.truelist$ and $E.falselist$, as above. L and S each also need a list of unfilled quadruples that must eventually be completed by backpatching. These lists are pointed to by the attributes $L.nextlist$ and $S.nextlist$. $S.nextlist$ is a pointer to a list of all conditional and unconditional jumps to the quadruple following the statement S in execution order, and $L.nextlist$ is defined simi-larly.

   In the code layout for $S \rightarrow$ **while** E **do** S_1 in Fig. 8.22(c), there are labels $S.begin$ and $E.true$ marking the beginning of the code for the complete state-ment S and the body S_1. The two occurrences of the marker nonterminal M in the following production record the quadruple numbers of these positions:

   $S \rightarrow$ **while** M_1 E **do** M_2 S_1

Again, the only production for M is $M \to \epsilon$ with an action setting attribute $M.quad$ to the number of the next quadruple. After the body S_1 of the while statement is executed, control flows to the beginning. Therefore, when we reduce **while** M_1 E **do** M_2 S_1 to S, we backpatch $S_1.nextlist$ to make all targets on that list be $M_1.quad$. An explicit jump to the beginning of the code for E is appended after the code for S_1 because control may also "fall out the bottom." $E.truelist$ is backpatched to go to the beginning of S_1 by making jumps on $E.truelist$ go to $M_2.quad$.

A more compelling argument for using $S.nextlist$ and $L.nextlist$ comes when code is generated for the conditional statement **if** E **then** S_1 **else** S_2. If control "falls out the bottom" of S_1, as when S_1 is an assignment, we must include at the end of the code for S_1 a jump over the code for S_2. We use another marker nonterminal to introduce this jump after S_1. Let nonterminal N be this marker with production $N \to \epsilon$. N has attribute $N.nextlist$, which will be a list consisting of the quadruple number of the statement goto _ that is generated by the semantic rule for N. We now give the semantic rules for the revised grammar.

(1) $S \to$ **if** E **then** M_1 S_1 N **else** M_2 S_2

> { $backpatch(E.truelist, \ M_1.quad)$;
> $backpatch(E.falselist, \ M_2.quad)$;
> $S.nextlist := merge(S_1.nextlist, \ merge(N.nextlist, \ S_2.nextlist))$ }

We backpatch the jumps when E is true to the quadruple $M_1.quad$, which is the beginning of the code for S_1. Similarly, we backpatch jumps when E is false to go to the beginning of the code for S_2. The list $S.nextlist$ includes all jumps out of S_1 and S_2, as well as the jump generated by N.

(2) $N \to \epsilon$ { $N.nextlist := makelist(nextquad)$;
                          $emit('\text{goto \_}')$ }

(3) $M \to \epsilon$ { $M.quad := nextquad$ }

(4) $S \to$ **if** E **then** M S_1 { $backpatch(E.truelist, \ M.quad)$;
                          $S.nextlist := merge(E.falselist, \ S_1.nextlist)$ }

(5) $S \to$ **while** M_1 E **do** M_2 S_1 { $backpatch(S_1.nextlist, \ M_1.quad)$;
                          $backpatch(E.truelist, \ M_2.quad)$;
                          $S.nextlist := E.falselist$
                          $emit('\text{goto}' \ M_1.quad)$ }

(6) $S \to$ **begin** L **end**   { $S.nextlist := L.nextlist$ }

(7) $S \to A$ { $S.nextlist := $ **nil** }

The assignment $S.nextlist := $ **nil** initializes $S.nextlist$ to an empty list.

(8) $L \to L_1 \ ; M \ S$ { $backpatch(L_1.nextlist, \ M.quad)$;
                          $L.nextlist := S.nextlist$ }

The statement following L_1 in order of execution is the beginning of S. Thus the $L_1.nextlist$ list is backpatched to the beginning of the code for S, which is given by $M.quad$.

(9) $L \rightarrow S$ $\qquad\qquad\qquad$ { $L.nextlist := S.nextlist$ }

Note that no new quadruples are generated anywhere in these semantic rules except for rules (2) and (5). All other code is generated by the semantic actions associated with assignment statements and expressions. What the flow of control does is cause the proper backpatching so that the assignments and boolean expression evaluations will connect properly.

Labels and Gotos

The most elementary programming language construct for changing the flow of control in a program is the label and goto. When a compiler encounters a statement like goto L, it must check that there is exactly one statement with label L in the scope of this goto statement. If the label has already appeared, either in a label-declaration statement or as the label of some source statement, then the symbol table will have an entry giving the compiler-generated label for the first three-address instruction associated with the source statement labeled L. For the translation we generate a goto three-address statement with that compiler-generated label as target.

When a label L is encountered for the first time in the source program, either in a declaration or as the target of a forward goto, we enter L into the symbol table and generate a symbolic label for L.

8.7 PROCEDURE CALLS

The procedure[6] is such an important and frequently used programming construct that it is imperative for a compiler to generate good code for procedure calls and returns. The run-time routines that handle procedure argument passing, calls, and returns are part of the run-time support package. We discussed the different kinds of mechanisms needed to implement the run-time support package in Chapter 7. In this section, we discuss the code that is typically generated for procedure calls and returns.

Let us consider a grammar for a simple procedure call statement.

$\quad$ (1) $\qquad S \rightarrow$ **call id** ($Elist$)
$\quad$ (2) $\qquad Elist \rightarrow Elist$, E
$\quad$ (3) $\qquad Elist \rightarrow E$

---

[6] We use the term procedure to include function. A function is a procedure that returns a value.

Calling Sequences

As discussed in Chapter 7, the translation for a call includes a calling sequence, a sequence of actions taken on entry to and exit from each procedure. While calling sequences differ, even for implementations of the same language, the following actions typically take place:

When a procedure call occurs, space must be allocated for the activation record of the called procedure. The arguments of the called procedure must be evaluated and made available to the called procedure in a known place. Environment pointers must be established to enable the called procedure to access data in enclosing blocks. The state of the calling procedure must be saved so it can resume execution after the call. Also saved in a known place is the return address, the location to which the called routine must transfer after it is finished. The return address is usually the location of the instruction that follows the call in the calling procedure. Finally, a jump to the beginning of the code for the called procedure must be generated.

When a procedure returns, several actions also must take place. If the called procedure is a function, the result must be stored in a known place. The activation record of the calling procedure must be restored. A jump to the calling procedure's return address must be generated.

There is no exact division of the run-time tasks between the calling and called procedure. Often the source language, the target machine, and the operating system impose requirements that favor one solution over another.

A Simple Example

Let us consider a simple example in which parameters are passed by reference and storage is statically allocated. In this situation, we can use the `param` statements themselves as placeholders for the arguments. The called procedure is passed a pointer in a register to the first of the `param` statements, and can obtain pointers to any of its arguments by using the proper offset from this base pointer. When generating three-address code for this type of call, it is sufficient to generate the three-address statements needed to evaluate those arguments that are expressions other than simple names, then follow them by a list of `param` three-address statements, one for each argument. If we do not want to mix the argument-evaluating statements with the `param` statements, we shall have to save the value of $E.place$, for each expression E in $\mathbf{id}(E, E, \ldots, E)$.[7]

A convenient data structure in which to save these values is a queue, a first-in first-out list. Our semantic routine for $Elist \rightarrow Elist$, E will include a step to store $E.place$ on a queue $queue$. Then, the semantic routine for

---

[7] If parameters are passed to the called procedure by putting them on a stack, as would normally be the case for dynamically allocated data, there is no reason not to mix evaluation and `param` statements. The `param` statement is replaced at code-generation time by code to push a parameter on the stack.

$S \rightarrow$ **call id** (*Elist*) will generate a param statement for each item on *queue*, causing these statements to follow the statements evaluating the argument expressions. Those statements were generated when the arguments themselves were reduced to *E*. The following syntax-directed translation incorporates these ideas.

(1) $S \rightarrow$ **call id** (*Elist*)
             {   **for** each item *p* on *queue* **do**
                     emit('param' *p*);
               emit('call' *id.place*) }

The code for *S* is the code for *Elist*, which evaluates the arguments, followed by a param *p* statement for each argument, followed by a **call** statement. A count of the number of parameters is not generated with the call statement but could be calculated in the same way we computed *Elist.ndim* in the previous section.

(2)   *Elist* $\rightarrow$ *Elist* , *E*
             {   append *E.place* to the end of *queue* }

(3)   *Elist* $\rightarrow$ *E*
             {   initialize *queue* to contain only *E.place* }

Here *queue* is emptied and then gets a single pointer to the symbol table location for the name that denotes the value of *E*.

EXERCISES

8.1 Translate the arithmetic expression a $*$ - (b + c) into
    a) a syntax tree
    b) postfix notation
    c) three-address code.

8.2 Translate the expression - (a + b) $*$ (c + d) + (a + b + c) into
    a) quadruples
    b) triples
    c) indirect triples.

8.3 Translate the executable statements of the following C program

```
main( )
{
    int i;
    int a[10];
    i = 1;
    while (i <= 10) {
        a[i] = 0; i = i + 1;
    }
}
```

    into

a) a syntax tree
b) postfix notation
c) three-address code.

*8.4 Prove that if all operators are binary, then a string of operators and operands is a postfix expression if and only if (1) there is exactly one fewer operator than operands, and (2) every nonempty prefix of the expression has fewer operators than operands.

8.5 Modify the translation scheme in Fig. 8.11 for computing the types and relative addresses of declared names to allow lists of names instead of single names in declarations of the form $D \rightarrow \textbf{id} : T$.

8.6 The *prefix* form of an expression in which operator θ is applied to expressions $e_1, e_2, \ldots, e_k$ is $\theta p_1 p_2 \cdots p_k$, where p_i is the prefix form of e_i.

a) Generate the prefix form of $a * - (b+c)$.

**b) Show that infix expressions cannot be translated into prefix form by translation schemes in which all actions are printing actions and all actions appear at the ends of right sides of productions.

c) Give a syntax-directed definition to translate infix expressions into prefix form. Which of the methods of Chapter 5 can you use?

8.7 Write a program to implement the syntax-directed definition for translating booleans to three-address code given in Fig. 8.24.

8.8 Modify the syntax-directed definition in Fig. 8.24 to generate code for the stack machine of Section 2.8.

8.9 The syntax-directed definition in Fig. 8.24 translates $E \rightarrow \textbf{id}_1 < \textbf{id}_2$ into the pair of statements

$$\textbf{if id}_1 < \textbf{id}_2 \textbf{ goto } \cdots$$
$$\textbf{goto } \cdots$$

We could translate instead into the single statement

$$\textbf{if id}_1 \geq \textbf{id}_2 \textbf{ goto } \_$$

and fall through the code when E is true. Modify the definition in Fig. 8.24 to generate code of this nature.

8.10 Write a program to implement the syntax-directed definition for flow-of-control statements given in Fig. 8.23.

8.11 Write a program to implement the backpatching algorithm given in Section 8.6.

8.12 Translate the following assignment statement into three-address code using the translation scheme in Section 8.3.

```
A[i,j] := B[i,j] + C[A[k,l]] + D[i+j]
```

*8.13 Some languages, such as PL/I, permit a list of names to be given a list of attributes and also permit declarations to be nested within one another. The following grammar abstracts the problem:

$$D \rightarrow \textit{namelist attrlist}$$
$$| \ (\ D \ ) \ \textit{attrlist}$$
$$\textit{namelist} \rightarrow \textbf{id} \ , \ \textit{namelist}$$
$$| \ \textbf{id}$$
$$\textit{attrlist} \rightarrow A \ \textit{attrlist}$$
$$| \ A$$
$$A \rightarrow \textbf{decimal} \ | \ \textbf{fixed} \ | \ \textbf{float} \ | \ \textbf{real}$$

The meaning of $D \rightarrow (D) \ \textit{attrlist}$ is that all names mentioned in the declaration inside parentheses are given the attributes on *attrlist*, no matter how many levels of nesting there are. Note that a declaration of n names and m attributes may cause nm pieces of information to be entered into the symbol table. Give a syntax-directed definition for declarations defined by this grammar.

8.14 In C, the for statement has the following form:

`for ( ` e_1 ` ; ` e_2 ` ; ` e_3 ` ) ` *stmt*

Taking its meaning to be

e_1;
`while ( ` e_2 ` ) {`
    stmt;
    e_3;
`}`

construct a syntax-directed definition to translate C-style for statements into three-address code.

8.15 The Pascal standard defines the statement

for $v :=$ *initial* **to** *final* **do** *stmt*

to have the same meaning as the following code sequence:

begin
    $t_1 :=$ *initial*; $t_2 :=$ *final*;
    if $t_1 \leq t_2$ **then begin**
        $v := t_1$;
        stmt
        while $v \neq t_2$ **do begin**
            $v := succ(v)$;
            stmt
        end
    end
end

a) Consider the following Pascal program:

```
program forloop(input, output);
     var i, initial, final: integer;
     begin
         read(initial, final);
         for i:= initial to final do
             writeln(i)
     end.
```

What behavior does this program have for *initial* = MAXINT − 5 and *final* = MAXINT, where MAXINT is the largest integer on the target machine.

*b) Construct a syntax-directed definition that generates correct three-address code for Pascal for-statements.

BIBLIOGRAPHIC NOTES

UNCOL (for Universal Compiler Oriented Language) is a mythical universal intermediate language, sought since the mid 1950's. Given an UNCOL, the committee report by Strong et al. [1958] showed how compilers could be constructed by hooking a front end for a given source language with a back end for a given target language. The bootstrapping techniques given in the report are routinely used to retarget compilers (see Section 11.2). Steel [1961] contains an original proposal for UNCOL.

A retargetable compiler consists of one front end that can be put together with several back ends to implement a given language on several machines. Neliac is an early example of a language with a retargetable compiler (Huskey, Halstead, and McArthur [1960]) written in its own language. See also Richards [1971] for a description of a retargetable compiler for BCPL, Nori et al. [1981] for Pascal, and Johnson [1979] for C. Newey, Poole, and Waite [1972] apply the idea of changing the back end to a macro processor, a text editor, and a Basic compiler.

The UNCOL ideal of implementing *n* languages on *m* machines by writing *n* front ends and *m* back ends, as opposed to *n*×*m* distinct compilers, has been approached in a number of ways. One approach is to retro-fit a front end for a new language onto an existing compiler. Feldman [1979b] describes the addition of a Fortran 77 front end to the C compilers by Johnson [1979] and Ritchie [1979]. Compiler organizations designed to accomodate multiple front ends and back ends are described by Davidson and Fraser [1984b], Leverett et al. [1980], and Tanenbaum et al. [1983].

The terms "union" and "intersection" abstract machines used by Davidson and Fraser [1984b] highlight the role of the set of allowable operators in an intermediate representation. The instruction set and addressing modes of an intersection machine are limited, so the front end does not have to make many choices when it generates intermediate code. Union machines provide alternative ways of implementing source-level constructs. Since all of the alternatives may not be implemented directly by all target machines, the richer instruction set of the union machine may allow dependence on the target machine to creep in. Similar remarks apply to other kinds of intermediate code, such as syntax trees and three-address code. Fraser and Hanson [1982] consider ways of expressing access to the run-time stack using machine-independent operations.

The implementation of Algol 60 is discussed in detail by Randell and Russell [1964] and Grau, Hill, and Langmaack [1967]. Freiburghouse [1969] discusses PL/I, Wirth [1971] Pascal, and Branquart et al. [1976] Algol 68.

Minker and Minker [1980] and Giegerich and Wilhelm [1978] discuss the generation of optimal code for boolean expressions. Exercise 8.15 is from Newey and Waite [1985].

CHAPTER 9

Code
Generation

The final phase in our compiler model is the code generator. It takes as input an intermediate representation of the source program and produces as output an equivalent target program, as indicated in Fig. 9.1. The code generation techniques presented in this chapter can be used whether or not an optimization phase occurs before code generation, as in some so-called "optimizing" compilers. Such a phase tries to transform the intermediate code into a form from which more efficient target code can be produced. We shall talk about code optimization in detail in the next chapter.

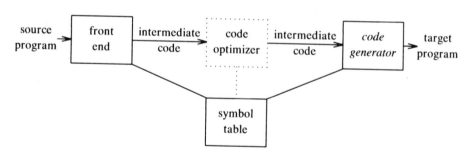

Fig. 9.1. Position of code generator.

The requirements traditionally imposed on a code generator are severe. The output code must be correct and of high quality, meaning that it should make effective use of the resources of the target machine. Moreover, the code generator itself should run efficiently.

Mathematically, the problem of generating optimal code is undecidable. In practice, we must be content with heuristic techniques that generate good, but not necessarily optimal, code. The choice of heuristics is important, in that a carefully designed code generation algorithm can easily produce code that is several times faster than that produced by a hastily conceived algorithm.

9.1 ISSUES IN THE DESIGN OF A CODE GENERATOR

While the details are dependent on the target language and the operating system, issues such as memory management, instruction selection, register allocation, and evaluation order are inherent in almost all code-generation problems. In this section, we shall examine the generic issues in the design of code generators.

Input to the Code Generator

The input to the code generator consists of the intermediate representation of the source program produced by the front end, together with information in the symbol table that is used to determine the run-time addresses of the data objects denoted by the names in the intermediate representation.

As we noted in the previous chapter, there are several choices for the intermediate language, including: linear representations such as postfix notation, three-address representations such as quadruples, virtual machine representations such as stack machine code, and graphical representations such as syntax trees and dags. Although the algorithms in this chapter are couched in terms of three-address code, trees, and dags, many of the techniques also apply to the other intermediate representations.

We assume that prior to code generation the front end has scanned, parsed, and translated the source program into a reasonably detailed intermediate representation, so the values of names appearing in the intermediate language can be represented by quantities that the target machine can directly manipulate (bits, integers, reals, pointers, etc.). We also assume that the necessary type checking has taken place, so type-conversion operators have been inserted wherever necessary and obvious semantic errors (e.g., attempting to index an array by a floating-point number) have already been detected. The code generation phase can therefore proceed on the assumption that its input is free of errors. In some compilers, this kind of semantic checking is done together with code generation.

Target Programs

The output of the code generator is the target program. Like the intermediate code, this output may take on a variety of forms: absolute machine language, relocatable machine language, or assembly language.

Producing an absolute machine-language program as output has the advantage that it can be placed in a fixed location in memory and immediately executed. A small program can be compiled and executed quickly. A number of "student-job" compilers, such as WATFIV and PL/C, produce absolute code.

Producing a relocatable machine-language program (object module) as output allows subprograms to be compiled separately. A set of relocatable object modules can be linked together and loaded for execution by a linking loader. Although we must pay the added expense of linking and loading if we produce relocatable object modules, we gain a great deal of flexibility in being able to compile subroutines separately and to call other previously compiled programs from an object module. If the target machine does not handle relocation automatically, the compiler must provide explicit relocation information to the loader to link the separately compiled program segments.

Producing an assembly-language program as output makes the process of code generation somewhat easier. We can generate symbolic instructions and use the macro facilities of the assembler to help generate code. The price paid is the assembly step after code generation. Because producing assembly code does not duplicate the entire task of the assembler, this choice is another reasonable alternative, especially for a machine with a small memory, where a compiler must use several passes. In this chapter, we use assembly code as the target language for readability. However, we should emphasize that as long as addresses can be calculated from the offsets and other information stored in the symbol table, the code generator can produce relocatable or absolute addresses for names just as easily as symbolic addresses.

Memory Management

Mapping names in the source program to addresses of data objects in run-time memory is done cooperatively by the front end and the code generator. In the last chapter, we assumed that a name in a three-address statement refers to a symbol-table entry for the name. In Section 8.2, symbol-table entries were created as the declarations in a procedure were examined. The type in a declaration determines the width, i.e., the amount of storage, needed for the declared name. From the symbol-table information, a relative address can be determined for the name in a data area for the procedure. In Section 9.3, we outline implementations of static and stack allocation of data areas, and show how names in the intermediate representation can be converted into addresses in the target code.

If machine code is being generated, labels in three-address statements have to be converted to addresses of instructions. This process is analogous to the "backpatching" technique in Section 8.6. Suppose that labels refer to quadruple numbers in a quadruple array. As we scan each quadruple in turn we can deduce the location of the first machine instruction generated for that quadruple, simply by maintaining a count of the number of words used for the instructions generated so far. This count can be kept in the quadruple array (in an extra field), so if a reference such as j: goto i is encountered, and i is less than j, the current quadruple number, we may simply generate a jump instruction with the target address equal to the machine location of the first instruction in the code for quadruple i. If, however, the jump is forward, so i exceeds j, we must store on a list for quadruple i the location of the first machine instruction generated for quadruple j. Then, when we process quadruple i, we fill in the proper machine location for all instructions that are forward jumps to i.

Instruction Selection

The nature of the instruction set of the target machine determines the difficulty of instruction selection. The uniformity and completeness of the instruction set are important factors. If the target machine does not support each data type in a uniform manner, then each exception to the general rule requires special handling.

Instruction speeds and machine idioms are other important factors. If we do not care about the efficiency of the target program, instruction selection is straightforward. For each type of three-address statement, we can design a code skeleton that outlines the target code to be generated for that construct. For example, every three-address statement of the form $x:=y+z$, where x, y, and z are statically allocated, can be translated into the code sequence

```
MOV y,R0   /* load y into register R0 */
ADD z,R0   /* add z to R0 */
MOV R0,x   /* store R0 into x */
```

Unfortunately, this kind of statement-by-statement code generation often produces poor code. For example, the sequence of statements

```
a := b + c
d := a + e
```

would be translated into

```
MOV b,R0
ADD c,R0
MOV R0,a
MOV a,R0
ADD e,R0
MOV R0,d
```

Here the fourth statement is redundant, and so is the third if a is not subsequently used.

The quality of the generated code is determined by its speed and size. A target machine with a rich instruction set may provide several ways of implementing a given operation. Since the cost differences between different implementations may be significant, a naive translation of the intermediate code may lead to correct, but unacceptably inefficient target code. For example, if the target machine has an "increment" instruction (INC), then the three-address statement $a:=a+1$ may be implemented more efficiently by the single instruction INC a, rather than by a more obvious sequence that loads a into a register, adds one to the register, and then stores the result back in a:

```
MOV   a, R0
ADD   #1, R0
MOV   R0, a
```

Instruction speeds are needed to design good code sequences but, unfortunately, accurate timing information is often difficult to obtain. Deciding which machine-code sequence is best for a given three-address construct may also require knowledge about the context in which that construct appears. Tools for constructing instruction selectors are discussed in Section 9.12.

Register Allocation

Instructions involving register operands are usually shorter and faster than those involving operands in memory. Therefore, efficient utilization of registers is particularly important in generating good code. The use of registers is often subdivided into two subproblems:

1. During *register allocation*, we select the set of variables that will reside in registers at a point in the program.

2. During a subsequent *register assignment* phase, we pick the specific register that a variable will reside in.

Finding an optimal assignment of registers to variables is difficult, even with single-register values. Mathematically, the problem is NP-complete. The problem is further complicated because the hardware and/or the operating system of the target machine may require that certain register-usage conventions be observed.

Certain machines require *register-pairs* (an even and next odd-numbered register) for some operands and results. For example, in the IBM System/370 machines integer multiplication and integer division involve register pairs. The multiplication instruction is of the form

        M   x, y

where x, the multiplicand, is the even register of an even/odd register pair. The multiplicand value is taken from the odd register of the pair. The multiplier y is a single register. The product occupies the entire even/odd register pair.

The division instruction is of the form

        D   x, y

where the 64-bit dividend occupies an even/odd register pair whose even register is x; y represents the divisor. After division, the even register holds the remainder and the odd register the quotient.

Now, consider the two three-address code sequences in Fig. 9.2(a) and (b), in which the only difference is the operator in the second statement. The shortest assembly-code sequences for (a) and (b) are given in Fig. 9.3.

R*i* stands for register *i*. (SRDA[1] R0,32 shifts the dividend into R1 and clears R0 so all bits equal its sign bit.) L, ST, and A stand for load, store and add, respectively. Note that the optimal choice for the register into which

---

[1] Shift Right Double Arithmetic.

```
t := a + b              t := a + b
t := t * c              t := t + c
t := t / d              t := t / d

   (a)                     (b)
```

Fig. 9.2. Two three-address code sequences.

```
L    R1, a          L     R0, a
A    R1, b          A     R0, b
M    R0, c          A     R0, c
D    R0, d          SRDA  R0, 32
ST   R1, t          D     R0, d
                    ST    R1, t

     (a)                  (b)
```

Fig. 9.3. Optimal machine-code sequences.

a is to be loaded depends on what will ultimately happen to t. Strategies for register allocation are discussed in Section 9.7.

Choice of Evaluation Order

The order in which computations are performed can affect the efficiency of the target code. Some computation orders require fewer registers to hold intermediate results than others, as we shall see. Picking a best order is another difficult, NP-complete problem. Initially, we shall avoid the problem by generating code for the three-address statements in the order in which they have been produced by the intermediate code generator.

Approaches to Code Generation

Undoubtedly the most important criterion for a code generator is that it produce correct code. Correctness takes on special significance because of the number of special cases that a code generator might face. Given the premium on correctness, designing a code generator so it can be easily implemented, tested, and maintained is an important design goal.

Section 9.6 contains a straightforward code-generation algorithm that uses information about subsequent uses of an operand to generate code for a register machine. It considers each statement in turn, keeping operands in registers as long as possible. The output of such a code generator can be improved by peephole optimization techniques such as those discussed in Section 9.9.

Section 9.7 presents techniques to make better use of registers by considering the flow of control in the intermediate code. The emphasis is on allocating registers for heavily used operands in inner loops.

Sections 9.10 and 9.11 present some tree-directed code-selection techniques that facilitate the construction of retargetable code generators. Versions of PCC, the portable C compiler, with such code generators have been moved to numerous machines. The availability of the UNIX operating system on a variety of machines owes much to the portability of PCC. Section 9.12 shows how code generation can be treated as a tree-rewriting process.

9.2 THE TARGET MACHINE

Familiarity with the target machine and its instruction set is a prerequisite for designing a good code generator. Unfortunately, in a general discussion of code generation it is not possible to describe the nuances of any target machine in sufficient detail to be able to generate good code for a complete language on that machine. In this chapter, we shall use as the target computer a register machine that is representative of several minicomputers. However, the code-generation techniques presented in this chapter have also been used on many other classes of machines.

Our target computer is a byte-addressable machine with four bytes to a word and n general-purpose registers, R0, R1, . . . , R$n-1$. It has two-address instructions of the form

op $source, destination$

in which op is an op-code, and $source$ and $destination$ are data fields. It has the following op-codes (among others):

MOV   (move $source$ to $destination$)
ADD   (add $source$ to $destination$)
SUB   (subtract $source$ from $destination$)

Other instructions will be introduced as needed.

The source and destination fields are not long enough to hold memory addresses, so certain bit patterns in these fields specify that words following an instruction contain operands and/or addresses. The source and destination of an instruction are specified by combining registers and memory locations with address modes. In the following description, $contents(a)$ denotes the contents of the register or memory address represented by a.

The address modes together with their assembly-language forms and associated costs are as follows:

MODE	FORM	ADDRESS	ADDED COST
absolute	M	M	1
register	R	R	0
indexed	$c(R)$	$c + contents(R)$	1
indirect register	*R	$contents(R)$	0
indirect indexed	*$c(R)$	$contents(c + contents(R))$	1

A memory location M or a register R represents itself when used as a source or destination. For example, the instruction

    MOV R0,M

stores the contents of register R0 into memory location M.

An address offset c from the value in register R is written as $c(R)$. Thus,

    MOV 4(R0),M

stores the value

$$contents(4 + contents(R0))$$

into memory location M.

Indirect versions of the last two modes are indicated by prefix *. Thus,

    MOV *4(R0),M

stores the value

$$contents(contents(4 + contents(R0)))$$

into memory location M.

A final address mode allows the source to be a constant:

MODE	FORM	CONSTANT	ADDED COST
literal	#c	c	1

Thus, the instruction

    MOV #1,R0

loads the constant 1 into register R0.

Instruction Costs

We take the cost of an instruction to be one plus the costs associated with the source and destination address modes (indicated as "added cost" in the table for address modes above). This cost corresponds to the length (in words) of the instruction. Address modes involving registers have cost zero, while those with a memory location or literal in them have cost one, because such operands have to be stored with the instruction.

If space is important, then we should clearly minimize instruction length. However, doing so has an important additional benefit. For most machines and for most instructions, the time taken to fetch an instruction from memory exceeds the time spent executing the instruction. Therefore, by minimizing the instruction length we also tend to minimize the time taken to perform the instruction as well.[2] Some examples follow.

---

[2] The cost criterion is meant to be instructive rather than realistic. Allowing a full word for an instruction simplifies the rule for determining the cost. A more accurate estimate of the time taken by an instruction would consider whether an instruction requires the value of an operand, as well

1.   The instruction MOV R0,R1 copies the contents of register R0 into register R1. This instruction has cost one, since it occupies only one word of memory.

2.   The (store) instruction MOV R5,M copies the contents of register R5 into memory location M. This instruction has cost two, since the address of memory location M is in the word following the instruction.

3.   The instruction ADD #1,R3 adds the constant 1 to the contents of register 3, and has cost two, since the constant 1 must appear in the next word following the instruction.

4.   The instruction SUB 4(R0),*12(R1) stores the value

$$contents(contents(12 + contents(R1))) - contents(contents(4 + R0))$$

into the destination *12(R1). The cost of this instruction is three, since the constants 4 and 12 are stored in the next two words following the instruction.

Some of the difficulties in generating code for this machine can seen by considering what code to generate for a three-address statement of the form a := b + c where b and c are simple variables in distinct memory locations denoted by these names. This statement can be implemented by many different instruction sequences. Here are a few examples:

1.   MOV   b, R0
     ADD   c, R0   cost = 6
     MOV   R0, a

2.   MOV   b, a
     ADD   c, a   cost = 6

Assuming R0, R1, and R2 contain the addresses of a, b, and c, respectively, we can use:

3.   MOV   *R1, *R0
     ADD   *R2, *R0   cost = 2

Assuming R1 and R2 contain the values of b and c, respectively, and that the value of b is not needed after the assignment, we can use:

4.   ADD   R2, R1
     MOV   R1, a   cost = 3

We see that in order to generate good code for this machine, we must utilize its addressing capabilities efficiently. There is a premium on keeping the *l*- or *r*-value of a name in a register, if possible, if it is going to be used in the near future.

---

as its address (found with the instruction), to be fetched from memory.

9.3 RUN-TIME STORAGE MANAGEMENT

As we saw in Chapter 7, the semantics of procedures in a language determines how names are bound to storage during execution. Information needed during an execution of a procedure is kept in a block of storage called an activation record; storage for names local to the procedure also appears in the activation record.

In this section, we discuss what code to generate to manage activation records at run time. In Section 7.3, two standard storage-allocation strategies were presented, namely, static allocation and stack allocation. In static allocation, the position of an activation record in memory is fixed at compile time. In stack allocation, a new activation record is pushed onto the stack for each execution of a procedure. The record is popped when the activation ends. Later in this section, we consider how the target code of a procedure can refer to data objects in activation records.

As we saw in Section 7.2, an activation record for a procedure has fields to hold parameters, results, machine-status information, local data, temporaries and the like. In this section, we illustrate allocation strategies using the machine-status field to hold the return address and the field for local data. We assume the other fields are handled as discussed in Chapter 7.

Since run-time allocation and deallocation of activation records occurs as part of the procedure call and return sequences, we focus on the following three-address statements:

1. `call`,
2. `return`,
3. `halt`, and
4. `action`, a placeholder for other statements.

For example, the three-address code for procedures c and p in Fig. 9.4 contains just these kinds of statements. The size and layout of activation records are communicated to the code generator via the information about names that is in the symbol table. For clarity, we show the layout in Fig. 9.4, rather than the form of the symbol-table entries.

We assume that run-time memory is divided into areas for code, static data, and a stack, as in Section 7.2 (the additional area for a heap in that section is not used here).

Static Allocation

Consider the code needed to implement static allocation. A `call` statement in the intermediate code is implemented by a sequence of two target-machine instructions. A `MOV` instruction saves the return address, and a `GOTO` transfers control to the target code for the called procedure:

```
MOV    #here +20,  callee.static_area
GOTO   callee.code_area
```

THREE-ADDRESS CODE
/* code for c */
action₁
call p
action₂
halt
/* code for p */
action₃
return

ACTIVATION RECORD
for c (64 bytes)

0:	return address
8:	arr
56:	i
60:	j

ACTIVATION RECORD
for p (88 bytes)

0:	return address
4:	buf
84:	n

Fig. 9.4. Input to a code generator.

The attributes *callee.static_area* and *callee.code_area* are constants referring to the address of the activation record and the first instruction for the called procedure, respectively. The source *#here + 20* in the MOV instruction is the literal return address; it is the address of the instruction following the GOTO instruction. (From the discussion in Section 9.2, the three constants plus the two instructions in the calling sequence cost 5 words or 20 bytes.)

The code for a procedure ends with a return to the calling procedure, except that the first procedure has no caller, so its final instruction is HALT, which presumably returns control to the operating system. A return from procedure *callee* is implemented by

GOTO *callee.static_area*

which transfers control to the address saved at the beginning of the activation record.

Example 9.1. The code in Fig. 9.5 is constructed from the procedures c and p in Fig. 9.4. We use the pseudo-instruction ACTION to implement the statement action, which represents three-address code that is not relevant for this discussion. We arbitrarily start the code for these procedures at addresses 100 and 200, respectively, and assume that each ACTION instruction takes 20 bytes. The activation records for the procedures are statically allocated starting at location 300 and 364, respectively.

The instructions starting at address 100 implement the statements

action₁; call p; action₂; halt

of the first procedure c. Execution therefore starts with the instruction ACTION₁ at address 100. The MOV instruction at address 120 saves the return address 140 in the machine-status field, which is the first word in the activation record of p. The GOTO instruction at address 132 transfers control to the first instruction in the target code of the called procedure.

```
                            /* code for c */
100:  ACTION₁
120:  MOV #140, 364         /* save return address 140 */
132:  GOTO 200              /* call p */
140:  ACTION₂
160:  HALT
      . . .

                            /* code for p */
200:  ACTION₃
220:  GOTO *364             /* return to address saved in location 364 */
      . . .

                            /* 300-363 hold activation record for c */
300:                        /* return address */
304:                        /* local data for c */
      . . .

                            /* 364-451 hold activation record for p */
364:                        /* return address */
368:                        /* local data for p */
```

Fig. 9.5. Target code for the input in Fig. 9.4.

Since 140 was saved at address 364 by the call sequence above, *364 represents 140 when the GOTO statement at address 220 is executed. Control therefore returns to address 140 and execution of procedure c resumes.   □

Stack Allocation

Static allocation can become stack allocation by using relative addresses for storage in activation records. The position of the record for an activation of a procedure is not known until run time. In stack allocation, this position is usually stored in a register, so words in the activation record can be accessed as offsets from the value in this register. The indexed address mode of our target machine is convenient for this purpose.

Relative addresses in an activation record can be taken as offsets from any known position in the activation record, as we saw in Section 7.3. For convenience, we shall use positive offsets by maintaining in a register SP a pointer to the beginning of the activation record on top of the stack. When a procedure call occurs, the calling procedure increments SP and transfers control to the called procedure. After control returns to the caller, it decrements SP, thereby deallocating the activation record of the called procedure.[3]

---

[3] With negative offsets, we could have SP point to the end of the stack and have the called procedure increment SP.

The code for the first procedure initializes the stack by setting SP to the start of the stack area in memory:

```
MOV #stackstart, SP          /* initialize the stack */
code for the first procedure
HALT                          /* terminate execution */
```

A procedure call sequence increments SP, saves the return address, and transfers control to the called procedure:

```
ADD #caller.recordsize, SP
MOV #here + 16, *SP          /* save return address */
GOTO callee.code_area
```

The attribute *caller.recordsize* represents the size of an activation record, so the ADD instruction leaves SP pointing to the beginning of the next activation record. The source *#here + 16* in the MOV instruction is the address of the instruction following the GOTO; it is saved in the address pointed to by SP.

The return sequence consists of two parts. The called procedure transfers control to the return address using

```
GOTO *0(SP)    /* return to caller */
```

The reason for using *0(SP) in the GOTO instruction is that we need two levels of indirection: 0(SP) is the address of the first word in the activation record and *0(SP) is the return address saved there.

The second part of the return sequence is in the caller, which decrements SP, thereby restoring SP to its previous value. That is, after the subtraction SP points to the beginning of the activation record of the caller:

```
SUB #caller.recordsize, SP
```

A broader discussion of calling sequences and the tradeoffs in the division of labor between the calling and called procedures appears in Section 7.3.

Example 9.2. The program in Fig. 9.6 is a condensation of the three-address code for the Pascal program discussed in Section 7.1. Procedure q is recursive, so more than one activation of q can be alive at the same time.

Suppose that the sizes of the activation records for procedures s, p, and q have been determined at compile time to be *ssize*, *psize* and *qsize*, respectively. The first word in each activation record will hold a return address. We arbitrarily assume that the code for these procedures starts at addresses 100, 200, and 300, respectively, and that the stack starts at 600. The target code for the program in Fig. 9.6 is as follows:

THREE-ADDRESS
CODE

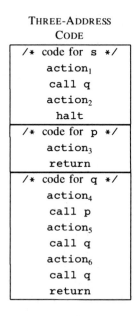

/* code for s */
action₁
call q
action₂
halt
/* code for p */
action₃
return
/* code for q */
action₄
call p
action₅
call q
action₆
call q
return

Fig. 9.6. Three-address code to illustrate stack allocation.

```
                    /* code for s */
100:  MOV #600, SP  /* initialize the stack */
108:  ACTION₁
128:  ADD #ssize, SP  /* call sequence begins */
136:  MOV #152, *SP   /* push return address */
144:  GOTO 300        /* call q */
152:  SUB #ssize, SP  /* restore SP */
160:  ACTION₂
180:  HALT
      . . .

                    /* code for p */
200:  ACTION₃
220:  GOTO *0(SP)     /* return */
      . . .

                    /* code for q */
300:  ACTION₄         /* conditional jump to 456 */
320:  ADD #qsize, SP
328:  MOV #344, *SP   /* push return address */
336:  GOTO 200        /* call p */
344:  SUB #qsize, SP
352:  ACTION₅
372:  ADD #qsize, SP
```

```
380:   MOV #396, *SP      /* push return address */
388:   GOTO 300           /* call q */
396:   SUB #qsize, SP
404:   ACTION₆
424:   ADD #qsize, SP
432:   MOV #448, *SP      /* push return address */
440:   GOTO 300           /* call q */
448:   SUB #qsize, SP
456:   GOTO *0(SP)        /* return */
          . . .

600:                      /* stack starts here */
```

We assume that ACTION$_4$ contains a conditional jump to the address 456 of the return sequence from q; otherwise, the recursive procedure q is condemned to call itself forever. In an example below, we consider an execution of the program in which the first call of q does not return immediately, but all subsequent calls do.

If *ssize*, *psize* and *qsize* are 20, 40, and 60, respectively, then SP is initialized to 600, the starting address of the stack, by the first instruction at address 100. SP holds 620 just before control transfers from s to q, because *ssize* is 20. Subsequently, when q calls p, the instruction at address 320 increments SP to 680, where the activation record for p begins; SP reverts to 620 after control returns to q. If the next two recursive calls of q return immediately, the maximum value of SP during this execution is 680. Note, however, that the last stack location used is 739, since the activation record for q starting at location 680 extends for 60 bytes.   □

Run-Time Addresses for Names

The storage-allocation strategy and the layout of local data in an activation record for a procedure determine how the storage for names is accessed. In Chapter 8, we assumed that a name in a three-address statement is really a pointer to a symbol-table entry for the name. This approach has a significant advantage; it makes the compiler more portable, since the front end need not be changed even if the compiler is moved to a different machine where a different run-time organization is needed (e.g., the display can be kept in registers instead of memory). On the other hand, generating the specific sequence of access steps while generating intermediate code can be of significant advantage in an optimizing compiler, since it lets the optimizer take advantage of details it would not even see in the simple three-address statement.

In either case, names must eventually be replaced by code to access storage locations. We thus consider some elaborations of the simple three-address copy statement x := 0. After the declarations in a procedure are processed, suppose the symbol-table entry for x contains a relative address 12 for x. First consider the case in which x is in a statically allocated area beginning at address *static*. Then the actual run-time address of x is *static* + 12. Although the compiler can eventually determine the value of *static* + 12 at compile time, the position of the static area may not be known when intermediate code to access the name is generated. In that case, it makes sense to generate three-address code to "compute" *static* + 12, with the understanding that this computation will be carried out during the code-generation phase, or possibly by the loader, before the program runs. The assignment x := 0 then translates into

```
static[12]  :=  0
```

If the static area starts at address 100, the target code for this statement is

```
MOV #0, 112
```

On the other hand, suppose our language is one like Pascal and that a display is used to access nonlocal names, as discussed in Section 7.4. Suppose also that the display is kept in registers, and that x is local to an active procedure whose display pointer is in register R3. Then we may translate the copy x := 0 into the three-address statements

```
t₁ :=  12  +  R3
*t₁ :=  0
```

in which t_1 contains the address of x. This sequence can be implemented by the single machine instruction

```
MOV #0, 12(R3)
```

Notice that the value in register R3 cannot be determined at compile time.

9.4 BASIC BLOCKS AND FLOW GRAPHS

A graph representation of three-address statements, called a flow graph, is useful for understanding code-generation algorithms, even if the graph is not explicitly constructed by a code-generation algorithm. Nodes in the flow graph represent computations, and the edges represent the flow of control. In Chapter 10, we use the flow graph of a program extensively as a vehicle to collect information about the intermediate program. Some register-assignment algorithms use flow graphs to find the inner loops where a program is expected to spend most of its time.

Basic Blocks

A *basic block* is a sequence of consecutive statements in which flow of control enters at the beginning and leaves at the end without halt or possibility of branching except at the end. The following sequence of three-address statements forms a basic block:

```
t₁ :=  a * a
t₂ :=  a * b
```

$$t_3 := 2 * t_2$$
$$t_4 := t_1 + t_3$$
$$t_5 := b * b$$
$$t_6 := t_4 + t_5$$

(9.1)

A three-address statement $x := y + z$ is said to *define* x and to *use* (or *reference*) y and z. A name in a basic block is said to be *live* at a given point if its value is used after that point in the program, perhaps in another basic block.

The following algorithm can be used to partition a sequence of three-address statements into basic blocks.

Algorithm 9.1. Partition into basic blocks.

Input. A sequence of three-address statements.

Output. A list of basic blocks with each three-address statement in exactly one block.

Method.

1. We first determine the set of *leaders*, the first statements of basic blocks. The rules we use are the following.

   i)   The first statement is a leader.
   ii) Any statement that is the target of a conditional or unconditional goto is a leader.
   iii) Any statement that immediately follows a goto or conditional goto statement is a leader.

2. For each leader, its basic block consists of the leader and all statements up to but not including the next leader or the end of the program.   □

Example 9.3. Consider the fragment of source code shown in Fig. 9.7; it computes the dot product of two vectors a and b of length 20. A list of three-address statements performing this computation on our target machine is shown in Fig. 9.8.

```
begin
    prod := 0;
    i := 1;
    do begin
        prod := prod + a[i] * b[i];
        i := i + 1
    end
    while i <= 20
end
```

Fig. 9.7. Program to compute dot product.

Let us apply Algorithm 9.1 to the three-address code in Fig. 9.8 to determine its basic blocks. Statement (1) is a leader by rule (i) and statement (3) is a leader by rule (ii), since the last statement can jump to it. By rule (iii) the statement following (12) (recall that Fig. 9.13 is just a fragment of a program) is a leader. Therefore, statements (1) and (2) form a basic block. The remainder of the program beginning with statement (3) forms a second basic block.   □

```
(1)    prod := 0
(2)    i := 1
(3)    t₁ := 4 * i
(4)    t₂ := a [ t₁ ]         /* compute a[i] */
(5)    t₃ := 4 * i
(6)    t₄ := b [ t₃ ]         /* compute b[i] */
(7)    t₅ := t₂ * t₄
(8)    t₆ := prod + t₅
(9)    prod := t₆
(10)   t₇ := i + 1
(11)   i := t₇
(12)   if i <= 20 goto (3)
```

Fig. 9.8. Three-address code computing dot product.

Transformations on Basic Blocks

A basic block computes a set of expressions. These expressions are the values of the names live on exit from the block. Two basic blocks are said to be *equivalent* if they compute the same set of expressions.

A number of transformations can be applied to a basic block without changing the set of expressions computed by the block. Many of these transformations are useful for improving the quality of code that will be ultimately generated from a basic block. In the next chapter, we show how a global code "optimizer" tries to use such transformations to rearrange the computations in a program in an effort to reduce the overall running time or space requirement of the final target program. There are two important classes of local transformations that can be applied to basic blocks; these are the structure-preserving transformations and the algebraic transformations.

Structure-Preserving Transformations

The primary structure-preserving transformations on basic blocks are:

1. common subexpression elimination
2. dead-code elimination
3. renaming of temporary variables
4. interchange of two independent adjacent statements

Let us now examine these transformations in a little more detail. For the time being, we assume basic blocks have no arrays, pointers, or procedure calls.

1. *Common subexpression elimination.* Consider the basic block

$$
\begin{aligned}
a &:= b + c \\
b &:= a - d \\
c &:= b + c \\
d &:= a - d
\end{aligned}
\qquad (9.2)
$$

The second and fourth statements compute the same expression, namely, $b+c-d$, and hence this basic block may be transformed into the equivalent block

$$
\begin{aligned}
a &:= b + c \\
b &:= a - d \\
c &:= b + c \\
d &:= b
\end{aligned}
\qquad (9.3)
$$

Note that although the first and third statements in (9.2) and (9.3) appear to have the same expression on the right, the second statement redefines b. Therefore, the value of b in the third statement is different from the value of b in the first, and the first and third statements do not compute the same expression.

2. *Dead-code elimination.* Suppose x is dead, that is, never subsequently used, at the point where the statement $x := y+z$ appears in a basic block. Then this statement may be safely removed without changing the value of the basic block.

3. *Renaming temporary variables.* Suppose we have a statement $t := b+c$, where t is a temporary. If we change this statement to $u := b+c$, where u is a new temporary variable, and change all uses of this instance of t to u, then the value of the basic block is not changed. In fact, we can always transform a basic block into an equivalent block in which each statement that defines a temporary defines a new temporary. We call such a basic block a *normal-form* block.

4. *Interchange of statements.* Suppose we have a block with the two adjacent statements

$$
\begin{aligned}
t_1 &:= b + c \\
t_2 &:= x + y
\end{aligned}
$$

Then we can interchange the two statements without affecting the value of the block if and only if neither x nor y is t_1 and neither b nor c is t_2. Notice that a normal-form basic block permits all statement interchanges that are possible.

Algebraic Transformations

Countless algebraic transformations can be used to change the set of expressions computed by a basic block into an algebraically equivalent set. The useful ones are those that simplify expressions or replace expensive operations by cheaper ones. For example, statements such as

```
x := x + 0
```

or

```
x := x * 1
```

can be eliminated from a basic block without changing the set of expressions it computes. The exponentiation operator in the statement

```
x := y ** 2
```

usually requires a function call to implement. Using an algebraic transformation, this statement can be replaced by the cheaper, but equivalent statement

```
x := y * y
```

Algebraic transformations are discussed in more detail in Section 9.9 on peephole optimization and in Section 10.3 on optimization of basic blocks.

Flow Graphs

We can add the flow-of-control information to the set of basic blocks making up a program by constructing a directed graph called a *flow graph*. The nodes of the flow graph are the basic blocks. One node is distinguished as *initial*; it is the block whose leader is the first statement. There is a directed edge from block B_1 to block B_2 if B_2 can immediately follow B_1 in some execution sequence; that is, if

1. there is a conditional or unconditional jump from the last statement of B_1 to the first statement of B_2, or

2. B_2 immediately follows B_1 in the order of the program, and B_1 does not end in an unconditional jump.

We say that B_1 is a *predecessor* of B_2, and B_2 is a *successor* of B_1.

Example 9.4. The flow graph of the program of Fig. 9.7 is shown in Fig. 9.9. B_1 is the initial node. Note that in the last statement, the jump to statement (3) has been replaced by an equivalent jump to the beginning of block B_2. □

Representation of Basic Blocks

Basic blocks can be represented by a variety of data structures. For example, after partitioning the three-address statements by Algorithm 9.1, each basic block can be represented by a record consisting of a count of the number of quadruples in the block, followed by a pointer to the leader (first quadruple)

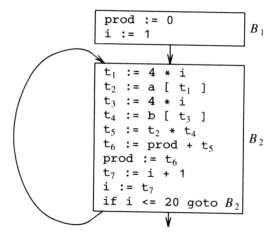

Fig. 9.9. Flow graph for program.

of the block, and by the lists of predecessors and successors of the block. An alternative is to make a linked list of the quadruples in each block. Explicit references to quadruple numbers in jump statements at the end of basic blocks can cause problems if quadruples are moved during code optimization. For example, if the block B_2 running from statements (3) through (12) in the intermediate code of Fig. 9.9 were moved elsewhere in the quadruple array or were shrunk, the (3) in `if i <= 20 goto (3)` would have to be changed. Thus, we prefer to make jumps point to blocks rather than quadruples, as we have done in Fig. 9.9.

It is important to note that an edge of the flow graph from block B to block B' does not specify the conditions under which control flows from B to B'. That is, the edge does not tell whether the conditional jump at the end of B (if there is a conditional jump there) goes to the leader of B' when the condition is satisfied or when the condition is not satisfied. That information can be recovered when needed from the jump statement in B.

Loops

In a flow graph, what is a loop, and how does one find all loops? Most of the time, it is easy to answer these questions. For example, in Fig. 9.9 there is one loop, consisting of block B_2. The general answers to these questions, however, are a bit subtle, and we shall examine them in detail in the next chapter. For the present, it is sufficient to say that a loop is a collection of nodes in a flow graph such that

1. All nodes in the collection are *strongly connected*; that is, from any node in the loop to any other, there is a path of length one or more, wholly within the loop, and

2. The collection of nodes has a unique *entry*, that is, a node in the loop such that the only way to reach a node of the loop from a node outside the loop is to first go through the entry.

A loop that contains no other loops is called an *inner* loop.

9.5 NEXT-USE INFORMATION

In this section, we collect next-use information about names in basic blocks. If the name in a register is no longer needed, then the register can be assigned to some other name. This idea of keeping a name in storage only if it will be used subsequently can be applied in a number of contexts. We used it in Section 5.8 to assign space for attribute values. The simple code generator in the next section applies it to register assignment. As a final application, we consider the assignment of storage for temporary names.

Computing Next Uses

The *use* of a name in a three-address statement is defined as follows. Suppose three-address statement i assigns a value to x. If statement j has x as an operand, and control can flow from statement i to j along a path that has no intervening assignments to x, then we say statement j *uses* the value of x computed at i.

We wish to determine for each three-address statement $x := y$ *op* z what the next uses of x, y, and z are. For the present, we do not concern ourselves with uses outside the basic block containing this three-address statement but we may, if we wish, attempt to determine whether or not there is such a use by the live-variable analysis technique of Chapter 10.

Our algorithm to determine next uses makes a backward pass over each basic block. We can easily scan a stream of three-address statements to find the ends of basic blocks as in Algorithm 9.1. Since procedures can have arbitrary side effects, we assume for convenience that each procedure call starts a new basic block.

Having found the end of a basic block, we scan backwards to the beginning, recording (in the symbol table) for each name x whether x has a next use in the block and if not, whether it is live on exit from that block. If the data-flow analysis discussed in Chapter 10 has been done, we know which names are live on exit from each block. If no live-variable analysis has been done, we can assume all nontemporary variables are live on exit, to be conservative. If the algorithms generating intermediate code or optimizing the code permit certain temporaries to be used across blocks, these too must be considered live. It would be a good idea to mark any such temporaries, so we do not have to consider all temporaries live.

Suppose we reach three-address statement i: $x := y$ *op* z in our backward scan. We then do the following.

1. Attach to statement i the information currently found in the symbol table

regarding the next use and liveness of **x**, **y**, and **z**.[4]

2. In the symbol table, set **x** to "not live" and "no next use."

3. In the symbol table, set **y** and **z** to "live" and the next uses of **y** and **z** to i. Note that the order of steps (2) and (3) may not be interchanged because **x** may be **y** or **z**.

If three-address statement i is of the form **x** := **y** or **x** := *op* **y**, the steps are the same as above, ignoring **z**.

Storage for Temporary Names

Although it may be useful in an optimizing compiler to create a distinct name each time a temporary is needed (see Chapter 10 for justification), space has to be allocated to hold the values of these temporaries. The size of the field for temporaries in the general activation record of Section 7.2 grows with the number of temporaries.

We can, in general, pack two temporaries into the same location if they are not live simultaneously. Since almost all temporaries are defined and used within basic blocks, next-use information can be applied to pack temporaries. For temporaries that are used across blocks, Chapter 10 discusses the data-flow analysis needed to compute liveness.

We can allocate storage locations for temporaries by examining each in turn and assigning a temporary to the first location in the field for temporaries that does not contain a live temporary. If a temporary cannot be assigned to any previously created location, add a new location to the data area for the current procedure. In many cases, temporaries can be packed into registers rather than memory locations, as in the next section.

For example, the six temporaries in the basic block (9.1) can be packed into two locations. These locations correspond to t_1 and t_2 in:

```
t₁ := a * a
t₂ := a * b
t₂ := 2 * t₂
t₁ := t₁ + t₂
t₂ := b * b
t₁ := t₁ + t₂
```

9.6 A SIMPLE CODE GENERATOR

The code-generation strategy in this section generates target code for a sequence of three-address statement. It considers each statement in turn, remembering if any of the operands of the statement are currently in registers, and taking advantage of that fact if possible. For simplicity, we assume that

---

[4] If **x** is not live, then this statement can be deleted; such transformations are considered in Section 9.8.

for each operator in a statement there is a corresponding target-language operator. We also assume that computed results can be left in registers as long as possible, storing them only (a) if their register is needed for another computation or (b) just before a procedure call, jump, or labeled statement.[5]

Condition (b) implies that everything must be stored just before the end of a basic block.[6] The reason we must do so is that, after leaving a basic block, we may be able to go to several different blocks, or we may go to one particular block that can be reached from several others. In either case, we cannot, without extra effort, assume that a datum used by a block appears in the same register no matter how control reached that block. Thus, to avoid a possible error, our simple code-generation algorithm stores everything when moving across basic-block boundaries as well as when procedure calls are made. Later we consider ways to hold some data in registers across block boundaries.

We can produce reasonable code for a three-address statement $a := b + c$ if we generate the single instruction ADD Rj, Ri with cost one, leaving the result a in register Ri. This sequence is possible only if register Ri contains b, Rj contains c, and b is not live after the statement; that is, b is not used after the statement.

If Ri contains b but c is in a memory location (called c for convenience), we can generate the sequence

        ADD   c, Ri   cost = 2

or

        MOV   c, Rj
                                  cost = 3
        ADD   Rj, Ri

provided b is not subsequently live. The second sequence becomes attractive if this value of c is subsequently used, as we can then take its value from register Rj. There are many more cases to consider, depending on where b and c are currently located and depending on whether the current value of b is subsequently used. We must also consider the cases where one or both of b and c is a constant. The number of cases that need to be considered further increases if we assume that the operator + is commutative. Thus, we see that code generation involves examining a large number of cases, and which case should prevail depends on the context in which a three-address statement is seen.

---

[5] However, to produce a *symbolic dump*, which makes available the values of memory locations and registers in terms of the source program's names for these values, it may be more convenient to have programmer-defined variables (but not necessarily compiler-generated temporaries) stored immediately upon calculation, should a program error suddenly cause a precipitous interrupt and exit.

[6] Note we are not assuming that the quadruples were actually partitioned into basic blocks by the compiler; the notion of a basic block is useful conceptually in any event.

Register and Address Descriptors

The code-generation algorithm uses descriptors to keep track of register contents and addresses for names.

1. A register descriptor keeps track of what is currently in each register. It is consulted whenever a new register is needed. We assume that initially the register descriptor shows that all registers are empty. (If registers are assigned across blocks, this would not be the case.) As the code generation for the block progresses, each register will hold the value of zero or more names at any given time.

2. An address descriptor keeps track of the location (or locations) where the current value of the name can be found at run time. The location might be a register, a stack location, a memory address, or some set of these, since when copied, a value also stays where it was. This information can be stored in the symbol table and is used to determine the accessing method for a name.

A Code-Generation Algorithm

The code-generation algorithm takes as input a sequence of three-address statements constituting a basic block. For each three-address statement of the form $x := y \ op \ z$ we perform the following actions:

1. Invoke a function *getreg* to determine the location L where the result of the computation $y \ op \ z$ should be stored. L will usually be a register, but it could also be a memory location. We shall describe *getreg* shortly.

2. Consult the address descriptor for y to determine y′, (one of) the current location(s) of y. Prefer the register for y′ if the value of y is currently both in memory and a register. If the value of y is not already in L, generate the instruction MOV y′,L to place a copy of y in L.

3. Generate the instruction OP z′,L where z′ is a current location of z. Again, prefer a register to a memory location if z is in both. Update the address descriptor of x to indicate that x is in location L. If L is a register, update its descriptor to indicate that it contains the value of x, and remove x from all other register descriptors.

4. If the current values of y and/or z have no next uses, are not live on exit from the block, and are in registers, alter the register descriptor to indicate that, after execution of $x := y \ op \ z$, those registers no longer will contain y and/or z, respectively.

If the current three-address statement has a unary operator, the steps are analogous to those above, and we omit the details. An important special case is a three-address statement $x := y$. If y is in a register, simply change the register and address descriptors to record that the value of x is now found only in the register holding the value of y. If y has no next use and is not live on exit from the block, the register no longer holds the value of y.

If y is only in memory, we could in principle record that the value of x is in the location of y, but this option would complicate our algorithm, since we could not then change the value of y without preserving the value of x. Thus, if y is in memory we use *getreg* to find a register in which to load y and make that register the location of x.

Alternatively, we can generate a MOV y, x instruction, which would be preferable if the value of x has no next use in the block. It is worth noting that most, if not all, copy instructions will be eliminated if we use the block-improving and copy-propagation algorithm of Chapter 10.

Once we have processed all three-address statements in the basic block, we store, by MOV instructions, those names that are live on exit and not in their memory locations. To do this we use the register descriptor to determine what names are left in registers, the address descriptor to determine that the same name is not already in its memory location, and the live variable information to determine whether the name is to be stored. If no live-variable information has been computed by data-flow analysis among blocks, we must assume all user-defined names are live at the end of the block.

The Function *getreg*

The function *getreg* returns the location L to hold the value of x for the assignment x := y *op* z. A great deal of effort can be expended in implementing this function to produce a perspicacious choice for L. In this section, we discuss a simple, easy-to-implement scheme based on the next-use information collected in the last section.

1. If the name y is in a register that holds the value of no other names (recall that copy instructions such as x := y could cause a register to hold the value of two or more variables simultaneously), and y is not live and has no next use after execution of x := y *op* z, then return the register of y for L. Update the address descriptor of y to indicate that y is no longer in L.

2. Failing (1), return an empty register for L if there is one.

3. Failing (2), if x has a next use in the block, or *op* is an operator, such as indexing, that requires a register, find an occupied register R. Store the value of R into a memory location (by MOV R, M) if it is not already in the proper memory location M, update the address descriptor for M, and return R. If R holds the value of several variables, a MOV instruction must be generated for each variable that needs to be stored. A suitable occupied register might be one whose datum is referenced furthest in the future, or one whose value is also in memory. We leave the exact choice unspecified, since there is no one proven best way to make the selection.

4. If x is not used in the block, or no suitable occupied register can be found, select the memory location of x as L.

A more sophisticated *getreg* function would also consider the subsequent uses of **x** and the commutativity of the operator *op* in determining the register to hold the value of **x**. We leave such extensions of *getreg* as exercises.

Example 9.5. The assignment d := (a – b) + (a – c) + (a – c) might be translated into the following three-address code sequence

```
t := a - b
u := a - c
v := t + u
d := v + u
```

with d live at the end. The code-generation algorithm given above would produce the code sequence shown in Fig. 9.10 for this three-address statement sequence. Shown alongside are the values of the register and address descriptors as code generation progresses. Not shown in the address descriptor is the fact that a, b, and c are always in memory. We also assume that t, u and v, being temporaries, are not in memory unless we explicitly store their values with a MOV instruction.

STATEMENTS	CODE GENERATED	REGISTER DESCRIPTOR	ADDRESS DESCRIPTOR
		registers empty	
t := a - b	MOV a, R0 SUB b, R0	R0 contains t	t in R0
u := a - c	MOV a, R1 SUB c, R1	R0 contains t R1 contains u	t in R0 u in R1
v := t + u	ADD R1, R0	R0 contains v R1 contains u	u in R1 v in R0

d := v + u	ADD R1, R0
	
	 MOV R0, d
		R0 contains d	d in R0
			
			 d in R0 and
			 memory

Fig. 9.10. Code sequence.

The first call of *getreg* returns R0 as the location in which to compute t. Since a is not in R0, we generate instructions MOV a, R0 and SUB b, R0. We now update the register descriptor to indicate that R0 contains t.

Code generation proceeds in this manner until the last three-address statement d := v + u has been processed. Note that R1 becomes empty because u has no next use. We then generate MOV R0, d to store the live variable d at the end of the block.

The cost of the code generated in Fig. 9.10 is 12. We could reduce this to

11 by generating MOV R0,R1 immediately after the first instruction and removing the instruction MOV a,R1, but to do so requires a more sophisticated code-generation algorithm. The reason for the savings is that it is cheaper to load R1 from R0 than from memory. □

Generating Code for Other Types of Statements

Indexing and pointer operations in three-address statements are handled in the same manner as binary operations. The table in Fig. 9.11 shows the code sequences generated for the indexed assignment statements a := b[i] and a[i] := b, assuming b is statically allocated.

STATEMENT	i IN REGISTER Ri		i IN MEMORY Mi		i IN STACK	
	CODE	COST	CODE	COST	CODE	COST
a:=b[i]	MOV b(Ri),R	2	MOV Mi,R MOV b(R),R	4	MOV Si(A),R MOV b(R),R	4
a[i]:=b	MOV b,a(Ri)	3	MOV Mi,R MOV b,a(R)	5	MOV Si(A),R MOV b,a(R)	5

Fig. 9.11. Code sequences for indexed assignments.

The current location of i determines the code sequence. Three cases are covered depending on whether i is in register Ri, whether i is in memory location Mi, or whether i is on the stack at offset Si and the pointer to the activation record for i is in register A. The register R is the register returned when the function *getreg* is called. For the first assignment, we would prefer to leave a in register R if a has a next use in the block and register R is available. In the second assignment, we assume a is statically allocated.

The table in Fig. 9.12 shows the code sequences generated for the pointer assignments a := *p and *p := a. Here, the current location of p determines the code sequence.

STATEMENT	p IN REGISTER Rp		p IN MEMORY Mp		p IN STACK	
	CODE	COST	CODE	COST	CODE	COST
a:=*p	MOV *Rp,a	2	MOV Mp,R MOV *R,R	3	MOV Sp(A),R MOV *R,R	3
*p:=a	MOV a,*Rp	2	MOV Mp,R MOV a,*R	4	MOV a,R MOV R,*Sp(A)	4

Fig. 9.12. Code sequences for pointer assignments.

Three cases are covered depending on whether p is initially in register Rp, whether p is in memory location Mp, or whether p is on the stack at offset Sp and the pointer to the activation record for p is in register **A**. The register R is the register returned when the function *getreg* is called. In the second assignment, we assume a is statically allocated.

Conditional Statements

Machines implement conditional jumps in one of two ways. One way is to branch if the value of a designated register meets one of the six conditions: negative, zero, positive, nonnegative, nonzero, and nonpositive. On such a machine a three-address statement such as if x < y goto z can be implemented by subtracting y from x in register R, and then jumping to z if the value in register R is negative.

A second approach, common to many machines, uses a set of *condition codes* to indicate whether the last quantity computed or loaded into a register is negative, zero, or positive. Often a compare instruction (CMP in our machine) has the desirable property that it sets the condition code without actually computing a value. That is, CMP x, y sets the condition code to positive if x > y, and so on. A conditional-jump machine instruction makes the jump if a designated condition $<$, $=$, $>$, $\leq$, $\neq$, or $\geq$ is met. We use the instruction CJ<= z to mean "jump to z if the condition code is negative or zero." For example, if x < y goto z could be implemented by

```
CMP     x, y
CJ<     z
```

If we are generating code for a machine with condition codes it is useful to maintain a condition-code descriptor as we generate code. This descriptor tells the name that last set the condition code, or the pair of names compared, if the condition code was last set that way. Thus we could implement

```
x := y + z
if x < 0 goto z
```

by

```
MOV     y, R0
ADD     z, R0
MOV     R0, x
CJ<     z
```

if we were aware that the condition code was determined by x after ADD z, R0.

9.7 REGISTER ALLOCATION AND ASSIGNMENT

Instructions involving only register operands are shorter and faster than those involving memory operands. Therefore, efficient utilization of registers is important in generating good code. This section presents various strategies for deciding what values in a program should reside in registers (register allocation) and in which register each value should reside (register assignment).

One approach to register allocation and assignment is to assign specific values in an object program to certain registers. For example, a decision can be made to assign base addresses to one group of registers, arithmetic computation to another, the top of the run-time stack to a fixed register, and so on.

This approach has the advantage that it simplifies the design of a compiler. Its disadvantage is that, applied too strictly, it uses registers inefficiently; certain registers may go unused over substantial portions of code, while unnecessary loads and stores are generated. Nevertheless, it is reasonable in most computing environments to reserve a few registers for base registers, stack pointers and the like, and to allow the remaining registers to be used by the compiler as it sees fit.

Global Register Allocation

The code-generation algorithm in Section 9.6 used registers to hold values for the duration of a single basic block. However, all live variables were stored at the end of each block. To save some of these stores and corresponding loads, we might arrange to assign registers to frequently used variables and keep these registers consistent across block boundaries (*globally*). Since programs spend most of their time in inner loops, a natural approach to global register assignment is to try to keep a frequently used value in a fixed register throughout a loop. For the time being, assume that we know the loop structure of a flow graph, and that we know what values computed in a basic block are used outside that block. The next chapter covers techniques for computing this information.

One strategy for global register allocation is to assign some fixed number of registers to hold the most active values in each inner loop. The selected values may be different in different loops. Registers not already allocated may be used to hold values local to one block as in Section 9.6. This approach has the drawback that the fixed number of registers is not always the right number to make available for global register allocation. Yet the method is simple to implement and it has been used in Fortran H, the optimizing Fortran compiler for the IBM-360 series machines (Lowry and Medlock [1969]).

In languages like C and Bliss, a programmer can do some register allocation directly by using register declarations to keep certain values in registers for the duration of a procedure. Judicious use of register declarations can speed up many programs, but a programmer should not do register allocation without first profiling the program.

Usage Counts

A simple method for determining the savings to be realized by keeping variable x in a register for the duration of loop L is to recognize that in our machine model we save one unit of cost for each reference to x if x is in a register. However, if we use the approach of the previous section to generate code for a block, there is a good chance that after x has been computed in a block it will remain in a register if there are subsequent uses of x in that block. Thus we count a savings of one for each use of x in loop L that is not preceded by an assignment to x in the same block. We also save two units if we can avoid a store of x at the end of a block. Thus if x is allocated a register, count a savings of two for each block of L for which x is live on exit and in which x is assigned a value.

On the debit side, if x is live on entry to the loop header, we must load x into its register just before entering loop L. This load costs two units. Similarly, for each exit block B of loop L at which x is live on entry to some successor of B outside of L, we must store x at a cost of two. However, on the assumption that the loop is iterated many times, we may neglect these debits since they occur only once each time we enter the loop. Thus an approximate formula for the benefit to be realized from allocating a register to x within loop L is:

$$\sum_{\text{blocks } B \text{ in } L} (\ use(x, B) + 2 * live(x, B)\ ) \qquad (9.4)$$

where $use(x, B)$ is the number of times x is used in B prior to any definition of x; $live(x, B)$ is 1 if x is live on exit from B and is assigned a value in B, and $live(x, B)$ is 0 otherwise. Note that (9.4) is approximate, because not all blocks in a loop are executed with equal frequency and also because (9.4) was based on the assumption that a loop is iterated "many" times. On other machines a formula analogous to (9.4), but possibly quite different from it, would have to be developed.

Example 9.6. Consider the basic blocks in the inner loop depicted in Fig. 9.13, where jump and conditional jump statements have been omitted. Assume registers R0, R1, and R2 are allocated to hold values throughout the loop. Variables live on entry into and on exit from each block are shown in Fig. 9.13 for convenience, immediately above and below each block, respectively. There are some subtle points about live variables that we address in Chapter 10. For example, notice that both e and f are live at the end of B_1, but of these, only e is live on entry to B_2 and only f on entry to B_3. In general, the variables live at the end of a block are the union of those live at the beginning of each of its successor blocks.

To evaluate (9.4) for $x = $ a we observe that a is live on exit from B_1 and is assigned a value there, but is not live on exit from B_2, B_3, or B_4. Thus, $\sum_{B \text{ in } L} 2*live(\text{a}, B) = 2$. Also, $use(\text{a}, B_1) = 0$, since a is defined in B_1 before any use. Also, $use(\text{a}, B_2) = use(\text{a}, B_3) = 1$ and $use(\text{a}, B_4) = 0$. Thus, $\sum_{B \text{ in } L} use(\text{a}, B) = 2$. Hence the value of (9.4) for $x = $ a is 4. That is, four units of cost can be saved by selecting a for one of the global registers. The values of (9.4) for b, c, d, e, and f are 6, 3, 6, 4, and 4, respectively.

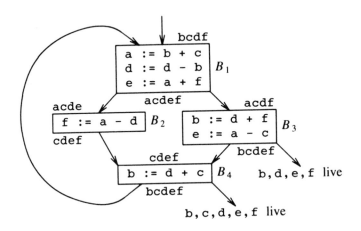

Fig. 9.13. Flow graph of an inner loop.

Thus we may select a, b, and d, for registers R0, R1, and R2, respectively. Using R0 for e or f instead of a would be another choice with the same apparent benefit. Fig. 9.14 shows the assembly code generated from Fig. 9.13, assuming that the strategy of Section 9.6 is used to generate code for each block. We do not show the generated code for the omitted conditional or unconditional jumps that end each block in Fig. 9.13, and we therefore do not show the generated code as a single stream, as it would appear in practice. It is worth noting that, if we did not adhere strictly to our strategy of reserving R0, R1, and R2, we could use

```
        SUB   R2, R0
        MOV   R0, f
```

for B_2, saving a unit since a is not live on exit from B_2. A similar saving could be realized at B_3.   □

Register Assignment for Outer Loops

Having assigned registers and generated code for inner loops, we may apply the same idea to progressively larger loops. If an outer loop L_1 contains an inner loop L_2, the names allocated registers in L_2 need not be allocated registers in $L_1 - L_2$. However, if name x is allocated a register in loop L_1 but not L_2, we must store x on entrance to L_2 and load x if we leave L_2 and enter a block of $L_1 - L_2$. Similarly, if we choose to allocate x a register in L_2 but not L_1 we must load x on entrance to L_2 and store x on exit from L_2. We leave as an exercise the derivation of a criterion for selecting names to be allocated registers in an outer loop L, given that choices have already been made for all loops nested within L.

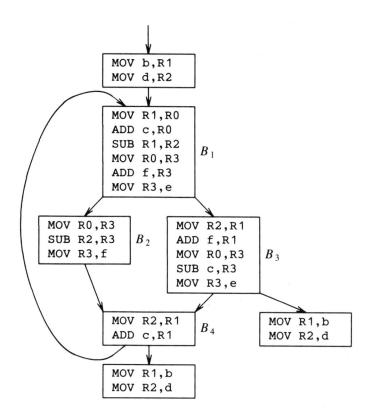

Fig. 9.14. Code sequence using global register assignment.

Register Allocation by Graph Coloring

When a register is needed for a computation but all available registers are in use, the contents of one of the used registers must be stored (*spilled*) into a memory location in order to free up a register. Graph coloring is a simple, systematic technique for allocating registers and managing register spills.

In this method, two passes are used. In the first, target-machine instructions are selected as though there were an infinite number of symbolic registers; in effect, names used in the intermediate code become names of registers and the three-address statements become machine-language statements. If access to variables requires instructions that use stack pointers, display pointers, base registers, or other quantities that assist access, then we assume that these quantities are held in registers reserved for each purpose. Normally, their use is directly translatable into an access mode for an address mentioned in a machine instruction. If access is more complex, the access must be broken into several machine instructions, and a temporary symbolic register (or several) may need to be created.

Once the instructions have been selected, a second pass assigns physical registers to symbolic ones. The goal is to find an assignment that minimizes the cost of the spills.

In the second pass, for each procedure a *register-interference graph* is constructed in which the nodes are symbolic registers and an edge connects two nodes if one is live at a point where the other is defined. For example, a register-interference graph for Figure 9.13 would have nodes for names a and d. In block B_1, a is live at the second statement, which defines d; therefore, in the graph there would be an edge between the nodes for a and d.

An attempt is made to color the register-interference graph using k colors, where k is the number of assignable registers. (A graph is said to be *colored* if each node has been assigned a color in such a way that no two adjacent nodes have the same color.) A color represents a register, and the coloring makes sure that no two symbolic registers that can interfere with each other are assigned the same physical register.

Although the problem of determining whether a graph is k-colorable is NP-complete in general, the following heuristic technique can usually be used to do the coloring quickly in practice. Suppose a node n in a graph G has fewer than k neighbors (nodes connected to n by an edge). Remove n and its edges from G to obtain a graph G'. A k-coloring of G' can be extended to a k-coloring of G by assigning n a color not assigned to any of its neighbors.

By repeatedly eliminating nodes having fewer than k edges from the register-interference graph, either we obtain the empty graph, in which case we can produce a k-coloring for the original graph by coloring the nodes in the reverse order in which they were removed, or we obtain a graph in which each node has k or more adjacent nodes. In the latter case a k-coloring is no longer possible. At this point a node is spilled by introducing code to store and reload the register. Then the interference graph is appropriately modified and the coloring process resumed. Chaitin [1982] and Chaitin et al. [1981] describe several heuristics for choosing the node to spill. A general rule is to avoid introducing spill code into inner loops.

9.8 THE DAG REPRESENTATION OF BASIC BLOCKS

Directed acyclic graphs (dags) are useful data structures for implementing transformations on basic blocks. A dag gives a picture of how the value computed by each statement in a basic block is used in subsequent statements of the block. Constructing a dag from three-address statements is a good way of determining common subexpressions (expressions computed more than once) within a block, determining which names are used inside the block but evaluated outside the block, and determining which statements of the block could have their computed value used outside the block.

A *dag for a basic block* (or just *dag*) is a directed acyclic graph with the following labels on nodes:

1. Leaves are labeled by unique identifiers, either variable names or

constants. From the operator applied to a name we determine whether the *l*-value or *r*-value of a name is needed; most leaves represent *r*-values. The leaves represent initial values of names, and we subscript them with 0 to avoid confusion with labels denoting "current" values of names as in (3) below.

2.   Interior nodes are labeled by an operator symbol.

3.   Nodes are also optionally given a sequence of identifiers for labels. The intention is that interior nodes represent computed values, and the identifiers labeling a node are deemed to have that value.

It is important not to confuse dags with flow graphs. Each node of a flow graph can be represented by a dag, since each node of the flow graph stands for a basic block.

```
(1)    t₁ := 4 * i
(2)    t₂ := a [ t₁ ]
(3)    t₃ := 4 * i
(4)    t₄ := b [ t₃ ]
(5)    t₅ := t₂ * t₄
(6)    t₆ := prod + t₅
(7)    prod := t₆
(8)    t₇ := i + 1
(9)    i := t₇
(10)   if i <= 20 goto (1)
```

Fig. 9.15. Three-address code for block B_2.

Example 9.7. Figure 9.15 shows the three-address code corresponding to block B_2 of Fig. 9.9. Statement numbers starting from (1) have been used for convenience. The corresponding dag is shown in Fig. 9.16. We discuss the significance of the dag after giving an algorithm to construct it. For the time being let us observe that each node of the dag represents a formula in terms of the leaves, that is, the values possessed by variables and constants upon entering the block. For example, the node labeled t_4 in Fig. 9.16 represents the formula

b [4 * i]

that is, the value of the word whose address is 4*i bytes offset from address b, which is the intended value of t_4.   □

Dag Construction

To construct a dag for a basic block, we process each statement of the block in turn. When we see a statement of the form x := y + z, we look for the

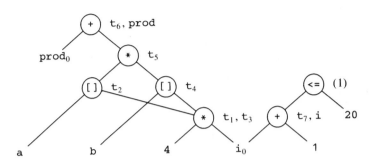

Fig. 9.16. Dag for block of Fig. 9.15.

nodes that represent the "current" values of y and z. These could be leaves, or they could be interior nodes of the dag if y and/or z had been evaluated by previous statements of the block. We then create a node labeled $+$ and give it two children; the left child is the node for y, the right the node for z. Then we label this node x. However, if there is already a node denoting the same value as $y + z$, we do not add the new node to the dag, but rather give the existing node the additional label x.

Two details should be mentioned. First, if x (not x_0) had previously labeled some other node, we remove that label, since the "current" value of x is the node just created. Second, for an assignment such as $x := y$ we do not create a new node. Rather, we append label x to the list of names on the node for the "current" value of y.

We now give the algorithm to compute a dag from a block. The algorithm is almost the same as Algorithm 5.1, except for the additional list of identifiers we attach to each node here. The reader should be warned that this algorithm may not operate correctly if there are assignments to arrays, if there are indirect assignments through pointers, or if one memory location can be referred to by two or more names, due to EQUIVALENCE statements or the correspondences between actual and formal parameters of a procedure call. We discuss the modifications necessary to handle these situations at the end of this section.

Algorithm 9.2. Constructing a dag.

Input. A basic block.

Output. A dag for the basic block containing the following information:

1. A *label* for each node. For leaves the label is an identifier (constants permitted), and for interior nodes, an operator symbol.

2. For each node a (possibly empty) list of attached identifiers (constants not permitted here).

Method. We assume the appropriate data structures are available to create nodes with one or two children, with a distinction between "left" and "right" children in the latter case. Also available in the structure is a place for a label for each node and the facility to create a linked list of attached identifiers for each node.

In addition to these components, we need to maintain the set of all identifiers (including constants) for which there is a node associated. The node could be either a leaf labeled by that identifier or an interior node with that identifier on its attached identifier list. We assume the existence of a function *node*(*identifier*), which, as we build the dag, returns the most recently created node associated with *identifier*. Intuitively, *node*(*identifier*) is the node of the dag that represents the value that *identifier* has at the current point in the dag construction process. In practice, an entry in the symbol-table record for *identifier* would indicate the value of *node*(*identifier*).

The dag construction process is to do the following steps (1) through (3) for each statement of the block, in turn. Initially, we assume there are no nodes, and *node* is undefined for all arguments. Suppose the "current" three-address statement is either (i) $x := y$ *op* z, (ii) $x := $ *op* y, or (iii) $x := y$.[7] We refer to these as cases (i), (ii), and (iii). We treat a relational operator like if $i <= 20$ goto as case (i), with x undefined.

1. If *node*(y) is undefined, create a leaf labeled y, and let *node*(y) be this node. In case (i), if *node*(z) is undefined, create a leaf labeled z and let that leaf be *node*(z).

2. In case (i), determine if there is a node labeled *op*, whose left child is *node*(y) and whose right child is *node*(z). (This check is to catch common subexpressions.) If not, create such a node. In either event, let n be the node found or created. In case (ii), determine whether there is a node labeled *op*, whose lone child is *node*(y). If not, create such a node, and let n be the node found or created. In case (iii), let n be *node*(y).

3. Delete x from the list of attached identifiers for *node*(x). Append x to the list of attached identifiers for the node n found in (2) and set *node*(x) to n.   □

Example 9.8. Let us return to the block of Fig. 9.15 and see how the dag of Fig. 9.16 is constructed for it. The first statement is $t_1 := 4 * i$. In step (1), we must create leaves labeled 4 and i_0. (We use the subscript 0, as before, to help distinguish labels from attached identifiers in pictures, but the subscript is not really part of the label.) In step (2), we create a node labeled *, and in step (3) we attach identifier t_1 to it. Figure 9.17(a) shows the dag at this stage.

---

[7] Operators are assumed to have at most two arguments. The generalization to three or more arguments is straightforward.

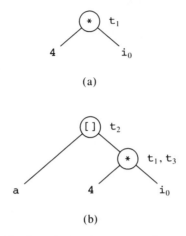

(a)

(b)

Fig. 9.17. Steps in the dag construction process.

For the second statement, $t_2 := a'[t_1]$, we create a new leaf labeled a and find the previously created $node(t_1)$. We also create a new node labeled [ ] to which we attach the nodes for a and t_1 as children.

For statement (3), $t_3 := 4 * i$, we determine that $node(4)$ and $node(i)$ already exist. Since the operator is $*$, we do not create a new node for statement (3), but rather append t_3 on the identifier list for node t_1. The resulting dag is shown in Fig. 9.17(b). The value-number method of Section 5.2 can be used to discover quickly that the node for $4 * i$ already exists.

We invite the reader to complete the construction of the dag. We mention only the steps taken for statement (9), $i := t_7$. Before statement (9), $node(i)$ is the leaf labeled i_0. Statement (9) is an instance of case (iii); therefore, we find $node(t_7)$, append i to its identifier list, and set $node(i)$ to $node(t_7)$. This is one of only two statements — the other is statement (7) — where the value of *node* changes for an identifier. It is this change that ensures that the new node for i is the left child of the <= operator node constructed for statement (10).   □

Applications of Dags

There are several pieces of useful information that we can obtain as we are executing Algorithm 9.2. First, note that we automatically detect common subexpressions. Second, we can determine which identifiers have their values used in the block; they are exactly those for which a leaf is created in step (1) at some time. Third, we can determine which statements compute values that could be used outside the block. They are exactly those statements S whose node n constructed or found in step (2) still has $node(x) = n$ at the end of the dag construction, where x is the identifier assigned by statement S. (Equivalently, x is still an attached identifier for n.)

Example 9.9. In Example 9.8, all statements meet the above constraint because the only times *node* is redefined — for prod and i — the previous value of *node* was a leaf. Thus all interior nodes can have their value used outside the block. Now, suppose we inserted before statement (9) a new statement *s* that assigned a value to i. At statement *s* we would create a node *m* and set *node*(i) = *m*. However, at statement (9) we would redefine *node*(i). Thus the value computed at statement *s* could not be used outside the block.   □

Another important use to which the dag may be put is to reconstruct a simplified list of quadruples taking advantage of common subexpressions and not performing assignments of the form x := y unless absolutely necessary. That is, whenever a node has more than one identifier on its attached list, we check which, if any, of those identifiers are needed outside the block. As we mentioned, finding live variables for the end of a block requires a data-flow analysis called "live-variable analysis" discussed in Chapter 10. However, in many cases we may assume no temporary name such as $t_1, t_2, \ldots, t_7$ in Fig. 9.15 is needed outside the block. (But beware of how logical expressions are translated; one expression may wind up spread over several basic blocks.)

We may in general evaluate the interior nodes of the dag in any order that is a topological sort of the dag. In a topological sort, a node is not evaluated until all of its children that are interior nodes have been evaluated. As we evaluate a node, we assign its value to one of its attached identifiers x, preferring one whose value is needed outside the block. We may not, however, choose x if there is another node *m* whose value was also held by x such that *m* has been evaluated and is still "live." Here, we define *m* to be live if its value is needed outside the block or if *m* has a parent which has not yet been evaluated.

If there are additional attached identifiers $y_1, y_2, \ldots, y_k$ for a node *n* whose values are also needed outside the block, we assign to them with statements $y_1 := x, y_2 := x, \ldots, y_k := x$. If *n* has no attached identifiers at all (this could happen if, say, *n* was created by an assignment to x, but x was subsequently reassigned), we create a new temporary name to hold the value of *n*. The reader should beware that in the presence of pointer or array assignments, not every topological sort of a dag is permissible; we shall attend to this matter shortly.

Example 9.10. Let us reconstruct a basic block from the dag of Fig. 9.16, ordering nodes in the same order as they were created: $t_1, t_2, t_4, t_5, t_6, t_7$, (1). Note that statements (3) and (7) of the original block did not create new nodes, but added labels t_3 and prod to the identifier lists of nodes t_1 and t_6, respectively. We assume none of the temporaries t_i are needed outside the block.

We begin with the node representing 4*i. This node has two identifiers attached, t_1 and t_3. Let us pick t_1 to hold the value 4*i, so the first reconstructed statement is

t_1 := 4 * i

just as in the original basic block. The second node considered is labeled t_2. The statement constructed from this node is

t_2 := a [t_1]

also as before. The node considered next is labeled t_4 from which we generate the statement

t_4 := b [t_1]

The latter statement uses t_1 as an argument rather than t_3 as in the original basic block, because t_1 is the name chosen to carry the value 4*i.

Next we consider the node labeled t_5 and generate the statement

t_5 := t_2 * t_4

For the node labeled t_6, prod, we select prod to carry the value, since that identifier and not t_6 will (presumably) be needed outside the block. Like t_3, temporary t_6 disappears. The next statement generated is

prod := prod + t_5

Similarly, we choose i rather than t_7 to carry the value i+1. The last two statements generated are

i := i + 1
if i <= 20 goto (1)

Note that the ten statements of Fig. 9.15 have been reduced to seven by taking advantage of the common subexpressions exposed during the dag construction process, and by eliminating unnecessary assignments. □

Arrays, Pointers, and Procedure Calls

Consider the basic block:

x := a[i]
a[j] := y   (9.5)
z := a[i]

If we use Algorithm 9.2 to construct the dag for (9.5), a[i] would become a common subexpression, and the "optimized" block would turn out to be

x := a[i]
z := x   (9.6)
a[j] := y

However, (9.5) and (9.6) compute different values for z in the case i = j and y ≠ a[i]. The problem is that when we assign to an array a, we may be changing the r-value of expression a[i], even though a and i do not change. It is therefore necessary that when processing an assignment to array a, we *kill* all nodes labeled [ ], whose left argument is a plus or minus a constant (possibly zero).[8] That is, we make these nodes ineligible to be given an additional identifier label, preventing them from being falsely recognized as common subexpressions. It is thus required that we keep a bit for each node telling whether or not it has been killed. Further, for each array a mentioned in the block, it is convenient to have a list of all nodes currently not killed but that must be killed should we assign to an element of a.

A similar problem occurs if we have an assignment such as *p:=w, where p is a pointer. If we do not know what p might point to, every node currently in the dag being built must be killed in the sense above. If node *n* labeled a is killed and there is a subsequent assignment to a, we must create a new leaf for a and use that leaf rather than *n*. We later consider the constraints on the order of evaluation caused by the killing of nodes.

In Chapter 10, we discuss methods whereby we could discover that p could only point to some subset of the identifiers. If p could only point to r or s, then only *node*(r) and *node*(s) must be killed. It is also conceivable that we could discover that i = j is impossible in block (9.5), in which case the node for a[i] need not be killed by a[j] := y. However, the latter type of discovery is not usually worth the trouble.

A procedure call in a basic block kills all nodes, since in the absence of knowledge about the called procedure, we must assume that any variable may be changed as a side effect. Chapter 10 discusses how we may establish that certain identifiers are not changed by a procedure call, and then nodes for these identifiers need not be killed.

If we intend to reassemble the dag into a basic block and may not want to use the order in which the nodes of the dag were created, then we must indicate in the dag that certain apparently independent nodes must be evaluated in a certain order. For example, in (9.5), the statement z := a[i] must follow a[j] := y, which must follow x := a[i]. Let us introduce certain edges *n → m* in the dag that do not indicate that *m* is an argument of *n*, but rather that evaluation of *n* must follow evaluation of *m* in any computation of the dag. The rules to be enforced are the following.

1. Any evaluation of or assignment to an element of array a must follow the previous assignment to an element of that array if there is one.

2. Any assignment to an element of array a must follow any previous evaluation of a.

3. Any use of any identifier must follow the previous procedure call or indirect assignment through a pointer if there is one.

4. Any procedure call or indirect assignment through a pointer must follow all previous evaluations of any identifier.

---

[8] Note that the argument of [ ] indicating the array name could be a itself, or an expression like a−4. In the latter case, the node a would be a grandchild, rather than a child of the node [ ].

That is, when reordering code, uses of an array a may not cross each other, and no statement may cross a procedure call or an assignment through a pointer.

9.9 PEEPHOLE OPTIMIZATION

A statement-by-statement code-generation strategy often produces target code that contains redundant instructions and suboptimal constructs. The quality of such target code can be improved by applying "optimizing" transformations to the target program. The term "optimizing" is somewhat misleading because there is no guarantee that the resulting code is optimal under any mathematical measure. Nevertheless, many simple transformations can significantly improve the running time or space requirement of the target program, so it is important to know what kinds of transformations are useful in practice.

A simple but effective technique for locally improving the target code is *peephole optimization*, a method for trying to improve the performance of the target program by examining a short sequence of target instructions (called the *peephole*) and replacing these instructions by a shorter or faster sequence, whenever possible. Although we discuss peephole optimization as a technique for improving the quality of the target code, the technique can also be applied directly after intermediate code generation to improve the intermediate representation.

The peephole is a small, moving window on the target program. The code in the peephole need not be contiguous, although some implementations do require this. It is characteristic of peephole optimization that each improvement may spawn opportunities for additional improvements. In general, repeated passes over the target code are necessary to get the maximum benefit. In this section, we shall give the following examples of program transformations that are characteristic of peephole optimizations:

- redundant-instruction elimination
- flow-of-control optimizations
- algebraic simplifications
- use of machine idioms

Redundant Loads and Stores

If we see the instruction sequence

(1) MOV   R0, a   (9.7)
(2) MOV   a, R0

we can delete instruction (2) because whenever (2) is executed, (1) will ensure that the value of a is already in register R0. Note that if (2) had a label[9] we

---

[9] One advantage of generating assembly code is that labels will be present, facilitating peephole optimizations such as this. If machine code is generated, and peephole optimization is desired, we can use a bit to mark the instructions that would have labels.

could not be sure that (1) was always executed immediately before (2) and so we could not remove (2). Put another way, (1) and (2) have to be in the same basic block for this transformation to be safe.

While target code such as (9.7) would not be generated if the algorithm suggested in Section 9.6 were used, it might be if a more naive algorithm like the one mentioned at the beginning of Section 9.1 were used.

Unreachable Code

Another opportunity for peephole optimization is the removal of unreachable instructions. An unlabeled instruction immediately following an unconditional jump may be removed. This operation can be repeated to eliminate a sequence of instructions. For example, for debugging purposes, a large program may have within it certain segments that are executed only if a variable debug is 1. In C, the source code might look like:

```
#define debug 0
  . . .
if ( debug ) {
      print debugging information
}
```

In the intermediate representation the if-statement may be translated as:

$$
\begin{array}{ll}
\texttt{if debug = 1 goto L1} & \\
\texttt{goto L2} & \\
\texttt{L1: print debugging information} & \text{(9.8)} \\
\texttt{L2:} &
\end{array}
$$

One obvious peephole optimization is to eliminate jumps over jumps. Thus, no matter what the value of debug, (9.8) can be replaced by:

$$
\begin{array}{ll}
\texttt{if debug} \neq \texttt{1 goto L2} & \\
\texttt{print debugging information} & \text{(9.9)} \\
\texttt{L2:} &
\end{array}
$$

Now, since debug is set to 0 at the beginning of the program,[10] constant propagation should replace (9.9) by

$$
\begin{array}{ll}
\texttt{if 0} \neq \texttt{1 goto L2} & \\
\texttt{print debugging information} & \text{(9.10)} \\
\texttt{L2:} &
\end{array}
$$

As the argument of the first statement of (9.10) evaluates to a constant **true**, it can be replaced by goto L2. Then all the statements that print debugging aids are manifestly unreachable and can be eliminated one at a time.

---

[10] To tell that debug has the value 0 we need to do a global "reaching definitions" data-flow analysis, as discussed in Chapter 10.

Flow-of-Control Optimizations

The intermediate code generation algorithms in Chapter 8 frequently produce jumps to jumps, jumps to conditional jumps, or conditional jumps to jumps. These unnecessary jumps can be eliminated in either the intermediate code or the target code by the following types of peephole optimizations. We can replace the jump sequence

```
        goto L1
        . . .

L1: goto L2
```

by the sequence

```
        goto L2
        . . .

L1: goto L2
```

If there are now no jumps to L1,[11] then it may be possible to eliminate the statement L1: goto L2 provided it is preceded by an unconditional jump. Similarly, the sequence

```
        if a < b goto L1
        . . .

L1: goto L2
```

can be replaced by

```
        if a < b goto L2
        . . .

L1: goto L2
```

Finally, suppose there is only one jump to L1 and L1 is preceded by an unconditional goto. Then the sequence

```
        goto L1
        . . .

L1: if a < b goto L2
L3:
```

$$(9.11)$$

may be replaced by

```
        if a < b goto L2
        goto L3
        . . .

L3:
```

$$(9.12)$$

While the number of instructions in (9.11) and (9.12) is the same, we

---

[11] If this peephole optimization is attempted, we can count the number of jumps to each label in the symbol-table entry for that label; a search of the code is not necessary.

sometimes skip the unconditional jump in (9.12), but never in (9.11). Thus, (9.12) is superior to (9.11) in execution time.

Algebraic Simplification

There is no end to the amount of algebraic simplification that can be attempted through peephole optimization. However, only a few algebraic identities occur frequently enough that it is worth considering implementing them. For example, statements such as

```
x := x + 0
```

or

```
x := x * 1
```

are often produced by straightforward intermediate code-generation algorithms, and they can be eliminated easily through peephole optimization.

Reduction in Strength

Reduction in strength replaces expensive operations by equivalent cheaper ones on the target machine. Certain machine instructions are considerably cheaper than others and can often be used as special cases of more expensive operators. For example, x^2 is invariably cheaper to implement as $x*x$ than as a call to an exponentiation routine. Fixed-point multiplication or division by a power of two is cheaper to implement as a shift. Floating-point division by a constant can be implemented (approximated) as multiplication by a constant, which may be cheaper.

Use of Machine Idioms

The target machine may have hardware instructions to implement certain specific operations efficiently. Detecting situations that permit the use of these instructions can reduce execution time significantly. For example, some machines have auto-increment and auto-decrement addressing modes. These add or subtract one from an operand before or after using its value. The use of these modes greatly improves the quality of code when pushing or popping a stack, as in parameter passing. These modes can also be used in code for statements like i:=i+1.

9.10 GENERATING CODE FROM DAGS

In this section, we show how to generate code for a basic block from its dag representation. The advantage of doing so is that from a dag we can more easily see how to rearrange the order of the final computation sequence than we can starting from a linear sequence of three-address statements or quadruples. Central to our discussion is the case where the dag is a tree. For this case we can generate code that we can prove is optimal under such criteria as program length or the fewest number of temporaries used. This algorithm for optimal code generation from a tree is also useful when the intermediate code is a parse tree.

Rearranging the Order

Let us briefly consider how the order in which computations are done can affect the cost of resulting object code. Consider the following basic block whose dag representation is shown in Fig. 9.18 (the dag happens to be a tree).

```
t₁ := a + b
t₂ := c + d
t₃ := e - t₂
t₄ := t₁ - t₃
```

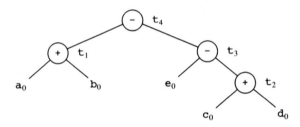

Fig. 9.18. Dag for basic block.

Note that the order is the one we would naturally obtain from a syntax-directed translation of the expression $(a+b)-(e-(c+d))$ by the algorithm of Section 8.3.

If we generate code for the three-address statements using the algorithm in Section 9.6 we get the code sequence of Fig. 9.19 (assuming two registers R0 and R1 are available, and only t_4 is live on exit).

```
MOV   a, R0
ADD   b, R0
MOV   c, R1
ADD   d, R1
MOV   R0, t₁
MOV   e, R0
SUB   R1, R0
MOV   t₁, R1
SUB   R0, R1
MOV   R1, t₄
```

Fig. 9.19. Code sequence.

On the other hand suppose we rearranged the order of the statements so that the computation of t_1 occurs immediately before that of t_4 as:

$$t_2 := c + d$$
$$t_3 := e - t_2$$
$$t_1 := a + b$$
$$t_4 := t_1 - t_3$$

Then, using the code-generation algorithm of Section 9.6, we get the code sequence of Fig. 9.20. (Again, only R0 and R1 are available.) By performing the computation in this order, we have been able to save two instructions, MOV R0, t_1 (which stores the value of R0 in memory location t_1) and MOV t_1, R1 (which reloads the value of t_1 in register R1).

```
MOV   c,  R0
ADD   d,  R0
MOV   e,  R1
SUB   R0, R1
MOV   a,  R0
ADD   b,  R0
SUB   R1, R0
MOV   R0, t₄
```

Fig. 9.20. Revised code sequence.

A Heuristic Ordering for Dags

The reason the above reordering improved the code was that the computation of t_4 was made to follow immediately after the computation of t_1, its left operand in the tree. That this arrangement is beneficial should be clear. The left argument for the computation of t_4 must be in a register for efficient computation of t_4, and computing t_1 immediately before t_4 ensures that will be the case.

In selecting an ordering for the nodes of a dag, we are only constrained to be sure that the order preserves the edge relationships of the dag. Recall from Section 9.8 that those edges can represent either the operator-operand relationship or implied constraints due to possible interactions among procedure calls, array assignments, or pointer assignments. We propose the following heuristic ordering algorithm, which attempts as far as possible to make the evaluation of a node immediately follow the evaluation of its leftmost argument. The algorithm of Fig. 9.21 produces the ordering in reverse.

Example 9.11. The algorithm of Fig. 9.21 applied to the tree of Fig. 9.18 yields the order from which the code of Fig. 9.20 was produced. For a more complete example, consider the dag of Fig. 9.22.

(1)   **while** unlisted interior nodes remain **do begin**
(2)   select an unlisted node n, all of whose parents have
               been listed;
(3)   list n;
(4)   **while** the leftmost child m of n has no unlisted parents
               and is not a leaf **do**
               /∗ since n was just listed, m is not yet listed ∗/
               begin
(5)   list m;
(6) $n := m$
               end
        end

Fig. 9.21. Node listing algorithm.

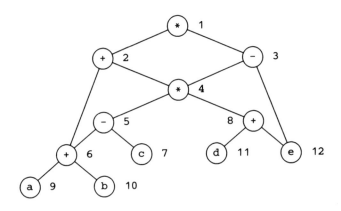

Fig. 9.22. A dag.

Initially the only node with no unlisted parents is 1, so we set $n=1$ at line
(2) and list 1 at line (3). Now the left argument of 1, which is 2, has its
parents listed, so we list 2 and set $n=2$ at line (6). Now at line (4) we find
the leftmost child of 2, which is 6, has an unlisted parent, 5. Thus we select a
new n at line (2), and node 3 is the only candidate. We list 3 and then
proceed down its left chain, listing 4, 5, and 6. This leaves only 8 among the
interior nodes, so we list that. The resulting list is 1234568 so the suggested
order of evaluation is 8654321. This ordering corresponds to the sequence of
three-address statements:

```
t8 := d + e
t6 := a + b
t5 := t6 - c
```

$$t_4 := t_5 * t_8$$
$$t_3 := t_4 - e$$
$$t_2 := t_6 + t_4$$
$$t_1 := t_2 * t_3$$

which will yield optimal code for the dag on our machine whatever the number of registers, if the code-generation algorithm of Section 9.6 is used. It should be noted that in this example our ordering heuristic never had any choices to make at step (2), but in general it may have many choices.   □

Optimal Ordering for Trees

It turns out that for the machine model of Section 9.2 we can give a simple algorithm to determine the optimal order in which to evaluate statements in a basic block when the dag representation of the block is a tree. Optimal order here means the order that yields the shortest instruction sequence, over all instruction sequences that evaluate the tree. This algorithm, modified to take into account register pairs and other target-machine vagaries, has been used in compilers for Algol, Bliss, and C.

The algorithm has two parts. The first part labels each node of the tree, bottom-up, with an integer that denotes the fewest number of registers required to evaluate the tree with no stores of intermediate results. The second part of the algorithm is a tree traversal whose order is governed by the computed node labels. The output code is generated during the tree traversal.

Intuitively, the algorithm works, given the two operands of a binary operator, by first evaluating the operand requiring more registers (the harder operand). If the register requirements of both operands are the same, either operand can be evaluated first.

The Labeling Algorithm

We use the term "left leaf" to mean a node that is a leaf and the leftmost descendant of its parent. All other leaves are referred to as "right leaves."

The labeling can be done by visiting nodes in a bottom-up order so that a node is not visited until all its children are labeled. The order in which parse tree nodes are created is suitable if the parse tree is used as intermediate code, so in this case, the labels can be computed as a syntax-directed translation. Figure 9.23 gives the algorithm for computing the label at node n. In the important special case that n is a binary node and its children have labels l_1 and l_2, the formula of line (6) reduces to

$$label(n) = \begin{cases} \max(l_1, l_2) & \text{if } l_1 \neq l_2 \\ l_1 + 1 & \text{if } l_1 = l_2 \end{cases}$$

Example 9.12. Consider the tree in Fig. 9.18. A postorder traversal[12] of the

---

[12] A postorder traversal recursively visits the subtrees rooted at children $n_1, n_2, \ldots, n_k$ of a node n, then n. It is the order in which nodes of a parse tree are created in a bottom-up parse.

(1)   **if** n is a leaf **then**
(2)   **if** n is the leftmost child of its parent **then**
(3) $label(n) := 1$
(4)   **else** $label(n) := 0$
      else begin /* n is an interior node */
(5)   let $n_1, n_2, \ldots, n_k$ be the children of n ordered by $label$,
            so $label(n_1) \geq label(n_2) \geq \cdots \geq label(n_k)$;
(6) $label(n) := \max_{1 \leq i \leq k} (label(n_i) + i - 1)$

   end

Fig. 9.23. Label computation.

nodes visits the nodes in the order a b t_1 e c d t_2 t_3 t_4. Postorder is always an appropriate order in which to do the label computations. Node a is labeled 1 since it is a left leaf. Node b is labeled 0 since it is a right leaf. Node t_1 is labeled 1 because the labels of its children are unequal and the maximum label of a child is 1. Figure 9.24 shows the labeled tree that results. It implies that two registers are needed to evaluate t_4 and, in fact, two registers are needed just to evaluate t_3.   □

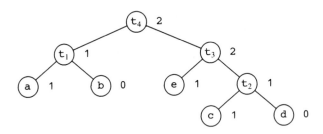

Fig. 9.24. Labeled tree.

Code Generation from a Labeled Tree

We now present the algorithm that takes as input a labeled tree T and produces as output a machine code sequence that evaluates T into R0. (R0 can then be stored into the appropriate memory location.) We assume T has only binary operators. The generalization to operators with an arbitrary number of operands is not hard, and it is left as an exercise.

   The algorithm uses the recursive procedure $gencode(n)$ to produce machine code evaluating the subtree of T with root n into a register. The procedure $gencode$ uses a stack $rstack$ to allocate registers. Initially, $rstack$ contains all available registers, which we assume are R0, R1, . . . , R($r-1$), in this order. A call of *gencode* may find a subset of the registers, perhaps in a different order, on *rstack*. When *gencode* returns, it leaves the registers on *rstack* in the same order it found them. The resulting code computes the value of the tree T in the top register on *rstack*.

The function *swap(rstack)* interchanges the top two registers on *rstack*. The use of *swap* is to make sure that a left child and its parent are evaluated into the same register.

The procedure *gencode* uses a stack *tstack* to allocate temporary memory locations. We assume *tstack* initially contains T0, T1, T2, ... In practice, *tstack* need not be implemented as a list, if we just keep track of that i such that Ti is currently on top. The contents of *tstack* is always a suffix of T0, T1, ...

The statement $X := pop(stack)$ means "pop *stack* and assign the value popped to X." Conversely, we use *push(stack, X)* to mean "push X onto *stack*;" *top(stack)* refers to the value on top of *stack*.

The code-generation algorithm is to call *gencode* on the root of T, where *gencode* is the procedure shown in Fig. 9.25. It can be explained by examining each of the five cases. For case 0, we have a subtree of the form

That is, n is a leaf and the leftmost child of its parent. Therefore we generate just a load instruction. In case 1, we have a subtree of the form

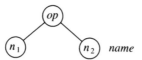

for which we generate code to evaluate n_1 into register $R = top(rstack)$ followed by the instruction *op name, R*. In case 2, we have a subtree of the form

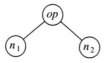

where n_1 can be evaluated without stores but n_2 is harder to evaluate (i.e., requires more registers) than n_1. For this case, we swap the top two registers on *rstack*, then evaluate n_2 into $R = top(rstack)$. We remove R from *rstack* and evaluate n_1 into $S = top(rstack)$. Note that S was the register initially on top of *rstack* at the beginning of case 2. We then generate the instruction *op R, S*, which produces the value of n (the node labeled *op*) in register S. Another call to *swap* leaves *rstack* as it was when this call of *gencode* began.

```
procedure gencode (n);
begin
/* case 0 */
if n is a left leaf representing operand name and n is
           the leftmost child of its parent then
       print 'MOV' ‖ name ‖ ',' ‖ top (rstack)
else if n is an interior node with operator op, left child n₁,
           and right child n₂ then
/* case 1 */
       if label (n₂) = 0 then begin
           let name be the operand represented by n₂;
           gencode (n₁);
           print op ‖ name ‖ ',' ‖ top (rstack)
       end
/* case 2 */
       else if 1 ≤ label (n₁) < label (n₂) and label (n₁) < r then begin
           swap (rstack);
           gencode (n₂);
           R := pop (rstack);  /* n₂ was evaluated into register R */
           gencode (n₁);
           print op ‖ R ‖ ',' ‖ top (rstack);
           push (rstack, R);
           swap (rstack)
       end
/* case 3 */
       else if 1 ≤ label (n₂) ≤ label (n₁) and label (n₂) < r then begin
           gencode (n₁);
           R := pop (rstack);  /* n₁ was evaluated into register R */
           gencode (n₂);
           print op ‖ top (rstack) ‖ ',' ‖ R;
           push (rstack, R)
       end
/* case 4,  both labels ≥ r, the total number of registers */
       else begin
           gencode (n₂);
           T := pop (tstack);
           print 'MOV' ‖ top (rstack) ‖ ',' ‖ T;
           gencode (n₁);
           push (tstack, T);
           print op ‖ T ‖ ',' ‖ top (rstack)
       end
   end
```

Fig. 9.25. The function *gencode*.

Case 3 is similar to case 2 except that here the left subtree is harder and is evaluated first. There is no need to *swap* registers here.

Case 4 occurs when both subtrees require r or more registers to evaluate without stores. Since we must use a temporary memory location, we first evaluate the right subtree into the temporary T, then the left subtree, and finally the root.

Example 9.13. Let us generate code for the labeled tree in Fig. 9.24 with *rstack* = R0, R1 initially. The sequence of calls to *gencode* and code printing steps is shown in Fig. 9.26. Shown alongside in brackets is the contents of *rstack* at the time of each call, with the top at the right end. The code sequence here is a permutation of that in Fig. 9.20.   □

```
gencode(t₄)      [R₁R₀]                      /* case 2 */
    gencode(t₃)      [R₀R₁]                  /* case 3 */
        gencode(e)       [R₀R₁]              /* case 0 */
        print MOV e,R₁
    gencode(t₂)      [R₀]                     /* case 1 */
        gencode(c)       [R₀]                /* case 0 */
        print MOV c,R₀
        print ADD d,R₀
        print SUB R₀,R₁
    gencode(t₁)      [R₀]                     /* case 1 */
        gencode(a)       [R₀]                /* case 0 */
        print MOV a,R₀
        print ADD b,R₀
    print SUB R₁,R₀
```

Fig. 9.26. Trace of *gencode* routine.

We can prove that *gencode* produces optimal code on expressions for our machine model, assuming that no algebraic properties of operators are taken into account and assuming there are no common subexpressions. The proof, left as an exercise, is based on showing that any code sequence must perform

1. an operation for each interior node,
2. a load for each leaf which is the leftmost child of its parent, and
3. a store for every node both of whose children have labels equal to or greater than r.

Since *gencode* produces exactly these steps, it is optimal.

Multiregister Operations

We can modify our labeling algorithm to handle operations like multiplication, division, or a function call, which normally require more than one register to perform. Simply modify step (6) of Fig. 9.23, the labeling algorithm, so *label(n)* is always at least the number of registers required by the operation. For example, if a function call is assumed to require all r registers, replace line (6) by $label(n) = r$. If multiplication requires two registers, in the binary case use

$$label(n) = \begin{cases} \max(2, l_1, l_2) & \text{if } l_1 \neq l_2 \\ l_1 + 1 & \text{if } l_1 = l_2 \end{cases}$$

where l_1 and l_2 are the labels of the children of n.

Unfortunately, this modification will not guarantee that a register-pair is available for a multiplication or division, or for multiple-precision operations. A useful trick on some machines is to pretend that multiplication and division require three registers. If *swap* is never used in *gencode*, then *rstack* will always contain consecutive high-numbered registers, $i, i+1, \ldots, r-1$ for some i. Thus the first three of these are sure to include a register pair. By taking advantage of the fact that many operations are commutative we can often avoid using case 2 of *gencode*, the case that calls *swap*. Also, even if *rstack* does not contain three consecutive registers at the top, we have a very good chance of finding a register-pair somewhere in *rstack*.

Algebraic Properties

If we may assume algebraic laws for various operators, we have the opportunity to replace a given tree T by one with smaller labels (to avoid stores in case 4 of *gencode*) and/or fewer left leaves (to avoid loads in case 0). For example, since + is normally regarded as being commutative, we may replace the tree of Fig. 9.27(a) by that of Fig. 9.27(b), reducing the number of left leaves by one and possibly lowering some labels as well.

Since + is usually treated as being associative as well as being commutative, we may take a cluster of nodes labeled + as in Fig. 9.27(c) and replace it by a left chain as in Fig. 9.27(d). To minimize the label of the root we need only arrange that T_{i_1} is one of T_1, T_2, T_3, and T_4 with a largest label and that T_{i_1} is not a leaf unless all of $T_1, \ldots, T_4$ are.

Common Subexpressions

When there are common subexpressions in a basic block, the corresponding dag will no longer be a tree. The common subexpressions will correspond to nodes with more than one parent, called *shared nodes*. We can no longer apply the labeling algorithm or *gencode* directly. In fact, common subexpressions make code generation markedly more difficult from a mathematical point of view. Bruno and Sethi [1976] showed that optimal code generation for dags on a one-register machine is NP-complete. Aho, Johnson, and Ullman [1977a] showed that even with an unlimited number of registers the problem remains NP-complete. The difficulty arises in trying to determine an optimal order in which to evaluate a dag in the cheapest way.

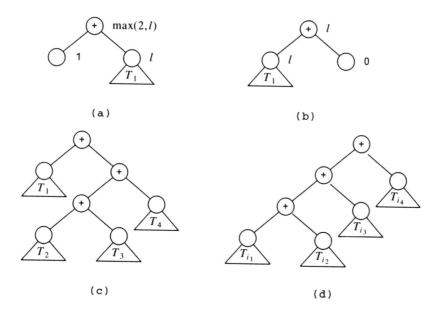

Fig. 9.27. Commutative and associative transformations.

In practice, we can obtain a reasonable solution if we partition the dag into a set of trees by finding for each root and/or shared node n, the maximal subtree with n as root that includes no other shared nodes, except as leaves. For example, the dag of Fig. 9.22 can be partitioned into the trees of Fig. 9.28. Each shared node with p parents appears as a leaf in at most p trees. Nodes with more than one parent in the same tree can be turned into as many leaves as necessary, so no leaf has multiple parents.

Once we have partitioned the dag into trees in this fashion, we can order the evaluation of the trees and use any of the preceding algorithms to generate code for each tree. The order of the trees must be such that shared values that are leaves of a tree must be available when the tree is evaluated. The shared quantities can be computed and stored into memory (or kept in registers if enough registers are available). While this process does not necessarily generate optimal code, it will often be satisfactory.

9.11 DYNAMIC PROGRAMMING CODE-GENERATION ALGORITHM

In the previous section, the procedure *gencode* produces optimal code from an expression tree using an amount of time that is a linear function of the size of the tree. This procedure works for machines in which all computation is done in registers and in which instructions consist of an operator applied to two registers or to a register and a memory location.

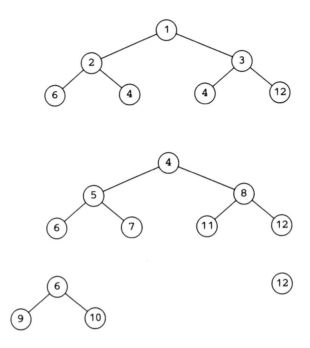

Fig. 9.28. Partition into trees.

An algorithm based on the principle of dynamic programming can be used to extend the class of machines for which optimal code can be generated from expression trees in linear time. The dynamic programming algorithm applies to a broad class of register machines with complex instruction sets.

A Class of Register Machines

The dynamic programming algorithm can be used to generate code for any machine with r interchangeable registers R0, R1, . . . , R$r-1$ and instructions of the form Ri := E where E is any expression containing operators, registers, and memory locations. If E involves one or more registers, then Ri must be one of those registers. This machine model includes the machine introduced in Section 9.2.

For example, the instruction ADD R0,R1 would be represented as R1 := R1 + R0. The instruction ADD *R0,R1 would be represented as R1 := R1 + ind R0 where ind stands for the indirection operator.

We assume a machine has a load instruction Ri := M, a store instruction M := Ri, and a register-to-register copy instruction Ri := Rj. For simplicity, we also assume every instruction costs one unit, although the dynamic programming algorithm can easily be modified to work even if each instruction has its own cost.

The Principle of Dynamic Programming

The dynamic programming algorithm partitions the problem of generating optimal code for an expression into subproblems of generating optimal code for the subexpressions of the given expression. As a simple example, consider an expression E of the form $E_1 + E_2$. An optimal program for E is formed by combining optimal programs for E_1 and E_2, in one or the other order, followed by code to evaluate the operator $+$. The subproblems of generating optimal code for E_1 and E_2 are solved similarly.

An optimal program produced by the dynamic programming algorithm has an important property. It evaluates an expression $E = E_1 \; op \; E_2$ "contiguously." We can appreciate what this means by looking at the syntax tree T for E:

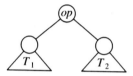

Here T_1 and T_2 are trees for E_1 and E_2, respectively.

Contiguous Evaluation

We say a program P evaluates a tree T *contiguously* if it first evaluates those subtrees of T that need to be computed into memory. Then, it evaluates the remainder of T either in the order T_1, T_2, and then the root, or in the order T_2, T_1, and then the root, in either case using the previously computed values from memory whenever necessary. As an example of noncontiguous evaluation, P might first evaluate part of T_1 leaving the value in a register (instead of memory), next evaluate T_2, and then return to evaluate the rest of T_1.

For the register machine defined above, we can prove that given any machine-language program P to evaluate an expression tree T, we can find an equivalent program P' such that

1. P' is of no higher cost than P,
2. P' uses no more registers than P, and
3. P' evaluates the tree in a contiguous fashion.

This result implies that every expression tree can be evaluated optimally by a contiguous program.

By way of contrast, machines with even-odd register pairs such as the IBM System/370 machines do not always have optimal contiguous evaluations. For these machines, we can give examples of expression trees in which an optimal machine language program must first evaluate into a register a portion of the left subtree of the root, then a portion of the right subtree, then another part of the left subtree, then another part of the right, and so on. This type of oscillation is unnecessary for an optimal evaluation of any expression tree using the general register machine.

The contiguous evaluation property defined above says that for any expression tree T there always exists an optimal program that consists of optimal programs for subtrees of the root, followed by an instruction to evaluate the root. This property allows us to use the dynamic programming algorithm to generate an optimal program for T.

The Dynamic Programming Algorithm

The dynamic programming algorithm proceeds in three phases. Suppose the target machine has r registers. In the first phase, compute bottom-up for each node n of the expression tree T an array C of costs, in which the ith component $C[i]$ is the optimal cost of computing the subtree S rooted at n into a register, assuming i registers are available for the computation, for $1 \leq i \leq r$. The cost includes whatever loads and stores are necessary to evaluate S in the given number of registers. It also includes the cost of computing the operator at the root of S. The zeroth component of the cost vector is the optimal cost of computing the subtree S into memory. The contiguous evaluation property ensures that an optimal program for S can be generated by considering combinations of optimal programs only for the subtrees of the root of S. This restriction reduces the number of cases that need to be considered.

To compute $C[i]$ at node n, consider each machine instruction $R := E$ whose expression E matches the subexpression rooted at node n. By examining the cost vectors at the corresponding descendants of n, determine the costs of evaluating the operands of E. For those operands of E that are registers, consider all possible orders in which the corresponding subtrees of T can be evaluated into registers. In each ordering, the first subtree corresponding to a register operand can be evaluated using i available registers, the second using $i-1$ registers, and so on. To account for node n, add in the cost of the instruction $R := E$ that was used to match node n. The value $C[i]$ is then the minimum cost over all possible orders.

The cost vectors for the entire tree T can be computed bottom up in time linearly proportional to the number of nodes in T. It is convenient to store at each node the instruction used to achieve the best cost for $C[i]$ for each value of i. The smallest cost in the vector for the root of T gives the minimum cost of evaluating T.

In the second phase of the algorithm, traverse T, using the cost vectors to determine which subtrees of T must be computed into memory. In the third phase, traverse each tree using the cost vectors and associated instructions to generate the final target code. The code for the subtrees computed into memory locations is generated first. These two phases can also be implemented to run in time linearly proportional to the size of the expression tree.

Example 9.14. Consider a machine having two registers R0 and R1, and the following instructions, each of unit cost:

```
Ri  := Mj
Ri  := Ri op Rj
Ri  := Ri op Mj
Ri  := Rj
Mi  := Ri
```

In these instructions, Ri is either R0 or R1, and Mj is a memory location.

Let us apply the dynamic programming algorithm to generate optimal code for the syntax tree in Fig. 9.29. In the first phase, we compute the cost vectors shown at each node. To illustrate this cost computation, consider the cost vector at the leaf a. $C[0]$, the cost of computing a into memory, is 0 since it is already there. $C[1]$, the cost of computing a into a register, is 1 since we can load it into a register with the instruction R0 := a. $C[2]$, the cost of loading a into a register with two registers available, is the same as that with one register available. The cost vector at leaf a is therefore $(0,1,1)$.

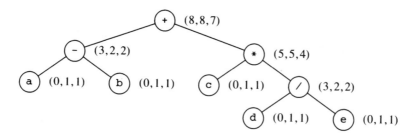

Fig. 9.29. Syntax tree for (a−b)+c*(d/e) with cost vector at each node.

Consider the cost vector at the root. We first determine the minimum cost of computing the root with one and two registers available. The machine instruction R0 := R0 + M matches the root, because the root is labeled with the operator +. Using this instruction, the minimum cost of evaluating the root with one register available is the minimum cost of computing its right subtree into memory, plus the minimum cost of computing its left subtree into the register, plus 1 for the instruction. No other way exists. The cost vectors at the right and left children of the root show that the minimum cost of computing the root with one register available is $5+2+1 = 8$.

Now consider the minimum cost of evaluating the root with two registers available. Three cases arise depending on which instruction is used to compute the root and in what order the left and right subtrees of the root are evaluated.

1. Compute the left subtree with two registers available into register R0, compute the right subtree with one register available into register R1, and use the instruction R0 := R0 + R1 to compute the root. This sequence has cost $2+5+1 = 8$.

2. Compute the right subtree with two registers available into R1, compute
    the left subtree with one register available into R0, and use the instruc-
    tion R0 := R0 + R1. This sequence has cost $4+2+1 = 7$.

3. Compute the right subtree into memory location M, compute the left sub-
    tree with two registers available into register R0, and use the instruction
    R0 := R0 + M. This sequence has cost $5+2+1 = 8$.

The second choice gives the minimum cost 7.

The minimum cost of computing the root into memory is determined by
adding one to the minimum cost of computing the root with all registers available; that is, we compute the root into a register and then store the result.
The cost vector at the root is therefore (8,8,7).

From the cost vectors we can easily construct the code sequence by making
a traversal of the tree. From the tree in Fig. 9.29, assuming two registers are
available, an optimal code sequence is

```
R0  :=  c
R1  :=  d
R1  :=  R1 / e
R0  :=  R0 * R1
R1  :=  a
R1  :=  R1 - b
R1  :=  R1 + R0
```
                                                                          □

This technique, originally developed in Aho and Johnson [1976], has been
used in a number of compilers, including the second version of S. C.
Johnson's portable C compiler, PCC2. The technique facilitates retargeting
because of the applicability of the dynamic programming technique to a broad
class of machines.

9.12 CODE-GENERATOR GENERATORS

Code generation involves picking an evaluation order for operations, assigning
registers to hold values, and selecting the appropriate target-language instructions to implement the operators in the intermediate representation. Even if
we assume the order of evaluation is given and registers are allocated by a
separate mechanism, the problem of deciding what instructions to use can be a
large combinatorial task, especially on a machine rich in addressing modes.
In this section, we present tree-rewriting techniques that can be used to construct the instruction selection phase of a code generator automatically from a
high-level specification of the target machine.

Code Generation by Tree Rewriting

Throughout this section, the input to the code-generation process will be a
sequence of trees at the semantic level of the target machine. The trees are
what we might get after inserting the run-time addresses into the intermediate

representation, as described in Section 9.3.

Example 9.15. Figure 9.30 contains a tree for the assignment statement
$a[i]:=b+1$ in which a and i are locals whose run-time addresses are given
as offsets $const_a$ and $const_i$ from SP, the register containing the pointer
to the beginning of the current activation record. The array a is stored on the
run-time stack. The assignment to $a[i]$ is an indirect assignment in which
the r-value of the location for $a[i]$ is set to the r-value of the expression
$b+1$. The address of array a is given by adding the value of the constant
$const_a$ to the contents of register SP; the value of i is in the location
obtained by adding the value of the constant $const_i$ to the contents of register SP. The variable b is a global in memory location mem_b. For simplicity,
we assume all variables are of type character.

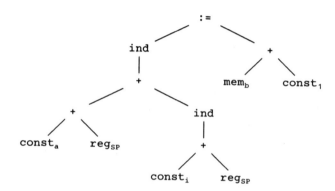

Fig. 9.30. Intermediate-code tree for $a[i]:=b+1$.

In the tree, the ind operator treats its argument as a memory address. As
the left child of an assignment operator, the ind node gives the location into
which the r-value on the right side of the assignment operator is to be stored.
If an argument of a + or ind operator is a memory location or a register,
then the contents of that memory location or register are taken as the value.
The leaves in the tree are type attributes with subscripts; the subscript indicates the value of the attribute.   □

The target code is generated during a process in which the input tree is
reduced into a single node by applying a sequence of tree-rewriting rules to
the tree. Each tree-rewriting rule is a statement of the form

    replacement ← *template* { *action* }

where

1. *replacement* is a single node,
2. *template* is a tree, and
3. *action* is a code fragment, as in a syntax-directed translation scheme.

A set of tree-rewriting rules is called a *tree-translation scheme*.

Each tree template represents a computation performed by the sequence of machine instructions emitted by the associated action. Usually, a template corresponds to a single machine instruction. The leaves of the template are attributes with subscripts, as in the input tree. Often, certain restrictions apply to the values of the subscripts in the templates; these restrictions are specified as semantic predicates that must be satisfied before the template is said to match. For example, a predicate might specify that the value of a constant fall in a certain range.

A tree-translation scheme is a convenient way to represent the instruction-selection phase of a code generator. As an example of a tree-rewriting rule, consider the rule for the register-to-register add instruction:

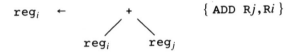

This rule is used as follows. If the input tree contains a subtree that matches this tree template, that is, a subtree whose root is labeled by the operator + and whose left and right children are quantities in registers i and j, then we can replace that subtree by a single node labeled reg_i and emit the instruction ADD Rj, Ri as output. More than one template may match a subtree at a given time; we shall describe shortly some mechanisms for deciding which rule to apply in cases of conflict. We assume register allocation is done before code selection.

Example 9.16. Figure 9.31 contains tree-rewriting rules for a few instructions of our target machine. These rules will be used in a running example throughout this section. The first two rules correspond to load instructions, the next two to store instructions, and the remainder to indexed loads and additions. Note that rule (8) requires the value of the constant to be one. This condition would be specified by a semantic predicate.   □

A tree-translation scheme works in the following way. Given an input tree, the templates in the tree-rewriting rules are applied to its subtrees. If a template matches, the matching subtree in the input tree is replaced with the replacement node of the rule and the action associated with the rule is done. If the action contains a sequence of machine instructions, the instructions are emitted. This process is repeated until the tree is reduced to a single node, or until no more templates match. The sequence of machine instructions generated as the input tree is reduced to a single node constitutes the output of the tree-translation scheme on the given input tree.

The process of specifying a code generator becomes similar to that of using a syntax-directed translation scheme to specify a translator. We write a tree-translation scheme to describe the instruction set of a target machine. In practice, we would like to find a scheme that causes a minimal-cost instruction

<table>
<tr><td>(1)</td><td>$\mathtt{reg}_i$</td><td>←</td><td>$\mathtt{const}_c$</td><td>{ MOV #c , Ri }</td></tr>
<tr><td>(2)</td><td>$\mathtt{reg}_i$</td><td>←</td><td>$\mathtt{mem}_a$</td><td>{ MOV a , Ri }</td></tr>
<tr><td>(3)</td><td>mem</td><td>←</td><td>
</td><td>{ MOV Ri , a }</td></tr>
<tr><td>(4)</td><td>mem</td><td>←</td><td>
</td><td>{ MOV Rj , *Ri }</td></tr>
<tr><td>(5)</td><td>$\mathtt{reg}_i$</td><td>←</td><td>
</td><td>{ MOV c(Rj) , Ri }</td></tr>
<tr><td>(6)</td><td>$\mathtt{reg}_i$</td><td>←</td><td>
</td><td>{ ADD c(Rj) , Ri }</td></tr>
<tr><td>(7)</td><td>$\mathtt{reg}_i$</td><td>←</td><td>
</td><td>{ ADD Rj , Ri }</td></tr>
<tr><td>(8)</td><td>$\mathtt{reg}_i$</td><td>←</td><td>
</td><td>{ INC Ri }</td></tr>
</table>

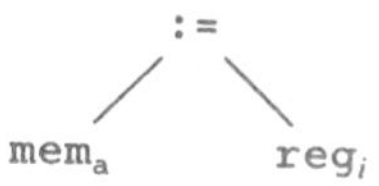

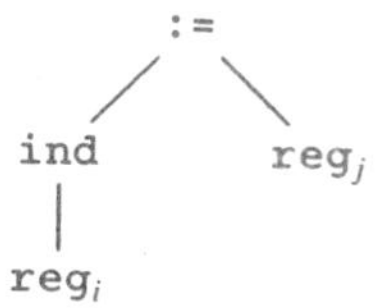

Fig. 9.31. Tree-rewriting rules for some target-machine instructions.

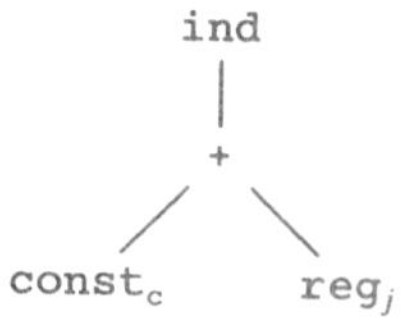

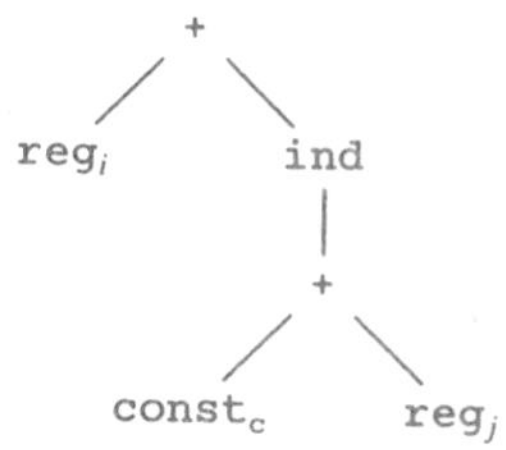

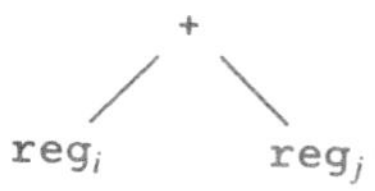

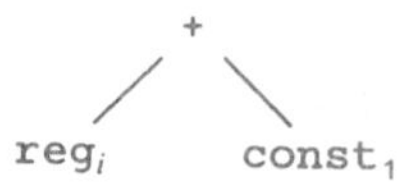

sequence to be generated for each input tree. Several tools are available to help build a code generator automatically from a tree-translation scheme.

Example 9.17. Let us use the tree-translation scheme in Fig. 9.31 to generate code for the input tree in Fig. 9.30. Suppose the first rule

$$(1) \quad reg_0 \quad \leftarrow \quad const_a \qquad \{ \text{ MOV \#a,R0 } \}$$

is applied to load the constant a into register R0. The label of the leftmost leaf then changes from $const_a$ to reg_0 and the instruction MOV #a,R0 is generated. The seventh rule

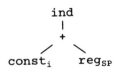

$$(7) \quad reg_0 \quad \leftarrow \qquad \qquad \{ \text{ ADD SP,R0 } \}$$

now matches the leftmost subtree with root labeled +. Using this rule, we rewrite this subtree as a single node labeled reg_0 and generate the instruction ADD SP,R0. Now the tree looks like

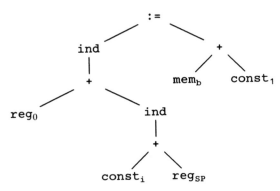

At this point, we could apply rule (5) to reduce the subtree

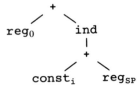

to a single node labeled reg_1. However, we can also use rule (6) to reduce the larger subtree

into a single node labeled reg_0 and generate the instruction ADD i(SP),R0.

Assuming it is more efficient to use a single instruction to compute the larger subtree rather than the smaller one, we choose the latter reduction to get

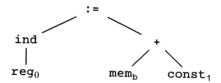

In the right subtree, rule (2) applies to the leaf mem_b. This rule generates an instruction to load b into register 1, say. Now, using rule (8) we can match the subtree

and generate the increment instruction INC R1. At this point, the input tree has been reduced to

This remaining tree is matched by rule (4), which reduces the tree to a single node and generates the instruction MOV R1, *R0.

In the process of reducing the tree to a single node, we generate the following code sequence:

```
MOV #a,R0
ADD SP,R0
ADD i(SP),R0
MOV b,R1
INC R1
MOV R1,*R0
```
□

Several aspects of this tree-reduction process need further explication. We have not specified how the tree-pattern matching is to be done. Nor have we specified an order in which the templates are matched or what to do if more than one template matches at a given time. Also, notice that if no template matches, then the code-generation process blocks. On the other extreme, it may be possible for a single node to be rewritten indefinitely, generating an infinite sequence of register move instructions or an infinite sequence of loads and stores.

One way to do the tree-pattern matching efficiently is to extend the multiple-keyword pattern-matching algorithm in Exercise 3.32 into a top-down tree-pattern matching algorithm. Each template can be represented by a set of strings, namely, by the set of paths from the root to the leaves. From these collections of strings, we can construct a tree-pattern matcher as in Exercise 3.32.

The ordering and multiple-match problems can be resolved by using tree-pattern matching in conjunction with the dynamic programming algorithm of the previous section. A tree-translation scheme can be augmented with cost information by associating with each tree-rewriting rule the cost of the sequence of machine instructions generated if that rule is applied.

In practice, the tree-rewriting process can be implemented by running the tree-pattern matcher during a depth-first traversal of the input tree and performing the reductions as the nodes are visited for the last time. If we run the dynamic programming algorithm concurrently, we can select an optimal sequence of matches using the cost information associated with each rule. We may need to defer deciding upon a match until the cost of all alternatives is known. Using this approach, a small, efficient code generator can be constructed quickly from a tree-rewriting scheme. Moreover, the dynamic programming algorithm frees the code-generator designer from having to resolve conflicting matches or decide upon an order for the evaluation.

Pattern Matching by Parsing

Another approach is to use an LR parser to do the pattern matching. The input tree can be treated as a string by using its prefix representation. For example, the prefix representation for the tree in Fig. 9.30 is

$$:= \text{ind } + + \text{const}_a \text{ reg}_{SP} \text{ ind } + \text{const}_i \text{ reg}_{SP} + \text{mem}_b \text{ const}_1$$

The tree-translation scheme can be converted into a syntax-directed translation scheme by replacing the tree-rewriting rules with the productions of a context-free grammar in which the right sides are prefix representations of the instruction templates.

Example 9.18. The syntax-directed translation scheme in Fig. 9.32 is based on the tree translation scheme in Fig. 9.31.   □

From the productions of the translation scheme we build an LR parser using one of the LR-parser construction techniques of Chapter 4. The target code is generated by emitting the machine instruction corresponding to each reduction.

A code-generation grammar is usually highly ambiguous, and some care needs to be given to how the parsing-action conflicts are resolved when the parser is constructed. In the absence of cost information, a general rule is to favor larger reductions over smaller ones. This means that in a reduce-reduce conflict, the longer reduction is favored; in a shift-reduce conflict, the shift move is chosen. This "maximal munch" approach causes a larger number of operations to be performed with a single machine instruction.

There are several aspects to using LR parsing in code generation. First, the

(1)	$reg_i \rightarrow const_c$	{ MOV #c , Ri }
(2)	$reg_i \rightarrow mem_a$	{ MOV a , Ri }
(3)	mem $\rightarrow$:= mem_a reg_i	{ MOV Ri , a }
(4)	mem $\rightarrow$:= ind reg_i reg_j	{ MOV Rj , *Ri }
(5)	$reg_i \rightarrow$ ind + $const_c$ reg_j	{ MOV c(Rj) , Ri }
(6)	$reg_i \rightarrow$ + reg_i ind + $const_c$ reg_j	{ ADD c(Rj) , Ri }
(7)	$reg_i \rightarrow$ + reg_i reg_j	{ ADD Rj , Ri }
(8)	$reg_i \rightarrow$ + reg_i $const_1$	{ INC Ri }

Fig. 9.32. Syntax-directed translation scheme constructed from Fig. 9.31.

parsing method is efficient and well understood, so reliable and efficient code generators can be produced using the algorithms described in Chapter 4. Second, it is relatively easy to retarget the resulting code generator; a code selector for a new machine can be constructed by writing a grammar to describe the instructions of the new machine. Third, the quality of the code generated can be made efficient by adding special-case productions to take advantage of machine idioms.

However, there are some difficulties as well. A left-to-right order of evaluation is fixed by the parsing method. Also, for some machines with large numbers of addressing modes, the machine-description grammar and resulting parser can become inordinately large. As a consequence, specialized techniques are necessary to encode and process the machine-description grammars. We must also be careful that the resulting parser does not block (has no next move) while parsing on an expression tree, because the grammar does not handle some operator patterns or the parser has made the wrong resolution of some parsing-action conflict. We must also make sure the parser does not get into an infinite loop of reductions of productions with single symbols on the right side. The looping problem can be solved using a state-splitting technique at the time the parser tables are generated (see Glanville [1977]).

Routines for Semantic Checking

The leaves in the input tree are type attributes with subscripts, where a subscript associates a value with an attribute. In a code-generation translation scheme, the same attributes appear, but often with restrictions on what values the subscripts can have. For example, a machine instruction may require that an attribute value fall in a certain range or that the values of two attributes be related.

These restrictions on attribute values can be specified as predicates that are invoked before a reduction is made. In fact, the general use of semantic actions and predicates can provide greater flexibility and ease of description than a purely grammatical specification of a code generator. Generic templates can be used to represent classes of instructions and the semantic actions can then be used to pick instructions for specific cases. For example, two forms of the addition instruction can be represented with one template:

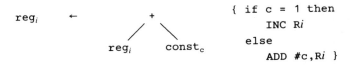

Parsing-action conflicts can be resolved by disambiguating predicates that can allow different selection strategies to be used in different contexts. A smaller description of a target machine is possible because certain aspects of the machine architecture, such as addressing modes, can be factored into the attributes. The complication in this approach is that it may become difficult to verify the accuracy of the attribute grammar as a faithful description of the target machine, although this problem is shared to some degree by all code generators.

EXERCISES

9.1 Generate code for the following C statements for the target machine of Section 9.2 assuming all variables are static. Assume three registers are available.
a) `x = 1`
b) `x = y`
c) `x = x + 1`
d) `x = a + b * c`
e) `x = a/(b+c) - d*(e+f)`

9.2 Repeat Exercise 9.1 assuming all variables are automatic (allocated on the stack).

9.3 Generate code for the following C statements for the target machine of Section 9.2 assuming all variables are static. Assume three registers are available.
a) `x = a[i] + 1`
b) `a[i] = b[c[i]]`
c) `a[i][j] = b[i][k] * c[k][j]`
d) `a[i] = a[i] + b[j]`
e) `a[i] += b[j]`

9.4 Do Exercise 9.1 using
a) the algorithm in Section 9.6
b) the procedure *gencode*
c) the dynamic programming algorithm of Section 9.11

9.5 Generate code for the following C statements

```
a) x = f(a) + f(a) + f(a)
b) x = f(a)/g(b,c)
c) x = f(f(a))
d) x = ++f(a)
e) *p++ = *q++
```

9.6 Generate code for the following C program

```
main()
{
    int i;
    int a[10];
    while (i <= 10)
        a[i] = 0;
}
```

9.7 Suppose that for the loop of Fig. 9.13 we choose to allocate three registers to hold a, b, and c. Generate code for the blocks of this loop. Compare the cost of your code with that in Fig. 9.14.

9.8 Construct the register-interference graph for the program in Fig. 9.13.

9.9 Suppose that for simplicity we automatically store all registers on the stack (or in memory if a stack is not used) before each procedure call and restore them after the return. How does this affect the formula (9.4) used to evaluate the utility of allocating a register to a given variable in a loop?

9.10 Modify the function *getreg* of Section 9.6 to return register-pairs when needed.

9.11 Give an example of a dag for which the heuristic for ordering the nodes of a dag given in Fig. 9.21 does not give the best ordering.

*9.12 Generate optimal code for the following assignment statements:
```
a) x := a + b * c
b) x := (a * -b) + (c - (d + e))
c) x := (a/b - c)/d
d) x := a + (b + c/d*e)/(f*g - h*i)
e) a[i,j] := b[i,j] - c[a[k,l]] * d[i+j]
```

9.13 Generate code for the following Pascal program:

```
program forloop(input, output);
    var i, initial, final: integer;
    begin
        read(initial, final);
        for i:= initial to final do
            writeln(i)
    end.
```

9.14 Construct the dag for the following basic block.

```
d := b * c
e := a + b
b := b * c
a := e - d
```

9.15 What are the legal evaluation orders and names for the values at the nodes for the dag of Exercise 9.14
a) assuming a, b and c are live at the end of the basic block?
b) assuming only a is live at the end?

9.16 In Exercise 9.15(b), if we are going to generate code for a machine with only one register, which evaluation order is best? Why?

9.17 We can modify the dag construction algorithm to take into account assignments to arrays and through pointers. When any element of an array is assigned, we assume a new value for that array is created. This new value is represented by a node whose children are the old value of the array, the value of the index into the array, and the value assigned. When an assignment through a pointer occurs, we assume we have created a new value for every variable that the pointer might have pointed to; the children of the node for each new value are the value of the pointer and the old value of the variable that might have been assigned. Using these assumptions, construct the dag for the following basic block:

```
a[i] := b
*p := c
d := a[j]
e := *p
*p := a[i]
```

Assume that (a) p can point anywhere, (b) p points to only b or d. Do not forget to show the implied order constraints.

9.18 If a pointer or array expression such as a[i] or *p is assigned and then used without the possibility of its value having changed in the interim, we can recognize and take advantage of the situation to simplify the dag. For example, in the code of Exercise 9.17, since p is not assigned between the second and fourth statements, the statement e := *p can be replaced by e := c, since we are sure that whatever p points to has the same value as c, even though we don't know what p points to. Revise the dag construction algorithm to take advantage of such inferences. Apply your algorithm to the code of Exercise 9.17.

**9.19 Devise an algorithm to generate optimal code for a sequence of three-address statements of the form a : = b + c on the n-register machine of Example 9.14. The statements must be executed in the order given. What is the time complexity of your algorithm?

BIBLIOGRAPHIC NOTES

The reader interested in overviews of code-generation research should consult Waite [1976a,b], Aho and Sethi [1977], Graham [1980 and 1984], Ganapathi, Fischer, and Hennessy [1982], Lunell [1983], and Henry [1984]. Code generation for Bliss is discussed by Wulf et al. [1975], for Pascal by Ammann [1977], and for PL.8 by Auslander and Hopkins [1982].

Program-usage statistics are useful for compiler design. Knuth [1971b] did an empirical study of Fortran programs. Elshoff [1976] provides some statistics on PL/I usage, and Shimasaki et al. [1980] and Carter [1982] analyze Pascal programs. The performance of several compilers on various computer instruction sets is discussed by Lunde [1977], Shustek [1978], and Ditzel and McLellan [1982].

Many of the heuristics for code generation proposed in this chapter have been used in various compilers. Freiburghouse [1974] discusses usage counts as an aid to generating good code for basic blocks. The strategy used in *getreg* of creating a free register by throwing out of a register the variable whose value will be unused for the longest time was shown optimal in a page-swapping context by Belady [1966]. Our strategy of allocating a fixed number of registers to hold variables for the duration of a loop was mentioned by Marill [1962] and used in the implementation of Fortran H by Lowry and Medlock [1969].

Horwitz et al. [1966] give an algorithm for optimizing the use of index registers in Fortran. Graph coloring as a register-allocation technique was proposed by J. Cocke, Ershov [1971], and Schwartz [1973]. The treatment of graph coloring in Section 9.7 follows Chaitin et al. [1981] and Chaitin [1982]. Chow and Hennessy [1984] describe a priority-based graph coloring algorithm for register allocation. Other approaches to register allocation are discussed by Kennedy [1972], Johnsson [1975], Harrison [1975], Beatty [1974], and Leverett [1982].

The labeling algorithm for trees in Section 9.10 is reminiscent of an algorithm for naming rivers: the confluence of a major river and a minor tributary continues to use the name of the major river; the confluence of two equal-sized rivers is given a new name. The labeling algorithm originally appeared in Ershov [1958]. Code-generation algorithms using this method have been proposed by Anderson [1964], Nievergelt [1965], Nakata [1967], Redziejowski [1969], and Beatty [1972]. Sethi and Ullman [1970] used the labeling method in an algorithm that they were able to prove generated optimal code for expression trees in a wide variety of situations. The procedure *gencode* in Section 9.10 is a modification of Sethi and Ullman's algorithm, due to

Stockhausen [1973]. Bruno and Lassagne [1975] and Coffman and Sethi [1983] give optimal code-generation algorithms for expression trees if the target machine has registers that must be used as a stack.

Aho and Johnson [1976] devised the dynamic programming algorithm described in Section 9.11. This algorithm was used as the basis of the code generator in S.C. Johnson's portable C compiler, PCC2, and was also used by Ripken [1977] in a compiler for the IBM 370 machine. Knuth [1977] generalized the dynamic programming algorithm to machines with asymmetric register classes, such as the IBM 7090 and the CDC 6600. In developing the generalization, Knuth viewed code generation as a parsing problem for context-free grammars.

Floyd [1961] gives an algorithm to handle common subexpressions in arithmetic expressions. The partition of dags into trees and the use of a procedure like *gencode* on the trees separately is from Waite [1976a]. Sethi [1975] and Bruno and Sethi [1976] show that the optimal code-generation problem for dags is NP-complete. Aho, Johnson, and Ullman [1977a] show that the problem remains NP-complete even with single-register and infinite-register machines. Aho, Hopcroft, and Ullman [1974] and Garey and Johnson [1979] discuss the significance of what it means for a problem to be NP-complete.

Transformations on basic blocks have been studied by Aho and Ullman [1972a] and by Downey and Sethi [1978]. Peephole optimization is discussed by McKeeman [1965], Fraser [1979], Davidson and Fraser [1980 and 1984a,b], Lamb [1981], and Giegerich [1983]. Tanenbaum, van Staveren, and Stevenson [1982] advocate using peephole optimization on intermediate code as well.

Code generation has been treated as a tree-rewriting process by Wasilew [1971], Weingart [1973], Johnson [1978], and Cattell [1980]. The tree-rewriting example in Section 9.12 is derived from Henry [1984]. Aho and Ganapathi [1985] proposed the combination of efficient tree-pattern matching with dynamic programming mentioned in the same section. Tjiang [1986] has implemented a code-generation language called Twig based on the tree-translation schemes in Section 9.12. Kron [1975], Huet and Levy [1979], and Hoffman and O'Donnell [1982] describe general algorithms for tree-pattern matching.

The Graham-Glanville approach to code generation by using an LR parser for instruction selection is described and evaluated in Glanville [1977], Glanville and Graham [1978], Graham [1980 and 1984], Henry [1984], and Aigrain et al. [1984]. Ganapathi [1980] and Ganapathi and Fischer [1982] have used attribute grammars to specify and implement code generators.

Other techniques for automating the construction of code generators have been proposed by Fraser [1977], Cattell [1980], and Leverett et al. [1980]. Compiler portability is also discussed by Richards [1971 and 1977]. Szymanksi [1978] and Leverett and Szymanski [1980] describe techniques for chaining span-dependent jump instructions. Yannakakis [1985] has a polynomial-time algorithm for Exercise 9.19.

CHAPTER 10

Code
Optimization

Ideally, compilers should produce target code that is as good as can be written by hand. The reality is that this goal is achieved only in limited cases, and with difficulty. However, the code produced by straightforward compiling algorithms can often be made to run faster or take less space, or both. This improvement is achieved by program transformations that are traditionally called *optimizations*, although the term "optimization" is a misnomer because there is rarely a guarantee that the resulting code is the best possible. Compilers that apply code-improving transformations are called *optimizing compilers*.

The emphasis in this chapter is on machine-independent optimizations, program transformations that improve the target code without taking into consideration any properties of the target machine. Machine-dependent optimizations, such as register allocation and utilization of special machine-instruction sequences (machine idioms) were discussed in Chapter 9.

The most payoff for the least effort is obtained if we can identify the frequently executed parts of a program and then make these parts as efficient as possible. There is a popular saying that most programs spend ninety per cent of their execution time in ten per cent of the code. While the actual percentages may vary, it is often the case that a small fraction of a program accounts for most of the running time. Profiling the run-time execution of a program on representative input data accurately identifies the heavily traveled regions of a program. Unfortunately, a compiler does not have the benefit of sample input data, so it must make its best guess as to where the program hot spots are.

In practice, the program's inner loops are good candidates for improvement. In a language that emphasizes control constructs like while and for statements, the loops may be evident from the syntax of the program; in general, a process called control-flow analysis identifies loops in the flow graph of a program.

This chapter is a cornucopia of useful optimizing transformations and techniques for implementing them. The best technique for deciding what transformations are worthwhile to put into a compiler is to collect statistics about the source programs and evaluate the benefit of a given set of optimizations on a representative sample of real source programs. Chapter 12 describes transformations that have proven useful in optimizing compilers for several different languages.

One of the themes of this chapter is data-flow analysis, a process of collecting information about the way variables are used in a program. The information collected at various points in a program can be related using simple set equations. We present several algorithms for collecting information using data-flow analysis and for effectively using this information in optimization. We also consider the impact of language constructs such as procedures and pointers on optimization.

The last four sections of this chapter deal with more advanced material. They cover some graph-theoretic ideas relevant to control-flow analysis and apply these ideas to data-flow analysis. The chapter concludes with a discussion of general-purpose tools for data-flow analysis and techniques for debugging optimized code. The emphasis throughout this chapter is on optimizing techniques that apply to languages in general. Some compilers that use these ideas are reviewed in Chapter 12.

10.1 INTRODUCTION

To create an efficient target language program, a programmer needs more than an optimizing compiler. In this section, we review the options available to a programmer and a compiler for creating efficient target programs. We mention the types of code-improving transformations that a programmer and a compiler writer can be expected to use to improve the performance of a program. We also consider the representation of programs on which transformations will be applied.

Criteria for Code-Improving Transformations

Simply stated, the best program transformations are those that yield the most benefit for the least effort. The transformations provided by an optimizing compiler should have several properties.

First, a transformation must preserve the meaning of programs. That is, an "optimization" must not change the output produced by a program for a given input, or cause an error, such as a division by zero, that was not present in the original version of the source program. The influence of this criterion pervades this chapter; at all times we take the "safe" approach of missing an opportunity to apply a transformation rather than risk changing what the program does.

Second, a transformation must, on the average, speed up programs by a measurable amount. Sometimes we are interested in reducing the space taken by the compiled code, although the size of code has less importance than it once had. Of course, not every transformation succeeds in improving every program, and occasionally an "optimization" may slow down a program slightly, as long as on the average it improves things.

Third, a transformation must be worth the effort. It does not make sense for a compiler writer to expend the intellectual effort to implement a code-improving transformation and to have the compiler expend the additional time compiling source programs if this effort is not repaid when the target programs are executed. Certain local or "peephole" transformations of the kind discussed in Section 9.9 are simple enough and beneficial enough to be included in any compiler.

Some transformations can only be applied after detailed, often time-consuming, analysis of the source program, so there is little point in applying them to programs that will be run only a few times. For example, a fast, nonoptimizing, compiler is likely to be more helpful during debugging or for "student jobs" that will be run successfully a few times and thrown away. Only when the program in question takes up a significant fraction of the machine's cycles does improved code quality justify the time spent running an optimizing compiler on the program.

Getting Better Performance

Dramatic improvements in the running time of a program — such as cutting the running time from a few hours to a few seconds — are usually obtained by improving the program at all levels, from the source level to the target level, as suggested by Fig. 10.1. At each level, the available options fall between the two extremes of finding a better algorithm and of implementing a given algorithm so that fewer operations are performed.

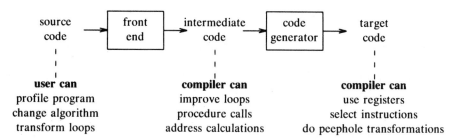

Fig. 10.1. Places for potential improvements by the user and the compiler.

Algorithmic transformations occasionally produce spectacular improvements in running time. For example, Bentley [1982] relates that the running time of a program for sorting N elements dropped from $2.02N^2$ microseconds to $12N\log_2 N$ microseconds when a carefully coded "insertion sort" was replaced by "quicksort."[1] For $N = 100$ the replacement speeds up the program by a

---

[1] See Aho, Hopcroft, and Ullman [1983] for a discussion of these sorting algorithms and their speeds.

factor of 2.5. For $N = 100,000$ the improvement is far more dramatic: the replacement speeds up the program by a factor of more than a thousand.

Unfortunately, no compiler can find the best algorithm for a given program. Sometimes, however, a compiler can replace a sequence of operations by an algebraically equivalent sequence, and thereby reduce the running time of a program significantly. Such savings are more common when algebraic transformations are applied to programs in very-high level languages, e.g., query languages for databases (see Ullman [1982]).

In this section and the next, a sorting program called quicksort will be used to illustrate the effect of various code-improving transformations. The C program in Fig. 10.2 is derived from Sedgewick [1978], where hand-optimization of such a program is discussed. We shall not discuss the algorithmic aspects of this program here — in fact, a[0] must contain the smallest and a[max] the largest element to be sorted for the program to work.

```
void quicksort(m,n)
int m,n;
{
    int i,j;
    int v,x;
    if ( n <= m ) return;
    /* fragment begins here */
    i = m-1; j = n; v = a[n];
    while(1) {
        do i = i+1; while ( a[i] < v );
        do j = j-1; while ( a[j] > v );
        if (i >= j ) break;
        x = a[i]; a[i] = a[j]; a[j] = x;
    }
    x = a[i]; a[i] = a[n]; a[n] = x;
    /* fragment ends here */
    quicksort(m,j); quicksort(i+1,n);
}
```

Fig. 10.2. C code for quicksort.

It may not be possible to perform certain code-improving transformations at the level of the source language. For example, in a language such as Pascal or Fortran, a programmer can only refer to array elements in the usual way, e.g., as b[i,j]. At the level of the intermediate language, however, new opportunities for code improvement may be exposed. Three-address code, for example, provides many opportunities for improving address calculations, especially in loops. Consider the three-address code for determining the value of a[i], assuming that each array element takes four bytes:

$$t_1 := 4*i; \quad t_2 := a[t_1]$$

Naive intermediate code will recalculate 4*i every time a[i] appears in the source program, and the programmer has no control over the redundant address calculations, because they are implicit in the implementation of the language, rather than being explicit in the code written by the user. In these situations, it behooves the compiler to clean them up. In a language like C, however, this transformation can be done at the source level by the programmer, since references to array elements can be systematically rewritten using pointers to make them more efficient. This rewriting is similar to transformations that optimizing compilers for Fortran traditionally apply.

At the level of the target machine, it is the compiler's responsibility to make good use of the machine's resources. For example, keeping the most heavily used variables in registers can cut running time significantly, often by as much as a half. Again, C allows a programmer to advise the compiler that certain variables be held in registers, but most languages do not. Similarly, the compiler can speed up programs significantly by choosing instructions that take advantage of the addressing modes of the machine to do in one instruction what naively we might expect to require two or three, as we discussed in Chapter 9.

Even if it is possible for the programmer to improve the code, it may be more convenient to have the compiler make some of the improvements. If a compiler can be relied upon to generate efficient code, then the user can concentrate on writing clear code.

An Organization for an Optimizing Compiler

As we have mentioned, there are often several levels at which a program can be improved. Since the techniques needed to analyze and transform a program do not change significantly with the level, this chapter concentrates on the transformation of intermediate code using the organization shown in Fig. 10.3. The code-improvement phase consists of control-flow and data-flow analysis followed by the application of transformations. The code generator, discussed in Chapter 9, produces the target program from the transformed intermediate code.

For convenience of presentation, we assume that the intermediate code consists of three-address statements. Intermediate code, of the sort produced by the techniques in Chapter 8, for a portion of the program in Fig. 10.2 is shown in Fig. 10.4. With other intermediate representations, the temporary variables $t_1, t_2, \ldots, t_{15}$ in Fig. 10.4 need not appear explicitly, as discussed in Chapter 8.

The organization in Fig. 10.3 has the following advantages:

1. The operations needed to implement high-level constructs are made explicit in the intermediate code, so it is possible to optimize them. For example, the address calculations for a[i] are explicit in Fig. 10.4, so the recomputation of expressions like 4*i can be eliminated as discussed in the next section.

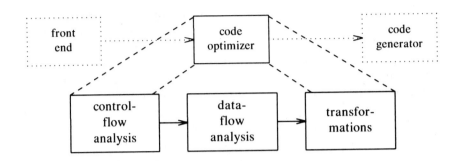

Fig. 10.3. Organization of the code optimizer.

(1)	$i := m-1$	(16)	$t_7 := 4*i$
(2)	$j := n$	(17)	$t_8 := 4*j$
(3)	$t_1 := 4*n$	(18)	$t_9 := a[t_8]$
(4)	$v := a[t_1]$	(19)	$a[t_7] := t_9$
(5)	$i := i+1$	(20)	$t_{10} := 4*j$
(6)	$t_2 := 4*i$	(21)	$a[t_{10}] := x$
(7)	$t_3 := a[t_2]$	(22)	goto (5)
(8)	if $t_3 < v$ goto (5)	(23)	$t_{11} := 4*i$
(9)	$j := j-1$	(24)	$x := a[t_{11}]$
(10)	$t_4 := 4*j$	(25)	$t_{12} := 4*i$
(11)	$t_5 := a[t_4]$	(26)	$t_{13} := 4*n$
(12)	if $t_5 > v$ goto (9)	(27)	$t_{14} := a[t_{13}]$
(13)	if $i >= j$ goto (23)	(28)	$a[t_{12}] := t_{14}$
(14)	$t_6 := 4*i$	(29)	$t_{15} := 4*n$
(15)	$x := a[t_6]$	(30)	$a[t_{15}] := x$

Fig. 10.4. Three-address code for fragment in Fig. 10.2.

2. The intermediate code can be (relatively) independent of the target
   machine, so the optimizer does not have to change much if the code generator is replaced by one for a different machine. The intermediate code
   in Fig. 10.4 assumes that each element of the array a takes four bytes.
   Some intermediate codes, e.g., P-code for Pascal, leave it to the code generator to fill in the size of array elements, so the intermediate code is
   independent of the size of a machine word. We could have done the
   same in our intermediate code if we replaced 4 by a symbolic constant.

In the code optimizer, programs are represented by flow graphs, in which edges indicate the flow of control and nodes represent basic blocks, as discussed in Section 9.4. Unless otherwise specified, a program means a single procedure. In Section 10.8, we discuss interprocedural optimization.

Example 10.1. Figure 10.5 contains the flow graph for the program in Fig. 10.4. B_1 is the initial node. All conditional and unconditional jumps to statements in Fig. 10.4 have been replaced in Fig. 10.5 by jumps to the block of which the statements are leaders.

In Fig. 10.5, there are three loops. B_2 and B_3 are loops by themselves. Blocks B_2, B_3, B_4, and B_5 together form a loop, with entry B_2.   □

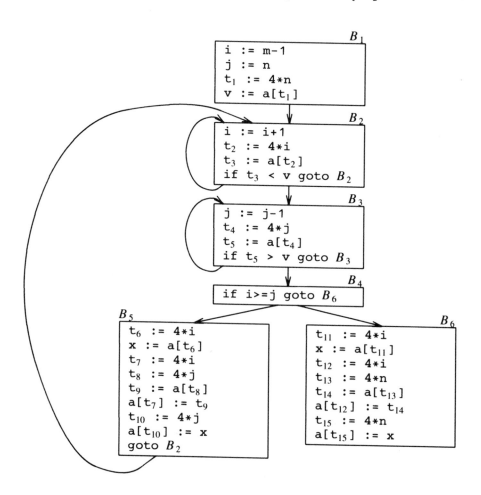

Fig. 10.5. Flow graph.

10.2 THE PRINCIPAL SOURCES OF OPTIMIZATION

In this section, we introduce some of the most useful code-improving transformations. Techniques for implementing these transformations are presented in subsequent sections. A transformation of a program is called *local* if it can be performed by looking only at the statements in a basic block; otherwise, it is called *global*. Many transformations can be performed at both the local and global levels. Local transformations are usually performed first.

Function-Preserving Transformations

There are a number of ways in which a compiler can improve a program without changing the function it computes. Common subexpression elimination, copy propagation, dead-code elimination, and constant folding are common examples of such function-preserving transformations. Section 9.8 on the dag representation of basic blocks showed how local common subexpressions could be removed as the dag for the basic block was constructed. The other transformations come up primarily when global optimizations are performed, and we shall discuss each in turn.

Frequently, a program will include several calculations of the same value, such as an offset in an array. As mentioned in Section 10.1, some of these duplicate calculations cannot be avoided by the programmer because they lie below the level of detail accessible within the source language. For example, block B_5 shown in Fig. 10.6(a) recalculates $4*i$ and $4*j$.

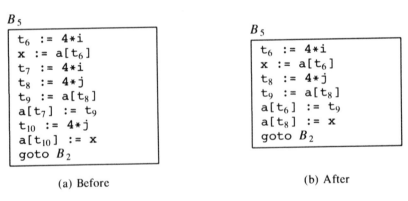

(a) Before   (b) After

Fig. 10.6. Local common subexpression elimination.

Common Subexpressions

An occurrence of an expression E is called a *common subexpression* if E was previously computed, and the values of variables in E have not changed since the previous computation. We can avoid recomputing the expression if we can use the previously computed value. For example, the assignments to t_7 and

t_{10} have the common subexpressions $4*i$ and $4*j$, respectively, on the right side in Fig. 10.6(a). They have been eliminated in Fig. 10.6(b), by using t_6 instead of t_7 and t_8 instead of t_{10}. This change is what would result if we reconstructed the intermediate code from the dag for the basic block.

Example 10.2. Figure 10.7 shows the result of eliminating both global and local common subexpressions from blocks B_5 and B_6 in the flow graph of Fig. 10.5. We first discuss the transformation of B_5 and then mention some subtleties involving arrays.

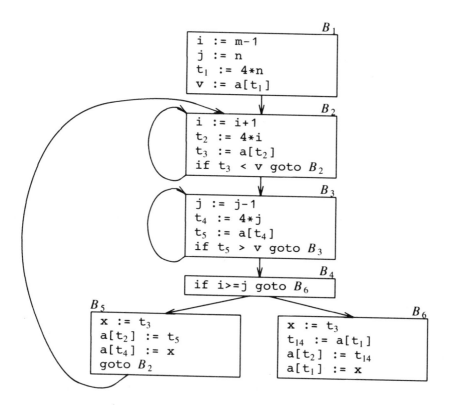

Fig. 10.7. B_5 and B_6 after common subexpression elimination.

After local common subexpressions are eliminated, B_5 still evaluates $4*i$ and $4*j$, as shown in Fig. 10.6(b). Both are common subexpressions; in particular, the three statements

$$t_8 := 4*j; \quad t_9 := a[t_8]; \quad a[t_8] := x$$

in B_5 can be replaced by

$$t_9 := a[t_4]; \quad a[t_4] := x$$

using t_4 computed in block B_3. In Fig. 10.7, observe that as control passes
from the evaluation of $4*j$ in B_3 to B_5, there is no change in j, so t_4 can be
used if $4*j$ is needed.

Another common subexpression comes to light in B_5 after t_4 replaces t_8.
The new expression $a[t_4]$ corresponds to the value of $a[j]$ at the source
level. Not only does j retain its value as control leaves B_3 and then enters
B_5, but $a[j]$, a value computed into a temporary t_5, does too because there
are no assignments to elements of the array a in the interim. The statements

$$t_9 := a[t_4]; \quad a[t_6] := t_9$$

in B_5 can therefore be replaced by

$$a[t_6] := t_5$$

Analogously, the value assigned to x in block B_5 of Fig. 10.6(b) is seen to
be the same as the value assigned to t_3 in block B_2. Block B_5 in Fig. 10.7 is
the result of eliminating common subexpressions corresponding to the values
of the source level expressions $a[i]$ and $a[j]$ from B_5 in Fig. 10.6(b). A
similar series of transformations has been done to B_6 in Fig. 10.7.

The expression $a[t_1]$ in blocks B_1 and B_6 of Fig. 10.7 is not considered a
common subexpression, although t_1 can be used in both places. After control
leaves B_1 and before it reaches B_6, it can go through B_5, where there are
assignments to a. Hence, $a[t_1]$ may not have the same value on reaching B_6
as it did on leaving B_1, and it is not safe to treat $a[t_1]$ as a common subexpression.   □

Copy Propagation

Block B_5 in Fig. 10.7 can be further improved by eliminating x using two new
transformations. One concerns assignments of the form $f:=g$ called *copy
statements*, or *copies* for short. Had we gone into more detail in Example
10.2, copies would have arisen much sooner, because the algorithm for eliminating common subexpressions introduces them, as do several other algorithms. For example, when the common subexpression in $c:=d+e$ is eliminated in Fig. 10.8, the algorithm uses a new variable t to hold the value of
$d+e$. Since control may reach $c:=d+e$ either after the assignment to a or
after the assignment to b, it would be incorrect to replace $c:=d+e$ by either
$c:=a$ or by $c:=b$.

The idea behind the copy-propagation transformation is to use g for f,
wherever possible after the copy statement $f:=g$. For example, the assignment $x:=t_3$ in block B_5 of Fig. 10.7 is a copy. Copy propagation applied to
B_5 yields:

$$
\begin{aligned}
&x := t_3 \\
&a[t_2] := t_5 \\
&a[t_4] := t_3 \\
&goto\ B_2
\end{aligned}
\qquad (10.1)
$$

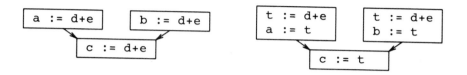

Fig. 10.8. Copies introduced during common subexpression elimination.

This may not appear to be an improvement, but as we shall see, it gives us the opportunity to eliminate the assignment to x.

Dead-Code Elimination

A variable is live at a point in a program if its value can be used subsequently; otherwise, it is dead at that point. A related idea is dead or useless code, statements that compute values that never get used. While the programmer is unlikely to introduce any dead code intentionally, it may appear as the result of previous transformations. For example, in Section 9.9 we discussed the use of debug that is set to true or false at various points in the program, and used in statements like

        if (debug) print ...   (10.2)

By a data-flow analysis, it may be possible to deduce that each time the program reaches this statement, the value of debug is false. Usually, it is because there is one particular statement

        debug := false

that we can deduce to be the last assignment to debug prior to the test (10.2), no matter what sequence of branches the program actually takes. If copy propagation replaces debug by false, then the print statement is dead because it cannot be reached. We can eliminate both the test and printing from the object code. More generally, deducing at compile time that the value of an expression is a constant and using the constant instead is known as *constant folding*.

One advantage of copy propagation is that it often turns the copy statement into dead code. For example, copy propagation followed by dead-code elimination removes the assignment to x and transforms (10.1) into:

        a[t₂] := t₅
        a[t₄] := t₃
        goto B₂

This code is a further improvement of block B_5 in Fig. 10.7.

Loop Optimizations

We now give a brief introduction to a very important place for optimizations, namely loops, especially the inner loops where programs tend to spend the bulk of their time. The running time of a program may be improved if we decrease the number of instructions in an inner loop, even if we increase the amount of code outside that loop. Three techniques are important for loop optimization: *code motion*, which moves code outside a loop; *induction-variable elimination*, which we apply to eliminate i and j from the inner loops B_2 and B_3 of Fig. 10.7; and, *reduction in strength*, which replaces an expensive operation by a cheaper one, such as a multiplication by an addition.

Code Motion

An important modification that decreases the amount of code in a loop is code motion. This transformation takes an expression that yields the same result independent of the number of times a loop is executed (a *loop-invariant computation*) and places the expression before the loop. Note that the notion "before the loop" assumes the existence of an entry for the loop. For example, evaluation of limit-2 is a loop-invariant computation in the following while-statement:

        while (i <= limit-2) /* statement does not change limit */

Code motion will result in the equivalent of

        t = limit-2;
        while (i <= t) /* statement does not change limit or t */

Induction Variables and Reduction in Strength

While code motion is not applicable to the quicksort example we have been considering, the other two transformations are. Loops are usually processed inside out. For example, consider the loop around B_3. Only the portion of the flow graph relevant to the transformations on B_3 is shown in Fig. 10.9.

Note that the values of j and t_4 remain in lock-step; every time the value of j decreases by 1, that of t_4 decreases by 4 because $4*j$ is assigned to t_4. Such identifiers are called *induction variables*.

When there are two or more induction variables in a loop, it may be possible to get rid of all but one, by the process of induction-variable elimination. For the inner loop around B_3 in Fig. 10.9(a), we cannot get rid of either j or t_4 completely; t_4 is used in B_3 and j in B_4. However, we can illustrate reduction in strength and illustrate a part of the process of induction-variable elimination. Eventually, j will be eliminated when the outer loop of B_2-B_5 is considered.

Example 10.3. As the relationship $t_4 = 4*j$ surely holds after such an assignment to t_4 in Fig. 10.9(a), and t_4 is not changed elsewhere in the inner loop around B_3, it follows that just after the statement j:=j-1 the

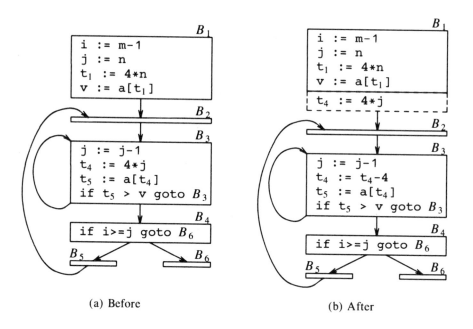

Fig. 10.9. Strength reduction applied to $4*j$ in block B_3.

relationship $t_4 = 4*j-4$ must hold. We may therefore replace the assignment $t_4 := 4*j$ by $t_4 := t_4-4$. The only problem is that t_4 does not have a value when we enter block B_3 for the first time. Since we must maintain the relationship $t_4 = 4*j$ on entry to the block B_3, we place an initialization of t_4 at the end of the block where j itself is initialized, shown by the dashed addition to block B_1 in Fig. 10.9(b).

The replacement of a multiplication by a subtraction will speed up the object code if multiplication takes more time than addition or subtraction, as is the case on many machines.   □

Section 10.7 discusses how induction variables can be detected and what transformations can be applied. We conclude this section with one more example of induction-variable elimination that treats i and j in the context of the outer loop containing B_2, B_3, B_4, and B_5.

Example 10.4. After reduction in strength is applied to the inner loops around B_2 and B_3, the only use of i and j is to determine the outcome of the test in block B_4. We know that the values of i and t_2 satisfy the relationship $t_2 = 4*i$, while those of j and t_4 satisfy the relationship $t_4 = 4*j$, so the test $t_2 >= t_4$ is equivalent to $i >= j$. Once this replacement is made, i in block B_2 and j in block B_3 become dead variables and the assignments to them in these blocks become dead code that can be eliminated, resulting in the flow graph shown in Fig. 10.10.   □

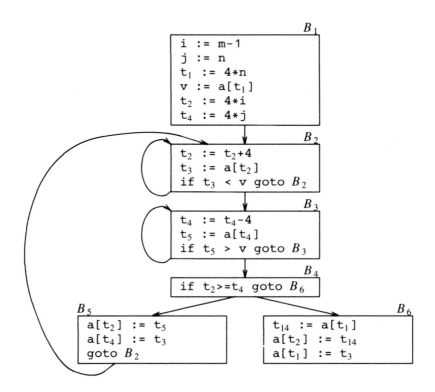

Fig. 10.10. Flow graph after induction-variable elimination.

The code-improving transformations have been effective. In Fig. 10.10, the number of instructions in blocks B_2 and B_3 has been reduced from 4 to 3 from the original flow graph in Fig. 10.5, in B_5 it has been reduced from 9 to 3, and in B_6 from 8 to 3. True, B_1 has grown from four instructions to six, but B_1 is executed only once in the fragment, so the total running time is barely affected by the size of B_1.

10.3 OPTIMIZATION OF BASIC BLOCKS

In Chapter 9, we saw a number of code-improving transformations for basic blocks. These included structure-preserving transformations, such as common subexpression elimination and dead-code elimination, and algebraic transformations such as reduction in strength.

Many of the structure-preserving transformations can be implemented by constructing a dag for a basic block. Recall that there is a node in the dag for each of the initial values of the variables appearing in the basic block, and there is a node n associated with each statement s within the block. The children of n are those nodes corresponding to statements that are the last definitions prior to s of the operands used by s. Node n is labeled by the operator applied at s, and also attached to n is the list of variables for which it is the last definition within the block. We also note those nodes, if any, whose values are live on exit from the block; these are the output nodes.

Common subexpressions can be detected by noticing, as a new node m is about to be added, whether there is an existing node n with the same children, in the same order, and with the same operator. If so, n computes the same value as m and may be used in its place.

Example 10.5. A dag for the block (10.3)

```
a := b + c
b := a - d
c := b + c
d := a - d
```
(10.3)

is shown in Fig. 10.11. When we construct the node for the third statement $c:=b+c$, we know that the use of b in $b+c$ refers to the node of Fig. 10.11 labeled $-$, because that is the most recent definition of b. Thus, we do not confuse the values computed at statements one and three.

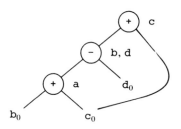

Fig. 10.11. Dag for basic block (10.3).

However, the node corresponding to the fourth statement $d:=a-d$ has the operator $-$ and the nodes labeled a and d_0 as children. Since the operator and the children are the same as those for the node corresponding to statement two, we do not create this node, but add d to the list of definitions for the node labeled $-$. □

It might appear that, since there are only three nodes in the dag of Fig. 10.11, block (10.3) can be replaced by a block with only three statements. In fact, if either b or d is not live on exit from the block, then we do not need to compute that variable, and can use the other to receive the value represented by the node labeled $-$ in Fig. 10.11. For example, if b is not live on exit, we could use:

```
a := b + c
d := a - d
c := d + c
```

However, if both b and d are live on exit, then a fourth statement must be used to copy the value from one to the other.[2]

Note that when we look for common subexpressions, we really are looking for expressions that are guaranteed to compute the same value, no matter how that value is computed. Thus, the dag method will miss the fact that the expression computed by the first and fourth statements in the sequence

$$
\begin{aligned}
a &:= b + c \\
b &:= b - d \\
c &:= c + d \\
e &:= b + c
\end{aligned}
\qquad (10.4)
$$

is the same, namely, b+c. However, algebraic identities applied to the dag, as discussed next, may expose the equivalence. The dag for this sequence is shown in Fig. 10.12.

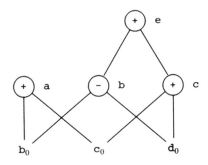

Fig. 10.12. Dag for basic block (10.4).

The operation on dags that corresponds to dead-code elimination is quite straightforward to implement. We delete from a dag any root (node with no ancestors) that has no live variables. Repeated application of this transformation will remove all nodes from the dag that correspond to dead code.

The Use of Algebraic Identities

Algebraic identities represent another important class of optimizations on basic blocks. In Section 9.9, we introduced some simple algebraic transformations that one might try during optimization. For example, we may apply arithmetic identities, such as

---

[2] In general, we have to be careful when reconstructing code from dags to choose the names of variables corresponding to nodes carefully. If a variable x is defined twice, or if it is assigned once and the initial value x_0 is also used, then we must make sure that we do not change the value of x until we have made all uses of the node whose value x previously held.

```
x + 0 = 0 + x = x
x - 0 = x
x * 1 = 1 * x = x
x / 1 = x
```

Another class of algebraic optimizations includes reduction in strength, that is, replacing a more expensive operator by a cheaper one as in

```
x ** 2 = x * x
2.0 * x = x + x
x / 2 = x * 0.5
```

A third class of related optimizations is constant folding. Here we evaluate constant expressions at compile time and replace the constant expressions by their values.[3] Thus the expression `2*3.14` would be replaced by `6.28`. Many constant expressions arise through the use of symbolic constants.

The dag-construction process can help us apply these and other more general algebraic transformations such as commutativity and associativity. For example, suppose `*` is commutative; that is, `x*y = y*x`. Before we create a new node labeled `*` with left child m and right child n, we check whether such a node already exists. We then check for a node having operator `*`, left child n and right child m.

The relational operators `<=`, `>=`, `<`, `>`, `=`, and `≠` sometimes generate unexpected common subexpressions. For example, the condition `x>y` can also be tested by subtracting the arguments and performing a test on the condition code set by the subtraction. (The subtraction can, however, introduce overflows and underflows while a compare instruction would not.) Thus, only one node of the dag need be generated for `x-y` and `x>y`.

Associative laws may also be applied to expose common subexpressions. For example, if the source code has the assignments

```
a := b + c
e := c + d + b
```

the following intermediate code might be generated:

```
a := b + c
t := c + d
e := t + b
```

If `t` is not needed outside this block, we can change this sequence to

```
a := b + c
e := a + d
```

---

[3] Arithmetic expressions should be evaluated the same way at compile time as they are at run time. K. Thompson has suggested an elegant solution to constant folding: compile the constant expression, execute the target code on the spot, and replace the expression with the result. Thus, the compiler does not need to contain an interpreter.

using both the associativity and commutativity of $+$.

The compiler writer should examine the language specification carefully to determine what rearrangements of computations are permitted, since computer arithmetic does not always obey the algebraic identities of mathematics. For example, the standard for Fortran 77 states that a compiler may evaluate any mathematically equivalent expression, provided that the integrity of parentheses is not violated. Thus, a compiler may evaluate `x*y-x*z` as `x*(y-z)` but it may not evaluate `a+(b-c)` as `(a+b)-c`. A Fortran compiler must therefore keep track of where parentheses were present in the source language expressions, if it is to optimize programs in accordance with the language definition.

10.4 LOOPS IN FLOW GRAPHS

Before considering loop optimizations, we need to define what constitutes a loop in a flow graph. We shall use the notion of a node "dominating" another to define "natural loops" and the important special class of "reducible" flow graphs. An algorithm for finding dominators and checking reducibility of flow graphs will be given in Section 10.9.

Dominators

We say node d of a flow graph *dominates* node n, written d *dom* n, if every path from the initial node of the flow graph to n goes through d. Under this definition, every node dominates itself, and the entry of a loop (as defined in Section 9.4) dominates all nodes in the loop.

Example 10.6. Consider the flow graph of Fig. 10.13, with initial node 1. The initial node dominates every node. Node 2 dominates only itself, since control can reach any other node along a path that begins $1 \rightarrow 3$. Node 3 dominates all but 1 and 2. Node 4 dominates all but 1, 2 and 3, since all paths from 1 must begin $1 \rightarrow 2 \rightarrow 3 \rightarrow 4$ or $1 \rightarrow 3 \rightarrow 4$. Nodes 5 and 6 dominate only themselves, since flow of control can skip around either by going through the other. Finally, 7 dominates 7, 8, 9, 10; 8 dominates 8, 9, 10; 9 and 10 dominate only themselves. □

A useful way of presenting dominator information is in a tree, called the *dominator tree*, in which the initial node is the root, and each node d dominates only its descendants in the tree. For example, Fig. 10.14 shows the dominator tree for the flow graph of Fig. 10.13.

The existence of dominator trees follows from a property of dominators; each node n has a unique *immediate dominator* m that is the last dominator of n on any path from the initial node to n. In terms of the *dom* relation, the immediate dominator m has that property that if $d \neq n$ and d *dom* n, then d *dom* m.

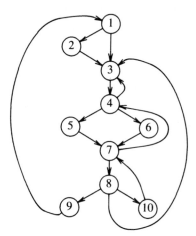

Fig. 10.13. Flow graph.

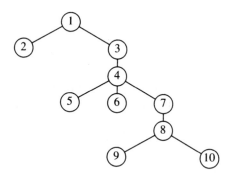

Fig. 10.14. Dominator tree for flow graph of Fig. 10.13.

Natural Loops

One important application of dominator information is in determining the loops of a flow graph suitable for improvement. There are two essential properties of such loops.

1. A loop must have a single entry point, called the "header." This entry point dominates all nodes in the loop, or it would not be the sole entry to the loop.

2. There must be at least one way to iterate the loop, i.e., at least one path back to the header.

A good way to find all the loops in a flow graph is to search for edges in the flow graph whose heads dominate their tails. (If $a \rightarrow b$ is an edge, b is the head and a is the *tail*.) We call such edges *back edges*.

Example 10.7. In Fig. 10.13, there is an edge $7 \rightarrow 4$, and 4 *dom* 7. Similarly, $10 \rightarrow 7$ is an edge, and 7 *dom* 10. The other edges with this property are $4 \rightarrow 3, 8 \rightarrow 3$, and $9 \rightarrow 1$. Note that these are exactly the edges that one would think of as forming loops in the flow graph.   □

Given a back edge $n \rightarrow d$, we define the *natural loop* of the edge to be d plus the set of nodes that can reach n without going through d. Node d is the header of the loop.

Example 10.8. The natural loop of the edge $10 \rightarrow 7$ consists of nodes 7, 8, and 10, since 8 and 10 are all those nodes that can reach 10 without going through 7. The natural loop of $9 \rightarrow 1$ is the entire flow graph. (Don't forget the path $10 \rightarrow 7 \rightarrow 8 \rightarrow 9$!)   □

Algorithm 10.1. Constructing the natural loop of a back edge.

Input. A flow graph G and a back edge $n \rightarrow d$.

Output. The set *loop* consisting of all nodes in the natural loop of $n \rightarrow d$.

Method. Beginning with node n, we consider each node $m \neq d$ that we know is in *loop*, to make sure that m's predecessors are also placed in *loop*. The algorithm is given in Fig. 10.15. Each node in *loop*, except for d, is placed once on *stack*, so its predecessors will be examined. Note that because d is put in the loop initially, we never examine its predecessors, and thus find only those nodes that reach n without going through d.   □

```
procedure insert(m);
if m is not in loop then begin
        loop := loop ∪ {m};
        push m onto stack
end;

/* main program follows */

stack := empty;
loop := { d };
insert(n);
while stack is not empty do begin
        pop m, the first element of stack, off stack;
        for each predecessor p of m do insert(p)
end
```

Fig. 10.15. Algorithm for constructing the natural loop.

Inner Loops

If we use the natural loops as "the loops," then we have the useful property that unless two loops have the same header, they are either disjoint or one is entirely contained (*nested within*) the other. Thus, neglecting loops with the same header for the moment, we have a natural notion of *inner loop*: one that contains no other loops.

When two loops have the same header, as in Fig. 10.16, it is hard to tell which is the inner loop. For example, if the test at the end of B_1 were

```
if a = 10 goto B2
```

probably the loop $\{B_0, B_1, B_3\}$ would be the inner loop. However, we could not be sure without a detailed examination of the code. Perhaps a is almost always 10, and it is typical to go around the $\{B_0, B_1, B_2\}$ loop many times before branching to B_3. Thus, we shall assume that when two natural loops have the same header, but neither is nested within the other, they are combined and treated as a single loop.

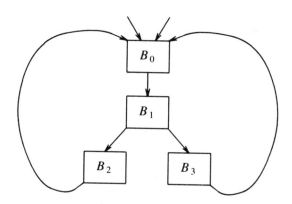

Fig. 10.16. Two loops with the same header.

Pre-Headers

Several transformations require us to move statements "before the header." We therefore begin treatment of a loop L by creating a new block, called the *preheader*. The preheader has only the header as successor, and all edges which formerly entered the header of L from outside L instead enter the preheader. Edges from inside loop L to the header are not changed. The arrangement is shown in Fig. 10.17. Initially, the preheader is empty, but transformations on L may place statements in it.

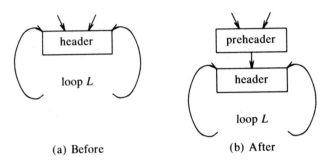

Fig. 10.17. Introduction of the preheader.

Reducible Flow Graphs

Flow graphs that occur in practice frequently fall into the class of reducible flow graphs defined below. Exclusive use of structured flow-of-control statements such as if-then-else, while-do, continue, and break statements produces programs whose flow graphs are always reducible. Even programs written using goto statements by programmers with no prior knowledge of structured program design are almost always reducible.

A variety of definitions of "reducible flow graph" have been proposed. The one we adopt here brings out one of the most important properties of reducible flow graphs; namely, that there are no jumps into the middle of loops from outside; the only entry to a loop is through its header. The exercises and bibliographic notes contain a brief history of the concept.

A flow graph G is *reducible* if and only if we can partition the edges into two disjoint groups, often called the *forward* edges and *back* edges, with the following two properties:

1. The forward edges form an acyclic graph in which every node can be reached from the initial node of G.

2. The back edges consist only of edges whose heads dominate their tails.

Example 10.9. The flow graph of Fig. 10.13 is reducible. In general, if we know the relation *dom* for a flow graph, we can find and remove all the back edges. The remaining edges must be the forward edges if the graph is reducible, and to check whether a flow graph is reducible it suffices to check that the forward edges form an acyclic graph. In the case of Fig. 10.13, it is easy to check that if we remove the five back edges $4 \rightarrow 3$, $7 \rightarrow 4$, $8 \rightarrow 3$, $9 \rightarrow 1$, and $10 \rightarrow 7$, whose heads dominate their tails, the remaining graph is acyclic. □

Example 10.10. Consider the flow graph of Fig. 10.18, whose initial node is 1. This flow graph has no back edges, since no head of an edge dominates the tail of that edge. Thus it could only be reducible if the entire graph were acyclic. But since it is not, the flow graph is not reducible. Intuitively, the reason this flow graph is not reducible is that the cycle 2-3 can be entered at

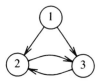

Fig. 10.18. A nonreducible flow graph.

two different places, nodes 2 and 3.   □

The key property of reducible flow graphs for loop analysis is that in such flow graphs every set of nodes that we would informally regard as a loop must contain a back edge. In fact, we need examine only the natural loops of back edges in order to find all loops in a program whose flow graph is reducible. In contrast, the flow graph of Fig. 10.18 appears to have a "loop" consisting of nodes 2 and 3, but there is no back edge of which this is the natural loop. In fact, that "loop" has two headers, 2 and 3, making application of many code-optimization techniques, such as those introduced in Section 10.2 for code motion and induction variable removal, not directly applicable.

Fortunately, nonreducible control-flow structures, such as that in Fig. 10.18, appear so rarely in most programs as to make the study of loops with more than one header of secondary importance. There are even languages, such as Bliss and Modula 2, that allow only programs with reducible flow graphs, and many other languages will yield only reducible flow graphs as long as we use no goto's.

Example 10.11. Returning again to Fig. 10.13, we note that the only "inner loop," that is, a loop with no subloops, is {7, 8, 10}, the natural loop of back edge 10 → 7. The set {4, 5, 6, 7, 8, 10} is the natural loop of 7 → 4. (Note that 8 and 10 can reach 7 via edge 10 → 7.) Our intuition that {4, 5, 6, 7} forms a loop is wrong, since 4 and 7 would both be entries from outside, violating our single-entry requirement. Put another way, there is no reason to assume that control spends much time going around the set of nodes {4, 5, 6, 7}; it is just as plausible that control passes to 8 from 7 more often than it does to 4. By including 8 and 10 in the loop, we are more certain of having isolated a heavily traveled region of the program.

It is wise to recognize, however, the danger in making assumptions about the frequency of branches. For example, if we moved an invariant statement out of 8 or 10 in loop {7, 8, 10}, and in fact, control followed edge 7 → 4 more frequently than 7 → 8, we would actually increase the number of times the moved statement was executed. We shall discuss methods to avoid this problem in Section 10.7.

The next larger loop is {3, 4, 5, 6, 7, 8, 10}, which is the natural loop of both edges 4 → 3 and 8 → 3. As before, our intuition that {3, 4} should be regarded as a loop violates the single header requirement. The last loop, the one for back edge 9 → 1, is the entire flow graph.   □

There are several additional useful properties of reducible flow graphs, which we shall introduce when we discuss the topics of depth-first search and interval analysis in Section 10.9.

10.5 INTRODUCTION TO GLOBAL DATA-FLOW ANALYSIS

In order to do code optimization and a good job of code generation, a compiler needs to collect information about the program as a whole and to distribute this information to each block in the flow graph. For example, we saw in Section 9.7 how knowing what variables are live on exit from each block could improve register usage. Section 10.2 suggested how we could use knowledge of global common subexpressions to eliminate redundant computations. Likewise, Sections 9.9 and 10.3 discussed how a compiler could take advantage of "reaching definitions," such as knowing where a variable like debug was last defined before reaching a given block, in order to perform transformations like constant folding and dead-code elimination. These facts are just a few examples of *data-flow information* that an optimizing compiler collects by a process known as *data-flow analysis*.

Data-flow information can be collected by setting up and solving systems of equations that relate information at various points in a program. A typical equation has the form

$$out[S] = gen[S] \cup (in[S] - kill[S]) \tag{10.5}$$

and can be read as, "the information at the end of a statement is either generated within the statement, or enters at the beginning and is not killed as control flows through the statement." Such equations are called *data-flow equations*.

The details of how data-flow equations are set up and solved depend on three factors.

1. The notions of generating and killing depend on the desired information, i.e., on the data-flow analysis problem to be solved. Moreover, for some problems, instead of proceeding along with the flow of control and defining $out[S]$ in terms of $in[S]$, we need to proceed backwards and define $in[S]$ in terms of $out[S]$.

2. Since data flows along control paths, data-flow analysis is affected by the control constructs in a program. In fact, when we write $out[S]$ we implicitly assume that there is unique end point where control leaves the statement; in general, equations are set up at the level of basic blocks rather than statements, because blocks do have unique end points.

3. There are subtleties that go along with such statements as procedure calls, assignments through pointer variables, and even assignments to array variables.

In this section, we consider the problem of determining the set of definitions reaching a point in a program and its use in finding opportunities for constant folding. Later in this chapter, algorithms for code motion and induction variable elimination will also use this information.

We initially consider programs constructed using **if** and **do-while** statements. The predictable control flow in these statements allows us to concentrate on the ideas needed to set up and solve data-flow equations. Assignments in this section are either copy statements or are of the form a:=b+c. In this chapter, we frequently use "+" as a typical operator. All that we say applies straightforwardly to other operators, including those with one operand, or with more than two operands.

Points and Paths

Within a basic block, we talk of the *point* between two adjacent statements, as well as the point before the first statement and after the last. Thus, block B_1 in Fig. 10.19 has four points: one before any of the assignments and one after each of the three assignments.

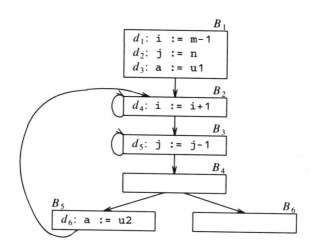

Fig. 10.19. A flow graph.

Now, let us take a global view and consider all the points in all the blocks. A *path* from p_1 to p_n is a sequence of points $p_1, p_2, \ldots, p_n$ such that for each i between 1 and $n-1$, either

1. p_i is the point immediately preceding a statement and p_{i+1} is the point immediately following that statement in the same block, or

2. p_i is the end of some block and p_{i+1} is the beginning of a successor block.

Example 10.12. In Fig. 10.19 there is a path from the beginning of block B_5 to the beginning of block B_6. It travels through the end point of B_5 and then through all the points in B_2, B_3, and B_4, in order, before it reaches the beginning of B_6.   □

Reaching Definitions

A *definition* of a variable x is a statement that assigns, or may assign, a value to x. The most common forms of definition are assignments to x and statements that read a value from an I/O device and store it in x. These statements certainly define a value for x, and they are referred to as *unambiguous* definitions of x. There are certain other kinds of statements that may define a value for x; they are called *ambiguous* definitions. The most usual forms of ambiguous definitions of x are:

1. A call of a procedure with x as a parameter (other than a by-value parameter) or a procedure that can access x because x is in the scope of the procedure. We also have to consider the possibility of "aliasing," where x is not in the scope of the procedure, but x has been identified with another variable that is passed as a parameter or is in the scope. These issues are taken up in Section 10.8.

2. An assignment through a pointer that could refer to x. For example, the assignment *q:=y is a definition of x if it is possible that q points to x. Methods for determining what a pointer could point to are also discussed in Section 10.8, but in the absence of any knowledge to the contrary, we must assume that an assignment through a pointer is a definition of every variable.

We say a definition d *reaches* a point p if there is a path from the point immediately following d to p, such that d is not "killed" along that path. Intuitively, if a definition d of some variable a reaches point p, then d might be the place at which the value of a used at p might last have been defined. We *kill* a definition of a variable a if between two points along the path there is a definition of a. Notice that only unambiguous definitions of a kill other definitions of a. Thus, a point can be reached by an unambiguous definition and an ambiguous definition of the same variable appearing later along one path.

For example, both the definitions i:=m-1 and j:=n in block B_1 in Fig. 10.19 reach the beginning of block B_2, as does the definition j:=j-1, provided there are no assignments to or reads of j in B_4, B_5, or the portion of B_3 following that definition. However, the assignment to j in B_3 kills the definition j:=n, so the latter does not reach B_4, B_5, or B_6.

By defining reaching definitions as we have, we sometimes allow inaccuracies. However, they are all in the "safe," or "conservative" direction. For example, notice our assumption that all edges of a flow graph can be traversed. This may not be true in practice. For example, for no values of a and b can control actually reach the assignment a:=4 in the following program fragment:

```
if a = b then a := 2
else if a = b then a := 4
```

To decide in general whether each path in a flow graph can be taken is an undecidable problem, and we shall not attempt to solve it.

A recurring theme in the design of code improving transformations is that we must make only conservative decisions in the face of any doubt, although conservative strategies may cause us to miss some transformations that we actually could make safely. A decision is *conservative* if it never leads to a change in what the program computes. In applications of reaching definitions, it is normally conservative to assume that a definition can reach a point even if it might not. Thus, we allow paths that may never be traversed in any execution of the program, and we allow definitions to pass through ambiguous definitions of the same variable.

Data-Flow Analysis of Structured Programs

Flow graphs for control-flow constructs such as do-while statements have a useful property: there is a single beginning point at which control enters and a single end point that control leaves from when execution of the statement is over. We exploit this property when we talk of the definitions reaching the beginning and end of statements with the following syntax

$$S \rightarrow \textbf{id} := E \mid S ; S \mid \textbf{if } E \textbf{ then } S \textbf{ else } S \mid \textbf{do } S \textbf{ while } E$$
$$E \rightarrow \textbf{id} + \textbf{id} \mid \textbf{id}$$

Expressions in this language are similar to those in intermediate code, but the flow graphs for statements have restricted forms that are suggested by the diagrams in Fig. 10.20. A primary purpose of this section is to study the data-flow equations summarized in Fig. 10.21.

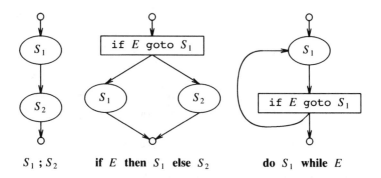

$S_1 ; S_2$ **if** E **then** S_1 **else** S_2 **do** S_1 **while** E

Fig. 10.20. Some structured control constructs.

We define a portion of a flow graph called a *region* to be a set of nodes N that includes a *header*, which dominates all other nodes in the region. All

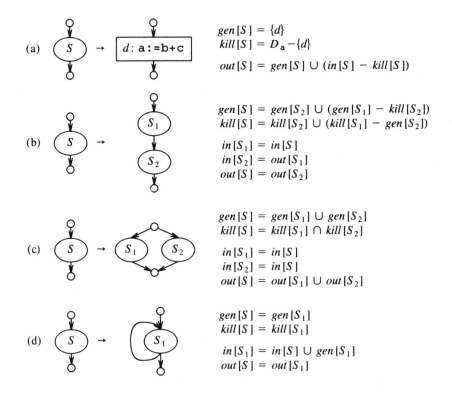

Fig. 10.21. Data-flow equations for reaching definitions.

edges between nodes in N are in the region, except (possibly) for some that enter the header.[4] The portion of a flow graph corresponding to a statement S is a region that obeys the further restriction that control can flow to just one outside block when it leaves the region.

As a technical convenience we assume that there are dummy blocks with no statements (indicated by open circles in Fig. 10.20) through which control flows just before it enters and just before it leaves the region. We say that the beginning points of the dummy blocks at the entry and exit of a statement's region are the *beginning* and *end* points, respectively, of the statement.

The equations in Fig. 10.21 are an inductive, or syntax-directed, definition of the sets $in[S]$, $out[S]$, $gen[S]$, and $kill[S]$ for all statements S. Sets $gen[S]$ and $kill[S]$ are synthesized attributes; they are computed bottom-up, from the smallest statements to the largest. Our desire is that definition d is in $gen[S]$

---

[4] A loop is a special case of a region that is strongly connected and includes all its back edges into the header.

if d reaches the end of S, independently of whether it reaches the beginning of S. Put another way, d must appear in S and reach the end of S via a path that does not go outside S. That is the justification for saying that $gen[S]$ is the set of definitions "generated by S."

Similarly, we intend that $kill[S]$ be the set of definitions that never reach the end of S, even if they reach the beginning. Thus, it makes sense to view these definitions as "killed by S." In order for definition d to be in $kill[S]$, every path from the beginning to the end of S must have an unambiguous definition of the same variable defined by d, and if d appears in S, then following every occurrence of d along any path must be another definition of the same variable.[5]

The rules for gen and $kill$, being synthesized translations, are relatively easy to understand. To begin, observe the rules in Fig. 10.21(a) for a single assignment of variable a. Surely that assignment is a definition of a, say definition d. Then d is the only definition sure to reach the end of the statement regardless of whether it reaches the beginning. Thus

$$gen[S] = \{d\}$$

On the other hand, d "kills" all other definitions of a, so we write

$$kill[S] = D_a - \{d\}$$

where D_a is the set of all definitions in the program for variable a.

The rule for a cascade of statements, illustrated in Fig. 10.21(b), is a bit more subtle. Under what circumstances is definition d generated by $S = S_1 ; S_2$? First of all, if it is generated by S_2, then it is surely generated by S. If d is generated by S_1, it will reach the end of S provided it is not killed by S_2. Thus, we write

$$gen[S] = gen[S_2] \cup (gen[S_1] - kill[S_2])$$

Similar reasoning applies to the killing of a definition, so we have

$$kill[S] = kill[S_2] \cup (kill[S_1] - gen[S_2])$$

For the if-statement, illustrated in Fig. 10.21(c), we note that if either branch of the "if" generates a definition, then that definition reaches the end of the statement S. Thus,

$$gen[S] = gen[S_1] \cup gen[S_2]$$

However, in order to "kill" definition d, the variable defined by d must be killed along any path from the beginning to the end of S. In particular, it must be killed along either branch, so

$$kill[S] = kill[S_1] \cap kill[S_2]$$

---

[5] In this introductory section, we are going to assume that all definitions are unambiguous. Section 10.8 deals with the modifications necessary to handle ambiguous definitions.

Lastly, consider the rules for loops, in Fig. 10.21(d). Simply stated, the loop does not affect *gen* or *kill*. If definition *d* is generated within S_1, then it reaches both the end of S_1 and the end of S. Conversely, if *d* is generated within S, it can only be generated within S_1. If *d* is killed by S_1, then going around the loop will not help; the variable of *d* gets redefined within S_1 each time around. Conversely, if *d* is killed by S, then it must surely be killed by S_1. We conclude that

$$gen[S] = gen[S_1]$$
$$kill[S] = kill[S_1]$$

Conservative Estimation of Data-Flow Information

There is a subtle miscalculation in the rules for *gen* and *kill* given in Fig. 10.21. We have made the assumption that the conditional expression E in the if and do statements are "uninterpreted;" that is, there exist inputs to the program that make their branches go either way. Put another way, we assume that any graph-theoretic path in the flow diagram is also an *execution path*, i.e., a path that is executed when the program is run with at least one possible input.

That is not always the case, and in fact we cannot decide in general whether a branch can be taken. Suppose, for example, that the expression E in an if-statement were always true. Then the path through S_2 in Fig. 10.21(c) could never be taken. This has two consequences. First, a definition generated by S_2 is not really generated by S, because there is no way to get from the beginning of S into the statement S_2. Second, no definition in $kill[S_1]$ can reach the end of S. Therefore, each such definition should logically be in $kill[S]$, even if it is not in $kill[S_2]$.

When we compare the computed *gen* with the "true" *gen* we discover that the true *gen* is always a subset of the computed *gen*. On the other hand, the true *kill* is always a superset of the computed *kill*. These containments hold even after we consider the other rules in Fig. 10.21. For example, if the expression E in a do-S-while-E statement can never be false, then we can never get out of the loop. Thus, the true *gen* is $\varnothing$, and every definition is "killed" by the loop. The case of a cascade of statements, in Fig. 10.21(b), where the inability to get out of S_1 or S_2 because of an infinite loop must be taken into account, is left as an exercise.

It is natural to wonder whether these differences between the true and computed *gen* and *kill* sets present a serious obstacle to data-flow analysis. The answer lies in the use intended for these data. In the particular case of reaching definitions, we normally use the information to infer that the value of a variable **x** at a point is limited to some small number of possibilities. For example, if we find that the only definitions of **x** reaching that point are of the form **x** := 1, we may infer that **x** has the value 1 at the point. Thus, we might decide to replace references to **x** by references to 1.

As a consequence, overestimating the set of definitions reaching a point does not seem serious; it merely stops us from doing an optimization that we could legitimately do. On the other hand, underestimating the set of definitions is a fatal error; it could lead us into making a change in the program that changes what the program computes. For example, we may think all reaching definitions of x give x the value 1, and so replace x by 1; but there is another undetected reaching definition that gives x the value 2. For the case of reaching definitions, then, we call a set of definitions *safe* or *conservative* if the estimate is a superset (not necessarily a proper superset) of the true set of reaching definitions. We call the estimate *unsafe* if it is not necessarily a superset of the truth.

For each data-flow problem we must examine the effect of inaccurate estimates on the kinds of program changes they may cause. We generally accept discrepancies that are *safe* in the sense that they may forbid optimizations that could legally be made, but not accept discrepancies that are *unsafe* in the sense that they may cause "optimizations" that do not preserve the externally observed behavior of the program. In each data-flow problem, either a subset or a superset of the true answer (but not both) is usually safe.

Returning now to the implications of safety on the estimation of *gen* and *kill* for reaching definitions, note that our discrepancies, supersets for *gen* and subsets for *kill* are both in the safe direction. Intuitively, increasing *gen* adds to the set of definitions that can reach a point, and cannot prevent a definition from reaching a place that it truly reached. Likewise, decreasing *kill* can only increase the set of definitions reaching any given point.

Computation of *in* and *out*

Many data-flow problems can be solved by synthesized translations similar to those used to compute *gen* and *kill*. For example, we may wish to determine, for each statement S, the set of variables that are defined within S. This information can be computed by equations analogous to those for *gen*, without even requiring sets analogous to *kill*. It can be used, for example, to determine loop-invariant computations.

However, there are other kinds of data-flow information, such as the reaching-definitions problem we have used as an example, where we also need to compute certain inherited attributes. It turns out that *in* is an inherited attribute, and *out* is a synthesized attribute depending on *in*. We intend that *in*[S] be the set of definitions reaching the beginning of S, taking into account the flow of control throughout the entire program, including statements outside of S or within which S is nested. The set *out*[S] is defined similarly for the end of S. It is important to note the distinction between *out*[S] and *gen*[S]. The latter is the set of definitions that reach the end of S without following paths outside S.

As a simple example of the difference, consider the cascade of statements in Fig. 10.21(b). A statement d may be generated in S_1 and therefore reach the beginning of S_2. If d is not in *kill*[S_2], d will reach the end of S_2, and therefore be in $out[S_2]$. However, d is not in $gen[S_2]$.

After computing $gen[S]$ and $kill[S]$ bottom-up, for all statements S, we may compute in and out starting at the statement representing the complete program, understanding that $in[S_0] = \varnothing$ if S_0 is the complete program. That is, no definitions reach the beginning of the program. For each of the four types of statements in Fig. 10.21, we may assume that $in[S]$ is known. We must use it to compute in for each of the substatements of S [which is trivial in cases (b)–(d) and irrelevant in case (a)]. Then, we recursively (top-down) compute out for each of the substatements S_1 or S_2, and use these sets to compute $out[S]$.

The simplest case is Fig. 10.21(a), where the statement is an assignment. Assuming we know $in[S]$, we compute out by equation (10.5), that is

$$out[S] = gen[S] \cup (in[S] - kill[S])$$

In words, a definition reaches the end of S if either it is generated by S (i.e., it is the definition d that is the statement), or it reaches the beginning of the statement and is not killed by the statement.

Suppose we have computed $in[S]$ and S is the cascade of two statements $S_1; S_2$, as in the second case of Fig. 10.21. We start by observing $in[S_1] = in[S]$. Then, we recursively compute $out[S_1]$, which gives us $in[S_2]$, since a definition reaches the beginning of S_2 if and only if it reaches the end of S_1. Now we can recursively compute $out[S_2]$, and this set is equal to $out[S]$.

Next, consider the if-statement of Fig. 10.21(c). As we have conservatively assumed that control can follow either branch, a definition reaches the beginning of S_1 or S_2 exactly when it reaches the beginning of S. That is,

$$in[S_1] = in[S_2] = in[S]$$

It also follows from the diagram in Fig. 10.21(c) that a definition reaches the end of S if and only if it reaches the end of one or both substatements; i.e.,

$$out[S] = out[S_1] \cup out[S_2]$$

We thus may use these equations to compute $in[S_1]$ and $in[S_2]$ from $in[S]$, recursively compute $out[S_1]$ and $out[S_2]$, then use these to compute $out[S]$.

Dealing With Loops

The last case, Fig. 10.21(d), presents special problems. Let us again assume we are given $gen[S_1]$ and $kill[S_1]$, having computed them bottom-up, and let us assume we are given $in[S]$, as we are in the process of performing a depth-first traversal of the parse tree. Unlike cases (b) and (c), we cannot simply use $in[S]$ as $in[S_1]$, because definitions inside S_1 that reach the end of S_1 are able to follow the arc back to the beginning of S_1, and therefore these definitions also are in $in[S_1]$. Rather, we have

$$in[S_1] = in[S] \cup out[S_1] \qquad (10.6)$$

We also have the obvious equation for $out[S]$:

$$out[S] = out[S_1]$$

which we can use once we have computed $out[S_1]$. However, it seems we cannot compute $in[S_1]$ by (10.6) until we have computed $out[S_1]$, and our general plan has been to compute out for a statement by first computing in for that statement.

Fortunately, there is a direct way to express out in terms of in; it is given by (10.5), or in this particular case:

$$out[S_1] = gen[S_1] \cup (in[S_1] - kill[S_1]) \qquad (10.7)$$

It is important to understand what is going on here. We do not really know that (10.7) is true about an arbitrary statement S_1; we only suspect that it should be true because it "makes sense" that a definition should reach the end of a statement if and only if it is either generated inside the statement or it reaches the beginning and is not killed. However, the only way we know to compute out for a statement is by the equations given in Fig. 10.21(a)–(c). We are going to assume (10.7) and derive the equations for in and out in Fig. 10.21(d). Then, we can use the equations of Fig. 10.21(a)—(d) to prove that (10.7) holds for an arbitrary S_1. We could then put these proofs together to make a valid proof by induction on the size of a statement S that the equations (10.7) and all the equations of Fig. 10.21 hold for S and all its substatements. We shall not do so; we leave the proofs as an exercise, but the reasoning we do follow here should prove instructive.

Even assuming (10.6) and (10.7) we are still not out of the woods. These two equations define a recurrence for $in[S_1]$ and $out[S_1]$ simultaneously. Let us write the equations as

$$I = J \cup O \qquad (10.8)$$
$$O = G \cup (I - K)$$

where I, O, J, G, and K correspond to $in[S_1]$, $out[S_1]$, $in[S]$, $gen[S_1]$, and $kill[S_1]$, respectively. The first two are variables; the other three are constants.

To solve (10.8), let us assume that $O = \varnothing$. We could then use the first equation in (10.8) to compute an estimate of I, that is,

$$I^1 = J$$

Next, we can use the second equation to get a better estimate of O:

$$O^1 = G \cup (I^1 - K) = G \cup (J - K)$$

Applying the first equation to this new estimate of O gives us:

$$I^2 = J \cup O^1 = J \cup G \cup (J - K) = J \cup G$$

If we then reapply the second equation, the next estimate of O is:

$$O^2 = G \cup (I^2 - K) = G \cup (J \cup G - K) = G \cup (J - K)$$

Note that $O^2 = O^1$. Thus, if we compute the next estimate of I, it will be equal to I^1, which will give us another estimate of O equal to O^1, and so on. Thus, the limiting values for I and O are those given for I^1 and O^1 above. We have thus derived the equations in Fig. 10.21(d), which are

$$in [S_1] = in [S] \cup gen [S_1]$$
$$out [S] = out [S_1]$$

The first of these equations is from the calculation above; the second follows from examination of the graph in Fig. 10.21(d).

A detail that remains is why we were entitled to start with the estimate $O = \emptyset$. Recall in our discussion of conservative estimates we suggested that sets like $out [S_1]$, which O stands for, should be overestimated rather than underestimated. In fact, if we were to start with $O = \{d\}$, where d is a definition appearing neither in J, G, or K, then d would wind up in the limiting values of both I and O.

Here, we must invoke the intended meanings of in and out. If such a d really belonged in $in [S_1]$, there would have to be a path from wherever d is located to the beginning of S_1 that showed how d reaches that point. If d is outside S, then d would have to be in $in [S]$, while if d were inside S (and therefore inside S_1) it would have to be in $gen [S_1]$. In the first case, d is in J and therefore placed in I by (10.8). In the second case, d is in G and again transmitted to I via O in (10.8). The conclusion is that starting with a too small estimate and building upward by adjoining more definitions to I and O is a safe way to estimate $in [S_1]$.

Representation of Sets

Sets of definitions, such as $gen [S]$ and $kill [S]$, can be represented compactly using bit vectors. We assign a number to each definition of interest in the flow graph. Then the bit vector representing a set of definitions will have 1 in position i if and only if the definition numbered i is in the set.

The number of a definition statement can be taken as the index of the statement in an array holding pointers to statements. However, not all definitions may be of interest during global data-flow analysis. For example, definitions of temporaries that are used only within a single block, as most temporaries generated for expression evaluation will be, need not be assigned numbers. Therefore, the numbers of definitions of interest will typically be recorded in a separate table.

A bit-vector representation for sets also allows set operations to be implemented efficiently. The union and intersection of two sets can be implemented by logical **or** and logical **and**, respectively, basic operations in most systems-oriented programming languages. The difference $A - B$ of sets A and B can be implemented by taking the complement of B and then using logical **and** to compute $A \wedge \neg B$.

Example 10.13. Figure 10.22 shows a program with seven definitions,

```
/* d₁ */    i := m-1;
/* d₂ */    j := n;
/* d₃ */    a := u1;
            do
/* d₄ */        i := i+1;
/* d₅ */        j := j-1;
                if e1 then
/* d₆ */            a := u2
                else
/* d₇ */            i := u3
            while e2
```

Fig. 10.22. Program for illustrating reaching definitions.

indicated by d_1 through d_7 in the comments to the left of the definitions. Bit vectors representing the *gen* and *kill* sets for the statements in Fig. 10.22 are shown to the left of syntax-tree nodes in Fig. 10.23. The sets themselves were computed by applying the data-flow equations in Fig. 10.21 to the statements represented by the syntax-tree nodes.

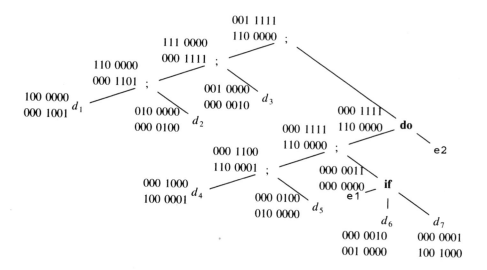

Fig. 10.23. The *gen* and *kill* sets at nodes in a syntax tree.

Consider the node for d_7 in the bottom-right corner of Fig. 10.23. The *gen* set $\{d_7\}$ is represented by 000 0001 and the *kill* set $\{d_1, d_4\}$ by 100 1000. That is, d_7 kills all the other definitions of i, its variable.

The second and third children of the **if** node represent the then and else parts, respectively, of the conditional. Note that the *gen* set 000 0011 at the **if** node is the union of the sets 000 0010 and 000 0001 at the second and third children. The *kill* set is empty because the definitions killed by the then and else parts are disjoint.

Data-flow equations for a cascade of statements are applied at the parent of the **if** node. The *kill* set at this node is obtained by

$$000\,0000 \cup (110\,0001 - 000\,0011) = 110\,0000$$

In words, nothing is killed by the conditional, and d_7, killed by the statement d_4, is generated by the conditional, so only d_1 and d_2 are in the *kill* set of the parent of the **if** node.

Now we can compute *in* and *out*, starting from the top of the parse tree. We assume the *in* set at the root of the syntax tree is empty. Thus *out* for the left child of the root is *gen* of that node, or 111 0000. This is also the value of the *in* set at the **do** node. From the data-flow equations associated with the **do** production in Fig. 10.21, the *in* set for the statement inside the **do** loop is obtained by taking the union of the *in* set 111 0000 at the **do** node and the *gen* set 000 1111 at the statement. The union yields 111 1111, so all definitions can reach the beginning of the loop body. However, at the point just before definition d_5, the *in* set is 011 1110, since definition d_4 kills d_1 and d_7. The balance of the *in* and *out* calculations are left as an exercise.   □

Local Reaching Definitions

Space for data-flow information can be traded for time, by saving information only at certain points and, as needed, recomputing information at intervening points. Basic blocks are usually treated as a unit during global flow analysis, with attention restricted to only those points that are the beginnings of blocks. Since there are usually many more points than blocks, restricting our effort to blocks is a significant savings. When needed, the reaching definitions for all points in a block can be calculated from the reaching definitions for the beginning of a block.

In more detail, consider a sequence of assignments $S_1 ; S_2 ; \cdots ; S_n$ in a basic block B. We refer to the beginning of B as point p_0, to the point between statements S_i and S_{i+1} as p_i, and to the end of the block as point p_n. The definitions reaching point p_j can be obtained from $in[B]$ by considering the statements $S_1 ; S_2 ; \cdots ; S_j$, starting with S_1 and applying the data-flow equations in Fig. 10.21 for cascades of statements. Initially, let $D = in[B]$. When S_i is considered, we delete from D the definitions killed by S_i and add the definitions generated by S_i. At the end, D consists of the definitions reaching p_j.

Use-Definition Chains

It is often convenient to store the reaching definition information as "use-definition chains" or "ud-chains," which are lists, for each use of a variable, of all the definitions that reach that use. If a use of variable a in block B is preceded by no unambiguous definition of a, then the ud-chain for that use of a is the set of definitions in $in[B]$ that are definitions of a. If there are unambiguous definitions of a within B preceding this use of a, then only the last such definition of a will be on the ud-chain, and $in[B]$ is not placed on the ud-chain. In addition, if there are ambiguous definitions of a, then all of these for which no unambiguous definition of a lies between it and the use of a are on the ud-chain for this use of a.

Evaluation Order

The techniques for conserving space during attribute evaluation, discussed in Chapter 5, also apply to the computation of data-flow information using specifications like the one in Fig. 10.21. Specifically, the only constraint on the evaluation order for the *gen*, *kill*, *in*, and *out* sets for statements is that imposed by dependencies between these sets. Having chosen an evaluation order, we are free to release the space for a set after all uses of it have occurred.

The data-flow equations of this section differ in one respect from semantic rules for attributes in Chapter 5: circular dependencies between attributes were not allowed in Chapter 5, but we have seen that data-flow equations may have circular dependencies, e.g., $in[S_1]$ and $out[S_1]$ depend on each other in 10.8. For the reaching-definitions problem, the data-flow equations can be rewritten to eliminate the circularity — compare the noncircular equations in Fig. 10.21 with 10.8. Once a noncircular specification is obtained, the techniques of Chapter 5 can be applied to obtain efficient solutions of data-flow equations.

General Control Flow

Data-flow analysis must take all control paths into account. If the control paths are evident from the syntax, then data-flow equations can be set up and solved in a syntax-directed manner, as in this section. When programs can contain goto statements, or even the more disciplined break and continue statements, the approach we have taken must be modified to take the actual control paths into account.

Several approaches may be taken. The iterative method in the next section works for arbitrary flow graphs. Since the flow graphs obtained in the presence of break and continue statements are reducible, such constructs can be handled systematically using the interval-based methods to be discussed in Section 10.10.

However, the syntax-directed approach need not be abandoned when break and continue statements are allowed. Before leaving this section we consider an example suggesting how break-statements can be accommodated, leaving the development of the ideas to Section 10.10.

Example 10.14. The break-statement within the **do-while** loop in Fig. 10.24 is equivalent to a jump to the end of the loop. How then are we to define the *gen* set for the following statement?

```
if e3 then a := u2
else begin i := u3; break end
```

We define the *gen* set to be $\{d_6\}$, where d_6 is the definition a:=u2, because d_6 is the only definition generated along the control paths from the beginning to the end points of the statement. Definition d_7, i.e., i:=u3, will get taken into account when the entire **do-while** loop is treated.

```
/* d₁ */     i := m-1;
/* d₂ */     j := n;
/* d₃ */     a := u1;
             do
/* d₄ */        i := i+1;
/* d₅ */        j := j-1;
             if e3 then
/* d₆ */           a := u2
             else begin
/* d₇ */              i := u3;
                   break
             end
          while e2
```

Fig. 10.24. Program containing a break-statement.

There is a programming trick that allows us to ignore the jump caused by the break-statement while we are processing the statements within the body of the loop: we take the *gen* and *kill* sets for a break-statement to be the empty set and U, the universal set of all definitions, respectively, as shown in Fig. 10.25. The remaining *gen* and *kill* sets shown in Fig. 10.25 are determined using the data-flow equations in Fig. 10.21, with the *gen* set shown above the *kill* set. Statements S_1 and S_2 represent sequences of assignments. The *gen* and *kill* sets at the do-node remain to be determined.

The end point of any sequence of statements ending in a break cannot be reached, so there is no harm in taking the *gen* set for the sequence to be $\varnothing$ and the *kill* set to be U; the result will still be a conservative estimate of *in* and *out*. Similarly, the end point of the if-statement can only be reached through the then part, and the *gen* and *kill* sets at the **if** node in Fig. 10.25 are indeed the same as those at its second child.

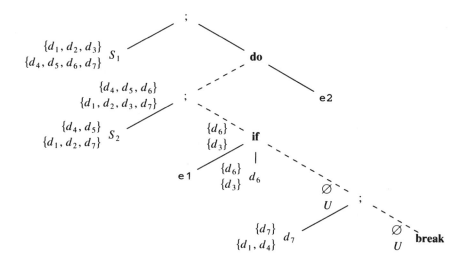

Fig. 10.25. Effect of a break-statement on *gen* and *kill* sets.

The *gen* and *kill* sets at the do-node must take into account all paths from the beginning to the end of the do-statement, so they are affected by the break-statement. Let us now compute two sets G and K, initially empty, as we traverse the dashed path from the do-node to the break-node. The intuition is that G and K represent the definitions generated and killed as control flows to the break-statement from the beginning of the loop body. The *gen* set for the do-while statement may then be determined by taking the union of G and the *gen* set for the loop body, because control can reach the end of the **do** either from the break-statement or by falling through the loop body. For the same reason, the *kill* set for the **do** is determined by taking the intersection of K and the *kill* set of the loop body.

Just before we reach the **if** node we have $G = gen[S_2] = \{d_4, d_5\}$ and $K = kill[S_2] = \{d_1, d_2, d_7\}$. At the **if** node we are interested in the case when control flows to the break-statement, so the then-part of the conditional has no effect on G and K. The next node along the dotted path is for a sequence of statements, so we compute new values of G and K. Writing S_3 for the statement represented by the left child of the sequence node (the one labeled d_7), we use

$$G := gen[S_3] \cup (G - kill[S_3])$$

$$K := kill[S_3] \cup (K - gen[S_3])$$

The values of G and K on reaching the break-statement are therefore $\{d_5, d_7\}$ and $\{d_1, d_2, d_4\}$, respectively.   □

10.6 ITERATIVE SOLUTION OF DATA-FLOW EQUATIONS

The method of the last section is simple and efficient when it applies, but for languages like Fortran or Pascal that permit arbitrary flow graphs, it is not sufficiently general. Section 10.10 discusses "interval analysis," a way to obtain the advantages of the syntax-directed approach to data-flow analysis for general flow graphs, at the expense of considerably more conceptual complexity.

Here, we shall discuss another important approach to solving data-flow problems. Instead of trying to use the parse tree to drive the calculation of *in* and *out* sets, we first build the flow graph, and then compute *in* and *out* for each node simultaneously. While discussing this new method, we shall also take the opportunity to introduce the reader to many different data-flow analysis problems, show some of their applications, and point out the differences among the problems.

The equations for many data-flow problems are similar in form in that information is being "generated" and "killed." However, there are two principal ways in which equations differ in detail.

1. The equations in the last section for reaching definitions are *forward* equations in the sense that the *out* sets are computed in terms of the *in* sets. We shall also see data-flow problems that are *backward* in that the *in* sets are computed from the *out* sets.

2. When there is more than one edge entering block *B*, the definitions reaching the beginning of *B* are the union of the definitions arriving along each of the edges. We therefore say that union is the *confluence operator*. In contrast, we shall consider problems like global available expressions, where intersection is the confluence operator, because an expression is only available at the beginning of *B* if it is available at the end of every predecessor of *B*. In Section 10.11 we shall see other examples of confluence operators.

In this section we shall see examples of both forward and backward equations with union and intersection taking turns as the confluence operator.

Iterative Algorithm for Reaching Definitions

For each basic block *B*, we can define *out* [*B*], *gen* [*B*], *kill* [*B*], and *in* [*B*], as in the last section, by noting that each block *B* may be viewed as a statement that is the cascade of one or more assignment statements. Assuming that *gen* and *kill* have been computed for each block, we can create two groups of equations, shown in (10.9) below, that relate *in* and *out*. The first group of equations follows from the observation that *in* [*B*] is the union of the definitions arriving from all predecessors of *B*. The second group are special cases of the general law (10.5) that we claim holds for all statements. These two groups are:

$$in[B] = \bigcup_{\substack{P \text{ a pred-}\\ \text{ecessor of } B}} out[P]$$

$$out[B] = gen[B] \cup (in[B] - kill[B])$$

(10.9)

If a flow graph has n basic blocks, we get $2n$ equations from (10.9). The $2n$ equations can be solved by treating them as recurrences for computing the in and out sets, just as the data-flow equations (10.6) and (10.5) for **do-while** statements were solved in the last section. In the last section we began with the empty set of definitions to be the starting estimate for all the out sets. Here we shall start with empty in sets, since we note from (10.9) that the in sets, being the union of out sets, will be empty if the out sets are. While we were able to agree that the equations (10.6) and (10.7) needed only one iteration, in the case of these more complex equations, we cannot *a priori* bound the number of iterations.

Algorithm 10.2. Reaching definitions.

Input. A flow graph for which $kill[B]$ and $gen[B]$ have been computed for each block B.

Output. $in[B]$ and $out[B]$ for each block B.

Method. We use an iterative approach, starting with the "estimate" $in[B] = \varnothing$ for all B and converging to the desired values of in and out. As we must iterate until the in's (and hence the out's) converge, we use a boolean variable *change* to record on each pass through the blocks whether any in has changed. The algorithm is sketched in Fig. 10.26.   □

```
            /*  initialize out on the assumption in[B] = ∅ for all B  */
(1)     for each block B do out[B] := gen[B];
(2)     change := true;          /*  to get the while-loop going  */
(3)     while change do begin
(4)         change := false;
(5)         for each block B do begin
(6)             in[B] :=   U   out[P];
                        P a prede-
                        cessor of B
(7)             oldout := out[B];
(8)             out[B] := gen[B] ∪ (in[B] - kill[B]);
(9)             if out[B] ≠ oldout then change := true
            end
        end
```

Fig. 10.26. Algorithm to compute *in* and *out*.

Intuitively, Algorithm 10.2 propagates definitions as far as they will go without being killed, in a sense simulating all possible executions of the program. The bibliographic notes contain references where formal proofs of the correctness of this and other data-flow analysis problems can be found.

We can see that the algorithm will eventually halt because $out[B]$ never decreases in size for any B; once a definition is added, it stays there forever. (The proof of this fact is left as an inductive exercise.) Since the set of all definitions is finite, there must eventually be a pass of the while-loop in which $oldout = out[B]$ for each B at line (9). Then *change* will remain **false** and the algorithm terminates. We are safe terminating then because if the out's have not changed, the in's will not change on the next pass. And, if the in's do not change, the out's cannot, so on all subsequent passes there can be no changes.

It may be shown that an upper bound on the number of times around the while-loop is the number of nodes in the flow graph. Intuitively, the reason is that if a definition reaches a point, it can do so along a cycle-free path, and the number of nodes in a flow graph is an upper bound on the number of nodes in a cycle-free path. Each time around the while-loop, the definition progresses by at least one node along the path in question.

In fact, if we properly order the blocks in the for-loop of line (5), there is empirical evidence that the average number of iterations on real programs is under 5 (see Section 10.10). Since the sets can be represented by bit vectors, and the operations on these sets can be implemented by logical operations on the bit vectors, Algorithm 10.2 is surprisingly efficient in practice.

Example 10.15. The flow graph of Fig. 10.27 has been derived from the program in Fig. 10.22 of the last section. We shall apply Algorithm 10.2 to this flow graph so the approaches of the two sections can be compared.

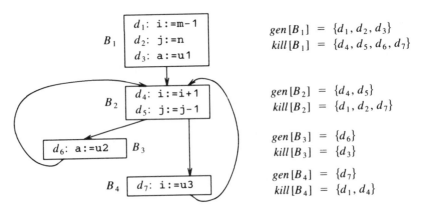

B_1	d_1: i:=m-1 d_2: j:=n d_3: a:=u1	$gen[B_1] = \{d_1, d_2, d_3\}$ $kill[B_1] = \{d_4, d_5, d_6, d_7\}$

$gen[B_1] = \{d_1, d_2, d_3\}$
$kill[B_1] = \{d_4, d_5, d_6, d_7\}$

B_2 d_4: i:=i+1 d_5: j:=j-1

$gen[B_2] = \{d_4, d_5\}$
$kill[B_2] = \{d_1, d_2, d_7\}$

d_6: a:=u2 B_3

$gen[B_3] = \{d_6\}$
$kill[B_3] = \{d_3\}$

B_4 d_7: i:=u3

$gen[B_4] = \{d_7\}$
$kill[B_4] = \{d_1, d_4\}$

Fig. 10.27. Flow graph for illustrating reaching definitions.

Only the definitions $d_1, d_2, \ldots, d_7$ defining i, j, and a in Fig. 10.27 are of interest. As in the last section, we shall represent sets of definitions by bit vectors, where bit i from the left represents definition d_i.

The loop of line (1) in Fig. 10.26 initializes $out[B] = gen[B]$ for each B, and these initial values of $out[B]$ are shown in the table in Fig. 10.28. The initial values ($\varnothing$) of each $in[B]$ are not computed or used, but are shown for completeness. Suppose the for-loop of line (5) is executed with $B = B_1, B_2, B_3, B_4$, in that order. With $B = B_1$, there are no predecessors for the initial node so $in[B_1]$ remains the empty set, represented by 000 0000; as a result, $out[B_1]$ remains equal to $gen[B_1]$. This value does not differ from $oldout$ computed at line (7), so we do not yet set $change$ to **true**.

Then we consider $B = B_2$ and compute

$$in[B_2] = out[B_1] \cup out[B_3] \cup out[B_4]$$

$$= 111\,0000 + 000\,0010 + 000\,0001 = 111\,0011$$

$$out[B_2] = gen[B_2] \cup (in[B_2] - kill[B_2])$$

$$= 000\,1100 + (111\,0011 - 110\,0001) = 001\,1110$$

This computation is summarized in Fig. 10.28. At the end of the first pass, $out[B_4] = 001\,0111$, reflecting the fact that d_7 is generated and that d_3, d_5, and d_6 reach B_4 and are not killed in B_4. From the second pass on there are no changes in any of the out sets, so the algorithm terminates. □

BLOCK B	INITIAL		PASS 1		PASS 2	
	$in[B]$	$out[B]$	$in[B]$	$out[B]$	$in[B]$	$out[B]$
B_1	000 0000	111 0000	000 0000	111 0000	000 0000	111 0000
B_2	000 0000	000 1100	111 0011	001 1110	111 1111	001 1110
B_3	000 0000	000 0010	001 1110	000 1110	001 1110	000 1110
B_4	000 0000	000 0001	001 1110	001 0111	001 1110	001 0111

Fig. 10.28. Computation of in and out.

Available Expressions

An expression x+y is *available* at a point p if every path (not necessarily cycle-free) from the initial node to p evaluates x+y, and after the last such evaluation prior to reaching p, there are no subsequent assignments to x or y. For available expressions we say that a block *kills* expression x+y if it assigns (or may assign) x or y and does not subsequently recompute x+y. A block *generates* expression x+y if it definitely evaluates x+y and does not subsequently redefine x or y.

Note that the notion of "killing" or "generating" an available expression is not exactly the same as that for reaching definitions. Nevertheless, these notions of "kill" and "generate" obey the same laws as they do for reaching definitions. We could compute them exactly as we did in Section 10.5, provided we modified the rules in 10.21(a) for a simple assignment statement.

The primary use of available expressions information is for detecting common subexpressions. For example, in Fig. 10.29, the expression 4*i in block B_3 will be a common subexpression if 4*i is available at the entry point of block B_3. It will be available if i is not assigned a new value in block B_2, or if, as in Fig. 10.29(b), 4*i is recomputed after i is assigned in B_2.

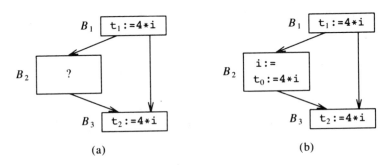

(a)   (b)

Fig. 10.29. Potential common subexpressions across blocks.

We can easily compute the set of generated expressions for each point in a block, working from beginning to end of the block. At the point prior to the block, assume no expressions are available. If at point p set A of expressions is available, and q is the point after p, with statement x:=y+z between them, then we form the set of expressions available at q by the following two steps.

1. Add to A the expression y+z.
2. Delete from A any expression involving x.

Note the steps must be done in the correct order, as x could be the same as y or z. After we reach the end of the block, A is the set of generated expressions for the block. The set of killed expressions is all expressions, say, y+z such that either y or z is defined in the block, and y+z is not generated by the block.

Example 10.16. Consider the four statements of Fig. 10.30. After the first, b+c is available. After the second, a-d becomes available, but b+c is no longer available, because b has been redefined. The third does not make b+c available again, because the value of c is immediately changed. After the last statement, a-d is no longer available, because d has changed. Thus no statements are generated, and all statements involving a, b, c, or d are killed.   □

We can find available expressions in a manner reminiscent of the way reaching definitions are computed. Suppose U is the "universal" set of all expressions appearing on the right of one or more statements of the program. For each block B, let $in[B]$ be the set of expressions in U that are available at the point just before the beginning of B. Let $out[B]$ be the same for the point following the end of B. Define $e\_gen[B]$ to be the expressions generated by B

STATEMENTS	AVAILABLE EXPRESSIONS
	.... none
a := b+c	
	.... only b+c
b := a−d	
	.... only a−d
c := b+c	
	.... only a−d
d := a−d	
	.... none

Fig. 10.30. Computation of available expressions.

and $e\_kill[B]$ to be the set of expressions in U killed in B. Note that in, out, e_gen, and e_kill can all be represented by bit vectors. The following equations relate the unknowns in and out to each other and the known quantities e_gen and e_kill.

$$out[B] = e\_gen[B] \cup (in[B] - e\_kill[B])$$

$$in[B] = \bigcap_{\substack{P \text{ a prede-} \\ \text{cessor of } B}} out[P] \quad \text{for } B \text{ not initial} \qquad (10.10)$$

$in[B_1] = \varnothing$ where B_1 is the initial block.

Equations (10.10) look almost identical to equations (10.9) for reaching definitions. The first difference is that in for the initial node is handled as a special case. This is justified on the grounds that nothing is available if the program has just begun at the initial node, even though some expression might be available along all paths to the initial node from elsewhere in the program. If we did not force $in[B_1]$ to be empty, we might erroneously deduce that certain expressions were available before the program started.

The second, and more important, difference is that the confluence operator is intersection rather than union. This operator is the proper one because an expression is available at the beginning of a block only if it is available at the end of all its predecessors. In contrast, a definition reaches the beginning of a block whenever it reaches the end of one or more of its predecessors.

The use of $\cap$ rather than $\cup$ makes equations (10.10) behave differently from (10.9). While neither set has a unique solution, for (10.9) it is the smallest solution that corresponds to the definition of "reaching," and we obtained that solution by starting with the assumption that nothing reached anywhere, and building up to the solution. In that way, we never assumed that a definition d could reach a point p unless an actual path propagating d to p could be found. In contrast, for equations (10.10) we want the largest possible solution, so we start with an approximation that is too large and work down.

It may not be obvious that by starting with the assumption "everything, i.e., the set U, is available everywhere" and eliminating only those expressions for which we can discover a path along which it is not available, we do reach a set of truly available expressions. In the case of available expressions, it is conservative to produce a subset of the exact set of available expressions, and this is what we do. The argument for subsets being conservative is that our intended use of the information is to replace the computation of an available expression by a previously computed value (see Algorithm 10.5 in the next section), and not knowing an expression is available only inhibits us from changing the code.

Example 10.17. We shall concentrate on a single block, B_2 in Fig. 10.31, to illustrate the effect of the initial approximation of $in[B_2]$ on $out[B_2]$. Let G and K abbreviate $gen[B_2]$ and $kill[B_2]$, respectively. The data-flow equations for block B_2 are:

$$in[B_2] = out[B_1] \cap out[B_2]$$

$$out[B_2] = G \cup (in[B_2] - K)$$

These equations have been rewritten as recurrences in Fig. 10.31, with I^j and O^j being the jth approximations of $in[B_2]$ and $out[B_2]$, respectively. The figure also shows that starting with $I^0 = \varnothing$ we get $O^1 = O^2 = G$, while starting with $I^0 = U$ we get a larger set for O^2. It so happens that $out[B_2]$ equals O^2 in each case, because the iterations each converge at the points shown.

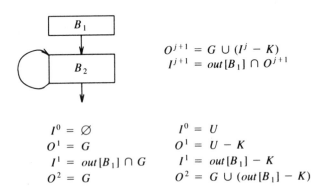

$$O^{j+1} = G \cup (I^j - K)$$
$$I^{j+1} = out[B_1] \cap O^{j+1}$$

$I^0 = \varnothing$	$I^0 = U$
$O^1 = G$	$O^1 = U - K$
$I^1 = out[B_1] \cap G$	$I^1 = out[B_1] - K$
$O^2 = G$	$O^2 = G \cup (out[B_1] - K)$

Fig. 10.31. Initializing the in sets to $\varnothing$ is too restrictive.

Intuitively, the solution obtained starting with $I^0 = U$ using

$$out[B_2] = G \cup (out[B_1] - K)$$

is more desirable, because it correctly reflects the fact that expressions in $out[B_1]$ that are not killed by B_2 are available at the end of B_2, just as the expressions generated by B_2 are.   □

Algorithm 10.3. Available expressions.

Input. A flow graph G with $e\_kill[B]$ and $e\_gen[B]$ computed for each block B. The initial block is B_1.

Output. The set $in[B]$ for each block B.

Method. Execute the algorithm of Fig. 10.32. The explanation of the steps is similar to that for Fig. 10.26.   □

```
in[B₁] := ∅;
out[B₁] := e_gen[B₁];   /* in and out never change for the initial node, B₁ */
for B ≠ B₁ do out[B] := U − e_kill[B];   /* initial estimate is too large */
change := true;
while change do begin
      change := false;
      for B ≠ B₁ do begin
          in[B] :=      ∩      out[P];
                    P a prede-
                    cessor of B
          oldout := out[B];
          out[B] := e_gen[B] ∪ (in[B] − e_kill[B]);
          if out[B] ≠ oldout then change := true
      end
end
```

Fig. 10.32. Available expressions computation.

Live-Variable Analysis

A number of code improving transformations depend on information computed in the direction opposite to the flow of control in a program; we shall consider some of these now. In *live-variable* analysis we wish to know for variable **x** and point p whether the value of **x** at p could be used along some path in the flow graph starting at p. If so, we say **x** is *live* at p; otherwise **x** is *dead* at p.

As we saw in Section 9.7, an important use for live-variable information comes when we generate object code. After a value is computed in a register, and presumably used within a block, it is not necessary to store that value if it is dead at the end of the block. Also, if all registers are full and we need another register, we should favor using a register with a dead value, since that value does not have to be stored.

Let us define $in[B]$ to be the set of variables live at the point immediately before block B and define $out[B]$ to be the same at the point immediately after the block. Let $def[B]$ be the set of variables definitely assigned values in B prior to any use of that variable in B, and let $use[B]$ be the set of variables whose values may be used in B prior to any definition of the variable. Then the equations relating *def* and *use* to the unknowns *in* and *out* are:

$$in[B] = use[B] \cup (out[B] - def[B])$$

$$out[B] = \bigcup_{\substack{S \text{ a suc-} \\ \text{cessor of } B}} in[S] \qquad (10.11)$$

The first group of equations says that a variable is live coming into a block if either it is used before redefinition in the block or it is live coming out of the block and is not redefined in the block. The second group of equations says that a variable is live coming out of a block if and only if it is live coming into one of its successors.

The relation between (10.11) and the reaching-definitions equations (10.9) should be noticed. Here, *in* and *out* have their roles interchanged, and *use* and *def* substitute for *gen* and *kill*, respectively. As for (10.9), the solution to (10.11) is not necessarily unique, and we want the smallest solution. The algorithm used for the minimum solution is essentially a backwards version of Algorithm 10.2. Since the mechanism for detecting changes to any of the *in*'s is so similar to the way we detected changes to *out*'s in Algorithms 10.2 and 10.3, we elide the details of checking for termination.

Algorithm 10.4. Live variable analysis.

Input. A flow graph with *def* and *use* computed for each block.

Output. *out*[B], the set of variables live on exit from each block *B* of the flow graph.

Method. Execute the program in Fig. 10.33. □

```
for each block B do in[B] := ∅;
while changes to any of the in's occur do
    for each block B do begin
        out[B] =      ∪      in[S]
                   S a suc-
                   cessor of B
        in[B] := use[B] ∪ (out[B] − def[B])
    end
```

Fig. 10.33. Live variable calculation.

Definition-Use Chains

A calculation done in virtually the same manner as live-variable analysis is *definition-use chaining* (du-chaining). We say a variable is *used* at statement *s* if its *r*-value may be required. For example, b and c (but not a) are used in each of the statements a:=b+c and a[b]:=c. The du-chaining problem is to compute for a point p the set of uses s of a variable, say $\mathbf{x}$, such that there is a path from p to s that does not redefine $\mathbf{x}$.

As with live variables, if we can compute $out[B]$, the set of uses reachable from the end of block B, then we can compute the definitions reached from any point p within block B by scanning the portion of block B that follows p. In particular, if there is a definition of variable $\mathbf{x}$ in the block, we can determine the *du-chain* for that definition, the list of all possible uses of that definition. The method is analogous to that discussed in Section 10.5 for computing ud-chains, and we leave it to the reader.

The equations for computing du-chaining information look exactly like (10.11) with substitution for *def* and *use*. In place of $use[B]$, take the set of *upwards exposed* uses in B, that is, the set of pairs $(s, \mathbf{x})$ such that s is a statement in B which uses variable $\mathbf{x}$ and such that no prior definition of $\mathbf{x}$ occurs in B. Instead of $def[B]$ take the set of pairs $(s, \mathbf{x})$ such that s is a statement which uses $\mathbf{x}$, s is not in B, and B has a definition of $\mathbf{x}$. These equations are solved by the obvious analog of Algorithm 10.4, and we shall not discuss the matter further.

10.7 CODE-IMPROVING TRANSFORMATIONS

Algorithms for performing the code-improving transformations introduced in Section 10.2 rely on data-flow information. In the last two sections, we have seen how this information can be collected. Here we consider common subexpression elimination, copy propagation, and transformations for moving loop invariant computations out of loops and for eliminating induction variables. For many languages, significant improvements in running time can be achieved by improving code in loops. When such transformations are implemented in a compiler, it is possible to perform some of the transformations together. However, we shall present the ideas underlying the transformations individually.

The emphasis in this section is on global transformations that use information about the program as a whole. As we saw in the last two sections, global data-flow analysis does not usually look at points within basic blocks. Global transformations are therefore not a substitute for local transformations; both must be performed. For example, when we perform global common subexpression elimination we shall only be concerned with whether an expression is generated by a block and not with whether it is recomputed several times within a block.

Elimination of Global Common Subexpressions

The available expressions data-flow problem discussed in the last section allows us to determine if an expression at point p in a flow graph is a common subexpression. The following algorithm formalizes the intuitive ideas presented in Section 10.2 for eliminating common subexpressions.

Algorithm 10.5. Global common subexpression elimination.

Input. A flow graph with available expression information.

Output. A revised flow graph.

Method. For every statement s of the form $x:=y+z$[6] such that $y+z$ is available at the beginning of s's block, and neither y nor z is defined prior to statement s in that block, do the following.

1. To discover the evaluations of $y+z$ that reach s's block, we follow flow graph edges, searching backward from s's block. However, we do not go through any block that evaluates $y+z$. The last evaluation of $y+z$ in each block encountered is an evaluation of $y+z$ that reaches s.

2. Create a new variable u.

3. Replace each statement $w:=y+z$ found in (1) by

   ```
   u := y+z
   w := u
   ```

4. Replace statement s by $x:=u$.   □

Some remarks about this algorithm are in order.

1. The search in step (1) of the algorithm for the evaluations of $y+z$ that reach statement s can also be formulated as a data-flow analysis problem. However, it does not make sense to solve it for all expressions $y+z$ and all statements or blocks, because too much irrelevant information is gathered. Rather we should perform a graph search on the flow graph for each relevant statement and expression.

2. Not all changes made by Algorithm 10.5 are improvements. We might wish to limit the number of different evaluations reaching s found in step (1), probably to one. However, copy propagation, to be discussed next, often allows benefit to be obtained even when several evaluations of $y+z$ reach s.

3. Algorithm 10.5 will miss the fact that $a*z$ and $c*z$ must have the same value in

   ```
   a := x+y          c := x+y
             vs.
   b := a*z          d := c*z
   ```

   because this simple approach to common subexpressions considers only the literal expressions themselves, rather than the values computed by expressions. Kildall [1973] presents a method for catching such equivalences on one pass; we shall discuss the ideas in Section 10.11. However, they can be caught with multiple passes of Algorithm 10.5, and

---

[6] Recall we continue to use + as a generic operator.

one might consider repeating it until no further changes occur. If a and c are temporary variables that are not used outside the block in which they appear, then the common subexpression (x+y)*z can be caught by treating the temporary variables specially, as in the next example.

Example 10.18. Suppose that there are no assignments to the array a in the flow graph of Fig. 10.34(a), so we can safely say that a[t_2] and a[t_6] are common subexpressions. The problem is to eliminate this common subexpression.

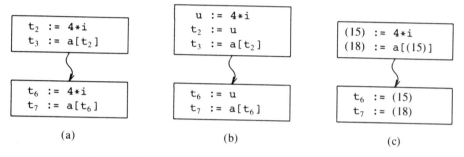

Fig. 10.34. Eliminating the common subexpression 4*i.

The common subexpression 4*i in Fig. 10.34(a) has been eliminated in Fig. 10.34(b). One way to determine that a[t_2] and a[t_6] are also common subexpressions is to replace t_2 and t_6 by u using copy propagation (to be discussed next); both expressions then become a[u], which can be eliminated by reapplying Algorithm 10.5. Note that the same new variable u is inserted in both blocks in Fig. 10.34(b), so local copy propagation is enough to convert both a[t_2] and a[t_6] to a[u].

There is another way, which takes into account the fact that temporary variables are inserted by the compiler and are used only within blocks they appear in. We shall look more closely at the way expressions are represented during the computation of available expressions to get around the fact that different temporary variables may represent the same expression. The recommended technique for representing sets of expressions is to assign a number to each expression and use bit vectors with bit *i* representing the expression numbered *i*. The value-numbering techniques of Section 5.2 can be applied during the numbering of expressions to treat temporary variables in a special way.

In more detail, suppose 4*i has value number 15. The expressions a[t_2] and a[t_6] will get the same value number if we use the value number 15 rather than the names of the temporary variables t_2 and t_6. Suppose the resulting value number is 18. Then bit 18 will represent both a[t_2] and a[t_6] during data-flow analysis, and we can determine that a[t_6] is available and can be eliminated. The resulting code is indicated in Fig. 10.34(c). We use (15) and (18) to represent temporaries corresponding to expressions with those value numbers. Actually, t_6 is useless and would be eliminated during local live variable analysis. Also t_7, being a temporary, would not be computed itself; rather, uses of t_7 would be replaced by uses of (18).   □

Copy Propagation

Algorithm 10.5 just presented, and various other algorithms such as induction-variable elimination discussed later in this section, introduce copy statements of the form x:=y. Copies may also be generated directly by the intermediate code generator, although most of these involve temporaries local to one block and can be removed by the dag construction discussed in Section 9.8. It is sometimes possible to eliminate copy statement s: x:=y if we determine all places where this definition of x is used. We may then substitute y for x in all these places, provided the following conditions are met by every such use u of x.

1. Statement s must be the only definition of x reaching u (that is, the ud-chain for use u consists only of s).

2. On every path from s to u, including paths that go through u several times (but do not go through s a second time), there are no assignments to y.

Condition (1) can be checked using ud-chaining information, but what of condition (2)? We shall set up a new data-flow analysis problem in which $in[B]$ is the set of copies s: x:=y such that every path from the initial node to the beginning of B contains the statement s, and subsequent to the last occurrence of s there are no assignments to y. The set $out[B]$ can be defined correspondingly, but with respect to the end of B. We say copy statement s: x:=y is *generated* in block B if s occurs in B and there is no subsequent assignment to y within B. We say s: x:=y is *killed* in B if x or y is assigned there and s is not in B. The notion that assignments to x "kill" x:=y is familiar from reaching definitions, but the idea that assignments to y do so is special to this problem. Note the important consequence of the fact that different assignments x:=y kill each other; $in[B]$ can contain only one copy statement with x on the left.

Let U be the "universal" set of all copy statements in the program. It is important to note that different statements x:=y are different in U. Define $c\_gen[B]$ to be the set of all copies generated in block B and $c\_kill[B]$ to be the set of copies in U that are killed in B. Then the following equations relate the quantities defined:

$$out[B] = c\_gen[B] \cup (in[B] - c\_kill[B])$$

$$in[B] = \bigcap_{\substack{P \text{ a prede-} \\ \text{cessor of } B}} out[P] \quad \text{for } B \text{ not initial} \tag{10.12}$$

$$in[B_1] = \varnothing \quad \text{where } B_1 \text{ is the initial block}$$

Equations 10.12 are identical to Equations 10.10, if c_kill is replaced by e_kill and c_gen by e_gen. Thus, 10.12 can be solved by Algorithm 10.3, and we shall not discuss the matter further. We shall, however, give an example that exposes some of the nuances of copy optimization.

Example 10.19. Consider the flow graph of Fig. 10.35. Here, $c\_gen[B_1] = \{x:=y\}$ and $c\_gen[B_3] = \{x:=z\}$. Also, $c\_kill[B_2] = \{x:=y\}$, since y is assigned in B_2. Finally, $c\_kill[B_1] = \{x:=z\}$ since x is assigned in B_1, and $c\_kill[B_3] = \{x:=y\}$ for the same reason.

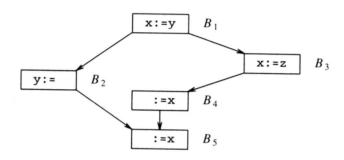

Fig. 10.35. Example flow graph.

The other c_gen's and c_kill's are $\varnothing$. Also, $in[B_1] = \varnothing$ by Equations 10.12. Algorithm 10.3 in one pass determines that

$$in[B_2] = in[B_3] = out[B_1] = \{x:=y\}$$

Likewise, $out[B_2] = \varnothing$ and

$$out[B_3] = in[B_4] = out[B_4] = \{x:=z\}$$

Finally, $in[B_5] = out[B_2] \cap out[B_4] = \varnothing$.

We observe that neither copy $x:=y$ nor $x:=z$ "reaches" the use of x in B_5, in the sense of Algorithm 10.5. It is true but irrelevant that both these definitions of x "reach" B_5 in the sense of reaching definitions. Thus, neither copy may be propagated, as it is not possible to substitute y (respectively z) for x in all uses of x that definition $x:=y$ (respectively $x:=z$) reaches. We could substitute z for x in B_4, but that would not improve the code.   □

We now specify the details of the algorithm to remove copy statements.

Algorithm 10.6. Copy propagation.

Input. A flow graph G, with ud-chains giving the definitions reaching block B, and with $c\_in[B]$ representing the solution to Equations 10.12, that is, the set of copies $x:=y$ that reach block B along every path, with no assignment to x or y following the last occurrence of $x:=y$ on the path. We also need du-chains giving the uses of each definition.

Output. A revised flow graph.

Method. For each copy s: x:=y do the following.

1. Determine those uses of x that are reached by this definition of x, namely, s: x:=y.

2. Determine whether for every use of x found in (1), s is in $c\_in[B]$, where B is the block of this particular use, and moreover, no definitions of x or y occur prior to this use of x within B. Recall that if s is in $c\_in[B]$, then s is the only definition of x that reaches B.

3. If s meets the conditions of (2), then remove s and replace all uses of x found in (1) by y.   □

Detection of Loop-Invariant Computations

We shall make use of ud-chains to detect those computations in a loop that are *loop-invariant*, that is, whose value does not change as long as control stays within the loop. As discussed in Section 10.4, a loop is a region consisting of a set of blocks with a header that dominates all the other blocks, so the only way to enter the loop is through the header. We also require that a loop have at least one way to get back to the header from any block in the loop.

If an assignment x:=y+z is at a position in the loop where all possible definitions of y and z are outside the loop (including the special case where y and/or z is a constant), then y+z is loop-invariant because its value will be the same each time x:=y+z is encountered, as long as control stays within the loop. All such assignments can be detected from the ud-chains, that is, a list of all definition points of y and z reaching assignment x:=y+z.

Having recognized that the value of x computed at x:=y+z does not change within the loop, suppose there is another statement v:=x+w, where w could only have been defined outside the loop. Then x+w is also loop-invariant.

We can use the above ideas to make repeated passes over the loop, discovering more and more computations whose value is loop-invariant. If we have both ud- and du-chains, we do not even have to make repeated passes over the code. The du-chain for definition x:=y+z will tell us where this value of x could be used, and we need only check among these uses of x, within the loop, that use no other definition of x. These loop-invariant assignments may be moved to the preheader, provided their operands besides x are also loop-invariant, as discussed in the next algorithm.

Algorithm 10.7. Detection of loop-invariant computations.

Input. A loop L consisting of a set of basic blocks, each block containing a sequence of three-address statements. We assume ud-chains, as computed in Section 10.5, are available for the individual statements.

Output. The set of three-address statements that compute the same value each time executed, from the time control enters the loop L until control next leaves L.

Method. We shall give a rather informal specification of the algorithm, trusting that the principles will be clear.

1. Mark "invariant" those statements whose operands are all either constant or have all their reaching definitions outside L.

2. Repeat step (3) until at some repetition no new statements are marked "invariant."

3. Mark "invariant" all those statements not previously so marked all of whose operands either are constant, have all their reaching definitions outside L, or have exactly one reaching definition, and that definition is a statement in L marked invariant.   □

Performing Code Motion

Having found the invariant statements within a loop, we can apply to some of them an optimization known as *code motion*, in which the statements are moved to the preheader of the loop. The following three conditions ensure that code motion does not change what the program computes. None of the conditions is absolutely essential; we have selected these conditions because they are easy to check and apply to situations that occur in real programs. We shall later discuss the possibility of relaxing the conditions.

The conditions for statement s: **x:=y+z** are:

1. The block containing s dominates all *exit* nodes of the loop, where an exit of a loop is a node with a successor not in the loop.

2. There is no other statement in the loop that assigns to **x**. Again, if **x** is a temporary assigned only once, this condition is surely satisfied and need not be checked.

3. No use of **x** in the loop is reached by any definition of **x** other than s. This condition too will be satisfied, normally, if **x** is a temporary.

The next three examples motivate the above conditions.

Example 10.20. Moving a statement that need not be executed within a loop to a position outside the loop can change what the program computes, as we show using Fig. 10.36. This observation motivates condition (1), since a statement that dominates all the exits cannot fail to be executed, assuming the loop does not run forever.

Consider the flow graph shown in Fig. 10.36(a). B_2, B_3, and B_4 form a loop with header B_2. Statement **i:=2** in B_3 is clearly loop-invariant. However, B_3 does not dominate B_4, the only loop exit. If we move **i:=2** to a newly created preheader B_6, as shown in Fig. 10.36(b), we may change the

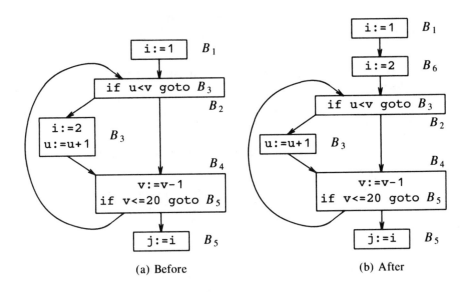

(a) Before   (b) After

Fig. 10.36. Example of illegal code motion.

value assigned to j in B_5, in those cases where B_3 never gets executed. For example, if u=30 and v=25 when B_2 is first entered, Fig. 10.36(a) sets j to 1 at B_5, since B_3 is never entered, while Fig. 10.36(b) sets j to 2.   □

Example 10.21. Condition (2) is required when there is more than one assignment to x in the loop. For example, the flow graph structure in Fig. 10.37 is the same as that in Fig. 10.36(a), and we have the option of creating a preheader B_6 as in Fig. 10.36(b).

Since B_2 in Fig. 10.37 dominates the exit B_4, condition (1) does not prevent i:=3 from being moved to the preheader B_6. However, if we do so, we shall set i to 2 whenever B_3 is executed, and i will have value 2 when we reach B_5, even if we follow a sequence such as $B_2 \rightarrow B_3 \rightarrow B_4 \rightarrow B_2 \rightarrow B_4 \rightarrow B_5$. For example, consider what happens if v is 22 and u is 21 when B_2 is first reached. If i:=3 is in B_2, we set j to 3 at B_5, but if i:=3 is removed to the preheader, we set j to 2.   □

Example 10.22. Now let us consider rule (3). The use k:=i in block B_4 of Fig. 10.38 is reached by i:=1 in block B_1, as well as by i:=2 in B_3. Thus, we could not move i:=2 to the preheader, because the value of k reaching B_5 would change in the case u>=v. For example, if u=v=0 then k is set to 1 in the flow graph of Fig. 10.38, but if i:=2 is moved to the preheader, we set k to 2 once and for all.   □

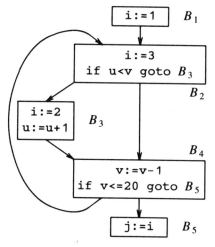

Fig. 10.37. Illustrating condition (2).   **Fig. 10.38.** Illustrating condition (3).

Algorithm 10.8. Code motion.

Input. A loop L with ud-chaining information and dominator information.

Output. A revised version of the loop with a preheader and (possibly) some statements moved to the preheader.

Method.

1. Use Algorithm 10.7 to find loop-invariant statements.

2. For each statement s defining x found in step (1), check:

    i)   that it is in a block that dominates all exits of L,
    ii) that x is not defined elsewhere in L, and
    iii) that all uses in L of x can only be reached by the definition of x in statement s.

3. Move, in the order found by Algorithm 10.7, each statement s found in (1) and meeting conditions (2i), (2ii), and (2iii), to a newly created preheader, provided any operands of s that are defined in loop L (in the case that s was found in step (3) of Algorithm 10.7) have previously had their definition statements moved to the preheader.   □

    To understand why no change to what the program computes can occur, conditions (2i) and (2ii) of Algorithm 10.8 assure that the value of x computed at s must be the value of x after any exit block of L. When we move s to the preheader, s will still be the definition of x that reaches the end of any exit block of L. Condition (2iii) assures that any uses of x within L did, and will continue to, use the value of x computed by s.

To see why the transformation cannot increase the running time of the program, we have only to note that condition (2i) ensures that s is executed at least once each time control enters L. After code motion, it will be executed exactly once in the preheader and not at all in L whenever control enters L.

Alternative Code Motion Strategies

We can relax condition (1) somewhat if we are willing to take the risk that we may actually increase the running time of the program a bit; of course, we never change what the program computes. The relaxed version of code-motion condition (1) [i.e., item 2(i) in Algorithm 10.8] is that we may move a statement s assigning x only if:

1'. The block containing s either dominates all exits of the loop, or x is not used outside the loop. For example, if x is a temporary variable, we can be sure (in many compilers) that the value will be used only in its own block. In general, live variable analysis is needed to tell if x is live at any exit from the loop.

If Algorithm 10.8 is modified to use condition (1'), occasionally the running time will increase slightly, but we can expect to do reasonably well on the average. The modified algorithm may move to the preheader certain computations that might not be executed in the loop. Not only does this risk slowing down the program significantly, it may also cause an error in certain circumstances. For example, the evaluation of a division x/y in a loop may be preceded by a test to see whether $y=0$. If we move x/y to the preheader, a division by zero may occur. For this reason, it is unwise to use condition (1') unless optimization may be inhibited by the programmer, or we apply the stricter condition (1) to division statements.

Even if none of conditions (2i), (2ii), and (2iii) of Algorithm 10.8 are met by an assignment $x:=y+z$, we can still take the computation $y+z$ outside a loop. Create a new temporary t, and set $t:=y+z$ in the preheader. Then replace $x:=y+z$ by $x:=t$ in the loop. In many cases we can then propagate out the copy statement $x:=t$, as discussed earlier in this section. Note that if condition (2iii) of Algorithm 10.8 is satisfied, that is, if all uses of x in loop L are defined at $x:=y+z$ (now $x:=t$), then we can surely remove statement $x:=t$ by replacing uses of x in L by uses of t and placing $x:=t$ after each exit of the loop.

Maintaining Data-Flow Information After Code Motion

The transformations of Algorithm 10.8 do not change ud-chaining information, since by conditions (2i), (2ii), and (2iii), all uses of the variable assigned by a moved statement s that were reached by s are still reached by s from its new position. Definitions of variables used by s are either outside L, in which case they reach the preheader, or they are inside L, in which case by step (3) they were moved to the preheader ahead of s.

If the ud-chains are represented by lists of pointers to pointers to statements (rather than by lists of pointers to statements), we can maintain ud-chains when we move statement s by simply changing the pointer to s when we move it. That is, we create for each statement s a pointer p_s, which always points to s. We put p_s on each ud-chain containing s. Then, no matter where we move s, we have only to change p_s, regardless of how many ud-chains s is on. Of course the extra level of indirection costs some compiler time and space.

If we represent ud-chains by a list of statement addresses (pointers to statements) we can still maintain ud-chains as we move statements. But then we need du-chains, as well, for efficiency. When we move s, we may go down its du-chain, changing the ud-chain of all uses that refer to s.

The dominator information is changed slightly by code motion. The preheader is now the immediate dominator of the header, and the immediate dominator of the preheader is the node that formerly was the immediate dominator of the header. That is, the preheader is inserted into the dominator tree as the parent of the header.

Elimination of Induction Variables

A variable x is called an *induction variable* of a loop L if every time the variable x changes values, it is incremented or decremented by some constant. Often, an induction variable is incremented by the same constant each time around the loop, as i in a loop headed by **for** $i := 1$ **to** 10. However, our methods deal with variables that are incremented or decremented zero, one, two, or more times as we go around a loop. The number of changes to an induction variable may even differ at different iterations.

A common situation is one in which an induction variable, say i, indexes an array, and some other induction variable, say t, whose value is a linear function of i, is the actual offset used to access the array. Often, the only use made of i is in the test for loop termination. We can then get rid of i by replacing its test by one on t.

The algorithms that follow deal with a restricted class of induction variables to simplify the presentation. Some extensions of the algorithms can be done by adding more cases, but others require theorems to be proved about expressions involving the usual arithmetic operators.

We shall look for *basic induction variables*, which are those variables i whose only assignments within loop L are of the form $i := i \pm c$, where c is a constant.[7] We then look for additional induction variables j that are defined only once within L, and whose value is a linear function of some basic induction variable i where j is defined.

---

[7] In our discussion of induction variables, "+" stands only for the addition operator, not a generic operator, and likewise for the other standard arithmetic operators.

Algorithm 10.9. Detection of induction variables.

Input. A loop L with reaching definition information and loop-invariant computation information (from Algorithm 10.7).

Output. A set of induction variables. Associated with each induction variable j is a triple (i, c, d), where i is a basic induction variable, and c and d are constants such that the value of j is given by $c*i+d$ at the point where j is defined. We say that j belongs to the *family* of i. The basic induction variable i belongs to its own family.

Method.

1. Find all basic induction variables by scanning the statements of L. We use the loop-invariant computation information here. Associated with each basic induction variable i is the triple $(i, 1, 0)$.

2. Search for variables k with a single assignment to k within L having one of the following forms:

   $$\texttt{k:=j*}b, \quad \texttt{k:=}b\texttt{*j}, \quad \texttt{k:=j/}b, \quad \texttt{k:=j}\pm b, \quad \texttt{k:=}b\pm\texttt{j}$$

   where b is a constant, and j is an induction variable, basic or otherwise.

   If j is basic, then k is in the family of j. The triple for k depends on the instruction defining it. For example, if k is defined by $\texttt{k:=j*}b$, then the triple for k is $(j, b, 0)$. The triples for the remaining cases can be determined similarly.

   If j is not basic, let j be in the family of i. Then our additional requirements are that

   (a) there is no assignment to i between the lone point of assignment to j in L and the assignment to k, and

   (b) no definition of j outside L reaches k.

   The usual case will be where the definitions of k and j are in temporaries in the same block, in which case it is easy to check. In general, reaching definitions information will provide the check we need if we analyze the flow graph of the loop L to determine those blocks (and therefore those definitions) on paths between the assignment to j and the assignment to k.

   We compute the triple for k from the triple (i, c, d) for j and the instruction defining k. For example, the definition $\texttt{k:=}b\texttt{*j}$ leads to $(i, b*c, b*d)$ for k. Note that the multiplications in $b*c$ and $b*d$ can be done as the analysis proceeds because b, c, and d are constants.   □

Once families of induction variables have been found, we modify the instructions computing an induction variable to use additions or subtractions rather than multiplications. The replacement of a more expensive instruction by a cheaper one is called *strength reduction*.

Example 10.23. The loop consisting of block B_2 in Fig. 10.39(a) has basic induction variable i, because the lone assignment to i in the loop increments its value by 1. The family of i contains t_2, because there is a single assignment to t_2, with right hand side 4*i. Thus the triple for t_2 is (i,4,0). Similarly, j is the only basic induction variable in the loop consisting of B_3, and t_4, with triple (j,4,0), is in the family of j.

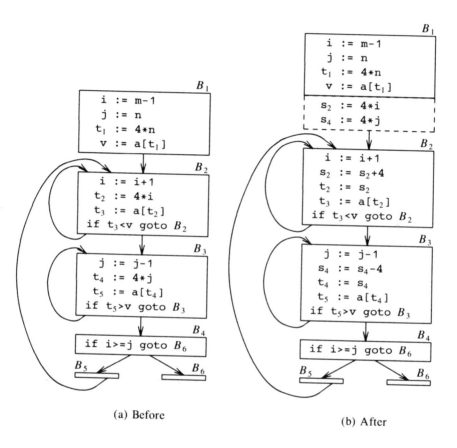

(a) Before   (b) After

Fig. 10.39. Strength reduction.

We can also look for induction variables in the outer loop with header B_2 and blocks B_2, B_3, B_4, B_5. Both i and j are basic induction variables in this larger loop. Again t_2 and t_4 are induction variables with triples (i,4,0) and (j,4,0), respectively.

The flow graph in Fig. 10.39(b) is obtained from that in Fig. 10.39(a) by applying the next algorithm. We shall discuss this transformation below.   □

Algorithm 10.10. Strength reduction applied to induction variables.

Input. A loop L with reaching definition information and families of induction variables computed using Algorithm 10.9.

Output. A revised loop.

Method. Consider each basic induction variable i in turn. For every induction variable j in the family of i with triple (i, c, d):

1. Create a new variable s (but if two variables j_1 and j_2 have the same triples, just create one new variable for both).

2. Replace the assignment to j by $j := s$.

3. Immediately after each assignment $i := i + n$ in L, where n is a constant, append:

   ```
   s := s + c*n
   ```

   where the expression $c*n$ is evaluated to a constant because c and n are constants. Place s in the family of i, with triple (i, c, d).

4. It remains to ensure that s is initialized to $c*i + d$ on entry to the loop. The initialization may be placed at the end of the preheader. The initialization consists of

   ```
   s := c*i    /* just s:=i if c is 1 */
   s := s+d    /* omit if d is 0 */
   ```

   Note that s is an induction variable in the family of i.   □

Example 10.24. Suppose we consider the loops in Fig. 10.39(a) inside-out. Since the treatment of inner loops containing B_2 and B_3 is very similar, we shall talk of the loop around B_3 only. In Example 10.23 we observed that the basic induction variable in the loop around B_3 is j, and the other induction variable is t_4 with triple $(j, 4, 0)$. In step (1) of Algorithm 10.10, a new variable s_4 is constructed. In step (2), the assignment $t_4 := 4*j$ is replaced by $t_4 := s_4$. Step (4) inserts the assignment $s_4 := s_4 - 4$ after the assignment $j := j - 1$, where the -4 is obtained by multiplying the -1 in the assignment to j and the 4 in the triple $(j, 4, 0)$ for t_4.

Since B_1 serves as a preheader for the loop, we may place the initialization of s_4 at the end of the block B_1 containing the definition of j. The added instructions are shown in the dashed extension to block B_1.

When the outer loop is considered, the flow graph looks as shown in Fig. 10.39(b). There are four variables, i, s_2, j, and s_4, that could be considered induction variables. However, step (3) of Algorithm 10.10 places the newly created variables in the families of i and j, respectively, to facilitate the elimination of i and j, using the next algorithm.   □

After strength reduction we find that the only use of some induction variables is in tests; we can replace a test of such an induction variable by that of another. For example, if i and t are induction variables such that the value of t is always four times the value of i, then the test $i>=j$ is equivalent to $t>=4*j$. After this replacement, it may be possible to eliminate i. Note however that if $t=-4*i$, then we need to change the relational operator as well, because $i>=j$ is equivalent to $t<=-4*j$. In the following algorithm we consider the case where the multiplicative constant is positive, leaving the generalization to negative constants as an exercise.

Algorithm 10.11. Elimination of induction variables.

Input. A loop L with reaching definition information, loop-invariant computation information (from Algorithm 10.7) and live variable information.

Output. A revised loop.

Method.

1. Consider each basic induction variable i whose only uses are to compute other induction variables in its family and in conditional branches. Take some j in i's family, preferably one such that c and d in its triple (i, c, d) are as simple as possible (i.e., we prefer $c = 1$ and $d = 0$), and modify each test that i appears in to use j instead. We assume in the following that c is positive. A test of the form if i **relop** x goto B, where x is not an induction variable, is replaced by

    ```
    r := c*x        /* r := x if c is 1 */
    r := r+d        /* omit if d is 0 */
    if j relop r goto B
    ```

    where r is a new temporary. The case if x **relop** i goto B is handled analogously. If there are two induction variables i_1 and i_2 in the test if i_1 **relop** i_2 goto B, then we check if both i_1 and i_2 can be replaced. The easy case is when we have j_1 with triple (i_1, c_1, d_1) and j_2 with triple (i_2, c_2, d_2), and $c_1 = c_2$ and $d_1 = d_2$. Then, i_1 **relop** i_2 is equivalent to j_1 **relop** j_2. In more complex cases, replacement of the test may not be worthwhile, because we may need to introduce two multiplicative steps and one addition, while as few as two steps may be saved by eliminating i_1 and i_2.

    Finally, delete all assignments to the eliminated induction variables from the loop L, as they will now be useless.

2. Now, consider each induction variable j for which a statement $j:=s$ was introduced by Algorithm 10.10. First check that there can be no assignment to s between the introduced statement $j:=s$ and any use of j. In the usual situation, j is used in the block in which it is defined, simplifying this check; otherwise, reaching definitions information, plus some graph analysis is needed to implement the check. Then replace all uses of j by uses of s and delete statement $j:=s$. □

Example 10.25. Consider the flow graph in Fig. 10.39(b). The inner loop around B_2 contains two induction variables i and s_2, but neither can be eliminated because s_2 is used to index into the array a and i is used in a test outside the loop. Similarly, the loop around B_3 contains induction variables j and s_4, but neither can be eliminated.

Let us apply Algorithm 10.11 to the outer loop. When the new variables s_2 and s_4 were created by Algorithm 10.10, as discussed in Example 10.24, s_2 was placed in the family of i and s_4 was placed in the family of j. Consider the family of i. The only use of i is in the test for loop termination in block B_4, so i is a candidate for elimination in step (1) of Algorithm 10.11. The test in block B_4 involves the two induction variables i and j. Fortunately, the families of i and j contain s_2 and s_4 with the same constants in their triples, because the triples are (i,4,0) and (j,4,0), respectively. The test i>=j can therefore be replaced by s_2>=s_4, allowing both i and j to be eliminated.

Step (2) of the Algorithm 10.11 applies copy propagation to the newly created variables, replacing t_2 and t_4 by s_2 and s_4, respectively.   □

Induction Variables with Loop-Invariant Expressions

In Algorithms 10.9 and 10.10 we can allow loop-invariant expressions instead of constants. However, the triple (i, c, d) for an induction variable j may then contain loop-invariant expressions rather than constants. The evaluation of these expressions should be done outside the loop L, in the preheader. Moreover, since the intermediate code requires there to be at most one operator per instruction, we must be prepared to generate intermediate code statements for the evaluation of the expressions. The replacement of tests in Algorithm 10.11 requires the sign of the multiplicative constant c to be known. For this reason it may be reasonable to restrict attention to cases in which c is a known constant.

10.8 DEALING WITH ALIASES

If two or more expressions denote the same memory address, we say that the expressions are *aliases* of one another. In this section we shall consider data-flow analysis in the presence of pointers and procedures, both of which introduce aliases.

The presence of pointers makes data-flow analysis more complex, since they cause uncertainty regarding what is defined and used. The only safe assumption if we know nothing about where pointer p can point to is to assume that an indirect assignment through a pointer can potentially change (i.e., define) any variable. We must also assume that any use of the data pointed to by a pointer, e.g., x:=*p, can potentially use any variable. These assumptions result in more live variables and reaching definitions than is realistic and fewer available expressions than is realistic. Fortunately, we can use data-flow analysis to pin down what a pointer might point to, thus allowing us to get more accurate information from our other data-flow analyses.

As for assignments with pointer variables, when we come to a procedure call, we may not have to make our worst-case assumption — that everything can be changed — provided, we can compute the set of variables that the procedure might change. As with all code optimizations we may still make errors on the conservative side. That is, the sets of variables whose values "may be" changed or used could properly include the variables that are actually changed or used in some execution of the program. We shall, as usual, simply try to come fairly close to the true sets of changed and used variables without working unduly hard or making an error that alters what the program does.

A Simple Pointer Language

For specificity, let us consider a language in which there are elementary data types (e.g., integers and reals) requiring one word each, and arrays of these types. Let there also be pointers to these elements and to arrays, but not to other pointers. We shall be content to know that a pointer p is pointing somewhere in array a, without concerning ourselves with what particular element of a is being pointed to. This grouping together of all elements of an array, as far as pointer targets are concerned, is reasonable. Typically, pointers will be used as cursors to run through an entire array, so a more detailed data-flow analysis, if we could accomplish it at all, would often tell us that at a particular point in the program, p might be pointing to any one of the elements of a anyway.

We must also make certain assumptions about which arithmetic operations on pointers are semantically meaningful. First, if pointer p points to a primitive (one word) data element, then any arithmetic operation on p produces a value that may be an integer, but not a pointer. If p points to an array, then addition or subtraction of an integer leaves p pointing somewhere in the same array, while other arithmetic operations on pointers produce a value that is not a pointer. While not all languages prohibit, say, moving a pointer from one array a to another array b by adding to the pointer, such action would depend on the particular implementation to make sure that array b followed a in storage. It is our point of view that an optimizing compiler should adhere only to the language definition in deciding what optimizations to perform. Each compiler implementer, however, must make a judgment on what specific optimizations the compiler should be allowed to do.

The Effects of Pointer Assignments

Under these assumptions, the only variables that could possibly be used as pointers are those declared to be pointers and temporaries that receive a value that is a pointer plus or minus a constant. We shall refer to all these variables as pointers. Our rules for determining what a pointer p can point to are as follows.

1. If there is an assignment statement s: p:=&a, then immediately after s, p points only to a. If a is an array, then p can point only to a after any assignment to p of the form p:=&a±c, where c is a constant.[8] As usual, &a is deemed to refer to the location of the first element of array a.

2. If there is an assignment statement s: p:=q±c, where c is an integer other than zero, and p and q are pointers, then immediately after s, p can point to any array that q could point to before s, but to nothing else.

3. If there is an assignment s: p:=q, then immediately after s, p can point to whatever q could point to before s.

4. After any other assignment to p, there is no object that p could point to; such an assignment is probably (depending on the semantics of the language) meaningless.

5. After any assignment to a variable other than p, p points to whatever it did before the assignment. Note that this rule assumes that no pointer can point to a pointer. Relaxing this assumption does not make matters particularly more difficult, and we leave the generalization to the reader.

We shall define $in[B]$, for block B, to be the function that gives for each pointer p the set of variables to which p could point at the beginning of B. Formally, $in[B]$ is a set of pairs of the form (p, a), where p is a pointer and a a variable, meaning that p might point to a. In practice, $in[B]$ might be represented as a list for each pointer, the list for p giving the set of a's such that (p, a) is in $in[B]$. We define $out[B]$ similarly for the end of B.

We specify a transfer function $trans_B$ that defines the effect of block B. That is, $trans_B$ is a function taking as argument a set of pairs S, each pair of the form (p, a) for p a pointer and a a nonpointer variable, and producing another set T. Presumably, the set to which $trans_B$ is applied will be $in[B]$ and the result of the application will be $out[B]$. We need only tell how to compute $trans$ for single statements; $trans_B$ will then be the composition of $trans_s$ for each statement s of block B. The rules for computing $trans$ are as follows.

1. If s is p:=&a or p:=&a±c in the case a is an array, then

$$trans_s(S) = (S - \{(p, b)\mid \text{any variable b}\}) \cup \{(p, a)\}$$

2. If s is p:=q±c for pointer q and nonzero integer c, then

$$trans_s(S) = (S - \{(p, b) \mid \text{any variable b}\})$$
$$\cup \{(p, b) \mid (q, b) \text{ is in } S \text{ and b is an array variable }\}$$

Note that this rule makes sense even if p = q.

3. If s is p:=q, then

---

[8] In this section, + stands for itself rather than a generic operator.

$$trans_s(S) = (S - \{(p, b) \mid \text{any variable } b\})$$
$$\cup \{(p, b) \mid (q, b) \text{ is in } S\}$$

4. If s assigns to pointer p any other expression, then

$$trans_s(S) = S - \{(p, b) \mid \text{any variable } b\}$$

5. If s is not an assignment to a pointer, then $trans_s(S) = S$.

We may now write the equations relating *in*, *out*, and *trans* as follows.

$$out[B] = trans_B(in[B])$$
$$in[B] = \bigcup_{\substack{P \text{ a pred-} \\ \text{ecessor of } B}} out[P] \qquad\qquad (10.13)$$

where if B consists of statements $s_1, s_2, \ldots, s_k$, then

$$trans_B(S) = trans_{s_k}(trans_{s_{k-1}}(\cdots (trans_{s_2}(trans_{s_1}(S))) \cdots)).$$

Equations 10.13 can be solved essentially like reaching definitions in Algorithm 10.2. We shall therefore not go into the details of the algorithm, but content ourselves with an example.

Example 10.26. Consider the flow graph of Fig. 10.40. We suppose a is an array and c is an integer; p and q are pointers. Initially, we set $in[B_1]$ to $\varnothing$. Then, $trans_{B_1}$ has the effect of removing any pairs with first component q, then adding the pair (q, c). That is, q is asserted to point to c. Thus

$$out[B_1] = trans_{B_1}(\varnothing) = \{(q, c)\}$$

Then, $in[B_2] = out[B_1]$. The effect of p:=&c is to replace all pairs with first component p by the pair (p, c). The effect of q:=&(a[2]) is to replace pairs with first component q by (q, a). Note that q:=&(a[2]) is actually an assignment of the form q:=&a+c for a constant c. We may now compute

$$out[B_2] = trans_{B_2}(\{(q, c)\}) = \{(p, c), (q, a)\}$$

Similarly, $in[B_3] = \{(q, c)\}$ and $out[B_3] = \{(p, a), (q, c)\}$.

Next, we find $in[B_4] = out[B_2] \cup out[B_3] \cup out[B_5]$. Presumably, $out[B_5]$ was initialized to $\varnothing$ and has not been changed on this pass yet. However, $out[B_2] = \{(p, c), (q, a)\}$ and $out[B_3] = \{(p, a), (q, c)\}$, so

$$in[B_4] = \{(p,a), (p,c), (q,a), (q,c)\}$$

The effect of p:=p+1 in B_4 is to discard the possibility that p does not point to an array. That is,

$$out[B_4] = trans_{B_4}(in[B_4]) = \{(p, a), (q, a), (q, c)\}$$

Note that whenever B_2 is executed, making p point to c, a semantically meaningless action takes place if p is used indirectly after p:=p+1 in B_4. Thus, this flow graph is not "realistic," but it does illustrate the inferences about pointers that we can make.

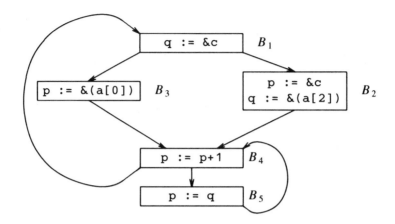

Fig. 10.40. Flow graph with pointer operations shown.

Continuing, $in[B_5] = out[B_4]$, and $trans_{B_5}$ copies the targets of q and gives them to p as well. Since q can point to a or c in $in[B_5]$,

$$out[B_5] = \{(p, a), (p, c), (q, a), (q, c)\}$$

On the next pass we find $in[B_1] = out[B_4]$, so $out[B_1] = \{(p, a),(q, c)\}$. This value is also the new $in[B_2]$ and $in[B_3]$, but these new values do not change $out[B_2]$ or $out[B_3]$, nor is $in[B_4]$ changed. We have thus converged to the desired answer.   □

Making Use of Pointer Information

Suppose $in[B]$ is the set of variables pointed to by each pointer at the beginning of block B and that we have a reference to pointer p inside block B. Starting with $in[B]$, apply $trans_s$ for each statement s of block B that precedes the reference to p. This computation tells us what p could point to at the particular statement where that information is important.

Suppose now that we have determined what each pointer could point to when that pointer is used in an indirect reference, either on the left or right of the assignment symbol. How can we use this information to get more accurate solutions to the usual data-flow problems? In each case we must consider in which direction errors are conservative, and we must utilize pointer information in such a way that only conservative errors are made. To see how this choice is made, let us consider two examples: reaching definitions and live variable analysis.

To calculate reaching definitions we can use Algorithm 10.2, but we need to know the values of *kill* and *gen* for a block. The latter quantities are computed as usual for statements that are not indirect assignments through pointers. An indirect assignment *p:=a is deemed to generate a definition of every variable b such that p could point to b. This assumption is conservative, because as discussed in Section 10.5, it is generally conservative to assume definitions reach a point while in reality they do not.

When we compute *kill*, we shall assume that `*p:=a` kills definitions of b only if b is not an array and is the only variable p could possibly point to. If p could point to two or more variables, then we do not assume definitions of either are killed. Again, we are being conservative because we permit definitions of b to pass through `*p:=a`, and thus reach wherever they can, unless we can prove that `*p:=a` redefined b. In other words, when there is doubt, we assume that a definition reaches.

For live variables we may use Algorithm 10.4, but we must reconsider how *def* and *use* are to be defined for statements of the form `*p:=a` and `a:=*p`. The statement `*p:=a` uses only a and p. We say it defines b only if b is the unique variable that p might point to. This assumption allows uses of b to pass through unless they are surely blocked by the assignment `*p:=a`. Thus we can never claim that b is dead at a point when it is in fact live. The statement `a:=*p` surely represents a definition of a. It also represents a use of p and a use of any variable that p could point to. By maximizing possible uses, we again maximize our estimate of live variables. By maximizing live variables, we are normally being conservative. For example, we might generate code to store a dead variable, but we shall never fail to store one that was live.

Interprocedural Data Flow Analysis

Until now, we have spoken of "programs" that are single procedures and therefore single flow graphs. We shall now see how to gather information from many interacting procedures. The basic idea is to determine how each procedure influences the *gen*, *kill*, *use*, or *def* information of the others, then to compute our data-flow information for each procedure independently as before.

During data-flow analysis we shall have to deal with aliases set up by parameters in procedure calls. As it is not possible for two global variables to denote the same memory address, at least one of a pair of aliases must be a formal parameter. Since formals may be passed to procedures, it is possible for two formals to be aliases.

Example 10.27. Suppose we have a procedure p, with two formal parameters x and y passed by reference. In Fig. 10.41, we see a situation in which b+x is computed in B_1 and B_3. Suppose that the only paths from blocks B_1 to B_3 go through B_2, and there are no assignments to b or x along any such path. Then, is b+x available at B_3? The answer depends on whether x and y could denote the same memory address. For example, there could be a call p(z,z), or perhaps a call of p(u,v), where u and v are formal parameters of another procedure q(u,v), and a call of q(z,z) is possible.

Similarly, it is possible for x and y to be aliases if x is a formal parameter, say of p(x,w), and y is a variable with a scope accessible to some procedure q that calls p, say with call p(y,t). Even more complicated situations could make x and y aliases of one another, and we shall shortly develop some general rules for determining all such pairs of aliases.   □

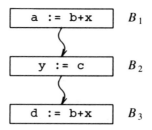

Fig. 10.41. Illustration of aliasing problems.

It will turn out in some situations that it is conservative not to regard variables as aliases of one another. For example, in reaching definitions, if we wish to assert that a definition of a is killed by a definition of b, we had better be sure that a and b are definitely aliases whenever the definition of b is executed. Other times it is conservative to regard variables as aliases of one another whenever there is doubt. Example 10.27 is one such case. If the available expression b+x is not to be killed by a definition of y, we had better be sure neither b nor x could be an alias of y.

A Model of Code with Procedure Calls

To illustrate how aliasing might be dealt with, let us consider a language that permits recursive procedures, any of which may refer to both local and global variables. The data available to a procedure consists of the globals and its own locals only; that is, there is no block structure to the language. Parameters are passed by reference. We require that all procedures have a flow graph with single *entry* (the initial node) and a single *return* node which causes control to pass back to the calling routine. We suppose for convenience that every node lies on some path from the entry to the return.

Now suppose we are in a procedure p and we come upon a call to procedure q(u,v). If we are interested in computing reaching definitions, available expressions or any of a number of other data-flow analyses, we must know whether q(u,v) might change the value of some variable. Note that we say "might" change, rather than "will" change. As with all data-flow problems, it is impossible to know for certain whether or not the value of a variable is changed. We can only find a set that includes all variables whose values do change and perhaps some that don't. By being careful, we can cut down on the latter class of variables, obtaining a good approximation to the truth and erring only on the conservative side.

The only variables whose values the call of $q(u,v)$ could define are the globals and the variables u and v, which might be local to p. Definitions of locals of q are of no consequence after the call returns. Even if $p = q$, it will be other copies of q's locals that change, and these copies disappear after the return. It is easy to determine which globals are explicitly defined by q; just see which have definitions in q, or are defined in a procedure call made by q. In addition, u and/or v, which may be global, change if q has a definition of its first and/or second formal parameter, respectively, or if these formal parameters are passed as actual parameters by q to another procedure that defines them. However, not every variable changed by a call to q need be defined explicitly by q or one of the procedures it calls, because variables may have aliases.

Computing Aliases

Before we can answer the question of what variables might change in a given procedure, we must develop an algorithm for finding aliases. The approach we shall use here is a simple one. We compute a relation $\equiv$ on variables that formalizes the notion "can be an alias of." In so doing we do not distinguish among occurrences of a variable in different calls to the same procedure, although we distinguish variables local to different procedures but having the same identifier.

To make things simpler, we do not try to differentiate the sets of aliases at different points in the program. Rather, if two variables could ever be aliases of one another we assume they always could be. Finally, we shall make the conservative assumption that $\equiv$ is transitive, so variables are grouped into equivalence classes, and two variables could be aliases of one another if and only if they are in the same class.

Algorithm 10.12. Simple alias computation.

Input. A collection of procedures and global variables.

Output. An equivalence relation $\equiv$ with the property that whenever there is a position in the program where x and y are aliases of one another, $x \equiv y$; the converse need not be true.

Method.

1. Rename variables, if necessary, so that no two procedures use the same formal parameter or local variable identifier, nor do a local, formal, or global share an identifier.

2. If there is a procedure $p(x_1, x_2, \ldots, x_n)$ and an invocation $p(y_1, y_2, \ldots, y_n)$ of that procedure, set $x_i \equiv y_i$ for all i. That is, each formal parameter can be an alias of any of its corresponding actual parameters.

3.   Take the reflexive and transitive closure of the actual-formal correspondences by adding

a) $x \equiv y$ whenever $y \equiv x$.
b) $x \equiv z$ whenever $x \equiv y$ and $y \equiv z$ for some y.   □

Example 10.28. Consider the sketch of the three procedures shown in Fig. 10.42, where parameters are assumed passed by reference. There are two globals, g and h, and two local variables, i for the procedure main and k for the procedure two. Procedure one has formals w and x, procedure two has formals y and z, and main has no formal parameters. Thus, no renaming of variables is necessary. We first compute the aliasing due to actual-formal correspondences.

The call of one by main makes $h \equiv w$ and $i \equiv x$. The first call of two by one makes $w \equiv y$ and $w \equiv z$. The second call makes $g \equiv y$ and $x \equiv z$.

The call of one by two makes $k \equiv w$ and $y \equiv x$. When we take the transitive closure of the alias relationships represented by $\equiv$, then we find in this example that all variables are possible aliases of one another.   □

```
global g, h;
    procedure main( );
        local i;
        g :=  ... ;
        one(h, i)
    end
    procedure one(w, x);
        x :=  ... ;
        two(w, w);
        two(g, x)
    end;
    procedure two(y, z);
        local k;
        h :=  ... ;
        one(k, y)
    end
```

Fig. 10.42. Sample procedures.

The aliasing computation of Algorithm 10.12 does not often result in such extensive aliasing as we found in Example 10.28. Intuitively, we would not often expect two different variables with dissimilar types to be aliases. Moreover, the programmer undoubtedly has conceptual types for his variables. For example, if the first formal parameter of a procedure p represents a velocity, it can be expected that the first argument in any call to p will also be thought of by the programmer as a velocity. Thus we intuitively expect most programs to produce small groups of possible aliases.

Data-Flow Analysis in the Presence of Procedure Calls

Let us consider, as an example, how available expressions can be calculated in the presence of procedure calls, where parameters are passed by reference. As in Section 10.6, we must determine when a variable could be defined, thus killing an expression, and we must determine when expressions are generated (evaluated).

We may define, for each procedure p, a set *change* [p], whose value is to be the set of global variables and formal parameters of p that might be changed during an execution of p. At this point, we do not count a variable as changed if a member of its equivalence class of aliases is changed.

Let *def* [p] be the set of formal parameters and globals having explicit definitions within p (not including those defined within procedures called by p). To write the equations for *change* [p], we have only to relate the globals and formals of p that are used as actual parameters in calls made by p to the corresponding formal parameters of the called procedures. We may write:

$$change\,[p] = def\,[p] \cup A \cup G \qquad\qquad (10.14)$$

where

1. $A = \{a \mid a$ is a global variable or formal parameter of p such that, for some procedure q and integer i, p calls q with a as the ith actual parameter and the ith formal parameter of q is in *change* [q]$\}$

2. $G = \{g \mid g$ is a global in *change* [q] and p calls q$\}$.

It should come as no surprise that Equation (10.14) may be solved for a set of procedures by an iterative technique. Although the solution is not unique, we only need the smallest one. We may converge to that solution by starting with a too-small approximation and iterating. The obvious too-small approximation with which to start is *change* [p] = *def* [p]. The details of the iteration are left as an exercise for the reader.

It is worth considering the order in which procedures should be visited in the above iteration. For example, if the procedures are not mutually recursive, then we can first visit procedures that do not call any other (there must be at least one). For these procedures, *change* = *def*. Next, we can compute *change* for those procedures that call only procedures which call nothing. We can apply (10.14) for this next group of procedures directly, since *change* [q] will be known for any q in (10.14).

This idea can be made more precise as follows. We draw a *calling graph*, whose nodes are procedures, with an edge from p to q if p calls q.[9] A

---

[9] Here we assume no procedure-valued variables. These complicate the construction of the calling graph, as we must determine the possible actuals corresponding to procedure-valued formals at the same time we construct the edges of the calling graph.

collection of procedures that are not mutually recursive will have an acyclic calling graph. In this case we can visit each node once.

We now give an algorithm for computing *change*.

Algorithm 10.13. Interprocedural analysis of changed variables.

Input. A collection of procedures p_1, p_2, . . . , p_n. If the calling graph is acyclic, we assume p_i calls p_j only if $j < i$. Otherwise, we make no assumption about which procedures call which.

Output. For each procedure p, we produce *change*[p], the set of global variables and formal parameters of p that may be changed explicitly by p with no aliasing.

Method.

1. Compute *def* [p] for each procedure p by inspection.
2. Execute the program of Fig. 10.43 to compute *change*.   □

```
(1)   for each procedure p do change[p]:=def[p]; /* initialize */
(2)   while changes to any change[p] occur do
(3)       for i := 1 to n do
(4)           for each procedure q called by pᵢ do begin
(5)               add any global variables in change[q] to change[pᵢ];
(6)               for each formal parameter x (the jth) of q do
(7)                   if x is in change[q] then
(8)                       for each call of q by pᵢ do
(9)                           if a, the jth actual parameter of the call,
                                  is a global or formal parameter of pᵢ
(10)                              then add a to change[pᵢ]
          end
```

Fig. 10.43. Iterative algorithm to compute *change*.

Example 10.29. Let us consider Fig. 10.42 again. By inspection, *def* [main] = {g}, *def* [one] = {x} and *def* [two] = {h}. These are the initial values of *change*. The calling graph of the procedures is shown in Fig. 10.44. We shall take two, one, main as the order in which we visit the procedures.

Consider p_i = two in the program of Fig. 10.42. Then q can only be procedure one in line (4). Since *change*[one] = {x} initially, nothing is added to *change*[two] at line (5). At lines (6) and (7) we need consider only the second formal parameter of procedure one, since the first actual parameter is local to two. In the only call of one by two, the second actual parameter is y, and its corresponding formal, x, is changed, so we set *change*[two] to {h, y} at line (10).

We now consider p_i = one. At line (4), q can only be procedure two.

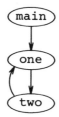

Fig. 10.44. Calling graph.

At line (5), h is a global in *change*[two], so we set *change*[one] = {h, x}. At lines (6) and (7), only the first formal parameter of two is in *change*[two], so we must add g and w to *change*[one] at line (10), these being the two first actual parameters in the calls of procedure two. Thus, *change*[one] = {g, h, w, x}.

Now consider main. Procedure one changes both its formals, so both h and i will be changed in the call of one by main. However, i is a local and need not be considered. Thus we set *change*[main] = {g, h}. Finally, we repeat the while-loop of line (2). On reconsidering two, we find that one modifies global g. Thus the call to one(k,y) causes g to be modified, so *change*[two] = {g, h, y}. No further changes occur in the iteration.   □

Use of Change Information

As an example of the way *change* can be used, consider the computation of global common subexpressions. Suppose we are computing available expressions for a procedure p, and we want to compute *a_kill*[B] for a block B. A definition of variable a must be deemed to kill any expression involving a or involving some x that could be an alias of a. However, a call in B to procedure q cannot kill an expression involving a unless a is an alias (remember a is an alias of itself) of some variable in *change*[q]. Thus, the information computed by Algorithms 10.12 and 10.13 can be used to construct a safe approximation to the set of expressions killed.

To compute available expressions in programs with procedure calls, we must also have a conservative way of estimating the set of expressions generated by a procedure call. To be conservative, we may assume a+b is generated by a call to q if and only if, on every path from q's entry to its return, we find a+b with no subsequent redefinition of a or b. When we look for occurrences of a+b, we must not accept x+y as such an occurrence unless we are sure that, in every call of q, x is an alias of a and y an alias of b.

We make this requirement because it is conservative to err by assuming that an expression is not available when it is. By the same token, we must assume a+b is killed by a definition of any z that could possibly be an alias of a or b. Thus the simplest way to compute available expressions for all nodes of all procedures is to assume that a call generates nothing, and that $a\_kill[B]$ for all blocks B is as computed above. As one does not expect many expressions to be generated by the typical procedure, this approach is good enough for most purposes.

A more complicated, and more accurate, alternative approach to the computation of available expressions is to compute $gen[p]$ for each procedure p iteratively. We may initialize $gen[p]$ to be the set of expressions available at the end of p's return node according to the method above. That is, no aliasing is permitted for generated expressions; a+b represents only itself, even if other variables could be aliases of a or b.

Now compute available expressions for all nodes of all procedures again. However, a call to q(a,b) generates those expressions in $gen[q]$ with a and b substituted for the corresponding formals of q. a_kill remains as before. A new value of $gen[p]$, for each procedure p, can be found by seeing what expressions are available at the end of p's return. This iteration may be repeated until we get no more changes in available expressions at any node.

10.9 DATA-FLOW ANALYSIS OF STRUCTURED FLOW GRAPHS

Gotoless programs have reducible flow graphs; so do programs encouraged by several programming methodologies. Several studies of large classes of programs have revealed that virtually all programs written by people have flow graphs that are reducible.[10] This observation is relevant for optimization purposes because we can find optimization algorithms that run significantly faster on reducible flow graphs. In this section we discuss a variety of flow-graph concepts, such as "interval analysis," that are primarily relevant to structured flow graphs. In essence, we shall apply the syntax-directed techniques developed in Section 10.5 to the more general setting where the syntax doesn't necessarily provide the structure, but the flow graph does.

Depth-First Search

There is a useful ordering of the nodes of a flow graph, known as *depth-first* ordering, which is a generalization of the depth-first traversal of a tree introduced in Section 2.3. A depth-first ordering can be used to detect loops in any flow graph; it also helps speed up iterative data-flow algorithms such as those discussed in Section 10.6. The depth-first ordering is created by starting at the initial node and searching the entire graph, trying to visit nodes as far away from the initial node as quickly as possible (*depth first*). The route of the search forms a tree. Before we give the algorithm, let us consider an example.

---

[10] "Written by people" is not redundant because we know of several programs that generate code with "rats' nests" of goto's. There is nothing wrong with this; the structure is in the input to these programs.

Example 10.30. One possible depth-first search of the flow graph in Fig. 10.45 is illustrated in Fig. 10.46. Solid edges form the tree; dashed edges are the other edges of the flow graph. The depth-first search of the flow graph corresponds to a preorder traversal of the tree, $1 \to 3 \to 4 \to 6 \to 7 \to 8 \to 10$, then back to 8, then to 9. We go back to 8 once more, retreating to 7, 6, and 4, and then forward to 5. We retreat from 5 back to 4, then back to 3 and 1. From 1 we go to 2, then retreat from 2, back to 1, and we have traversed the entire tree in preorder. Note that we have not yet explained how the tree is selected from the flow graph.   □

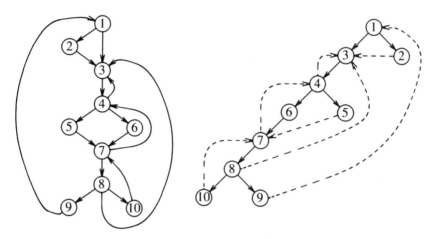

Fig. 10.45. Flow graph   **Fig. 10.46.** Depth-first presentation

The *depth-first ordering* of the nodes is the reverse of the order in which we last visit the nodes in the preorder traversal.

Example 10.31. In Example 10.30, the complete sequence of nodes visited as we traverse the tree is

  1, 3, 4, 6, 7, 8, 10, 8, 9, 8, 7, 6, 4, 5, 4, 3, 1, 2, 1.

In this list, mark the last occurrence of each number to get

  1, 3, 4, 6, 7, 8, <u>10</u>, 8, <u>9</u>, <u>8</u>, <u>7</u>, <u>6</u>, 4, <u>5</u>, <u>4</u>, <u>3</u>, 1, <u>2</u>, <u>1</u>

The depth-first ordering is the sequence of marked numbers in reverse order. Here, this sequence happens to be 1, 2, . . . , 10. That is, initially the nodes were numbered in depth-first order.   □

We now give an algorithm that computes a depth-first ordering of a flow graph by constructing and traversing a tree rooted at the initial node, trying to make paths in the tree as long as possible. Such a tree is called a *depth-first spanning tree (dfst)*. It is this algorithm that was used to construct Fig. 10.46 from Fig. 10.45.

Algorithm 10.14. Depth-first spanning tree and depth-first ordering.

Input. A flow graph *G*.

Output. A *dfst T* of *G* and an ordering of the nodes of *G*.

Method. We use the recursive procedure *search(n)* of Fig. 10.47; the algorithm is to initialize all nodes of *G* to "unvisited," then call $search(n_0)$, where n_0 is the initial node. When we call *search(n)*, we first mark *n* "visited," to avoid adding *n* to the tree twice. We use *i* to count from the number of nodes of *G* down to 1, assigning depth-first numbers *dfn[n]* to nodes *n* as we go. The set of edges *T* forms the depth-first spanning tree for *G*, and they are called *tree edges*.   □

```
        procedure search(n);
        begin
(1)         mark n "visited";
(2)         for each successor s of n do
(3)             if s is "unvisited" then begin
(4)                 add edge n → s to T;
(5)                 search(s)
                end;
(6)         dfn[n] := i;
(7)         i := i −1
        end;

        /* main program follows */

(8)   T := empty;   /* set of edges */
(9)   for each node n of G do mark n "unvisited";
(10)  i := number of nodes of G;
(11)  search(n₀)
```

Fig. 10.47. Depth-first search algorithm.

Example 10.32. Consider Fig. 10.47. We set *i* to 10 and call *search(1)*. At line (2) of *search* we must consider each successor of node 1. Suppose we consider *s* = 3 first. Then we add edge 1 → 3 to the tree and call *search(3)*. In *search(3)* we add edge 3 → 4 to *T* and call *search(4)*.

Suppose in *search(4)* we choose *s* = 6 first. Then we add edge 4 → 6 to *T* and call *search(6)*. This in turn causes us to add 6 → 7 to *T* and call *search(7)*. Node 7 has two successors, 4 and 8. But 4 was already marked "visited" by *search(4)*, so we do nothing when *s* = 4. When *s* = 8 we add edge 7 → 8 to *T* and call *search(8)*. Suppose we then choose *s* = 10. We add edge 8 → 10 and call *search(10)*.

Now 10 has a successor, 7, but 7 is already marked "visited," so in *search(10)*, we fall through to step (6) in Fig. 10.47, setting *dfn*[10] = 10 and

$i = 9$. This completes the call to *search*(10), so we return to *search*(8). We now set $s = 9$ in *search*(8), add edge $8 \rightarrow 9$ to T and call *search*(9). The only successor of 9, node 1, is already "visited," so we set $dfn[9] = 9$ and $i = 8$. Then we return to *search*(8). The last successor of 8, node 3, is "visited," so we do nothing for $s = 3$. At this point, we have considered all successors of 8, so we set $dfn[8] = 8$ and $i = 7$, returning to *search*(7).

All of 7's successors have been considered, so we set $dfn[7] = 7$ and $i = 6$, returning to *search*(6). Similarly, 6's successors have been considered, so we set $dfn[6] = 6$ and $i = 5$, and we return to *search*(4). Successor 3 of 4 has been "visited," but 5 has not, so we add $4 \rightarrow 5$ to the tree and call *search*(5), which results in no further calls, as successor 7 of 5 has been "visited." Thus, $dfn[5] = 5$, i is set to 4, and we return to *search*(4). We have completed consideration of the successors of 4, so we set $dfn[4] = 4$ and $i = 3$, returning to *search*(3). Then we set $dfn[3] = 3$ and $i = 2$ and return to *search*(1).

The final steps are to call *search*(2) from *search*(1), set $dfn[2] = 2$, $i = 1$, return to *search*(1), set $dfn[1] = 1$ and $i = 0$. Note that we chose a numbering of the nodes such that $dfn[i] = i$, but that relation need not hold for an arbitrary graph, or even for another depth-first ordering of the graph of Fig. 10.45. □

Edges in a Depth-First Presentation of a Flow Graph

When we construct a *dfst* for a flow graph, the edges of the flow graph fall into three categories.

1. There are edges that go from a node m to an ancestor of m in the tree (possibly to m itself). These edges we shall term *retreating* edges. For example, $7 \rightarrow 4$ and $9 \rightarrow 1$ are retreating edges in Fig. 10.46. It is an interesting and useful fact that if the flow graph is reducible, then the retreating edges are exactly the back edges of the flow graph,[11] independent of the order in which successors are visited in step (2) of Fig. 10.47. For any flow graph, every back edge is retreating, although if the graph is nonreducible there will be some retreating edges that are not back edges.

2. There are edges, called *advancing edges*, that go from a node m to a proper descendant of m in the tree. All edges in the *dfst* itself are advancing edges. There are no other advancing edges in Fig. 10.46, but, for example, if $4 \rightarrow 8$ were an edge, it would be in this category.

3. There are edges $m \rightarrow n$ such that neither m nor n is an ancestor of the other in the *dfst*. Edges $2 \rightarrow 3$ and $5 \rightarrow 7$ are the only such examples in Fig. 10.46. We call these edges *cross edges*. An important property of

---

[11] Recall, the back edges of a flow graph are those whose heads dominate their tails.

cross edges is that if we draw the *dfst* so children of a node are drawn from left to right in the order in which they were added to the tree, then all cross edges travel from right to left.

It should be noted that $m \to n$ is a retreating edge if and only if $dfn[m] \geq dfn[n]$. To see why, note that if m is a descendant of n in the *dfst*, then $search(m)$ terminates before $search(n)$, so $dfn[m] \geq dfn[n]$. Conversely, if $dfn[m] \geq dfn[n]$, then $search(m)$ terminates before $search(n)$, or $m = n$. But $search(n)$ must have begun before $search(m)$ if there is an edge $m \to n$, or else the fact that n is a successor of m would have made n a descendant of m in the *dfst*. Thus the time $search(m)$ is active is a subinterval of the time $search(n)$ is active, from which it follows that n is an ancestor of m in the *dfst*.

Depth of a Flow Graph

There is an important parameter of flow graphs called the *depth*. Given a depth-first spanning tree for the graph, the depth is the largest number of retreating edges on any cycle-free path.

Example 10.33. In Fig. 10.46, the depth is 3, since there is a path

$$10 \to 7 \to 4 \to 3$$

with three retreating edges, but no cycle-free path with four or more retreating edges. It is a coincidence that the "deepest" path here has only retreating edges; in general we may have a mixture of retreating, advancing, and cross edges in a "deepest" path.   □

We can prove the depth is never greater than what one would intuitively call the depth of loop nesting in the flow graph. If a flow graph is reducible, we may replace "retreating" by "back" in the definition of "depth," since the retreating edges in any *dfst* are exactly the back edges. The notion of depth then becomes independent of the *dfst* actually chosen.

Intervals

The division of a flow graph into intervals serves to put a hierarchical structure on the flow graph. That structure in turn allows us to apply the rules for syntax-directed data-flow analysis whose development began in Section 10.5.

Intuitively, an "interval" in a flow graph is a natural loop plus an acyclic structure that dangles from the nodes of that loop. An important property of intervals is that they have *header* nodes that dominate all the nodes in the interval; that is, every interval is a region. Formally, given a flow graph G with initial node n_0, and a node n of G, the *interval with header n*, denoted $I(n)$, is defined as follows.

1. n is in $I(n)$.
2.   If all the predecessors of some node $m \neq n_0$ are in $I(n)$, then m in is $I(n)$.
3.   Nothing else is in $I(n)$.

We therefore may build I(n) by starting with n, and adding nodes m by rule (2). It does not matter in which order we add two candidates m because once a node's predecessors are all in I(n), they remain in I(n), and each candidate will eventually be added by rule (2). Eventually, no more nodes can be added to I(n), and the resulting set of nodes is the interval with header n.

Interval Partitions

Given any flow graph G, we can partition G into disjoint intervals as follows.

Algorithm 10.15. Interval analysis of a flow graph.

Input. A flow graph G with initial node n_0.

Output. A partition of G into a set of disjoint intervals.

Method. For any node n, we compute I(n) by the method sketched above:

> I(n) := {n};
> **while** there exists a node $m \neq n_0$,
>   all of whose predecessors are in I(n) **do**
>   I(n) := I(n) $\cup$ {m}

The particular nodes that are headers of intervals in the partition are chosen as follows. Initially, no nodes are "selected."

> construct I(n_0) and "select" all nodes in that interval;
> **while** there is a node m, not yet "selected,"
>   but with a selected predecessor **do**
>   construct I(m) and "select" all nodes in that interval   □

Once a candidate m has a predecessor p selected, m can never be added to some interval not containing p. Thus, candidate m's remain candidates until they are selected to head their own interval. Thus, the order in which interval headers m are picked in Algorithm 10.15 does not affect the final partition into intervals. Also, as long as all nodes are reachable from n_0, it can be shown by induction on the length of a path from n_0 to n that node n will eventually either be put in some other node's interval, or will become a header of its own interval, but not both. Thus, the set of intervals constructed in Algorithm 10.15 truly partition G.

Example 10.34. Let us find the interval partition for Fig. 10.45. We start by constructing I(1), because node 1 is the initial node. We can add 2 to I(1) because 2's only predecessor is 1. However, we cannot add 3 because it has predecessors, 4 and 8, that are not yet in I(1), and similarly, every other node except 1 and 2 has predecessors not yet in I(1). Thus, I(1) = {1,2}.

We may now compute I(3) because 3 has some "selected" predecessors, 1 and 2, but 3 is not itself in an interval. However, no node can be added to I(3), so I(3) = {3}. Now 4 is a header because it has a predecessor, 3, in an interval. We can add 5 and 6 to I(4) because these have only 4 as a predecessor but no other nodes can be added; e.g., 7 has predecessor 10.

Next, 7 becomes a header, and we can add 8 to I(7). Then, we can add 9 and 10, because these have only 8 as predecessor. Thus, the intervals in the partition of Fig. 10.45 are:

$$I(1) = \{1,2\} \qquad I(4) = \{4,5,6\}$$
$$I(3) = \{3\} \qquad\quad I(7) = \{7,8,9,10\}$$
□

Interval Graphs

From the intervals of one flow graph G, we can construct a new flow graph $I(G)$ by the following rules.

1. The nodes of $I(G)$ correspond to the intervals in the interval partition of G.

2. The initial node of $I(G)$ is the interval of G that contains the initial node of G.

3. There is an edge from interval I to a different interval J if and only if in G there is an edge from some node in I to the header of J. Note that there could not be an edge entering some node n of J other than the header, from outside J, because then there would be no way n could have been added to J in Algorithm 10.15.

We may apply Algorithm 10.15 and the interval graph construction alternately, producing the sequence of graphs G, $I(G)$, $I(I(G))$, ... Eventually, we shall come to a graph each of whose nodes is an interval all by itself. This graph is called the *limit flow graph* of G. It is an interesting fact that a flow graph is reducible if and only if its limit flow graph is a single node.[12]

Example 10.35. Fig. 10.48 shows the result of applying the interval construction repeatedly to Fig. 10.45. The intervals of that graph were given in Example 10.34, and the interval graph constructed from these is in Fig. 10.48(a). Note that the edge $10 \rightarrow 7$ in Fig. 10.45 does not cause an edge from the node representing $\{7,8,9,10\}$ to itself in Fig. 10.48(a), because the interval graph construction explicitly excluded such loops. Also note that the flow graph of Fig. 10.45 is reducible because its limit flow graph is a single node.
□

Node Splitting

If we reach a limit flow graph that is other than a single node, we can proceed further only if we split one or more nodes. If a node n has k predecessors, we may replace n by k nodes, $n_1, n_2 , \ldots , n_k$. The ith predecessor of n becomes the predecessor of n_i only, while all successors of n become

---
[12] In fact, this definition is historically the original definition.

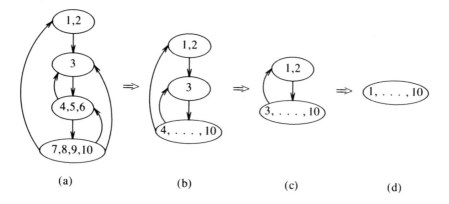

Fig. 10.48. Interval graph sequence.

successors of all of the n_i's.

If we apply Algorithm 10.15 to the resulting graph, each n_i has a unique predecessor, and so it will surely become part of that predecessor's interval. Thus, one node splitting plus one round of interval partitioning results in a graph with fewer nodes. As a consequence, the construction of interval graphs, interspersed when necessary with node splitting, must eventually attain a graph of a single node. The significance of this observation will become clear in the next section, when we design data-flow analysis algorithms that are driven by these two operations on graphs.

Example 10.36. Consider the flow graph of Fig. 10.49(a), which is its own limit flow graph. We may split node 2 into $2a$ and $2b$, with predecessors 1 and 3, respectively. This graph is shown in Fig. 10.49(b). If we apply interval partitioning twice, we get the sequence of graphs shown in Fig. 10.49(c) and (d), leading to a single node.   □

T_1 - T_2 Analysis

A convenient way to achieve the same effect as interval analysis is to apply two simple transformations to flow graphs.

T_1: If n is a node with a loop, i.e., an edge $n \to n$, delete that edge.

T_2: If there is a node n, not the initial node, that has a unique predecessor, m, then m may *consume* n by deleting n and making all successors of n (including m, possibly) be successors of m.

Some interesting facts about the T_1 and T_2 transformations are:

1. If we apply T_1 and T_2 to a flow graph G in any order, until a flow graph results for which no applications of T_1 or T_2 are possible, then a unique flow graph results. The reason is that a candidate for loop removal by T_1

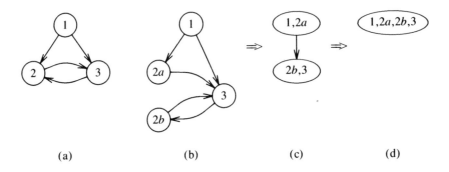

Fig. 10.49. Node splitting followed by interval partitioning.

or consumption by T_2 remains a candidate, even if some other application of T_1 or T_2 is made first.

2. The flow graph resulting from exhaustive application of T_1 and T_2 to G is the limit flow graph of G. The proof is somewhat subtle and left as an exercise. As a consequence, another definition of "reducible flow graph" is one that can be converted to a single node by T_1 and T_2.

Example 10.37. In Fig. 10.50 we see a sequence of T_1 and T_2 reductions starting from a flow graph that is a renaming of Fig. 10.49(b). In Fig. 10.50(b), c has consumed d. Note that the loop on cd in Fig. 10.50(b) results from the edge $d \rightarrow c$ in Fig. 10.50(a). That loop is removed by T_1 in Fig. 10.50(c). Also note that when a consumes b in Fig. 10.50(d), the edges from a and b to the node cd become a single edge.   □

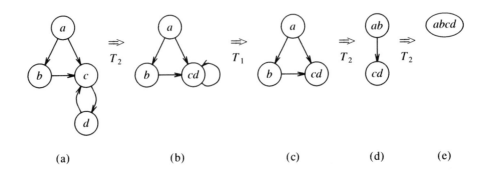

Fig. 10.50. Reduction by T_1 and T_2.

Regions

Recall from Section 10.5 that a region in a flow graph is a set of nodes N that includes a header, which dominates all the other nodes in a region. All edges between nodes in N are in the region, except (possibly) for some of those that enter the header. For example, every interval is a region, but there are regions that are not intervals because, for example, they may omit some nodes an interval would include, or they may omit some edges back to the header. There are also regions much larger than any interval, as we shall see.

As we reduce a flow graph G by T_1 and T_2, at all times the following conditions are true:

1. A node represents a region of G.

2. An edge from a to b represents a set of edges. Each such edge is from some node in the region represented by a to the header of the region represented by b.

3. Each node and edge of G is represented by exactly one node or edge of the current graph.

To see why these observations hold, notice first that they hold trivially for G itself. Every node is a region by itself, and every edge represents only itself. Suppose we apply T_1 to some node n representing a region R, while the loop $n \rightarrow n$ represents some set of edges E, all of which must enter the header of R. If we add the edges E to region R, it is still a region, so after removing the edge $n \rightarrow n$, the node n represents R and the edges of E, which preserves conditions (1)–(3) above.

If we instead use T_2 to consume node b by node a, let a and b represent regions R and S respectively. Also, let E be the set of edges represented by the edge $a \rightarrow b$. We claim R, S, and E together form a region whose header is the header of R. To prove this, we must verify that the header of R dominates every node in S. If not, then there must be some path to the header of S that does not end with an edge of E. Then the last edge of this path would have to be represented in the current flow graph by some other edge entering b. But there can be no such edge, or T_2 cannot be used to consume b.

Example 10.38. The node labeled cd in Fig. 10.50(b) represents the region shown in Fig. 10.51(a), which was formed by having c consume d. Note that the edge $d \rightarrow c$ is not part of the region; in Fig. 10.50(b) that edge is represented by the loop on cd. However, in Fig. 10.50(c), the edge $cd \rightarrow cd$ has been removed, and the node cd now represents the region shown in Fig. 10.51(b).

In Fig. 10.50(d), node cd still represents the region of Fig. 10.51(b), while node ab represents the region of Fig. 10.51(c). The edge $ab \rightarrow cd$ in Fig. 10.50(d) represents the edges $a \rightarrow c$ and $b \rightarrow c$ of the original flow graph in Fig. 10.50(a). When we apply T_2 to reach Fig. 10.50(e), the remaining node represents the entire flow graph, Fig. 10.50(a).   □

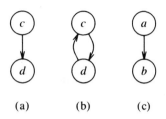

(a)   (b)   (c)

Fig. 10.51. Some regions.

We should observe that the property of T_1 and T_2 reduction mentioned above holds also for interval analysis. We leave as an exercise the fact that as we construct $I(G)$, $I(I(G))$, and so on, each node in each of these graphs represents a region, and each edge a set of edges satisfying property (2) above.

Finding Dominators

We close this section with an efficient algorithm for a concept that we have used frequently, and will continue to use in developing the theory of flow graphs and data-flow analysis. We shall give a simple algorithm for computing the dominators of every node n in a flow graph, based on the principle that if $p_1, p_2, \ldots, p_k$ are all the predecessors of n, and $d \neq n$, then d *dom* n if and only if d *dom* p_i for each i. The method is akin to forward data-flow analysis with intersection as the confluence operator (e.g., available expressions), in that we take an approximation to the set of dominators of n and refine it by repeatedly visiting all the nodes in turn.

In this case, the initial approximation we choose has the initial node dominated only by the initial node, and everything dominating everything besides the initial node. Intuitively, the reason this approach works is that dominator candidates are ruled out only when we find a path that proves, say, m. *dom* n is false. If we cannot find such a path, from the initial node to n avoiding m, then m really is a dominator of n.

Algorithm 10.16. Finding dominators.

Input. A flow graph G with set of nodes N, set of edges E and initial node n_0.

Output. The relation *dom*.

Method. We compute $D(n)$, the set of dominators of n, iteratively by the procedure in Fig. 10.52. At the end, d is in $D(n)$ if and only if d *dom* n. The reader may supply the details regarding how changes to $D(n)$ are detected; Algorithm 10.2 will serve as a model.

One can show that $D(n)$ computed at line (5) of Fig. 10.52 is always a subset of the current $D(n)$. Since $D(n)$ cannot get smaller indefinitely, we must eventually terminate the while-loop. A proof that, after convergence, $D(n)$ is

(1) $D(n_0) := \{n_0\}$;
(2)   **for** n in $N - \{n_0\}$ **do** $D(n) := N$;

      /* end initialization */

(3)   **while** changes to any $D(n)$ occur **do**
(4)   **for** n in $N - \{n_0\}$ **do**
(5) $D(n) := \{n\} \cup \underset{\substack{p \text{ a pred-}\\ \text{ecessor of } n}}{\cap} D(p)$;

Fig. 10.52. Dominator computing algorithm.

the set of dominators of n is left for the interested reader. The algorithm of Fig. 10.52 is quite efficient, as $D(n)$ can be represented by a bit vector and the set operations of line (5) can be done with logical **and** and **or**.   □

Example 10.39. Let us return to the flow graph of Fig. 10.45, and suppose in the for-loop of line (4) nodes are visited in numerical order. Node 2 has only 1 for a predecessor, so $D(2) := \{2\} \cup D(1)$. Since 1 is the initial node, $D(1)$ was assigned $\{1\}$ at line (1). Thus, $D(2)$ is set to $\{1, 2\}$ at line (5).

   Then node 3, with predecessors 1, 2, 4, and 8, is considered. Line (5) gives us $D(3) = \{3\} \cup (\{1\} \cap \{1,2\} \cap \{1,2, \ldots , 10\}) = \{1,3\}$. The remaining calculations are:

$$D(4) = \{4\} \cup (D(3) \cap D(7)) = \{4\} \cup (\{1,3\} \cap \{1,2, \ldots , 10\}) = \{1,3,4\}$$

$$D(5) = \{5\} \cup D(4) = \{5\} \cup \{1,3,4\} = \{1,3,4,5\}$$

$$D(6) = \{6\} \cup D(4) = \{6\} \cup \{1,3,4\} = \{1,3,4,6\}$$

$$D(7) = \{7\} \cup (D(5) \cap D(6) \cap D(10))$$

$$= \{7\} \cup (\{1,3,4,5\} \cap \{1,3,4,6\} \cap \{1,2, \ldots , 10\}) = \{1,3,4,7\}$$

$$D(8) = \{8\} \cup D(7) = \{8\} \cup \{1,3,4,7\} = \{1,3,4,7,8\}$$

$$D(9) = \{9\} \cup D(8) = \{9\} \cup \{1,3,4,7,8\} = \{1,3,4,7,8,9\}$$

$$D(10) = \{10\} \cup D(8) = \{10\} \cup \{1,3,4,7,8\} = \{1,3,4,7,8,10\}$$

   The second pass through the while-loop is seen to produce no changes, so the above values yield the relation *dom*.   □

10.10 EFFICIENT DATA-FLOW ALGORITHMS

In this section we shall consider two ways to use flow-graph theory to speed data-flow analysis. The first is an application of depth-first ordering to reduce the number of passes that the iterative algorithms of Sections 10.6 take, and the second uses intervals or the T_1 and T_2 transformations to generalize the syntax-directed approach of Section 10.5.

Depth-First Ordering in Iterative Algorithms

In all the problems studied so far, such as reaching definitions, available expressions, or live variables, any event of significance at a node will be propagated to that node along an acyclic path. For example, if a definition d is in $in[B]$, then there is some acyclic path from the block containing d to B such that d is in the in's and out's all along that path. Similarly, if an expression x+y is not available at the entrance to block B, then there is some acyclic path that demonstrates that fact; either the path is from the initial node and includes no statement that kills or generates x+y, or the path is from a block that kills x+y and along the path there is no subsequent generation of x+y. Finally, for live variables, if x is live on exit from block B, then there is an acyclic path from B to a use of x, along which there are no definitions of x.

The reader should check that in each of these cases, paths with cycles add nothing. For example, if a use of x is reached from the end of block B along a path with a cycle, we can eliminate that cycle to find a shorter path along which the use of x is still reached from B.

If all useful information propagates along acyclic paths, we have an opportunity to tailor the order in which we visit nodes in iterative data-flow algorithms so that after relatively few passes through the nodes, we can be sure information has passed along all the acyclic paths. In particular, statistics gathered in Knuth [1971b] show that typical flow graphs have a very low *interval depth*, which is the number of times one must apply the interval partition to reach the limit flow graph; an average of 2.75 was found. Furthermore, it can be shown that the interval depth of a flow graph is never less than what we have called the "depth," the maximum number of retreating edges on any acyclic path. (If the flow graph is not reducible, the depth may depend on the depth-first spanning tree chosen.)

Recalling our discussion of the depth-first spanning tree in the previous section, we note that if $a \rightarrow b$ is an edge, then the depth-first number of b is less than that of a only when the edge is a retreating edge. Thus, replace line (5) of Fig. 10.26, which tells us to visit each block B of the flow graph for which we are computing reaching definitions, by:

for each block B in depth-first order **do**

Suppose we have a path along which a definition d propagates, such as

$$3 \rightarrow 5 \rightarrow 19 \rightarrow 35 \rightarrow 16 \rightarrow 23 \rightarrow 45 \rightarrow 4 \rightarrow 10 \rightarrow 17$$

where integers represent the depth-first numbers of the blocks along the path. Then the first time through the loop of lines (5)–(9) in Fig. 10.26, d will propagate from $out[3]$ to $in[5]$ to $out[5]$, and so on, up to $out[35]$. It will not reach $in[16]$ on that round, because as 16 precedes 35, we had already computed $in[16]$ by the time d was put in $out[35]$. However, the next time we run through the loop of lines (5)–(9), when we compute $in[16]$, d will be included because it is in $out[35]$. Definition d will also propagate to $out[16]$, $in[23]$, and so on, up to $out[45]$, where it must wait because $in[4]$ was already computed.

On the third pass, d travels to $in[4]$, $out[4]$, $in[10]$, $out[10]$, and $in[17]$, so after three passes we establish that d reaches block 17.[13]

It should not be hard to extract the general principle from this example. If we use depth-first order in Fig. 10.26, then the number of passes needed to propagate any reaching definition along any acyclic path is no more than one greater than the number of edges along that path that go from a higher numbered block to a lower numbered block. Those edges are exactly the retreating edges, so the number of passes needed is one plus the depth. Of course Algorithm 10.2 does not detect the fact that all definitions have reached wherever they can reach for one more pass, so the upper bound on the number of passes taken by that algorithm with depth-first block ordering is actually two plus the depth, or 5 if we believe the results of Knuth [1971b] to be typical.

The depth-first order is also advantageous for available expressions (Algorithm 10.3), or any data flow problem that we solved by propagation in the forward direction. For problems like live variables, where we propagate backwards, the same average of five passes can be achieved if we chose the reverse of the depth-first order. Thus, we may propagate a use of a variable in block 17 backwards along the path

$$3 \rightarrow 5 \rightarrow 19 \rightarrow 35 \rightarrow 16 \rightarrow 23 \rightarrow 45 \rightarrow 4 \rightarrow 10 \rightarrow 17$$

in one pass to $in[4]$, where we must wait for the next pass to in order reach $out[45]$. On the second pass it reaches $in[16]$, and on the third pass it goes from $out[35]$ to $out[3]$. In general, one plus the depth passes suffices to carry the use of a variable backward, along any acyclic path, if we choose the reverse of depth-first order to visit the nodes in a pass, because then, uses propagate along any decreasing sequence in a single pass.

Structure-Based Data-Flow Analysis

With a bit more effort, we can implement data-flow algorithms that visit nodes (and apply data-flow equations) no more times than the interval depth of the flow graph, and frequently the average node will be visited even fewer times than that. Whether the extra effort results in a true time savings has not been firmly established, but a technique like this one, based on interval analysis, has been used in several compilers. Further, the ideas exposed here apply to syntax-directed data-flow algorithms for all sorts of structured control statements, not just the **if** $\cdots$ **then** and **do** $\cdots$ **while** discussed in Section 10.5, and these have also appeared in several compilers.

We shall base our algorithm on the structure induced on flow graphs by the T_1 and T_2 transformations. As in Section 10.5, we are concerned with the definitions that are generated and killed as control flows through a region. Unlike the regions defined by if or while statements, a general region can have multiple exits, so for each block B in region R we shall compute sets

---

[13] Definition d also reaches $out[17]$, but that is irrelevant to the path in question.

$gen_{R,B}$ and $kill_{R,B}$ of definitions generated and killed, respectively, along paths within the region from the header to the end of block B. These sets will be used to define a *transfer function* $trans_{R,B}(S)$ that tells for any set S of definitions, what set of definitions reach the end of block B by traveling along paths wholly within R, given that all and only the definitions in S reach the header of R.

As we have seen in Sections 10.5 and 10.6, the definitions reaching the end of block B fall into two classes.

1. Those that are generated within R and propagate to the end of B independent of S.

2. Those that are not generated in R, but that also are not killed along some path from the header of R to the end of B, and therefore are in $trans_{R,B}(S)$ if and only if they are in S.

Thus, we may write *trans* in the form:

$$trans_{R,B}(S) = gen_{R,B} \cup (S - kill_{R,B})$$

The heart of the algorithm is a way to compute $trans_{R,B}$ for progressively larger regions defined by some (T_1, T_2)-decomposition of a flow graph. For the moment, we assume that the flow graph is reducible, although a simple modification allows the algorithm to work for nonreducible graphs as well.

The basis is a region consisting of a single block, B. Here the transfer function of the region is the transfer function of the block itself, since a definition reaches the end of the block if and only if it is either generated by the block or is in the set S and not killed. That is,

$$gen_{B,B} = gen[B]$$

$$kill_{B,B} = kill[B]$$

Now, let us consider the construction of a region R by T_2; that is, R is formed when R_1 consumes R_2, as suggested in Fig. 10.53. First, note that within region R there are no edges from R_2 back to R_1 since any edge from R_2 to the header of R_1 is not a part of R. Thus any path totally within R goes (optionally) through R_1 first, then (optionally) through R_2, but cannot then return to R_1. Also note that the header of R is the header of R_1. We may conclude that within R, R_2 does not affect the transfer function of nodes in R_1; that is,

$$gen_{R,B} = gen_{R_1,B}$$

$$kill_{R,B} = kill_{R_1,B}$$

for all B in R_1.

For B in R_2, a definition can reach the end of B if any of the following conditions hold.

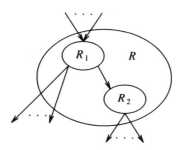

Fig. 10.53. Region building by T_2.

1. The definition is generated within R_2.

2. The definition is generated within R_1, reaches the end of some predecessor of the header of R_2, and is not killed going from the header of R_2 to B.

3. The definition is in the set S available at the header of R_1, not killed going to some predecessor of the header of R_2, and not killed going from the header of R_2 to B.

Hence, the definitions reaching the ends of those blocks in R_1 that are predecessors of the header of R_2 play a special role. In essence, we see what happens to a set S entering the header of R_1 as its definitions try to reach the header of R_2, via one of its predecessors. The set of definitions that reach one of the predecessors of the header of R_2 becomes the input set for R_2, and we apply the transfer functions for R_2 to that set.

Thus, let G be the union of $gen_{R_1,P}$ for all predecessors P of the header of R_2, and let K be the intersection of $kill_{R_1,P}$ for all those predecessors P. Then if S is the set of definitions that reach the header of R_1, the set of definitions that reach the header of R_2 along paths staying wholly within R is $G \cup (S-K)$. Therefore, the transfer function in R for those blocks B in R_2 may be computed by

$$gen_{R,B} = gen_{R_2,B} \cup (G - kill_{R_2,B})$$

$$kill_{R,B} = kill_{R_2,B} \cup (K - gen_{R_2,B})$$

Next, consider what happens when a region R is built from a region R_1 using transformation T_1. The general situation is shown in Fig. 10.54; note that R consists of R_1 plus some back edges to the header of R_1 (which is also the header of R, of course). A path going through the header twice would be cyclic and, as we argued earlier in the section, need not be considered. Thus, all definitions generated at the end of block B are generated in one of two ways.

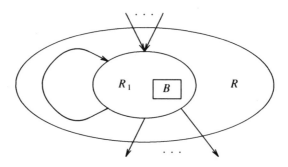

Fig. 10.54. Region building by T_1.

1. The definition is generated within R_1 and does not need the back edges incorporated into R in order to reach the end of B.

2. The definition is generated somewhere within R_1, reaches a predecessor of the header, follows one back edge, and is not killed going from the header to B.

If we let G be the union of $gen_{R_1,P}$ for all predecessors of the header in R, then

$$gen_{R,B} \;=\; gen_{R_1,B} \;\cup\; (G - kill_{R_1,B})$$

A definition is killed going from the header to B if and only if it is killed along all acyclic paths, so the back edges incorporated into R do not cause more definitions to be killed. That is,

$$kill_{R,B} \;=\; kill_{R_1,B}$$

Example 10.40. Let us reconsider the flow graph of Fig. 10.50, whose (T_1, T_2)-decomposition is shown in Fig. 10.55, with the regions of the decomposition named. We also show in Fig. 10.56 some hypothetical bit vectors representing three definitions and whether they are generated or killed by each of the blocks in Fig. 10.55.

Starting from the inside out, we note that for single-node regions, which we call A, B, C, and D, *gen* and *kill* are given by the table in Fig. 10.56. We may then proceed to region R, which is formed when C consumes D by T_2. Following the rules for T_2 above, we note that *gen* and *kill* do not change for C, that is,

$$gen_{R,C} = gen_{C,C} = 000$$
$$kill_{R,C} = kill_{C,C} = 010$$

For node D, we have to find in region C the union of *gen* for all the predecessors of the header of the region D. Of course the header of region D is node

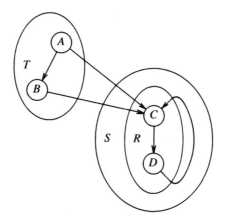

Fig. 10.55. Decomposition of a flow graph.

BLOCK	gen	kill
A	100	010
B	010	101
C	000	010
D	001	000

Fig. 10.56. *gen* and *kill* information for blocks in Fig. 10.55.

D, and there is only one predecessor of that node in region C, namely, the node C. Thus,

$$gen_{R,D} = gen_{D,D} \cup (gen_{C,C} - kill_{D,D}) = 001 + (000 - 000) = 001$$
$$kill_{R,D} = kill_{D,D} \cup (kill_{C,C} - gen_{D,D}) = 000 + (010 - 001) = 010$$

Now, we build region S from region R by T_1. The *kill*'s don't change, so we have

$$kill_{S,C} = kill_{R,C} = 010$$
$$kill_{S,D} = kill_{R,D} = 010$$

To compute the *gen*'s for S we note that the only back edge to the header of S that is incorporated going from R to S is the edge $D \rightarrow C$. Thus,

$$gen_{S,C} = gen_{R,C} \cup (gen_{R,D} - kill_{R,C}) = 000 + (001 - 010) = 001$$
$$gen_{S,D} = gen_{R,D} \cup (gen_{R,D} - kill_{R,D}) = 001 + (001 - 010) = 001$$

The computation for region T is analogous to that for region R and we obtain

$$gen_{T,A} = 100$$
$$kill_{T,A} = 010$$
$$gen_{T,B} = 010$$
$$kill_{T,B} = 101$$

Finally, we compute *gen* and *kill* for region U, the entire flow graph. Since U is constructed when T consumes S by transformation T_2, the values of *gen* and *kill* for nodes A and B do not change from what was just given above. For C and D, we note that the header of S, node C, has two predecessors in region T, namely A and B. Therefore, we compute

$$G = gen_{T,A} \cup gen_{T,B} = 110$$
$$K = kill_{T,A} \cap kill_{T,B} = 000$$

Then we may compute

$$gen_{U,C} = gen_{S,C} \cup (G - kill_{S,C}) = 101$$
$$kill_{U,C} = kill_{S,C} \cup (K - gen_{S,C}) = 010$$
$$gen_{U,D} = gen_{S,D} \cup (G - kill_{S,D}) = 101$$
$$kill_{U,D} = kill_{S,D} \cup (K - gen_{S,D}) = 010 \qquad \qquad \square$$

Having computed $gen_{U,B}$ and $kill_{U,B}$ for each block B, where U is the region consisting of the entire flow graph, we essentially have computed $out[B]$ for each block B. That is, if we look at the definition of $trans_{U,B}(S) = gen_{U,B} \cup (S - kill_{U,B})$, we note that $trans_{U,B}(\varnothing)$ is exactly $out[B]$. But $trans_{U,B}(\varnothing) = gen_{U,B}$. Thus, the completion of the structure-based reaching definition algorithm is to use the *gen*'s as the *out*'s, and compute the *in*'s by taking the union of the *out*'s of the predecessors. These steps are summarized in the following algorithm.

Algorithm 10.17. Structure-based reaching definitions.

Input. A reducible flow graph G and sets of definitions $gen[B]$ and $kill[B]$ for each block B of G.

Output. $in[B]$ for each block B.

Method.

1.   Find the (T_1, T_2)-decomposition for G.

2.   For each region R in the decomposition, from the inside out, compute $gen_{R,B}$ and $kill_{R,B}$ for each block B in R.

3.   If U is the name of the region consisting of the entire graph, then for each block B, set $in[B]$ to the union, over all predecessors P of block B, of $gen_{U,P}$. $\qquad \square$

Some Speedups to the Structure-Based Algorithm

First, notice that if we have a transfer function $G \cup (S - K)$, the function is not changed if we delete from K some members of G. Thus, when we apply T_2, instead of using the formulas

$$gen_{R,B} = gen_{R_2,B} \cup (G - kill_{R_2,B})$$

$$kill_{R,B} = kill_{R_2,B} \cup (K - gen_{R_2,B})$$

we can replace the second by

$$kill_{R,B} = kill_{R_2,B} \cup K$$

thus saving an operation for each block in region R_2.

Another useful idea is to notice that the only time we apply T_1 is after we have first consumed some region R_2 by R_1, and there are some back edges from R_2 to the header of R_1. Instead of first making changes in R_2 because of the T_2 operation, and then making changes in R_1 and R_2 due to the T_1 operation, we can combine the two sets of changes if we do the following.

1. Using the T_2 rule, compute the new transfer function for those nodes in R_2 that are predecessors of the header of R_1.

2. Using the T_1 rule, compute the new transfer function for all the nodes of R_1.

3. Using the T_2 rule, compute the new transfer function for all the nodes of R_2. Note that feedback due to the application of T_1 has reached the predecessors of R_2 and is passed to all of R_2 by the T_2 rule; there is no need to apply the T_1 rule for R_2.

Handling Nonreducible Flow Graphs

If the (T_1, T_2)-reduction of a flow graph stops at a limit flow graph that is not a single node, then we must perform a node splitting. Splitting a node of the limit flow graph corresponds to duplicating the entire region represented by that node. For example, in Fig. 10.57 we suggest the effect that node splitting might have on an original nine-node flow graph that was partitioned by T_1 and T_2 into three regions connected by some edges.

As mentioned in the previous section, by alternating splits with sequences of reductions, we are guaranteed to reduce the flow graph to a single node. The result of the splits is that some of the nodes of the original graph will have more than one copy in the region represented by the one-node graph. We may apply Algorithm 10.17 to this region with little change. The only difference is that when we split a node, the *gen*'s and *kill*'s for the nodes of the original graph in the region represented by the split node must be duplicated. For example, whatever the values of *gen* and *kill* are for the nodes in the two-node region of Fig. 10.57 on the left become *gen* and *kill* for each of the corresponding nodes in both two-node regions on the right. At the final step,

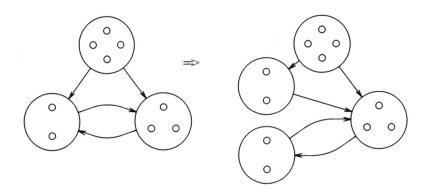

Fig. 10.57. Splitting a nonreducible flow graph.

when we compute the *in*'s for all the nodes, those nodes of the original graph that have several representatives in the final region have their *in*'s computed by taking the union of the *in*'s of all their representatives.

In the worst case, splitting of nodes could exponentiate the total number of nodes represented by all the regions. Thus, if we expect many flow graphs to be nonreducible, we probably should not use structure-based methods. Fortunately, nonreducible flow graphs are sufficiently rare that we can generally ignore the cost of node splitting.

10.11 A TOOL FOR DATA-FLOW ANALYSIS

As we have pointed out before, there are strong similarities among the various data-flow problems studied. The data-flow equations of Section 10.6 were seen to be distinguished by:

1. The transfer function used, which in each case studied was of the form $f(X) = A \cup (X - B)$. For example, $A = kill$ and $B = gen$ for reaching definitions.

2. The confluence operator, which in all cases so far has been either union or intersection.

3. The direction of propagation of information: forward or backward.

Since these distinctions are not great, it should not be surprising that all these problems can be treated in a unified way. Such an approach was described in Kildall [1973], and a tool to simplify the implementation of data-flow problems was implemented by Kildall and used by him in several compiler projects. It has not seen widespread use, probably because the amount of labor saved by the system is not as great as that saved by tools like parser generators. However, we should be aware of what can be done not only because it does suggest a simplification for implementers of optimizing compilers, but also because it helps to unify the various ideas we have seen so far in this chapter. Further, this section suggests how more powerful data-flow analysis strategies, ones that provide more precise information than the algorithms mentioned so far, can be developed.

Data-Flow Analysis Frameworks

We shall describe frameworks that model forward propagation problems. If we consider only the iterative type of solution to data-flow problems, then the direction of flow makes no difference; we can reverse the direction of edges and make some minor adjustments to account for the initial node, and then treat a backward problem as if it were forward. Structure-based algorithms are somewhat different; the forward and backward problems are not solved in quite the same way because the reverse of a reducible flow graph need not be reducible. However, the treatment of backward problems will be left as an exercise, and we shall restrict ourselves to forward problems only.

A *data-flow analysis framework* consists of:

1. A set V of *values* to be propagated. The values of *in* and *out* are members of V.

2. A set F of *transfer functions* from V to V.

3. A binary *meet operation* $\wedge$, on V, to represent the confluence operator.

Example 10.41. For reaching definitions, V consists of all subsets of the set of definitions in the program. The set F is the set of all functions of the form $f(X) = A \cup (X - B)$, where A and B are sets of definitions, i.e., members of V; A and B are what we called *gen* and *kill*, respectively. Finally, the operation $\wedge$ is union.

For available expressions, V consists of all subsets of the set of expressions computed by the program, and F is the set of expressions of the same form as above, but where A and B are now sets of expressions. The meet operation is intersection, of course. □

Example 10.42. Kildall's approach is not limited to the simple examples with which we have been dealing, although the complexity, both in terms of computation time and intellectual difficulty, rises. The exercises suggest a very powerful example, where the data-flow information computed tells us in essence, all pairs of expressions that have the same value at a point. However, we shall get some of the flavor of this example by giving a method for telling which variables have constant values in a way that captures more information than reaching definitions. Our new framework understands, for example, that when **x** is defined by d: **x:=x+1**, and **x** had a constant value before assignment, it does so afterward.

In contrast, using reaching definitions for constant propagation we would see that statement d was a possible definition of **x**, and assume therefore that **x** did not have a constant value. Of course, in one pass the right side of

d: $\mathbf{x:=x+1}$ might be replaced by a constant, and then another round of constant propagation could detect that uses of the $\mathbf{x}$ defined at d were actually uses of a constant.

In the new framework, the set V is the set of all mappings from the variables of the program to a particular set of values. That set of values consists of

1. All constants.

2. The value *nonconst*, which means that the variable in question has been determined not to have a constant value. The value *nonconst* would be assigned to variable $\mathbf{x}$ if, say, during data-flow analysis we discovered two paths along which the values 2 and 3, respectively, were assigned to $\mathbf{x}$, or a path along which the previous definition of $\mathbf{x}$ was a read statement.

3. The value *undef*, which means that nothing may yet be asserted about the variable in question, presumably because early in the execution of the data-flow analysis, no definition of the variable has been discovered to reach the point in question.

Note that *nonconst* and *undef* are not the same; they are essentially opposites. The first says we have seen so many ways a variable could be defined that we know it is not constant. The second says we have seen so little about the variable, that we cannot say anything at all.

The meet operation is defined by the following table. We let μ and ν be two members of V; that is, μ and ν both map each variable to a constant, to *undef*, or to *nonconst*. Then the function $\rho = \mu \wedge \nu$ is defined in Fig. 10.58, where we give the value of $\rho(\mathbf{x})$ in terms of the values of $\mu(\mathbf{x})$ and $\nu(\mathbf{x})$ for each variable $\mathbf{x}$. In that table, c is an arbitrary constant, and d is another constant definitely not equal to c. For example, if $\mu(\mathbf{x}) = c$ and $\nu(\mathbf{x}) = d$, a different constant, then apparently $\mathbf{x}$ takes the values c and d along two different paths, and at the confluence of those paths, $\mathbf{x}$ has no constant value; hence the choice $\rho(\mathbf{x}) = $ *nonconst*. As another example, if along one path, nothing is known about $\mathbf{x}$, reflected by $\mu(\mathbf{x}) = $ *undef*, and along another path, $\mathbf{x}$ is believed to have the value c, then after the confluence of these paths, we can only assert that $\mathbf{x}$ has the value c. Of course, later discovery of another path to the point of confluence, along which $\mathbf{x}$ has a value besides c, will change the assigned value for $\mathbf{x}$ after the confluence to *nonconst*.

Finally, we must design the set of functions F that reflect the transfer of information from the beginning to the end of any block. The description of this set of functions is complicated, although the ideas are straightforward. We shall therefore give a "basis" for the set of functions by describing the functions that represent single definition statements, and the entire set of functions can then be constructed by composing functions from this basis set to reflect blocks with more than one definition statement.

$v(\mathbf{x})$	$\mu(\mathbf{x})$			
	nonconst	*c*	$d\,(\neq c)$	*undef*
nonconst	*nonconst*	*nonconst*	*nonconst*	*nonconst*
c	*nonconst*	*c*	*nonconst*	*c*
undef	*nonconst*	*c*	*d*	*undef*

Fig. 10.58. $\rho(\mathbf{x})$ in terms of $\mu(\mathbf{x})$ and $v(\mathbf{x})$.

1. The identity function is in F; this function reflects any block that has no definition statements. If I is the identity function, and μ is any mapping from variables to values, then $I(\mu) = \mu$. Note that μ itself need not be the identity; it is arbitrary.

2. For each variable $\mathbf{x}$ and constant c there is a function f in F such that for every mapping μ in V, we have $f(\mu) = v$, where $v(\mathbf{w}) = \mu(\mathbf{w})$ for all $\mathbf{w}$ other than $\mathbf{x}$, and $v(\mathbf{x}) = c$. These functions reflect the action of an assignment statement $\mathbf{x}:=c$.

3. For each three (not necessarily distinct) variables $\mathbf{x}$, $\mathbf{y}$, and $\mathbf{z}$, there is a function f in F such that for every mapping μ in V, we have $f(\mu) = v$. The mapping v is defined by: for every $\mathbf{w}$ besides $\mathbf{x}$ we have $v(\mathbf{w}) = \mu(\mathbf{w})$, and $v(\mathbf{x}) = \mu(\mathbf{y}) + \mu(\mathbf{z})$. If either $\mu(\mathbf{y})$ or $\mu(\mathbf{z})$ is *nonconst*, then the sum is *nonconst*. If either $\mu(\mathbf{y})$ or $\mu(\mathbf{z})$ is *undef*, but neither is *nonconst*, then the result is *undef*. This function expresses the effect of the assignment $\mathbf{x}:=\mathbf{y}+\mathbf{z}$. As usual in this chapter, + may be thought of as a generic operator; here an obvious modification is necessary if the operator is unary, ternary, or higher, and another obvious modification is needed to take into account effect of a copy statement, $\mathbf{x}:=\mathbf{y}$.

4. For each variable $\mathbf{x}$ there is a function f in F such that for each μ, $f(\mu) = v$, where $v(\mathbf{w}) = \mu(\mathbf{w})$ for all $\mathbf{w}$ other than $\mathbf{x}$, and $v(\mathbf{x}) = \textit{nonconst}$. This function reflects a definition by reading $\mathbf{x}$, since after a read statement, $\mathbf{x}$ surely must be assumed not to have any particular constant value.   □

The Axioms of Data-Flow Analysis Frameworks

In order to make the kinds of data-flow algorithms that we have seen so far work for an arbitrary framework, we need to assume some things about the set V, the set of functions F, and the meet operator $\wedge$. Our basic assumptions are listed below, although some data-flow algorithms need additional assumptions.

1. F has an identity function I, such that $I(\mu) = \mu$ for all μ in V.

2. F is closed under composition; that is, for any two functions f and g in F, the function h defined by $h(\mu) = g(f(\mu))$ is in F.

3. $\wedge$ is an associative, commutative, and idempotent operation. These three properties are expressed algebraically as

$$\mu \wedge (v \wedge \rho) = (\mu \wedge v) \wedge \rho$$

$$\mu \wedge v = v \wedge \mu$$

$$\mu \wedge \mu = \mu$$

for all μ, v, and ρ in V.

4.   There is a *top element* $\top$ in V, satisfying the law

$$\top \wedge \mu = \mu$$

for all μ in V.

Example 10.43. Let us consider reaching definitions. F surely has the identity, the function where *gen* and *kill* are both the empty set. To show closure under composition, suppose we have two functions

$$f_1(X) = G_1 \cup (X - K_1)$$
$$f_2(X) = G_2 \cup (X - K_2)$$

Then

$$f_2(f_1(X)) = G_2 \cup ((G_1 \cup (X - K_1)) - K_2)$$

We may verify that the right side of the above is algebraically equal to

$$(G_2 \cup (G_1 - K_2)) \cup (X - (K_1 \cup K_2))$$

If we let $K = K_1 \cup K_2$ and $G = (G_2 \cup (G_1 - K_2))$, then we have shown that the composition of f_1 and f_2, which is $f(X) = G \cup (X - K)$, is of the form that makes it a member of F.

As for the meet operator, which is union, it is easy to check that union is associative, commutative, and idempotent. The "top" element turns out to be the empty set in this case, since $\phi \cup X = X$ for any set X.

When we consider available expressions, we find that the same arguments used for reaching definitions also show that F has an identity and is closed under composition. The meet operator is now intersection, but this operator too is associative, commutative, and idempotent. The top element makes more intuitive sense this time; it is the set E of all expressions in the program, since for any set X of expressions, $E \cap X = X$.   □

Example 10.44. Let us consider the constant computation framework introduced in Example 10.42. The set of functions F was designed to include the identity and to be closed under composition. To check the algebraic laws for

$\wedge$, it suffices to show that they apply for each variable x. As an instance, we shall check idempotence. Let $v = \mu \wedge \mu$, that is, for all x, $v(x) = \mu(x) \wedge \mu(x)$. It is simple to check by cases that $v(x) = \mu(x)$. For example, if $\mu(x) = nonconst$, then $v(x) = nonconst$, since the result of pairing *nonconst* with itself in Fig. 10.58 is *nonconst*.

Finally, the top element is the mapping τ defined by $\tau(x) = undef$ for all variables x. We can check from Fig. 10.58 that for any mapping μ and any variable x, if v is the function $\tau \wedge \mu$, then $v(x) = \mu(x)$, since the result of pairing *undef* with any value in Fig. 10.58 is that other value. □

Monotonicity and Distributivity

We need another condition to make the iterative algorithm for data-flow analysis work. This condition, called monotonicity, says informally that if you take any function f from the set F, and if you apply f to two members of V, one "bigger" than the other, then the result of applying f to the bigger is not less than what you get by applying f to the smaller.

To make the notion of "bigger" precise, we define a relation $\leq$ on V by

$$\mu \leq v \text{ if and only if } \mu \wedge v = \mu$$

Example 10.45. In the reaching definition framework, where meet is union and members of V are sets of definitions, $X \leq Y$ means $X \cup Y = X$, that is, X is a superset of Y. Thus, $\leq$ looks "backward;" smaller elements of V are supersets of larger ones.

For available expressions, where meet is intersection, things work "right," and $X \leq Y$ means that $X \cap Y = X$; i.e., X is a subset of Y. □

Note from Example 10.45 that $\leq$ in our sense need not have all the properties of $\leq$ on integers. It is true that $\leq$ is transitive; the reader may prove, as an exercise in using the axioms for $\wedge$, that $\mu \leq v$ and $v \leq \rho$ imply $\mu \leq \rho$. However, $\leq$ in our sense is not a total order. For example, in the available expressions framework, we can have two sets X and Y, neither of which is a subset of the other, in which case neither $X \leq Y$ nor $Y \leq X$ would be true.

It often helps to draw the set V in a *lattice diagram*, which is a graph whose nodes are the elements of V, and whose edges are directed downward, from X to Y if $Y \leq X$. For example, Fig. 10.59 shows the set V for a reaching definitions data-flow problem where there are three definitions, d_1, d_2, and d_3. Since $\leq$ is "superset of," an edge is directed downward from any subset of these three definitions to each of its supersets. Since $\leq$ is transitive, we conventionally omit the edge from X to Y if there is another path from X to Y left in the diagram. Thus, although $\{d_1, d_2, d_3\} \leq \{d_1\}$, we do not draw this edge since it is represented by the path through $\{d_1, d_2\}$, for example.

It is also useful to note that we can read the meet off such diagrams, since $X \wedge Y$ is always the highest Z for which there are paths downward to Z from both X and Y. For example, if X is $\{d_1\}$ and Y is $\{d_2\}$, then Z in Fig. 10.59 is $\{d_1, d_2\}$, which makes sense, because the meet operator is union. It is also

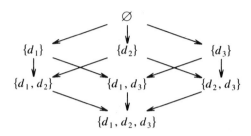

Fig. 10.59. Lattice of subsets of definitions.

true that the top element will appear at the top of the lattice diagram; that is, there is a path downward from $\top$ to each element.

Now, we can define a framework $(F, V, \wedge)$ to be *monotone* if

$$\mu \leq \nu \text{ implies } f(\mu) \leq f(\nu) \tag{10.15}$$

for all μ and ν in V, and f in F.

There is an equivalent way to define monotonicity:

$$f(\mu \wedge \nu) \leq f(\mu) \wedge f(\nu) \tag{10.16}$$

for all μ and ν in V and f in F. It is useful to jump back and forth between these two equivalent definitions, so we shall sketch a proof of their equivalence, leaving for the reader some simple observations to verify, using the definition of $\leq$ and the associative, commutative, and idempotent laws for $\wedge$.

Let us assume (10.15) and show why (10.16) holds. First, note that for any μ and ν, $\mu \wedge \nu \leq \mu$ and $\mu \wedge \nu \leq \nu$ both hold; it is a simple proof, left for the reader, to prove these facts by proving, for any x and y, that $(x \wedge y) \wedge y = x \wedge y$. Thus, by (10.15), $f(\mu \wedge \nu) \leq f(\mu)$ and $f(\mu \wedge \nu) \leq f(\nu)$. We leave it to the reader to verify the general law that

$$x \leq y \text{ and } x \leq z \text{ imply } x \leq y \wedge z$$

Letting x be $f(\mu \wedge \nu)$, $y = f(\mu)$, and $z = f(\nu)$, we have (10.16).

Conversely, let us assume (10.16) and prove (10.15). We suppose $\mu \leq \nu$ and use (10.16) to conclude $f(\mu) \leq f(\nu)$, thus proving (10.15). Equation (10.16) tells us $f(\mu \wedge \nu) \leq f(\mu) \wedge f(\nu)$. But since $\mu \leq \nu$ is assumed, $\mu \wedge \nu = \mu$, by definition. Thus (10.16) says $f(\mu) \leq f(\mu) \wedge f(\nu)$. As a general rule the reader may show that

$$\text{if } x \leq y \wedge z \text{ then } x \leq z$$

Thus, (10.16) implies $f(\mu) \leq f(\nu)$, and we have proved (10.15).

Often, a framework obeys a condition stronger than (10.16), which we call the *distributivity condition*:

$$f(\mu \wedge \nu) = f(\mu) \wedge f(\nu)$$

for all μ and ν in V and f in F. Certainly, if $x = y$, then $x \wedge y = x$ by idempotence, so $x \leq y$. Thus, distributivity implies monotonicity.

Example 10.46. Consider the reaching definitions framework. Let X and Y be sets of definitions, and let f be a function defined by $f(Z) = G \cup (Z - K)$ for some sets of definitions G and K. Then we can verify that the reaching definitions framework satisfies the distributivity condition, by checking that

$$G \cup ((X \cup Y) - K) = (G \cup (X - K)) \cup (G \cup (Y - K))$$

Drawing a Venn diagram makes the proof of the above relationship transparent, although it looks complicated.   □

Example 10.47. Let us show that the constant computation framework is monotone, but not distributive. First, it helps to apply the $\wedge$ operation and the $\leq$ relationship to the elements appearing in the table of Fig. 10.58. That is, let us define

$$
\begin{aligned}
nonconst \wedge c &= nonconst &&\text{for any constant } c \\
c \wedge d &= nonconst &&\text{for constants } c \neq d \\
c \wedge undef &= c &&\text{for any constant } c \\
nonconst \wedge undef &= nonconst \\
x \wedge x &= x &&\text{for any value } x
\end{aligned}
$$

Then Fig. 10.58 can be interpreted as saying that $\rho(a) = \mu(a) \wedge \nu(a)$.

We can determine what the $\leq$ relationship on values is from the $\wedge$ operation. We find

$$
\begin{aligned}
nonconst &\leq c &&\text{for any constant } c \\
c &\leq undef &&\text{for any constant } c \\
nonconst &\leq undef
\end{aligned}
$$

This relationship is shown in the lattice diagram of Fig. 10.60, where the c_i's are intended to suggest all possible constants. Note that that figure is not $\leq$ on elements of V; rather it is a relation on the set of values for $\mu(a)$ for individual variables a. The elements of V may be thought of as vectors of such values, one component for each variable, and the lattice diagram for V can be extrapolated from Fig. 10.60 if we remember that $\mu \leq \nu$ holds if and only if $\mu(a) \leq \nu(a)$ for all a; i.e., if the vectors representing μ and ν have each component related by $\leq$, and the relationship is in the same direction in each component.

Thus, to say $\mu \leq \nu$ is to say that whenever $\mu(a)$ is a constant c, $\nu(a)$ is either that constant or *undef*, and whenever $\mu(a)$ is *undef*, so is $\nu(a)$. A careful examination of the various functions f that are associated with the different kinds of definition statements enables us to verify that if $\mu \leq \nu$, then $f(\mu) \leq f(\nu)$, thus proving (10.15) and showing monotonicity. For example, if f is associated with assignment a:=b+c, only $\mu(a)$ and $\nu(a)$ change, so we have to check that if $\mu \leq \nu$ — i.e., $\mu(x) \leq \nu(x)$, for all x — then

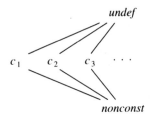

Fig. 10.60. Lattice diagram for values of variables.

$[f(\mu)](a) \leq [f(\nu)](a)$.[14] We must consider all possible values of $\mu(b)$, $\mu(c)$, $\nu(b)$, and $\nu(c)$, subject to the constraints that $\mu(b) \leq \nu(b)$ and $\mu(c) \leq \nu(c)$. For example, if

$$\mu(b) = nonconst$$
$$\nu(b) = 2$$
$$\mu(c) = 3$$
$$\nu(c) = undef$$

then $[f(\mu)](a) = nonconst$ and $[f(\nu)](a) = undef$. Since $nonconst \leq undef$, we have made the check in one case. The other cases are left as an exercise for the reader.

Now, we must check our claim that the constant computation framework is not distributive. For this part, let f be the function associated with the assignment a:=b+c, and let $\mu(b) = 2$, $\mu(c) = 3$, $\nu(b) = 3$, and $\nu(c) = 2$. Let $\rho = \mu \wedge \nu$. Then $\mu(b) \wedge \nu(b) = 2 \wedge 3 = nonconst$. Similarly, $\mu(c) \wedge \nu(c) = nonconst$. Equivalently, $\rho(b) = \rho(c) = nonconst$. It follows that $[f(\rho)](a) = nonconst$, since the sum of two nonconstant values is presumed to be nonconstant.

On the other hand, $[f(\mu)](a) = 5$, since given b = 2 and c = 3, the assignment a:=b+c sets a to 5. Similarly, $[f(\nu)](a) = 5$. Thus, $[f(\mu) \wedge f(\nu)](a) = 5$. We now see that $\rho(a) = [f(\mu \wedge \nu)](a) \neq [f(\mu) \wedge f(\nu)](a)$, so the distributivity condition is violated.

Intuitively, the reason we get a distributivity violation is that the constant computation framework is not powerful enough to remember all invariants, in particular, the fact that along paths whose effects on variables are described by either μ or ν, the equation b+c = 5 holds, even though neither b nor c are themselves constant. We could devise more complicated frameworks to avoid this particular problem, although the payoff from doing so is not clear. Fortunately, monotonicity is adequate for the iterative data-flow algorithm to "work," as we shall next see.   □

---

[14] We have to be careful reading an expression like $[f(\mu)](a)$. It says, we apply f to μ to get some mapping $f(\mu)$, which we call μ'. Then, we apply μ' to a, and the result is one of the values in the diagram of Fig. 10.60.

Meet-Over-Paths Solutions to Data-Flow Problems

Let us imagine that a flow graph has associated with each of its nodes a transfer function, one of the functions in the set F. For each block B, let f_B be the transfer function for B.

Consider any path $P = B_0 \rightarrow B_1 \rightarrow \cdots \rightarrow B_k$ from the initial node B_0 to some block B_k. We can define the *transfer function for P* to be the composition of $f_{B_0}, f_{B_1}, \ldots, f_{B_{k-1}}$. Note that f_{B_k} is not part of the composition, reflecting the point of view that this path is taken to reach the beginning of block B_k, not its end.

We have assumed that the values in V represent information about data used by the program, and that the confluence operator $\wedge$ tells how that information is combined when paths converge. It also makes sense to see the top element as representing "no information," since a path carrying the top element yields to any other path, as far as what information is carried after confluence of the paths. Thus, if B is a block in the flow graph, the information entering B should be computable by considering every possible path from the initial node to B and seeing what happens along that path, starting out with no information. That is, for each path P from B_0 to B, we compute $f_P(\top)$ and take the meet of all the resulting elements.

In principle, this meet could be over an infinite number of different values, since there are an infinite number of different paths. In practice, it is often adequate to consider only acyclic paths, and even when it is not, as for the constant computation framework discussed above, there are usually other reasons we can find to make this infinite meet be finite for any particular flow graph.

Formally, we define the *meet-over-paths solution* to a flow graph to be

$$mop(B) = \bigwedge_{\substack{\text{paths } P \\ \text{from } B_0 \text{ to } B}} f_P(\top)$$

The *mop* solution to a flow graph makes sense when we realize that as far as information reaching block B is concerned, the flow graph may as well be the one suggested in Fig. 10.61, where the transfer function associated with each of the (possibly infinite number of) paths $P_1, P_2, \ldots$, in the original flow graph has been given an entirely separate path to B. In Fig. 10.61, the information reaching B is given by the meet over all paths.

Conservative Solutions to Flow Problems

When we try to solve the data-flow equations that come from an arbitrary framework, we may or may not be able to obtain the *mop* solution easily. Fortunately, as with the concrete examples of data-flow frameworks in Sections 10.5 and 10.6, there is a safe direction in which to err, and the iterative data-flow algorithm we discussed in those sections turns out always to provide us with a safe solution. We say a solution $in[B]$ is a *safe solution* if $in[B] \leq mop(B)$ for all blocks B.

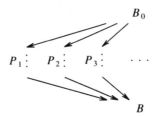

Fig. 10.61. Graph showing the set of all possible paths to B.

Despite what the reader might imagine, we did not pull this definition out of thin air. Recall that in any flow graph, the set of *apparent* paths to a node (those that are paths in the flow graph) can be a proper subset of the *real* paths, those that are taken on some execution of the program corresponding to this flow graph. In order that the result of the data-flow analysis be usable for whatever purpose we intend it, the data must still be safe if we modify the flow graph by deleting some paths, since we cannot in general distinguish real paths from apparent paths that are not real.

Suppose among the infinite set of paths suggested in Fig. 10.61, x is the meet of $f_P(\top)$ taken over all real paths P that are followed on some execution. Also, let y be the meet of $f_P(\top)$ over all other paths P. Thus, $mop(B)$ is $x \wedge y$. Then the true answer to our data-flow problem at node B is x, but the *mop* solution is $x \wedge y$. Recall that $x \wedge y \leq y$, since $(x \wedge y) \wedge y = x \wedge y$. Thus, the *mop* solution is $\leq$ the true solution.

While we may prefer the "true" solution to the data-flow problem, we shall almost surely have no efficient way to tell exactly which paths are real and which are not, so we are forced to accept the *mop* solution as the closest feasible solution. Thus, whatever use we make of the data-flow information must be consistent with the possibility that the solution we obtain is $\leq$ the true solution. Once we accept that, we should also be able to accept a solution that is $\leq$ the *mop* (and therefore $\leq$ the true solution). Such solutions are easier to obtain than the *mop* for those frameworks that are monotone but not distributive. For distributive frameworks, like those of Section 10.6, the simple iterative algorithm computes the *mop* solution.

The Iterative Algorithm for General Frameworks

There is an obvious generalization of Algorithm 10.2 that works for a large variety of frameworks. The iterative algorithm requires that the framework be monotone, and it requires finiteness, in the sense that the meet over the infinite set of paths suggested in Fig. 10.61 is equivalent to a meet over a finite subset. We shall give the algorithm and then discuss the ways in which we could assure finiteness. However, one common guarantee of finiteness is the one we have had all along: propagation along acyclic paths is sufficient.

Algorithm 10.18. Iterative solution to general data-flow frameworks.

Input. A data-flow graph, a set of "values" V, a set of functions F, a meet operation $\wedge$, and an assignment of a member of F to each node of the flow graph.

Output. A value $in[B]$ in V for each node of the flow graph.

Method. The algorithm is given in Fig. 10.62. As with the familiar iterative data-flow algorithms, we compute in and out for each node by successive approximations. We assume that f_B is the function in F associated with block B; that function plays the role of gen and $kill$ in Section 10.6.   □

```
1)    for each node B do /* initialize, assuming in[B] = ⊤ */
2)        out[B] := f_B[⊤];
3)    while changes to any out occur do
4)        for each block B, in depth-first order do begin
5)            in[B] :=      ⋀      out[P];
                        predecessors
                          P of B
              /* in above, the meet of an empty set is ⊤ */
6)            out[B] := f_B(in[B])
          end
```

Fig. 10.62. Iterative algorithm for general frameworks.

A Data-Flow Analysis Tool

We can now see the way the ideas of this section can be applied to a tool for data-flow analysis. Algorithm 10.18 depends for its working on the following subroutines.

1. A routine to apply a given f_B in F to a given value in V. This routine is used in lines (2) and (6) of Fig. 10.62.

2. A routine to apply the meet operator to two values in V; this routine is needed zero or more times in line (5).

3. A routine to tell whether two values are equal. This test is not made explicitly in Fig. 10.62, but it is implicit in the test for change in any of the values of out.

We also need to have specific data type declarations for F and V, so we can pass arguments to the routines mentioned above. The values of in and out in Fig. 10.62 are also of the type declared for V. Finally, we need a routine that will take the ordinary representation of the contents of a basic block, that is, a list of statements, and produce an element of F, the transfer function for that block.

Example 10.48. For the reaching definitions framework, we might first build a table that identified each statement of the given flow graph with a unique integer from 1 up to some maximum m. Then, the type of V could be bit vectors of length m. F could be represented by pairs of bit vectors of that size, i.e., by the *gen* and *kill* sets. The routine to construct the *gen* and *kill* bit vectors, given the statements of a block and the table associating definition statements with bit-vector positions, is straightforward, as are the routines to compute meets (logical or of bit vectors), compare bit vectors for equality, and apply functions defined by a *gen-kill* pair to bit vectors.   □

The data-flow analysis tool is thus little more than an implementation of Fig. 10.62 with calls to the given subroutines whenever a meet, function application, or comparison is needed. The tool would support a fixed representation of flow graphs, and thus be able to perform tasks like finding all the predecessors of a node, finding the depth-first ordering of the flow graph, or applying to each block the routine that computes the function in F associated with that block. The advantage of using such a tool is that the graph-manipulation and convergence-checking aspects of Algorithm 10.18 do not have to be rewritten for each data-flow analysis that we do.

Properties of Algorithm 10.18

We should make clear the assumptions under which Algorithm 10.18 actually works and exactly what the algorithm converges to when it does converge. First, if the framework is monotone and converges, then we claim the result of the algorithm is that $in[B] \leq mop(B)$ for all blocks B. The intuitive reason is that along any path $P = B_0, B_1, \ldots, B_k$ from the initial node to $B = B_k$, we can show by induction on i that the effect of the path from B_0 to B_i is felt after at most i iterations of the while-loop in Fig. 10.62. That is, if P_i is the path $B_0, \ldots, B_i$, then after i rounds, $in[B_i] \leq f_{P_i}(\top)$. Thus, when and if the algorithm converges, $in[B]$ will be $\leq f_P(\top)$ for every path P from B_0 to B. Using the rule that if $x \leq y$ and $x \leq z$, then $x \leq y \wedge z$,[15] we can show that $in[B] \leq mop(B)$.

When the framework is distributive, we can show Algorithm 10.18 does in fact converge to the *mop* solution. The essential idea is to prove that at all times during the running of the algorithm, $in[B]$ and $out[B]$ are each equal to the meet of $f_P(\top)$ for some set of paths P to the beginning and end of B, respectively. However, we show in the next example that need not be the case when the framework is monotone but not distributive.

Example 10.49. Let us exploit the example of nondistributivity of the

---

[15] There is the technicality that we must in principle show this rule not just for two values, y and z (from which follows the rule that if $x \leq y_i$ for any finite set of y_i's then $x \leq \wedge_i y_i$) but that the same rule holds for an infinite number of y_i's. However, in practice, whenever we get convergence of Algorithm 10.18, we shall find a finite number of paths such that the meet over all paths is equal to the meet over this finite set.

constant computation framework discussed in Example 10.47; the relevant flow graph is shown in Fig. 10.63. The mappings μ and ν coming out of B_2 and B_4 are the ones from Example 10.47. Mapping ρ, entering B_5, is $\mu \wedge \nu$, and σ is the mapping coming out of B_5, setting a to *nonconst*, even though every real path (and every apparent path), computes $a = 5$ after B_5.

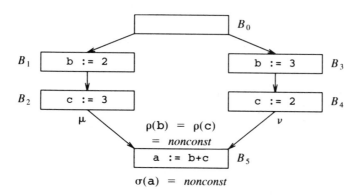

Fig. 10.63. Example of solution less than *mop* solution.

The problem, intuitively, is that Algorithm 10.18, dealing with a nondistributive framework, behaves as if some sequences of nodes that are not even apparent paths (paths in the flow graph), were real paths. Thus, in Fig. 10.63, the algorithm behaves as if paths like $B_0 \rightarrow B_1 \rightarrow B_4 \rightarrow B_5$ or $B_0 \rightarrow B_3 \rightarrow B_2 \rightarrow B_5$ were real paths, setting b and c to a combination of values that do not sum to five.   □

Convergence of Algorithm 10.18

There are various ways that we could prove Algorithm 10.18 converges for a particular framework. Probably the most common case is where only acyclic paths are needed, i.e., we can show that the meet over acyclic paths is the same as the *mop* solution, over all paths. If that is the case, not only does the algorithm converge, it will normally do so very rapidly, in two more passes than the depth of the flow graph, as we discussed in Section 10.10.

On the other hand, frameworks like our constant computation example require more than acyclic paths be considered. For example, Fig. 10.64 shows a simple flow graph where we have to consider the path $B_1 \rightarrow B_2 \rightarrow B_2 \rightarrow B_3$ to realize that x does not have a constant value on entering B_3.

However, for constant computations, we can reason that Algorithm 10.18 converges as follows. First of all, it is easy to show for an arbitrary monotone framework that $in[B]$ and $out[B]$, for any block B, form a nonincreasing sequence, in the sense that the new value for one of these variables is always $\leq$ the old value. If we recall Fig. 10.60, the lattice diagram for the values of mappings applied to variables, we realize that for any variable, the value of

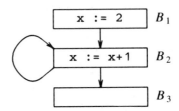

Fig. 10.64. Flow graph requiring cyclic path be included in *mop*.

in[*B*] or *out*[*B*] can only drop twice, once from *undef* to a constant, and once from that constant to *nonconst*.

Suppose there are *n* nodes and *v* variables. Then on every iteration of the while-loop in Fig. 10.62, at least one variable must have its value drop in some *out*[*B*], or the algorithm converges, and even infinite iteration of the while-loop will not change the values of the *in*'s or *out*'s. Thus, the number of iterations is limited to $2nv$; if that number of changes occurs, then every variable must have reached *nonconst* at every block of the flow graph.

Fixing the Initialization

In some data-flow problems, there is a discrepancy between what Algorithm 10.18 gives us as a solution and what we intuitively want. Recall that for available expressions, $\wedge$ is intersection, so $\top$ must be the set of all expressions. Since Algorithm 10.18 initially assumes *in*[*B*] is $\top$ for each block *B*, including the initial node, the *mop* solution produced by Algorithm 10.18 is actually the set of expressions that, assuming they are available at the initial node (which they are not), would be available on entrance to block *B*.

The difference, of course, is that there might be paths from the initial node to *B* along which an expression x+y is neither generated nor killed. Algorithm 10.18 would say x+y is available, when in fact it is not, because no variable along that path can be found to hold its value. The fixup is simple. We can either modify Algorithm 10.18 so that for the available expression framework, *in*[B_0] is set and held equal to the empty set, or we can modify the flow graph by introducing a dummy initial node, a predecessor of the real initial node, that kills every expression.

10.12 ESTIMATION OF TYPES

We now come to a data-flow problem that is more challenging than the frameworks of the previous section. Various languages, ranging from APL to SETL to the many dialects of Lisp, do not require that the types of variables be declared, and even permit the same variable to hold values of different types at different times. Serious attempts to compile such languages into efficient code have used data-flow analysis to infer the types of variables, since code to, say, add two integers, is far more efficient than a call to a general routine that can add two objects of a variety of types (e.g., integer, real, vector).

Our first guess might be that computing types of variables is something like computing reaching definitions. We can associate a set of possible types with each variable at each point. The confluence operator is union on sets of types, since if variable x has set S_1 of possible types on one path and set S_2 on another, then x has any of the types in $S_1 \cup S_2$ after the confluence of the paths. As control passes through a statement, we may be able to make some inferences about the types of variables based on the operators in the statement, the possible types of their operands, and the types they produce as results. Example 6.6, which dealt with an operator that could multiply both integers and complex numbers, was an example of this sort of inference.

Unfortunately, there are at least two problems with this approach.

1. The set of possible types for a variable may be infinite.

2. Type determination usually requires both forward and backward propagation of information to obtain precise estimates of possible types. Thus, even the framework of Section 10.11 is not general enough to do justice to the problem.

Before considering point (1), let us examine some of the kinds of inferences about types that can be made in familiar languages.

Example 10.50. Consider the statements

```
i := a[j]
k := a[i]
```

Suppose at first we do not know anything about the types of the variables a, i, j, and k. However, let us suppose that the array accessing operator [ ] requires an integer argument. By examining the first statement we may infer that j is an integer at that point, and a is an array of elements of some type. Then, the second statement tells us that i is an integer.

Now, we may propagate inferences backward. If i was computed to be an integer in the first statement, then the type of expression a[i] must be integer, which means that a must be an array of integers. We can then reason forward again to discover that the value assigned to k by the second statement must also be an integer. Notice it is impossible to discover that the elements of a are integers by reasoning only forward or only backward.   □

Dealing with Infinite Type Sets

There are numerous examples of pathological cases where the set of possible types for a variable really is infinite. For example, SETL allows a statement like

```
x := { x }
```

to be executed inside a loop. If we start out knowing only that x could be an integer, then after we consider one iteration of the loop, we realize x could be either an integer or a set of integers. After considering a second iteration we find that x could also be a set of sets of integers, and so on.

A similar problem could occur in a typeless version of a conventional language like C, where the statement

    x = &x

with the initial possibility that x is an integer leads us to discover that x can have any type of the form

    pointer to pointer to $\cdots$ pointer to integer

The traditional way to deal with such problems is to reduce the set of possible types to a finite number. The general idea is to group the infinite number of possible types into a finite number of classes, generally keeping the simpler types by themselves, and grouping the most complicated, and hopefully the rarest, types into large classes. When we do so, we have to exercise judgement as to how we make inferences about the interaction between types and operators. The following example suggests what can be done.

Example 10.51. Let us continue the example of Chapter 6, where we used the operator $\rightarrow$ as a type constructor for functions. Here, our set of types will include the basic type *int*, and all types of the form $\tau \rightarrow \sigma$, representing the type of a function with domain type τ and range type σ, where τ and σ are types in our set. Thus, our set of types is infinite, including such types as

$$(int \rightarrow int) \rightarrow ((int \rightarrow int) \rightarrow int)$$

To reduce this set to a finite number of classes, we shall restrict a type expression to have only one function type constructor $\rightarrow$, by replacing subexpressions in a type expression containing at least one occurrence of $\rightarrow$ by the name *func*. Thus, there are five different types:

  int
  int $\rightarrow$ *int*
  int $\rightarrow$ *func*
  func $\rightarrow$ *int*
  func $\rightarrow$ *func*

We shall represent sets of types as bit vectors of length five, with the positions corresponding to the five types in the order listed above. Thus, 01111 represents the type for any function application, i.e., for anything but *int*. Note that this is in a sense the type of *func*, since a *func* may not be an integer.

The basic assignment statement for our model is

    x := f(y)

Knowing the possible types of f and y, we can determine the possible types

of **x** by looking up the type in the table of Fig. 10.65. If **f** can be of any
type in the set S_1 and y of any type in set S_2, we take each pair τ in S_1 and σ
in S_2 and look up the entry in the row for τ and the column for σ, which we
call $\tau(\sigma)$. We then take the union of the results of all these lookups to get the
set of possible types for **x**.

τ	σ				
	int	*int→int*	*int→func*	*func→int*	*func→func*
int	00000	00000	00000	00000	00000
int→int	10000	00000	00000	00000	00000
int→func	01111	00000	00000	00000	00000
func→int	00000	10000	10000	10000	10000
func→func	00000	01111	01111	01111	01111

Fig. 10.65. The value of $\tau(\sigma)$.

For example, if $\tau = int \rightarrow func$ and $\sigma = int$, then $\tau(\sigma) = 01111$. That is,
the result of applying a mapping of type $int \rightarrow func$ to an int is a *func*, which
means a mapping of any of the four types besides *int*. We cannot tell which
because our smearing of an infinite number of types into five classes precludes
our knowing.

For a second example, let τ be as before and $\sigma = int \rightarrow int$. Then
$\tau(\sigma) = 00000$ because the domain type of τ is definitely unequal to the type
σ, and therefore the mapping is inapplicable.   □

A Simple Type System

To illustrate the ideas behind our type-inference algorithms, we introduce a
simple type system and language based on Example 10.51. The types are the
five illustrated in that example. The statements of our language are of three
kinds.

1. **read x**. A value of **x** is read from the input, and presumably, nothing
    is known about its type.

2. **x := f(y)**. The value of **x** is set to be that obtained by applying func-
    tion **f** to value **y**. What is known about the type of **x** after the assign-
    ment is summarized in Fig. 10.65.

3. **use x as τ**. When we go through such a statement, we may assume
    that the program is correct, and therefore, the type of **x** can only be τ
    both before and after the statement. The value and type of **x** are not
    affected by the statement.

We infer types by performing a data-flow analysis on a flow graph of a program consisting of statements of these three types. For simplicity, we assume

that all blocks consist of a single statement. The values of *in* and *out* for blocks are mappings from variables to sets of the five types from Example 10.51.

Initially, each *in* and *out* maps every variable to the set of all five types. As we propagate information, we reduce the set of types associated with certain variables at certain points, until at some time we cannot reduce any of these sets any further. The resulting sets will be assumed to indicate the possible types of each variable at each point. That assumption is conservative, since a type is eliminated only if we can prove (given that the program is correct) that the type is impossible. Normally, we expect to take advantage of the fact that some types are impossible, not that they are possible, so "too large" is the safe direction for errors.

We use two schemes to modify the *in*'s and *out*'s: a "forward" scheme and a "backward" scheme. The forward scheme uses the statement in a block B and the value of *in*$[B]$ to restrict *out*$[B]$,[16] and the backward scheme does the opposite. In each scheme, the confluence operator is "variable-wise union," in the sense that the confluence of two mappings α and β is that mapping γ such that for all variables **x**,

$$\gamma[\mathbf{x}] = \alpha[\mathbf{x}] \cup \beta[\mathbf{x}]$$

The Forward Scheme

Let us suppose we have a block B with *in*$[B]$ the mapping μ and *out*$[B]$ the mapping ν. The forward scheme lets us restrict ν. The rules for restricting ν depend upon what instruction is found in block B, naturally.

1. If the statement is read **x**, then any type could be read. If we already know something about the type of **x** after the read, we must not forget it during this forward pass, so we simply do not change $\nu(\mathbf{x})$ on the forward pass. For all other variables **y**, we set

    $$\nu(\mathbf{y}) := \nu(\mathbf{y}) \cap \mu(\mathbf{y})$$

2. Now suppose the statement is use **x** as τ. After this statement, τ is the only possible type for **x**. If we already know that type τ is impossible for **x**, then there is no possible type for **x** after the statement. These observations can be summarized by:

---

[16] It is worth noting that in traditional forward data-flow schemes, we did not restrict *out*, but rather computed it anew from *in* each time. We could do this because *in*'s and *out*'s always changed in one direction, either always growing or always shrinking. However, in a problem like type inference, where we alternately perform forward and backward passes, we may have a situation where the backward pass has left *out* much smaller than we can justify by applying the forward rules to *in*. Thus, we must not accidentally raise *out* on the forward pass, only to have it lowered again (but perhaps not as far) on the backward pass. A similar remark applies to the backward pass; we must restrict *in*, not recompute it.

$$\nu(\mathbf{x}) := \nu(\mathbf{x}) \cap \{\tau\}$$
$$\nu(\mathbf{y}) := \nu(\mathbf{y}) \cap \mu(\mathbf{y}) \quad \text{for } \mathbf{y} \neq \mathbf{x}$$

3. Now, consider the case that the statement is $\mathbf{x} := \mathbf{f}(\mathbf{y})$. The only possible types for $\mathbf{x}$ after the statement are those that

    i)   are possible according to the present value of ν, and

    ii) are the result of applying a mapping of some type τ to type σ, and τ and σ are types that $\mathbf{f}$ and $\mathbf{y}$, respectively, could have before the statement is executed.

    Formally,

    $$\nu(\mathbf{x}) := \nu(\mathbf{x}) \cap \{\rho \mid \rho = \tau(\sigma), \tau \text{ is in } \mu(\mathbf{f}), \text{ and } \sigma \text{ is in } \mu(\mathbf{y})\}$$

    We may also make some inferences about the types of $\mathbf{f}$ and $\mathbf{y}$, since on the assumption of program correctness, $\mathbf{f}$ cannot have a type that doesn't apply to some type of $\mathbf{y}$, and $\mathbf{y}$ cannot have a type that cannot serve as the argument type for some possible type of $\mathbf{f}$. That is, if $\mathbf{f} \neq \mathbf{x}$ then

    $$\nu(\mathbf{f}) := \nu(\mathbf{f}) \cap \{\tau \text{ in } \mu(\mathbf{f}) \mid \text{for some } \sigma \text{ in } \mu(\mathbf{y}), \tau(\sigma) \neq \varnothing\}$$

    if $\mathbf{y} \neq \mathbf{x}$ then

    $$\nu(\mathbf{y}) := \nu(\mathbf{y}) \cap \{\sigma \text{ in } \mu(\mathbf{y}) \mid \text{for some } \tau \text{ in } \mu(\mathbf{f}), \tau(\sigma) \neq \varnothing\}$$

    for all other $\mathbf{z}$,

    $$\nu(\mathbf{z}) := \nu(\mathbf{z}) \cap \mu(\mathbf{z})$$

The Backward Scheme

Now let us consider how, in a backward pass, we can restrict μ based on what ν tells us and what the statement tells us.

1. If the statement is `read` $\mathbf{x}$, it is easy to see that no new inferences about impossible types before the statement can be made, so $\mu(\mathbf{x})$ does not change. However, for all $\mathbf{y} \neq \mathbf{x}$, we may propagate information backward by setting $\mu(\mathbf{y}) := \mu(\mathbf{y}) \cap \nu(\mathbf{y})$.

2. If we have the statement `use` $\mathbf{x}$ `as` τ, then we can make the same sort of inference we made in the forward direction; $\mathbf{x}$ can only have type τ before the statement, and any other variable's types are those that are believed possible both before and after the statement. That is:

    $$\mu(\mathbf{x}) := \mu(\mathbf{x}) \cap \{\tau\}$$
    $$\mu(\mathbf{y}) := \mu(\mathbf{y}) \cap \nu(\mathbf{y}) \quad \text{for } \mathbf{y} \neq \mathbf{x}$$

3. As before, the most complex case is a statement of the form $\mathbf{x} := \mathbf{f}(\mathbf{y})$. To begin, nothing new can be inferred about $\mathbf{x}$ before the statement, unless $\mathbf{x}$ happens to be one of $\mathbf{f}$ or $\mathbf{y}$. Thus, $\mu(\mathbf{x})$ is not changed except by the following rules concerning $\mathbf{f}$ and $\mathbf{y}$. Next, note that as in the forward rules, we may make inferences from the fact that the types of $\mathbf{f}$ and $\mathbf{y}$ must be compatible before the statement. However, if $\mathbf{f} \neq \mathbf{x}$, we may

also restrict $\mu(\mathbf{f})$ to the types in $\nu(\mathbf{f})$, and an analogous statement holds about $\mathbf{y}$. On the other hand, if $\mathbf{f} = \mathbf{x}$, then the types of $\mathbf{f}$ after the statement are unrelated to the types of $\mathbf{f}$ before, so no such restriction is permitted. Again, an analogous statement holds if $\mathbf{y} = \mathbf{x}$. It is useful to define a special mapping, just for $\mathbf{f}$ and $\mathbf{y}$, to reflect this decision. Thus, we define:

if $\mathbf{f} = \mathbf{x}$ then $\mu_1(\mathbf{f}) := \mu(\mathbf{f})$ else $\mu_1(\mathbf{f}) := \mu(\mathbf{f}) \cap \nu(\mathbf{f})$
if $\mathbf{y} = \mathbf{x}$ then $\mu_1(\mathbf{y}) := \mu(\mathbf{y})$ else $\mu_1(\mathbf{y}) := \mu(\mathbf{y}) \cap \nu(\mathbf{y})$

Now, we can restrict $\mathbf{f}$ and $\mathbf{y}$ to those types that are compatible with the other's set of types. At the same time, we can restrict the types of $\mathbf{f}$ and $\mathbf{y}$ based on the fact that they must not only be compatible, but must yield a type that ν says $\mathbf{x}$ may have. Thus, we define:

$$\mu(\mathbf{f}) := \{\tau \text{ in } \mu_1(\mathbf{f}) \mid \text{for some } \sigma \text{ in } \mu_1(\mathbf{y}), \tau(\sigma) \cap \nu(\mathbf{x}) \neq \varnothing\}$$

$$\mu(\mathbf{y}) := \{\sigma \text{ in } \mu_1(\mathbf{y}) \mid \text{for some } \tau \text{ in } \mu_1(\mathbf{f}), \tau(\sigma) \cap \nu(\mathbf{x}) \neq \varnothing\}$$

$$\mu(\mathbf{z}) := \mu(\mathbf{z}) \cap \nu(\mathbf{z}) \text{ for } \mathbf{z} \text{ not equal to } \mathbf{x}, \mathbf{y}, \text{ or } \mathbf{f}$$

Before proceeding to the type determination algorithm, let us recall from our discussion of reaching definitions in Section 10.5 that if we start with the false assumption that some definition d is available at some point in a loop, we may erroneously propagate that fact around the loop, leaving us with a set of reaching definitions that is larger than necessary. A similar problem can occur in type determination, where the assumption that a variable can have a certain type "proves" itself as we go around a loop. Therefore, we shall introduce a 33rd value, in addition to the 32 sets of types from Example 10.51, that a mapping μ may assign to a variable, the value *undef*. This use of *undef* is similar to its use in the constant propagation framework of the previous section.

During confluence, the value *undef* yields to any other value, i.e., it acts like the type 00000. On the other hand, when intersecting sets of types, e.g., computing $\mu(\mathbf{x}) \cap \nu(\mathbf{x})$, the value *undef* also yields to any other set of types; that is, it functions like the type 11111. Thus, for example, when we read a value of a variable $\mathbf{x}$, the fact that the "type" of $\mathbf{x}$ was thought to be *undef* after the read is overruled, and the type of $\mathbf{x}$ becomes 11111.

Algorithm 10.19.

Input. A flow graph whose blocks are single statements of the three types (read, assignment, and use-as) mentioned above.

Output. A set of types for each variable at each point. The set is conservative, in the sense that any real computation must lead to a type in the set.

Method. We compute a mapping $in[B]$ and a mapping $out[B]$ for each block B. Each mapping sends the program's variables to sets of types in the type system introduced in Example 10.51. Initially, all mappings send each variable to *undef*.

We then make alternate forward and backward passes through the flow graph, until consecutive forward and backward passes both fail to make any changes. The forward pass is performed by:

> **for** each block B in depth-first order **do begin**
> $\qquad in[B] := \bigcup\limits_{pred.\ P\ of\ B} out[P];$
> $\qquad out[B] :=$ function of $in[B]$ and $out[B]$ as defined above
> **end**

The backward pass is:

> **for** each block B in reverse depth-first order **do begin**
> $\qquad out[B] := \bigcup\limits_{succ.\ S\ of\ B} in[S];$
> $\qquad in[B] :=$ function of $in[B]$ and $out[B]$ as defined above
> **end**   □

Example 10.52. Consider the simple straight-line program shown in Fig. 10.66. We are interested in four mappings, which we designate μ_1 through μ_4. Each μ_i is both $out[B_i]$ and $in[B_{i+1}]$. Technically, B_1 is not supposed to have two statements, because we have assumed blocks are single statements in this section. However, we are not concerned with what happens before the end of B_1, because all variables can have any type there.

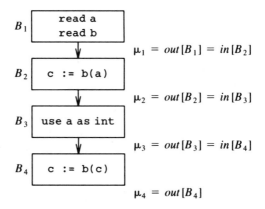

Fig. 10.66. Example program.

It turns out that we need five passes before convergence occurs and another two to detect that convergence has occurred. These passes are summarized in Fig. 10.67(a)–(e). The first pass is forward. When considering B_2, we discover that b cannot be an integer, because it is used as a mapping. We also discover that a is used as an integer in B_3, and therefore can only be mapped to *int* in μ_3 and μ_4. These observations are summarized in Fig. 10.67(a).

	a	b	c
μ_1	11111	11111	*undef*
μ_2	11111	01111	11111
μ_3	10000	01111	11111
μ_4	10000	01111	11111

(a) FORWARD

	a	b	c
μ_1	10000	01100	*undef*
μ_2	10000	01111	11111
μ_3	10000	01111	11111
μ_4	10000	01111	11111

(b) BACKWARD

	a	b	c
μ_1	10000	01100	*undef*
μ_2	10000	01100	11111
μ_3	10000	01100	11111
μ_4	10000	01100	11111

(c) FORWARD

	a	b	c
μ_1	10000	01000	*undef*
μ_2	10000	01100	10000
μ_3	10000	01100	10000
μ_4	10000	01100	11111

(d) BACKWARD

	a	b	c
μ_1	10000	01000	*undef*
μ_2	10000	01000	10000
μ_3	10000	01000	10000
μ_4	10000	01000	10000

(e) FORWARD

Fig. 10.67. Simulation of Algorithm 10.19 on flow graph of Fig. 10.66.

The second pass, shown in Fig. 10.67(b), is backward. On this pass, when considering B_2, we know that a must be an integer when b is applied to it. Thus, the type of b could only be *int → int* or *int → func*. On the third pass, which is forward, this restriction on the type of b propagates all the way down the flow graph, as shown in Fig. 10.67(c).

The fourth pass, backward, is shown in Fig. 10.67(d). Here, the fact that c is an argument of b in B_3 tells us that c can only be an integer. Also, when we consider B_2, we find that the result of b(a) can only be of the type of c, which is *int*. This fact rules out the possibility that b is of type *int → func*. Finally, in Fig. 10.67(e), we see how on the fifth pass, forward, these facts about b and c propagate. On further passes, no new inferences can be made. In this case, we have reduced the sets of possible types to single types for each variable at each point; a and c are integers, and b is a mapping from integers to integers. In general, we might be left with several possible types for a variable at a point.   □

10.13 SYMBOLIC DEBUGGING OF OPTIMIZED CODE

A *symbolic debugger* is a system that allows us to look at a program's data while that program is running. The debugger is usually called when a program error, such as an overflow, occurs or when certain statements, indicated by the programmer in the source code, are reached. Once invoked, the symbolic debugger allows the programmer to examine, and possibly change, any of the variables that are currently accessible to the running program.

In order for a user command like "show me the current value of a" to be intelligible to the debugger, it must have available certain information.

1. There must be a way to associate an identifier like a with the location it represents. Thus, the portion of the symbol table that assigns to each variable a location, e.g., a place in a global data area or in an activation record for some procedure, must be recorded by the compiler and preserved for the debugger to use. For example, this information might be encoded into the load module for the program.

2. There must be scope information, so we can disambiguate references to an identifier that is declared more than once, and so that we can tell, given we are in some procedure p, what other procedures' data is accessible and how do we find that data on the stack or other run-time structure. Again, this information must be taken from the symbol table of the compiler and preserved for future use by the debugger.

3. We must know where we are in the program when the debugger is invoked. This information is embedded by the compiler in the call to the debugger when the compiler handles a user-declared invocation of the debugger. It is also obtained from the exception handler when a run-time error causes the debugger to be called.

4. In order that program-location information, mentioned in (3), make sense to the user, there must be a table associating each machine language statement with the source statement from which it came. This table can be prepared by the compiler as it generates code.

While the design of a symbolic debugger is interesting in its own right, we shall consider only the difficulties that occur when trying to write a symbolic debugger for an optimizing compiler. At first glance, it might seem that there is no need to debug an optimized program. In the normal development cycle, as the user debugs a program, a fast, nonoptimizing compiler is used until the user is satisfied that the source program is correct. Only then is an optimizing compiler used.

Unfortunately, a program may run correctly with a nonoptimizing compiler, and then fail, with the same input data, when compiled by the optimizing compiler. For example, a bug may exist in the optimizing compiler, or, by reordering operations, the optimizing compiler may introduce an overflow or underflow. Also, even "nonoptimizing" compilers may do some simple transformations, like elimination of local common subexpressions or reordering of code within a basic block, that make a big difference in how hard it is to design a symbolic debugger. Thus, we need to consider what algorithms and data structures to use in a symbolic debugger for an optimizing compiler that transforms basic blocks in arbitrary ways.

Deducing Values of Variables in Basic Blocks

For simplicity, assume that both the source and object code are sequences of intermediate statements. Treating the source as intermediate code presents no problems, since the latter is more general than the former. For example, the user may only be allowed to put breaks (calls to the debugger) between source statements, but here we allow breaks after any intermediate statement. Treating the object code as intermediate code is questionable only if the optimizer breaks a single intermediate statement into several machine statements that get separated. For example, for some reason, we may compile the two intermediate statements

```
u := v + w
x := y + z
```

into code where the two additions are performed in different registers and interleaved. If that is the case, we can treat the loads and stores of registers as if the registers were temporaries in intermediate code, for example:

```
r1 := v
r2 := y
r1 := r1 + w
r2 := r2 + z
 u := r1
 x := r2
```

Several problems occur when interacting with the user about a block, where the user thinks the source block is being executed, but in fact, an optimized version of that block is running:

1. Suppose we are executing the program that results from "optimizing" some basic block of the source program, and while executing statement a:=b+c, an overflow occurs. We must tell the user that an error has occurred in one of the source statements. Since b+c may be a common subexpression appearing in two or more of the source statements, to which statement do we charge the error?

2. A harder problem occurs if the user of the debugger wants to see the "current" value of some variable d. In the optimized program, d may last have been assigned at some statement s. But in the source program, s may come after the statement at which the debugger was invoked, so the value of d that is available to the debugger is not the one that the user thinks is the "current" value of d according to the listing of the

source code. Similarly, s may precede the statement invoking the debugger, but in the source there is another assignment to d between them, so the value of d available to the debugger is out of date. Is it possible to make the correct value of d available to the user? For example, could it be the value of some other variable in the optimized version, or could it be computed from the values of other variables?

3.   Finally, if the user places a break after some statement of the source code, when should control be given to the debugger during the running of the optimized code?

One solution might be to run the unoptimized version of the block along with the optimized version, to make the correct value of each variable available at all times. We reject this "solution," because the subtlest of bugs, especially compiler-introduced bugs, may disappear when the instructions that caused the problem are separated from one another in time or space.

The solution we adopt is to provide enough information about each block to the debugger that it can at least answer the question: is it possible to provide the correct value of variable a, and if so, how? The structure we use to embody this information is the dag of the basic block, annotated with information about which variables hold the value corresponding to a node in the dag, at what times in both the source and optimized programs. The notation

  a: $i - j$

attached to a node means that the value represented by that node is stored in variable a from the beginning of statement i through the portion of statement j just before its assignment occurs. If $j = \infty$, then a holds this value until the end of the block.

Example 10.53. In Fig. 10.68(a) we see a basic block of source code, and in Fig. 10.68(b) is a possible "optimized" version of that code. Figure 10.69 shows the dag for either block, with indications of the ranges in which the variables hold those values in both the source and optimized code. Primes are used to indicate that a statement range is in the optimized code. For example, the node labeled + is the value of c in the source code from the beginning of statement (2) until just before the assignment in statement (3). It is also the value of d in the source from the beginning of statement (3) until the end. In addition, the same node is the value of d in the optimized code from statement (2′) until the end.   □

Now we can answer the first question raised above. Suppose that an error, such as overflow, occurs while executing statement j' of the optimized code. Since the same value would be computed by any source statement that computes the same dag node as statement j', it makes sense to report to the user that the error occurred at the first source statement computing this node. Thus, in Example 10.53, if the error occurred at statement 1′, 2′, 3′, or 4′, we would report that it occurred at statement 1, 5, 3, and 6, respectively. No

$$
\begin{array}{llll}
(1) & c := a+b & (1') & d := a+b \\
(2) & d := c & (2') & t := b*e \\
(3) & c := c-e & (3') & a := d-e \\
(4) & a := d-e & (4') & b := d/t \\
(5) & b := b*e & (5') & c := a \\
(6) & b := d/b & &
\end{array}
$$

$$
\qquad\qquad (a) \qquad\qquad\qquad\qquad (b)
$$

Fig. 10.68. Source and optimized code.

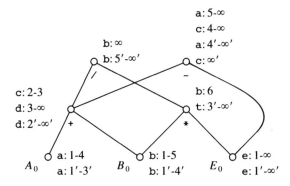

Fig. 10.69. Annotated dag.

error can occur at statement $5'$, because no value is computed. We defer details of how corresponding statements are computed until Example 10.54, below.

We can also answer the second question. Suppose we are at statement j' of the optimized code, and the user is told that control is at statement i of the source, where an error occurred. If the user asks to see the value of a variable x, we must find a variable y (frequently, but not always, y is x) such that the value of x at statement i of the source is the same dag node as y at statement j' in the optimized code. We inspect the dag to see what node represents the value of x at i, and we may read off from that node all the variables of the object program that ever have that value, to see if one of them holds this value at j'.

If so, we are done; if not, we may still compute the value of x at i from other variables at j'. Let n be the node for x at time i. Then we may consider the children of n, say m and p, to see if both these nodes represent the value of some variable at time j. If, say, there is a variable for m, but none for p, we may consider the children of p, recursively. Ultimately, we either find a way to compute the value of x at time i or conclude that there is no such way. If we find a way to compute the values of m and p, then we compute them and apply the operator at n to compute the value of x at time i.[17]

Example 10.54. Suppose that when executing the code of Fig. 10.68(b), an error occurs at statement $2'$. The statement was computing the node labeled *∗* in Fig. 10.69, and the first source statement computing that value is statement 5. Thus we report an error in statement 5.

In Fig. 10.70, we have tabulated the dag node corresponding to each variable in both the source and optimized code, at the beginning of statements 5 and $2'$, respectively; nodes are indicated by their label, either an operator symbol or an initial value symbol like A_0. We also indicate how to compute the value at time 5 from the values of variables at time $2'$. For example, if the user asks for the value of a, the value of the node labeled – is given. No variable has that value at time $2'$, but fortunately, there are variables, d and e, that hold the value of each of the children of node – at time $2'$, so we may print the value of a by computing the value of d-e.   □

VARIABLE	VALUE AT		OBTAIN BY
	TIME $2'$	TIME 5	
a	A_0	–	d-e
b	B_0	B_0	b
c	undefined	–	d-e
d	+	+	d
e	E_0	E_0	e
t	undefined		

Fig. 10.70. Values of variables at times $2'$ and 5.

Now let us answer the third question: how to handle debugger calls inserted by the user. In a sense the answer is trivial; if the user asks for a break after statement i in the source program, we can halt execution at the beginning of the block. If the user wants to see the value of some variable x after statement i, we consult the annotated dag to see what node represents the desired value of x, and we compute that value from the initial values of variables for that block.

On the other hand, we can leave less work for the debugger, and also avoid

---

[17] A subtlety occurs if the computation of the value of node n causes another error. We must then report to the user that the error actually occurred earlier, at the first source statement computing the value of n.

some situations where attempts to compute a value lead to errors that must be announced to the user, if we postpone the call to the debugger to as late a time as possible. It is easy to compute the last statement j' in the optimized program, such that we call the debugger after j' and pretend to the user that the call was made after statement i of the source program. To find j', let S be the set of nodes of the dag that correspond to the value of some variable of the source program immediately after statement i. We may be asked by the user to compute any value in S. Thus, we may break after statement j' of the optimized code only if for each node n in S there is some $k' > j'$ such that some variable is associated with node n at time k' in the optimized code. For then we know that the value of n is either available immediately after statement j', or it will be computed sometime after statement j'. In the former case, it is trivial to compute the value of n if we break after j', while in the latter case, we know that the values available after j' are sufficient to compute n somehow.

Example 10.55. Consider the source and optimized code of Fig. 10.68 again, and suppose that the user inserts a break after statement (3) of the source code. To find the set S, inspect the dag of Fig. 10.69, and see which nodes have source-program variables attached to them at time 4. These nodes are the ones labeled A_0, B_0, E_0, +, and − in that figure.

Now, we look at the dag again to find the largest j' such that each of the nodes in S has some variable of the optimized code attached to it at a time strictly greater than j'. The nodes labeled +, −, and E_0 present no problem, since their values are carried by variables d, a, and e, respectively, at time ∞'. Nodes A_0 and B_0 do limit the value of j', and the earliest of these to lose its value is A_0, whose value is destroyed by statement 3'. Thus, $j' = 2'$ is the largest possible value of j'; that is, if the user asks for a break after source statement 3, we can give him the break after statement 2'.   □

The reader should be aware of a subtlety in Example 10.55, for which no really good solution exists. If we run the optimized code through statement 2' before we call the debugger, an error in the computation of b*e at statement 2' (for example, an underflow) may cause the debugger to be invoked before the intended call. However, since the computation corresponding to statement 2' doesn't occur until statement 5 in the source program, we are going to tell the user that the error occurred at statement 5. It will be somewhat mysterious to the user how we got to statement 5 without calling the debugger at statement 3. Probably the best solution to this problem is not to allow j' to be so large that there is a statement k' of the optimized code, with $k' \leq j'$, such that the source code does not compute the value computed by k' until after the statement i at which the break was placed.

Effects of Global Optimization

When our compiler performs global optimizations, there are harder problems for the symbolic debugger to solve, and frequently, no way to find the correct value of a variable at a point exists. Two important transformations that do not cause significant trouble are induction-variable elimination and global common subexpression elimination; in each case the problem can be localized to a few blocks and treated in the manner discussed above.

Induction-Variable Elimination

If we eliminate a source program induction variable i in favor of some member of i's family, say t, then there is some linear function relating i and t. Moreover, if we follow the methods of Section 10.7, the optimized code will change t in exactly those blocks in which i is changed, so the linear relationship between i and t always holds. Thus, after taking into account reordering of statements within a block that assigns to t (and in the source, assigns to i), we can provide the user with the "current" value of i by a linear transformation on t.

We have to be careful if i is not defined prior to the loop, since t surely will be assigned before loop entry, and we might thus provide a value for i at a point in the program where the user expects i to be undefined. Fortunately, it is usual for a source-program variable that is an induction variable to be initialized prior to the loop, and only compiler-generated variables (whose values the user cannot ask for) will be undefined on entry to the loop. If that is not the case for some induction variable i, then we have a problem similar to that for code motion, to be discussed below.

Global Common Subexpression Elimination

If we perform a global common subexpression elimination for expression a+b, we also affect a limited number of blocks in simple ways. If t is the variable used to hold the value of a+b, then at certain blocks computing a+b we might replace

```
c := a+b
```

by

```
t := a+b
c := t
```

This sort of change can be handled by the methods for basic blocks already discussed.

In other blocks, a use such as d:=a+b may be replaced by a use d:=t. To handle this situation by previous methods, we have only to note in the dag for this block that the value of t remains for all time at the value of the node for a+b (which will appear in the dag for the source code, but would not otherwise appear in the dag for the optimized code).

Code Motion

Other transformations are not so easy to handle. For example, suppose we move a statement

s: a:=b+c

out of a loop because it is loop-invariant. If we call the debugger within the loop, we do not know whether statement s would have been executed yet in the source program, and thus we cannot know whether the current value of a is the one the user would see in the source program.

One possibility is to insert into the optimized code a new variable that, within the loop, indicates whether a has been assigned in the loop, (which can only occur at the old position of statement s). However, this strategy may not always be suitable, because for absolute reliability, only the real code, not a version of the code constructed specially for debugging purposes, should be used.

There is a common special case where we can do better, however. Suppose that the block B containing statement s in the source program divides the loop into two sets of nodes: those that dominate B and those dominated by it. Moreover, assume that all predecessors of the header are dominated by B, as suggested in Fig. 10.71. Then the first time through the blocks that dominate B, we may assume a has not been assigned in the loop, while the first time through the blocks that B dominates, a has been assigned at statement s. Of course, the second and subsequent times through the loop, a has surely been assigned at s.

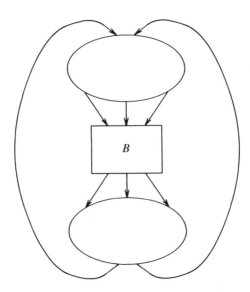

Fig. 10.71. A block that divides a loop into two parts.

If the call to the debugger is caused by a run-time error, there is a good chance that the error is exposed the first time through the loop. If that is the case, then we have only to know whether we are above B or below it in Fig. 10.71. Then we know whether the value of a is that defined at s, in which case we can just print the value of a produced by the optimized code, or whether the value of a is that which a had on entry to the loop in the source version of the program. In the latter case, there is little we can do, except if

1. the debugger has reaching definition information available to it, for both the source and optimized program,

2. there is a unique definition of a that reaches the header in the source program, and

3. that definition is also the unique definition of some variable x that reaches the point where the debugger was called.

If all these conditions hold, then we can print the value of x and say it is the value of a.

The reader should be aware that this line of reasoning does not hold if the debugger was called by a user-inserted break point, for then we cannot have any reason to suspect that we are going around the loop for the first time. However, if user-inserted breaks are being used, then it might also be reasonable to insert code into the optimized program to help the debugger tell whether this is the first time through the loop, a solution that we mentioned earlier but suggested might not be suitable because it tampered with the optimized code.

EXERCISES

10.1 Consider the matrix multiplication program in Fig. 10.72.

```
begin
    for i := 1 to n do
        for j := 1 to n do
            c[i,j] := 0;
    for i := 1 to n do
        for j := 1 to n do
            for k := 1 to n do
                c[i,j] := c[i,j] + a[i,k] * b[k,j]
end
```

Fig. 10.72. Matrix multiplication program.

a) Assuming a, b, and c are allocated static storage and there are four bytes per word in a byte-addressed memory, produce three-address statements for the program in Fig. 10.72.

b) Generate target-machine code from the three-address statements.

c) Construct a flow graph from the three-address statements.

d) Eliminate the common subexpressions from each basic block.

e) Find the loops in the flow graph.

f) Move the loop-invariant computations out of the loops.

g) Find the induction variables of each loop and eliminate them where possible.

h) Generate target-machine code from the flow graph in (g). Compare the code with that produced in (b).

10.2 Compute reaching definitions and ud-chains for the original flow graph from Exercise 10.1(c) and the final flow graph from 10.1(g).

10.3 The program of Fig. 10.73 counts the primes from 2 to n using the sieve method on a suitably large array.

```
begin
    read n;
    for i := 2 to n do
        a[i] := true;    /* initialize  */
    count := 0;
    for i := 2 to n ** .5 do
        if a[i] then    /* i is a prime */
            begin
                count := count + 1;
                for j := 2 * i to n by i do
                    a[j] := false
                    /* j is divisible by i */
            end;
    print count
end
```

Fig. 10.73. Program to calculate primes.

a) Translate the program of Fig. 10.73 into three-address statements assuming a is allocated static storage.

b) Generate target-machine code from the three-address statements.

c) Construct a flow graph from the three-address statements.

d) Show the dominator tree for the flow graph in (a).

e) For the flow graph in (c), indicate the back edges and their natural loops.

f) Move the invariant computations out of loops using Algorithm 10.7.

g) Eliminate induction variables wherever possible.

   h) Propagate out copy statements wherever possible.

   i) Is loop jamming possible? If so, do it.

   j) On the assumption that n will always be even, unroll inner loops once each. What new optimizations are now possible?

10.4 Repeat Exercise 10.3 on the assumption that a is allocated dynamic storage, with ptr a pointer to the first word of a.

10.5 For the flow graph of Fig. 10.74 compute:

   a) ud- and du-chains,

   b) live variables at the end of each block,

   c) available expressions.

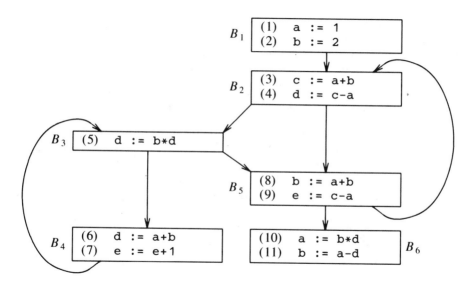

Fig. 10.74. Flow graph.

10.6 Is any constant folding possible in Fig. 10.74? If so, do it.

10.7 Are there any common subexpressions in Fig. 10.74? If so, eliminate them.

10.8 An expression e is said to be *very busy* at point p if no matter what path is taken from p, the expression e will be evaluated before any of its operands are defined. Give a data-flow algorithm in the style of Section 10.6 to find all very busy expressions. What confluence operator do you use, and does propagation run forward or backward? Apply your algorithm to the flow graph in Fig. 10.74.

∗**10.9** If expression e is very busy at point p we can *hoist* e by computing it at p and preserving its value for subsequent use. (Note: This optimization does not usually save time, but may save space.) Give an algorithm to hoist very busy expressions.

10.10 Are there any expressions that may be hoisted in Fig. 10.74? If so, hoist them.

10.11 Where possible, propagate out any copy steps introduced in the modifications of Exercises 10.6, 10.7, and 10.10.

10.12 An *extended basic block* is a sequence of blocks $B_1, \ldots, B_k$ such that for $1 \le i < k$, B_i is the only predecessor of B_{i+1}, and B_1 does not have a unique predecessor. Find the extended basic block ending at each node in
a) Fig. 10.39,
b) the flow graph constructed in Exercise 10.1(c),
c) Fig. 10.74.

∗**10.13** Give an algorithm that runs in time $O(n)$ on an n-node flow graph to find the extended basic block ending at each node.

10.14 We can do some interblock code optimization without any data-flow analysis by treating each extended basic block as if it were a basic block. Give algorithms to do the following optimizations within an extended basic block. In each case, indicate what effect on other extended basic blocks a change within one extended basic block can have.
a) Common subexpression elimination.
b) Constant folding.
c) Copy propagation.

10.15 For the flowgraph of Exercise 10.1(c):
a) Find a sequence of T_1 and T_2 reductions for the graph.
b) Find the sequence of interval graphs.
c) What is the limit flow graph? Is the flow graph reducible?

10.16 Repeat Exercise 10.15 for the flow graph of Fig. 10.74.

∗∗**10.17** Show that the following conditions are equivalent (they are alternative definitions of "reducible flow graph").
a) The limit of T_1-T_2 reduction is a single node.
b) The limit of interval analysis is a single node.
c) The flow graph can have its edges divided into two classes; one forms an acyclic graph and the other, the "back" edges, consists of edges whose heads dominate their tails.
d) The flow graph has no subgraph of the form shown in Fig. 10.75. Here, n_0 is the initial node, and n_0, a, b, and c are all distinct, with the exception that $a = n_0$ is possible. The arrows represent

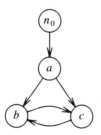

Fig. 10.75. Forbidden subgraph for reducible flow graphs.

node-disjoint paths (except for the endpoints, of course).

10.18 Give algorithms to compute (a) available expressions and (b) live variables for the language with pointers discussed in Section 10.8. Be sure to make conservative assumptions about *gen, kill, use,* and *def* in (b).

10.19 Give an algorithm to compute reaching definitions interprocedurally using the model of Section 10.8. Again, be sure you make conservative approximations to the truth.

10.20 Suppose parameters are passed by value instead of by reference. Can two names be aliases of one another? What if copy-restore linkage is used?

10.21 What is the depth of the flow graph in Exercise 10.1(c)?

**10.22 Prove that the depth of a reducible flow graph is never less than the number of times interval analysis must be performed to produce a single node.

*10.23 Generalize the structure-based data-flow analysis algorithm of Section 10.8 to a general data-flow framework in the sense of Section 10.11. What assumptions about F and $\wedge$ do you have to make to ensure that your algorithm works?

*10.24 An interesting and powerful data-flow analysis framework is obtained by imagining that the "values" to be propagated are all the possible partitions of expressions so that two expressions are in the same class only if they have the same value. To avoid having to list all of the infinity of possible expressions, we can represent such values by listing only the minimal expressions that are equivalent to some other expression. For example, if we execute the statements

```
A := B
C := A + D
```

then we have the following minimal equivalences: $A \equiv B$, and

C ≡ A+D. From these follow other equivalences, such as C ≡ B+D and A+E ≡ B+E, but there is no need to list these explicitly.

a) What is the appropriate meet, or confluence, operator for this framework?

b) Give a data structure to represent values and an algorithm to implement the meet operator.

c) What are the appropriate functions to associate with statements? Explain the effect that the function associated with assignments such as A:=B+C should have on a partition.

d) Is this framework distributive? Monotone?

10.25 How would you use the data gathered by the framework of Exercise 10.24 to perform

a) common subexpression elimination?

b) copy propagation?

c) constant folding?

*10.26 Give formal proofs of the following about the relation $\le$ on lattices.

a) $a \le b$ and $a \le c$ implies $a \le (b \wedge c)$.

b) $a \le (b \wedge c)$ implies $a \le b$.

c) $a \le b$ and $b \le c$ implies $a \le c$.

d) $a \le b$ and $b \le a$ implies $a = b$.

**10.27 Show that the following condition is necessary and sufficient for the iterative data-flow algorithm, with depth-first ordering, to converge within 2 plus the depth passes. For all functions f and g and value a:

$$f(g(a)) \ge f(a) \wedge g(a) \wedge a$$

10.28 Show that the reaching definitions and available expressions frameworks satisfy the condition of Exercise 10.27. Note: In fact, these frameworks converge in 1 plus the depth passes.

**10.29 Is the condition of Exercise 10.27 implied by monotonicity? By distributivity? Vice versa?

10.30 We see in Fig. 10.76 two basic blocks, the first "initial" code and the second an optimized version.

a) Construct the dags for the blocks of Fig. 10.76(a) and (b). Verify that, on the assumption only J is live on exit, these two blocks are equivalent.

b) Annotate the dag with the times at which each variable's value is known at each node.

c) Indicate, for an error occurring at each of statements (1′) through (4′), at which statement of Fig. 10.76(a) we should say an error occurs.

1)	E := A+B		1')	E := A+B
2)	F := E-C		2')	E := E-C
3)	G := F*D		3')	F := E*D
4)	H := A+B		4')	J := E+F
5)	I := I-C			
6)	J := I+G			
	(a) INITIAL			(b) OPTIMIZED

Fig. 10.76. Initial and optimized code.

d) For each of the errors in part (c), indicate for which variables of Fig. 10.76(a) it is possible to compute a value, and how we do so.

e) Suppose we allowed ourselves to use algebraically valid laws like "if $a + b = c$ then $a = c - b$." Would your answer to (d) change?

10.31 Generalize Example 10.14 to account for an arbitrary set of break statements. Also, generalize it to allow continue statements, which do not break the inner loop but proceed directly to the next iteration of the loop. Hint: Use the techniques developed in Section 10.10 for reducible flow graphs.

10.32 Show that in Algorithm 10.3 the *in* and *out* sets of definitions never decrease. Similarly, show that in Algorithm 10.4 these sets of expressions never increase.

10.33 Generalize Algorithm 10.9 for the elimination of induction variables to the case where multiplicative constants can be negative.

10.34 Generalize the algorithm for determining what pointers can point to, from Section 10.8, to the case where pointers are permitted to point to other pointers.

*10.35 When estimating each of the following sets, tell whether too-large or too-small estimates are conservative. Explain your answer in terms of the intended use of the information.

a) Available expressions.

b) Variables changed by a procedure.

c) Variables not changed by a procedure.

d) Induction variables belonging to a given family.

e) Copy statements reaching a given point.

*10.36 Refine Algorithm 10.12 to compute the aliases of a given variable at a given point.

*10.37 Modify Algorithm 10.12 for the cases that parameters are passed

a) by value,

b) by copy-restore.

*10.38 Prove that Algorithm 10.13 converges to a superset (not necessarily proper) of the truly changed variables.

*10.39 Generalize Algorithm 10.13 to determine changed variables in the case that procedure-valued variables are permitted.

*10.40 Prove that in each interval graph each node represents a region of the original flow graph.

10.41 Prove that Algorithm 10.16 correctly computes the set of dominators of each node.

*10.42 Modify Algorithm 10.17 (structure-based reaching definitions) to compute reaching definitions for designated small regions only, without requiring that the whole flow graph be present in memory at once. Be sure your result is conservative. Adapt your algorithm to available expressions. Which is more likely to provide useful information?

*10.43 In Section 10.10 we proposed a speedup to Algorithm 10.17 based on combining a T_1 with a T_2 reduction. Prove the correctness of the modification.

10.44 Generalize the iterative method of Section 10.11 to backward-flowing problems.

**10.45 Prove that when Algorithm 10.18 converges, the resulting solution is $\leq$ the *mop* solution by showing that for every path P of length i, then after i iterations, $in[B_i] \leq f_P[\top]$.

10.46 In Fig. 10.77 is a flow graph of a program in the hypothetical language introduced in Section 10.12. Find the best estimate of the types of each variable using Algorithm 10.19.

BIBLIOGRAPHIC NOTES

Additional information about code optimization may be found in Cocke and Schwartz [1970], Abel and Bell [1972], Schaefer [1973], Hecht [1977], and Muchnick and Jones [1981]. Allen [1975] provides a bibliography on program optimization.

Many optimizing compilers are described in the literature. Ershov [1966] discusses an early compiler that used sophisticated optimization techniques. Lowry and Medlock [1969] and Scarborough and Kolsky [1980] detail the construction of optimizing compilers for Fortran. Busam and Englund [1969] and Metcalf [1982] describe additional techniques for Fortran optimization. Wulf et al. [1975] discuss the design of an influential optimizing compiler for Bliss.

Allen et al. [1980] describe a system that was built to experiment with

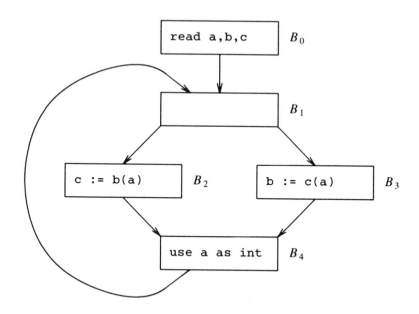

Fig. 10.77. Example program for type inference.

program optimizations. Cocke and Markstein [1980] report on the effectiveness of various optimizations for a PL/I-like language. Anklam, Cutler, Heinen and MacLaren [1982] describe the implementation of optimizing transformations that were used in compilers for PL/I and C. Auslander and Hopkins [1982] report on a compiler for a variant of PL/I that uses a simple algorithm to produce low-level intermediate code that is then improved by global optimizing transformations. Freudenberger, Schwartz, and Sharir [1983] describe experiences with an optimizer for SETL. Chow [1983] reports on experiments with a portable, machine-independent, optimizer for Pascal. Powell [1984] describes a portable, machine-independent, optimizing compiler for Modula-2.

The systematic study of data-flow analysis techniques begins with Allen [1970] and Cocke [1970], since published together as Allen and Cocke [1976], although various data-flow analysis methods were in use before then.

Syntax-directed data-flow analysis, as introduced in Section 10.5, has been used in Bliss (Wulf et al. [1975], Geschke [1972]), SIMPL (Zelkowitz and Bail [1974]), and Modula-2 (Powell [1984]). Additional discussions of this family of algorithms appears in Hecht and Schaffer [1975], Hecht [1977], and Rosen [1977].

The iterative approach to data-flow analysis discussed in Section 10.6 has been traced to Vyssotsky (see Vyssotsky and Wegner [1963]), who used the method in a 1962 Fortran compiler. The use of depth-first ordering to improve the efficiency is from Hecht and Ullman [1975].

The interval-analysis approach to data-flow analysis was pioneered by Cocke [1970]. Kennedy [1971] originates the use of interval analysis for backward flow problems, like live variables. There is reason to believe, following Kennedy [1976], that interval-based methods are somewhat more efficient than iterative ones, if the language being optimized tends to produce few, if any, nonreducible flow graphs. The variant used here, based on T_1 and T_2, is from Ullman [1973]. A somewhat faster version that takes advantage of the fact that most regions have a single exit was given in Graham and Wegman [1976].

The original definition of a reducible flow graph, one that becomes a single node under iterated interval analysis, is from Allen [1970]. Equivalent characterizations are found in Hecht and Ullman [1972, 1974], Kasyanov [1973], and Tarjan [1974b]. Node splitting for nonreducible flow graphs is from Cocke and Miller [1969].

The idea that structured flow of control is modeled by reducible flow graphs is expressed in Kosaraju [1974], Kasami, Peterson, and Tokura [1973], and Cherniavsky, Henderson, and Keohane [1976]. Baker [1977] describes their use in a program-structuring algorithm.

The lattice-theoretic approach to iterative data-flow analysis began with Kildall [1973]. Tennenbaum [1974] and Wegbreit [1975] are similar formulations. The efficient version of Kildall's algorithm, in which depth-first order is used, is from Kam and Ullman [1976].

While Kildall assumed the distributivity condition (which his frameworks such as the constant computation framework of Example 10.42 do not actually satisfy), the adequacy of monotonicity was perceived in a number of papers giving data-flow algorithms, such as Tennenbaum [1974], Schwartz [1975a, b], Graham and Wegman [1976], Jones and Muchnick [1976], Kam and Ullman [1977], and Cousot and Cousot [1977].

Since different algorithms require differing assumptions about the data, the theory of what properties are needed for certain algorithms was developed by Kam and Ullman [1977], Rosen [1980], and Tarjan [1981].

Another direction that followed from Kildall's paper was improving the algorithms for dealing with the particular data-flow problems (e.g., Example 10.42) he introduced. One key idea is that the lattice elements need not be treated as atomic, but we can exploit the fact that they are really mappings from variables to values. See Reif and Lewis [1977] and Wegman and Zadeck [1985]. Also, Kou [1977] exploits the idea for more conventional problems.

Kennedy [1981] is a survey of data-flow analysis techniques, and Cousot [1981] surveys lattice-theoretic ideas.

Gear [1965] introduced the basic loop optimizations of code motion and a limited form of induction-variable elimination. Allen [1969] is a fundamental paper on loop optimization; Allen and Cocke [1972] and Waite [1976b] are more extensive surveys of techniques in the area. Morel and Renvoise [1979] describe an algorithm that simultaneously eliminates redundant and invariant computations from loops.

The discussion of induction-variable elimination in Section 10.7 is based on Lowry and Medlock [1969]. See Allen, Cocke, and Kennedy [1981] for more powerful algorithms.

An algorithm for some of the loop problems not discussed in detail here, such as finding whether there is a path from a to b that does not go through c, can be solved by an efficient algorithm of Wegman [1983].

The use of dominators, both for loop discovery and for performing code motion was pioneered by Lowry and Medlock [1969], although they attribute the general idea to Prosser [1959]. Algorithm 10.16 for finding dominators was discovered independently by Purdom and Moore [1972] and Aho and Ullman [1973a]. The use of depth-first ordering to speed the algorithm is from Hecht and Ullman [1975], while the asymptotically most efficient way to do the job is from Tarjan [1974a]. Lengauer and Tarjan [1979] describe an efficient algorithm for finding dominators that is suitable for practical use.

The study of aliasing and interprocedural analysis begins with Spillman [1971] and Allen [1974]. Some more powerful methods than those of Section 10.8 have been developed. In general, they deal with the alias relation at each point of the program to avoid some of the impossible alias pairs that our simple algorithm "discovers." These works include Barth [1978], Banning [1979], and Weihl [1980]. See also Ryder [1979] on the construction of calling graphs.

An issue similar to interprocedural analysis, the effect of exceptions on the data-flow analysis of programs, is discussed by Hennessy [1981].

The fundamental paper of determination of types by data-flow analysis is Tennenbaum [1974], on which our discussion of Section 10.12 is based. Kaplan and Ullman [1980] give a more powerful algorithm for type detection.

The discussion of symbolic debugging of optimized code in Section 10.13 is from Hennessy [1982].

There have been a number of papers that attempt to evaluate the improvement due to various optimizations. The value of an optimization appears to be highly dependent on the language being compiled. The reader may wish to consult the classic study of Fortran optimization in Knuth [1971b], or the papers by Gajewska [1975], Palm [1975], Cocke and Kennedy [1976], Cocke and Markstein [1980], Chow [1983], Chow and Hennessy [1984], and Powell [1984].

Another topic in optimization that we have not covered here is the optimization of "very high-level" languages, such as the set-theoretic language SETL, where we are really changing the underlying algorithms and data structures. One central optimization in this area is generalized induction-variable elimination, as in Earley [1975b], Fong and Ullman [1976], Paige and Schwartz [1977], and Fong [1979].

Another key step in optimization for very high-level languages is the selection of data structures; this topic is covered in Schwartz [1975a, b], Low and Rovner [1976], and Schonberg, Schwartz, and Sharir [1981].

We also have not touched on issues in incremental code optimization, where small modifications to the program do not require a complete reoptimization. Ryder [1983] discusses incremental data-flow analysis, while Pollock and Soffa [1985] attempt to do incremental optimization of basic blocks.

Finally, we should mention some of the many other ways that data-flow analysis techniques have been used. Backhouse [1984] uses it on the transition graphs associated with parsers to perform error recovery. Harrison [1977] and Suzuki and Ishihata [1977] discuss its use in compile-time array-bounds checking.

One of the most significant uses of data-flow analysis outside code optimization is in the area of static (compile-time) checking for program errors. Fosdick and Osterweil [1976] is a fundamental paper, while Osterweil [1981], Adrion, Bronstad, and Cherniavsky [1982], and Freudenberger [1984] give some more recent developments.

CHAPTER 11

Want to Write
a Compiler?

Having seen the principles, techniques, and tools of compiler design, suppose we want to write a compiler. With some advance planning the implementation can proceed more quickly and smoothly than otherwise. This brief chapter raises some implementation issues that arise in compiler construction. Much of the discussion is focussed around writing compilers using the UNIX operating system and its tools.

11.1 PLANNING A COMPILER

A new compiler may be for a new source language, or produce new target code, or both. Using the framework espoused in this book, we ultimately obtain a design for a compiler that consists of a set of modules. Several diverse factors impact the design and implementation of these modules.

Source Language Issues

The "size" of a language affects the size and number of the modules. Although there is no precise definition for the size of a language, it is apparent that a compiler for a language like Ada or PL/I is bigger and harder to implement than a compiler for a little language like Ratfor (a "rational" Fortran preprocessor, Kernighan [1975]) or EQN (a language for typesetting mathematics).

Another important factor is the extent to which the source language will change during the course of compiler construction. Although the source language specification may look immutable, few languages remain the same for the life of a compiler. Even a mature language evolves, albeit slowly. Fortran, for example, has changed considerably from the language it was in 1957; the looping, Hollerith, and conditional statements in Fortran 77 are quite different from those in the original language. Rosler [1984] reports on the evolution of C.

A new, experimental language, on the other hand, may undergo dramatic change as it is implemented. One way to create a new language is to evolve a compiler for a working prototype of the language into one that satisfies the needs of a certain group of users. Many of the "little" languages initially developed on the UNIX system like AWK and EQN were created this way.

Consequently, a compiler writer might anticipate at least some amount of change in the definition of the source language over the lifetime of a compiler. Modular design and use of tools can help the compiler writer cope with this change. For example, using generators to implement the lexical analyzer and parser of a compiler allows the compiler writer to accommodate syntactic changes in the language definition more readily than when the lexical analyzer and parser are written directly in code.

Target Language Issues

The nature and limitations of the target language and run-time environment have to be carefully considered, for they too have a strong influence on the compiler design and on what code generation strategies it should use. If the target language is new, the compiler writer is well advised to make sure that it is correct and that its timing sequences are well understood. A new machine or a new assembler may have bugs that a compiler is likely to uncover. Bugs in the target language can greatly aggravate the task of debugging the compiler itself.

A successful source language is likely to be implemented on several target machines. If a language persists, compilers for the language will need to generate code for several generations of target machines. Further evolution in machine hardware seems certain, so retargetable compilers are likely to have an edge. Consequently, the design of the intermediate language is important, as is confining machine-specific details to a small number of modules.

Performance Criteria

There are several aspects to compiler performance: compiler speed, code quality, error diagnostics, portability, and maintainability. The tradeoffs between these criteria are not so clear cut, and the compiler specification may leave many of these parameters unspecified. For example, is compilation speed of greater importance than the speed of the target code? How important are good error messages and error recovery?

Compiler speed can be achieved by reducing the number of modules and passes as much as possible, perhaps to the point of generating machine language directly in one pass. However, this approach may not produce a compiler that generates high quality target code, nor one that is particularly easy to maintain.

There are two aspects to portability: retargetability and rehostability. A retargetable compiler is one that can be modified easily to generate code for a new target language. A rehostable compiler is one that can be moved easily to run on a new machine. A portable compiler may not be as efficient as a compiler designed for a specific machine, because the single-machine compiler can safely make specific assumptions about the target machine that a portable compiler cannot.

11.2 APPROACHES TO COMPILER DEVELOPMENT

There are several general approaches that a compiler writer can adopt to implement a compiler. The simplest is to retarget or rehost an existing compiler. If there is no suitable existing compiler, the compiler writer might adopt the organization of a known compiler for a similar language and implement the corresponding components, using component-generation tools or implementing them by hand. It is relatively rare that a completely new compiler organization is required.

No matter what approach is adopted, compiler writing is an exercise in software engineering. Lessons from other software efforts (see for example Brooks [1975]) can be applied to enhance the reliability and maintainability of the final product. A design that readily accommodates change will allow the compiler to evolve with the language. The use of compiler-building tools can be a significant help in this regard.

Bootstrapping

A compiler is a complex enough program that we would like to write it in a friendlier language than assembly language. In the UNIX programming environment, compilers are usually written in C. Even C compilers are written in C. Using the facilities offered by a language to compile itself is the essence of *bootstrapping*. Here we shall look at the use of bootstrapping to create compilers and to move them from one machine to another by modifying the back end. The basic ideas of bootstrapping have been known since the mid 1950's (Strong et al. [1958]).

Bootstrapping may raise the question, "How was the first compiler compiled?" which sounds like, "What came first, the chicken or the egg?" but is easier to answer. For an answer we consider how Lisp became a programming language. McCarthy [1981] notes that in late 1958 Lisp was used as a notation for writing functions; they were then hand-translated into assembly language and run. The implementation of an interpreter for Lisp occurred unexpectedly. McCarthy wanted to show that Lisp was a notation for describing functions "much neater than Turing machines or the general recursive definitions used in recursive function theory," so he wrote a function $eval[e, a]$ in Lisp that took a Lisp expression e as an argument. S. R. Russell noticed that $eval$ could serve as an interpreter for Lisp, hand-coded it, and thus created a programming language with an interpreter. As mentioned in Section 1.1, rather than generating target code, an interpreter actually performs the operations of the source program.

For bootstrapping purposes, a compiler is characterized by three languages: the source language S that it compiles, the target language T that it generates code for, and the implementation language I that it is written in. We represent the three languages using the following diagram, called a *T-diagram*, because of its shape (Bratman [1961]).

Within text, we abbreviate the above T-diagram as $S_I T$. The three languages S, I, and T may all be quite different. For example, a compiler may run on one machine and produce target code for another machine. Such a compiler is often called a *cross-compiler*.

Suppose we write a cross-compiler for a new language L in implementation language S to generate code for machine N; that is, we create $L_S N$. If an existing compiler for S runs on machine M and generates code for M, it is characterized by $S_M M$. If $L_S N$ is run through $S_M M$, we get a compiler $L_M N$, that is, a compiler from L to N that runs on M. This process is illustrated in Fig. 11.1 by putting together the T-diagrams for these compilers.

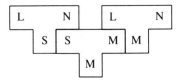

Fig. 11.1. Compiling a compiler.

When T-diagrams are put together as in Fig. 11.1, note that the implementation language S of the compiler $L_S N$ must be the same as the source language of the existing compiler $S_M M$ and that the target language M of the existing compiler must be that same as the implementation language of the translated form $L_M N$. A trio of T-diagrams such as Fig. 11.1 can be thought of as an equation

$$L_S N + S_M M = L_M N$$

Example 11.1. The first version of the EQN compiler (see Section 12.1) had C as the implementation language and generated commands for the text formatter TROFF. As shown in the following diagram, a cross-compiler for EQN, running on a PDP-11, was obtained by running $EQN_C TROFF$ through the C compiler $C_{11} 11$ on the PDP-11.

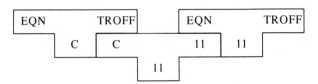

□

One form of bootstrapping builds up a compiler for larger and larger subsets of a language. Suppose a new language L is to be implemented on machine M. As a first step we might write a small compiler that translates a subset S of L into the target code for M; that is, a compiler $S_M M$. We then use the subset S to write a compiler $L_S M$ for L. When $L_S M$ is run through $S_M M$, we obtain an implementation of L, namely, $L_M M$. Neliac was one of the first languages to be implemented in its own language (Huskey, Halstead, and McArthur [1960]).

Wirth [1971] notes that Pascal was first implemented by writing a compiler in Pascal itself. The compiler was then translated "by hand" into an available low-level language without any attempt at optimization. The compiler was for a subset "(>60 per cent)" of Pascal; several bootstrapping stages later a compiler for all of Pascal was obtained. Lecarme and Peyrolle-Thomas [1978] summarize methods that have been used to bootstrap Pascal compilers.

For the advantages of bootstrapping to be realized fully, a compiler has to be written in the language it compiles. Suppose we write a compiler $L_L N$ for language L in L to generate code for machine N. Development takes place on a machine M, where an existing compiler $L_M M$ for L runs and generates code for M. By first compiling $L_L N$ with $L_M M$, we obtain a cross-compiler $L_M N$ that runs on M, but produces code for N:

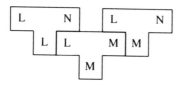

The compiler $L_L N$ can be compiled a second time, this time using the generated cross-compiler:

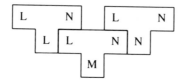

The result of the second compilation is a compiler $L_N N$ that runs on N and generates code for N. The are a number of useful applications of this two-step process, so we shall write it as in Fig. 11.2.

Example 11.2. This example is motivated by the development of the Fortran H compiler (see Section 12.4). "The compiler was itself written in Fortran and bootstrapped three times. The first time was to convert from running on the IBM 7094 to System/360 — an arduous procedure. The second time was to optimize itself, which reduced the size of the compiler from about 550K to about 400K bytes" (Lowry and Medlock [1969]).

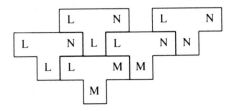

Fig. 11.2. Bootstrapping a compiler.

Using bootstrapping techniques, an optimizing compiler can optimize itself. Suppose all development is done on machine M. We have $S_S M$, a good optimizing compiler for a language S written in S, and we want $S_M M$, a good optimizing compiler for S written in M.

We can create $S_{M\ddagger} M\ddagger$, a quick-and-dirty compiler for S on M that not only generates poor code, but also takes a long time to do so. ($M\ddagger$ indicates a poor implementation in M. $S_{M\ddagger} M\ddagger$ is a poor implementation of a compiler that generates poor code.) However, we can use the indifferent compiler $S_{M\ddagger} M\ddagger$ to obtain a good compiler for S in two steps:

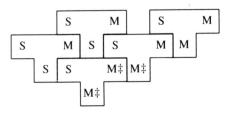

First, the optimizing compiler $S_S M$ is translated by the quick-and-dirty compiler to produce $S_{M\ddagger} M$, a poor implementation of the optimizing compiler, but one that does produce good code. The good optimizing compiler $S_M M$ is obtained by recompiling $S_S M$ through $S_{M\ddagger} M$.   □

Example 11.3. Ammann [1981] describes how a clean implementation of Pascal was obtained by a process similar to that of Example 11.2. Revisions to Pascal led to a fresh compiler being written in 1972 for the CDC 6000 series machines. In the following diagram, O represents "old" Pascal and P represents the revised language.

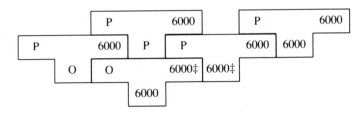

A compiler for revised Pascal was written in old Pascal and translated into $P_{6000}\ddagger6000$. As in Example 11.2, the symbol $\ddagger$ marks a source of inefficiency. The old compiler did not generate sufficiently efficient code. "Therefore, the compiler speed of [$P_{6000}\ddagger6000$] was rather moderate and its storage requirements quite high (Ammann [1981])." Revisions to Pascal were small enough that the compiler P_O6000 could be hand-translated with little effort into P_p6000 and run through the inefficient compiler $P_{6000}\ddagger6000$ to obtain a clean implementation.   □

11.3 THE COMPILER-DEVELOPMENT ENVIRONMENT

In a real sense, a compiler is just a program. The environment in which this program is developed can affect how quickly and reliably the compiler is implemented. The language in which the compiler is implemented is equally as important. Although compilers have been written in languages like Fortran, a clear choice for most compiler writers is a systems-oriented language like C.

If the source language itself is a new systems-oriented language, then it makes good sense to write the compiler in its own language. Using the bootstrapping techniques discussed in the previous section, compiling the compiler helps debug the compiler.

The software-construction tools in the programming environment can greatly facilitate the creation of an efficient compiler. In writing a compiler, it is customary to partition the overall program into modules, where each module may be processed in quite different ways. A program that manages the processing of these modules is an indispensable aid to the compiler writer. The UNIX system contains a command called *make* (Feldman [1979a]) that manages and maintains the modules making up a computer program; *make* keeps track of the relationships between the modules of the program, and issues only those commands needed to make the modules consistent after changes are made.

Example 11.4. The command *make* reads the specification of what tasks need to be done from a file called makefile. In Section 2.9, we constructed a translator by compiling seven files with a C compiler, each depending on a global header file global.h. To show how the task of putting the compiler together can be done by *make*, suppose we call the resulting compiler trans. The makefile specification might look like:

```
OBJS = lexer.o parser.o emitter.o symbol.o\
        init.o error.o main.o

trans:  $(OBJS)
        cc $(OBJS) -o trans

lexer.o parser.o emitter.o symbol.o\
        init.o error.o main.o:  global.h
```

The equal sign on the first line makes OBJS on the left stand for the seven
object files on the right. (Long lines can be split by placing a backslash at the
end of the continued portion.) The colon on the second line says trans on
its left depends on all the files in OBJS. Such a dependency line can be followed by a command to "make" the file to the left of the colon. The third
line therefore says that the target program trans is created by linking the
object files lexer.o, parser.o, . . . , main.o. However, *make* knows
that it must first create the object files; it automatically does this by looking
for the corresponding source files lexer.c, parser.c, . . . , main.c,
and compiling each with the C compiler to create the corresponding object
files. The last line of makefile says that all seven object files depend on
the global header file global.h.

The translator is created by just typing the command *make*, which causes
the following commands to be issued:

```
cc -c lexer.c
cc -c parser.c
cc -c emitter.c
cc -c symbol.c
cc -c init.c
cc -c error.c
cc -c main.c
cc lexer.o parser.o emitter.o symbol.o\
        init.o error.o main.o -o trans
```

Subsequently, a compilation will be redone only if a dependent source file is
changed after the last compilation. Kernighan and Pike [1984] contains examples of the use of *make* to facilitate the construction of a compiler.   □

A profiler is another useful compiler-writing tool. Once the compiler is
written, a profiler can be used to determine where the compiler spending its
time as it compiles a source program. Identification and modification of the
hot spots in the compiler can speed up the compiler by a factor of two or
three.

In addition to software-development tools, a number of tools have been
developed specifically for the compiler-development process. In Section 3.5,
we described the generator Lex that can be used to automatically produce a
lexical analyzer from a regular-expression specification of a lexical analyzer; in
Section 4.9, we described a generator Yacc that can be used to automatically
produce an LR parser from a grammatical description of the syntax of the
language. The *make* command described above will automatically invoke Lex
and Yacc wherever needed. In addition to lexical-analyzer generators and
parser generators, attribute-grammar generators and code-generator generators
have been created to help build compiler components. Many of these
compiler-construction tools have the desirable property that they will catch
bugs in the specification of the compiler.

There has been some debate on the efficiency and convenience of program generators in compiler construction (Waite and Carter [1985]). The observed fact is that well-implemented program generators are a significant aid in producing reliable compiler components. It is much easier to produce a correct parser using a grammatical description of the language and a parser generator, than implementing a parser directly by hand. An important issue, however, is how well these generators interface with one another and with other programs. A common mistake in the design of a generator is to assume that it is the center of the design. A better design has the generator produce subroutines with clean interfaces that can be called by other programs (Johnson and Lesk [1978]).

11.4 TESTING AND MAINTENANCE

A compiler must generate correct code. Ideally, we would like to have a computer mechanically verify that a compiler faithfully implements its specification. Several papers do discuss the correctness of various compiling algorithms but unfortunately, compilers are rarely specified in such a manner that an arbitrary implementation can be mechanically checked against a formal specification. Since compilers are usually rather complex functions, there is also the issue of verifying that the specification itself is correct.

In practice, we must resort to some systematic method of testing the compiler in order to increase our confidence that it will work satisfactorily in the field. One approach used successfully by many compiler writers is the "regression" test. Here we maintain a suite of test programs, and whenever the compiler is modified, the test programs are compiled using both the new and the old versions of the compiler. Any differences in the target programs produced by the two compilers are reported to the compiler writer. The UNIX system command *make* can also be used to automate the testing.

Choosing the programs to include in the test suite is a difficult problem. As a goal, we would like the test programs to exercise every statement in the compiler at least once. It usually requires great ingenuity to find such a test suite. Exhaustive test suites have been constructed for several languages (Fortran, TEX, C, etc.). Many compiler writers add to the regression tests programs that have exposed bugs in previous versions of their compiler; it is frustrating to have an old bug reappear because of a new correction.

Performance testing is also important. Some compiler writers check that new versions of the compiler generate code that is approximately as good as the previous version by doing timing studies as part of the regression test.

Maintenance of a compiler is another important problem, particularly if the compiler is going to be run in different environments, or if people involved in the compiler project come and go. A crucial element in being able to maintain a compiler is good programming style and good documentation. The authors know of one compiler that was written using only seven comments, one of which read "This code is cursed." Needless to say, such a program is somewhat difficult to maintain by anyone except perhaps the original writer.

Knuth [1984b] has developed a system called WEB that addresses the problem of documenting large programs written in Pascal. WEB facilitates literate programming; the documentation is developed at the same time as the code, not as an afterthought. Many of the ideas in WEB can be applied equally well to other languages.

CHAPTER 12

A Look at
Some Compilers

This chapter discusses the structure of some existing compilers for a text-formatting language, Pascal, C, Fortran, Bliss, and Modula 2. Our intent is not to advocate the designs presented here to the exclusion of others, but rather to illustrate the variety that is possible in the implementation of a compiler.

The compilers for Pascal were chosen because they influenced the design of the language itself. The compilers for C were chosen because C is the primary programming language on the UNIX operating system. The Fortran H compiler was chosen because it has significantly influenced the development of optimization techniques. BLISS/11 was chosen to illustrate the design of a compiler whose goal is to optimize space. The DEC Modula 2 compiler was chosen because it uses relatively simple techniques to produce excellent code, and was written by one person in a few months.

12.1 EQN, A PREPROCESSOR FOR TYPESETTING MATHEMATICS

The set of possible inputs to a number of computer programs can be viewed as a little language. The structure of the set can be described by a grammar, and syntax-directed translation can be used to precisely specify what the program does. Compiler technology can then be applied to implement the program.

One of the first compilers for little languages in the UNIX programming environment was EQN by Kernighan and Cherry [1975]. As described briefly in Section 1.2, EQN takes input like "E sub 1" and generates commands for the text formatter TROFF to produce output of the form "E_1".

The implementation of EQN is sketched in Fig. 12.1. Macro preprocessing (see Section 1.4) and lexical analysis are done together. The token stream after lexical analysis is translated during parsing into text-formatting commands. The translator is constructed using the parser generator Yacc, described in Section 4.9.

The approach of treating the input to EQN as a language and applying compiler technology to construct a translator has several benefits noted by the authors.

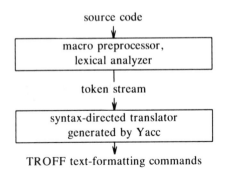

source code

macro preprocessor,
lexical analyzer

token stream

syntax-directed translator
generated by Yacc

TROFF text-formatting commands

Fig. 12.1. EQN implementation.

1. *Ease of implementation.* "Construction of a working system sufficient to try out significant examples required perhaps a person-month."

2. *Language evolution.* A syntax-directed definition facilitates changes in the input language. Over the years EQN has evolved in response to user needs.

The authors conclude by observing that "defining a language, and building a compiler for it using a compiler/compiler seems like the only sensible way to do business."

12.2 COMPILERS FOR PASCAL

The design of Pascal and the development of the first compiler for it "were interdependent," as Wirth [1971] notes. It is therefore instructive to examine the structure of the compilers for the language written by Wirth and his colleagues. The first (Wirth [1971]) and the second compilers (Ammann [1981, 1977]) generated absolute machine code for the CDC 6000 series machines. Portability experiments with the second compiler led to the Pascal-P compiler that generates code, called P-code, for an abstract stack machine (Nori et al. [1981]).

Each of the above compilers is a one-pass compiler organized around a recursive-descent parser, like the "baby" front end in Chapter 2. Wirth [1971] observes that "it turned out to be relatively easy to mould the language according to [the restrictions of the parsing method]." The organization of the Pascal-P compiler is shown in Fig. 12.2.

The basic operations of the abstract stack machine used by the Pascal-P compiler reflect the needs of Pascal. Storage for the machine is organized into four areas:

1. code for the procedures,
2. constants,

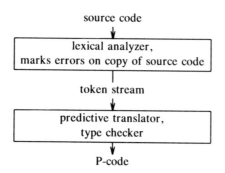

Fig. 12.2. Pascal-P compiler.

3.   a stack for activation records, and
4.   a heap for data allocated by applying the **new** operator.[1]

Since procedures may be nested in Pascal, the activation record for a procedure contains both access and control links. A procedure call is translated into a "mark stack" instruction for the abstract machine, with the access and control links as parameters. The code for a procedure refers to the storage for a local name using a displacement from an end of the activation record. Storage for nonlocals is referred to by a pair, consisting of the number of access links to be traversed and a displacement, as in Section 7.4. The first compiler used a display for efficient access to nonlocals.

Ammann [1981] draws the following conclusions from the experience with writing the second compiler. On the one hand, the one-pass compiler was easy to implement and generated modest input/output activity (the code for a procedure body is compiled in memory and written out as a unit to secondary storage). On the other hand, the one-pass organization "imposes severe restrictions on the quality of the generated code and suffers from relatively high storage requirements."

12.3 THE C COMPILERS

C is a general-purpose programming language designed by D. M. Ritchie and is used as the primary programming language on the UNIX operating system (Ritchie and Thompson [1974]). UNIX itself is written in C and has been moved to a number of machines, ranging from micro-processors to large mainframes, by first moving a C compiler. This section briefly describes the overall structure of the compiler for the PDP-11 by Ritchie [1979] and the PCC family of portable C compilers by Johnson [1979]. Three-quarters of the

---

[1] Bootstrapping is facilitated by the fact that the compiler, written in the subset it compiles, uses the heap like a stack, so a simple heap manager can be used initially.

code in PCC is independent of the target machine. All these compilers are essentially two-pass; the PDP-11 compiler has an optional third pass that does optimization on the assembly-language output, as indicated in Fig. 12.3. This peephole optimization phase eliminates redundant or inaccessible statements.

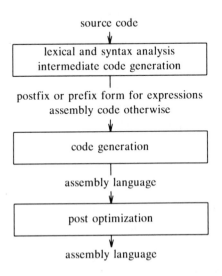

Fig. 12.3. Pass structure of C compilers.

Pass I of each compiler does lexical analysis, syntax analysis, and intermediate code generation. The PDP-11 compiler uses recursive descent to parse everything except expressions, for which operator precedence is used. The intermediate code consists of postfix notation for expressions and assembly code for control-flow statements. PCC uses an LALR(1) parser generated by Yacc. Its intermediate code consists of prefix notation for expressions and assembly code for other constructs. In each case, storage allocation for local names is done during the first pass, so these names can be referred to using offsets into an activation record.

Within the back end, expressions are represented by syntax trees. In the PDP-11 compiler, code generation is implemented by a tree walk, using a strategy similar to the labeling algorithm in Section 9.10. Modifications to that algorithm have been made to assure that register pairs are available for operations that need them and to take advantage of operands that are constants.

Johnson [1978] reviews the influence of theory on PCC. In both PCC and PCC2, a subsequent version of the compiler, code for expressions is generated by tree rewriting. The code generator in PCC examines a source language statement at a time, repeatedly finding maximal subtrees that can be computed without stores, using the available registers. Labels computed as in Section

9.10 identify subexpressions to be computed and stored in temporaries. Code to evaluate and store the values represented by these subtrees is generated by the compiler as the subtrees are selected. The rewriting is more evident in PCC2, whose code generator is based on the dynamic programming algorithm of Section 9.11.

Johnson and Ritchie [1981] describe the influence of the target machine on the design of activation records and the procedure call/return sequence. The standard library function `printf` can have a variable number of arguments, so the design of the calling sequence on some machines is dominated by the need to allow variable-length argument lists.

12.4 THE FORTRAN H COMPILERS

The original Fortran H compiler written by Lowry and Medlock [1969] was an extensive and fairly powerful optimizing compiler built using methods that largely predate those described in this book. Several attempts at increased performance have been made; an "extended" version of the compiler was developed for the IBM/370, and an "enhanced" version was developed by Scarborough and Kolsky [1980]. Fortran H offers the user the choice of no optimization, register optimization only, or full optimization. A sketch of the compiler in the case that full optimization is performed appears in Fig. 12.4.

The source text is treated in four passes. The first two perform lexical and syntactic analysis, producing quadruples. The next pass incorporates code optimization and register optimization and the final pass generates object code from the quadruples and register assignments.

The lexical analysis phase is somewhat unusual, since its output is not a stream of tokens but a stream of "operator-operand pairs," which are roughly equivalent to an operand token together with the preceding nonoperator token. It should be noted that in Fortran, like most languages, we never have two consecutive operand tokens such as identifiers or constants; rather, two such tokens are always separated by at least one punctuation token.

For example, the assignment statement

```
A = B(I) + C
```

would be translated into the sequence of pairs:

"assignment statement"	A
=	B
(s	I
)	—
+	C

The lexical analysis phase distinguishes between a left parenthesis whose job is to introduce a list of parameters or subscripts from one whose job is to group operands. Thus, the symbol "(s" is intended to represent a left parenthesis used as a subscripting operator. Right parentheses never have an operand

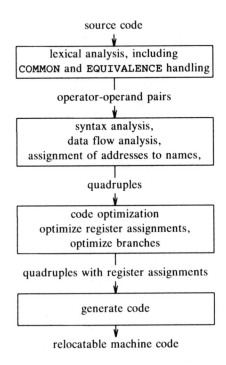

source code

lexical analysis, including
COMMON and EQUIVALENCE handling

operator-operand pairs

syntax analysis,
data flow analysis,
assignment of addresses to names,

quadruples

code optimization
optimize register assignments,
optimize branches

quadruples with register assignments

generate code

relocatable machine code

Fig. 12.4. Outline of Fortran H compiler.

following, and Fortran H does not distinguish the two roles for right
parentheses.

Associated with lexical analysis is the processing of COMMON and
EQUIVALENCE statements. It is possible at this stage to map out each COM-
MON block of storage, as well as the storage blocks associated with the subroutines, and to determine the location of each variable mentioned by the program in one of these static storage areas.

Since Fortran has no structured control statements like while-statements,
parsing, except for expressions, is quite straightforward, and Fortran H simply
uses an operator-precedence parser for expressions. Some very simple local
optimizations are performed during the generation of quadruples; for example,
multiplications by powers of 2 are replaced by left-shift operations.

Code Optimization in Fortran H

Each subroutine is partitioned into basic blocks, and the loop structure is
deduced by finding flow-graph edges whose heads dominate their tails, as
described in Section 10.4. The compiler performs the following optimizations.

1. *Common subexpression elimination.* The compiler looks for local common subexpressions and for expressions that are common to a block *B* and one or more blocks that *B* dominates. Other instances of common subexpressions are not detected. Further, the detection of common subexpressions is done one expression at a time, rather than using the bit-vector method described in Section 10.6. Interestingly, in developing the "enhanced" version of the compiler, the authors found that a major speedup was possible by using bit-vector methods.

2. *Code motion.* Loop-invariant statements are removed from loops essentially as described in Section 10.7.

3. *Copy propagation.* Again, this is done one copy statement at a time.

4. *Induction variable elimination.* This optimization is performed only for variables that are assigned once in the loop. Instead of using the "family" approach described in Section 10.7, multiple passes through the code are made to detect induction variables that belong to the family of some other induction variable.

Although data flow analysis is done in a one-at-a-time style, the values corresponding to what we have called *in* and *out* are stored as bit vectors. However, in the original compiler, a limit of length 127 was placed on these vectors, so large programs have only the most frequently used of their variables involved in optimizations. The enhanced version increases the limit but does not remove it.

Algebraic Optimizations

As Fortran is frequently used for numerical calculations, algebraic optimization is dangerous, since transformations of expressions can, in computer arithmetic, introduce overflows or losses of precision that are not visible if we take an idealized view of algebraic simplification. However, algebraic transformations involving integers are generally safe, and the enhanced version of the compiler does some of this optimization in the case of array references only.

In general, an array reference like A(I,J,K) involves an offset calculation in which an expression of the form $a\mathtt{I} + b\mathtt{J} + c\mathtt{K} + d$ is computed; the exact values of the constants depend on the location of A and the dimensions of the array. If, say, I and K were constants, either numerical constants or loop-invariant variables, then the compiler applies the commutative and associative law to get an expression $b\mathtt{J} + e$, where $e = a\mathtt{I} + c\mathtt{K} + d$.

Register Optimization

Fortran H divides registers into three classes. These sets of registers are used for local register optimization, global register optimization, and "branch optimization." The exact number of registers in each class can be adjusted by the compiler, within limits.

Global registers are allocated on a loop-by-loop basis to the most frequently referenced variables in that loop. A variable that qualifies for a register in one loop L, but not in the loop immediately containing L, is loaded in the pre-header of L and stored on exit from L.

Local registers are used within a basic block to hold the results of one statement until it is used in a subsequent statement or statements. Only if not enough local registers exist is a temporary value stored. The compiler tries to compute new values in the register holding one of its operands, if that operand is subsequently dead. In the enhanced version, an attempt is made to recognize the situation where global registers may be exchanged with other registers to increase the number of times that an operation can take place in the register holding one of its operands.

Branch optimization is an artifact of the IBM/370 instruction set, which puts a significant premium on jumping only to locations that can be expressed as the contents of some register, plus a constant in the range 0 to 4095. Thus, Fortran H allocates some registers to hold addresses in the code space, at intervals of 4096 bytes, to allow efficient jumps in all but extremely large programs.

12.5 THE BLISS/11 COMPILER

This compiler implements the systems programming language Bliss on a PDP-11 (Wulf et al. [1975]). In a sense, it is an optimizing compiler from a world that has ceased to exist, a world where memory space was at enough of a premium that it made sense to perform optimizations whose sole purpose was to reduce space rather than time. However, most of the optimizations performed by the compiler save time as well, and descendants of this compiler are in use today.

The compiler is worth our attention for several reasons. Its optimization performance is strong, and it performs a number of transformations found almost nowhere else. Further, it pioneered the "syntax-directed" approach to optimization, as discussed in Section 10.5. That is, the language Bliss was designed to produce only reducible flow graphs (it has no goto's). Thus, it was possible for data flow analysis to be performed on the parse tree directly, rather than on a flow graph.

The compiler operates in a single pass, with one procedure completely processed before the next is read in. The designers view the compiler as composed of five modules, as shown in Fig. 12.5.

LEXSYNFLO performs lexical analysis and parsing. A recursive-descent parser is used. As BLISS permits no goto-statements, all flow graphs of BLISS procedures are reducible. In fact, the syntax of the language enables us to build the flow graph, and determine loops and loop entries, as we parse. LEXSYNFLO does so, and also determines common subexpressions and a variant of ud- and du-chains, taking advantage of the structure of reducible flow graphs. Another important job of LEXSYNFLO is to detect groups of

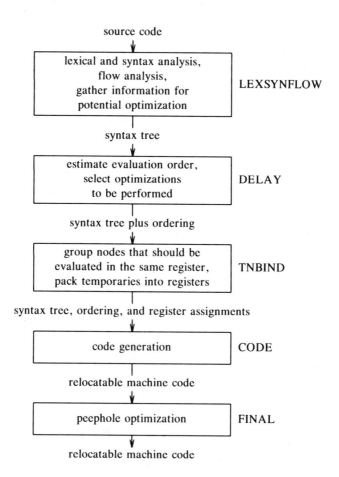

source code

| lexical and syntax analysis,
flow analysis,
gather information for
potential optimization | LEXSYNFLOW |

syntax tree

| estimate evaluation order,
select optimizations
to be performed | DELAY |

syntax tree plus ordering

| group nodes that should be
evaluated in the same register,
pack temporaries into registers | TNBIND |

syntax tree, ordering, and register assignments

| code generation | CODE |

relocatable machine code

| peephole optimization | FINAL |

relocatable machine code

Fig. 12.5. The BLISS/11 compiler.

similar expressions. These are candidates for replacement by a single subroutine. Note that this replacement makes the program run more slowly but can save space.

The module DELAY examines the syntax tree to determine which particular instances of the usual optimizations, such as invariant code motion and elimination of common subexpressions, are actually likely to produce a profit. The order of expression evaluation is determined at this time, based on the labeling strategy of Section 9.10, modified to take into account registers that are unavailable because they are used to preserve the values of common subexpressions. Algebraic laws are used to determine whether reordering of computations should be done. Conditional expressions are evaluated either numerically or by control flow, as discussed in Section 8.4, and DELAY decides which mode is cheaper in each instance.

TNBIND considers which temporary names should be bound to registers. Both registers and memory locations are allocated. The strategy used is to first group nodes of the syntax tree that should be assigned the same register. As discussed in Section 9.6, there is an advantage to evaluating a node in the same register as one of its parents. Next, the advantage to be gained by keeping a temporary in a register is estimated by a calculation favoring those that are used several times over a short span. Registers are then assigned until used up, packing the most advantageous nodes into registers first. CODE converts the tree, with its ordering and register assignment information, to relocatable machine code.

This code is then repeatedly examined by FINAL which performs peephole optimization until no further improvement results. The improvements made include elimination of (conditional or unconditional) jumps to jumps and complementation of conditionals, as discussed in Section 9.9.

Redundant or unreachable instructions are eliminated (these could have resulted from other FINAL optimizations). Merging of similar code sequences on the two paths of a branch is attempted, as is local propagation of constants. A number of other local optimizations, some quite machine-dependent are attempted. An important one is replacement, where possible, of jump instructions by PDP-11 "branches," which require one word but are limited in their range to 128 words.

12.6 MODULA-2 OPTIMIZING COMPILER

This compiler, described in Powell [1984], was developed with the intent of producing good code, using optimizations that provide a high payoff for little effort; the author describes his strategy as looking for the "best simple" optimizations. Such a philosophy can be difficult to carry out; without experimentation and measurement, it is hard to decide what the "best simple" optimizations are in advance, and some of the decisions made in the Modula-2 compiler are probably inappropriate for a compiler providing maximum optimization. Nevertheless, the strategy did achieve the author's goal of producing excellent code with a compiler that was written in a few months by one person. The five passes of the front end of the compiler are sketched in Fig. 12.6.

The parser was generated using Yacc, and it produces syntax trees in two passes, since Modula variables do not have to be declared before use. An attempt to make this compiler compatible with existing facilities was made. The intermediate code is P-code for compatibility with many Pascal compilers. The procedure call format for this compiler agrees with that of the Pascal and C compilers running under Berkeley UNIX, so procedures written in the three languages can be integrated easily.

The compiler does not do data-flow analysis. Rather, Modula-2, like Bliss, is a language that can produce only reducible flow graphs, so the methodology

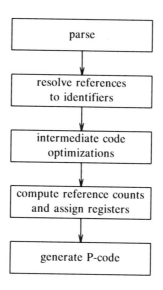

Fig. 12.6. Modula-2 compiler passes.

of Section 10.5 can be used here as well. In fact, the Modula compiler goes beyond the Bliss-11 compiler in the way it takes advantage of the syntax. Loops are identified by their syntax; i.e., the compiler looks for while- and for-constructs. Invariant expressions are detected by the fact that none of their variables are defined in the loop, and these are moved to a loop header. The only induction variables that are detected are those in the family of a for-loop index. Global common subexpressions are detected when one is in a block that dominates the block of the other, but this analysis is done an expression at a time, rather than with bit vectors.

The register allocation strategy is similarly designed to do reasonable things without being exhaustive. In particular, it considers as candidates for allocation to a register only:

1. temporaries used during the evaluation of an expression (these receive first priority),

2. values of common subexpressions,

3. indices and limit values in for-loops,

4. the address of E in an expression of the form with E do, and

5. simple variables (characters, integers, and so on) local to the current procedure.

An attempt is made to estimate the value of keeping each variable in classes (2)–(5) in a register. It is assumed that a statement is executed 10^d times if it is nested within d loops. However, variables referenced no more than twice are not considered eligible; others are ranked in order of estimated use and assigned to a register if one is available after assigning expression temporaries and higher-ranked variables.

A
Programming
Project

A.1 INTRODUCTION

This appendix suggests programming exercises that can be used in a programming laboratory accompanying a compiler-design course based on this book. The exercises consist of implementing the basic components of a compiler for a subset of Pascal. The subset is minimal, but allows programs such as the recursive sorting procedure in Section 7.1 to be expressed. Being a subset of an existing language has certain utility. The meaning of programs in the subset is determined by the semantics of Pascal (Jensen and Wirth [1975]). If a Pascal compiler is available, it can be used as a check on the behavior of the compiler written as an exercise. The constructs in the subset appear in most programming languages, so corresponding exercises can be formulated using a different language if a Pascal compiler is not available.

A.2 PROGRAM STRUCTURE

A program consists of a sequence of global data declarations, a sequence of procedure and function declarations, and a single compound statement that is the "main program." Global data is to be allocated static storage. Data local to procedures and functions is allocated storage on a stack. Recursion is permitted, and parameters are passed by reference. The procedures read and write are assumed supplied by the compiler.

Fig. A.1 gives an example program. The name of the program is example, and input and output are the names of the files used by read and write, respectively.

A.3 SYNTAX OF A PASCAL SUBSET

Listed below is an LALR(1) grammar for a subset of Pascal. The grammar can be modified for recursive-descent parsing by eliminating left recursion as described in Sections 2.4 and 4.3. An operator-precedence parser can be

```
program example(input, output);
var x, y: integer;
function gcd(a, b: integer): integer;
begin
    if b = 0 then gcd := a
    else gcd := gcd(b, a mod b)
end;

begin
    read(x, y);
    write(gcd(x, y))
end.
```

Fig. A.1. Example program.

constructed for expressions by substituting out for **relop**, **addop**, and **mulop**, and eliminating ε-productions.

The addition of the production

   statement → **if** *expression* **then** *statement*

introduces the "dangling-else" ambiguity, which can be eliminated as discussed in Section 4.3 (see also Example 4.19 if predictive parsing is used).

There is no syntactic distinction between a simple variable and the call of a function without parameters. Both are generated by the production

   factor → **id**

Thus, the assignment a := b sets a to the value returned by the function b, if b has been declared to be a function.

program →
        program id (*identifier_list*) ;
        declarations
        subprogram_declarations
        compound_statement
        .

identifier_list →
        id
        | *identifier_list* , **id**

declarations →
        declarations **var** *identifier_list* : *type* ;
        | ε

type →
        standard_type
        | **array** [**num** .. **num**] **of** *standard_type*

standard_type →
    integer
    | **real**

subprogram_declarations →
    subprogram_declarations subprogram_declaration ;
    | ε

subprogram_declaration →
    subprogram_head declarations compound_statement

subprogram_head →
    function id *arguments* : *standard_type* ;
    | **procedure id** *arguments* ;

arguments →
    (*parameter_list*)
    | ε

parameter_list →
    identifier_list : *type*
    | *parameter_list* ; *identifier_list* : *type*

compound_statement →
    begin
    optional_statements
    end

optional_statements →
    statement_list
    | ε

statement_list →
    statement
    | *statement_list* ; *statement*

statement →
    variable **assignop** *expression*
    | *procedure_statement*
    | *compound_statement*
    | **if** *expression* **then** *statement* **else** *statement*
    | **while** *expression* **do** *statement*

variable →
    id
    | **id** [*expression*]

procedure_statement →
    id
    | **id** (*expression_list*)

expression_list →
    expression
    | *expression_list* , *expression*

expression →
    simple_expression
    | *simple_expression* **relop** *simple_expression*

simple_expression →
    term
    | *sign term*
    | *simple_expression* **addop** *term*

term →
    factor
    | *term* **mulop** *factor*

factor →
    id
    | **id** (*expression_list*)
    | **num**
    | (*expression*)
    | **not** *factor*

sign →
    + | –

A.4 LEXICAL CONVENTIONS

The notation for the specifying tokens is from Section 3.3.

1. Comments are surrounded by { and }. They may not contain a {. Comments may appear after any token.

2. Blanks between tokens are optional, with the exception that keywords must be surrounded by blanks, newlines, the beginning of the program, or the final dot.

3. Token **id** for identifiers matches a letter followed by letters or digits:

    letter → [a-zA-Z]
    digit → [0-9]
      id → **letter** (**letter** | **digit**)*

The implementer may wish to put a limit on identifier length.

4. Token **num** matches unsigned integers (see Example 3.5):

             digits → **digit digit***
      optional_fraction → . **digits** | ϵ
    optional_exponent → (E (+ | – | ϵ) **digits**) | ϵ
                num → **digits optional_fraction optional_exponent**

5. Keywords are reserved and appear in boldface in the grammar.

6. The relation operators (**relop**'s) are: =, <>, <, <=, >=, and >. Note that <> denotes ≠.

7. The **addop**'s are +, -, and or.

8. The **mulop**'s are *, /, div, mod, and and.

9. The lexeme for token **assignop** is :=.

A.5 SUGGESTED EXERCISES

A programming exercise suitable for a one-term course is to write an interpreter for the language defined above, or for a similar subset of another high-level language. The project involves translating the source program into an intermediate representation such as quadruples or stack machine code and then interpreting the intermediate representation. We shall propose an order for the construction of the modules. The order is different from the order in which the modules are executed in the compiler because it is convenient to have a working interpreter to debug the other compiler components.

1. *Design a symbol-table mechanism.* Decide on the symbol-table organization. Allow for information to be collected about names, but leave the symbol-table record structure flexible at this time. Write routines to:

i) Search the symbol table for a given name, create a new entry for that name if none is present, and in either case return a pointer to the record for that name.

ii) Delete from the symbol table all names local to a given procedure.

2. *Write an interpreter for quadruples.* The exact set of quadruples may be left open at this time but they should include the arithmetic and conditional jump statements corresponding to the set of operators in the language. Also include logical operations if conditions are evaluated arithmetically rather than by position in the program. In addition, expect to need "quadruples" for integer-to-real conversion, for marking the beginning and end of procedures, and for parameter passing and procedure calls.

It is also necessary at this time to design the calling sequence and runtime organization for the programs being interpreted. The simple stack organization discussed in Section 7.3 is suitable for the example language, because no nested declarations of procedures are permitted in the language; that is, variables are either global (declared at the level of the entire program) or local to a simple procedure.

For simplicity, another high-level language may be used in place of the interpreter. Each quadruple can be a statement of a high-level language such as C, or even Pascal. The output of the compiler is then a sequence of C statements that can be compiled on an existing C compiler. This approach enables the implementer to concentrate on the run-time organization.

3. *Write the lexical analyzer.* Select internal codes for the tokens. Decide how constants will be represented in the compiler. Count lines for later use by an error-message handler. Produce a listing of the source program if desired. Write a program to enter the reserved words into the symbol table. Design your lexical analyzer to be a subroutine called by the parser, returning a pair (token, attribute value). At present, errors detected by your lexical analyzer may be handled by calling an error-printing routine and halting.

4. *Write the semantic actions.* Write semantic routines to generate the quadruples. The grammar will need to be modified in places to make the translation easier. Consult Sections 5.5 and 5.6 for examples of how to modify the grammar usefully. Do semantic analysis at this time, converting integers to reals when necessary.

5. *Write the parser.* If an LALR parser generator is available, this will simplify the task considerably. If a parser generator handling ambiguous grammars, like Yacc, is available, then nonterminals denoting expressions can be combined. Moreover, the "dangling-else" ambiguity can be resolved by shifting whenever a shift/reduce conflict occurs.

6. *Write the error-handling routines.* Be prepared to recover from lexical and syntactic errors. Print error diagnostics for lexical, syntactic, and semantic errors.

7. *Evaluation.* The program in Fig. _FIB.1_ can serve as a simple test routine. Another test program can be based on the Pascal program in Fig. 7.1. The code for function `partition` in the figure corresponds to the marked fragment in the C program of Fig. 10.2. Run your compiler through a profiler, if one is available. Determine the routines in which most of the time is being spent. What modules would have to be modified in order to increase the speed of your compiler?

A.6 EVOLUTION OF THE INTERPRETER

An alternative approach to constructing an interpreter for the language is to start by implementing a desk calculator, that is, an interpreter for expressions. Gradually add constructs to the language until an interpreter for the entire language is obtained. A similar approach is taken in Kernighan and Pike [1984]. A proposed order for adding constructs is:

1. *Translate expressions into postfix notation.* Using either recursive-descent parsing, as in Chapter 2, or a parser generator, familiarize yourself with the programming environment by writing a translator from simple arithmetic expressions into postfix notation.

2. *Add a lexical analyzer.* Allow for keywords, identifiers, and numbers to appear in the translator constructed above. Retarget the translator to produce either code for a stack machine or quadruples.

3. *Write an interpreter for the intermediate representation.* As discussed in

Section A.5, a high-level language may be used in place of the interpreter. For the moment, the interpreter need only support arithmetic operations, assignments, and input-output. Extend the language by allowing global variable declarations, assignments, and calls of procedures read and write. These constructs allow the interpreter to be tested.

4. *Add statements.* A program in the language now consists of a main program without subprogram declarations. Test both the translator and the interpreter.

5. *Add procedures and functions.* The symbol table must now allow the scopes of identifiers to be limited to procedure bodies. Design a calling sequence. Again, the simple stack organization of Section 7.3 is adequate. Extend the interpreter to support the calling sequence.

A.7 EXTENSIONS

There are a number of features that can be added to the language without greatly increasing the complexity of compilation. Among these are:

1. multidimensional arrays
2 for- and case-statements
3. block structure
4. record structures

If time permits, add one or more of these extensions to your compiler.

Bibliography

ABEL, N. E. AND J. R. BELL [1972]. "Global optimization in compilers," *Proc. First USA-Japan Computer Conf.*, AFIPS Press, Montvale, N. J.

ABELSON, H. AND G. J. SUSSMAN [1985]. *Structure and Interpretation of Computer Programs*, MIT Press, Cambridge, Mass.

ADRION, W. R., M. A. BRANSTAD, AND J. C. CHERNIAVSKY [1982]. "Validation, verification, and testing of computer software," *Computing Surveys* **14:2**, 159-192.

AHO, A. V. [1980]. "Pattern matching in strings," in Book [1980], pp. 325-347.

AHO, A. V. AND M. J. CORASICK [1975]. "Efficient string matching: an aid to bibliographic search," *Comm. ACM* **18:6**, 333-340.

AHO, A. V. AND M. GANAPATHI [1985]. "Efficient tree pattern matching: an aid to code generation," *Twelfth Annual ACM Symposium on Principles of Programming Languages*, 334-340.

AHO, A. V., J. E. HOPCROFT, AND J. D. ULLMAN [1974]. *The Design and Analysis of Computer Algorithms*, Addison-Wesley, Reading, Mass.

AHO, A. V., J. E. HOPCROFT, AND J. D. ULLMAN [1983]. *Data Structures and Algorithms*, Addison-Wesley, Reading, Mass.

AHO, A. V. AND S. C. JOHNSON [1974]. "LR parsing," *Computing Surveys* **6:2**, 99-124.

AHO, A. V. AND S. C. JOHNSON [1976]. "Optimal code generation for expression trees," *J. ACM* **23:3**, 488-501.

AHO, A. V., S. C. JOHNSON, AND J. D. ULLMAN [1975]. "Deterministic parsing of ambiguous grammars," *Comm. ACM* **18:8**, 441-452.

AHO, A. V., S. C. JOHNSON, AND J. D. ULLMAN [1977a]. "Code generation for expressions with common subexpressions," *J. ACM* **24:1**, 146-160.

AHO, A. V., S. C. JOHNSON, AND J. D. ULLMAN [1977b]. "Code generation for machines with multiregister operations," *Fourth ACM Symposium on Principles of Programming Languages*, 21-28.

AHO, A. V., B. W. KERNIGHAN, AND P. J. WEINBERGER [1979]. "Awk – a pattern scanning and processing language," *Software—Practice and Experience* **9:4**, 267-280.

AHO, A. V. AND T. G. PETERSON [1972]. "A minimum distance error-correcting parser for context-free languages," *SIAM J. Computing* **1:4**, 305-312.

AHO, A. V. AND R. SETHI [1977]. "How hard is compiler code generation?" Lecture Notes in Computer Science **52**, Springer-Verlag, Berlin, 1-15.

AHO, A. V. AND J. D. ULLMAN [1972a]. "Optimization of straight line code," *SIAM J. Computing* **1:1**, 1-19.

AHO, A. V. AND J. D. ULLMAN [1972b]. *The Theory of Parsing, Translation and Compiling,* Vol. I: *Parsing*, Prentice-Hall, Englewood Cliffs, N. J.

AHO, A. V. AND J. D. ULLMAN [1973a]. *The Theory of Parsing, Translation and Compiling,* Vol. II: *Compiling*, Prentice-Hall, Englewood Cliffs, N. J.

AHO, A. V. AND J. D. ULLMAN [1973b]. "A technique for speeding up LR(k) parsers," *SIAM J. Computing* **2:2**, 106-127.

AHO, A. V. AND J. D. ULLMAN [1977]. *Principles of Compiler Design*, Addison-Wesley, Reading, Mass.

AIGRAIN, P., S. L. GRAHAM, R. R. HENRY, M. K. MCKUSICK, AND E. PELEGRI-LLOPART [1984]. "Experience with a Graham-Glanville style code generator," *ACM SIGPLAN Notices* **19:6**, 13-24.

ALLEN, F. E. [1969]. "Program optimization," *Annual Review in Automatic Programming* **5**, 239-307.

ALLEN, F. E. [1970]. "Control flow analysis," *ACM SIGPLAN Notices* **5:7**, 1-19.

ALLEN, F. E. [1974]. "Interprocedural data flow analysis," *Information Processing 74*, North-Holland, Amsterdam, 398-402.

ALLEN, F. E. [1975]. "Bibliography on program optimization," RC-5767, IBM T. J. Watson Research Center, Yorktown Heights, N. Y.

ALLEN, F. E., J. L. CARTER, J. FABRI, J. FERRANTE, W. H. HARRISON, P. G. LOEWNER, AND L. H. TREVILLYAN [1980]. "The experimental compiling system," *IBM. J. Research and Development* **24:6**, 695-715.

ALLEN, F. E. AND J. COCKE [1972]. "A catalogue of optimizing transformations," in Rustin [1972], pp. 1-30.

ALLEN, F. E. AND J. COCKE [1976]. "A program data flow analysis procedure," *Comm. ACM* **19:3**, 137-147.

ALLEN, F. E., J. COCKE, AND K. KENNEDY [1981]. "Reduction of operator strength," in Muchnick and Jones [1981], pp. 79-101.

AMMANN, U. [1977]. "On code generation in a Pascal compiler," *Software—Practice and Experience* **7:3**, 391-423.

AMMANN, U. [1981]. "The Zurich implementation," in Barron [1981], pp. 63-82.

ANDERSON, J. P. [1964]. "A note on some compiling algorithms," *Comm. ACM* **7:3**, 149-150.

ANDERSON, T., J. EVE, AND J. J. HORNING [1973]. "Efficient LR(1) parsers," *Acta Informatica* **2:1**, 12-39.

ANKLAM, P., D. CUTLER, R. HEINEN, JR., AND M. D. MACLAREN [1982]. *Engineering a Compiler*, Digital Press, Bedford, Mass.

ARDEN, B. W., B. A. GALLER, AND R. M. GRAHAM [1961]. "An algorithm for equivalence declarations," *Comm. ACM* **4:7**, 310-314.

AUSLANDER, M. A. AND M. E. HOPKINS [1982]. "An overview of the PL.8 compiler," *ACM SIGPLAN Notices* **17:6**, 22-31.

BACKHOUSE, R. C. [1976]. "An alternative approach to the improvement of LR parsers," *Acta Informatica* **6:3**, 277-296.

BACKHOUSE, R. C. [1984]. "Global data flow analysis problems arising in locally least-cost error recovery," *TOPLAS* **6:2**, 192-214.

BACKUS, J. W. [1981]. "Transcript of presentation on the history of Fortran I, II, and III," in Wexelblat [1981], pp. 45-66.

BACKUS, J. W., R. J. BEEBER, S. BEST, R. GOLDBERG, L. M. HAIBT, H. L. HERRICK, R. A. NELSON, D. SAYRE, P. B. SHERIDAN, H. STERN, I. ZILLER, R. A. HUGHES, AND R. NUTT [1957]. "The Fortran automatic coding system," *Western Joint Computer Conference*, 188-198. Reprinted in Rosen [1967], pp. 29-47.

BAKER, B. S. [1977]. "An algorithm for structuring programs," *J. ACM* **24:1**, 98-120.

BAKER, T. P. [1982]. "A one-pass algorithm for overload resolution in Ada," *TOPLAS* **4:4**, 601-614.

BANNING, J. P. [1979]. "An efficient way to find the side effects of procedure calls and aliases of variables," *Sixth Annual ACM Symposium on Principles of Programming Languages*, 29-41.

BARRON, D. W. [1981]. *Pascal – The Language and its Implementation*, Wiley, Chichester.

BARTH, J. M. [1978]. "A practical interprocedural data flow analysis algorithm," *Comm. ACM* **21:9**, 724-736.

BATSON, A. [1965]. "The organization of symbol tables," *Comm. ACM* **8:2**, 111-112.

BAUER, A. M. AND H. J. SAAL [1974]. "Does APL really need run-time checking?" *Software—Practice and Experience* **4:2**, 129-138.

BAUER, F. L. [1976]. "Historical remarks on compiler construction," in Bauer and Eickel [1976], pp. 603-621. Addendum by A. P. Ershov, pp. 622-626.

BAUER, F. L. AND J. EICKEL [1976]. *Compiler Construction: An Advanced Course,* 2nd Ed., Lecture Notes in Computer Science **21**, Springer-Verlag, Berlin.

BAUER, F. L. AND H. WOSSNER [1972]. "The 'Plankankül' of Konrad Zuse: A forerunner of today's programming languages," *Comm. ACM* **15:7**, 678-685.

BEATTY, J. C. [1972]. "An axiomatic approach to code optimization for expressions," *J. ACM* **19:4**, 714-724. Errata **20** (1973), p. 180 and 538.

BEATTY, J. C. [1974]. "Register assignment algorithm for generation of highly optimized object code," *IBM J. Research and Development* **5:2**, 20-39.

BELADY, L. A. [1966]. "A study of replacement algorithms for a virtual storage computer," *IBM Systems J.* **5:2**, 78-101.

BENTLEY, J. L. [1982]. *Writing Efficient Programs*, Prentice-Hall, Englewood Cliffs, N. J.

BENTLEY, J. L., W. S. CLEVELAND, AND R. SETHI [1985]. "Empirical analysis of hash functions," manuscript, AT&T Bell Laboratories, Murray Hill, N. J.

BIRMAN, A. AND J. D. ULLMAN [1973]. "Parsing algorithms with backtrack," *Information and Control* **23:1**, 1-34.

BOCHMANN, G. V. [1976]. "Semantic evaluation from left to right," *Comm. ACM* **19:2**, 55-62.

BOCHMANN, G. V. AND P. WARD [1978]. "Compiler writing system for attribute grammars," *Computer J.* **21:2**, 144-148.

BOOK, R. V. [1980]. *Formal Language Theory*, Academic Press, New York.

BOYER, R. S. AND J S. MOORE [1977]. "A fast string searching algorithm," *Comm. ACM* **20:10**, 262-272.

BRANQUART, P., J.-P. CARDINAEL, J. LEWI, J.-P. DELESCAILLE, AND M. VANBEGIN [1976]. *An Optimized Translation Process and its Application to Algol 68*, Lecture Notes in Computer Science, **38**, Springer-Verlag, Berlin.

BRATMAN, H. [1961]. "An alternate form of the 'Uncol diagram'," *Comm. ACM* **4:3**, 142.

BROOKER, R. A. AND D. MORRIS [1962]. "A general translation program for phrase structure languages," *J. ACM* **9:1**, 1-10.

BROOKS, F. P., JR. [1975]. *The Mythical Man-Month*, Addison-Wesley, Reading, Mass.

BROSGOL, B. M. [1974]. *Deterministic Translation Grammars*, Ph. D. Thesis, TR 3-74, Harvard Univ., Cambridge, Mass.

BRUNO, J. AND T. LASSAGNE [1975]. "The generation of optimal code for stack machines," *J. ACM* **22:3**, 382-396.

BRUNO, J. AND R. SETHI [1976]. "Code generation for a one-register machine," *J. ACM* **23:3**, 502-510.

BURSTALL, R. M., D. B. MacQUEEN, AND D. T. SANNELLA [1980]. "Hope: an experimental applicative language," *Lisp Conference*, P.O. Box 487, Redwood Estates, Calif. 95044, 136-143.

BUSAM, V. A. AND D. E. ENGLUND [1969]. "Optimization of expressions in Fortran," *Comm. ACM* **12:12**, 666-674.

CARDELLI, L. [1984]. "Basic polymorphic typechecking," Computing Science Technical Report 112, AT&T Bell Laboratories, Murray Hill, N. J.

CARTER, L. R. [1982]. *An Analysis of Pascal Programs*, UMI Research Press, Ann Arbor, Michigan.

CARTWRIGHT, R. [1985]. "Types as intervals," *Twelfth Annual ACM Symposium on Principles of Programming Languages*, 22-36.

CATTELL, R. G. G. [1980]. "Automatic derivation of code generators from machine descriptions," *TOPLAS* **2:2**, 173-190.

CHAITIN, G. J. [1982]. "Register allocation and spilling via graph coloring," *ACM SIGPLAN Notices* **17:6**, 201-207.

CHAITIN, G. J., M. A. AUSLANDER, A. K. CHANDRA, J. COCKE, M. E. HOPKINS, AND P. W. MARKSTEIN [1981]. "Register allocation via coloring," *Computer Languages* **6**, 47-57.

CHERNIAVSKY, J. C., P. B. HENDERSON, AND J. KEOHANE [1976]. "On the equivalence of URE flow graphs and reducible flow graphs," *Proc. 1976 Conference on Information Sciences and Systems*, Johns Hopkins Univ., 423-429.

CHERRY, L. L. [1982]. "Writing tools," *IEEE Trans. on Communications* **COM-30:1**, 100-104.

CHOMSKY, N. [1956]. "Three models for the description of language," *IRE*

Trans. on Information Theory **IT-2:3**, 113-124.

CHOW, F. [1983]. *A Portable Machine-Independent Global Optimizer*, Ph. D. Thesis, Computer System Lab., Stanford Univ., Stanford, Calif.

CHOW, F. AND J. L. HENNESSY [1984]. "Register allocation by priority-based coloring," *ACM SIGPLAN Notices* **19:6**, 222-232.

CHURCH, A. [1941]. *The Calculi of Lambda Conversion*, Annals of Math. Studies, No. 6, Princeton University Press, Princeton, N. J.

CHURCH, A. [1956]. *Introduction to Mathematical Logic*, Vol. I, Princeton University Press, Princeton, N. J.

CIESINGER, J. [1979]. "A bibliography of error handling," *ACM SIGPLAN Notices* **14:1**, 16-26.

COCKE, J. [1970]. "Global common subexpression elimination," *ACM SIGPLAN Notices* **5:7**, 20-24.

COCKE, J. AND K. KENNEDY [1976]. "Profitability computations on program flow graphs," *Computers and Mathematics with Applications* **2:2**, 145-159.

COCKE, J. AND K. KENNEDY [1977]. "An algorithm for reduction of operator strength," *Comm. ACM* **20:11**, 850-856.

COCKE, J. AND J. MARKSTEIN [1980]. "Measurement of code improvement algorithms," *Information Processing 80*, 221-228.

COCKE, J. AND J. MILLER [1969]. "Some analysis techniques for optimizing computer programs," *Proc. 2nd Hawaii Intl. Conf. on Systems Sciences*, 143-146.

COCKE, J. AND J. T. SCHWARTZ [1970]. *Programming Languages and Their Compilers: Preliminary Notes, Second Revised Version*, Courant Institute of Mathematical Sciences, New York.

COFFMAN, E. G., JR. AND R. SETHI [1983]. "Instruction sets for evaluating arithmetic expressions," *J. ACM* **30:3**, 457-478.

COHEN, R. AND E. HARRY [1979]. "Automatic generation of near-optimal linear-time translators for non-circular attribute grammars," *Sixth ACM Symposium on Principles of Programming Languages*, 121-134.

CONWAY, M. E. [1963]. "Design of a separable transition diagram compiler," *Comm. ACM* **6:7**, 396-408.

CONWAY, R. W. AND W. L. MAXWELL [1963]. "CORC – the Cornell computing language," *Comm. ACM* **6:6**, 317-321.

CONWAY, R. W. AND T. R. WILCOX [1973]. "Design and implementation of a diagnostic compiler for PL/I," *Comm. ACM* **16:3**, 169-179.

CORMACK, G. V. [1981]. "An algorithm for the selection of overloaded functions in Ada," *ACM SIGPLAN Notices* **16:2** (February) 48-52.

CORMACK, G. V., R. N. S. HORSPOOL, AND M. KAISERSWERTH [1985]. "Practical perfect hashing," *Computer J.* **28:1**, 54-58.

COURCELLE, B. [1984]. "Attribute grammars: definitions, analysis of dependencies, proof methods," in Lorho [1984], pp. 81-102.

COUSOT, P. [1981]. "Semantic foundations of program analysis," in Muchnick and Jones [1981], pp. 303-342.

COUSOT, P. AND R. COUSOT [1977]. "Abstract interpretation: a unified lattice model for static analysis of programs by construction or approximation of fixpoints," *Fourth ACM Symposium on Principles of Programming Languages*, 238-252.

CURRY, H. B. AND R. FEYS [1958]. *Combinatory Logic,* Vol. 1, North-Holland, Amsterdam.

DATE, C. J. [1986]. *An Introduction to Database Systems,* 4th Ed., Addison-Wesley, Reading, Mass.

DAVIDSON, J. W. AND C. W. FRASER [1980]. "The design and application of a retargetable peephole optimizer," *TOPLAS* **2:2**, 191-202. Errata **3:1** (1981) 110.

DAVIDSON, J. W. AND C. W. FRASER [1984a]. "Automatic generation of peephole optimizations," *ACM SIGPLAN Notices* **19:6**, 111-116.

DAVIDSON, J. W. AND C. W. FRASER [1984b]. "Code selection through object code optimization," *TOPLAS* **6:4**, 505-526.

DEREMER, F. [1969]. *Practical Translators for LR(k) Languages,* Ph. D. Thesis, M.I.T., Cambridge, Mass.

DEREMER, F. [1971]. "Simple LR(k) grammars," *Comm. ACM* **14:7**, 453-460.

DEREMER, F. AND T. PENNELLO [1982]. "Efficient computation of LALR(1) look-ahead sets," *TOPLAS* **4:4**, 615-649.

DEMERS, A. J. [1975]. "Elimination of single productions and merging of nonterminal symbols in LR(1) grammars," *J. Computer Languages* **1:2**, 105-119.

DENCKER, P., K. DURRE, AND J. HEUFT [1984]. "Optimization of parser tables for portable compilers," *TOPLAS* **6:4**, 546-572.

DERANSART, P., M. JOURDAN, AND B. LORHO [1984]. "Speeding up circularity tests for attribute grammars," *Acta Informatica* **21**, 375-391.

DESPEYROUX, T. [1984]. "Executable specifications of static semantics," in Kahn, MacQueen, and Plotkin [1984], pp. 215-233.

DIJKSTRA, E. W. [1960]. "Recursive programming," *Numerische Math.* **2**,

312-318. Reprinted in Rosen [1967], pp. 221-228.

DIJKSTRA, E. W. [1963]. "An Algol 60 translator for the X1," *Annual Review in Automatic Programming* **3**, Pergamon Press, New York, 329-345.

DITZEL, D. AND H. R. MCLELLAN [1982]. "Register allocation for free: the C machine stack cache," *Proc. ACM Symp. on Architectural Support for Programming Languages and Operating Systems*, 48-56.

DOWNEY, P. J. AND R. SETHI [1978]. "Assignment commands with array references," *J. ACM* **25:4**, 652-666.

DOWNEY, P. J., R. SETHI, AND R. E. TARJAN [1980]. "Variations on the common subexpression problem," *J. ACM* **27:4**, 758-771.

EARLEY, J. [1970]. "An efficient context-free parsing algorithm," *Comm. ACM* **13:2**, 94-102.

EARLEY, J. [1975a]. "Ambiguity and precedence in syntax description," *Acta Informatica* **4:2**, 183-192.

EARLEY, J. [1975b]. "High level iterators and a method of data structure choice," *J. Computer Languages* **1:4**, 321-342.

ELSHOFF, J. L. [1976]. "An analysis of some commercial PL/I programs," *IEEE Trans. Software Engineering* **SE2:2**, 113-120.

ENGELFRIET, J. [1984]. "Attribute evaluation methods," in Lorho [1984], pp. 103-138.

ERSHOV, A. P. [1958]. "On programming of arithmetic operations," *Comm. ACM* **1:8** (August) 3-6. Figures 1-3 appear in **1:9** (September 1958), p. 16.

ERSHOV, A. P. [1966]. "Alpha – an automatic programming system of high efficiency," *J. ACM* **13:1**, 17-24.

ERSHOV, A. P. [1971]. *The Alpha Automatic Programming System*, Academic Press, New York.

ERSHOV, A. P. AND C. H. A. KOSTER [1977]. *Methods of Algorithmic Language Implementation*, Lecture Notes in Computer Science **47**, Springer-Verlag, Berlin.

FANG, I. [1972]. "FOLDS, a declarative formal language definition system," STAN-CS-72-329, Stanford Univ.

FARROW, R. [1984]. "Generating a production compiler from an attribute grammar," *IEEE Software* **1** (October) 77-93.

FARROW, R. AND D. YELLIN [1985]. "A comparison of storage optimizations in automatically-generated compilers," manuscript, Columbia Univ.

FELDMAN, S. I. [1979a]. "Make – a program for maintaining computer programs," *Software—Practice and Experience* **9:4**, 255-265.

FELDMAN, S. I. [1979b]. "Implementation of a portable Fortran 77 compiler using modern tools," *ACM SIGPLAN Notices* **14:8**, 98-106.

FISCHER, M. J. [1972]. "Efficiency of equivalence algorithms," in Miller and Thatcher [1972], pp. 153-168.

FLECK, A. C. [1976]. "The impossibility of content exchange through the by-name parameter transmission technique," *ACM SIGPLAN Notices* **11:11** (November) 38-41.

FLOYD, R. W. [1961]. "An algorithm for coding efficient arithmetic expressions," *Comm. ACM* **4:1**, 42-51.

FLOYD, R. W. [1963]. "Syntactic analysis and operator precedence," *J. ACM* **10:3**, 316-333.

FLOYD, R. W. [1964]. "Bounded context syntactic analysis," *Comm. ACM* **7:2**, 62-67.

FONG, A. C. [1979]. "Automatic improvement of programs in very high level languages," *Sixth Annual ACM Symposium on Principles of Programming Languages*, 21-28.

FONG, A. C. AND J. D. ULLMAN [1976]. "Induction variables in very high-level languages," *Third Annual ACM Symposium on Principles of Programming Languages*, 104-112.

FOSDICK, L. D. AND L. J. OSTERWEIL [1976]. "Data flow analysis in software reliability," *Computing Surveys* **8:3**, 305-330.

FOSTER, J. M. [1968]. "A syntax improving program," *Computer J.* **11:1**, 31-34.

FRASER, C. W. [1977]. *Automatic Generation of Code Generators*, Ph. D. Thesis, Yale Univ., New Haven, Conn.

FRASER, C. W. [1979]. "A compact, machine-independent peephole optimizer," *Sixth Annual ACM Symposium on Principles of Programming Languages*, 1-6.

FRASER, C. W. AND D. R. HANSON [1982]. "A machine-independent linker," *Software—Practice and Experience* **12**, 351-366.

FREDMAN, M. L., J. KOMLOS, AND E. SZEMEREDI [1984]. "Storing a sparse table with $O(1)$ worst case access time," *J. ACM* **31:3**, 538-544.

FREGE, G. [1879]. "Begriffsschrift, a formula language, modeled upon that of arithmetic, for pure thought," in Heijenoort [1967], 1-82.

FREIBURGHOUSE, R. A. [1969]. "The Multics PL/I compiler," *AFIPS Fall Joint Computer Conference* **35**, 187-208.

FREIBURGHOUSE, R. A. [1974]. "Register allocation via usage counts," *Comm. ACM* **17:11**, 638-642.

FREUDENBERGER, S. M. [1984]. "On the use of global optimization algorithms for the detection of semantic programming errors," NSO-24, New York Univ.

FREUDENBERGER, S. M., J. T. SCHWARTZ, AND M. SHARIR [1983]. "Experience with the SETL optimizer," *TOPLAS* **5:1**, 26-45.

GAJEWSKA, H. [1975]. "Some statistics on the usage of the C language," AT&T Bell Laboratories, Murray Hill, N. J.

GALLER, B. A. AND M. J. FISCHER [1964]. "An improved equivalence algorithm," *Comm. ACM* **7:5**, 301-303.

GANAPATHI, M. [1980]. *Retargetable Code Generation and Optimization using Attribute Grammars*, Ph. D. Thesis, Univ. of Wisconsin, Madison, Wis.

GANAPATHI, M. AND C. N. FISCHER [1982]. "Description-driven code generation using attribute grammars," *Ninth ACM Symposium on Principles of Programming Languages*, 108-119.

GANAPATHI, M., C. N. FISCHER, AND J. L. HENNESSY [1982]. "Retargetable compiler code generation," *Computing Surveys* **14:4**, 573-592.

GANNON, J. D. AND J. J. HORNING [1975]. "Language design for programming reliability," *IEEE Trans. Software Engineering* **SE-1:2**, 179-191.

GANZINGER, H., R. GIEGERICH, U. MONCKE, AND R. WILHELM [1982]. "A truly generative semantics-directed compiler generator," *ACM SIGPLAN Notices* **17:6** (June) 172-184.

GANZINGER, H. AND K. RIPKEN [1980]. "Operator identification in Ada," *ACM SIGPLAN Notices* **15:2** (February) 30-42.

GAREY, M. R. AND D. S. JOHNSON [1979]. *Computers and Intractability: A Guide to the Theory of NP-Completeness*, Freeman, San Francisco.

GEAR, C. W. [1965]. "High speed compilation of efficient object code," *Comm. ACM* **8:8**, 483-488.

GESCHKE, C. M. [1972]. *Global Program Optimizations*, Ph. D. Thesis, Dept. of Computer Science, Carnegie-Mellon Univ.

GIEGERICH, R. [1983]. "A formal framework for the derivation of machine-specific optimizers," *TOPLAS* **5:3**, 422-448.

GIEGERICH, R. AND R. WILHELM [1978]. "Counter-one-pass features in one-pass compilation: a formalization using attribute grammars," *Information Processing Letters* **7:6**, 279-284.

GLANVILLE, R. S. [1977]. *A Machine Independent Algorithm for Code*

Generation and its Use in Retargetable Compilers, Ph. D. Thesis, Univ. of California, Berkeley.

GLANVILLE, R. S. AND S. L. GRAHAM [1978]. "A new method for compiler code generation," *Fifth ACM Symposium on Principles of Programming Languages*, 231-240.

GRAHAM, R. M. [1964]. "Bounded context translation," *AFIPS Spring Joint Computer Conference* **40**, 205-217. Reprinted in Rosen [1967], pp. 184-205.

GRAHAM, S. L. [1980]. "Table-driven code generation," *Computer* **13:8**, 25-34.

GRAHAM, S. L. [1984]. "Code generation and optimization," in Lorho [1984], pp. 251-288.

GRAHAM, S. L., C. B. HALEY, AND W. N. JOY [1979]. "Practical LR error recovery," *ACM SIGPLAN Notices* **14:8**, 168-175.

GRAHAM, S. L., M. A. HARRISON, AND W. L. RUZZO [1980]. "An improved context-free recognizer," *TOPLAS* **2:3**, 415-462.

GRAHAM, S. L. AND S. P. RHODES [1975]. "Practical syntactic error recovery," *Comm. ACM* **18:11**, 639-650.

GRAHAM, S. L. AND M. WEGMAN [1976]. "A fast and usually linear algorithm for global data flow analysis," *J. ACM* **23:1**, 172-202.

GRAU, A. A., U. HILL, AND H. LANGMAACK [1967]. *Translation of Algol 60*, Springer-Verlag, New York.

HANSON, D. R. [1981]. "Is block structure necessary?" *Software—Practice and Experience* **11**, 853-866.

HARRISON, M. C. [1971]. "Implementation of the substring test by hashing," *Comm. ACM* **14:12**, 777-779.

HARRISON, W. [1975]. "A class of register allocation algorithms," RC-5342, IBM T. J. Watson Research Center, Yorktown Heights, N. Y.

HARRISON, W. [1977]. "Compiler analysis of the value ranges for variables," *IEEE Trans. Software Engineering* **3:3**.

HECHT, M. S. [1977]. *Flow Analysis of Computer Programs*, North-Holland, New York.

HECHT, M. S. AND J. B. SHAFFER [1975]. "Ideas on the design of a 'quad improver' for SIMPL-T, part I: overview and intersegment analysis," Dept. of Computer Science, Univ. of Maryland, College Park, Md.

HECHT, M. S. AND J. D. ULLMAN [1972]. "Flow graph reducibility," *SIAM J. Computing* **1**, 188-202.

HECHT, M. S. AND J. D. ULLMAN [1974]. "Characterizations of reducible flow graphs," *J. ACM* **21**, 367-375.

HECHT, M. S. AND J. D. ULLMAN [1975]. "A simple algorithm for global data flow analysis programs," *SIAM J. Computing* **4**, 519-532.

HEIJENOORT, J. VAN [1967]. *From Frege to Gödel*, Harvard Univ. Press, Cambridge, Mass.

HENNESSY, J. [1981]. "Program optimization and exception handling," *Eighth Annual ACM Symposium on Principles of Programming Languages*, 200-206.

HENNESSY, J. [1982]. "Symbolic debugging of optimized code," *TOPLAS* **4:3**, 323-344.

HENRY, R. R. [1984]. *Graham-Glanville Code Generators*, Ph. D. Thesis, Univ. of California, Berkeley.

HEXT, J. B. [1967]. "Compile time type-matching," *Computer J.* **9**, 365-369.

HINDLEY, R. [1969]. "The principal type-scheme of an object in combinatory logic," *Trans. AMS* **146**, 29-60.

HOARE, C. A. R. [1962a]. "Quicksort," *Computer J.* **5:1**, 10-15.

HOARE, C. A. R. [1962b]. "Report on the Elliott Algol translator," *Computer J.* **5:2**, 127-129.

HOFFMAN, C. M. AND M. J. O'DONNELL [1982]. "Pattern matching in trees," *J. ACM* **29:1**, 68-95.

HOPCROFT, J. E. AND R. M. KARP [1971]. "An algorithm for testing the equivalence of finite automata," TR-71-114, Dept. of Computer Science, Cornell Univ. See Aho, Hopcroft, and Ullman [1974], pp. 143-145.

HOPCROFT, J. E. AND J. D. ULLMAN [1969]. *Formal Languages and Their Relation to Automata*, Addison-Wesley, Reading, Mass.

HOPCROFT, J. E. AND J. D. ULLMAN [1973]. "Set merging algorithms," *SIAM J. Computing* **2:3**, 294-303.

HOPCROFT, J. E. AND J. D. ULLMAN [1979]. *Introduction to Automata Theory, Languages, and Computation*, Addison-Wesley, Reading, Mass.

HORNING, J. J. [1976]. "What the compiler should tell the user," in Bauer and Eickel [1976].

HORWITZ, L. P., R. M. KARP, R. E. MILLER, AND S. WINOGRAD [1966]. "Index register allocation," *J. ACM* **13:1**, 43-61.

HUET, G. AND G. KAHN (EDS.) [1975]. *Proving and Improving Programs*, Colloque IRIA, Arc-et-Senans, France.

HUET, G. AND J.-J. LEVY [1979]. "Call-by-need computations in nonambiguous linear term rewriting systems," Rapport de Recherche 359, INRIA Laboria, Rocquencourt.

HUFFMAN, D. A. [1954]. "The synthesis of sequential machines," *J. Franklin Inst.* **257**, 3-4, 161, 190, 275-303.

HUNT, J. W. AND M. D. MCILROY [1976]. "An algorithm for differential file comparison," Computing Science Technical Report 41, AT&T Bell Laboratories, Murray Hill, N. J.

HUNT, J. W. AND T. G. SZYMANSKI [1977]. "A fast algorithm for computing longest common subsequences," *Comm. ACM* **20:5**, 350-353.

HUSKEY, H. D., M. H. HALSTEAD, AND R. MCARTHUR [1960]. "Neliac — a dialect of Algol," *Comm. ACM* **3:8**, 463-468.

ICHBIAH, J. D. AND S. P. MORSE [1970]. "A technique for generating almost optimal Floyd-Evans productions for precedence grammars," *Comm. ACM* **13:8**, 501-508.

INGALLS, D. H. H. [1978]. "The Smalltalk-76 programming system design and implementation," *Fifth Annual ACM Symposium on Principles of Programming Languages*, 9-16.

INGERMAN, P. Z. [1967]. "Panini-Backus form suggested," *Comm. ACM* **10:3**, 137.

IRONS, E. T. [1961]. "A syntax directed compiler for Algol 60," *Comm. ACM* **4:1**, 51-55.

IRONS, E. T. [1963]. "An error correcting parse algorithm," *Comm. ACM* **6:11**, 669-673.

IVERSON, K. [1962]. *A Programming Language*, Wiley, New York.

JANAS, J. M. [1980]. "A comment on "Operator identification in Ada" by Ganzinger and Ripken," *ACM SIGPLAN Notices* **15:9** (September) 39-43.

JARVIS, J. F. [1976]. "Feature recognition in line drawings using regular expressions," *Proc. 3rd Intl. Joint Conf. on Pattern Recognition*, 189-192.

JAZAYERI, M., W. F. OGDEN, AND W. C. ROUNDS [1975]. "The intrinsic exponential complexity of the circularity problem for attribute grammars," *Comm. ACM* **18:12**, 697-706.

JAZAYERI, M. AND D. POZEFSKY [1981]. "Space-efficient storage management in an attribute grammar evaluator," *TOPLAS* **3:4**, 388-404.

JAZAYERI, M. AND K. G. WALTER [1975]. "Alternating semantic evaluator," *Proc. ACM Annual Conference*, 230-234.

JENSEN, K. AND N. WIRTH [1975]. *Pascal User Manual and Report*, Springer-

Verlag, New York.

JOHNSON, S. C. [1975]. "Yacc – yet another compiler compiler," Computing Science Technical Report 32, AT&T Bell Laboratories, Murray Hill, N. J.

JOHNSON, S. C. [1978]. "A portable compiler: theory and practice," *Fifth Annual ACM Symposium on Principles of Programming Languages*, 97-104.

JOHNSON, S. C. [1979]. "A tour through the portable C compiler," AT&T Bell Laboratories, Murray Hill, N. J.

JOHNSON, S. C. [1983]. "Code generation for silicon," *Tenth Annual ACM Symposium on Principles of Programming Languages*, 14-19.

JOHNSON, S. C. AND M. E. LESK [1978]. "Language development tools," *Bell System Technical J.* **57:6**, 2155-2175.

JOHNSON, S. C. AND D. M. RITCHIE [1981]. "The C language calling sequence," Computing Science Technical Report 102, AT&T Bell Laboratories, Murray Hill, N. J.

JOHNSON, W. L., J. H. PORTER, S. I. ACKLEY, AND D. T. ROSS [1968]. "Automatic generation of efficient lexical processors using finite state techniques," *Comm. ACM* **11:12**, 805-813.

JOHNSSON, R. K. [1975]. *An Approach to Global Register Allocation*, Ph. D. Thesis, Carnegie-Mellon Univ., Pittsburgh, Pa.

JOLIAT, M. L. [1976]. "A simple technique for partial elimination of unit productions from LR(k) parser tables," *IEEE Trans. on Computers* **C-25:7**, 763-764.

JONES, N. D. [1980]. *Semantics Directed Compiler Generation*, Lecture Notes in Computer Science **94**, Springer-Verlag, Berlin.

JONES, N. D. AND C. M. MADSEN [1980]. "Attribute-influenced LR parsing," in Jones [1980], pp. 393-407.

JONES, N. D. AND S. S. MUCHNICK [1976]. "Binding time optimization in programming languages," *Third ACM Symposium on Principles of Programming Languages*, 77-94.

JOURDAN, M. [1984]. "Strongly noncircular attribute grammars and their recursive evaluation," *ACM SIGPLAN Notices* **19:6**, 81-93.

KAHN, G., D. B. MACQUEEN, AND G. PLOTKIN [1984]. *Semantics of Data Types*, Lecture Notes in Computer Science **173**, Springer-Verlag, Berlin.

KAM, J. B. AND J. D. ULLMAN [1976]. "Global data flow analysis and iterative algorithms," *J. ACM* **23:1**, 158-171.

KAM, J. B. AND J. D. ULLMAN [1977]. "Monotone data flow analysis frameworks," *Acta Informatica* **7:3**, 305-318.

KAPLAN, M. AND J. D. ULLMAN [1980]. "A general scheme for the automatic inference of variable types," *J. ACM* **27:1**, 128-145.

KASAMI, T. [1965]. "An efficient recognition and syntax analysis algorithm for context-free languages," AFCRL-65-758, Air Force Cambridge Research Laboratory, Bedford, Mass.

KASAMI, T., W. W. PETERSON, AND N. TOKURA [1973]. "On the capabilities of while, repeat, and exit statements," *Comm. ACM* **16:8**, 503-512.

KASTENS, U. [1980]. "Ordered attribute grammars," *Acta Informatica* **13:3**, 229-256.

KASTENS, U., B. HUTT, AND E. ZIMMERMANN [1982]. *GAG: A Practical Compiler Generator*, Lecture Notes in Computer Science **141**, Springer-Verlag, Berlin.

KASYANOV, V. N. [1973]. "Some properties of fully reducible graphs," *Information Processing Letters* **2:4**, 113-117.

KATAYAMA, T. [1984]. "Translation of attribute grammars into procedures," *TOPLAS* **6:3**, 345-369.

KENNEDY, K. [1971]. "A global flow analysis algorithm," *Intern. J. Computer Math. Section A* **3**, 5-15.

KENNEDY, K. [1972]. "Index register allocation in straight line code and simple loops," in Rustin [1972], pp. 51-64.

KENNEDY, K. [1976]. "A comparison of two algorithms for global flow analysis," *SIAM J. Computing* **5:1**, 158-180.

KENNEDY, K. [1981]. "A survey of data flow analysis techniques," in Muchnick and Jones [1981], pp. 5-54.

KENNEDY, K. AND J. RAMANATHAN [1979]. "A deterministic attribute grammar evaluator based on dynamic sequencing," *TOPLAS* **1:1**, 142-160.

KENNEDY, K. AND S. K. WARREN [1976]. "Automatic generation of efficient evaluators for attribute grammars," *Third ACM Symposium on Principles of Programming Languages*, 32-49.

KERNIGHAN, B. W. [1975]. "Ratfor – a preprocessor for a rational Fortran," *Software—Practice and Experience* **5:4**, 395-406.

KERNIGHAN, B. W. [1982]. "PIC – a language for typesetting graphics," *Software—Practice and Experience* **12:1**, 1-21.

KERNIGHAN, B. W. AND L. L. CHERRY [1975]. "A system for typesetting mathematics," *Comm. ACM* **18:3**, 151-157.

KERNIGHAN, B. W. AND R. PIKE [1984]. *The UNIX Programming Environment*, Prentice-Hall, Englewood Cliffs, N. J.

KERNIGHAN, B. W. AND D. M. RITCHIE [1978]. *The C Programming Language*, Prentice-Hall, Englewood Cliffs, N. J.

KILDALL, G. [1973]. "A unified approach to global program optimization," *ACM Symposium on Principles of Programming Languages*, 194-206.

KLEENE, S. C. [1956]. "Representation of events in nerve nets," in Shannon and McCarthy [1956], pp. 3-40.

KNUTH, D. E. [1962]. "A history of writing compilers," *Computers and Automation* (December) 8-18. Reprinted in Pollack [1972], pp. 38-56.

KNUTH, D. E. [1964]. "Backus Normal Form vs. Backus Naur Form," *Comm. ACM* **7:12**, 735-736.

KNUTH, D. E. [1965]. "On the translation of languages from left to right," *Information and Control* **8:6**, 607-639.

KNUTH, D. E. [1968]. "Semantics of context-free languages," *Mathematical Systems Theory* **2:2**, 127-145. Errata **5:1** (1971) 95-96.

KNUTH, D. E. [1971a]. "Top-down syntax analysis," *Acta Informatica* **1:2**, 79-110.

KNUTH, D. E. [1971b]. "An empirical study of FORTRAN programs," *Software—Practice and Experience* **1:2**, 105-133.

KNUTH, D. E. [1973a]. *The Art of Computer Programming:* Vol. 1, 2nd. Ed., *Fundamental Algorithms*, Addison-Wesley, Reading, Mass.

KNUTH, D. E. [1973b]. *The Art of Computer Programming:* Vol. 3, *Sorting and Searching*, Addison-Wesley, Reading, Mass.

KNUTH, D. E. [1977]. "A generalization of Dijkstra's algorithm," *Information Processing Letters* **6**, 1-5.

KNUTH, D. E. [1984a]. *The TEXbook*, Addison-Wesley, Reading, Mass.

KNUTH, D. E. [1984b]. "Literate programming," *Computer J.* **28:2**, 97-111.

KNUTH, D. E. [1985,1986]. *Computers and Typesetting*, Vol. 1: TEX, Addison-Wesley, Reading, Mass. A preliminary version has been published under the title, "*TEX: The Program*."

KNUTH, D. E., J. H. MORRIS, AND V. R. PRATT [1977]. "Fast pattern matching in strings," *SIAM J. Computing* **6:2**, 323-350.

KNUTH, D. E. AND L. TRABB PARDO [1977]. "Early development of programming languages," *Encyclopedia of Computer Science and Technology* **7**, Marcel Dekker, New York, 419-493.

KORENJAK, A. J. [1969]. "A practical method for constructing LR(k) processors," *Comm. ACM* **12:11**, 613-623.

KOSARAJU, S. R. [1974]. "Analysis of structured programs," *J. Computer and System Sciences* **9:3**, 232-255.

KOSKIMIES, K. AND K.-J. RAIHA [1983]. "Modelling of space-efficient one-pass translation using attribute grammars," *Software—Practice and Experience* **13**, 119-129.

KOSTER, C. H. A. [1971]. "Affix grammars," in Peck [1971], pp. 95-109.

KOU, L. [1977]. "On live-dead analysis for global data flow problems," *J. ACM* **24:3**, 473-483.

KRISTENSEN, B. B. AND O. L. MADSEN [1981]. "Methods for computing LALR(k) lookahead," *TOPLAS* **3:1**, 60-82.

KRON, H. [1975]. *Tree Templates and Subtree Transformational Grammars*, Ph. D. Thesis, Univ. of California, Santa Cruz.

LALONDE, W. R. [1971]. "An efficient LALR parser generator," Tech. Rep. 2, Computer Systems Research Group, Univ. of Toronto.

LALONDE, W. R. [1976]. "On directly constructing LR(k) parsers without chain reductions," *Third ACM Symposium on Principles of Programming Languages*, 127-133.

LALONDE, W. R., E. S. LEE, AND J. J. HORNING [1971]. "An LALR(k) parser generator," *Proc. IFIP Congress 71* **TA-3**, North-Holland, Amsterdam, 153-157.

LAMB, D. A. [1981]. "Construction of a peephole optimizer," *Software—Practice and Experience* **11**, 638-647.

LAMPSON, B. W. [1982]. "Fast procedure calls," *ACM SIGPLAN Notices* **17:4** (April) 66-76.

LANDIN, P. J. [1964]. "The mechanical evaluation of expressions," *Computer J.* **6:4**, 308-320.

LECARME, O. AND M.-C. PEYROLLE-THOMAS [1978]. "Self-compiling compilers: an appraisal of their implementation and portability," *Software—Practice and Experience* **8**, 149-170.

LEDGARD, H. F. [1971]. "Ten mini-languages: a study of topical issues in programming languages," *Computing Surveys* **3:3**, 115-146.

LEINIUS, R. P. [1970]. *Error Detection and Recovery for Syntax Directed Compiler Systems*, Ph. D. Thesis, University of Wisconsin, Madison.

LENGAUER, T. AND R. E. TARJAN [1979]. "A fast algorithm for finding dominators in a flowgraph," *TOPLAS* **1**, 121-141.

LESK, M. E. [1975]. "Lex – a lexical analyzer generator," Computing Science Technical Report 39, AT&T Bell Laboratories, Murray Hill, N. J.

LEVERETT, B. W. [1982]. "Topics in code generation and register allocation," CMU CS-82-130, Computer Science Dept., Carnegie-Mellon Univ., Pittsburgh, Pennsylvania.

LEVERETT, B. W., R. G. G. CATTELL, S. O. HOBBS, J. M. NEWCOMER, A. H. REINER, B. R. SCHATZ, AND W. A. WULF [1980]. "An overview of the production-quality compiler-compiler project," *Computer* **13:8**, 38-40.

LEVERETT, B. W. AND T. G. SZYMANSKI [1980]. "Chaining span-dependent jump instructions," *TOPLAS* **2:3**, 274-289.

LEVY, J. P. [1975]. "Automatic correction of syntax errors in programming languages," *Acta Informatica* **4**, 271-292.

LEWIS, P. M., II, D. J. ROSENKRANTZ, AND R. E. STEARNS [1974]. "Attributed translations," *J. Computer and System Sciences* **9:3**, 279-307.

LEWIS, P. M., II, D. J. ROSENKRANTZ, AND R. E. STEARNS [1976]. *Compiler Design Theory*, Addison-Wesley, Reading, Mass.

LEWIS, P. M., II AND R. E. STEARNS [1968]. "Syntax-directed transduction," *J. ACM* **15:3**, 465-488.

LORHO, B. [1977]. "Semantic attribute processing in the system Delta," in Ershov and Koster [1977], pp. 21-40.

LORHO, B. [1984]. *Methods and Tools for Compiler Construction*, Cambridge Univ. Press.

LORHO, B. AND C. PAIR [1975]. "Algorithms for checking consistency of attribute grammars," in Huet and Kahn [1975], pp. 29-54.

LOW, J. AND P. ROVNER [1976]. "Techniques for the automatic selection of data structures," *Third ACM Symposium on Principles of Programming Languages*, 58-67.

LOWRY, E. S. AND C. W. MEDLOCK [1969]. "Object code optimization," *Comm. ACM* **12**, 13-22.

LUCAS, P. [1961]. "The structure of formula translators," *Elektronische Rechenanlagen* **3**, 159-166.

LUNDE, A. [1977]. "Empirical evaluation of some features of instruction set processor architectures," *Comm. ACM* **20:3**, 143-153.

LUNELL, H. [1983]. *Code Generator Writing Systems*, Ph. D. Thesis, Linköping University, Linköping, Sweden.

MACQUEEN, D. B., G. P. PLOTKIN, AND R. SETHI [1984]. "An ideal model of recursive polymorphic types," *Eleventh Annual ACM Symposium on Principles of Programming Languages*, 165-174.

MADSEN, O. L. [1980]. "On defining semantics by means of extended attribute grammars," in Jones [1980], pp. 259-299.

MARILL, T. [1962]. "Computational chains and the simplification of computer programs," *IRE Trans. Electronic Computers* **EC-11:2**, 173-180.

MARTELLI, A. AND U. MONTANARI [1982]. "An efficient unification algorithm," *TOPLAS* **4:2**, 258-282.

MAUNEY, J. AND C. N. FISCHER [1982]. "A forward move algorithm for LL and LR parsers," *ACM SIGPLAN Notices* **17:4**, 79-87.

MAYOH, B. H. [1981]. "Attribute grammars and mathematical semantics," *SIAM J. Computing* **10:3**, 503-518.

McCARTHY, J. [1963]. "Towards a mathematical science of computation," *Information Processing 1962*, North-Holland, Amsterdam, 21-28.

McCARTHY, J. [1981]. "History of Lisp," in Wexelblat [1981], pp. 173-185.

McCLURE, R. M. [1965]. "TMG – a syntax-directed compiler," *Proc. 20th ACM National Conf.*, 262-274.

McCRACKEN, N. J. [1979]. *An Investigation of a Programming Language with a Polymorphic Type Structure*, Ph. D. Thesis, Syracuse University, Syracuse, N. Y.

McCULLOUGH, W. S. AND W. PITTS [1943]. "A logical calculus of the ideas immanent in nervous activity," *Bulletin of Math. Biophysics* **5**, 115-133.

McKEEMAN, W. M. [1965]. "Peephole optimization," *Comm. ACM* **8:7**, 443-444.

McKEEMAN, W. M. [1976]. "Symbol table access," in Bauer and Eickel [1976], pp. 253-301.

McKEEMAN, W. M., J. J. HORNING, AND D. B. WORTMAN [1970]. *A Compiler Generator*, Prentice-Hall, Englewood Cliffs, N. J.

McNAUGHTON, R. AND H. YAMADA [1960]. "Regular expressions and state graphs for automata," *IRE Trans. on Electronic Computers* **EC-9:1**, 38-47.

MEERTENS, L. [1983]. "Incremental polymorphic type checking in B," *Tenth ACM Symposium on Principles of Programming Languages*, 265-275.

METCALF, M. [1982]. *Fortran Optimization*, Academic Press, New York.

MILLER, R. E. AND J. W. THATCHER (EDS.) [1972]. *Complexity of Computer Computations*, Academic Press, New York.

MILNER, R. [1978]. "A theory of type polymorphism in programming," *J. Computer and System Sciences* **17:3**, 348-375.

MILNER, R. [1984]. "A proposal for standard ML," *ACM Symposium on Lisp and Functional Programming*, 184-197.

MINKER, J. AND R. G. MINKER [1980]. "Optimization of boolean expressions – historical developments," *A. of the History of Computing* **2:3**, 227-238.

MITCHELL, J. C. [1984]. "Coercion and type inference," *Eleventh ACM Symposium on Principles of Programming Languages*, 175-185.

MOORE, E. F. [1956]. "Gedanken experiments in sequential machines," in Shannon and McCarthy [1956], pp. 129-153.

MOREL, E. AND C. RENVOISE [1979]. "Global optimization by suppression of partial redundancies," *Comm. ACM* **22**, 96-103.

MORRIS, J. H. [1968a]. *Lambda-Calculus Models of Programming Languages*, Ph. D. Thesis, MIT, Cambridge, Mass.

MORRIS, R. [1968b]. "Scatter storage techniques," *Comm. ACM* **11:1**, 38-43.

MOSES, J. [1970]. "The function of FUNCTION in Lisp," *SIGSAM Bulletin* **15** (July) 13-27.

MOULTON, P. G. AND M. E. MULLER [1967]. "DITRAN – a compiler emphasizing diagnostics," *Comm. ACM* **10:1**, 52-54.

MUCHNICK, S. S. AND N. D. JONES [1981]. *Program Flow Analysis: Theory and Applications*, Prentice-Hall, Englewood Cliffs, N. J.

NAKATA, I. [1967]. "On compiling algorithms for arithmetic expressions," *Comm. ACM* **10:8**, 492-494.

NAUR, P. (ED.) [1963]. "Revised report on the algorithmic language Algol 60," *Comm. ACM* **6:1**, 1-17.

NAUR, P. [1965]. "Checking of operand types in Algol compilers," *BIT* **5**, 151-163.

NAUR, P. [1981]. "The European side of the last phase of the development of Algol 60," in Wexelblat [1981], pp. 92-139, 147-161.

NEWEY, M. C., P. C. POOLE, AND W. M. WAITE [1972]. "Abstract machine modelling to produce portable software – a review and evaluation," *Software—Practice and Experience* **2:2**, 107-136.

NEWEY, M. C. AND W. M. WAITE [1985]. "The robust implementation of sequence-controlled iteration," *Software—Practice and Experience* **15:7**, 655-668.

NICHOLLS, J. E. [1975]. *The Structure and Design of Programming Languages*, Addison-Wesley, Reading, Mass.

NIEVERGELT, J. [1965]. "On the automatic simplification of computer code," *Comm. ACM* **8:6**, 366-370.

NORI, K. V., U. AMMANN, K. JENSEN, H. H. NAGELI, AND CH. JACOBI [1981]. "Pascal P implementation notes," in Barron [1981], pp. 125-170.

OSTERWEIL, L. J. [1981]. "Using data flow tools in software engineering," in Muchnick and Jones [1981], pp. 237-263.

PAGER, D. [1977a]. "A practical general method for constructing LR(k) parsers," *Acta Informatica* **7**, 249-268.

PAGER, D. [1977b]. "Eliminating unit productions from LR(k) parsers," *Acta Informatica* **9**, 31-59.

PAI, A. B. AND R. B. KIEBURTZ [1980]. "Global context recovery: a new strategy for syntactic error recovery by table-driven parsers," *TOPLAS* **2:1**, 18-41.

PAIGE, R. AND J. T. SCHWARTZ [1977]. "Expression continuity and the formal differentiation of algorithms," *Fourth ACM Symposium on Principles of Programming Languages*, 58-71.

PALM, R. C., JR. [1975]. "A portable optimizer for the language C," M. Sc. Thesis, MIT, Cambridge, Mass.

PARK, J. C. H., K. M. CHOE, AND C. H. CHANG [1985]. "A new analysis of LALR formalisms," *TOPLAS* **7:1**, 159-175.

PATERSON, M. S. AND M. WEGMAN [1978]. "Linear unification," *J. Computer and System Sciences* **16:2**, 158-167.

PECK, J. E. L. [1971]. *Algol 68 Implementation*, North-Holland, Amsterdam.

PENNELLO, T. AND F. DeREMER [1978]. "A forward move algorithm for LR error recovery," *Fifth Annual ACM Symposium on Principles of Programming Languages*, 241-254.

PENNELLO, T., F. DeREMER, AND R. MEYERS [1980]. "A simplified operator identification scheme for Ada," *ACM SIGPLAN Notices* **15:7** (July-August) 82-87.

PERSCH, G., G. WINTERSTEIN, M. DAUSSMANN, AND S. DROSSOPOULOU [1980]. "Overloading in preliminary Ada," *ACM SIGPLAN Notices* **15:11** (November) 47-56.

PETERSON, W. W. [1957]. "Addressing for random access storage," *IBM J. Research and Development* **1:2**, 130-146.

POLLACK, B. W. [1972]. *Compiler Techniques*, Auerbach Publishers, Princeton, N. J.

POLLOCK, L. L. AND M. L. SOFFA [1985]. "Incremental compilation of locally optimized code," *Twelfth Annual ACM Symposium on Principles of Programming Languages*, 152-164.

POWELL, M. L. [1984]. "A portable optimizing compiler for Modula-2," *ACM SIGPLAN Notices* **19:6**, 310-318.

PRATT, T. W. [1984]. *Programming Languages: Design and Implementation,* 2nd Ed., Prentice-Hall, Englewood Cliffs, N. J.

PRATT, V. R. [1973]. "Top down operator precedence," *ACM Symposium on Principles of Programming Languages,* 41-51.

PRICE, C. E. [1971]. "Table lookup techniques," *Computing Surveys* **3:2**, 49-65.

PROSSER, R. T. [1959]. "Applications of boolean matrices to the analysis of flow diagrams," *AFIPS Eastern Joint Computer Conf.,* Spartan Books, Baltimore, Md., 133-138.

PURDOM, P. AND C. A. BROWN [1980]. "Semantic routines and LR(k) parsers," *Acta Informatica* **14:4**, 299-315.

PURDOM, P. W. AND E. F. MOORE [1972]. "Immediate predominators in a directed graph," *Comm. ACM* **15:8**, 777-778.

RABIN, M. O. AND D. SCOTT. [1959]. "Finite automata and their decision problems," *IBM J. Research and Development* **3:2**, 114-125.

RADIN, G. AND H. P. ROGOWAY [1965]. "NPL: Highlights of a new programming language," *Comm. ACM* **8:1**, 9-17.

RAIHA, K.-J. [1981]. *A Space Management Technique for Multi-Pass Attribute Evaluators,* Ph. D. Thesis, Report A-1981-4, Dept. of Computer Science, University of Helsinki.

RAIHA, K.-J. AND M. SAARINEN [1982]. "Testing attribute grammars for circularity," *Acta Informatica* **17**, 185-192.

RAIHA, K.-J., M. SAARINEN, M. SARJAKOSKI, S. SIPPU, E. SOISALON-SOININEN, AND M. TIENARI [1983]. "Revised report on the compiler writing system HLP78," Report A-1983-1, Dept. of Computer Science, University of Helsinki.

RANDELL, B. AND L. J. RUSSELL [1964]. *Algol 60 Implementation,* Academic Press, New York.

REDZIEJOWSKI, R. R. [1969]. "On arithmetic expressions and trees," *Comm. ACM* **12:2**, 81-84.

REIF, J. H. AND H. R. LEWIS [1977]. "Symbolic evaluation and the global value graph," *Fourth ACM Symposium on Principles of Programming Languages,* 104-118.

REISS, S. P. [1983]. "Generation of compiler symbol processing mechanisms from specifications," *TOPLAS* **5:2**, 127-163.

REPS, T. W. [1984]. *Generating Language-Based Environments,* MIT Press, Cambridge, Mass.

REYNOLDS, J. C. [1985]. "Three approaches to type structure," *Mathematical Foundations of Software Development*, Lecture Notes in Computer Science **185**, Springer-Verlag, Berlin, 97-138.

RICHARDS, M. [1971]. "The portability of the BCPL compiler," *Software— Practice and Experience* **1:2**, 135-146.

RICHARDS, M. [1977]. "The implementation of the BCPL compiler," in P. J. Brown (ed.), *Software Portability: An Advanced Course*, Cambridge University Press.

RIPKEN, K. [1977]. "Formale beschreibun von maschinen, implementierungen und optimierender maschinen-codeerzeugung aus attributierten programmgraphe," TUM-INFO-7731, Institut für Informatik, Universität München, Munich.

RIPLEY, G. D. AND F. C. DRUSEIKIS [1978]. "A statistical analysis of syntax errors," *Computer Languages* **3**, 227-240.

RITCHIE, D. M. [1979]. "A tour through the UNIX C compiler," AT&T Bell Laboratories, Murray Hill, N. J.

RITCHIE, D. M. AND K. THOMPSON [1974]. "The UNIX time-sharing system," *Comm. ACM* **17:7**, 365-375.

ROBERTSON, E. L. [1979]. "Code generation and storage allocation for machines with span-dependent instructions," *TOPLAS* **1:1**, 71-83.

ROBINSON, J. A. [1965]. "A machine-oriented logic based on the resolution principle," *J. ACM* **12:1**, 23-41.

ROHL, J. S. [1975]. *An Introduction to Compiler Writing*, American Elsevier, New York.

ROHRICH, J. [1980]. "Methods for the automatic construction of error correcting parsers," *Acta Informatica* **13:2**, 115-139.

ROSEN, B. K. [1977]. "High-level data flow analysis," *Comm. ACM* **20**, 712-724.

ROSEN, B. K. [1980]. "Monoids for rapid data flow analysis," *SIAM J. Computing* **9:1**, 159-196.

ROSEN, S. [1967]. *Programming Systems and Languages*, McGraw-Hill, New York.

ROSENKRANTZ, D. J. AND R. E. STEARNS [1970]. "Properties of deterministic top-down grammars," *Information and Control* **17:3**, 226-256.

ROSLER, L. [1984]. "The evolution of C — past and future," *AT&T Bell Labs Technical Journal* **63:8**, 1685-1699.

RUSTIN, R. [1972]. *Design and Optimization of Compilers*, Prentice-Hall,

Englewood Cliffs, N.J.

RYDER, B. G. [1979]. "Constructing the call graph of a program," *IEEE Trans. Software Engineering* **SE-5:3**, 216-226.

RYDER, B. G. [1983]. "Incremental data flow analysis," *Tenth ACM Symposium on Principles of Programming Languages*, 167-176.

SAARINEN, M. [1978]. "On constructing efficient evaluators for attribute grammars," *Automata, Languages and Programming, Fifth Colloquium*, Lecture Notes in Computer Science **62**, Springer-Verlag, Berlin, 382-397.

SAMELSON, K. AND F. L. BAUER [1960]. "Sequential formula translation," *Comm. ACM* **3:2**, 76-83.

SANKOFF, D. AND J. B. KRUSKAL (EDS.) [1983]. *Time Warps, String Edits, and Macromolecules: The Theory and Practice of Sequence Comparison*, Addison-Wesley, Reading, Mass.

SCARBOROUGH, R. G. AND H. G. KOLSKY [1980]. "Improved optimization of Fortran object programs," *IBM J. Research and Development* **24:6**, 660-676.

SCHAEFER, M. [1973]. *A Mathematical Theory of Global Program Optimization*, Prentice Hall, Englewood Cliffs, N. J.

SCHONBERG, E., J. T. SCHWARTZ, AND M. SHARIR [1981]. "An automatic technique for selection of data representations in SETL Programs," *TOPLAS* **3:2**, 126-143.

SCHORRE, D. V. [1964]. "Meta-II: a syntax-oriented compiler writing language," *Proc. 19th ACM National Conf.*, D1.3-1 - D1.3-11.

SCHWARTZ, J. T. [1973]. *On Programming: An Interim Report on the SETL Project*, Courant Inst., New York.

SCHWARTZ, J. T. [1975a]. "Automatic data structure choice in a language of very high level," *Comm. ACM* **18:12**, 722-728.

SCHWARTZ, J. T. [1975b]. "Optimization of very high level languages," *Computer Languages*. Part I: "Value transmission and its corollaries," **1:2**, 161-194; part II: "Deducing relationships of inclusion and membership," **1:3**, 197-218.

SEDGEWICK, R. [1978]. "Implementing Quicksort programs," *Comm. ACM* **21**, 847-857.

SETHI, R. [1975]. "Complete register allocation problems," *SIAM J. Computing* **4:3**, 226-248.

SETHI, R. AND J. D. ULLMAN [1970]. "The generation of optimal code for arithmetic expressions," *J. ACM* **17:4**, 715-728.

SHANNON, C. AND J. MCCARTHY [1956]. *Automata Studies*, Princeton University Press.

SHERIDAN, P. B. [1959]. "The arithmetic translator-compiler of the IBM Fortran automatic coding system," *Comm. ACM* **2:2**, 9-21.

SHIMASAKI, M., S. FUKAYA, K. IKEDA, AND T. KIYONO [1980]. "An analysis of Pascal programs in compiler writing," *Software—Practice and Experience* **10:2**, 149-157.

SHUSTEK, L. J. [1978]. "Analysis and performance of computer instruction sets," SLAC Report 205, Stanford Linear Accelerator Center, Stanford University, Stanford, California.

SIPPU, S. [1981]. "Syntax error handling in compilers," Rep. A-1981-1, Dept. of Computer Science, Univ. of Helsinki, Helsinki, Finland.

SIPPU, S. AND E. SOISALON-SOININEN [1983]. "A syntax-error-handling technique and its experimental analysis," *TOPLAS* **5:4**, 656-679.

SOISALON-SOININEN, E. [1980]. "On the space optimizing effect of eliminating single productions from LR parsers," *Acta Informatica* **14**, 157-174.

SOISALON-SOININEN, E. AND E. UKKONEN [1979]. "A method for transforming grammars into LL(k) form," *Acta Informatica* **12**, 339-369.

SPILLMAN, T. C. [1971]. "Exposing side effects in a PL/I optimizing compiler," *Information Processing 71*, North-Holland, Amsterdam, 376-381.

STEARNS, R. E. [1971]. "Deterministic top-down parsing," *Proc. 5th Annual Princeton Conf. on Information Sciences and Systems*, 182-188.

STEEL, T. B., JR. [1961]. "A first version of Uncol," *Western Joint Computer Conference*, 371-378.

STEELE, G. L., JR. [1984]. *Common LISP*, Digital Press, Burlington, Mass.

STOCKHAUSEN, P. F. [1973]. "Adapting optimal code generation for arithmetic expressions to the instruction sets available on present-day computers," *Comm. ACM* **16:6**, 353-354. Errata: **17:10** (1974) 591.

STONEBRAKER, M., E. WONG, P. KREPS, AND G. HELD [1976]. "The design and implementation of INGRES," *ACM Trans. Database Systems* **1:3**, 189-222.

STRONG, J., J. WEGSTEIN, A. TRITTER, J. OLSZTYN, O. MOCK, AND T. STEEL [1958]. "The problem of programming communication with changing machines: a proposed solution," *Comm. ACM* **1:8** (August) 12-18. Part 2: **1:9** (September) 9-15. Report of the Share Ad-Hoc committee on Universal Languages.

STROUSTRUP, B. [1986]. *The C++ Programming Language*, Addison-Wesley, Reading, Mass.

SUZUKI, N. [1981]. "Inferring types in Smalltalk," *Eighth ACM Symposium on Principles of Programming Languages*, 187-199.

SUZUKI, N. AND K. ISHIHATA [1977]. "Implementation of array bound checker," *Fourth ACM Symposium on Principles of Programming Languages*, 132-143.

SZYMANSKI, T. G. [1978]. "Assembling code for machines with span-dependent instructions," *Comm. ACM* **21:4**, 300-308.

TAI, K. C. [1978]. "Syntactic error correction in programming languages," *IEEE Trans. Software Engineering* **SE-4:5**, 414-425.

TANENBAUM, A. S., H. VAN STAVEREN, E. G. KEIZER, AND J. W. STEVENSON [1983]. "A practical tool kit for making portable compilers," *Comm. ACM* **26:9**, 654-660.

TANENBAUM, A. S., H. VAN STAVEREN, AND J. W. STEVENSON [1982]. "Using peephole optimization on intermediate code," *TOPLAS* **4:1**, 21-36.

TANTZEN, R. G. [1963]. "Algorithm 199: Conversions between calendar date and Julian day number," *Comm. ACM* **6:8**, 443.

TARHIO, J. [1982]. "Attribute evaluation during LR parsing," Report A-1982-4, Dept. of Computer Science, University of Helsinki.

TARJAN, R. E. [1974a]. "Finding dominators in directed graphs," *SIAM J. Computing* **3:1**, 62-89.

TARJAN, R. E. [1974b]. "Testing flow graph reducibility," *J. Computer and System Sciences* **9:3**, 355-365.

TARJAN, R. E. [1975]. "Efficiency of a good but not linear set union algorithm," *JACM* **22:2**, 215-225.

TARJAN, R. E. [1981]. "A unified approach to path problems," *J. ACM* **28:3**, 577-593. And "Fast algorithms for solving path problems," *J. ACM* **28:3** 594-614.

TARJAN, R. E. AND A. C. YAO [1979]. "Storing a sparse table," *Comm. ACM* **22:11**, 606-611.

TENNENBAUM, A. M. [1974]. "Type determination in very high level languages," NSO-3, Courant Institute of Math. Sciences, New York Univ.

TENNENT, R. D. [1981]. *Principles of Programming Languages*, Prentice-Hall International, Englewood Cliffs, N. J.

THOMPSON, K. [1968]. "Regular expression search algorithm," *Comm. ACM* **11:6**, 419-422.

TJIANG, S. W. K. [1986]. "Twig language manual," Computing Science

Technical Report 120, AT&T Bell Laboratories, Murray Hill, N. J.

Токuda, T. [1981]. "Eliminating unit reductions from LR(k) parsers using minimum contexts," *Acta Informatica* **15**, 447-470.

Trickey, H. W. [1985]. *Compiling Pascal Programs into Silicon*, Ph. D. Thesis, Stanford Univ.

Ullman, J. D. [1973]. "Fast algorithms for the elimination of common subexpressions," *Acta Informatica* **2**, 191-213.

Ullman, J. D. [1982]. *Principles of Database Systems*, 2nd Ed., Computer Science Press, Rockville, Md.

Ullman, J. D. [1984]. *Computational Aspects of VLSI*, Computer Science Press, Rockville, Md.

Vyssotsky, V. and P. Wegner [1963]. "A graph theoretical Fortran source language analyzer," manuscript, AT&T Bell Laboratories, Murray Hill, N. J.

Wagner, R. A. [1974]. "Order-n correction for regular languages," *Comm. ACM* **16:5**, 265-268.

Wagner, R. A. and M. J. Fischer [1974]. "The string-to-string correction problem," *J. ACM* **21:1**, 168-174.

Waite, W. M. [1976a]. "Code generation," in Bauer and Eickel [1976], 302-332.

Waite, W. M. [1976b]. "Optimization," in Bauer and Eickel [1976], 549-602.

Waite, W. M. and L. R. Carter [1985]. "The cost of a generated parser," *Software—Practice and Experience* **15:3**, 221-237.

Wasilew, S. G. [1971]. *A Compiler Writing System with Optimization Capabilities for Complex Order Structures*, Ph. D. Thesis, Northwestern Univ., Evanston, Ill.

Watt, D. A. [1977]. "The parsing problem for affix grammars," *Acta Informatica* **8**, 1-20.

Wegbreit, B. [1974]. "The treatment of data types in EL1," *Comm. ACM* **17:5**, 251-264.

Wegbreit, B. [1975]. "Property extraction in well-founded property sets," *IEEE Trans. on Software Engineering* **1:3**, 270-285.

Wegman, M. N. [1983]. "Summarizing graphs by regular expressions," *Tenth Annual ACM Symposium on Principles of Programming Languages*, 203-216.

Wegman, M. N. and F. K. Zadeck [1985]. "Constant propagation with conditional branches," *Twelfth Annual ACM Symposium on Principles of*

Programming Languages, 291-299.

WEGSTEIN, J. H. [1981]. "Notes on Algol 60," in Wexelblat [1981], pp. 126-127.

WEIHL, W. E. [1980]. "Interprocedural data flow analysis in the presence of pointers, procedure variables, and label variables," *Seventh Annual ACM Symposium on Principles of Programming Languages*, 83-94.

WEINGART, S. W. [1973]. *An Efficient and Systematic Method of Code Generation*, Ph. D. Thesis, Yale University, New Haven, Connecticut.

WELSH, J., W. J. SNEERINGER, AND C. A. R. HOARE [1977]. "Ambiguities and insecurities in Pascal," *Software—Practice and Experience* **7:6**, 685-696.

WEXELBLAT, R. L. [1981]. *History of Programming Languages*, Academic Press, New York.

WIRTH, N. [1968]. "PL 360 – a programming language for the 360 computers," *J. ACM* **15:1**, 37-74.

WIRTH, N. [1971]. "The design of a Pascal compiler," *Software—Practice and Experience* **1:4**, 309-333.

WIRTH, N. [1981]. "Pascal-S: A subset and its implementation," in Barron [1981], pp. 199-259.

WIRTH, N. AND H. WEBER [1966]. "Euler: a generalization of Algol and its formal definition: Part I," *Comm. ACM* **9:1**, 13-23.

WOOD, D. [1969]. "The theory of left factored languages," *Computer J.* **12:4**, 349-356.

WULF, W. A., R. K. JOHNSSON, C. B. WEINSTOCK, S. O. HOBBS, AND C. M. GESCHKE [1975]. *The Design of an Optimizing Compiler*, American Elsevier, New York.

YANNAKAKIS, M. [1985]. private communication.

YOUNGER, D. H. [1967]. "Recognition and parsing of context-free languages in time n^3," *Information and Control* **10:2**, 189-208.

ZELKOWITZ, M. V. AND W. G. BAIL [1974]. "Optimization of structured programs," *Software—Practice and Experience* **4:1**, 51-57.

Index